To my sons Dallas, Wes, Tim, and Roy who provided encouragement and especially to my wife, Susan, whose sacrifice and love made this textbook possible.
— **Kenneth E. Clow**

I would like to dedicate my efforts and contributions to the book to my wife Pam, children, Jessica, Daniel, and David, and grandchildren, Danielle and Rile.
— **Donald Baack**

Brief Contents

Contents

vii

Preface

We created *Integrated Advertising, Promotion, and Marketing Communications,* in part, to deal with what we believed were three problems with the integrated marketing communications course. First, we thought the textbooks available did not always practice exactly what they preached: They included large sections on advertising and marketing communications, but these two key ingredients were not completely blended together. Without this integration, students would be unable to see why everyone made such a fuss about integrated marketing communications. We wanted to provide a more carefully *integrated* marketing communications text.

Second, we discovered that some instructors had a tough time reconciling teaching and learning materials with a project-heavy course. Almost everyone teaching the course assigns projects to help students put their knowledge to work. This reliance on projects raises three problems. First, the textbooks now available may not recognize that this is a project-heavy course. Second, when textbooks do mention projects, it is possible to provide more materials to help the student in preparing these projects. Third, because doing even simple projects has turned into such an adventure, textbooks do not take projects very far—projects are not extended from one chapter to another. These three problems have made this project-driven course a challenge for the instructor to teach and a frustration for the student to learn. We wanted to provide a text that was *integrated* with student projects.

Third, we found that integrated marketing communications texts sometimes have disjointed supplements packages. Too often, we have heard professors complain that there

JAVANET INTERNET CAFÉ

The IMC Plan Pro software disk provided with your textbook contains four sample IMC plans as well as the template you will use to design a plan. Each section of this textbook highlights a different sample IMC plan. Section 1 features JavaNet Internet Café's sample plan.

Studying the sample IMC plan with the chapter material will help you learn how to create your own IMC plan while focusing on the information provided in the chapter itself. For example, Chapter 1 notes that an effective integrated marketing communications program begins with the precise assessment of several factors. First, the nature of the company must be clearly understood. Second, the potential customer base must be identified. And third, the key message which is to be delivered to everyone must be established. Everyone includes company employees, suppliers and partners, advertising agencies and other marketing organizations, and customers. These tasks are carried out in the JavaNet Internet Café example.

Read the Executive Summary (Section 1.0) for the JavaNet Internet Café example provided on the IMC Plan Pro disk. JavaNet is an Internet café seeking to take advantage of high quality coffee, combined with quality Internet access, for several distinct consumer groups. This information forms the foundation for what is to follow throughout the plan. Success in building a strong, clear voice for a company starts with knowing who you are, what you do, and how you intend to carry out the plan.

were unpleasant surprises teaching with these supplements. We wanted to provide a more useful and *integrated* supplements package.

This, then, was the mandate for the first edition of *Integrated Advertising, Promotion, and Marketing Communications:* Provide a true integrated marketing communications text that integrated student projects that were so necessary for the course and that integrated the supplements used to teach the course. Hopefully we have accomplished this by providing an integrated text, building a running project into every chapter, and providing commercial software to bring this project to fruition, and putting together a supplements package ourselves.

WHAT IS NEW IN THE SECOND EDITION?

Based on extensive review from users of our textbook and professionals in the field, we have made the following improvements to the text:

▶ **Improved organization.** We have reorganized the chapters in response to feedback from various constituents. In the foundations section of the text (Part 1), the chapter regarding promotions opportunities analysis (Chapter 5) has been moved. It now follows the presentations regarding consumer buying behavior and business-to-business buyer behavior (Chapters 3 and 4).

Also, the chapter regarding media selection (Chapter 9) has been moved to follow presentations on advertising management (Chapter 6) and advertising design (Chapters 7 and 8). Although all of these activities must be integrated, it will be easier for students to understand the role of media selection after they have a better understanding of the advertising function.

▶ **Enhanced discussion of customer relationship management (CRM).** A section of Chapter 12 describes the concept of CRM and how it is being used by businesses. CRM is designed to be a cost effective method of interacting with customers to better serve key customers and generate higher profits for the firm. When combined with information regarding database marketing, CRM programs are effective methods of integrating communications with members of various target markets.

▶ **A new chapter (Chapter 15) devoted to small business ventures and IMC programs.** Promotional activities are challenging for small business owners who work with limited budgets. While the same tools are available, the manner in which the promotional tools are integrated is often different. The central message of this chapter is how a small business using a limited budget can speak with a clear and memorable voice to potential customers.

---

12 Personal Selling, Database Marketing, and Customer Relationship Management

15 IMC for Small Businesses and Entrepreneurial Ventures

▶ **A new approach to integrating ethics into IMC programs.** The first edition of this text contained a stand-alone chapter on regulations and ethics. This edition features ethics vignettes in each chapter. The vignettes are designed to identify key issues from the chapter and lead to discussion regarding ethical concerns. The legal issues associated with advertising regulation have been moved to Chapter 13 where they are discussed in conjunction with public relations. Having already covered the major forms of marketing communications, students are better able to understand the role of regulations at this point in the course.

▶ **Greater emphasis on branding.** Brand management is presented throughout the text where it is applicable to the IMC issue involved. This discussion builds on materials presented in Chapter 2 regarding corporate image, brand management, brand equity, and brand parity.

▶ **Enhanced visual appeal.** This edition contains a substantially greater number of ads than the previous version. These new ads make the book more visually appealing while at the same time provide students with examples of various advertising and promotional tactics. We are especially indebted to Shannon Wyczynski from the Joplin Globe, who gave us access to numerous ads that support Chapter 15 regarding small business IMC programs.

awareness of the company. The objective defines how the trade show booth will be constructed and manned. For example, if the goal is to generate awareness, then the exhibit should include an attention-getting feature. Bright lights, characters in colorful costumes, and music are ways to attract attention. If instead the goal is to generate customer interest in company products, then the products should be displayed in a manner that makes it easy for prospective customers to examine them. Also, the booth should be manned by personnel with expertise and product knowledge.

Sponsorships can be another creative way to locate customers and place the name of the company in the consumer's mind. For a small business, a sponsorship program should be a local event or organization. It is important to make sure the image is consistent with the IMC theme of the sponsoring company. When established carefully, various goals may be reached, such as winning new customers or creating a positive image to attract new employees.[12]

Cost is a concern with sponsorships; however, there are many options. A restaurant or dairy store can sponsor a little league baseball or soccer team at a low cost. A furniture store may develop a relationship with an art gallery without spending significant funds. The primary objective in a sponsorship is to make certain the right people are exposed to [...] does not make sense to sponsor [...]. For example, sponsoring an [...] aimed at teenagers.

This award-winning ad ("Best Use of 4-color" and "Best of Show," Missouri Press Association Award Ceremony) is an excellent method for creating brand awareness of an automobile Web site.
Source: Used with permission of the *Joplin Globe, Joplin, Missouri.*

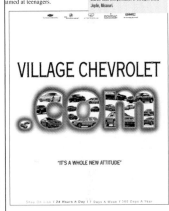

An advertisement for the Magnolia House informing customers of the type of merchandise the company sells.
Source: Used with permission of the *Joplin Globe, Joplin, Missouri.*

A Cut-N-Heaven understands the needs of their customers.
Source: Used with permission of the *Joplin Globe, Joplin, Missouri.*

For Your Fairy Dogmother, the major factor in the decision to purchase the service was convenience. Once customers discovered that Your Fairy Dogmother would come to their homes, it was easy to decide to give the company a try. Also, the company's name suggested that the family dog would be treated with extra special care. By understanding and then defining the needs of her customers, Otto has been able to develop a successful small business.[6]

Through careful research, marketing professionals in businesses such as Your Fairy Dogmother, VIPdesk, and Geeks On Call have been able to identify a target market. Demographic characteristics are vital, but the research must go beyond demographics to include psychographic and purchasing behavior information. Understanding the attitudes, interests, and opinions of individuals in the target market is important in developing a product. It is also important in developing an IMC plan that will reach those consumers.

Creating a Clearly Defined Product

A clearly defined product means that everyone knows exactly what the company intends to deliver. As Leslie Godwin, a career and life-transition counselor pointed out, it is just as important to say what your company *won't do* as what it will do.[7] She noted that a psychotherapist participating in a new group of doctors with a business card that says, "Specializes in treating children, adults, adolescents, groups, and individuals" is overstating the professional's talents. Compared to an ob/gyn who claims she specializes in "women struggling with menopause," the differences are obvious. One professional is trying to be all things to all people. The other has more logically spelled out a form of expertise that would be attractive to a specific set of people.

Any form of new company is liable to fall into the trap of trying to please every potential customer. Unfortunately, this leads to no clear sense of identity for employees, customers, and company leaders. A simple question to ask is, "What do we do well?" The goal is to feature that good, service, or skill.

Once the product is clearly defined, it is important to carefully create a brand name, logo, and other word-based marketing elements such as the company's slogan and advertising tag line. These items must communicate the nature of the clearly defined good or service, or other efforts will not be as likely to succeed. Brand names such as The Pasta House Co. or Champion Dry Cleaners clearly spell out to customers what the business is all about. While VIPdesk and Geeks On Call are easy to remember, it is less clear to consumers exactly what type of service is being provided. These companies will have to expend greater effort in defining the business so that customers see the advantage in giving the firm a try.

Developing a Unique Market Niche

This process is also known as having a **unique selling position (USP)**. A USP is some feature that allows the newly formed company to stand alone and be distinct from all other competitors. This may be based on price, the offer of a service not previously available, or some other feature that is not easily duplicated in the market. VIPdesk, which is used by 10.5 million people, offers services via the Internet, phone, or through a wireless device. No other

JAVANET INTERNET CAFÉ

The IMC Plan Pro software disk provided with your textbook contains four sample IMC plans as well as the template you will use to design a plan. Each section of this textbook highlights a different sample IMC plan. Section 1 features JavaNet Internet Café's sample plan.

Studying the sample IMC plan with the chapter material will help you learn how to create your own IMC plan while focusing on the information provided in the chapter itself. For example, Chapter 1 notes that an effective integrated marketing communications program begins with the precise assessment of several factors. First, the nature of the company must be clearly understood. Second, the potential customer base must be identified. And third, the key message which is to be delivered to everyone must be established. Everyone includes company employees, suppliers and partners, advertising agencies and other marketing organizations, and customers. These tasks are carried out in the JavaNet Internet Café example.

Read the Executive Summary (Section 1.0) for the JavaNet Internet Café example provided on the IMC Plan Pro disk. JavaNet is an Internet café seeking to take advantage of high quality coffee, combined with quality Internet access, for several distinct consumer groups. This information forms the foundation for what is to follow throughout the plan. Success in building a strong, clear voice for a company starts with knowing who you are, [...]

Conducting a Promotions Opportunity Analysis for Your Product

Each of the products listed in Chapter 1 has various kinds of competitors. In order to build a complete and solid IMC program, it is important to begin by following each of the steps of the promotions opportunity analysis. Also, to succeed, you need to identify key target markets for your item. This includes both consumer markets and business-to-business opportunities. In addition, it will be important to consider the possible international customers as you proceed. Go to the Prentice-Hall Web site at www.prenhall.com/clow or access the IMC Plan Pro disk that accompanied this textbook to develop a market analysis for your product by completing the exercise for Chapter 5.

We have enhanced the projects part of the text by doing two key things:

▶ **"Building Your IMC Campaign" exercises now begin in the chapter-opening vignette and tie everything together at the end of the chapter.** We found that waiting until the end of the chapter to introduce the campaign project left too many loose ends. We now introduce the project at the beginning of the chapter and return to it at the end.

▶ **New IMC Plan Pro Sample Cases.** New sample IMC plans have been added to the IMC Plan Pro CD-ROM that accompanies the textbook. These new samples cover a variety of businesses, letting students see multiple ways of developing an IMC Plan.

Finally, we have enhanced the supplements part of the teaching package by adding an exciting new supplement and adding to our video offerings.

In all, we think these improvements and additions help to make *Integrated Advertising, Promotion, and Marketing Communication* the most integrated and effective IMC teaching and learning package available.

THE STUDENT INTEGRATED LEARNING PACKAGE

To learn the material properly, students must first have a text that engages them. Next, students must go outside of the text and learn by doing. Because of this, we have created the following features with the student in mind:

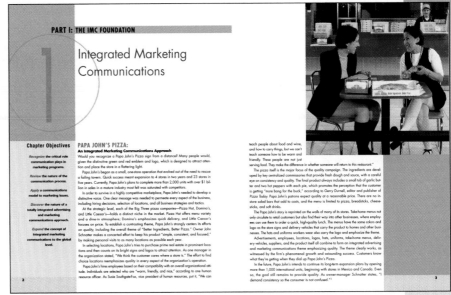

> **Lead-in vignettes.** Each chapter begins with a vignette that is related to the topic being presented. The majority of the vignettes revolve around success stories in companies students will recognize, such as Starbucks and Papa John's Pizza. In this edition, new vignettes have been introduced including features on the Dell dude and the AFLAC duck to keep the stories fresh and recognizable.

> **Business-to-business marketing concepts.**
A large number of marketing students are likely to hold jobs that emphasize sales to other businesses. Therefore, business-to-business components have been incorporated in many of the discussions throughout the text. Examples, cases, text illustrations, and Internet exercises have been woven into the materials. Also a complete examination of business-to-business buyer behavior is provided in Chapter 4.

> **International marketing discussions.** Students are curious about the world around them, especially in light of the events of September 11, 2001. Many marketing texts address international issues as an add-on. While there are some separate discussions of international issues, this book features international concerns where they correlate with the materials being presented. Further international cases are found in several chapters. These end-of-chapter features lead students to discover a more integrated approach to advertising, promotions, and marketing communications in both domestic and international markets.

INTEGRATED LEARNING EXPERIENCE

Visual images are an important feature of any attempt to market a product globally. Access the Sun Microsystems marketing resource center at www.sun.com/smrc, and the "advertising" section of that center. Next, go to the "International Gallery" part of the site. Examine the advertisements for Sun that appear in various countries throughout the world. What are the similarities? What are the differences? To obtain more information, access the "Outdoor," "Radio," and "TV" sections. To view an ad agency's perspective, access Leo Burnett Agency at www.leoburnett.com. At the "Work" section, look at the examples of the agency's various print, television, or other media advertisements. What are the differences in the ads across the various countries?

COMMUNICATION ACTION

Hewlett-Packard

An excellent example of an integrated marketing communications program is provided by the software systems engineering division (SESD) of Hewlett-Packard. This group initiated its IMC process through workshops designed to help HP's employees better understand the dilemmas faced by its customers. These workshops were directed by representatives from sales, product marketing, engineering, and customer support departments within HP. Each had a different perspective of the customer and provided valuable input into the various dilemmas faced by end users. The team approach allowed everyone to see the customer from a more holistic perspective.

Based on input from these departments, a creative strategy emerged with a strong focus on customer needs. The theme "we understand" was adopted. HP's marketing emphasis centered on the idea that members of the company understood the issues, pressures, and constraints that software developers faced. Knowing about unrealistic deadlines, hidden-code errors, and other problems and how to cope with these issues was the key. HP's leaders believed they could solve transition problems for customers by moving to object-oriented programming and simultaneously developing multiple applications of company software. The theme was integrated into all of HP's marketing programs. It was launched in an advertising campaign, then reinforced in three direct mailings. The same message was used in trade show handouts and displays. HP's Web site was redesigned around the same principle.

The "we understand" idea served as an umbrella that all marketing strategies and tactics would then utilize. The integrated approach allowed HP to speak with one voice regardless of the communication method customers encountered when they contacted the firm. This more fully integrated program was more than just the theme, however. It began with effective communication within and built outward to the point where HP's end users (other business) could see and experience a real difference in the products and services that were being provided.

Source: P. Griffeth Lindell, "You Need an Integrated Attitude to Develop IMC," Marketing News, 31, no. 11 (May 26, 1997), p. 6.

▶ **"Communication Action" box.** In each chapter, one key illustration of the subject matter in a real-world setting is presented as a "Communication Action" box. These features include business-to-business, consumer, and international examples. In addition, interviews of professionals from the worlds of advertising and marketing are presented as "Communication Action" boxes in some chapters.

▶ **Key Terms glossary.** In the end-of-chapter materials that follow the text, a glossary of key terms and their definitions is provided. The terms are displayed in the order that they appear in the chapter. When combined with the subject and author index included at the end of the book, there is ready access to each new term that is used.

CRITICAL THINKING EXERCISES

Discussion Questions

1. The marketing director for a furniture manufacturer is assigned the task of developing an integrated marketing communications program to emphasize the furniture's natural look. Discuss the problems the director may encounter in developing this message and in ensuring that consumers understand the message correctly. Refer to the communication process in Figure 1.1 for ideas. What type of noise may interfere with the communication process?

2. Referring to Exercise 1, assume the director wants to develop an integrated marketing communications program emphasizing a theme focused on the furniture's natural look. This theme applies to all of their markets, that is, both retailers and consumers. Using Figure 1.4 as a guide, briefly discuss each element of the integrated marketing communications plan and how to incorporate it into an overall theme.

3. The marketing director for a manufacturer of automobile tires wants to integrate its marketing program internationally.

Should the director use a standardization or adaptation approach? How could the company be certain that its marketing program would effectively be integrated among the different countries where it sells tires?

4. Look up each of the following companies on the Internet. For each company, discuss how effective its Web site is in communicating an overall message. Also, discuss how well the marketing team integrates the material on the Web site. How well does the Web site integrate the company's advertising with other marketing communications?

   a. Revlon (www.revlon.com)
   b. Reebok (www.reebok.com)
   c. J.B. Hunt (www.jbhunt.com)
   d. United Airlines (www.ual.com)
   e. Steamboat Resorts (www.steamboatresorts.com)

▶ **Discussion and Critical Thinking Exercises.** The end-of-chapter materials also contain several short scenarios and exercises to help students review chapter concepts by applying them in various settings. Internet exercises lead students to Web sites where advertisements can be assessed for quality. Innovative approaches, such as asking students to prepare and evaluate various kinds of advertisements and advertising campaigns, are also suggested.

CASE 2

JENNY'S HAIR SALON

Jenny Burns finished high school in the late 1980s. She had no real interest in college. She loved fashion, style, and "glamour." Moving out on her own meant trying to find a job that would accommodate her love of trendy things. She decided to become a hairstylist. After taking all the courses and gaining her cosmetology license, Jenny worked for two years at an independent salon, which went out of business when the owner developed health problems.

After careful deliberation, and with some help from an SBA loan, Jenny opened her own salon on the outskirts of Grand Lake, Oklahoma. The building boom had just taken over the area, and she was convinced she would make a good living because of the growing population and bustle of activities present, especially in the summertime.

The new business, "Jenny's Hair Salon," was started. She used newspaper advertisements, radio spots, and coupons in a local advertising pamphlet to announce her grand opening. Her location was visible and accessible to residents of the major town near the lake, Grove, Oklahoma. Unfortunately, there was no quality sign maker in town, so Jenny had to rely on a portable flashing sign to present the name of her business.

When the business opened, Jenny was able to attract a solid clientele, because she was one of only two salons in town. The other business tended to

▶ **Cases.** At the conclusion of each chapter, two cases are available as assignments or to generate discussion. These cases assist student learning by providing plausible scenarios that require thought and review of chapter materials. The short cases are designed to help students conceptually understand chapter components as well as larger, more general marketing issues.

▶ **Integrated Learning Experiences.** At key points in each chapter, the text guides students to the Internet to access information that ties into the subject matter covered in the text. These places are marked in the book and are also highlighted on the Instructor's Teaching CD-ROM, making it possible for the instructor to go directly to a Web site while using PowerPoint slides.

INTEGRATED LEARNING EXPERIENCE

The use of animation in advertisements has increased in popularity because of computer technology sophistication. Even the Green Giant and the Pillsbury Doughboy are still popular. Each has a Web site. The Green Giant is available at **www.greengiant.com**. Be sure to check out "The Green Giant Around the World." The Doughboy is at **www.doughboy.com**. Notice that Pillsbury created both animations. To get an insight into the mind of an animation creative, read Vince Backeberg's 3D Site at **www.teleport.com/~v3d/index.html**. If you are interested in adding animation to your Web site, or when a business wants to add animation, Animation Factory at **www.camelotdesign.com** contains several thousand free animations. Free animation also is available at the Animation Library at **www.animationlibrary.com**.

▶ **Building Your IMC Campaign exercises.** At the beginning of each chapter, we reference one of the sample IMC programs to illustrate the materials presented in that chapter. At the conclusion of each chapter, students are given an exercise designed to lead them through the development of their own personalized IMC programs, from start to finish. These exercises help students understand chapter materials and apply them to an ongoing company.

▶ **IMC Plan Pro.** Each book contains a CD-ROM disk containing the IMC Plan Pro program. This commercial software produced by Palo Alto software serves as a valuable supplement for students during the course and as a professional tool after graduation.

Using these materials will expose students to an integrated learning package.

THE INSTRUCTOR'S INTEGRATED TEACHING PACKAGE

The best way to teach IMC is with an integrated teaching package. We have prepared all of the supplements to make sure everything works together. The textbook includes the following instructional supplements:

▶ **PowerPoint Presentation.** The PowerPoint presentation features print advertisements, slides that build concepts over several steps, discussion questions, Web links, and video snippets. The print ads not only include ads from the text but also additional ads. The slides, Website links, video clips, and questions form a coherent presentation for the class. The print advertisements are accompanied by questions or captions relating them to the concepts within the chapter. Integrated Learning Experiences take the class to Websites referenced in the text. The end of every chapter's PowerPoint set includes materials regarding the IMC campaign. These files are available on the Instructor's Resource CD-ROM, and a download version may be found on the Companion Website.

NEW

▶ **Website.** The Companion Website contains chapter objectives, faculty resources, and links to company sites referenced in the text. Study guide questions for each chapter are available, and students can receive e-mail results, complete with grade reports, directly from professors. The Companion Website also includes details and information to direct students through the process of building an IMC campaign, and serves as an alternative for those who desire not to use the IMC Plan Pro disk. For faculty, the PowerPoint slides, Instructor's Manual, and other resources may be accessed.

▶ **Instructor's Manual.** This resource provides support and suggestions for instructors. A complete outline is provided for each chapter, including key words and their definitions, important themes, references to text figures, and the Implications for Marketing Professionals materials. Review questions, discussion questions, and application questions are all answered thoroughly by the authors, and the chapter-opening vignettes are also explained. A separate IMC section offers guidance and solutions for the "Building an IMC Campaign" activities.

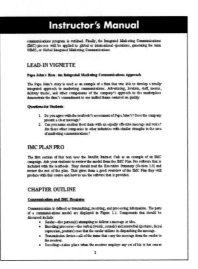

▶ **Test Item File.** A test item file containing over 1,400 true-false, multiple-choice, and short-answer questions is available. It includes page references and difficulty level so that instructors can provide greater feedback to students. The test item file itself is available in print and electronic formats. The new TestGen-EQ test generation software is a computerized package that allows instructors to custom design, save, and generate classroom tests. The test program permits instructors to edit, add, or delete questions from the test bank; analyze test results; and organize a database of tests and student results. The new software allows for greater flexibility and ease of use. It provides many options for organizing and displaying tests, along with a search and sort feature.

▶ **Instructor's Resource CD-ROM.** The Instructor's Resource CD-ROM contains additional presentation materials for instructors to bring into class, including figures from the book, a version of the electronic test bank, and advertisements not found in the text. This is in addition to inclusion of the electronic files for the Instructor's Manual and full PowerPoint Presentation.

▶ **Advertisement transparencies.** Many of the ads shown in the text are reproduced as transparencies, as well as additional ads not found in the text.

▶ **The Prentice-Hall Advertising Video Library.** A video library is available for use in the classroom. Using today's popular news magazine format, students are taken on location and behind closed doors. Each news story profiles a well-known or up-and-coming company leading the way in its industry. Teaching materials to accompany the video library are available on the Companion Website.

ORGANIZATION OF THE TEXTBOOK

Part I: The IMC Foundation

Being heard in a cluttered marketplace is one of the major obstacles most firms face. The past decade has introduced numerous new ways to vend products and many new venues to promote those products. The key to an effective advertising, promotions, and integrated marketing communications program is to develop the one clear voice that will be heard over the din of so many ads and marketing tactics. Meeting this challenge involves bringing together every aspect of the firm's marketing efforts, and having them focus as a team on one message.

Chapter One, Integrated Marketing Communications, presents a basic model of communication and describes how it applies to marketing goods and services. An overview of the entire IMC approach is presented containing four parts: the foundation, advertising tools, promotional tools, and integration tools.

Chapter Two, Corporate Image and Brand Management, describes the elements of corporate image and brand management. The role of the brand name, package, label, company logos, and other branding issues are described.

Chapter Three, Consumer Buyer Behavior, reviews the steps of the consumer buyer behavior process. Individual decision-making models are identified. Tactics to influence buyers are also described.

Chapter Four, Business-to-Business Buyer Behavior, is a presentation of buying decisions made in business-to-business marketing relationships. The roles played by members of the buying center are noted. Methods that can be used to reach individual members are suggested.

Chapter Five, Promotions Opportunity Analysis, discusses the nature of a promotions opportunity analysis program. Market segmentation in consumer and business-to-business settings is also presented.

Part II: IMC Advertising Tools

Chapter Six, Advertising Management, describes the overall process of managing an ad campaign. Selection criteria used in choosing an agency are provided.

Chapter Seven, Advertising Design: Theoretical Frameworks and Types of Appeals, analyzes the various kinds of appeals that can be used in creating ads. Sex, fear, rational approaches, and other methods are noted. Advantages and appropriate usage of each type of appeal is discussed.

Chapter Eight, Advertising Design: Message Strategies and Executional Frameworks, explains the individual executional frameworks that are available, such as the slice-of-life, demonstration, and testimonial forms. Also, sources and spokespersons are analyzed.

Chapter Nine, Advertising Media Selection, completes the advertising section by reviewing the various media that are available, including both more conventional methods such as television and radio as well as more recent venues including the Internet and guerilla marketing programs.

Part III: IMC Promotional Tools

A fully integrated marketing communications program requires the inclusion of other company activities. Many customers are persuaded to make purchases through the use of marketing tactics other than advertising. This is also true in the business-to-business sector. This is the focus of Part Three.

Chapter Ten, Trade Promotions, details the various kinds of trade promotions that are useful to marketing teams. Advantages and costs of each are defined.

Chapter Eleven, Consumer Promotions, notes the connections between consumer promotions, advertisements, and effective IMC programs. Benefits and costs of consumer promotions tactics are identified.

Chapter Twelve, Personal Selling, Database Marketing, and Customer Relationship Management, examines personal selling, database management, and customer relationship management programs. All of these buyer-focused activities must be integrated with other communications that consumers experience.

Chapter Thirteen, Public Relations, Regulations, and Sponsorship Programs, notes the importance of quality public relations efforts and the role of government and industry regulations within the integrated marketing communications plan. Individual sponsorship programs are noted in light of their contributions and costs.

Part IV: IMC Integration Tools

The strings that tie together a complete IMC program include other important marketing activities as well as the assessment of the levels of success of a company's efforts. This final section provides information about the Internet, special concerns for small businesses, and assessment programs.

Chapter Fourteen, Internet Marketing, gives special attention to Internet marketing and e-commerce programs. This form of marketing must be carefully integrated with other company activities.

Chapter Fifteen, IMC for Small Businesses and Entrepreneurial Ventures, is devoted to the special IMC challenges for small businesses and entrepreneurial companies. Limited budgets and limited customer awareness must be overcome to successfully build and sustain a new firm.

Chapter Sixteen, Evaluating an Integrated Marketing Program, is the assessment chapter. Managers who are faced with accountability issues require quality methods for analyzing the effectiveness of their IMC programs. This chapter describes the tools that are available.

ACKNOWLEDGMENTS

We would like to thank the following individuals who assisted in the development of the second edition of this text through their careful and thoughtful reviews:

Robert W. Armstrong, University of North Alabama

Jerome Christa, Coastal Carolina University

Stefanie Garcia, University of Central Florida

Robert J. Gulovsen, Washington University – Saint Louis

Sreedhar Kavil, St. John's University

Tom Laughon, Florida State University

William C. Lesch, University of North Dakota

James M. Maskulka, Lehigh University

Darrel D. Muehling, Washington State University

Esther S. Page-Wood, Western Michigan University

Venkatesh Shankar, University of Maryland

Albert J. Taylor, Austin Peay State University

Jerald Weaver, SUNY—Brockport

We are grateful to these reviewers of the first edition:

Craig Andrews, Marquette University

Ronald Bauerly, Western Illinois University

Mary Ellen Campbell, University of Montana

Les Carlson, Clemson University

Newell Chiesl, Indiana State University

John Cragin, Oklahoma Baptist College

J. Charlene Davis, Trinity University

Steven Edwards, Michigan State University

P. Everett Fergenson, Iona College

James Finch, University of Wisconsin—La Crosse

Thomas Jensen, University of Arkansas

Russell W. Jones, University of Central Oklahoma

Dave Kurtz, University of Arkansas

Monle Lee, Indiana University—South Bend

Ron Lennon, Barry University

Charles L. Martin, Wichita State University

Robert D. Montgomery, University of Evansville

S. Scott Nadler, University of Alabama

Ben Oumlil, University of Dayton

Melodie R. Phillips, Middle Tennessee State University

Don Roy, Middle Tennessee State University

Elise Sautter, New Mexico State University

Janice E. Taylor, Miami University

Robert L. Underwood, Bradley University

Robert Welch, California State University—Long Beach

While there were many individuals who helped us with advertising programs, we want to thank a few who were especially helpful. These include Ethel Uy of the Bozell Advertising Agency for giving us access to the "Got Milk" advertisements. Erin Flowers assisted us with a number of Procter & Gamble product ads, and Cynthia Miller assisted us in obtaining the Bijan advertisements. Cynthia also gave us insights into the work of creatives. Special thanks goes to Kerri Martin of BWM motorcycles and Gretchen Hoag of Publics Technology for taking time to share with us their thoughts concerning their work and the IMC process. And, as mentioned earlier, we are deeply indebted to the staff at the *Joplin Globe* for providing so many local advertisements.

On a personal note, we would like to thank Leah Johnson, who signed us for the first edition of the book. Bruce Kaplan and Katie Stevens are our current editors, and they have rendered insightful opinions and given us a great deal of quality advice as the second edition moved forward. We would also like to thank the entire Prentice Hall production team.

Kenneth Clow would like to thank the secretarial staff at the University of North Carolina at Pembroke and the University of Louisiana at Monroe. Both worked with him to ensure the work on this second edition continued while he was transitioning to a new job. He is especially thankful to his sons Dallas, Wes, Tim, and Roy who always provided encouragement and support.

Donald Baack would like to thank Mimi Morrison for her continual assistance in all his work at Pittsburg State University. Henry Crouch was most gracious in his role of department chair, and Christine Fogliasso has followed him nicely. Both made this work much easier. Dan Baack, his son, also contributed to this work.

We would like to especially thank our wives, Susan Clow and Pam Baack, for being patient and supportive during those times when we were swamped by the work involved in completing this edition. They have been enthusiastic and understanding throughout this entire journey.

Integrated Advertising, Promotion, & Marketing Communications

1 Integrated Marketing Communications

Chapter Objectives

Recognize the critical role communication plays in marketing programs.

Review the nature of the communication process.

Apply a communications model to marketing issues.

Discover the nature of a totally integrated advertising and marketing communications approach.

Expand the concept of integrated marketing communications to the global level.

PAPA JOHN'S PIZZA:

An Integrated Marketing Communications Approach

Would you recognize a Papa John's Pizza sign from a distance? Many people would, given the distinctive green and red emblem and logo, which is designed to attract attention and place the store in a flattering light.

Papa John's began as a small, one-store operation that evolved out of the need to rescue a failing tavern. Quick success meant expansion to 4 stores in two years and 23 stores in five years. Currently, Papa John's plans to complete more than 2,000 units with over $1 billion in sales in a mature industry most felt was saturated with competitors.

In order to survive in a highly competitive marketplace, Papa John's needed to develop a distinctive voice. One clear message was needed to permeate every aspect of the business, including hiring decisions, selection of locations, and all business strategies and tactics.

At the strategic level, each of the Big Three pizza companies—Pizza Hut, Domino's, and Little Caesar's—holds a distinct niche in the market. Pizza Hut offers menu variety and a dine-in atmosphere; Domino's emphasizes quick delivery, and Little Caesar's focuses on price. To establish a contrasting theme, Papa John's strongly centers its efforts on *quality,* including the overall theme of "Better Ingredients, Better Pizza." Owner John Schnatter makes a concerted effort to keep his product "simple, consistent, and focused," by making personal visits to as many locations as possible each year.

In selecting locations, Papa John's tries to purchase prime real estate in prominent locations and then counts on its bright signs and logos to attract attention. As one manager in the organization stated, "We think the customer cares where a store is." The effort to find choice locations reemphasizes quality in every aspect of the organization's operation.

Papa John's hires employees based on their compatibility with an overall organizational attitude. Individuals are selected who are "warm, friendly, and nice," according to one human resource officer. As Susie Southgate-Fox, vice president of human resources, put it, "We can

teach people about food and wine, and how to carry things, but we can't teach someone how to be warm and friendly. These people are not just serving food. They make the difference in whether someone will return to this restaurant."

The pizza itself is the major focus of the quality campaign. The ingredients are developed by key centralized commissaries that provide fresh dough and sauce, with a careful eye on consistency and quality. The final product always includes a small tub of garlic butter and two hot peppers with each pie, which promotes the perception that the customer is getting "more bang for the buck," according to Gerry Durnell, editor and publisher of *Pizza Today.* Papa John's patrons expect quality at a reasonable price. There are no in-store salad bars that add to costs, and the menu is limited to pizza, breadsticks, cheesesticks, and soft drinks.

The Papa John's story is reprinted on the walls of many of its stores. Take-home menus not only circulate to retail customers but also find their way into other businesses, where employees can use them to order a quick, high-quality lunch. The menus have the same colors and logo as the store signs and delivery vehicles that carry the product to homes and other businesses. The hats and uniforms workers wear also carry the logo and emphasize the theme.

Advertisements, employees, locations, logos, hats, uniforms, take-home menus, delivery vehicles, suppliers, and the product itself all combine to form an integrated advertising and marketing communications theme emphasizing quality. The theme clearly works, as witnessed by the firm's phenomenal growth and astounding success. Customers know what they're getting when they dial up Papa John's Pizza.

In the future, Papa John's intends to continue its long-term expansion plans by opening more than 1,000 international units, beginning with stores in Mexico and Canada. Even so, the goal still remains to provide quality. As owner-manager Schnatter states, "I demand consistency so the consumer is not confused."[1]

3

JAVANET INTERNET CAFÉ

The IMC Plan Pro software disk provided with your textbook contains four sample IMC plans as well as the template you will use to design a plan. Each section of this textbook highlights a different sample IMC plan. Section 1 features JavaNet Internet Café's sample plan.

Studying the sample IMC plan with the chapter material will help you learn how to create your own IMC plan while focusing on the information provided in the chapter itself. For example, Chapter 1 notes that an effective integrated marketing communications program begins with the precise assessment of several factors. First, the nature of the company must be clearly understood. Second, the potential customer base must be identified. And third, the key message which is to be delivered to everyone must be established. Everyone includes company employees, suppliers and partners, advertising agencies and other marketing organizations, and customers. These tasks are carried out in the JavaNet Internet Café example.

Read the Executive Summary (Section 1.0) for the JavaNet Internet Café example provided on the IMC Plan Pro disk. JavaNet is an Internet café seeking to take advantage of high quality coffee, combined with quality Internet access, for several distinct consumer groups. This information forms the foundation for what is to follow throughout the plan. Success in building a strong, clear voice for a company starts with knowing who you are, what you do, and how you intend to carry out the plan.

overview

The global marketplace consists of an increasingly complex arena of competitors within a rapidly changing international environment. New companies are formed on a daily basis, from small businesses, to Internet-based operations, to expanding global conglomerates originating from major takeovers and mergers. At the same time, a wide variety of venues beckon company leaders to invest their advertising and marketing dollars. From approaches as simple as using billboards to methods as complex as establishing global Web sites, the number and ways to reach out to customers continually increases.

In the face of these sophisticated and cluttered market conditions, firms try to be heard. They attempt to speak with clear voices about the natures of their operations and the benefits associated with the firm's goods and services. With so many choices available, and so many media bombarding potential customers with messages, it is vital that what should be communicated is reaching buyers in a clear and consistent manner.

Two important consequences emerge from this turbulent new marketing context. First, *accountability* is a primary concern to advertising agencies and for company leaders that hire those agencies. Currently, company leaders recognize that they cannot spend unlimited dollars on marketing and advertising. The funds must be spent wisely, and marketing managers increasingly demand *tangible results* from advertising campaigns. A coupon program, contest, rebate program, or advertising campaign must yield measurable gains in sales, brand awareness, or customer loyalty in order to be considered successful.

The second issue, which is tied to the first, is a change in the nature of the job of *account executive* in advertising agencies and marketing companies. With increasing demands for accountability, the advertising or marketing account manager is now on the hot seat. He or she must respond to the more careful scrutiny placed on individual marketing efforts. As a result, the increased responsibility has generated a new job description for the account manager. Rather than simply serving as a go-between working with the people who prepare commercials and the company, the account manager is increasingly expected to be involved in the strategic development of the marketing plan and to make sure efforts are garnering tangible results.

Another person facing greater accountability is the brand or product manager. The *brand manager* is responsible for the management of a specific brand or line of products. When sales of a brand slow down, it is the responsibility of the brand manager to find ways to boost them. He or she also must coordinate efforts so that every marketing endeavor used to promote the brand speaks with one voice. The brand manager must work diligently to make sure the advertising agency, the trade promotion specialist, the consumer promotion specialist, and any other individual or agency involved conveys the same message to customers. The brand manager must be a master at organizing the activities of many individuals while integrating each marketing campaign.

Previously, creatives were often the most visible individuals in promotional efforts. *Creatives* are the individuals who develop the actual advertising and promotional campaigns. Most creatives are employed by advertising agencies. Others work within individual companies or as freelancers. Creatives have seen their roles change as well, particularly in this era in which attracting attention to a company, product, or service is such a difficult task. Creatives are being asked to contribute to the strategic marketing direction of the firm, to develop effective advertisements, and to share accountability (in both rewards given as bonuses and lost accounts when campaigns fail) with the account manager.

This new partnership between account executives, brand managers, and creatives moves many advertising and marketing agencies into the realm of developing totally integrated communications programs in order to succeed. As the field evolves, this trend toward a more integrated approach to all advertising and marketing communications efforts can be expected to continue. This textbook is devoted to explaining marketing communications from the strategic perspective of the decision makers both inside and outside the firm. Various topics are viewed from the vantage point of the key individuals involved, such as the account manager, brand manager, creative, media buyer, and even the Web master.

In this first chapter, the nature of an integrated advertising and marketing communications program is examined. First, communication processes are described. This process builds the foundation for an integrated marketing program. Then, a totally integrated marketing communications program is outlined. Finally, the integrated marketing communications process is applied to global or international operations, generating the term *GIMC,* or globally integrated marketing communications.

COMMUNICATION AND IMC PROGRAMS

Communication is defined as transmitting, receiving, and processing information. This definition suggests that when a person, group, or organization attempts to transfer an idea or message, the receiver (another person or group) must be able to process that information effectively. Communication occurs when the message that was sent reaches its destination in a form that is understood by the intended audience.[2] A model of communication is shown in Figure 1.1.

An illustration can be useful in demonstrating the communication process used to market a variety of goods and services. Assume someone plans to buy a new pair of athletic shoes. The **senders** are companies that manufacture and sell shoes. New Balance, Asics, Reebok, and Skechers all try to garner the customer's attention. In most cases, these firms hire advertising agencies to construct messages. An account manager serves as a major contact between the shoe company and the ad agency. In other situations the firm may have its own in-house marketing group.

Encoding the message is the second step in the communication of a marketing idea. Someone must take the idea and transform it into an attention-getting form, through an advertisement or some other verbal or nonverbal medium. An advertising *creative* usually performs this role. The shoe advertisements shown are examples of encoding.

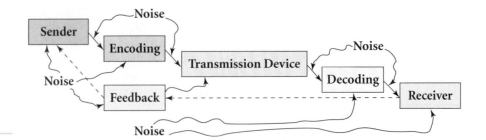

FIGURE 1.1
The Communication Process

Messages travel to audiences through various **transmission devices**. The third stage of the marketing communication process occurs when a channel or medium delivers the message. The channel may be a television carrying an advertisement, a billboard, a Sunday paper with a coupon placed in it, or a letter to the purchasing agent of a large retail store.[3] The shoe ads were transmitted through various magazines.

Decoding occurs when the message touches the receiver's senses in some way. Some consumers will hear and see a television ad. Others will handle and read a coupon offer. It is even possible to "smell" a message. A well-placed perfume sample may entice a buyer to purchase both the magazine containing the sample and the perfume being advertised. Those interested in purchasing shoes pay closer attention to advertisements and other information about shoes such as the brands being offered.

Various advertisements for shoes.
Courtesy of New Balance Athletic Shoes Inc.
Photograph by Paul Wakefield; ASICS Tiger
Corporation; Reebok International; Skechers USA Inc.

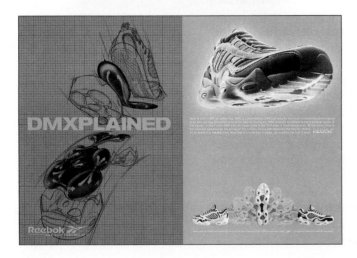

Study the shoe advertisements, then answer the following questions:

1. Which advertisement attracts your attention the most? Why?
2. Which advertisement is the least appealing? Why?
3. How important is the brand name in each ad? Why?
4. What is the major message of each individual advertisement?
5. What makes each advertisement effective or ineffective?
6. Discuss the pros and cons of each advertisement with other students.

Those who discussed the advertisements with other students probably discovered that the same advertisement was interpreted differently by each member of the group. In other words, the message that was decoded may not have been the same one the various companies meant to send. Quality marketing communication occurs when customers (the **receivers**) decode or understand the message as it was intended by the sender. In the case of the shoe ads, effective marketing communications depends upon receivers getting the right message and responding in the desired fashion (shopping, buying, telling their friends about the shoes, etc.).

Examining the Web sites listed in the Integrated Learning Experience provides additional insights into how each company encodes its messages. A comparison of the materials on the Web sites with the shoe advertisements should lead to the conclusion that the two messages go together. If they do not, the IMC program is not completely developed or fully integrated.

INTEGRATED LEARNING EXPERIENCE

How do companies integrate their ads with their Web sites? Access each of the following company Web sites, and compare the appearance and content of the Web site to the shoe advertisements shown both on the site and in this book. Using the communication model presented in Figure 1.1, examine how well they communicate to consumers accessing their site.

Reebok (www.reebok.com)
New Balance (www.newbalance.com)
Asics (www.asicstiger.com)
Skechers (www.skechers.com)

S T O P

There are other difficulties in making certain marketing communications efforts are efficient and effective. In Figure 1.1, notice that **noise** interferes with the communication process. Noise is anything that distorts or disrupts a message. It can occur at any stage in the process. Examples of noise are shown in Figure 1.2.

Between Individuals	Between Companies
▶ Age	▶ Poor selling techniques
▶ Gender	▶ Unfocused advertising
▶ Social status	▶ Poor media choices
▶ Personality	▶ Failure to find correct contact persons

Within Companies

▶ Poor downward flow (orders, procedures)
▶ Poor lateral flow (communication between departments)
▶ Poor upward flow (computers, telephone systems, intranet systems)
▶ Information not stored for future use or poor retrieval system

FIGURE 1.2
Barriers to Communication

Feedback takes the forms of purchases, inquiries, complaints, questions, visits to the store, and hits on a Web site. Each indicates the message has reached the receiver and that the receiver is now responding.

The most common form of noise in the marketing communication process is **clutter**. Modern consumers are exposed to hundreds of marketing messages per day. Most are tuned out. Clutter includes:

▶ Eight minutes of commercials per half hour of television and radio programs

▶ A Sunday newspaper jammed with advertising supplements

▶ An endless barrage of billboards on a major street

▶ The inside of a bus or subway car papered with ads

▶ Web sites and servers loaded with commercials

Account managers, creatives, brand managers, and others involved in the marketing process must effectively utilize the communications model displayed in Figure 1.1. They constantly must work to make sure that the proper audiences receive their messages, while encountering as little noise as possible. In the case of athletic shoes, increases in market share, sales, and brand loyalty are common outcomes the marketing team tries to achieve.

Communication with consumers and other businesses requires more than simply creating attractive advertisements. In the next section, the nature of a fully developed integrated marketing communications program is described. An effective IMC process integrates numerous marketing activities into a single package, making it possible for companies to reach their target markets and other audiences more effectively.

INTEGRATED MARKETING COMMUNICATIONS

An integrated marketing communications program is based on the foundation provided by the communications model. Some marketing scholars argue that the integrated marketing communications (IMC) approach is a recent phenomenon. Others suggest the name is new, but the concept has been around for a long time. They note that the importance of effectively coordinating all marketing functions and promotional activities has been described in the marketing literature for many years.[4]

Although IMC programs have been described in several ways, the consensus is to define them as follows: **Integrated marketing communications (IMC)** is the coordination and integration of all marketing communication tools, avenues, and sources within a company into a seamless program that maximizes the impact on consumers and other end users at a minimal cost. This integration affects all of a firm's business-to-business, marketing channel, customer-focused, and internally directed communications.

Before further examining the IMC concept, it is helpful to consider the traditional framework of marketing from which it originated. The **marketing mix** is the starting point for such an analysis. As shown in Figure 1.3, promotion is one of the four components of the mix that contains another series of marketing functions. Traditionally, promotional activities include advertising, sales promotions, and personal selling activities. The sales promotion area normally includes both sales and trade promotions, with sales promotions

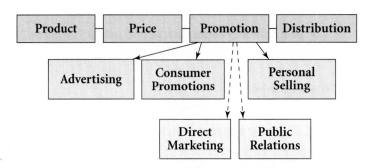

FIGURE 1.3
Traditional Marketing Mix

aimed at end users or consumers of goods and services and trade promotions directed toward distributors and retailers. Within the context of promotions, some add direct-marketing and public relations programs, as depicted in Figure 1.3. Others include them within the three major components of advertising, sales promotions, and personal selling.

An IMC plan begins with the development and coordination of the marketing mix, elements of prices, products, distribution methods, and promotions. This textbook primarily deals with the promotions component of the marketing mix. Keep in mind, however, that to present a unified message the four elements of the marketing mix must blend together.

AN INTEGRATED MARKETING COMMUNICATIONS PLAN

Integrated marketing begins with the development of a master marketing plan. The marketing plan is the basis of the total integrated communication design. The plan provides for the coordination of efforts in all components of the marketing mix. The purpose of the plan is to achieve harmony in relaying messages to customers and other publics. Planning also should integrate all key promotional efforts, which in turn keeps the company's total communication program in synch.

Figure 1.4 lists the primary steps required to complete a marketing plan. The first step is a *situational analysis,* which is the process of examining factors from the organization's internal and external environments. The analysis identifies external environmentally-generated marketing problems and opportunities; internal company strengths and weaknesses are also considered during this step. When the situation is fully understood, the second step is to define primary *marketing objectives.* These objectives normally are spelled out in the areas of sales, market share, competitive position, and desired customer actions. Based on these marketing objectives, a *marketing budget* is prepared and *marketing strategies* are finalized. The marketing strategies include the ingredients of the marketing mix plus all positioning, differentiation, and branding strategies the firm wants to use. From these strategies, *marketing tactics* emerge to guide the day-by-day steps necessary to support marketing strategies. The final step in the marketing plan is the *evaluation of performance.* These six steps are similar to those prescribed by management strategists attempting to integrate all company activities into one consistent effort. When properly designed and followed, they provide guidance to company leaders and marketing experts as they try to make certain the firm's total communications package is fully integrated.

Once the marketing plan has been established, the firm can prepare its integrated marketing communications program. This textbook's prime goal is to demonstrate this process. Figure 1.5 illustrates this view of the IMC model.

IMC COMPONENTS

Figure 1.5 outlines the topics presented in the remainder of this textbook. A brief description of each aspect of IMC follows. As shown, the foundation of an IMC program consists of careful consideration of the company's image as well as the buyers to be served and the markets in which they are located. Advertising programs build on this foundation, as do the other elements of the promotional mix. Finally, the integration tools located at

▶ **Situation analysis**

▶ **Marketing objectives**

▶ **Marketing budget**

▶ **Marketing strategies**

▶ **Marketing tactics**

▶ **Evaluation of performance**

FIGURE 1.4
The Marketing Plan

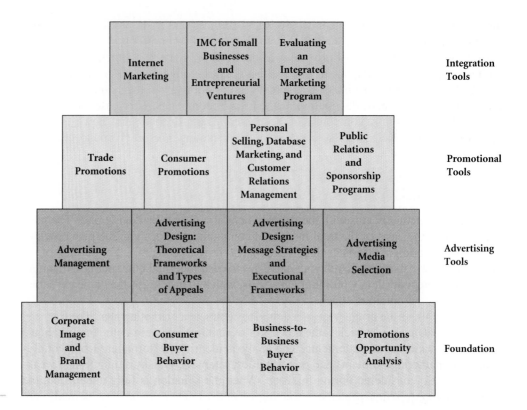

FIGURE 1.5
An IMC Plan

the peak of the pyramid help the company's marketing team make certain that all of the elements within the plan are consistent and effective.

The Foundation

The first section of this text builds the foundation for an effective IMC program. Chapter 2 describes the *corporate image* and *brand management* elements. Strengthening the firm's image and brands answers the key question, "Who are we?" From there it is possible to identify target markets.

Chapter 3 examines *consumer buyer behavior.* The steps of the purchasing process can be used to explain how individuals make choices. Marketers identify which motives lead to purchase decisions and which factors affect those decisions. Then, the IMC program can be designed in a manner which best influences consumer choices.

Chapter 4 identifies *business-to-business buyer behavior.* Knowing how to reach purchasing managers and other decision makers within target businesses is another critical element in the development of a totally integrated communications plan. Discovering viable business-to-business marketing opportunities plays a vital role in maintaining a fully developed IMC plan.

Chapter 5 describes the *promotions opportunity analysis* element of the IMC program. This task includes identifying all target markets. Consumer market segments are often distinguished by demographics, income, social class, and various psychographic variables. Business markets can also be segmented by understanding the demographics of the company's buying team, noting who the end users will be, as well as by determining the benefits other businesses expect to receive from the products and services they buy.

Advertising Tools

The second section of this text is devoted to advertising issues. *Advertising management,* as described in Chapter 6, addresses the major functions of advertising and directs the general path the company will take. Media selection and advertising design (Chapters 7 through 9) involve matching the message, media, and audience, so that the right people see and/or hear the ads. Many appeals can be used, including those oriented toward fear, humor, sex, music, and logic. These should be conveyed by attractive, credible, likable, and authoritative sources. Effective advertising is based on the foundation built by understanding consumer buyer behaviors and business buyer behaviors. Advertising must reinforce or project a specific brand and firm image, which evolves out of the marketing plan at the center of the IMC process.

Promotional Tools

The next level of activity includes the more traditional marketing elements of trade promotions, consumer promotions, and personal selling. When marketing managers carefully design all of the steps taken up to this point, the firm is in a better position to integrate consumer and trade promotions in conjunction with personal selling tactics. Messages presented in the advertising campaign can be reinforced in the trade and consumer promotions. *Trade promotions,* as described in Chapter 10, include contests, incentives, vendor support programs, and other fees and discounts that help the retailer promote the product. *Consumer promotions* are directly oriented to end users and include coupons, contests, premiums, refunds, rebates, free samples, and so forth. The advertisement for Papa John's pizza illustrates the use of consumer promotions. Consumer promotions are the subject of Chapter 11. Chapter 12 reviews *personal selling* techniques. The goal is to fully integrate all communications so that advertising messages are repeated and reinforced by the sales staff. Chapter 13 examines *public relations* and *sponsorship programs.*

The use of consumer promotion by Papa John's.
Source: Courtesy of Papa John's International.

Integration Tools

The "top" level of the IMC program includes all of the integration tools needed to make sure all customers are effectively being served. Chapter 14 explains the nature of *Internet marketing* in terms of e-commerce activities and other functions that can be performed online. Chapter 15 is devoted to *small businesses* and *entrepreneurial ventures.* All of the IMC tasks are included in managing a small business, however, the emphasis changes due to special challenges such as limited funds for promotions.

The last chapter (16) in this textbook explains how to *evaluate an integrated marketing program.* It is vital to make decisions about how a communication program will be evaluated *prior to* any promotional campaign so materials may be designed accordingly. A promotional evaluation process holds everything together and drives the entire IMC process as much as does developing the core business plan. Fully integrated marketing requires a careful linkage between planning and evaluation processes; one cannot occur without the other.

The Internet is an important communication tool for companies such as WeddingChannel.com.
Source: Courtesy of Wedding Channel.com.

INTEGRATED MARKETING COMMUNICATIONS

Morals, Ethics, and IMC

Morals are beliefs or principles that individuals hold concerning what is right and what is wrong. **Ethics** are principles that serve as guidelines for both individuals and organizations. Marketing and marketing communications are activities in which ethics and morals must play key roles.

In each chapter of this textbook, key ethical issues will be described. At the most general level, there are several major ethical concerns which have been raised regarding marketing programs. These are:

1. Marketing causes people to buy more than they can afford.
2. Marketing overemphasizes materialism.
3. Marketing increases the costs of goods and services.
4. Advertising perpetuates stereotyping of males, females, and various minorities.
5. Marketers create offensive advertisements.
6. Marketing creates advertisements linked to bad habits and intimate subjects.
7. Marketers use unfair tactics.
8. Marketers prepare deceptive and misleading advertisements.
9. Advertising of professional services is unethical.
10. Advertising to children is unethical.
11. Salespeople use too many deceptive practices.

While reading about the nature of an IMC program, consider these ethical issues. As part of a career in marketing, employees may be forced to deal with many of these criticisms. The time to start thinking about an ethical and moral basis for work is now.

Refining the IMC Program

Integrated marketing communications is more than a plan or a simple marketing function. IMC should be an overall organizational process. To be successful, every part of the marketing operation must be included. Organizations that have not developed an IMC approach will discover that it takes time to get things established. A study by American Productivity & Quality Center of Houston of the best integrated marketing firms indicates that four stages are involved in cultivating an integrated marketing communications system.[5]

The first stage is to identify, coordinate, and manage all forms of external communication. The objective is to bring all of the company's brands and strategic business units or divisions under one umbrella. During this stage of IMC development, the firm needs to be sure all advertisements, brochures, and promotional materials use the same logos, colors, and themes, as was the case in the Papa John's Pizza program noted at the beginning of this chapter. Effort must be made to coordinate all advertising and public relations activities. These programs should be integrated with sales promotions, direct-marketing efforts, and all other external marketing programs.

In the second stage, the firm's goal must be to extend the scope of communication to include everyone touched by the organization. Thus, all external communications should mesh with internal messages sent to employees and departments. External contacts made during public relations events or with outside advertising agencies must be consistent with what is being communicated internally. This spreads the IMC umbrella over all the groups that have contact with the firm and includes employees along with every external organization, such as distributors, retailers, dealers, product package designers, and so forth.

An advertisement by Guess directed toward females using a partially nude male.

An advertisement by Guess directed toward males using sexual suggestiveness.

Technology comes to the forefront in the third stage. Firms begin to apply information technology to their IMC programs. Databases must be developed summarizing each customer's activities, purchases, and interactions with the company. This step is critical to the development of an IMC program because now customer input is being gathered. This vital information becomes part of the overall IMC decision-making process.

The last stage of IMC development occurs when the organization treats IMC as an investment and not a departmental function. Firms reaching this stage, such as Dow Chemical, FedEx, and Hewlett-Packard, take these databases and use them to calculate and establish a customer value for each of their customers. The companies recognize that not all customers are equal. In contrast to a typical marketing program designed to win customers by sending the same marketing message to each one, Dow Chemical, FedEx, and Hewlett-Packard are able to allocate sales and marketing communication resources to those customers with the greatest potential for return, based on previous calculations of customer values. This process helps them understand each customer's worth and treat each individual as a unique customer.

Other noteworthy aspects of IMC programs emerged from the American Productivity & Quality Center's study.[6]

Source: Courtesy of PhotoEdit. Photograph by Michael Newman.

We're about to reveal a Saturn trade secret. But first, raise your right hand and repeat after us, "I promise that what I'm about to hear will stay with me for the rest of my life." Promise? Okay, here goes: Treat people the same way you would like to be treated.

Which got us to thinking one day, what would a service area be without pinups?

Not *those* pinups, but rather pictures of Saturn owners. That way, when people brought their cars in for an oil change or something, we'd be able to place a name with a face.

Think about it. *Hey you* is not exactly the most endearing greeting, especially to someone who took the time to shop at your place and who spent their hard-earned money on one of your cars. *Hi, Yvonne* or *Hi, Steve* doesn't seem like it would be asking too much. It's certainly how we would like to be greeted if we were bringing in our car. Of course, it would go even further if our name were Steve, but hopefully you get the point.

A DIFFERENT KIND of COMPANY. A DIFFERENT KIND of CAR.

Saturn's theme of building relationships with customers is directed to both external and internal publics.

The best companies worked hard at developing both interpersonal and cross-functional communications. Not only was communication opened up within the typical marketing department, but communication lines were opened between the marketing department and other functional departments. Every employee in the company became a part of the communication and customer orientation.

To make sure that customer input is obtained outside of compiling databases, the best IMC companies involved customers in their planning processes. Consumer goods companies invited consumers and business-to-business firms invited target members of other businesses. As a result, the potentially adversarial relationship between buyers and sellers was replaced with a cooperative, "let's work together" mentality.

The final facet present in successful IMC companies was their understanding of the natures of their customers. These firms took the stance that customers should be considered customers of the whole company, not just the SBU, operating division, or outlet in which they are doing business. Seeing a patron as a customer of the total company encourages the cross-selling of goods and services. This approach allows a firm such as ServiceMaster, which provides janitorial services to various companies, to cross-sell various pest control and lawn services to those same organizations. This mode of thinking suggests selling across countries when the firm is a multinational operation. Thus, a customer who buys from Hewlett-Packard in the United States is an excellent prospect in other countries where both companies are operating businesses. When firms think in these terms, they are able to spend marketing dollars wisely. When company leaders fail to grasp this concept, they often spend additional marketing dollars in order to gain new customers.

INTEGRATED LEARNING EXPERIENCE

STOP

The American Productivity & Quality Center has uncovered many leading-edge practices in the areas of sales, marketing, and integrated communications. Examine what it considers to be the best practices under the "Sales and Marketing at APQC" section at (**www.apqc.org**). Also examine the Web sites of Dow Chemical (**www.dow.com**), FedEx (**www.fedex.com**), and Hewlett-Packard (**www.hp.com**) to see why the American Productivity & Quality Center considers them excellent examples of firms using the IMC approach.

THE VALUE OF IMC PLANS

Why are IMC programs so crucial to marketing success? Figure 1.6 shows several items that are linked to the increasing importance of integrated advertising and marketing communications programs. The major force compelling firms to seek greater integration of advertising and marketing communications is *information technology.* Computers, the World Wide Web, and telecommunications are swiftly moving the

COMMUNICATION ACTION

Hewlett-Packard

An excellent example of an integrated marketing communications program is provided by the software systems engineering division (SESD) of Hewlett-Packard. This group initiated its IMC process through workshops designed to help HP's employees better understand the dilemmas faced by its customers. These workshops were directed by representatives from sales, product marketing, engineering, and customer support departments within HP. Each had a different perspective of the customer and provided valuable input into the various dilemmas faced by end users. The team approach allowed everyone to see the customer from a more holistic perspective.

Based on input from these departments, a creative strategy emerged with a strong focus on customer needs. The theme "we understand" was adopted. HP's marketing emphasis centered on the idea that members of the company understood the issues, pressures, and constraints that software developers faced. Knowing about unrealistic deadlines, hidden-code errors, and other problems and how to cope with these issues was the key. HP's leaders believed they could solve transition problems for customers by moving to object-oriented programming and simultaneously developing multiple applications of company software. The theme was integrated into all of HP's marketing programs. It was launched in an advertising campaign, then reinforced in three direct mailings. The same message was used in trade show handouts and displays. HP's Web site was redesigned around the same principle.

The "we understand" idea served as an umbrella that all marketing strategies and tactics would then utilize. The integrated approach allowed HP to speak with one voice regardless of the communication method customers encountered when they contacted the firm. This more fully integrated program was more than just the theme, however. It began with effective communication within and built outward to the point where HP's end users (other business) could see and experience a real difference in the products and services that were being provided.

Source: P. Griffeth Lindell, "You Need an Integrated Attitude to Develop IMC," *Marketing News,* 31, no. 11 (May 26, 1997), p. 6.

---

world into an information age where businesses and most consumers have access to an abundance of marketing information. The challenge for marketers in the future is not gathering information, but rather sifting through an avalanche of statistics, ideas, and messages and putting them together in a format company leaders can use. When this is accomplished, business leaders are better able to make intelligent, informed decisions about how to market products.

Technology makes it possible not only for companies to study customers but also for customers to study companies. In addition, quality information technology provides numerous other advantages and opportunities.

▶ **Development of information technology**

▶ **Changes in channel power**

▶ **Increase in competition (global competitors)**

▶ **Maturing markets**

▶ **Brand parity**

▶ **Integration of information by consumers**

▶ **Decline in effectiveness of mass-media advertising**

FIGURE 1.6
Factors Affecting the Value of IMC Programs

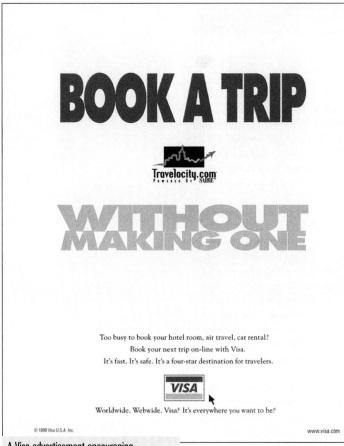

A Visa advertisement encouraging consumers to book vacations over the Internet.

Source: Courtesy of Visa USA Inc. © 1999 Visa USA Inc. All Rights Reserved. Used by Permission.

Information Technology

Technology allows instant communications between business executives and their employees, even when workers are dispersed throughout the world. Through computer technology, huge amounts of data and information about customers can quickly be gathered. Advanced statistical software helps analyze these data files in a matter of hours or even minutes. Because of the connections between financial (credit card, banking) and business firms, purchasing data can easily be collected. Using this information, demographic and psychographic information about consumers can be correlated with the items they buy, when they make purchases, and where they make purchases. Marketers can quickly determine who is buying a company's products and identify the best communication channels to reach those customers.

In the past, predicting the purchasing behaviors of consumers was accomplished by using test markets, attitudinal research, and intention-to-buy surveys. Although these methods are excellent means of obtaining information about consumers, they often are slow, costly, and sometimes inaccurate.

Today, predicting purchase behavior is more accurate because of the development of the UPC (universal product code) bar coding system and point-of-purchase systems. This technology was originally used to help control and evaluate inventory requirements. With computer scanning of every sale, retailers have been able to develop an inventory control system that did not rely as heavily on human counting of merchandise. Stockrooms were reduced and, in some cases, eliminated altogether as retailers shifted from stocking merchandise to selling merchandise.

Changes in Channel Power

Technological developments also served as catalysts for changes in channel power.[7] Typical market channels are:

Producer → Wholesaler → Retailer → Consumer

and

Producer → Business Agent → Business Merchant → Business User

With the advancement of the World Wide Web and information technology, the power is expected to shift more to the consumer.[8] Currently, consumers can obtain information about products and services from their homes or businesses and purchase almost anything over the Internet. For example, the VISA advertisement in this section encourages consumers to book hotel rooms, air travel, and car rentals over the Internet. The sale of products through the Internet has grown at a tremendous rate. In fact, beginning in 1997 these sales doubled three years in a row. In 1998, the Internet generated over $300 billion worth of business in the U.S. economy alone. Sales of books, automobiles, and other goods and services account for approximately one percent of the GDP in the United States.[9]

To illustrate the impact of this change on the channel members, suppose an individual is in the market for a new stereo. First she goes to the Internet and searches for information. She then identifies several possible brands and narrows them down to three. Next she travels to a local mall and investigates the three brands. Asking questions of the salesclerks helps her gather additional product information. Going home, she then logs onto the Web sites of the three manufacturers to learn about warranties and company policies. Having gathered sufficient information to make a decision, she can utilize Internet sources or a catalog to finalize the purchase either via the Web or by telephone. Within three days, the new stereo arrives complete with a money-back guarantee if she is not satisfied.

The same process applies to business-to-business purchasing activities. Buyers who shop on behalf of organizations, and other company members seeking business-to-business services, will be able to tap into the same resources (Web sites, databases) to help them make purchasing decisions. The same type of shift in channel power is likely to take place in the business-to-business sector.

Increases in Competition

Information technology has dramatically changed the marketplace in other ways. Consumers can purchase goods and services from anywhere in the world. Competition no longer comes from the company just down the street—it can come from a firm 10,000 miles away that can supply a product faster and cheaper. People want quality, but they also want low price. The company that delivers on both quality and price gets the business, regardless of location, because advancements in logistics make it possible for purchases to arrive almost anywhere in a matter of days.

In this type of mature market, the only way one firm can gain sales is to take customers away from another firm. Integrating advertising and other marketing communications becomes extremely important in such an environment. Advertising alone is not enough to maintain sales. This situation is further complicated for manufacturers when retailers hold stronger channel power and control the flow of merchandise to consumers. In that situation, manufacturers have to invest in trade promotions (dealer incentives, slotting allowances, discounts, etc.) to keep their products in various retail outlets. Encouraging retailers to promote a manufacturer's brand or prominently display it for consumer viewing requires even greater promotional dollars. Manufacturers also must invest heavily in consumer promotions to keep end users loyal to their companies and encourage them to purchase their brands because they know that the more they promote their own products, the more attractive those products become to retailers.

At the same time, retailers, equipped with scanner data, are quick to pull the plug on promotions that don't work.[10] To gain prominence for a product at the retail level requires a manufacturer to coordinate all advertising, trade promotions, and sales promotions as part of a larger integrated marketing communications effort. Retailers must also focus on IMC efforts to maintain customer loyalty to their stores and to maintain positive relationships with manufacturers. The net result is a strong case for the importance of understanding and creating a quality IMC program, at every level of the marketing chain.

Because of increased competition, medical centers such as Georgetown must use television advertising to promote health services.

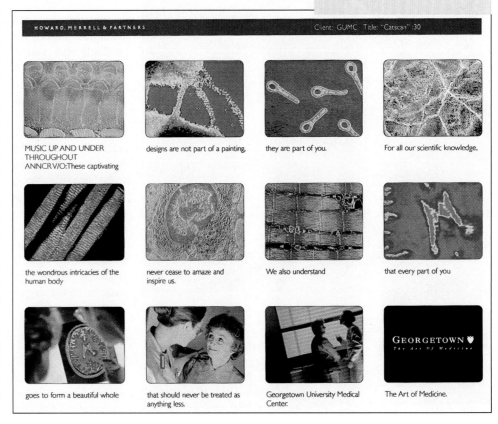

HOWARD, MERRELL & PARTNERS · Client: GUMC Title: "Catscan" :30

MUSIC UP AND UNDER THROUGHOUT
ANNCR V/O:These captivating

designs are not part of a painting,

they are part of you.

For all our scientific knowledge,

the wondrous intricacies of the human body

never cease to amaze and inspire us.

We also understand

that every part of you

goes to form a beautiful whole

that should never be treated as anything less.

Georgetown University Medical Center.

GEORGETOWN ♥
The Art Of Medicine

The Art of Medicine.

Brand Parity

The increase in national and global competition has resulted in multiple brands being available, and many of these products have nearly identical benefits for consumers. When consumers believe that many brands offer the same set of attributes, the result is called **brand parity**. From the consumer's perspective, this means shoppers will purchase from a *group* of accepted brands rather than one specific brand. When brand parity is present, quality is often not a major concern because consumers believe there are only minor quality differences among brands. If consumers view quality levels of products to be the same, they often base purchase decisions on other criteria such as price, availability, or a specific promotional deal. The net effect is that brand loyalty has experienced a steady decline.[11] This decline in brand loyalty is partly due to the proliferation of product choices.

In response, marketers must generate messages in a voice that expresses a clear difference. They must build some type of perceived brand superiority for their company and its products or services. They must convince consumers that their product or service is not the same as the competition's. A quality IMC program is, in part, designed to help regain the benefits of a strong brand name.

Integration of Information

In today's marketplace, consumers have a variety of choices regarding how they interpret information sent by a firm. There are many ways in which consumers can integrate the information they receive about various goods and services.[12]

Consumers now have the opportunity to obtain additional information. They may go to the Internet and read about companies and their competitors. Realizing this, many companies now list their Internet addresses on their advertisements to encourage consumers to visit their Web sites. In the McCormick's ad notice their address www.mccormick.com. The Web site contains additional information about McCormick seasonings along with ideas and recipes for consumers. Web users can discuss products and companies in chat rooms with other consumers to get other viewpoints. They may travel to a retail store and discuss various options with a salesclerk or consult independent sources of information such as *Consumer Reports*.

It is logical to conclude that because consumers integrate information they receive, marketers should also be concerned about integration. Company leaders need to make sure that every contact point projects the same message. **Contact points** are the places in which a customer may interact with or acquire additional information about a firm. These points may be direct or indirect, planned or unplanned. An effective IMC program seeks to establish a consistent message about the nature of the company, its products, and the benefits that result from making a purchase from the organization.

Decline in the Effectiveness of Mass-Media Advertising

In the past decade, the influence of mass-media advertising on the public has dramatically declined. Inventions such as the VCR and cable television now make it possi-

Many companies such as McCormick now list their Web addresses on advertisements to encourage customers to visit company Web sites.
Source: Courtesy of McCormick & Co., Inc.

YOUR CLIENT CUT YOUR DEADLINE.
AT LEAST DINNER CAN GO ON AS PLANNED.

CHICKEN DIJON

Delicious Dijon sauce. Savory chicken breasts. All the makings of a mouth-watering meal, in just 25 minutes. So no matter what they do at work, it won't hurt your dinner plans. Look for it in our color-coded Meal Idea Center. For more chicken ideas, look for the yellow packages or click to www.mccormick.com.

McCormick
The taste you trust

Positive Responses

▶ **Get amused by the ads (26%)**

▶ **Sit and watch commercials (19%)**

Negative Responses

▶ **Get annoyed at the number of ads (52%)**

▶ **Get up and do something else (45%)**

▶ **Switch channels (39%)**

▶ **Talk to others in the room (34%)**

▶ **Turn down the sound on TV (19%)**

▶ **Read (11%)**

▶ **Use the computer (5%)**

FIGURE 1.7
Viewer Activities During TV Commercials

Source: Jennifer Lach, "Commercial Overload," *American Demographics,* 21, no. 9 (September 1999), p. 20.

ble for consumers to watch programs without commercials. They can record shows and zap out advertisements. Using the remote while watching television means it is likely that, during the commercial, the consumer is surfing through other channels to see what else is on. Thus, many television advertisements are not seen, even by people watching a particular program. In a recent survey conducted by Roper Starch Worldwide, only 19 percent of viewers stated that they watch commercials during a program. Figure 1.7 identifies the results of this Roper research. The rise in popularity of cable TV and satellite dishes means consumers have a wider variety of viewing choices. As a result, the number of people tuned to the major national networks has declined.[13] To help overcome this problem, it is vital to integrate all market communications with advertising tactics.[14]

Many firms use advertising agencies to assist in their marketing efforts, therefore, it is helpful to examine how these agencies have addressed the issue of IMC. Until 1970, almost all advertising agencies focused only on the advertising aspect of marketing. Currently, many advertising agencies are spending substantial amounts of time assisting clients in the development of integrated marketing communication programs.[15] In addition to developing advertisements, many advertising agencies help create consumer promotion materials and direct-marketing programs, along with other types of marketing communications. As integration within a company occurs, more advertising agencies are working across a company's strategic business units to carefully integrate and coordinate every aspect of the marketing effort.

INTEGRATED LEARNING EXPERIENCE

Information is one key to developing a successful integrated marketing communications program. Two valuable sources for marketers are the Web sites of Roper Starch Worldwide at **www.roper.com** and BrandEra at **www.brandera.com**. By accessing the "In the News" section along with the press releases, you can read recent consumer research reports prepared by Roper Starch Worldwide. Although many research projects are proprietary, others have been released to the public and are available to you. At the BrandEra.com Web site, in the "Daily Digest" section, the BrandEra staff provides a brief synopsis and critique of recent news events in marketing. The division of these sections into three categories—creatives, marketers, and advertisers—makes it possible to keep up with recent news events in each specific area.

There's one thing AT&T international long distance customers will never have to worry about.

These days, things seem to go obsolete before you can get them out of the box.
Not so with AT&T International Long Distance. We're continually upgrading our Worldwide Intelligent Network, before you have time to even think about it.
When we saw that global events were affecting telephone traffic, we expanded our Network Operations Center. Now events are continually monitored 24 hours a day, and traffic is routed accordingly.
We also anticipated the growing demand for international voice, data and fax transmission, by developing the first transpacific and transatlantic fiber-optic cable systems.
© 1989 AT&T

So you'll enjoy fast international connections with unsurpassed clarity.
We could list other examples of advances you'll never have to think about.
But why not call 1 800 222-0400 ext.1277, and let the innovations speak for themselves.

AT&T
The right choice.

An advertisement by AT&T directed to international long-distance customers.

GLOBALLY INTEGRATED MARKETING COMMUNICATIONS

The same trend that exists among advertising agencies in the United States also occurs in the international arena. Instead of being called IMC, however, it is known as GIMC, or a globally integrated marketing communications program.[16] The goal is still the same—to coordinate marketing efforts. The challenges are greater due to larger national and cultural differences in target markets.

In the past, marketers could employ two different strategies for global companies. One was to *standardize the product and message* across countries. The goal of this approach was generating economies of scale in production while creating a global product using the same promotional theme. The language would be different, but the basic marketing message would be the same.

The second approach to global marketing was called **adaptation**. Products and marketing messages were designed for and adapted to individual countries. Thus, the manner in which a product was marketed in France was different than in Italy, India, or Australia.

The GIMC approach is easier to apply when a company has relied on the **standardization** method; however, GIMC can and should be used with either adaptation or standardization.[17] To reduce costs, careful coordination of marketing efforts should occur across countries. Even when a firm uses the adaptation strategy, marketers can learn from each other. Members of every company's marketing department should not feel like they have to reinvent the wheel. Synergy can occur between countries. More important, learning can occur. As telecommunications continue to expand, contacts between peoples of different countries are much more frequent, even when inadvertent. A commercial targeted for customers in France may be viewed by citizens of Spain because of satellite technologies. It is advisable to transmit a consistent theme, even when there are differences in local messages.

In terms of marketing, perhaps the best philosophy to follow is "think globally but act locally." As noted previously, in order to fully utilize the power of GIMC, marketing messages should be designed with a global theme in mind, so the same general message is heard throughout the world. At the same time, when marketers design or encode messages for local markets, they need to have the freedom to tailor or alter the message so that it fits the local culture and the target market. In other words, Pepsi may wish to portray a global image around a theme of "Generation Next," but how the final message is conveyed to each country often varies. Development of a GIMC is the final extension to an IMC plan. With its completion, companies are able to compete more effectively both at home and abroad.

SUMMARY

A new era is evolving in the fields of advertising, promotions, and marketing communications. Marketing departments and advertising agencies, as well as individual account managers, brand managers, and creatives are encountering stronger pressures to be accountable for expenditures of marketing communications dollars. Company leaders expect tangible results from promotional campaigns and other marketing programs. As a result, new partnerships form between account executives, creatives, and the companies that hire them. The duties of the account manager have expanded in the direction of a more strategically oriented approach to the advertising and marketing communications. Those preparing to become advertising or promotions professionals must be aware of both accountability issues and the new aspects of these jobs.[18]

Communication is transmitting, receiving, and processing information. It is a two-way street in which a sender must establish a clear connection with a receiver. Effective communication is the glue holding the relationship between two firms together. When communication breaks down, conflicts, misunderstandings, and other problems may develop between those same organizations.

The components of the communication process include the sender, an encoding process, the transmission device, the decoding process, and the receiver. Noise is anything that distorts or disrupts the flow of information from the sender to the receiver.

In the marketing arena, senders are companies seeking to transmit ideas to consumers, employees, other companies, retail outlets, and others. Encoding devices are the means of transmitting information, and include advertisements, public relations efforts, press releases, sales activities, promotions, and a wide variety of additional verbal and nonverbal cues sent out to receivers. Transmission devices are the media and spokespersons who carry the message. Decoding occurs when the receivers (customers, retailers, etc.) encounter the message. Noise takes many forms in marketing, most notably the clutter of an overabundance of messages in every available channel.

Integrated marketing communications (IMC) takes advantage of the effective management of the communications channel. Within the marketing mix of products, prices, distribution systems, and promotions, firms that speak with one clear voice are able to coordinate and integrate all marketing tools. The goal is to have a strong positive impact on consumers, businesses, and other end users.

IMC plans are vital to achieve success. Reasons for their importance begin with the explosion of information technologies. Changes in channel power have shifted from manufacturers to retailers and in the future to consumers. Firms must adjust in order to maintain a strong market standing, and IMC programs can assist in this effort. New levels of competition drive marketers to better understand their customers and be certain those end users are hearing a clear and consistent message from the firm. As consumers develop a stronger sense of brand parity, whereby no real differences in product-service quality are perceived, marketers must recreate a situation in which their brand holds a distinct advantage over others. This is difficult, because consumers now can collect and integrate information about products from a wide variety of sources, including technological outlets (Internet Web sites) and interpersonal (sales reps) sources. Quality IMC programs help maintain the strong voice companies need to be certain their messages are heard. An additional challenge is the decline in effectiveness of mass-media advertising. IMC helps company leaders find new ways to contact consumers with a unified message.

When a firm is involved in an international setting, a GIMC, or globally integrated marketing communications system, can be of great value. By developing one strong theme and then adapting that theme to individual countries, the firm conveys a message that integrates international operations into a more coherent package.

The majority of this text explains the issues involved in establishing an effective IMC program. The importance of business-to-business marketing efforts is noted, because many firms market their wares as much to other companies as they do to consumers. Successful development of an IMC program should help firms remain profitable and vibrant, even when the complexities of the marketplace make these goals much more difficult to reach.

REVIEW QUESTIONS

1. Define *communication*. Why does it play such a crucial role in business?

2. What are the parts of an individual human communications model?

3. Who are the typical senders in marketing communications? Who are the typical receivers?

4. Name the transmission devices, both human and nonhuman, that carry marketing messages. How can the human element become a problem?

5. Define *clutter*. Name some of the standard forms in marketing communications.

6. Define *integrated marketing communications*.

7. What are the four parts of the marketing mix?

8. What steps are required to write a marketing plan?

9. Describe a promotional analysis.

10. Describe firm and brand image.

11. What are the three main components of advertising?

12. Why has the growth of information technology made IMC programs so important for marketing efforts?

13. What reasons were given to explain the growth of IMC plans and their importance?

14. What is channel power? How has it changed in the past few decades?

15. What is brand parity? How is it related to successful marketing efforts?

16. What is a GIMC? Why is it important for multinational firms?

17. What is the difference between *standardization* and *adaptation* in GIMC programs?

18. How has the job of an advertising account executive changed? How has the job of a creative changed? How has the job of a brand manager changed? How do the three jobs interact in this new environment?

KEY TERMS

communication transmitting, receiving, and processing information.

senders the person(s) attempting to deliver a message or idea.

encoding the verbal (words, sounds) and nonverbal (gestures, facial expressions, posture) cues that the sender utilizes in dispatching the message.

transmission devices all of the items that carry the message from the sender to the receiver.

decoding takes place when the receiver employs any set of his or her senses (hearing, seeing, feeling, etc.) in the attempt to capture the message.

receivers the intended audience for a message.

noise anything that distorts or disrupts a message.

feedback information the sender obtains from the receiver regarding the receiver's perception or interpretation of a message.

clutter exists when consumers are exposed to hundreds of marketing messages per day, and most are tuned out.

integrated marketing communications (IMC) the coordination and integration of all marketing communication tools, avenues, and sources within a company into a seamless program that maximizes the impact on consumers and other end users at a minimal cost. This affects all of a firm's business-to-business, marketing channel, customer-focused, and internally oriented communications.

marketing mix consists of products, prices, places (the distribution system), and promotions.

morals beliefs or principles that individuals hold concerning what is right and what is wrong.

ethics principles that serve as guidelines for both individuals and organizations.

brand parity occurs when there is the perception that most products and services are essentially the same.

contact points the places in which a customer may interact with or acquire additional information about a firm.

adaptation occurs when products and marketing messages are designed for and adapted to individual countries.

standardization when a firm standardizes its products and market offerings across countries with the goal of generating economies of scale in production while using the same promotional theme.

CRITICAL THINKING EXERCISES

Discussion Questions

1. The marketing director for a furniture manufacturer is assigned the task of developing an integrated marketing communications program to emphasize the furniture's natural look. Discuss the problems the director may encounter in developing this message and in ensuring that consumers understand the message correctly. Refer to the communication process in Figure 1.1 for ideas. What type of noise may interfere with the communication process?

2. Referring to Exercise 1, assume the director wants to develop an integrated marketing communications program emphasizing a theme focused on the furniture's natural look. This theme applies to all of their markets, that is, both retailers and consumers. Using Figure 1.4 as a guide, briefly discuss each element of the integrated marketing communications plan and how to incorporate it into an overall theme.

3. The marketing director for a manufacturer of automobile tires wants to integrate its marketing program internationally.

Should the director use a standardization or adaptation approach? How could the company be certain that its marketing program would effectively be integrated among the different countries where it sells tires?

4. Look up each of the following companies on the Internet. For each company, discuss how effective its Web site is in communicating an overall message. Also, discuss how well the marketing team integrates the material on the Web site. How well does the Web site integrate the company's advertising with other marketing communications?

   a. Revlon (www.revlon.com)

   b. Reebok (www.reebok.com)

   c. J.B. Hunt (www.jbhunt.com)

   d. United Airlines (www.ual.com)

   e. Steamboat Resorts (www.steamboatresorts.com)

Pick Your Product

An effective integrated marketing communications program involves pulling together the thoughts and ideas described in each of the 16 chapters of this book. To help you understand how the process unfolds, the assignment is to pick a product to promote and then use the concepts presented in each chapter to develop an IMC program. Here are your product choices:

- Individual-size bottled water
- A new ink pen
- Chopsticks
- A baseball
- A perfume or cologne
- A purse
- An errand running and reminder service
- An e-trade service for NASDAQ stocks

Visit the Prentice-Hall Web site that has been built for this campaign exercise at **www.prenhall.com/clow** or access the IMC Plan Pro disk that accompanied this textbook.

In addition to picking a product, in this chapter's exercise you will be asked to relate your product to the communications model described in Chapter 1, along with other basic IMC concepts.

BUILDING AN
IMC
CAMPAIGN

IMC PlanPro

CASE 1

MARKETING MINI-CDS

Craft-tech Technologies was on the verge of a major expansion. The company's management team invested heavily in compact disk technology and created what they believed was a viable product for the mini-CD marketplace. Company leaders were certain mini-CDs soon would outsell the traditional-size version, giving them inroads into numerous markets, including the:

▶ Music industry

▶ Computer industry

▶ CD player market (both Walkman and larger versions for home use)

The company's president, Merv Watson, contacted a full-service advertising agency. Merv asked the agency manager, Susan Ashbacher, to describe the meaning of full service. Susan responded, "We will take care of every aspect of your company's integrated marketing communications program. We'll either prepare the material ourselves, or outsource it and manage the process."

Merv was still confused. "What exactly does that mean?" he asked.

Susan handed him a worksheet (Figure 1.8). She responded, "We will sit down with you and figure out your company's primary message. Do you want to represent yourself as a high-quality leader in technology? Or is your focus more toward this particular product, and how you serve that niche better than anyone else? What we'll ask you to do is define yourself, and then we'll help you develop a marketing program to get that message out."

Merv studied the worksheet. He was amazed to see all of the items listed. Noting his interest, Susan said, "Every single thing on that page should speak with the same voice. Every one of your customers, from businesses to end users, should know your main message. Your customers should buy from you because they have confidence in your brand. We want to make sure you stand out. After all, it's pretty crowded out there in the world of technology."

▶ Company logo

▶ Product brand name and company name

▶ Business cards

▶ Letterhead

▶ Carry home bags (paper or plastic)

▶ Wrapping paper

▶ Coupons

▶ Promotional giveaways (coffee mugs, pens, pencils, calendars)

▶ Design of booth for trade shows

▶ Advertisements (billboards, space used on cars and busses, television, radio, magazines, and newspapers)

▶ Toll free 800 or 888 number

▶ Company database

▶ Cooperative advertising with other businesses

▶ Personal selling pitches

▶ Characteristics of target market buyers

▶ Characteristics of business buyers

▶ Sales incentives provided to sales force (contests, prizes, bonuses and commissions)

▶ Internal messages

▶ Company magazines and newspapers

▶ Statements to shareholders

▶ Speeches by company leaders

▶ Public relations releases

▶ Sponsorship programs

▶ Web site

FIGURE 1.8
Items to Be Included in an IMC Program

(continued)

Merv hired Susan, and the process began. The IMC program was to integrate a marketing plan to other businesses, individual users, and international markets.

1. What image or theme should Craft-tech Technologies portray?
2. Design an IMC approach and state how it will affect all of the items shown in Figure 1.8.
3. Choose another product or service. Consider every IMC aspect of that product or service as you read the following chapters.

CASE 2

JENNY'S HAIR SALON

Jenny Burns finished high school in the late 1980s. She had no real interest in college. She loved fashion, style, and "glamour." Moving out on her own meant trying to find a job that would accommodate her love of trendy things. She decided to become a hairstylist. After taking all the courses and gaining her cosmetology license, Jenny worked for two years at an independent salon, which went out of business when the owner developed health problems.

After careful deliberation, and with some help from an SBA loan, Jenny opened her own salon on the outskirts of Grand Lake, Oklahoma. The building boom had just taken over the area, and she was convinced she would make a good living because of the growing population and bustle of activities present, especially in the summertime.

The new business, "Jenny's Hair Salon," was started. She used newspaper advertisements, radio spots, and coupons in a local advertising pamphlet to announce her grand opening. Her location was visible and accessible to residents of the major town near the lake, Grove, Oklahoma. Unfortunately, there was no quality sign maker in town, so Jenny had to rely on a portable flashing sign to present the name of her business.

When the business opened, Jenny was able to attract a solid clientele, because she was one of only two salons in town. The other business tended to attract an older crowd, leaving Jenny with both younger women and some younger men. She was able to convince some people in the community to bring their children to her salon, although she used only word of mouth to entice them.

Two major problems made Jenny's Hair Salon less profitable in later years. The first was increasing competition. Stores such as Wal-Mart added salon outlets, and one chain, Perfect Cuts, attracted both customers and new graduates of the nearest cosmetology school.

The second problem was Jenny's inability to pay competitive wages. Her best workers left for "greener pastures," even though they often spent their last days on the job at Jenny's Salon in tears, wishing they could stay. Jenny is considering adding new specialties, such as tanning booths, massages, manicures, and pedicures to her lines, but knows these will increase her overhead and the wages she would have to pay.

Most of all, Jenny is uncertain about her best target market. She spends her time cutting hair rather than developing a coherent marketing scheme. She knows winters are her worst time of year because tourists are scarce and locals, who are mostly retirees, tend to stay home due to inclement weather or patronize the other nonchain salon.

Jenny needs to attract and keep some high-quality hairstylists and entice some of her former customers back into the fold. She knows customer loyalty to her main stylists made her business much more successful in the early years.

1. How can Jenny succeed in this increasingly competitive environment?
2. Would an IMC program be helpful to Jenny? Why or why not?

ENDNOTES

1. Carolyn Walkup, "John Schnatter," *Nation's Restaurant News,* 31, no. 4 (January 1997), pp. 182–84; Zachary Schiller, "Papa John's: From a Broom Closet in a Bar to 485 Pizza Restaurants," *Business Week* (May 23, 1994), p. 94; Carolyn Walkup, "People— The Single Point of Difference—Hiring Them," *Nation's Restaurant News,* 30, no. 4 (October 6, 1997), pp. 106–8; Nancy Brumback, "Moving Up," *Restaurant Business,* 96, no. 8 (April 15, 1997), pp. 94–97.

2. Donald Baack, "Communication Processes," *Organizational Behavior,* Ch. 13 (1998), pp. 313–37.

3. David Gianatasio, "Too Bad for Converse," *Adweek, Eastern Edition,* 39, no. 3 (January 19, 1998), p. 3; Mark Tedesci, "The End of an Era?" *Sporting Goods Business,* 31, no. 3 (February 4, 1998), p. 24.

4. James G. Hutton, "Integrated Marketing Communications and the Evolution of Marketing Thought," *Journal of Business Research,* 37 (November 1996), pp. 155–62.

5. Don Schultz, "Invest in Integration," *Industry Week,* 247, no. 10 (May 18, 1998), p. 20.

6. Ibid.

7. Based on Don E. Schultz, "The Inevitability of Integrated Communications," *Journal of Business Research,* 37 (November 1996), pp. 139–46.

8. Ibid.

9. "Internet Economy Generates $300 Billion in Revenue," *The Robesonian* (June 10, 1999), p. 8.

10. Kathleen Kerwin, "Kicking the Rebate Habit," *Business Week,* (August 1, 1994), pp. 28–29; Douglas Lavin and Oscar Suris, "No Rebate on That New Car? Just Wait a Month," *Wall Street Journal, Eastern Edition,* 225, no. 22 (February 1, 1995), p. B1.

11. Adam Shell, "Brand Loyalty? Fuggedaboudit!" *Adweek, Eastern Edition,* 38, no. 19 (May 12, 1997), p. 40.

12. Based on Schultz, "The Inevitability of Integrated Communications."

13. Patricia Sellers, "Winning Over the New Consumer," *Fortune* (July 29, 1991), pp. 113–24; Jennifer Lach, "Commercial Overload," *American Demographics,* 21, no. 9 (September 1999), p. 20.

14. P. Griffith Lindell, "You Need an Integrated Attitude to Develop IMC," *Marketing News,* 31, no. 11 (May 26, 1997), p. 6.

15. Don E. Schultz and Philip J. Kitchen, "Integrated Marketing Communications in U.S. Advertising Agencies: An Exploratory Study," *Journal of Advertising Research* (September–October 1997), pp. 7–18.

16. Stephen J. Gould, Dawn B. Lerman, and Andreas F. Grein, "Agency Perceptions and Practices on Global IMC," *Journal of Advertising Research* (January–February 1999), pp. 7–26.

17. Ibid.

18. Laura Petrecca, "Agencies Urged to Show the Worth of Their Work," *Advertising Age,* 68, no. 15 (April 14, 1997), pp. 2–3; Joseph A. Tradii, "Get the Most from Your Agency," *Marketing News,* 28, no. 22 (October 24, 1994), p. 4; Pete Millard, "Gauging Ad Success: Bean Counters Eclipse Agency Creatives," *Business Journal Serving Greater Milwaukee: Marketing Resource Guide,* 14, no. 29 (April 18, 1997), p. 4; Robert L. Gustafson, "Better Leaders Make Better Account Execs," *Indianapolis Business Journal,* 16, no. 15 (March 4, 1996), p. 15; John Bissell, "Agency Creatives: A Strategic Resource?" *Brandweek,* 39, no. 19 (May 11, 1998), p. 18.

Corporate Image and Brand Management

Chapter Objectives

Understand **the nature of a corporation's image and why it is important.**

Develop **tactics and plans to build an effective corporate image.**

Discover **the advantages of a quality logo, package, and label.**

Cultivate **effective brand names, family brands, brand extensions, flanker brands, co-brands, private brands, brand equity, and brand recognition.**

Recognize **the importance of effective brand and product positioning, and utilize strategies to help establish a positive position.**

DELL'S DUDE BUILDS BRAND AWARENESS

"Dude, you're getting a Dell" undoubtedly became one of the most recognized phrases from the advertising world as the new millennium began to unfold. The pitch, made by Steven, the Dell guy, helped the company increase sales by 16.5 percent during the first three quarters of 2001. Over the life of the campaign, Dell has reported a 100 percent increase in consumer traffic to phone and Web sites. In the same time period, overall personal computer sales were down 31 percent.

Steven is actually actor Ben Curtis. He was first hired at the age of 20 by Dell's former New York advertising agency, Lowe Worldwide. Curtis is a Tennessee native who moved to the Big Apple to study acting at New York University. He answered a call to play a 12- to 17-year-old teenager in the original commercial and was hired on the spot, even though most of his previous acting experience was limited to high school productions.

The original ads focused on people who had not purchased the company's products, with Steven (Curtis) admonishing the poor soul, "Dude, you should have gotten a Dell." When Dell decided to launch a new $200 million campaign, a new agency was hired, DDB Chicago. Using both the "Dude, you're getting a Dell," and the "Easy as Dell" tagline, the campaign moved forward.

Dell's marketing team recognized the importance of matching the advertising with quality products and quality service. Online purchases and those made over the phone are rapidly filled. The customer service department maintains a friendly and helpful atmosphere, one in which a problem is resolved as quickly as possible. Additional sales have allowed Dell to lower prices on several models, making it possible to compete effectively with Gateway and other providers in the personal computer marketplace.

By mid-2002, Steven's character had practically reached cult status. Numerous features have appeared about Steven and Ben Curtis in media as diverse as CNN, *USA Today*, the *Today Show*, ABC's *20/20 Downtown*, the Sundance Movie Festival, *Advertising Age*, and the *Wall Street Journal*. Recognition and recall of the Dell name increased dramatically and, more importantly, the appeal is not limited to a single group. Dell and Steven receive fan mail from a spectrum of people ranging from teenage girls to senior citizens.

Curtis believes the appeal of the character is in the combination of energy and humor. *Ad Age* columnist and ABC News consultant Bob Garfield muses, "This campaign is so odd in so many ways. I mean, let's start with surfer-dude? He's sort of like *Leave It to Beaver* meets *Bill and Ted's Excellent Adventure*." However, the Steven character, which strongly connects with the younger generation, is helping drive sales. "It's very seldom that a single advertising campaign can make such a dramatic difference for a brand. But this campaign has."

Todd Wasserman of *Brandweek Magazine* concludes, "There's nothing else going on right now that people are talking about like this in the advertising world." Still, Curtis knows the run will end sooner or later. Life after Steven, he hopes, will include appearances either on television or in independent films. He has already been labeled as a "breakout star" by *Entertainment Weekly*, "Gen X's answer to 'Where's the Beef'" by the *Wall Street Journal*, and "loveable" by *USA Today*. Much in the same manner as the "Wazzup" campaign for Budweiser, the Dell company will ride the popularity of the spokesperson for as long as possible. Then, it will be time to look for the next advertising icon.[1]

JAVANET INTERNET CAFÉ

Building an effective IMC program can only move forward when the firm is grounded in a strong image and works toward building powerful brands. This part of the IMC foundation guides not only the marketing team but also managers from other areas. There are three levels of goals to reach when preparing an IMC model: (1) corporate image, (2) brand development, and (3) brand positioning.

In the JavaNet Internet Café example provided on the IMC Plan Pro disk, these three goals are shown in sections 3.1, 3.2, and 3.3. Read this portion of the campaign. Note that JavaNet's corporate image is based on quality in terms of the products, services, and facility atmospherics. The brand is designed to represent an upscale cyber café. JavaNet's position is based on an inviting environment to consume coffee and bakery goods and to relax with friends both in the store and on the Internet. Price is not the main feature—quality is the key.

o v e r v i e w

One of the most critical ingredients in the successful development of an integrated marketing communications plan is effective management of an organization's image. A firm's **image** is based on the feelings consumers and businesses have about an organization as well as evaluations of individual brands. Advertising, sales promotions, trade promotions, personal selling, and other marketing activities are all part of the larger umbrella of the firm's general image. If the image of either the organization or one of its brands becomes tarnished, sales revenues and profits often plummet, and rebuilding or revitalizing that image is a momentous task.

Developing and maintaining a quality image is one key responsibility being assigned to both brand managers and account executives at the agency level. Image has a "bottom line" that can even be assigned a value on accounting statements. Advertising managers and other marketing experts are expected to perform services that sell products in the short term and build image over time. Advertising creatives must think of both goals as they design individual ads and more elaborate campaigns.

In the overall IMC program, image first becomes a concern as part of the promotions opportunity process (see Chapter 5). Image is connected to company strengths and weaknesses. A strong image can be combined with an opportunity discovered in the external environment to create a major strategic advantage for the firm. A complete analysis of a firm's image and the strengths of its individual brands can be connected to a forceful effort to make solid connections with end use consumers and business-to-business accounts. As part of the IMC planning process, image and brand ideas can be related to various consumer and business buyer behaviors, thereby establishing a consistent message with all of the individuals who may purchase a company's goods and services.

The first part of this chapter examines the many facets of managing a corporation's image. The second part addresses the issues associated with developing and promoting the various forms of brand names. Brand equity and brand parity and also discussed in detail. Brand names, company logos, (e.g., McDonald's arches, the Nike swoosh, etc.), packages, and labels are closely tied to a firm's image.

THE CORPORATE IMAGE

Effective marketing communication begins with the establishment of a clearly defined corporate image. This image summarizes what the company stands for and how well its position has been established. Whether it is the "good hands" of Allstate Insurance or the "good neighbors" at State Farm Insurance, the goal of image management is to create a stable impression in the minds of clients and customers (in the case of insurance companies, helpfulness, safety, and security are most prevalent).

More important than what organizational officials believe about the company is what consumers believe about the company. Corporate names such as IBM, Apple Computers, General Motors, Nike, and Enron all conjure images in the minds of consumers. Although the specific version of the image varies from person to person or business to business, the overall or most general image of a firm is determined by the conglomerate view of all publics. This image influences customers either positively or negatively as they make purchase decisions.

Components of a Corporate Image

Consumers see many things as they encounter a company or organization. The goods or services offered are only part of the total picture. For example, personal views associated with General Motors consist of evaluations of the vehicles the organization produces, the dealerships that sell them, the factories where vehicles are built, and the advertisements used to persuade customers. In addition, the corporation's image includes assessments of the employees who work at the company's headquarters, factories, and dealerships. In fact, the mechanic trying to repair a GM vehicle at a local Mr. Goodwrench garage may become a major part of a specific customer's image of General Motors. Every aspect of General Motors, from the literature provided to the finished products sold, is a component in GM's image.

Further, as shown in the Figure 2.1, a corporate image contains many invisible and intangible elements. A policy of a pharmaceutical or cosmetic company that prohibits

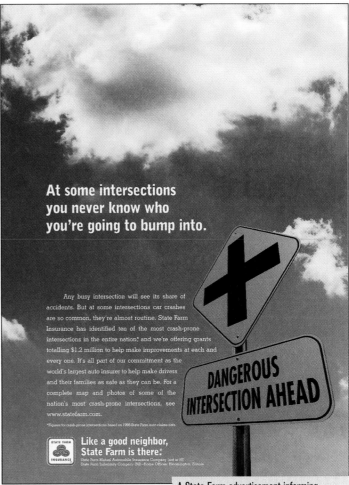

A State Farm advertisement informing consumers about the company's goal of making driving safer.
Source: Courtesy of State Farm Insurance Companies. © State Farm Mutual Automobile Insurance Company, 1999. Used by permission.

Tangible Elements	Intangible Elements
1. Goods and services sold 2. Retail outlets where the product is sold 3. Factories where the product is produced 4. Advertising, promotions, and other forms of communications 5. Corporate name and logo 6. Packages and labels 7. Employees	1. Corporate, personnel, and environmental policies 2. Ideals and beliefs of corporate personnel 3. Culture of country and location of company 4. Media reports

FIGURE 2.1
Components of a Corporate Image

animal testing becomes integrated into consumer attitudes toward the firm. Personnel policies and practices impact the firm's image, as Texaco recently learned when employee lawsuits regarding discrimination in hiring and promotion practices emerged. The business philosophies of Bill Gates at Microsoft and of Ross Perot at EDS affect the images consumers have of the two companies. The beliefs and attitudes consumers hold concerning the country of Japan influence their viewpoints of firms such as Sony and Toyota. Further, negative events or attitudes, such as were revealed regarding relationships with black patrons of Denny's restaurants, can stain or damage long-term perceptions of a firm's overall image.

The Role of a Corporate Image—Consumer Perspective

From a consumer's perspective, the corporate image serves several useful functions. These include:

- Assurance regarding purchase decisions of familiar products in unfamiliar settings
- Assurance concerning purchases where there is little previous experience
- Reduction of search time in purchase decisions
- Psychological reinforcement and social acceptance

A well-known corporate image provides consumers with positive assurance of what they can expect from the firm. A can of Coke or Pepsi purchased in Anchorage, Alaska, has a comparable taste to one purchased in Liverpool, England, or Kuala Lumpur, Malaysia. McDonald's serves the same or similar value meals in San Francisco as the ones sold in Minneapolis or Paris. Consumers on vacation know that if they purchase a product from Wal-Mart in Texas, they can return one that is defective to a local store in Toronto, Canada, or Mexico City, Mexico.

This assurance increases in importance when consumers purchase goods or services with which they have little experience. For example, consider a family on vacation. Often travelers in another state or country look for signs or logos of companies from their native area. Purchasing from a familiar corporation is perceived to be a "safer" strategy than purchasing from an unknown. Patronizing a hotel or restaurant that the consumer has never heard of will be seen as riskier than would be utilizing a familiar one. Vacationers in Brazil may never have stayed in a Holiday Inn, but because they have heard of the name, they feel it is a lower-risk alternative than staying in an unknown hotel.

A significant role that the corporate image plays for the consumer is the reduction of search time. Purchasing products from a familiar firm can save a consumer considerable energy. An individual loyal to Ford automobiles spends fewer hours searching for a new car than does one with no loyalty toward a particular automobile manufacturer. The same principle holds in purchasing low-cost items such as groceries. A great deal of search time is saved when a consumer purchases brands and items from the same corporation, such as Kellogg or Nabisco.

For many individuals, purchasing from a highly recognized company provides psychological reinforcement and social acceptance. The psychological reinforcement comes from customers feeling that they made wise purchasing choices, and that the products or services will perform well. The social acceptance is derived from the consumer's knowledge that many other individuals have also purchased from the well-known firm. More importantly, other people, such as family and friends, are likely to accept the choice.

The Role of a Corporate Image— Business-to-Business Perspective

Corporate image is a crucial element of the business-to-business marketplace. Purchasing from a well-known company reduces the feelings of risk that are part of the buying process. A firm with a well-established image makes the choice easier for business customers who often seek to reduce search time during the decision-making process. Also, a form of psychological reinforcement and social acceptance exists, because company buyers who make quality purchases receive praise from organizational leaders and others involved in the process. Once again, a strong company image or brand name can make the difference in a choice between competitors.

Brand image is especially important when expanding internationally. Foreign businesses are likely to feel more comfortable making transactions with a business from a different country with a established corporate image. Risk and uncertainty are reduced when the buyer knows something about the seller. Therefore, a company such as IBM can expand into a new country and more quickly gain the confidence of consumers and businesses.

The Role of a Corporate Image—Company Perspective

From the viewpoint of the firm itself, a highly reputable image generates many benefits. These include:

▶ Extension of positive consumer feelings to new products

▶ The ability to charge a higher price or fee

▶ Consumer loyalty leading to more frequent purchases

▶ Positive word-of-mouth endorsements

▶ The ability to attract quality employees

▶ More favorable ratings by financial observers and analysts

A quality corporate image provides the basis for the development of new goods and services. When consumers are already familiar with the corporate name and image, the introduction of a new product becomes much easier, because long-term customers are willing to give something new a try. Customers normally transfer their trust in and beliefs about the corporation to a new product.

A strong corporate image allows a company to charge more for their products and services. Most customers believe they "get what they pay for," which means higher quality is often associated with higher prices. This, in turn, can lead to better markup margins and greater profits for the firm with a strong corporate image that can charge higher prices.

Further, firms with well-developed images have customers who are more loyal. A higher level of customer loyalty results in patrons purchasing more products over time. This is, in part, because less substitution purchasing takes place (such as when other companies offer discounts, sales, and other enticements to switch brands).

Heightened levels of customer loyalty are often associated with positive word-of-mouth endorsements of the company and its products. These favorable comments about the firm help generate additional sales and attract new customers. Most consumers have more faith in the personal references they receive than in communication that comes from any form of advertising or promotion.

Another advantage of a strong corporate image is that it attracts quality employees. Just as consumers are drawn to strong firms, potential workers will apply for jobs at companies with solid reputations. Consequently, recruiting costs are reduced because of lower employee turnover, and fewer advertising expenditures are needed to entice new applicants.

An additional value of a strong corporate reputation is a more favorable rating by Wall Street analysts. A strong corporate image can also lead to

The strong General Mills brand name makes the introduction of new products easier.

more favorable evaluations by financial institutions. This is especially helpful when a company tries to get capital financing. Further, legislators and government entities tend to act in a more supportive manner toward companies with strong and positive reputations. Lawmakers are less inclined to pursue actions that may hurt the business. Regulatory agencies are less likely to investigate rumors of wrongdoing.

Building a strong corporate image provides tangible and intangible benefits. Both customers and organizations benefit from a well-known firm that has an established reputation in the community or area it serves. Organizational leaders devote considerable amounts of time and energy to building and maintaining a positive organizational image. Companies expect advertising account managers and their creatives to help design marketing programs that take advantage of the benefits of a strong corporate image.

S T O P

INTEGRATED LEARNING EXPERIENCE

Using Yahoo! Shopping, choose a product category. Look at the brands and the stores listed in that product category. Why were those particular brands chosen? Are any brands missing? How important is a well-known, well-established brand name to consumers? What about when the firm attempts to sell goods to another business?

PROMOTING THE DESIRED IMAGE

Communicating the proper image is critical to an organization's success. Organizational leaders try to understand the nature of the company's current image in order to make sure that future communications that promote the image are successfully transmitted. Marketing experts should make sure all constituencies correctly discern the nature of the company's image. This includes customers, suppliers, and employees. In addition, other consumers, especially noncustomers of the firm, should be approached to ascertain their views of the company. Once those in the firm understand how others currently view them, they can make decisions about the image they wish to portray in the future.

In making decisions about the image to be projected, marketers should remember four things:

BMW Motorcycles carefully plans all of its communication materials to ensure a consistent brand image is projected.

1. The image being projected must accurately portray the firm and coincide with the products and services being sold.

2. Reinforcing or rejuvenating a current image that is consistent with the view of consumers is easier to accomplish than changing a well-established image.

3. It is very difficult to change the images people hold about a given company. In some cases, modifying or developing a new image simply cannot be done.

4. Any negative or bad press can quickly destroy an image that took years to build. Reestablishing or rebuilding the firm's image takes a great deal of time once its reputation has been damaged.

COMMUNICATION ACTION

An Interview with a Brand Manager

Being an effective brand manager is a difficult task. One person who has taken the challenge is Kerri L. Martin, brand manager for BMW Motorcycles. We asked Kerri to describe her work. Here was her answer:

> The responsibilities of my job as brand manager fall into two very different yet linked areas, strategic and tactical. While on one hand I'm responsible for leading the brand's long-term identity and strategic positioning, on the other hand I'm also responsible for guiding all tactical marketing consumer communications programs and materials. It's my job to assure that all communications that touch the consumer are integrated, speaking in one tone and voice, and visually complementary of each other.

Beyond this more general description, Kerri noted her main duties.

> On a daily basis I could be involved in one or more of the following: new product launches, ad campaign marketing, media planning, point-of-purchase merchandising, co-op advertising, budgets, and general administration.

The company is quite attentive to the idea of developing a consistent theme to reach potential customers. Kerri stated it this way:

> BMW Motorcycles are the Indisputable Mark of a Real Ride. [We] . . . broadly communicate, in powerful terms, the reality that the most passionate riders, real riders, recognize the extraordinary characteristics of the BMW motorcycle. It is not a "two-wheeled car," but the result of the finest motorcycle design and manufacturing in the world over the last 75 years. The end result is a motorcycle that offers true synchronicity between the rider and the machine.

Kerri reported that her department is acutely aware of the importance of brand management, brand development, and integration of brand strategies with an overall IMC approach. She described the process this way:

> The building of a brand is a long-term proposition, not an overnight miracle. A brand is not just a logo, a unique product, or the latest ad campaign. Instead it is multi-dimensional and flows from a set of values. I believe that branding should be a companywide focus that differentiates the product from its competition in both marketing communications and operations. At all sets in the relationship with your customer and contact points, you're building brand loyalty. In the long run, this loyalty becomes the backbone of your brand.

The IMC approach to brand development helps ensure stability in the process. At BMW, the firm reflects many of the ideas reported in Chapter 1 of this text. Listen to Kerri talk about its approach:

> Today, more than ever in history, consumers are bombarded with marketing messages everywhere they go. Buy this, do this, visit us, go there, be here . . . it goes on and on. With such a crowded marketplace, marketers must be careful not to confuse customers any more than they already are. Thus, it's critical that a brand have one voice and communicate in that one voice in everything they do. With increased segmentation, you can no longer be all things to all people. Pick a USP (Unique Selling Proposition) and stick with it. It's important to be conscious of everything you put out there for the public to absorb, right down to the shirts that your event staff wear and the manner in which customers are treated when they call your customer service department to ask a question.

BMW Motorcycles works with the Merkley Newman Harty agency. The agency highlights a "governing brand idea," which is very similar to BMW's notion of a unique selling proposition. Although BMW uses Merkley Newman Harty as its "agency of record," Kerri stays highly involved in the brand management process.

> I manage another handful of agencies which specialize in defined areas, such as events, collateral, the Internet, merchandising co-op program administration, telemarketing, and sales promotion. The key to successfully managing each of these agencies so that one brand message is consistently conveyed in all marketing efforts is communication. It's extremely important that each of these other marketing partners buys into and understands the brand positioning as thoroughly as our primary agency of record. Therefore, I spend a lot of time working closely with them on all projects and bring them up to speed quickly when there are new developments on our product offering, industry and consumer research, media direction, creative strategy shifts, and so forth.

Through Kerri's efforts and those of the staff at BMW and all of the agencies involved, the company has a strong brand name and maintains a strong position in the marketplace. If there is one thing to note, it may be that Kerri would remind every student reading this text that "EVERYTHING COMMUNICATES!"

Let's just say tailgaters aren't a problem.

Motorcycles

An image-building advertisement for BMW Motorcycles.

Source: Courtesy of BMW of North America, LLC. © 1999 BMW of North America, Inc. All Rights Reserved. The BMW trademark and logo are registered. This advertisement is reproduced with the permission of BMW of North America, Inc. for promotional purposes only.

Creating the Right Image

Company leaders are often willing to spend substantial amounts of money to create the proper image for a firm. For example, when British Airways expanded into a low-cost operation and customers could buy tickets directly, the advertising department spent nearly $60 million to achieve the desired image. The outcome was the brand name *Go* for the subsidiary. At the same time, the firm tried to move away from close connotations with the country of Great Britain in its overall image management program. As a result, British Airways removed the U.K. flag from all its planes. British Airways' goal was to maintain the image of being a safe and secure method of travel, with easy access in the *Go* program.[2]

In contrast, Singapore Airlines accentuates its national identity by using the "Singapore Girl" in every advertisement. The image goal of Singapore Airlines is to stress quality service. Industry experts agree that although methods vary, the key for all airline images is to be simple, international, and easily translatable, emphasizing safety and security to reassure potential passengers.[3]

In each industry, the right image reaches all target markets and conveys a clear message about the unique nature of the organization and its products. This image must portray the nature of the firm accurately and logically fit with the products and services that organization offers. The advertisement for BMW Motorcycles in this section is designed to further the image that "BMW Motorcycles are the indisputable mark of a real ride," according to BMW brand manager Kerri Martin. The Communication Action Box contains more information about how Martin works to create the desired image for the BMW Motorcycles. Once the image is established, other promotions can be built around that reputation to increase long-term customer loyalty and future sales.

Rejuvenating an Image

Reinforcing or rejuvenating a current image consistent with the view of consumers is easier to accomplish than is changing a well-established image. McDonald's discovered that projecting a more grown-up Ronald McDonald (playing golf and being involved in other more adult activities) did not radically change the overall image, which is primarily oriented toward children, nor did it help the company sell the Arch Delux line of hamburgers.

An example of an organization that has more effectively rejuvenated its image is Radio Shack. As technology has become more sophisticated, it has only become more "mystical" to a large number of consumers, and Radio Shack is in the business of technology. Therefore, it was important to demystify that technology for average people. The slogan "You've got questions, we've got answers" helps the company reach people who want the advantages of new technologies but are at the same time intimidated by them.

Rejuvenating an image helps a firm sell new products and can attract new customers. At the same time, reinforcing previous aspects of an image assists the company in retaining loyal patrons comfortable with the firm's original image. The key to successful image reengineering is to keep consistent with a previous image while at the same time building to incorporate new elements to expand the firm's target audience.[4]

Changing an Image

It is very difficult to change the images people hold regarding a given company. Company leaders must carefully consider what they wish to change, why they wish to make a change, and how they intend to accomplish the task. Changing an image is most necessary when target markets have begun to shrink or disappear, or the firm's image no longer matches industry trends and consumer expectations.

Another competitor in the airline industry, the Soviet-owned Aeroflot, was aware of its poor safety image. Company officials decided to use humor to change this image, so they adopted a flying elephant as its symbol. This form of self-mocking is designed to let customers know Aeroflot has identified and is trying to fix any safety-related problems. Aeroflot's leaders then hope to move toward a more positive image in future years.[5] Changing an image requires more than one well-made ad or press release. It must begin with internal company publics and move outward to suppliers, other businesses, and then the public.[6]

Conveying an Image to Business Customers

Officials from many companies believe corporate advertising sends important signals to other businesses. Image advertising helps build a reputation not only with the general public but also with other firms. Robert Worcester, chairman of MORI, a British market research group, reports that the more a company advertises, the more it is admired. Opinion Research Corporation, a U.S. firm, noted that "knowing a company very well" is a key reason to award new business. Therefore, image advertising is a crucial ingredient in business-to-business marketing. Stephen Greyser, from the Harvard Business School, states that corporate image advertising should be aimed at three constituencies: opinion formers (customers, politicians, investors), employees, and *other businesses.*[7]

INTEGRATED LEARNING EXPERIENCE

Web sites are an important element of a company's image. Access the Web sites of the following companies to get a feel for the image each company tries to project.

www.kelloggs.com
www.nabisco.com
www.ibm.com
www.bmwmotorcycles.com
www.britishairways.com
www.singaporeair.com

Is the image projected on the Web site consistent with the image portrayed in the company's advertisements? Several consulting firms specialize in helping businesses project a consistent image to their stakeholders. One such firm is Corporate Images, Inc. Access this Web site at **www.corporate-images.com** to see services that might be beneficial to a business attempting to establish a sound corporate image.

CORPORATE NAMES AND LOGOS

A corporate name is the overall banner under which all other operations occur. According to David Placek, president and founder of Lexicon, Inc., "The corporate name is really the cornerstone of a company's relationship with its customers. It sets an attitude and tone and is the first step toward a personality."[8] When AT&T spun off its $26 billion systems and technology business, company officials examined over 700 names including the acronym AGB, which stood for Alexander Graham Bell. The name Lucent Technologies was finally chosen because it conveyed the idea of something glowing with light, which executives at AT&T felt would be a better image going into the twenty-first century than an acronym such as AGB.[9]

A critical corollary to the corporate name is the corporate logo. Both must be carefully chosen, be compatible, and say the correct thing about the company. Most organizations spend millions of dollars on selecting and promoting corporate names and logos. For example, Taco Bell spends more money on its permanent media such as signs that carry its name and logo than it does on advertising.[10] Consumers are flooded with hundreds of advertisements daily. Strong corporate names and logos can aid in memory recall of specific brands and even specific advertisements. They help consumers in the retail store by making shopping easier and faster. Search time is reduced when consumers can look for specific corporate products that are easily identified by logos and names.[11]

Quality logos and corporate names should meet four tests. They should: (1) be easily recognizable, (2) be familiar, (3) elicit a consensual meaning among those in the firm's target market, and (4) evoke positive feelings.[12]

Logos are especially important for in-store shopping. Pictures can be processed in the mind faster than words; thus, corporate logos are easily recognizable by consumers. To be advantageous to companies, logo recognition must occur at two levels. First, consumers remember seeing the logo in the past. It is stored in memory, and when it is seen at the store, the memory is jogged. Second, the logo reminds consumers of the brand or corporate name. This reminder should elicit positive feelings regarding either the brand name or corporate manufacturer.

Successful logos elicit shared meanings across consumers. The notion that a logo can elicit a consensual meaning among customers is known as **stimulus codability**. Logos with high stimulus codability easily evoke consensually held meanings within a culture or subculture (such as the Prudential Rock). Logos with a high degree of codability are more easily recognized, such as Apple, General Electric, and Budweiser. Logos with a low degree of codability must spend more money on advertising so recognition comes through familiarity rather than the stimulus codability. For example, Nike spent a considerable amount of resources making its swoosh recognizable to those in various target markets, because the swoosh itself did not conjure any specific image of the firm early in its life.

Image is an all-encompassing umbrella that projects the overall nature of the corporation. Firms seek to create the proper image, rejuvenate that image when necessary, change it in extreme circumstances, and extend it into all aspects of advertising, including plans to build stronger relations with other businesses. Corporate names and logos, brands, and the many components of an organization's operations, from manufacturing to service, are all part of the image of the firm.

BRANDING

Many of the characteristics and benefits of a corporate image apply to brands as well. The primary difference between the two is that of scope. **Brands** are names generally assigned to a product or service or a group of complementary products while a corporate image covers every aspect of the company. A company such as Procter & Gamble carries many brands such as Tide, Cheer, and Bold laundry detergents; Crest and Gleem toothpastes; and Old Spice, Secret, and Sure deodorants. As with a well-known corporate image, an effective brand name allows a company to charge more for its products, which in turn increases gross margins. Strong brands provide customers with assurances of quality and reduction of search time in the purchasing process.

In mature markets, few tangible distinctions exist between competing brands. If a substantial product improvement appears, competitors usually quickly copy it. Thus, only minor differences exist and in many product categories even minor variations are hard to find. When brand names and labels are removed, consumers often find it difficult to distinguish between products.

If many competing brands are not really different, then why are there such huge differences in market share? This primarily is due to the difference in what is **salient** for customers. A particular brand is salient for consumers if they are aware of the brand, have it in their consideration sets (things they consider when making purchases), regard the product and brand as a good value, buy it or use it on a regular basis, and recommend it to other consumers.[13] A brand name develops strength in the marketplace when many consumers choose the brand because they consider it salient, memorable, and noteworthy.

Developing a Strong Brand Name

Developing a strong brand begins with discovering why consumers buy a brand and why they rebuy the brand. Questions to be asked include:

▷ What are the most compelling benefits?

▷ What emotions are elicited by the brand either during or after the purchase?

▷ What one word best describes the brand?

▷ What is important to consumers in the purchase of the product?

Once the answers to these questions are known, a company is ready to develop a stronger brand position.

Two important processes help establish stronger brand prestige. First, the brand name must be prominently promoted through repetitious type ads. Because of the colossal number of brands and the myriad of advertisements consumers encounter, repetition is essential to capture the individual's attention and to store the message in his or her knowledge structures. Second, the brand name must be associated with its most prominent characteristic.[14] For example, many consumers associate Crest with "cavity prevention." Coca-Cola seeks to associate its name with a product that is "refreshing." For Volvo, the impression is "safety." For BMW, it is "performance driving."

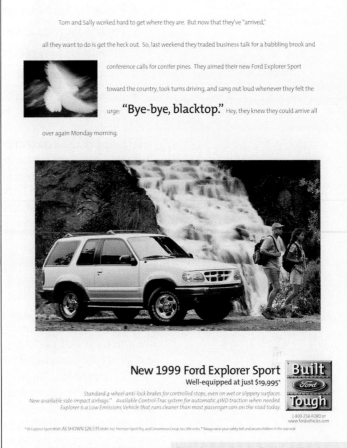

This advertisement by Ford is designed to convince consumers that the brand stands for "built tough."

Source: Courtesy of Ford Motor Company.

Brands develop histories. They have personalities. They include strengths, weaknesses, and flaws. Many brands produce family trees.

A **family brand** is one in which a company offers a series or group of products under one brand name. For example, Black & Decker has its name on numerous power tools. The advantage of a family brand is that consumers usually transfer the image associated with the brand name to any new products added to current lines. Thus, when Black & Decker offers a new power tool, it automatically assumes the reputation associated with the Black & Decker name. These transfer associations occur as long as the new product is within the same product category. When additional products are not related to the brand's core merchandise, the transfer of loyalty may not occur as easily.

The goal of branding is to set a product apart from its competitors. Market researchers must seek to identify the "one thing" the brand can stand for, that consumers recognize, and that is salient to consumers. When these tasks are successfully completed, more powerful brand recognition occurs. Notice the Ford advertisement in this section. In developing the brand for its SUVs and trucks, Ford has tried to convey to consumers that its vehicles are durable and tougher than the competition's.

Once brand recognition is achieved, the next step is to prolong its success. The secret to a long brand life is finding one unique selling point and sticking with it. A company that attempts to change the concept associated with a brand often confuses consumers and, in the long run, hurts its overall corporate image.

An example of brand image confusion may be found in American Express's attempt to move into the discount brokerage business. American Express officials hoped to take advantage of a high-quality image associated with the company's credit card service through a

> ◗ **Protect the product inside.**
> ◗ **Provide for ease of shipping, moving, and handling.**
> ◗ **Provide for easy placement on store shelves.**
> ◗ **Prevent or reduce the possibility of theft.**
> ◗ **Prevent tampering (drugs and foods).**

FIGURE 2.2
Traditional Elements of a Package

highly visible and expensive advertising campaign. The clash between serving as a low-cost discount brokerage and a high-quality credit card service confused consumers, and low sales resulted even as overall stock purchases grew, especially for competing firms such as Charles Schwab and E*TRADE. Consequently, American Express pulled back and moved to lower-cost direct-mail and online advertising in the attempt to salvage the project. When the brand does not match the corporation's image, it becomes more difficult to succeed.[15]

PACKAGING

The company's name, the logo, and a brand all appear as part of the package and/or label associated with the product. These elements should be consistently tied in with all other aspects of an IMC program. When a consumer picks up a product at the store, the company has its last opportunity to make an impression on that buyer. Traditionally, the primary purposes of packaging were those shown in Figure 2.2. Now, however, packages and labels are increasingly viewed as a key part of a company's marketing program.[16]

The Reynolds company recognized the value of a tie-in with packaging during the early 2000s. The entire wraps category was experiencing declining sales. The marketing team at Reynolds discovered that consumers enjoy using products that make them feel like experts. The firm created a new brand message that Reynolds was a "helper in the kitchen." This new brand message was extended and reinforced in ads showing how to use the product to prepare foods as well as by printing recipes into the design on the package. When tied to the perception that Reynolds was the premium brand in the marketplace, strong sales were continued.[17]

Most retail purchase decisions are made based on familiarity with a brand or product at the retail store. Consequently, a unique package that is attractive or captures the buyer's attention increases the chances the product will be purchased, sometimes as an impulse buy. For many years, wine makers strongly resisted the use of marketing tactics for fear of being perceived as having questionable quality. Products such as Blue Nun, Ripple, and Boone's farm were major marketing successes yet did not enjoy reputations for high quality. Recently, however, some wineries have begun to accept the value of a quality package. Many Australian wineries captured market share based on the knowledge that men (who are more likely to make the wine purchase) look at a wine's country of origin, followed by grape variety, and finally aesthetics. Since Australian wine is perceived as new, different, and of sufficient quality, especially in the Shriraz lines, attractive bottles were used featuring names such as Vale, Valley, Hill, and Cloudy Bay with images of mountain peaks and vineyards receding in the distance. Bottle color is crucial, because buyers prefer dark, warm, and intense colors (red and blue). These changes and the successes of the Australians have caused French and German wine makers to change their packages and labels to compete.[18] The Republic of Tea made similar inroads by featuring a bottle for green tea that was dome-shaped like the Taj Mahal.[19]

New Trends in Packaging

Some of the new trends in packaging are based on changes in the ways in which consumers use products (see Figure 2.3). In the foods market, foods that are fast, convenient, and portable are selling quickly. The package must accommodate these needs.[20]

Consumers also want packages that are eye-catching and contemporary. When Nestle created a new line of products called Nescafé Original, one primary consideration was a new package. While it was designed to meet the needs of content protection and

> ▶ **Meets consumer needs for speed, convenience, and portability.**
>
> ▶ **Must be contemporary and striking.**
>
> ▶ **Must be designed for ease of use.**

FIGURE 2.3
New Trends in Packaging

storage, it was also made to stand out through a unique geometrical set of shapes designed to appeal to younger consumers, and it was met with great success.[21]

The trend in international markets is much the same as in the United States. Ease of use is a key feature. When shipping products overseas, the buyer must feel reassured the package will not break or become contaminated.[22]

Labels

Labels on packages serve several functions. First, they must meet legal requirements. This includes identifying the product contained in the package and any other specific information about content, such as nutritional information on foods. The Food and Drug Administration (FDA) regulates food labels in the United States. Also, many times warranties and guarantees are printed on the label.

More importantly, the label represents another marketing opportunity. Many times a label is the only distinguishing feature of a product, such as a 12-ounce bottle of beer or a 1-gallon container of milk. An attractive label is an attention-getting device that may draw the consumer to the product. This feature is vitally important in the U.S. as well as other nations. For example, many Asian purchases are in part driven by the appeal of the label.[23] The company's logo and the brand name must appear prominently. Labels often contain special offers and other tie-ins, such as a box of cereal with a toy contained inside. The consumer is notified of the offer on the label.

Labels often carry terms designed to build consumer interest and confidence in making the purchase. Word such as "gourmet," "natural," "premium," "adult formula," and "industrial strength" make the product seem like a better buy. At the same time, consumers are used to such puffery. A private label brand is often plain, with low attractiveness, matching the buyer's perception that the price is being held down by lesser use of marketing tools.[24]

In general, a company's image, brand, logo, and theme should carry through to the design of the package and label. Doing so allows the marketing team one more chance to make the sale when the consumer is in the store making a final purchasing decision.

BRAND EQUITY

A strong brand name gives businesses several advantages associated with what is called brand equity. **Brand equity** is the set of characteristics unique to a brand that allows the company to charge a higher price and retain a greater market share than would otherwise be expected for an undifferentiated product. Such strength provides power to the company as it deals with retailers. This power, in turn, leads to an improved position in terms of shelf space and displays. Brand equity also influences wholesalers by affecting what they stock and which brands they encourage their customers to purchase. Wholesalers often will stock several brands but place greater emphasis on high-equity brands.

In business-to-business markets, brand equity often allows a company to charge a higher price. Equity also influences selections in the buying decision-making process. Products with strong brand equity are often selected over products with low brand equity or brands that firms know little about. The same scenario is present in international markets. Brand equity opens doors of foreign firms, brokers, and retailers and provides privileges that products with low brand equity cannot obtain.

Brand equity is a strong weapon that might dissuade consumers from looking for a cheaper product or for special deals or incentives to purchase another brand. Brand equity prevents erosion of a product's market share, even when there is a proliferation of brands coupled with endless promotional maneuvers by competitors. Additional benefits of brand equity are displayed in Figure 2.4.

1. **Allows manufacturers to charge more for their products**
2. **Creates higher gross margins**
3. **Provides power with retailers and wholesalers**
4. **Captures additional retail shelf space**
5. **Serves as a weapon against consumers switching due to sales promotions**
6. **Prevents erosion of market share**

FIGURE 2.4
Benefits of Brand Equity

Steps to Building Brand Equity

Brand-name recognition and recall can be built through repetitious advertising. Building brand equity, however, goes beyond mere brand recognition. Kmart has a high brand recognition but has fallen behind Wal-Mart and Target in terms of brand equity. To build brand equity requires the following six steps.[25] The previous section discussed the first three:

1. Research and analyze what it would take to make the brand distinctive.
2. Decide what makes the brand unique.
3. Boldly communicate the unique selling point of the brand.
4. Spend no more than 30 percent of the communication budget on *driving sales,* which includes techniques such as coupons, sweepstakes, premiums, and price-off incentives.
5. Make domination the goal.
6. Deliver on the promise or uniqueness being communicated.

The first three steps cultivate brand recognition. The last three steps build brand equity. Brand equity cannot be built without brand recognition. To develop brand equity, a firm must create messages that express the product's unique selling point and establish strong, positive consumer feelings. The firm should spend only a small portion of its communications budget on sales-driven techniques (coupons, sweepstakes, premiums, and price-off incentives). Although these techniques increase sales, they tend to affect brand image adversely.

Brand equity involves *domination,* consumers' strongly held view that the brand is number one in its product category. Domination can take place in a geographic region or in a smaller product category or market niche. Domination is associated with any product benefit that consumers desire. In each case, the brand must be viewed as number one in some way by consumers. For instance, with toothpastes, the number-one cavity fighter is Crest. For automobiles, the number-one car in terms of safety is Volvo.

Perhaps the most critical aspect of brand equity is delivering on the promise. If Crest promotes itself as the cavity fighter, then it must deliver on that promise. Consumers have to believe that Crest does a better job of preventing cavities than does any other brand of toothpaste. Recently, Buick launched a massive campaign designed to displace Volvo's position by making Buick known as the safest automobile. Buick's attack on Volvo's "safety" position is based on the premise that Volvo is not delivering the highest degree of safety due to the firm's recent cost-cutting measures. Still, for Buick to become viewed as the safest automobile, the company must demonstrate that its cars have surpassed Volvo's safety record.

The Mazda automobile company is attempting to move its image away from being price based and toward being a producer of stylish designs in performance cars. In the effort to simplify and clarify this image, the firm focuses advertisements on the overall company name rather than on individual products, ending with the tag line "Mazda: Get in, be moved." The program extends from new-product introductions, to advertisements, to advice given in a handbook to local dealerships, each stressing the simple consistent message about the organization and its products. The ultimate goal is stronger brand equity, which will occur only if Mazda does indeed produce and deliver stylish performance cars.[26]

Success Factors

Several key elements are linked to successful brand development. When they succeed, the company is able to realize the benefits shown in Figure 2.4. The success factors include:

▶ Continuing commitment to the brand

▶ Understanding the market the brand reaches

▶ Leveraging the effects of penetration[27]

Commitment to the brand means working hard to increase market penetration. **Market penetration** may be defined as the number of households within an area that purchased a product as a percentage of households that bought in that product's category. In simple terms, if one of every five households in a country buys a Toyota, and that number can be increased to two of every five, then the brand is growing in terms of success.

To capture a greater number of households in a target area means thoroughly understanding the market the brand reaches. In the competition for graham crackers, Keebler must fend off Nabisco, Honey Maid, plus smaller private label products. If Keebler is able to discover that people want higher quality crackers and are willing to pay a premium for that quality, the company can develop ads with Keebler elves stressing the high quality of the product. On the other hand, if Honey Maid discovers customers are primarily interested in price, the company must differentiate the product from private labels while at the same time stressing the value and price difference between Honey Maid and the other, higher-priced cracker makers. Brand equity means customers will buy a given product because a distinguishable difference (an advantage) exists.

Leveraging the effects of penetration means two things: (1) building effective expansion programs, and (2) fending off attacks. The Four Seasons resort chain provides an excellent example of an expansion program. The chain of high quality resorts has strong brand equity within the well-heeled North American baby boomer cohort. Four Seasons has leveraged this equity by expanding into the second-home marketplace, where an individual can have a Four Seasons second home year-round or purchase a share of ownership in "Four Seasons Residence Clubs." The luxury and reputation of this service was leveraged from the brand equity built in the travel lodge industry.[28] The Toyota Corolla and Chevrolet Prizm are built side by side in the New United Motor Manufacturing Plant in California. Toyota, due to strong brand equity, spends about $750 less in buyer incentives to support the Corolla and sells three times as many cars. Of every 107,000 prospects for a Mercedes automobile, 100,000 make purchases. It takes nearly 500,000 prospective customers to sell 100,000 Oldsmobiles or Mercury cars. Isuzu must attract 1,300,000 prospects to sell 100,000 cars. The equity in a brand name allows for greater leveraging of the brand as it expands into new products.[29]

It is equally important to fend off attacks. Victoria's Secret was forced to defend its brand when a pornography shop owner tried to create a company with the name Victor's Secret and then later Victor's Little Secret. Through legal action the company was able to argue that Victor was trying to capitalize on the brand equity associated with Victoria's Secret. The legal basis was the Federal Trademark Dilution Act, which recognizes the great investments companies make into building a brand. Thus, Bugs Bunny may not be used to sell carrots without infringing on the rights of Warner Brothers. Even in small communities, it is important to differentiate and defend a brand.[30]

Measuring Brand Equity

To discover whether or not brand equity exists is a difficult task. **Brand metrics** are measures of returns on branding investments. Attitudinal measures associated with branding may be used to track awareness, recall, and recognition. To increase their

CORPORATE IMAGE AND BRAND MANAGEMENT

Ethical Issues and Branding

Two ethical issues that routinely appear in the area of brand management are brand infringement and deceptive branding. Each poses a dilemma to consumers, the government, and marketing professionals who do not wish to engage in unethical practices.

Brand infringement occurs when a company creates a brand name that closely resembles a popular or successful brand, such as when the Korrs beer company was formed. In that case, courts deemed the brand an intentional infringement, and the name was abandoned.

The problem of brand infringement becomes more complex when a brand is so well established that it may be considered a generic term, such as a Kleenex tissue or a Xerox copy. Band-Aid encountered the problem in the 1970s, forcing the marketing team to make sure the product was identified as "Band-Aid Brand Strips" rather than simply "band aids," to keep the competition from being able to use the name.

Deceptive branding occurs when a company creates a brand simply to mask the real organization. For example, the Lucky Dog Telephone Company is owned by AT&T. While some would argue that it is unethical to create a brand simply to deceive consumers from knowing the real identity of the company, others would say it is a solid business practice to attract as many different customers as possible.

power, these factors can be tied with other variables such as awareness coupled with intent-to-buy, or awareness tacked to usage of either the product class (mustard) or the brand (Kraft, Grey Poupon).[31] At the level of awareness, recall, and recognition, it is critical to remember that a brand can be recalled for negative as well as positive reasons.[32]

In Quebec, a group of advertising agencies developed a new study, called Equi*Marques, to display the importance of brand equity to their clients. The measure shows that American products, which are the recipients of greater marketing investments, score higher than Quebec-based brands in many instances. In other words, U.S. firms have an advantage in Quebec due to brand equity. The head of the study, Paul Paré, noted, "If Quebec brands want to penetrate the U.S. market, they'll find themselves up against players who invest much more in marketing," and called for a "quiet revolution" in the classroom and the board room to fend off this disadvantage.[33]

Brand equity has also been studied on a global scale. The primary features of brand equity include the consumers' sensory, utilitarian, symbolic, and economic needs at the national and global level. Global brand equity exists when there is a cohesive image of the brand across nations and cultures. There is only limited preliminary research regarding how to build that cohesion.[34]

In general, the IMC program is not complete until a strong brand name has been established, the company builds brand equity, and the company is able to leverage that equity as it expands into other products and services. The very beginning of brand development is internal: Employees must know and understand the unique features of the product and brand. From there the company can build outward through positive publicity, advertisements, and word-of-mouth endorsements by satisfied customers.[35]

STOP

INTEGRATED LEARNING EXPERIENCE

A major consulting firm that has been a leader in extending marketing knowledge is the Boston Consulting Group. Access this Web site at **www.bcg.com**. Under the "Branding" section, read about the Boston Consulting Group's current thinking on the subject. Two other firms that assist companies with branding are Lexicon Branding, Inc. at **www.lexicon-branding.com** and Corporate Branding at **www.corebrand.com**.

> ▶ **Family brands**—a group of related products sold under one name.
>
> ▶ **Brand extension**—the use of an established brand name on products or services not related to the core brand.
>
> ▶ **Flanker brand**—the development of a new brand sold in the same category as another product.
>
> ▶ **Co-branding**—the offering of two or more brands in a single marketing offer.
>
> ▶ **Ingredient branding**—the placement of one brand within another brand.
>
> ▶ **Cooperative branding**—the joint venture of two or more brands into a new product or service.
>
> ▶ **Complementary branding**—the marketing of two brands together for co-consumption.
>
> ▶ **Private brands**—proprietary brands marketed by an organization and sold within the organization's outlets.

FIGURE 2.5
Types of Brands

BRAND EXTENSIONS AND FLANKER BRANDS

To leverage the equity built in its brands, firms often enter new markets using a brand extension strategy. Figure 2.5 identifies the types of brand strategies firms can utilize. **Brand extension** is the use of an established brand name on goods or services not related to the core brand. For example, Nike has been successful in extending its brand name to a line of clothing. Black & Decker has been somewhat successful in extending its brand name to a line of small kitchen appliances. Less successful was the brand extension of Singer in Europe from sewing machines to refrigerators, ranges, and televisions.

An alternative to brand extension is the development of a flanker brand. A **flanker brand** is the development of a new brand by a company in a good or service category it currently has a brand offering. For example, Procter & Gamble's primary laundry detergents are Cheer and Tide. Still, the company has introduced a number of additional brands such as Ivory Snow. In total, P&G offers 11 different brands of detergents in North America; 16 in Latin America; 12 in Asia; and 17 in Europe, the Middle East, and Africa. Table 2.1 lists Procter & Gamble's various brands of laundry detergents, cosmetics, and hair care products. The company's marketing team introduced these flanker brands to appeal to target markets that Procter & Gamble believed its main brand in each product category was not reaching. Thus, using a set of flanker brands can help a company offer a more complete line of products. This creates a barriers to entry for competing firms.

Sometimes a flanker brand is introduced when a company's leaders feel that offering the product under the current brand name may adversely affect the current brand. For example, Hallmark created a flanker brand known as Shoebox Greetings. These cards sell in discount stores as well as Hallmark outlets; however, the Hallmark brand sells only in its named retail stores. Shoebox Greeting's cards are lower priced and allow Hallmark to attract a larger percentage of the market. Firms often use this type of strategy in high-end markets

A brand extension of the Skin-So-Soft bath line to a line of Skin-So-Soft Bug Guard products.

"...ain't no bugs on me"

Let's talk AVON

As America's #1 DEET-free repellent, AVON Skin-So-Soft Bug Guard Plus helps keep your family bite-free and worry-free. Proven as effective as OFF!® Skintastic IV®*

Bug your AVON Representative or call 1-800 FOR AVON or visit at avon.com

Product Category	North America	Latin America	Asia	Europe, Middle East, and Africa
Laundry and cleaning brands	Bold	Ace	Ariel	Ace
	Bounce	Ariel	Bonus	Alo
	Cheer	Bold	Bounce	Ariel
	Downy	Downy	Cheer	Azurit
	Dreft	Duplex	Doll	Bold
	Dryel	InExtra	Ezee	Bonux
	Era	Limay	Gaofuli	Bounce
	Gain	Magia Blanca	Lanxiang	Dash
	Ivory Snow	ODD Fases	Panda	Daz
	Oxydol	Pop	Perla	Dreft
	Tide	Quanto	Tide	Fairy
		Rapido	Trilo	Lenor
		Rindex		Maintax
		Romtensid		Myth
		Supremo		Rei
		Tide		Tide
				Tix
Cosmetics	Cover Girl	Cover Girl	Cover Girl	Cover Girl
	Max Factor	Max Factor	Max Factor	Max Factor
	Oil of Olay			Ellen Betrix
Hair care	Head & Shoulders	Drene	Head & Shoulders	Head & Shoulders
	Mediker	Head & Shoulders	Mediker	Mediker
	Pantene Pro-V	Pantene Pro-V	Pantene Pro-V	Pantene Pro-V
	Physique	Pert Plus	Rejoy–Rejoice	Rejoy–Rejoice
	Rejoy–Rejoice		Pert Plus	Pert Plus
	Pert Plus		Vidal Sassoon	Vidal Sassoon
	Vidal Sassoon			

TABLE 2.1

Brands Sold by Procter & Gamble

that want to compete in low-end markets. It is also used in international expansion. For example, Procter & Gamble sells Ariel laundry detergent in Latin America, Asia, Europe, the Middle East, and Africa, but not in North America. Offering different brands for specific markets is a common flanker brand strategy that helps a firm expand in an international market using more than its current brands.

INTEGRATED LEARNING EXPERIENCE

Brand extensions and flanker branding are common leverage strategies for large corporations. Access the following company Web sites. Examine their various product categories and the brands they offer in each category.

Marriott Hotels (www.marriott.com)
Procter & Gamble (www.pg.com)
Sara Lee Corporation (www.saralee.com)
VF Corporation (www.vfc.com)

CO-BRANDING

Locating Subway's Sandwich Shops in convenience stores, Little Caesar's in Kmart outlets, and McDonald's in Wal-Mart stores is a co-branding trend that has recently mushroomed. **Co-branding** can take three forms: ingredient branding, cooperative branding, and complementary branding. **Ingredient branding** is the placement of one brand within another brand, such as Intel microprocessors in Compaq computers. **Cooperative brand-**

ing is the joint venture of two or more brands into a new product or service. Study the advertisement featuring a cooperating branding venture by American Airlines, Citibank, and MasterCard in this section. **Complementary branding** is the marketing of two brands together to encourage co-consumption or co-purchases, such as Seagram's 7 encouraging 7-Up as a compatible mixer or Oreo milkshakes sold in Dairy Queen stores.[36]

Co-branding succeeds when it builds the brand equity of both brands. For example, when Monsanto created NutraSweet, consumer trust was built by placing the NutraSweet logo on venerable brands consumers trusted, such as Diet Coke, Wrigley's Chewing Gum (Wrigley's Extra), and Crystal Light. The strategy worked so well that NutraSweet is now the standard of quality in the sweetener industry.[37]

Conversely, there can be risks in co-branding. If the relationship fails to do well in the marketplace, normally both brands suffer. To reduce the risk of failure, co-branding should be undertaken only with well-known brands. Co-branding of goods and services that are highly compatible generally will be less risky. Ingredient and cooperative branding tend to be less risky than complementary branding because both companies have more at stake and devote greater resources to ensure success.

For small companies and brands that are not as well known, co-branding is an excellent strategy. The difficult task is finding a well-known brand willing to take on a lesser-known product as a co-brand. Yet, if such an alliance can be made, the co-brand relationship often

An example of cooperative branding.
Source: Courtesy of Citibank.

builds brand equity for the lesser-known brand, as in the case of NutraSweet. Co-branding also provides access to distribution channels that may be difficult to obtain either because of lack of size or dominance by the major brands.

PRIVATE BRANDS

Private brands (also known as *private labels*) are proprietary brands marketed by an organization and normally distributed exclusively within the organization's outlets. Over the last 50 years, private brands have experienced a roller coaster ride in terms of popularity and sales. To many individuals, private brands carry the connotation of a lower price and inferior quality. Historically, the primary audience for private labels was price-sensitive individuals. Not surprisingly, private labels often experience a growth in sales during recessions.

An advertisement by Dell with both Microsoft and Intel brands included in the ad.

1. Improved quality
2. Priced 25% below manufacturer's brands
3. Loyalty toward retail outlets increased while loyalty toward specific brands decreased
4. Increase in advertising of private brands
5. Increase in quality of in-store displays of private brands

FIGURE 2.6
Changes in Private Brands

Over the past few years, several changes have occurred in the private brand arena, which Figure 2.6 summarizes. First, the quality levels of private label products have improved. In some cases, the quality is perceived to be equal to or better than that of national brands. For example, consumers perceive Nike's clothing merchandise and Gap's private label of clothing to be of excellent quality.

Second, although private labels still tend to be priced around 25 percent lower than national brands, some private labels are priced higher. These higher prices are due to the perceived increase in product quality.

A third major difference is that loyalty toward stores has been gaining while loyalty toward individual brands has been declining. Rather than going to outlets that sell specific brands, many shoppers go to specific stores. They are willing to buy from the brands offered by that store. Because of this increase in store loyalty, many department stores and specialty stores see an opportunity to expand their private brands. Store displays of private brands are now as attractive as those of national brands.

The fourth change in private labeling is in the area of advertising. Because of the increase in the image of private labels, many firms now advertise their brands. Although most advertising is still done within the scope of the store's promotion, some advertising is being designed apart from the store. The purpose of this latter approach is to establish the name as a bona fide brand that can effectively compete with national products. Recently, Sears launched a series of advertisements featuring its Kenmore and Craftsman brands. The emphasis on Sears has been reduced to simply informing consumers where to purchase Kenmore and Craftsman items. Kmart heavily promotes its private lines of Chic, Jacyln Smith, Kathy Ireland, Expressions, Route 66, and Sesame Street. Wal-Mart now has 14 private labels of clothing alone, including labels such as Basic Image, Bobbie Brooks, Catalina, Jordache, and Kathy Lee.

Private labeling has exploded in the area of active lifestyle–related clothing. The successes of Nike, Reebok, and Adidas apparel lines have enticed another sports retailer to create a competing private label. By creating fresh, original private label products, the store competes against other manufacturer brands. Retailers make higher margins from these lower-priced (but still premium) goods.

Some manufacturers have responded aggressively to the inroads made by private labels in the clothing industry. For example, Wrangler and Lee have increased their advertising budgets to restore their brand-name advantage and want to make sure they offer the proper mix of jeans to cooperating stores. They also sew more private label apparel for various retailers. Other partnerships between manufacturers and retailers looking to carry private brands will undoubtedly follow.[38]

Another approach manufacturers have taken to reduce the negative impact of private labels is to expand their own offerings. Sara Lee Corporation—which owns a number of branded apparel companies such as Bali, Playtex, Champion, Ocean, and Hanes—has expanded into the active wear market with the Hanes Sport casual collection. The surge in popularity of active lifestyle clothing has created an increase in sales of other related products such as the sports underwear featured in the advertisement. Hanes Sport manufactures products for women, men, and children in order to slow the surge of private label entries into the market.

INTEGRATED LEARNING EXPERIENCE

Private labels are an important source of revenue for many retail stores and manufacturers. The Private Label Manufacturers' Association promotes manufacturers that produce private labels. From the Web site at **www.plma.com**, identify the press updates, store brands, and upcoming events that illustrate the importance of private labels for both retailers and manufacturers.

BRAND MANAGEMENT DURING RECESSIONS

A **recession** is a phase in which the gross national product (GNP) declines for two consecutive quarters. In most economies, a recession occurs once every four to five years. During a recession, brand managers face the issue of selecting an appropriate response. When the economy is in a slump, prices often rise, layoffs occur, and consumers curb spending. Marketing experts must decide if advertising budgets should be cut and money shifted to promotions that drive sales. Although this strategy may negatively affect profits, it normally prevents market share erosion.

Poor economic conditions do not affect all product categories equally. Luxury goods, such as real estate, furniture, and automobiles, may be strongly affected. Necessity goods, such as food, medicine, and gasoline, may not experience as strong of an impact. Manufacturers and retailers often encounter substitute buying. In other words consumers hunt for lower-priced alternatives. Thus, hamburger is purchased rather than steak, Kool-Aid rather than Pepsi or Coke, and so forth.

The best approach for coping with a recession depends on a brand's product category. Also, the brand's unique selling point and position in the marketplace are factors. A brand that has promoted itself as the "cheapest" or "lowest-cost" alternative should not change during a recession. In fact, the firm may wish to emphasize such a position.

Building market share is difficult (although not impossible) during recessions, because consumers often become more choosy in their purchases. They are sometimes less willing to experiment and try new brands. Consumers tend to stick with brands they can trust and that provide them with a feeling of security. For example, Levi-Strauss normally projects its brand from a "value-added perspective," which helped it gain market share in Europe, the United States, and Asia during recent recessions.[39]

At the same time, during slow economic times, many companies try to gain on their competitors in terms of both market share and brand equity. In a recent recession, Levi-Strauss promoted itself as a choice that illustrated individuality and self-confidence. This approach often works during a recession because it bolsters an individual's confidence that he or she made a solid decision during a time that the economy is slumping. Levi-Strauss also invested in targeted promotional activities including pop concerts and sponsorships that promoted a sense of

Hanes Sport is one of many companies that has introduced new products into the active lifestyle wear market.
Source: Courtesy of Sara Lee Corporation.

belonging and feeling good. Both a sense of belonging and feeling good appear to be important to consumers during slower economic periods.[40]

Another way to gain a competitive advantage during a recession is to increase consumer awareness at a relatively low cost. Many companies cut advertising expenditures during poor economic times. As a result, various media make attractive offers to those willing to advertise. Recent studies in Japan, Asia, and the United States indicated that companies that increased advertising expenditures during recessions always gained in sales, market share, and operating profits. Recessions can be good times to attract new users and encourage brand switching. Because people need to feel secure during recessions, individuals are more willing to switch to a brand they perceive to be a lower risk. Effective advertising helps firms take advantage of this opportunity.[41]

POSITIONING

Another important element in corporate and brand image management is its position. **Positioning** is the process of creating a perception in the consumer's mind regarding the nature of a company and its products relative to the competition. Position is created by variables such as the quality of products, prices charged, methods of distribution, image, and other factors. Positioning consists of two important elements: (1) It is established relative to the competition, and (2) it exists in the minds of consumers. Although a firms attempts to position its products through advertising and other marketing communications, consumers ultimately determine the position of the firm's products. To be effective, firms must either reinforce what consumers already believe about a product and its brand name or shift the consumer's view toward a more desirable position. The former strategy is certainly easier to accomplish than the latter. The goal of positioning is to find that niche in a consumer's mind that a product can occupy.

To prevent cannibalism, Campbell's Soups must position each version of its V8 juice for individual target markets.
Source: Courtesy of Campbell Soup Company.

Positioning is vital for companies such as Procter & Gamble, VF Corporation, Sara Lee Corporation, and Campbell's Soups, because it helps prevent cannibalism among various brands within a product category. For example, Campbell's Soups produces five different types of V8 juice. The one pictured is marketed to individuals concerned about calories and fat content. Campbell's offers a low-sodium version of V8 for individuals on a low-sodium diet, a spicy hot version for consumers who want something with more taste or who need a mixer, and a calcium-enriched version for those who desire more calcium, potassium, or vitamins A and C.

Effective positioning can be achieved in seven different ways. Although companies may try two or three approaches, such efforts generally result in confusing the customer. The best method is to use one of these approaches consistently.

An *attribute* is a product trait or characteristic that sets it apart from other products. Ultra Brite positions itself by the attribute that it makes teeth their brightest. Ultra Brite has chosen a different attribute (whitening) to make a distinction in the consumer's mind because other toothpastes focus more on cavity prevention. In the advertisement shown, Sony is promoting the attribute of its projector having a stronger light to its business customers.

Using *competitors* to garner a position in the consumer's mind is another common tactic, whereby one brand is contrasted to show the position of another. For example, in an effort to gain market share, Avis ran a series of advertisements comparing itself to Hertz. Avis admitted

An advertisement by Echo positioning the automobile on the basis of high gas mileage.

A business-to-business advertisement positioned based on the product's attributes.

Source: Courtesy of Sony Electronics, Inc.

the company was not number one, then went on to explain the advantage that second place brought to consumers, because Avis was willing to "try harder" for business.

Use or application positioning involves creating a memorable set of uses for a product. Arm and Hammer has long utilized this approach in the attempt to convince consumers to use its baking soda as a deodorizer in the refrigerator. Arm & Hammer has also been featured as a co-brand in toothpaste, creating yet another use for the product.

Businesses on the extremes of the price range often use the *price–quality relationship*. At the top end, businesses emphasize high quality while at the bottom end, low prices are emphasized. Hallmark Cards cost more but are for those who "only want to send the very best." Other firms seek to be a "low-price leader," with no corresponding statement about quality.

A *product user* positioning strategy distinguishes a brand or product by clearly specifying who might use it. Apple Computers originally positioned itself as the computer for educational institutions. Although this strategy helped it grow rapidly, Apple had a difficult time convincing businesses to use its computers in the business arena. Apple had done such a good job with its original positioning strategy that changing people's view was virtually impossible.

Sometimes firms seek to position themselves in a particular *product class.* Orange juice was long considered part of the breakfast drink product class. Years ago, those in the industry decided to create advertisements designed to move orange juice into a new product class, with slogans such as "it's not just for breakfast anymore." If this repositioning is successful, then consumers would consider orange juice at any time during the day. Such a move would be somewhat successful if orange juice is viewed as a "healthy" drink. On the other hand, if the product class is beverages, then orange juice suddenly competes with giants such as Pepsi and Coke and is much less likely to succeed.

The Kenmore appliance brand uses a similar strategy. By seeking to make Kenmore a distinct product class (appliances) separate from retail, Sears tries to take advantage of product class positioning.

Identifying a product with a *cultural symbol* is difficult but, if done successfully, can become a strong competitive advantage for a firm. Chevrolet uses this type of positioning strategy. Chevrolet is advertised as being as American as baseball and apple pie during the summer. Playboy has evolved into an entertainment empire by becoming a cultural symbol, albeit a controversial one. In its advertisement, Stetson attempts to identify its cologne with the American cowboy and the spirit of the West. The ad copy reads that "The attraction is legendary." The purpose of placing this ad in *Glamour* magazine was to entice women to purchase the product for the men in their lives.

Other Elements of Positioning

Brand positioning is never completely fixed and can be changed. For instance, Gillette, traditionally firmly entrenched with men, has recently launched a massive campaign to position itself in the women's market. The company distributes new products (the Sensor Excel razor and Satin Care shave gel) through direct-marketing efforts such as mailings to consumer homes and free samples in homeroom bags for 14- and 15-year-old girls at school. The positions of the women's products are to be established through ads asking "Are you ready?" with the tagline "Yes, I am!" Gillette designed the campaign to encourage women to view its products as a key part of being physically and psychologically ready for anything. This positioning supports the position of Gillette's men's razors, marketed through the "Best a man can get" slogan.[42]

Understanding how consumers view a product is important to successfully position it. Industry analysts discovered that many consumers perceived the Lexus automobile to be distant and cold. According to Scott Gilbert, co-chairman of Team One Advertising Agency, the Lexus had "been criticized at times for not having enough soul." Current ads, in response, are dedicated to communicating the emotional connection between a Lexus driver and his or her car.[43]

Brand positioning also applies to business-to-business marketing efforts. Crowne Plaza, a sub-brand of Holiday Inn, has developed a positioning strategy for upscale business travelers based on attributes. The goal is to provide the services and amenities that business travelers desire along with those relevant to their jobs. At the same time, the company does not provide amenities that might be considered extravagant, so that the room can be charged to an expense account.[44]

The SubmitOrder.com ad positions the company as the business solution for those involved in e-commerce. A visit to the firm's Web site at www.submitorder.com indicates the firm offers multiple

An advertisement by Stetson using the cultural symbolism of the cowboy as the positioning strategy.
Source: Courtesy of J.B. Stetson Company.

THE ATTRACTION IS LEGENDARY

services such as brand development, IT management, data mining, e-distribution services, and customer response services.

Effective positioning is important in the international arena and must be included in the marketing plan when a firm expands into other countries. Often the positioning strategy used in one country will not work in another. Marketing experts carefully analyze the competition as well as the consumers or businesses that are potential customers. After this analysis, the firm is better able to choose a positioning strategy. Although the positioning strategy may need to be modified for each country, the company's overall theme and the brand image should be consistent.

Finally, in positioning products, it is important to be sure that the positioning strategy chosen is relevant to consumers and provides them with a benefit they consider useful in decision making. Aunt Jemima learned the hard way that although the company itself occupied a unique, strong position in the marketplace, sales of frozen waffles, a new product, could not be based on one attribute, a resealable storage bag. The attribute was not important to consumers in the decision process. This was because the product itself, the waffles, had a poor taste relative to fresh waffles.[45]

Brand positioning is a critical part of image and brand-name management. Consumers have an extensive set of purchasing options, which means they can try products with specific advantages or attributes. Effective positioning, by whatever tactic chosen, increases sales and strengthens the long-term positions of both individual products and the total organization.

An advertisement for SubmitOrder.com featuring positioning by product class.
Source: Courtesy of SubmitOrder.com Inc.

SUMMARY

An effective integrated marketing communications plan must emphasize, as part of the program, an effective company or corporate image. This image consists of consumer and business-to-business feelings toward the overall organization as well as evaluations of each individual brand the firm carries. An image has both tangible and intangible components. Tangible ingredients include products, advertisements, names, logos, and services provided. Intangible elements consist of policies and practices that change or enhance the company's image in the consumer's mind.

A well-developed and well-established image benefits both customers and the company in many ways.

Creating an effective image is a difficult task. It is important to know how all publics view the firm before seeking to build or enhance an image. Rejuvenating the image involves reminding customers of their previous conceptions of the company while at the same time expanding into a closely related area of concern. Once an image is strongly pressed into the minds of customers, it becomes difficult, if not impossible, to change.

A corporate name is the overall banner under which all other operations occur. The corporate logo accompanying the name is the symbol used to identify a company and its brands, helping to convey the overall corporate image. The firm's name and image are important not only to general customers but also to any firms that may make purchases from or conduct business with a manufacturer or service provider.

Brands are names given to products or services, or groups of complementary products. Effective brands give the firm an advantage, especially in mature markets containing fewer actual products or where service differences exist. Strong brands convey the most compelling benefits of the product, elicit proper consumer emotions, and help create loyalty. There are many versions of brands, including family brands, flanker brands, and co-brands. In each, brand equity is built by domination, or the recognition that the brand has one key advantage or characteristic.

Recently, private brands or private labels have become an important component in the success rates of both producers and retailers. Consumers now view private brands as having quality equal to or close to that of more famous manufacturer brand names. At the same time, customers expect price advantages in private label products. Consequently, effective management of brands and products includes creating a mix of offerings that both end users and retailers recognize as a beneficial range of choices.

Brand name management is crucial during recessions. Consumers may be more cautious about switching brands during slow economic periods. At the same time, firms that promote and emphasize key features (safety, low cost, confidence) may be able to build sales, create loyalty, and gain share during recessionary periods.

Positioning is the relative psychological location of the good or service as compared to its competitor's in the views of customers. Marketing managers must select a positioning strategy that highlights the best features of the company's products or services. Positioning is never fixed, because markets evolve over time. Positioning can be established with both the general public and business-to-business customers.

REVIEW QUESTIONS

1. What is meant by "corporate image"? What are the tangible aspects of a corporate image?
2. How does a corporation's image help customers? How does it help the specific company?
3. How will company leaders know they have created the "right" image for their firm?
4. What is a corporate logo? What are the characteristics of an effective corporate logo?
5. What is meant by the term *stimulus codability?*
6. What is the difference between a brand name and a corporation's overall image?
7. What are the characteristics of a strong and effective brand name?
8. What is the difference between brand equity and brand recognition?
9. Why is brand equity important? How is it measured?
10. Describe the use of brand extension and flanker brand strategies.
11. Name and describe three types of co-brands.
12. How has private branding, or private labeling, changed in the past decade?
13. Describe effective brand management during recessions.
14. What is product–brand positioning? Give examples of various types of positioning strategies.

KEY TERMS

image overall consumer perceptions or end user feelings toward a company along with its products and services.

corporate logo the symbol used to identify a company and its brands, helping to convey the overall corporate image.

stimulus codability items that easily evoke consensually held meanings within a culture or subculture.

brands names generally assigned to a product or service or a group of complementary products.

salient when consumers are aware of the brand, have it in their consideration sets (things they consider when making purchases), regard the product and brand as a good value, buy it or use it on a regular basis, and recommend it to other consumers.

family brand when a company offers a series or group of products under one brand name.

brand equity a set of brand assets that add to the value assigned to a product.

market penetration the number of households within an area that purchased a product as a percentage of total households that bought in that product's category.

brand metrics measures of returns on brand investments.

brand extension the use of an established brand name on products or services not related to the core brand.

flanker brand the development of a new brand by a company in a product or service category it currently has a brand offering.

co-branding offering two or more brands in a single marketing effort.

ingredient branding a form of co-branding in which the name of one brand is placed within another brand.

cooperative branding a form of co-branding in which two firms create a joint venture of two or more brands into a new product or service.

complementary branding a form of co-branding in which the marketing of two brands together encourages co-consumption or co-purchases.

private brands (also known as *private labels*) proprietary brands marketed by an organization and normally distributed exclusively within the organization's outlets.

recession a phase in which the gross national product (GNP) declines for two consecutive quarters.

positioning the process of creating a perception in the consumer's mind about the nature of a company and its products relative to the competition. It is created by the quality of products, prices charged, methods of distribution, image, and other factors.

CRITICAL THINKING EXERCISES

Discussion Questions

1. Dalton Office Supply Company has been in operation for over 50 years and was the predominant office supply company in its region during that time. Approximately 85 percent of Dalton's business is based on providing materials to other businesses. Only 15 percent comes from walk-in customers. Recently, low-cost providers such as Office Depot have cut into Dalton's market share. Surveys of consumers indicate that Dalton has an image of being outdated and pricey. Consumers did report that Dalton's customer service was above average. What image should Dalton project to regain its market share? Outline a plan to rejuvenate the company's image.

2. Henry and Becky Thompson plan to open a new floral and gift shop in Orlando, Florida. They want to project an image of being trendy, upscale, and fashionable. They are trying to decide on a name and logo. What should be the name of their company? What kind of logo should they develop?

3. Go to a local retail store. Choose five packages that are effective. Describe the reasons they are effective. Choose five labels that were effective at capturing attention. What features were the attention-getting aspects of the label?

4. Suppose Terminix Pest Control wants to expand through co-branding. To gather more information about Terminix, access its Web site at **www.terminix.net**. What type of co-branding would you suggest? Which companies should Terminix contact?

5. Look up one of the following companies on the Internet. Discuss the image conveyed by the Web site. What positioning strategy does it use? What changes or improvements could it make?

   a. Scuba world (**www.scubaworld.com**)

   b. Union Pacific Railroad (**www.uprr.com**)

   c. Bicycle Museum of America (**www.bicyclemuseum.com**)

   d. Metro Dynamics (**www.metrodynamics.com**)

   e. Canyon Beach Wear (**www.canyonbeachwear.com**)

Developing a Brand Name and an Image Management Program

One of the major challenges your product and company faces is brand equity. People may not perceive any great difference between items; therefore, a strong brand name is vital to success. If the product or service is part of larger company operations, the image of that firm also plays a key role as you develop your IMC campaign. The Web site **www.prenhall.com/clow** or access the IMC Plan Pro disk that accompanied this textbook provides an exercise to help you create an effective brand and a positive image for the firm. Remember, your firm's image is important not only domestically but also in the international arena.

BUILDING AN
IMC
CAMPAIGN
IMC PlanPro!

CASE 1

"For sale," read the sign in front of Dave's Scuba Shop. Dave Dishman, who loved his business, sadly had to admit that he could not continue operating with the kinds of losses he had been experiencing. He was left to ponder what had gone wrong.

From what he could tell, Dave's problems came in three areas: turnover, inconsistency, and bad public relations. He had tried to deal with all of the issues, but with no success.

The company began with a promising opening weekend. Dave set up shop on the south side of Arlington, Texas, with a small store containing basic scuba equipment items for sale and the offer to make repairs and provide routine maintenance for scuba gear. Early traffic through the store was encouraging, partly due to radio remote features of a local disk jockey, who was an avid diver.

In the first year, Dave sponsored a dive and also provided funds for a diving-for-charity event. He was trying to build a name for his store as the center of activity when it came to diving in the region. He posted billboards promoting his outlet as where the "best scuba gear and repair" could be found.

The first bad break came when Dave's key repairman, John, had to quit. John was a first-class repairman who took the time to do a job right. He never compromised on the quality of a repair, even if the store lost money on the deal. John's wife, who was their major source of income, had gotten a promotion, which meant they had to move. John's talent was easily transferred to another city. Consequently, he agreed to move on.

Dave tried three new maintenance and repair workers in the next six months. Two were male, one was female, and all three were unacceptable. There was either sloppy work to contend with, or the work took too long. Dave had to soothe the feelings of many unhappy customers during that time period.

Because Dave couldn't find a good repair person, he decided to do all of the repair work personally. He hired a sales rep to run the front of the store. Mimi was an attractive snorkeling enthusiast. Her only drawback was a great interest in talking about diving rather than selling gear. She was not highly productive in terms of other chores, such as checking out the drawer or restocking shelves. Dave ended up spending longer hours at night fixing things in the "front room." He was also inclined to make mistakes when he was tired, meaning even some of his repairs were suspect.

Word around town was that customers would get an overpriced diving suit with marginal service at Dave's Scuba Shop. Business slowed, and Dave was forced to terminate Mimi, leaving him to run the entire operation himself. Mimi quickly began spreading rumors that Dave was a "jerk," not a good thing to happen in a tightly knit diving community.

Dave decided to try big discounts. He cut prices on all of his products and took out several ads showing how his products were comparably priced with those in major discount stores. To offset his margin losses on scuba equipment, Dave raised the price for his repairs. He soon was spending too much time on the sales floor and not enough in the repair room.

Finally Dave found a competent maintenance person. He could again focus on selling. He lowered the rates for his repair business, but word around town was that his was the highest price in the area.

Dave tried getting more involved in the diving community to offset the negative image Mimi was creating. He had some limited success, enticing a few former customers to come back.

By then Dave pretty well knew that there was insufficient demand to continue operations in the same way. He was at a loss about how to proceed. Before he could even offer a new program, his rent was three months' overdue and several suppliers had "cut him off" until he paid some back bills. He knew the store's credit rating was ruined. Even the utility companies were unhappy.

At that point, Dave had no choice. He had lost his investment and knew his store was about to become one of those nameless and faceless statistics of failed entrepreneurial ventures.

1. What image did Dave try to establish in his store?
2. What image did Dave's Scuba Shop end up projecting?
3. What could Dave have done to maintain and improve the image of his store and his company?
4. Could Dave's Scuba Shop have been salvaged? How?

CASE 2

THE CANDIDATE

Sheila Patterson wanted to make a career change. Sheila had been a paralegal for the past 10 years and decided to run for circuit clerk of Gastonia County in Illinois. The job essentially involved managing a group of individuals responsible for sending out tax forms and collecting county taxes on vehicles and property.

The trick to getting the job, however, was that Sheila would need to win an election. Local politics are among the most shady and divisive that take place, especially when a good-paying job is at stake. During other elections over the past decade, Sheila was aware that one candidate had seen her billboard ads changed from "Democratic" party to "Communist" party in the middle of the night by a rival. Another black candidate had reported to the media that someone had scrawled the word *nigger* on several campaign posters, and then used the sympathy and backlash vote to win a district election for city council.

The other main issue was name awareness. In the most recent election, a local police chief who had been fired for illegal activities at his last two jobs had his name splashed all over the media for several years. In spite of the negative news about his work habits, the man ran for county sheriff, counting on voters to remember his name and little more. The strategy worked, and the county now is run by a less-than-ethical law enforcer.

Sheila would be running against an incumbent whose primary advantages were that he had his name sent out on tax mailings every December, meaning he had strong name recognition, and that the gentleman was a member of the Republican-Party, the stronger political party in the area. She knew these two obstacles would be difficult to overcome.

Sheila's major edges in the race were that her opponent would be complacent and not campaign very hard (he had won three times previously) and that she had a major "war chest" to spend on the election. She had carefully raised funds for the past year and would be able to spend three times as much on campaign ads.

Sheila wasn't sure if being female would be an advantage or a disadvantage. In her focus groups, some felt the term *clerk* is readily associated with a female. Others believed that her opponent could capitalize on the management aspects of the job, which was most associated with males.

The primary question Sheila had was about image. She knew the crooked sheriff had won but still wasn't sure a bad image was better than no image at all. On the other hand, she was not sure what kind of image to promote. Her choices were, of course, to make a strong positive case about her

(continued)

skills and qualifications or to go negative and claim her opponent simply was doing a poor job. There was some evidence that he was unpopular with his staff and that the state auditor had criticized some of his practices for being "sloppy" at best.

Still, Sheila knew the risks of going negative. First, she was divorced and had had a few minor brushes with the law over traffic tickets and reckless driving a few years ago. Her friends warned her that a negative campaign would make her look worse and damage her own image in what could turn into a tight race. At the same time, Sheila knew she only had six months to make people aware of her name and image, and to persuade them to vote against an incumbent, when many people vote only along party lines or for names they recognize.

1. What are the brand image issues in this case?

2. What kinds of ads should Sheila develop for this race?

3. Is there anything else Sheila could do to enhance her chances of winning?

4. Is "no image" better than a negative image in the politics of your hometown? Defend your reasoning with examples.

5. Based on the information given, develop a campaign theme to help Sheila win.

6. Can a politician's name have brand equity? Why or why not?

ENDNOTES

1. "Who Is Steven?" (www.dell.com/us/en/dhs/topics/segtopic_steven_whois.htm, June 15, 2002), "Dude, Meet the Dell Guy," (www.cnn.com/2002/SHOWBIZ/TV/01/31/dell.guy, January 31, 2002), ABC News Moneyscope, "Meet the Dell Dude: Surfer Geek Helps PC Maker Boost Sales," (www.abcnews.go.com/sections/business/dailynews/dell_dude_020124.html, January 24, 2002).

2. Alexandra Lennane, "Speaking for Themselves," *Airfinance Journal* (March 1998), p. 204.

3. Ibid.

4. Christopher Palmeri, "Radio Shack Redux," *Forbes* (March 23, 1998), pp. 54–56.

5. Lennane, "Speaking for Themselves," p. 204.

6. Jennifer McFarland, "Branding from the Inside Out, and from the Outside In," *Harvard Management Update,* 7, issue 2 (February 2002), pp. 3–4.

7. "Puffed Up," *The Economist* (March 21, 1998), p. 82.

8. Paul McNamara, "The Name Game," *Network World* (April 20, 1998), pp. 77–78.

9. Ibid.

10. James R. Shennan Jr., "Permanent Media Can Generate a Long Lasting Image," *Hotel and Motel Management*, 201 (1986), p. 30.

11. David J. Morrow, "An Image Makeover," *International Business*, 5, no. 3 (1992), pp. 66–68.

12. Pamela W. Henderson and Joseph A. Cote, "Guidelines for Selecting or Modifying Logos," *Journal of Marketing* (April 1998), pp. 14–30.

13. Andrew Ehrenberg, Neil Barnard, and John Scriven, "Differentiation or Salience," *Journal of Advertising Research* (November–December 1997), pp. 7–14.

14. Chuck Pettis, "Making Ignorance an Opportunity," *MC Technology Marketing Intelligence* (February 1998), pp. 52–53; David Marting, "Branding: Finding That 'One Thing,'" *Brandweek* (February 16, 1998), p. 18.

15. Stephen E. Frank, "American Express Image Fails to Deliver Success for Its Discount-Brokerage Unit," *Wall Street Journal* (May 5, 1997), p. C1.

16. Doris Walczyk, "Packaging should be a Critical Element in the Branding Scheme," *Marketing News,* 35, issue 23 (August 2001), pp. 14–17.

17. Ibid.

18. Victoria Moore and Frances Stonor Saunders, "Message on a Bottle," *New Statesman,* 130, issue 4538 (May 21, 2001), pp. 49–53.

19. Sarah Theodore, "Can You Judge a Beverage by its Package?," *Beverage Industry,* 92, issue 2 (February 2001), pp. 36–39.

20. Pamela Accetta, "Packaging Prowess," *Dairy Field,* 184, issue 10 (October 2001), p. 54.

21. *Food Manufacture,* "A Sleek Look For Nescafe," 76, issue 11 (November 2001), p. 21.

22. Michael Kahn, "Super Convenience," *Frozen Food Age,* 49, issue 6 (January 2001), p. 16.

23. Ibid.

24. Linda Bren, "Choosing Pet Food by the Label," *Consumers' Research Magazine,* 84, issue 6 (June 2001), pp. 22–27.

25. Marsha Lindsay, "Five Ways to Build Brand Equity," *Electrical World* (March 1998), p. 15.

26. Frank S. Washington, "Brand Advertising Pulls Consumers from the Clutter," *Auto Marketing* (April 6, 1998), p. S10.

27. Allan L. Baldinger, Edward Blair, and Raj Echambadi, "Why Brands Grow," *Journal of Advertising Research,* 42, issue 41 (January/February 2002), pp. 7–15.

28. Jeannette Hanna, "How To Expand Your Brand," *Marketing Magazine,* 107, issue 13 (April 1, 2002), pp. 15–20.

29. Anjan Chatterjee, Matthew E. Jauchius, Hans-Werner Kass, and Aurobind Satpathy, "Revving Up Auto Branding," *McKinsey Quarterly,* issue 1 (2002), pp. 134–44.

30. Maxine Lans Retsky, "Victor's Little Secret May be in Jeopardy," *Marketing News,* 36, issue 11 (May 27, 2002), p. 6

31. Don E. Schultz, "Mastering Brand Metrics," *Marketing Management,* 11, issue 3 (May/June 2002), pp. 8–9.

32. Daniel Baack and Mark N. Hatala, "Predictors of Brand Rating and Brand Recall: An Empirical Investigation," *Regional Business Review,* 17 (1998), pp. 17–34.

33. Danny Kucharsky, "AAPQ Study Highlights Brand Value," *Marketing Magazine,* 107, issue 13, (April 1, 2002), p. 3.

34. Ming H. Hsieh, "Identifying Brand Image Dimensionality and Measuring the Degree of Brand Globalization: A Cross-National Study," *Journal of International Marketing,* 10, issue 2 (2002), pp. 46–68.

35. Jennifer McFarland, "Branding from the Inside Out and from the Outside In," pp. 3–4.

36. Stephanie Thompson, "Brand Buddies," *Brandweek* (February 23, 1998), pp. 22–30.

37. Ibid.

38. Mark Henricks, "Private Labeling: Who Said the Stores Would Get Tired of Manufacturing. . ." *Apparel Industry Magazine* (March 1998), pp. 20–28.

39. Prashun Dutt, "Brand Management During Recession," *Asian Business* (May 1998), pp. 32–34.

40. Ibid.

41. Ibid.

42. Pat Sloan, "Gillette Bets $80 Mil on Women," *Advertising Age* (May 4, 1998), p. 63.

43. Kathy Tyrer, "Lexus Makes an Emotional Appeal: New Team One Campaign Hopes to Dispel Cold, Distant Image," *Adweek* Eastern Edition (September 8, 1997), p. 5.

44. "The New Address for the Savvy Traveler," *Lodging Hospitality* (April 1998), pp. 74–78.

45. Marc Schwimmer, "Relevance Is a Key, but Relative Factor" *Brandweek* (January 2, 1998), p. 14.

Consumer Buyer Behavior

3

Chapter Objectives

Learn **how to take advantage of each stage in the consumer purchase decision-making process.**

Target **advertisements and other marketing communications to meet the emotional and logical needs of consumers.**

Refine **knowledge about how attitudes and values are reflected in buyer behaviors.**

Discover **the traditional factors that affect consumer purchasing decisions.**

Understand **how new trends in society affect purchasing processes.**

STARBUCKS CREATES A NEW COFFEE CULTURE

Is it possible to convince ordinary Americans who routinely open 3-pound "value" cans of coffee, shovel the grounds into a paper filter, push a button, and go about their business to suddenly change their ways? Will they be willing to spend $2 or more per day on the same item? Will this eventually evolve into a $1,400 per year habit of a *latte* and a *scone* each day? The answers to these questions, according to Starbucks, is "absolutely!"

Starbucks began as a coffee importing firm. Howard Schultz, an employee in the organization, toured Italy in the early 1980s and watched as crowds of city dwellers began each morning with a stop at a coffee bar. Schultz tried to convince the owners of Starbucks to do something similar in the United States and was roundly rejected. Quitting the firm and launching out on his own quickly turned into a lucrative decision for Schultz. He raised money from a variety of investors and opened a café in Seattle using the name *Il Giornale*. Success came rapidly. Schultz wound up buying the original importing business and renaming his cafés Starbucks.

Within 15 years, Starbucks Coffee Company expanded to over 1,200 retail outlets. The firm achieved this remarkable growth because of several key marketing ideas. The product itself, locations, employees, sourcing, and effective marketing communications all worked together to help the firm prosper in a saturated marketplace. The nonchalance of major competitors was also a factor.

The product itself, coffee, had been a rather banal commodity for most consumers. Purchase price was traditionally the primary decision variable. Starbucks needed to convince prospective buyers of the difference in its offerings. By studying the basics of coffee (flavor, acidity, and body), the company's leadership sought the best beans in the world. Then, other aspects of the product changed, including steaming milk and brewing coffee in a plunger pot. *Espresso* is an acquired taste for most consumers. To reach the market,

Starbucks offers it both straight and diluted in creamy drinks such as *caffe latte,* which is *espresso* mixed with steamed milk and covered with a topping of milk foam. Other products include *cappuccino* and *caffe mocha.* When any one of these Starbucks products is sold, the basic ingredient, coffee, is never more than an hour old.

Locations are key ingredients in Starbucks's success. Cafés must be easily accessible on commuter routes and in other places where people can gather to socialize. In each café there are numerous enticements, including jazz music in the background and other merchandise to examine, such as stainless steel thermoses, commuter mugs, filters, natural hairbrushes for cleaning coffee grinders, and home *espresso* machines.

Starbucks attracts employees who enjoy coffee. They are retained through a variety of motivational programs including buy-in options. Workers are called *baristas,* Italian for "bar person." Starbucks continually encourages these *baristas* to provide high-quality, pleasant service to patrons. Extensive training helps ensure they become experts in all aspects of coffee vending. The company also insists on a diverse workforce reflecting the makeup of the local community.

Starbucks holds a major advantage of sourcing. The firm is vertically integrated and relies on quality suppliers from around the world. Each region grows beans with distinct flavors for coffee connisseurs, and Starbucks brings all of the flavors to a single location for purchase.

The most impressive aspect of Starbucks may be its marketing communications program. The firm had to convince price-conscious buyers to shift away from old purchasing decision rules in order to part with a great deal more money each day. Starbucks also needed to convince some consumers to develop a habit that, to many, seemed like a bad one because of the caffeine involved.

To achieve these goals, Starbucks noted two primary target markets. The first was the younger, grunge-dominated Generation X types inhabiting the Seattle area. Many people of this generation found coffee shops to be an alternative to the bar scene and made purchases accordingly. Coffee-shop regulars tend to hang out for longer periods of time, reading, talking, and listening to the background music. Next, the baby boom generation became a target as people in their 40s and 50s began consuming less alcohol and looking for other products with a degree of "snob appeal." Coffee became an excellent choice. The most loyal boomer customers can discuss coffees such as Jamaican Blue Mountain with as much sophistication as they used to describe wines such as Chateauneuf-du-Pape. Starbucks customers appear to agree that this more expensive but higher-quality coffee makes regular joe seem almost distasteful.

Coffee giants Maxwell House (owned by General Foods) and Folgers (owned by Procter & Gamble) simply ignored the potential of gourmet coffee. The idea of vending coffee in a café seemed so far-fetched to these firms that they did not view Starbucks as a threat, even as Seattle became known as "Latteland." Failing to see the growing market for whole bean coffee as a retail product led to lost market share. In 1990, gourmet coffee companies had a 13.5 percent share of the market. By 1991, the share was up to 17.1 percent. The trend has continued through the new millennium. Today Starbucks easily has as much name recognition and more brand loyalty compared to its major competitors.

Starbucks has continued to expand through business-to-business marketing efforts based on the strength of the company's name. New customers include United Airlines, the Holland America cruise line, Chicago's Wrigley Field, and an alliance with Barnes & Noble bookstores. What started as essentially a small blip on the competitive radar is now a major force in the coffee industry. Consumers continue to happily part with extra dollars to support coffee habits that represent something far more complex than simply buying a beverage in the morning. Starbucks has created a whole new coffee culture.[1]

JAVANET INTERNET CAFÉ

The IMC foundation consists of many components, including a clear understanding of the firm's target markets and customer base. It is not enough to know who buys products. The marketing team must also understand why they buy and how they buy. Only then can advertisements and other promotional devices be structured to reach the group effectively. Every step of the purchasing process, from problem recognition to post-purchase feelings, represents an opportunity to build a relationship with a customer.

Read sections 2.1.4 and 2.2 of the JavaNet Internet Café example from the IMC Plan Pro disk. Notice the extensive discussion regarding the various types of computer users and café visitors. The secret to building a successful IMC program is to create one clear voice and message that reaches all of these groups yet can be tailored to the individual needs of each group. Thus, senior novice computer users will be just as pleased to discover a pleasant environment and helpful employees as high-tech teenagers and college students.

One of the most common practices in the behavioral and social sciences is *modeling* various activities and behaviors. Marketing experts can utilize models to understand and manage a number of critical factors. Modeling helps researchers develop sophisticated approaches to effectively recognize and react to customer attitudes, preferences, and desires.

In this chapter, an important marketing model appears. It characterizes the processes consumers go through as they make purchasing decisions (Figure 3.1). The model is useful in explaining consumer buyer behaviors as well as recent factors that have affected the choices being made by individuals making purchases.

A primary goal of an integrated marketing communications program must be to develop an effective method of persuading consumers to purchase a particular product or service. Therefore, this chapter reviews *consumer buyer behavior* from an IMC perspective. When consumer purchasing decisions are more fully understood, it becomes possible to develop better marketing communications programs.

CONSUMER PURCHASING PROCESSES

Marketing managers constantly endeavor to influence consumer decisions. In an era in which they are directly accountable for results of individual campaigns, these marketing experts must carefully develop messages that will entice buyers to purchase the products being featured in a timely fashion. Therefore, it is helpful to step back and look at a traditional model of the process. Figure 3.1 highlights the five steps in the consumer decision-making process: (1) problem recognition, (2) information search, (3) evaluation of alternatives, (4) the purchase decision, and (5) postpurchase evaluation. A detailed analysis of each of these steps follows.

PROBLEM RECOGNITION

The first step in the consumer decision-making process is the recognition of a problem. A problem is present when a consumer's desired state is different than his or her actual state. In other words, it is the recognition of a need or a want. For instance, after a long day at work, a consumer might go home to look in the refrigerator for food. If there isn't any, then a need is present. Other times, food is in the refrigerator, but it is not the kind the consumer wants. Again, the consumer's current state is different than his or her desired state. In both situations, the consumer identifies a problem.

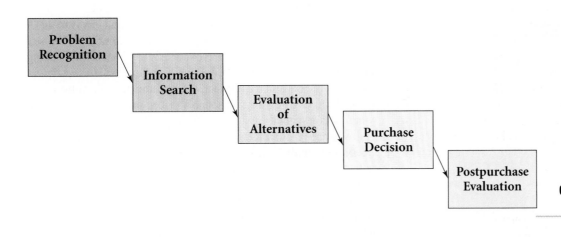

FIGURE 3.1
Consumer Decision-Making Process

An advertisement by Bell to trigger problem recognition using the heading "Does your kid have hundred dollar feet and a ten dollar head?"
Source: Courtesy of Bell Helmets.

A Neutrogena ad designed to convince consumers that the product should be the first choice when selecting an anti-wrinkle cream.
Source: Courtesy of Neutrogena Corporation.

Recognition of a problem is not always a cognitive event, in which a person actively thinks about a need. Simply seeing and smelling cookies at a bakery triggers a reflex or desire to have them (a want). The consumer must then move forward to satisfy the need or want that exists.

INFORMATION SEARCH

Once a need or want is recognized, the consumer conducts a search for information. This begins with an *internal search;* the consumer mentally recalls images of products that might fulfill or meet the need. Often, the individual remembers how the need was satisfied in the past. If a particular brand was chosen and the experience with that brand was positive, the consumer may repeat the purchase decision. When this happens, further evaluation of alternatives is not necessary. On the other hand, if the previous experience was not positive, the consumer will conduct a more in-depth internal search. Exposures to other brands from past experiences and memories are then considered.

Many motives are present in internal searches. Dissatisfaction with the last purchase is not the only reason an individual conducts a search. He or she may want to try a new brand or product for novelty or variety. For instance, a consumer who normally eats at Taco Bell decides to go to Hardee's instead because she wants to try something different. Further, a consumer expands an information search after hearing about a new or a different brand from a friend or because of a positive response to an advertisement.

When conducting the internal search, consumers utilize what is known as an evoked set. An **evoked set** consists of the set of brands a consumer considers during the information search and evaluation processes. The set does not normally contain every brand the consumer has experienced. The consumer often removes from the evoked set brands that have been tried that did not provide a positive experience. The consumer also usually eliminates brands he or she knows little about. During the information search process, the consumer reduces the number of brands to a subset that is mentally manageable.

A major objective of creatives and brand managers is to make sure that a given brand becomes part of a consumer's evoked set. When the brand is part of the evoked set, the chances of its being purchased are greatly increased. A high level of *brand equity* increases the odds that a product will become part of a consumer's evoked set. High-quality, reasonably priced products and services, when accompanied by attractive and powerful advertising messages, greatly enhance the odds that the good or service will become a finalist in the purchasing decision. The Neutrogena advertisement shown in this section uses "#1" four times to persuade consumers that Neutrogena is the number-one anti-wrinkle cream. If the ad accomplishes this, consumers who want an anti-wrinkle cream will recall Neutrogena as part of their evoked sets and may view the product as the first or best choice.

Following an internal search, consumers make mental decisions about *external searches.* If the customer has sufficient information internally, he or she moves on to the next step of the decision-making process: evaluating the alternatives. When the consumer feels uncertain about the right brand to purchase, an external search takes place.

External information comes from many sources. They include friends, relatives, expert consumers, books, magazines, newspapers, advertisements, exposures to public relations activities, in-store displays, salespeople, and searching the Internet. The amount of time a consumer spends on an external search depends on four factors: (1) ability, (2) motivation, (3) costs, and (4) benefits.[2]

The first factor that determines how extensively a consumer searches for information is the *ability to search.* Ability depends on the person's educational level combined with specific knowledge of the product category and the brands being offered. An individual's level of education and the tendency to conduct external searches are closely connected. That is, educated individuals are more likely to spend time searching for information. They are also more inclined to visit stores prior to making a decision.

Consumers with extensive knowledge about individual brands and product categories can conduct more involved external searches. For example, someone who knows a great deal about cameras has a more sophisticated ability to examine information than does someone who knows little about cameras. In addition, people with more comprehensive knowledge of a product area often collect additional data even when they are not in the market for the product.[3]

The degree to which an external search takes place also depends on the customer's level of motivation. The greater the motivation, the greater the extent of external search. Motivation is determined by the consumer's:

▶ Level of involvement

▶ Need for cognition

▶ Level of shopping enthusiasm

Individuals are motivated to search for information when their involvement levels are high. **Involvement** is the extent to which a stimulus or task is relevant to a consumer's existing needs, wants, or values. The more important a product is to a consumer, the more likely he or she will engage in an external search. The amount of involvement is based on several factors. The cost of the item is a primary concern. Also, the importance the item holds for the consumer is a key variable. Involvement may be enduring or situational. *Enduring involvement* occurs in a purchase situation that always is important to a consumer. *Situational involvement* is based on a particular temporary situation. For example, clothes for many male consumers may not be high-involvement decisions (low enduring involvement), but picking a tux for a high school prom is more likely to include greater levels of involvement (higher situational involvement).

The **need for cognition** is a personality characteristic an individual displays when he or she engages in and enjoys mental activities. These mental exercises have a positive impact on the information search process. People with high needs for cognition gather more information and search more thoroughly than do individuals with a lower need for cognition.

The search also depends on a person's enthusiasm for shopping. Customers who like to shop undertake a more in-depth search for details about products and services.

Products such as kitchen flooring tend to create high involvement decisions requiring higher levels of information search.
Source: Courtesy of Howard, Merrell & Partners.

Do You Know Anybody Who Has Time To Pamper A Kitchen Floor? Neither Do We.

Like most women today, you probably have a mountain of details to contend with. Like a full-time job, or being a full-time Mom. Or both.

So the last thing you need is a floor that needs extra attention.

Any vinyl floor that can't take the heat should get out of the kitchen. That's why you'll find Congoleum vinyl floors are designed to stand up to the kind of wear and tear that your family dishes out.

You'll also find our colors and patterns last over the long haul. (After all, what good is a floor that lasts for years, if it goes out of style in two?)

So for the name of the nearest Congoleum Design Studio retailer call 1-800-934-3567, Ext.109.

Congoleum
Floors For The Way You Live.

© 1994 Congoleum

Jayco. Because You're You!

Sure, you've got a lot in common with other RVers. You love to travel. Meet new friends. Share the fun and excitement of the Great Outdoors.

But you're also unique. You have your own style, your own needs, and your own budget.

Jayco understands this. Which is why we make all kinds of RVs: travel trailers, fifth wheels, fold-down camping trailers, mini motorhomes, and truck campers, each offering a variety of floorplans and decor styles. Each unique, with its own *marks of distinction*.

We offer a wide range of prices, too...from our elegant top-of-the-line Designer Series™ models, to our attractive, mid-priced Jay Series™, to our economical, value-intensive Express Series™. Of course, Jayco always gives you more for your money, whichever series you select. That's our proudest *mark of distinction*.

So see your Jayco dealer today. He's got just the RV that says you're you!

Jayco®
SHARE THE PRIDE!
For the name of your nearest Jayco dealer, call, toll-free, 1-800-447-4700, U.S. and Canada.
Jayco, Inc. • P.O. Box 460 • Middlebury, IN • 46540

The high cost of a recreational vehicle means a consumer will normally conduct an extensive search for information, which would include reading advertisements such as this one for Jayco's model.
Source: Courtesy of Jayco, Inc.

Involvement, need for cognition, and enthusiasm for shopping determine the individual's motivation to search for information.[4]

The final factors that influence an information search are the *perceived costs* and the *perceived benefits* of the search. Higher perceived benefits increase the tendency to search. One benefit that a consumer often looks for while examining external information is the ability to reduce purchase risk. This means that by obtaining additional information, a customer can lower the chances of making a mistake in the purchasing selection.

The cost of the search consists of several items:

▶ The actual cost of the good or service

▶ The subjective costs associated with the search, including time spent and anxiety experienced while making a decision

▶ The opportunity cost of foregoing other activities to search for information (e.g., going shopping instead of playing golf or watching a movie)

As would be expected, the greater the perceived subjective cost of the external information search, the less likely the consumer will conduct a search.[5]

The four factors that make up an external search (ability, motivation, costs, and benefits) are normally all considered at the same time. When the perceived cost of a search is low and the perceived benefit high, a consumer has a higher motivation to search for information. A consumer with a minimal amount of product knowledge and a low level of education is less likely to undertake an external search, because the consumer lacks the ability to find the right information.

From a marketing communication perspective, the search process is an important time to reach the consumer with information about a particular brand. The consumer's goal in making the effort to perform an external search is to acquire information leading to a better or more informed decision. The goal of marketers during this stage is to provide information that allows consumers to make the correct decision. Because consumers have not yet made the purchase decision, this is an ideal time for marketers to influence their decision-making processes. The key is to provide the right information at the right time, about costs, benefits, quality, price, image, and any other advantage the company can gain as consumers make comparisons between products. Marketing experts need to consider three additional concepts as they study the information search process: (1) attitudes and values, (2) information processing models, and (3) cognitive mapping.

INTEGRATED LEARNING EXPERIENCE

Consumers or businesses conduct external searches when they lack sufficient internal knowledge to make wise purchase decisions. Assume you have $50,000 to $70,000 to spend on a sailboat. Access the following four Web sites:

www.multihulls.com
www.yachtworld.com
www.2hulls.com
www.boatshow.com

Select a sailboat in your price range. Why did you select that particular brand? What features are attractive to you? Do you want to consider any additional information before making an actual purchase? Would you consider any other sources of information in addition to these Web sites?

STOP

Attitudes and Values

To fully understand the role of information processing in consumer purchasing decisions, it is helpful to review attitudes and values and how they relate to marketing communications. An **attitude** is a mental position taken toward a topic, person, or event that influences the holder's feelings, perceptions, learning processes, and subsequent behaviors.[6] From a marketing communications perspective, attitudes drive purchases. If a consumer has a positive attitude toward a brand, the propensity to actually purchase that brand is higher. If a consumer appreciates an advertisement, the probability of purchasing the product it features increases.

An attitude consists of three components: (1) affective, (2) cognitive, and (3) conative.[7] The *affective* component contains the feelings or emotions a person has about the object, topic, or idea. The *cognitive* component refers to a person's mental images, understanding, and interpretations of the person, object, or issue. The *conative* component is an individual's intentions, actions, or behavior. The most common sequence of events as an attitude forms is as follows:

Cognitive → Affective → Conative

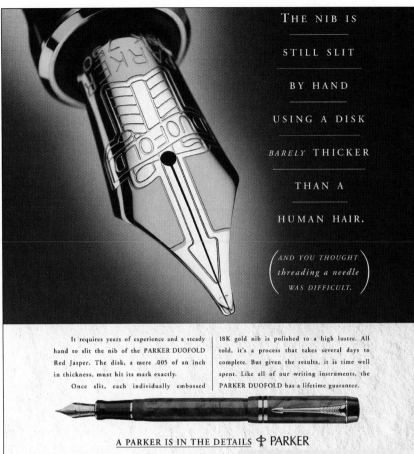

This Parker advertisement uses a cognitive appeal.
Source: Courtesy of Parker Pens.

In other words, a person first develops an understanding about an idea or object. In the case of marketing, these ideas center on the nature of the good or service. Thoughts about the product emerge from watching or reading an advertisement. They may result from exposures to information from other sources, such as the Internet or a friend's referral. Eventually, these thoughts become either positive or negative. Most people judge crime as bad and helping others as good. Consumers make positive or negative evaluations about companies and their products and services. For instance, some consumers may have negative views of credit cards while others see them as helpful and convenient.

The affective part of the attitude is the general feeling or emotion a person attaches to the idea. In the case of goods and services, the product, its name, and other features all can generate emotions. For example, what are your emotional reactions to these goods and services?

▶ Cough medicine

▶ Diaper wipes

▶ Laxatives

▶ Baseball and apple pie

▶ *Sports Illustrated*'s annual swimsuit issue

▶ Condoms

What emotions and thoughts emerge when you think about diaper wipes? Now, examine the Pampers diaper wipe advertisement shown in this section. What emotions does the ad solicit? Does the picture in the ad change your emotions? As you consider the items listed and this ad, some of your emotions or attitudes about them are relatively benign. Others are more strongly held. It is likely cough medicine does not evoke much of an emotional response, but the swimsuit issue or condoms may generate a much stronger reaction.

Some things can be rough.

Her wipe shouldn't be one of them.
Do you think your wipe is gentle enough? Pampers is.
You can count on Pampers wipes to always be feathery soft.

Pamper the skin they're in.

DMB&B

What emotions does this ad for Pampers Wipes elicit?

Source: Courtesy of D'Arcy Masius Benton & Bowles Inc. © Procter & Gamble Productions, Inc. 1999. Photograph by Penny Gentjeu.

The decision and action tendencies are the conative part of the attitude. Therefore, if a person feels strongly enough about the swimsuit issue, he or she may cancel a subscription to *Sports Illustrated* or buy extra copies for friends. Many times attitudes are not held that strongly. Some may feel favorably about a topic, such as green marketing, yet not be moved to change their purchasing behaviors.

Attitudes can develop in other ways. An alternative process may be:

Affective → Conative → Cognitive

In marketing, advertisements and other communications often appeal first to the emotions or feelings of consumers. The goal is to get a consumer to "like" a product and then make the purchase (the conative component). The cognitive understanding of the product follows. For example, a young woman may be exposed to a feminine hygiene product advertisement featuring soft, gentle images of nature that actually does not show the physical product. Still, the ad conjures favorable emotions. The person eventually purchases the product and finally learns more about it by using it and reading directions, instructions, and other information on the package or label.

Some attitudes result from a third combination of the components, as follows:

Conative → Cognitive → Affective

Purchases that require little thought, have a low price, or do not require a great deal of emotional involvement might follow this path. For instance, while shopping for groceries, a customer may notice a new brand of cookies on sale. The person may have never even seen the brand or flavor before but, because it is on sale, decides to give it a try. As the consumer eats the cookies, he or she develops a greater understanding of the product's taste, texture, and other qualities. Finally, the consumer reads the package to learn more about contents, including how many calories were devoured in one short gulp. Then the buyer finally establishes feeling toward the cookies that will affect future cookie purchases.

No matter which path is taken to develop attitudes, each component is present to some extent. Some attitudes are relatively trivial (e.g., "I like table tennis, even though I hardly ever get to play"). Others are staunchly held, such as "*I hate cigarette smoking!*" Both are associated with feelings toward things, including products in the marketplace, that may eventually result in behaviors (purchases).

Attitudes are shaped, in part, by an individual's personal values. **Values** are strongly held beliefs about various topics or concepts. Values contribute to attitudes and lead to the judgments that guide personal behaviors. Values tend to be enduring and normally form during childhood, although they can change as a person ages and experiences life.

Figure 3.2 lists some of the more common personal values that personality theorists recognize. Individuals hold these values to differing degrees. Factors that affect their impact on the person include the individual's personality, temperament, environment, and culture. These values will be discussed in greater detail in Chapter 8 in the context of advertising design. By appealing to basic values, marketers hope to convince prospective customers that their products can help them achieve a desirable outcome. At the same time, creatives know marketing communications are much more effective in changing a person's attitude about a product than they are in changing a consumer's value structure.

In terms of consumer decision-making processes, both attitudes and values help marketing experts. If a product or service can be tied to a relatively universal value, such as patriotism, then the firm can take advantage of the linkage to present a positive image of

- ▶ Comfortable life
- ▶ Equality
- ▶ Excitement
- ▶ Freedom
- ▶ Fun, exciting life
- ▶ Happiness
- ▶ Inner peace
- ▶ Mature love
- ▶ Personal accomplishment

- ▶ Pleasure
- ▶ Salvation
- ▶ Security
- ▶ Self-fulfillment
- ▶ Self-respect
- ▶ Sense of belonging
- ▶ Social acceptance
- ▶ Wisdom

FIGURE 3.2
Personal Values

the product. A recent advertisement for Lucky Brand jeans uses the slogan "Always America's favorite" and the fact that "every pair [is] American made" in the attempt to tie into the patriotism value.

Attitudes may also be helpful. For example, most people consider being put on hold to be a nuisance. Therefore, a marketing creative may be able to tap into that attitude and use it to present a product or service in a more favorable light. The manner in which individuals process such information further affects decisions and is described next.

INTEGRATED LEARNING EXPERIENCE

Almost everyone has an opinion about tattoos and body jewelry. Some attitudes are positive whereas others are negative. Few are neutral. Examine the following Web sites:

www.imaginetattoos.com
www.tattoos.com
www.risingdragon.com
www.bme.freeq.com

Did these sites have any impact on your attitude toward tattoos and body jewelry? Which of the businesses would you be most inclined to patronize? What factors in the Web site affected or reinforced your attitude? To which of the personal values listed in Figure 3.2 does each Web site seem to appeal?

Information Processing Models

The ultimate goal of an integrated marketing communications program is to positively influence the attitudes of consumers and to persuade them to buy a particular good or service. A common tool used in simulating decision-making processes is the **elaboration likelihood model (ELM)**.[8] The ELM is based on the belief that individuals take the time to consider persuasive communication messages designed to change consumer attitudes.

Information processing occurs along two routes in an ELM. The first is the *central processing route*. When a consumer cognitively processes a message, giving a high degree of attention to the message's major or core elements, then the pathway is the central processing route. For example, a core message from KFC is "We do chicken right!" Attitudes adopted through the central route (believing KFC does indeed do chicken right) are more firmly held, longer lasting, and resistant to change. Further, attitudes based on exposures to advertisements are excellent predictors of subsequent buyer behaviors. A young man or woman who has developed the attitude that Marines are indeed "The few, The proud" is more likely to enlist.

The alternate route of processing the information is the *peripheral route.* Individuals follow this path when they pay attention to other, more marginal cues embedded in a communication message. In a television advertisement, peripheral cues can be music, actors, and the background (beach, mountains, forests). When a car salesperson attempts to persuade a customer to purchase an automobile, the peripheral cues include the salesperson's clothes, appearance, demeanor, and tone of voice.

Consumers using the peripheral route pay less attention to the primary message or argument, focusing instead on one or more peripheral cues. The attitude that develops is based on these peripheral cues. For instance, a person who dislikes André Aggassi may develop a negative attitude toward a product he endorses without even listening to or considering what he says about it. Attitudes formed by using the peripheral route tend to be less rigid, less resistant to change, and are poorer predictors of subsequent behaviors than are messages processed through the central route.

Two factors determine the route consumers choose: (1) motivation and (2) ability. Just as motivation impacts the information search itself, it also influences the manner in which information is processed. The more motivated an individual is to search for information, the greater the tendency to process the information using the central route. Highly motivated consumers pay closer attention to the core message argument of an advertisement or sales pitch than they do to peripheral cues.

The second factor, ability, is a consumer's intrinsic desire to use his or her cognitive skills. Individuals who enjoy thinking tend to cognitively process more of the elements of the environment around them. These people pay more attention to the primary message arguments in advertisements and are more inclined to use the central route to process marketing information.

This Caress advertisement was designed with the idea that consumers will view the picture using a hedonic, experiential model (HEM) process.
Source: Courtesy of Lever Brothers Company.

You've never been caressed like this before.

Caress® Moisturizing Body Wash, Bath Salts, Body Spray, and Foaming Bath Gel. Each comes in three fragrances.

BEFORE YOU DRESS, CARESS.

Repetition is an important key when individuals process messages using the peripheral route. The more often a consumer sees a particular advertisement or marketing communication, the better the chance is that he or she will process the message argument. With a greater number of exposures to the same advertisement or communication, peripheral cues tend to become less important as customers attend more to the core message.

The elaboration likelihood model assumes consumers make rational purchase decisions, yet clearly not all purchase decisions are rational. Some purchase decisions are made on the spur of the moment and are highly irrational. They can be made because someone wants to "have fun" or to pursue a particular feeling, emotion, or fantasy. These behaviors are more accurately portrayed using the **hedonic, experiential model (HEM)**.[9] Hedonism is the tendency to maximize pleasure while minimizing pain. Following hedonic impulses often means ignoring longer-term consequences of behaviors while giving in to short-term pleasure.

Information processing using the HEM model uses the same two routes discussed previously: (1) the central route and (2) the peripheral route. The primary difference is in the appeal or content of the message argument. With the ELM approach, the consumer ordinarily pays attention to the elements of message argument pertaining to prices, company attributes, and product qualities or functions. With the HEM approach, the consumer pays attention to elements of the message related to emotions, feelings, fun, and new or unusual experiences. Price advantages and making wise purchases are less important.

Both the ELM and HEM methods of viewing consumer decision-making processes help marketing experts. Account managers direct creatives to focus on one type of appeal or another, based on the product type and target market. For example, one campaign selling life insurance may focus on a rational, cognitive element, with the message directed toward long-term financial security based on careful investments. The creative probably will develop a more serious and intellectual approach to such a campaign. A second campaign may emphasize the more emotional aspects of life insurance, such as showing love, care, and concern for family members. The creative, in that case, should probably design an ad with richer peripheral images, including music and set design elements.

Consumers use cognitive mapping to assess and evaluate information.
Source: Courtesy of PhotoEdit. Photograph by Mary Kate Denny.

Another important ingredient in understanding attitudes and persuasion is the connections people make when they recall events or things. Cognitive maps help explain the linkages individuals rely on as they think about various ideas.

Cognitive Mapping

The manner in which consumers store information and relate that information to previous experiences and other memories can be explained by yet another model. Knowing how people store, retrieve, and evaluate information is a useful tool for companies developing marketing communications. Also, studying how memory works can assist marketers in designing effective advertisements and promotional campaigns.

Cognitive maps are simulations of the knowledge structures embedded in an individual's brain.[10] These structures contain a person's assumptions, beliefs, interpretations of facts, feelings, and attitudes about the larger world. People use their knowledge structures to help them interpret new information and to determine an appropriate response to fresh information or a novel situation. Figure 3.3 is a hypothetical cognitive map for an individual thinking about a Ruby Tuesday restaurant.

Based on the cognitive structures illustrated in Figure 3.3, when this customer thinks about Ruby Tuesday, she connects images of it to other restaurants offering fast food and others that provide dine-in services. In this case, the individual recognizes Ruby Tuesday as a dine-in establishment. The consumer also believes that Ruby Tuesday offers excellent service, but that the service is slow. Next, when the person thinks of slow service, her thoughts turn to Mel's Diner. When she thinks of excellent service, she recalls

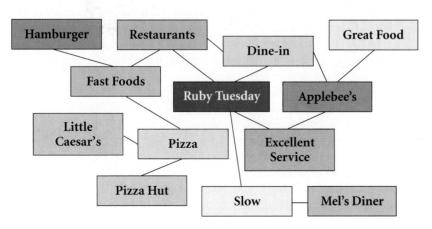

FIGURE 3.3
Cognitive Map for Ruby Tuesday

Applebee's. Besides these initial linkages, other features of cognitive maps are present. These include:

▶ Levels and layers

▶ Factors that affect existing linkages

▶ Situations in which a message has no current linkages

Concerning *levels and layers,* remember that Figure 3.3 is a simplified form of a cognitive map. Cognitive structures contain many linkages and can exist on several levels. For instance, one level of cognition is the map with the linkages in Figure 3.3. At another level, the cognitive map is more spatial and conjures images of the actual physical location of Ruby Tuesday along with the surrounding businesses. A third cognitive map (or another level) of Ruby Tuesday considers the interior of the restaurant along with other linkages that occur at that level. The consumer can even have a cognitive map of Ruby Tuesday oriented toward its employees and a relationship she had with an employee who is a friend. Therefore, cognitive processing occurs on many levels using highly complex mechanisms.

The second element of cognitive maps occurs when the person encounters a message with *linkages that already exist.* When consumers process these types of information as they view advertisements or read direct-marketing pieces, the result is often a multifaceted set of reactions and responses. As a marketing communication item reaches a consumer, several options about how to handle the message surface. If the new information is consistent with current information, then the new information primarily serves to strengthen an existing linkage. For example, when a consumer views a Ruby Tuesday ad promoting great service, the result may be that the ad will strengthen an existing belief, because the consumer already concluded that Ruby Tuesday has great service.

A different response can occur in other situations including times when a *message has no current linkages.* For example, if a consumer sees an advertisement featuring Ruby Tuesday seafood selection, and the consumer did not know that Ruby Tuesday offers seafood, a different reaction occurs. In order for this information to remain in the consumer's mind and to become linked to Ruby Tuesday, the customer must create a new linkage between previous Ruby Tuesday images with other images of seafood.

Hearing something once usually is not enough to cause it to be retained in a person's memory because of the difference between short-term recall and long-term memory. The cognitive mapping process explains knowledge structures embedded in a person's long-term memory. Ordinarily, information is retained in short-term memory for only a few seconds. As stimuli reach an individual's senses, short-term memory processes them. Short-term memory can retain five to nine bits of information. These new messages are either soon forgotten or eventually added to long-term memory. When a message is repeated, an individual is more likely to remember it, because it will be processed into long-term memory and fitted into previously developed cognitive maps.

As a result, when a company attempts to introduce consumers to a new brand, the advertisements and other marketing messages should repeat the name of the product several times during the presentation. This repetition improves the chances of its recall at a later time. To illustrate how this works, consider what happens when a person gives a phone number to a friend. To help remember it, the individual repeats the number several times to place it into longer-term recall.

Another way a consumer can process information is to link the message to a new concept. For example, if a consumer sees an advertisement from Ruby Tuesday emphasizing that it has great food but has never thought about the restaurant in terms of quality food, that linkage is not currently present. If the advertisement persuades the consumer, she may construct a linkage between Ruby Tuesday and good food without even traveling to the restaurant. If she does not believe the message, she will ignore or forget the information, and no new linkage evolves. A third possibility is that the consumer recalls the advertisement at a later time and decides to try Ruby Tuesday. If the food is great, then the link is established at that point. If it is not, the consumer continues thinking that Ruby Tuesday does not offer good food.

From a marketing perspective, it is easier to strengthen linkages that already exist; adding new linkages or modifying linkages is much more difficult. Regardless of how the information is presented, repetition is important due to the limitations of the short-term memory. Keep in mind that consumers are exposed to hundreds of messages a day. Only a few are processed into long-term memory. Chapter 8 describes this issue in more detail. Advertising techniques that can be used to get and hold a consumer's attention are presented at that point.

This advertisement by Sunkist is designed to establish a new linkage between Sunkist lemon juice and a salt substitute.
Source: Courtesy of Sunkist.

Cognitive mapping and persuasion techniques designed to change attitudes or tap into strongly held values are two key ingredients in any IMC program. It is important first to understand the needs and attitudes of the target market. Then, structure messages to fill those needs and to capture consumers' attention by exposing them to messages that will travel effectively through a core processing channel or peripheral channels, either through solid reasoning or alluring emotional appeals.

Further, creatives should attempt to design ads that reach the linkages consumers have already made between a product and other key ideas. For example, a longtime linkage existed between Cadillac and quality, as evidenced by the advertising and promotional phrase "This product is the *Cadillac* . . . [of all products in the market]." Common linkages exist between products and ideas such as quality, value, low cost, expense, fun, sex, danger, practical, exotic, and many others. Carefully planned marketing campaigns look for linkages to entice the consumer to buy a given product and to believe in (or be loyal to) that product in the future. At that point, the company is ahead of the game as consumers consider their various purchasing alternatives.

INTEGRATED LEARNING EXPERIENCE

The two models of information processing discussed in this chapter are the elaboration likelihood model (ELM) and the hedonic, experiential model (HEM). Examine the Web sites:

Fox (www.fox.com)
Carnival Cruise Line (www.carnival.com)
Merrill Lynch (www.ml.com)
Intel (www.intel.com)
Campbell Soup (www.campbellsoup.com)
IBM (www.ibm.com)

For each site, which model is predominant in the processing of information? What peripheral cues does it provide? What is the purpose of the peripheral cues in each site?

STOP

EVALUATION OF ALTERNATIVES

The third step in the decision-making process is the evaluation of alternatives. Three models portray the nature of the evaluation process: (1) the evoked set approach, (2) the multiattribute approach, and (3) affect referral.

The Evoked Set Method

A person's evoked set consists of the brands he or she considers in a purchasing situation. Two additional components of evoked sets are part of the evaluation of purchase alternatives: (1) the inept set and (2) the inert set. The **inept set** consists of the brands that are part of a person's memory that are *not considered* because they elicit negative feelings. These negative sentiments are normally caused by a bad experience with a vendor or particular brand. They may originate from negative comments made by a friend or by seeing an advertisement that the potential customer did not like.

The **inert set** holds the brands that the consumer is aware of but the individual has neither negative nor positive feelings about the products. Using the terms from cognitive mapping, these brands have not been entered into any map or have only weak linkages to other ideas. The lack of knowledge about these brands usually eliminates them as alternatives. In other words, in most purchase situations, the only brands considered are those that are strongly present in the evoked set.

The Multiattribute Approach

In evaluating alternatives, another method consumers use is the multiattribute approach. The key to understanding this model is noting that consumers often examine sets of attributes across sets of products or brands. The multiattribute model assumes that a consumer's attitude toward a brand is determined by the:

▶ Consumer's beliefs about a brand's performance on each attribute

▶ Importance of each attribute to the consumer[11]

The higher a brand is rated on attributes that are important to the consumer, the more likely it becomes that the brand will be purchased. Table 3.1 notes products along with some of the characteristics that affect their selection, each with potentially a lesser or greater value to individual consumers. An illustration of this concept is found in the case named "Buying a Television? It's Not That Simple" at the end of this chapter.

Affect Referral

A third model used in the evaluation of purchase alternatives is known as **affect referral**. With this method, a consumer chooses the brand he or she likes the best. The individual does not evaluate the other brands and often does not even think about which attributes are

---

TABLE 3.1

The Multiattribute Model

Product	Characteristics				
Computer	Price	Style	Service contract	Software	Memory-storage
Telephone	Price	Style	Speed dial	Caller ID	Cordless feature
Car	Price	Style	Safety	Room	Other features
T-bone steak	Price	Age	Fat content	Degree cooked	Seasonings
Sunglasses	Price	Style	UV protection	Durability	Prescription lenses
Sofa	Price	Style	Foldout bed	Stain resistance	Color
Credit card	Interest rate	Fees	Billing cycle	Access to ATM	Credit limit

Consider each item. Which characteristic is most important to you personally? Least important?

important. Instead, the consumer simply buys the brand he or she likes. Toothpaste, catsup, soft drinks, and milk are some of the products consumers normally select using this method. The types of purchases are those with low levels of involvement and those made frequently.

Two things explain why consumers rely on affect referral. First, it saves mental energy. A quick choice is easier than going through the mental process of evaluating all the possible alternatives. Some purchases basically don't deserve much effort, and the affect referral model is useful in those situations.

Second, the multiattribute model may have been utilized previously. The person has already spent a great deal of time considering various product attributes, deciding which are most critical, and reaching a decision about the product with the greatest number of advantages. Therefore, going through the process again would be "reinventing the wheel." For example, in purchasing jeans, a teenager may have spent considerable time evaluating styles, prices, colors, durability levels, and "fit" of various brands. After making the purchase, this consumer continues to purchase that same brand as long as the experience remains positive and reinforces the evaluation made.

Using one or more of these three processes (evoked set, multiattribute approach, or affect referral), the individual eventually completes the evaluation of alternatives. At that time, the person stores the knowledge for future use and recalls it when the time comes to make a purchase or moves immediately on to purchasing behavior.

THE PURCHASE DECISION

The fourth step in the consumer decision-making process is the purchase decision. Most of the time the consumer purchases the brand chosen during the evaluation of alternatives stage. Keep in mind that evaluations often occur at a retail store, and the purchase decision immediately follows the evaluation. Occasionally, however, the consumer makes a different purchase decision. There are several possible reasons for a shift away from the evaluation process. These include:

- A temporary change in the consumer's situation
- A desire for variety
- An impulse purchase
- An advertisement, consumer promotion, or some other marketing material
- The influence of a friend or relative

Each of these possibilities is briefly described next.

Situational Changes

Consumers may not always buy the brands they evaluated as best because of changes in the situation at the time of the purchase. If they are short on money, they may choose a cheaper brand to "get them by" until they can afford their first choice. Or this may mean buying a smaller quantity just to tide them over (e.g., a 10-ounce bag of chips versus the 16-ounce size). If the weather is bad, they may purchase a brand from a store that is closer to avoid making a longer trip. When a store is out of their favorite brand, they may substitute another product or brand rather than going without. At times a sales promotion deal may influence them to buy a different brand, especially for low-cost or low-involvement items.

Desire for Variety

A consumer will also purchase a different brand to satisfy an internal need for variety. Individuals tend to get tired of "the same old thing" and want something different as a result. Those who routinely drink Diet Coke occasionally buy a different brand—just to have something different.

Seeking variety does not mean an individual's attitude or past evaluation of various options has changed. Rather, the person decides to purchase an inferior brand merely for the sake of variety. The alternative purchase is essentially a one-time exception to a decision made previously.

Impulse Decisions

The "best" alternative may sometimes be ignored in favor of an impulse buy. Impulse purchases normally occur at the store while the consumer is shopping. Some consumers view a product displayed and make an immediate decision to buy it. Candy bars, gum, and magazines usually are offered near checkout registers because consumers purchase these items on impulse. In retail stores such as Wal-Mart or Target, other low-price items appear in the same place, including batteries, small toys, pens, pencils, and so forth.

Impulse purchases occur for more expensive items as well. Clothes are sometimes purchased in this manner. Further, when people travel on vacations, their pocket money essentially takes on a different value. Consequently, T-shirts, memorabilia, and other gift shop–type items become impulse buys. People also make impulsive decisions when Christmas shopping. Retailers are fully aware of the numbers and types of impulse purchases their customers make. Items that cause impulse buys usually are displayed at the front of the store, on center aisles, and in other key places.

Advertisements, Consumer Promotions, and Other Marketing Materials

At times consumers may also alter purchasing decisions after seeing an advertisement or receiving some type of consumer promotion. For example, an individual writes "lunch meat" on a shopping list and will have a specific brand in mind while traveling to the store. On the other hand, when a person sees an ad, such as the Carl Buddig advertisement with a 60-cent coupon shown in this section, he or she may alter the purchase decision. If this coupon were placed at the store next to the lunch meat section, the change in purchase decision could occur at that instant. The same is true for other marketing materials. An outdoor sign for Wendy's viewed just as a person exits a highway could alter the person's restaurant choice.

The Impact of Friends and Family

Finally, friends, relatives, and other people can alter purchases. At a restaurant, a person may conclude that a particular red wine is the best the restaurant offers and routinely purchases it. On another occasion, the same person, when out with business associates in a social setting, may be more inclined to order a more expensive wine in order to impress those associates. He may purchase the wine even though it is more expensive, but at the same time, in the consumer's mind, is inferior or not the best-tasting choice. Consumers make similar decisions when they buy products because they know their parents will like them better or to suit the needs and tastes of friends.

Remember, these four cases are the exceptions. Ordinarily a person who has thought about a decision and evaluated the alternatives chooses the best available option. Only unusual circumstances lead to differing purchasing decisions. Even then, the purchase process is not complete. One further item remains.

POSTPURCHASE EVALUATION

The final step in the consumer decision-making process is the postpurchase evaluation phase. During this time, a consumer evaluates the purchase. This review is the comparison of what he or she expected with what actually occurred. If the product or service meets his or her expectations, then the shopper is satisfied. If the product or service does not meet those expectations, then the indi-

Firms can use a consumer promotion to alter consumer purchase decisions.
Source: Courtesy of Carl Buddig & Company.

vidual experiences dissatisfaction. Sometimes the reaction is not based on using the product but rather takes place immediately following the physical purchase.

In situations where there is high involvement, a socially visible purchasing experience, or if the product or service is expensive, consumers often experience doubt after purchases. This is known as **postpurchase cognitive dissonance**. This form of dissonance is most likely when the consumer has spent a substantial amount of time searching for information and evaluating the different alternatives. Because of the investment in time, money, and ego, it is natural for a consumer to question a decision. To reduce the tension or sense of disharmony associated with cognitive dissonance, consumers continue to pay attention to advertisements and other marketing materials. These communications, along with other endorsements and reassurances (including those made by the sales agent) can help the individual believe a good decision was made.

In making postpurchase evaluations, consumers often compare the brand they chose with those they did not. For example, if a consumer purchased a new stereo, undoubtedly several brands were evaluated before the purchase decision. It may have been a very tough decision, and the consumer could have viewed two or three brands as being just about equal to one another. After the purchase, the consumer could be exposed to numerous advertisements by the competitor and none by the firm selling the chosen brand. If so, this increases the level of dissonance.

Gaining a new customer costs five to six times more than keeping a current one. Because of this, marketing executives work diligently to retain current customers. Consider the impact of postpurchase evaluations in the banking industry. In a national survey, 90 percent of the sample said they were satisfied or very satisfied with their bank. Seventy-six percent said they were likely or very likely to recommend the bank to a friend. Word-of-mouth communication has a very strong impact on service purchases; consequently, having a friend recommend a bank can be instrumental in gaining new customers.[12]

The importance of the postpurchase stage should not be underestimated. An effective integrated marketing communications plan addresses postpurchase evaluations and the potential for cognitive dissonance. Advertisements depicting satisfied customers giving positive testimonials serve this purpose. Comparative ads showing the advantages of the chosen brand over competing brands can be successful in reassuring customers. Phone calls by sales and customer service representatives may be used to reassure customers that they have made good purchase decisions and verify that all of their expectations were met. Direct-mail pieces can be designed to reach customers following a purchase. These items provide consumers with additional product information while reassuring them about the purchase. People like to believe they make quality decisions.

In summary, marketing professionals can take advantage of every step of the consumer purchasing decision-making process. First, they can both identify times when needs are likely to occur (problem recognition) and spur additional needs for goods or services by making products appear attractive and desirable. Second, they can try to be certain that a given brand becomes part of the individual's evoked set as the consumer searches internally and externally for information. Third, they design messages to reach a salient information processing channel as the consumer evaluates alternatives. Fourth, they can develop final persuasion tactics for the key moments when the purchase decision is actually made, including the aesthetics of the store, the techniques the sales representative uses, and the ease of physically making the purchase (no waiting lines, credit availability, etc.). Fifth and finally, marketing communications must address postpurchase dissonance issues. Marketers constantly need to reassure customers that they have made wise choices with their dollars and decisions. Then, the IMC program works effectively in conjunction with the consumer's decision-making process.

THE CONSUMER BUYING ENVIRONMENT

Utilizing the standard steps consumers employ to make purchasing decisions remains an effective tool for studying marketing communications. At the same time, the environment in which purchases are made rapidly changes and constantly evolves. It is important to examine these new features of the purchasing climate. In this section, two factors are

> ▶ **Demographics (age, gender, income, etc.)**
> ▶ **Heredity and home environment**
> ▶ **Family life cycle**
> ▶ **Life-changing events**
> ▶ **Cultural environment**
> ▶ **Social environment**
> ▶ **Situational environment**

FIGURE 3.4
Traditional Factors Affecting Consumer Purchasing Behavior

examined: first, traditional factors that affect consumer buying decisions, and second, recent trends influencing purchasing habits.

TRADITIONAL FACTORS

To understand the consumer buying process, marketers should be reminded of the traditional elements of the buying environment. Purchases are often affected by the environment in which they take place. Figure 3.4 lists factors that impact buying behavior. Each of these factors will now be described in greater detail.

Demographics

A complete discussion of demographic segmentation is presented in Chapter 5. There are many demographic variables, including age, gender, income level, race, and geographic area that distinguish buyer types. These may be identified in a manner that will help the marketing team create communications that appeal to individual groups. The RCA ad in this section specifically targets a particular group, teenagers. It is important, however, to recognize that demographic groups vary. For example, the 8- to 14-year-old market in Europe tends to be quite affluent in terms of spending power; however, they resent being treated as American teens with accents. Promotions are more likely to be effective than other marketing methods. Such cultural considerations must come into play whenever a business identifies targets in other countries.[13]

An advertisement targeted to a specific demographic group–teenagers.
Source: Courtesy of RCA

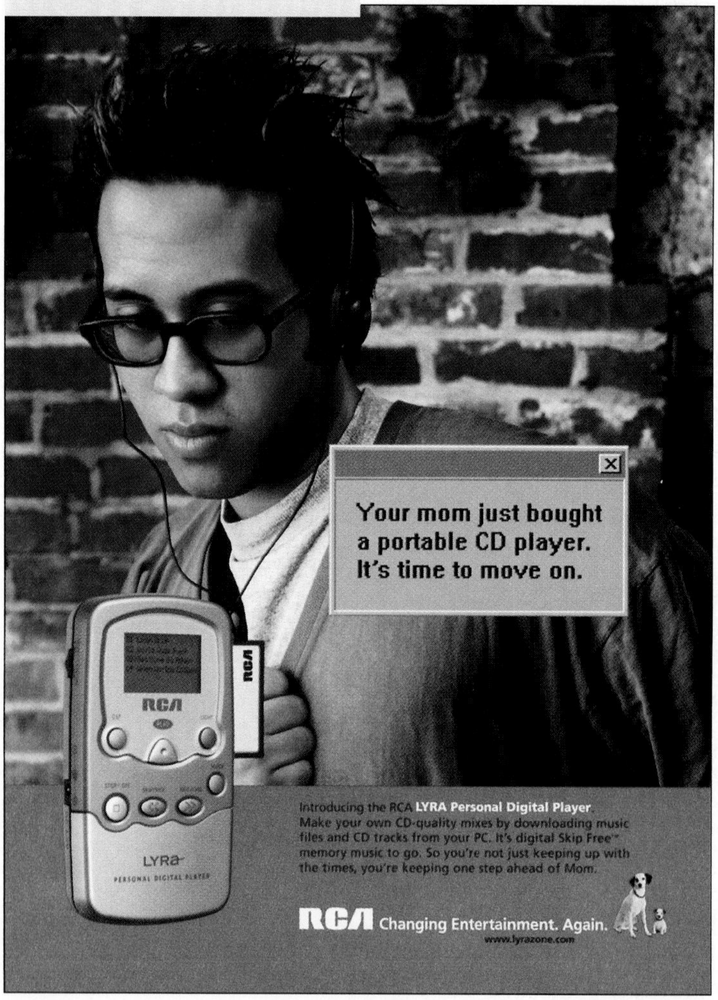

Your mom just bought a portable CD player. It's time to move on.

Introducing the RCA **LYRA** Personal Digital Player
Make your own CD-quality mixes by downloading music files and CD tracks from your PC. It's digital Skip Free™ memory music to go. So you're not just keeping up with the times, you're keeping one step ahead of Mom.

RCA Changing Entertainment. Again.
www.lyrazone.com

Heredity and Home Environment

Heredity and the home environment are important influences on an individual's purchasing behavior. Children often display purchasing behaviors similar to those of their parents and other family members. Many attitudes and values are transmitted at home and become strongly held, potentially lifelong features of the consumer's personality.

Family Life Cycle

The family life cycle affects purchasing behaviors. Some relatively standard stages in the life cycle of the family include:

▶ Being single (bachelorhood)
▶ Newlyweds with no children
▶ First families (with young children)

CONSUMER BUYER BEHAVIOR

IMC and Children: Should There Be Limits?

One of the emerging marketing controversies is the ethical acceptability of advertising to children. Children represent a tremendous level of spending and buying power (over $20 billion annually). The question is about the tactics used to reach them.

Mary Pipher, clinical psychologist and author of *The Shelter of Each Other,* suggests that, "No one ad is so bad, but the combination of 400 ads per day creates in children a combination of narcissism, entitlement, and dissatisfaction." Ads to children use multiple tactics, including building brand awareness through images and logos, featuring toys and collectibles, developing tie-ins with movies, and extensive use of children's television programs. Characters such as Barney, Ronald McDonald, and Harry Potter vend everything from food to toys to clothes.

With so many potential venues to sell directly to children and to put pressure on their parents, many company leaders have begun to believe it is best to "get them while they're young." From a larger, societal perspective, however, the question remains as to whether such impressionable young minds should be subjected to everything from *Star Wars* to Joe Camel, and beyond. Many marketing professionals will grapple with the drive for sales versus concern that the impact on young people may not be ideal.

- ▶ Full nest (with growing and teenage children)
- ▶ Empty nest (children have moved out)
- ▶ Remaining partner (following death of a spouse)

Each of these stages creates unique marketing opportunities. An example is shown in the Communication Action Box "Marketing to First Families."

Life-Changing Events

Life-changing events also influence consumer buyer behaviors. Some of the more prominent life changes that impact or modify purchasing behaviors include divorce, remarriage, death of a spouse, a spouse renewing or starting a second career, having a parent move into the home, and a major illness in a family member.

One of the main events that drastically affects purchasing behaviors is divorce and remarriage. Remarried divorcees represent about 10 percent of the population. These individuals tend to develop a new outlook on life that alters many things, including their purchasing patterns. This group, called *second chancers,* is usually between the ages of 40 and 59 and has a higher household income.

Second chancers are more content with life than are average adults. They tend to be happy with their new families but also have a different focus in life. They spend less time trying to please others and more time seeking fuller, more enriching lives for themselves and their children or spouse. Entertainment and vacation services especially appeal to this group.[14]

An advertisement directed to first families and the arrival of a new baby.
Source: Courtesy of State Farm Insurance Companies. © State Farm Mutual Automobile Insurance Company, 1997. Used by permission.

COMMUNICATION ACTION

Marketing to First Families

First families are those in which couples have started having children. To qualify as a first family, the oldest child is still not a teenager. In this group, children are the central focus. First family parents are willing to buy their kids just about anything. In various surveys, 60 percent say they put the needs and wants of their children ahead of their own.

About 50 percent of first families have dual incomes. Although parents of young children are family oriented, they also are wrapped up in their careers. Almost 80 percent report that one key to happiness is being able to support their family financially.

The demands of providing for their children leads nearly 60 percent of first family parents to say they don't have enough leisure time. This compares unfavorably to the 44 percent of the population as a whole that desires more free time. Dual-career families are the most likely to report they do not have enough time for rest and relaxation.

The dynamics of an involved family life combined with long hours of work lead first family parents to desire convenience and time-saving features from their products and services. Financial strains cause them to look for bargains and buy products they perceive to be better values. Reaching parents with marketing messages can often be a challenge. The average workweek for husbands is over 50 hours per week and for wives, 40-plus hours. Both must also spend time commuting. When they are at home, one or both parents are often involved in a child's activities, such as soccer, PTA, music lessons, parent–teacher conferences, and so forth.

Consequently, IMC programs must seek out the places to expose such parents to advertisements. Drive-time radio spots and later-night television programming offer some contacts. Creative companies often find places where these families' children will be to advertise to the adults. Bathroom walls in fast-food outlets, fences surrounding soccer fields, and billboards on well-traveled commuter routes may be keys to reaching these frazzled and busy members of the community.

Source: Robert Scally, "The Customer Connection: First Families," *Discount Store News,* 37, no. 20 (October 26, 1998), pp. 85–87.

Each of these groups presents unique marketing opportunities. Care of the elderly, especially following the loss of a spouse, should spark a major increase in products and services as the baby boom generation continues to grow older.

Cultural, Social, and Situational Environments

Other factors that shape consumer buying behaviors include the culture, social setting, and situational environment in which a consumer lives. For instance, a person near the ocean is more likely to develop a taste for seafood. Also, individuals often prefer food, clothing, and music that reflects their ethnic heritage. The cultural background in which a person is raised normally impacts purchasing choices.

Socially visible products such as furniture, automobiles, clothing, and housing affect other buyer behaviors. In one survey, 64 percent of a sample of teenagers said their friends had the greatest influence on clothing purchases, and that the influence was higher than that of parents or the media.[15] The need for social acceptance is used to market a wide variety of products and services, ranging from things as minor as perfume or cologne to items as expensive and involved as vacations in the Bahamas.

Many situational factors affect purchasing behavior. These temporary factors change a consumer's thought processes just as a purchase is about to be made. For example, something as simple as bad weather can change a person's behavior; the consumer avoids a trip that involves a great deal of driving or where access to the store is inconvenient. Further, a great tragedy or major news story, such as the September 11 attacks, caused many consumers to buy newspapers or magazines seeking with additional information.

Other Factors Affecting Purchases

In addition to the environment surrounding consumers, people buy various items for several other reasons. Consumer purchasing decisions are based on a number of factors, some of which are found in Figure 3.5. For example, people buy goods and services because of the utility present in those articles. **Utility** is the value or expected value associated with an item. A product has utility either directly (drinking Kool-Aid to satisfy thirst and to get a sugar buzz) or indirectly (thinking that wearing the Tommy Hilfiger brand causes people to assume the consumer is well-off financially and has a strong sense of fashion). Services also have utility. For instance, an instant teller card from a bank has the utility of 24-hour access to cash, plus the ability to conduct other transactions when the bank is closed. People exchange money, in part, for the utility present in the goods and services they purchase.

Other reasons consumers purchase products or services include the drive to satisfy physical, psychological, social, and emotional needs. Few goods are purchased solely because of their physical attributes; a consumer does not purchase deodorant because of the chemicals in the product. Rather, the purchase is made to satisfy social needs, due to the fear that body odor offends others and due to the belief that smelling good is attractive to others. Automobiles are purchased as much because of psychological issues as they are for their physical attributes.

To be effective in reaching consumers, marketing communication messages must go beyond physical descriptions of the product or service. Instead, messages should focus on the needs the product can satisfy. To illustrate this principle, consider an ad for chewing gum. Simply showing people munching on a given brand probably won't sell much product. Instead, chewing gum commercials emphasize fun, excitement, sexiness, love, romance, and so forth.

An epistemic need is the human desire to obtain knowledge. Some epistemic needs are related to novelty or curiosity. One might satisfy a certain curiosity about celebrities by touring a Planet Hollywood or Hard Rock Café facility. The Rainforest Café appeals to the concept of novelty because its unique atmosphere sets it apart from other dining spots. Restaurants currently can satisfy basic needs for knowledge by offering computer online services while people dine or sip a beverage. In each case, the marketing approach fits the product or service with the customer's desire for knowledge.

An advertisement directed to women, especially women without husbands.
Source: Courtesy of State Farm Insurance Companies. © State Farm Mutual Automobile Insurance Company, 1997. Used by permission.

> ▶ **Products–services provide utility**
> ▶ **To satisfy physical needs**
> ▶ **To satisfy psychological needs**
> ▶ **To satisfy social needs**
> ▶ **To satisfy emotional needs**
> ▶ **To satisfy epistemic needs**

FIGURE 3.5
Common Reasons Purchases Are Made

NEW TRENDS

To conclude this chapter on consumer buyer behavior, it is important to note some of the more recent trends affecting purchasing patterns listed in Figure 3.6.

Changes in Cultural Values and Attitudes

As mentioned previously, values and attitudes affect many purchasing decisions. Values tend to form during childhood and remain strongly held through life. At the same time, cultural values shift. Some of the attitudes and values shifting at a cultural level include those associated with:

▶ Sexual orientation

▶ Use of profanity in public arenas (television programs)

▶ Tolerance of nudity

▶ Living arrangements (unmarried couples)

▶ Views about the end of life, including assisted suicide and "do not resuscitate" orders

▶ Racial tolerance and acceptance of diversity in society

At that same time, there is considerable intolerance, as witnessed by the wide-ranging number of hate Web sites and paramilitary organizations.

Values in a society continually change and are sometimes dichotomous. For example, as the median age of the population increases (the aging of the baby boom generation), modifications in values are readily evident. While being tolerant of sexuality and other more "liberal" concepts, millions of Americans are, at the same time, returning to more "traditional" values and embracing some form of religion or spirituality. After decades of materialism and self-indulgence, many baby boomers are searching for meaning. Even younger members of society are changing. Many have embraced greater levels of temperance in terms of drugs, alcohol, and sex.[16]

The restructuring of values in society presents three challenges for marketing experts. The first is to monitor for changes so that the company is aware of what is happening in society. The second is to create products and services compatible with changing values. The third is to design marketing messages that reflect and build on the values target markets and individual customers hold.

▶ **Changes in cultural values and attitudes**

▶ **Time pressures and busy lifestyle**

▶ **Cocooning**

▶ **Indulgences and pleasure binges**

▶ **Desire for excitement and fantasy**

▶ **Emphasis on health**

▶ **Clanning**

FIGURE 3.6
Recent Trends Affecting
Consumer Buying Behavior

Time Pressures

Active, busy lifestyles have had a dramatic impact on consumer behaviors. In one survey, 44 percent of the respondents stated that they would prefer additional free time over more money. Almost 60 percent indicated they have less leisure time now than in the past. Many consumers focus less on material possessions and more on experiences such as vacations, entertainment, events with friends and family, and dining out.[17]

Time pressures account for increases in sales of convenience items, such as microwave ovens, drive-through dry cleaning establishments, and one-stop shopping outlets, most notably Wal-Mart's Supercenters. People on the go utilize cell phones and answering machines to make sure they don't miss messages during their busy days.

Cocooning

One of the side effects of a busy and hectic lifestyle is cocooning. The stress of long hours at work with additional hours spent fighting commuter traffic has led many individuals to retreat and cocoon in their homes once they arrive. A major element of cocooning is making the home environment as soothing as possible. Evidence of cocooning includes major expenditures on elaborate homes, extensive and expensive sound systems, satellite systems with big-screen televisions, swimming pools, saunas, hot tubs, gourmet kitchens with large dining rooms, decks and porches, and moving to the country or to a gated theme community.

At the same time, shopping, going out on the town, and even visiting with neighbors is out.[18] Many advertisements emphasize cocooning aspects of shops and services. Recently, Internet ads focused on the utility of shopping at home during the Christmas season to offer the consumer a method to avoid the hustle and bustle of the holidays.

Indulgences and Pleasure Binges

Some people handle stress through occasional indulgences or pleasure binges such as expensive dinners out and smaller luxury purchases. Pleasure binges also include "getaway" weekends in resorts and on short cruises. These self-rewarding activities make the consumer feel that all the work and effort is "worth it." The implications for marketing experts are to note the indulgence aspects of products. Recently Clairol's Herbal Essence shampoo and conditioner commercials play to the emotions of pleasure and self-indulgence, with the "yes, Yes, YES!" approach.

Excitement and Fantasy

Many people respond to stress through exciting adventures. From theme parks to virtual reality playrooms, consumers enjoy the mental relaxation of experiencing things that seem almost unreal. Many gambling establishments cater to these more exotic types of vacations. IMAX theaters generate a much more exciting experience than do normal movie theaters. As the technology of fantasy continues to develop, more firms enter the marketplace to profit from consumer desires to "get away from it all."

Emphasis on Health

The U.S. population continues to age. Two outcomes of this trend are a blossoming interest in health and maintaining one's youthful appearance. Many consumers manage their health by trying to develop a balanced lifestyle. This includes a regular emphasis on nutrition, exercise, and staying active without feeling too guilty about an occasional overindulgence. Marketers often create messages about the healthy aspects of products. These goods include vitamins, food products, exercise machines, stress management programs, and herbal remedies. Booming sales of all of these products indicate many people have a growing fascination with a healthy lifestyle.

Clanning

In spite of cocooning efforts, people still feel social needs. To maintain their social lives people occasionally visit friends and relatives. Also, many adults enjoy coffee or *cappuccino* at places such as Starbucks, as noted in the chapter-opening vignette. There, consumers socialize for limited periods while indulging in a low-cost perk.[19] A close circle of friends has replaced wide-ranging contacts and the elaborate social lives that were part of the youthful experiences of many baby boomers and members of Generation X.

INTEGRATED LEARNING EXPERIENCE

STOP

A current trend for many companies is the development of marketing messages for specific demographic, ethnic, or lifestyle groups. This allows for a more targeted message than possible for the mass audience. Examine the **www.women.com** Web site. What information does this site provide about women's purchase behaviors? How do they differ from those of men? Because many times their lifestyles are different, marketing to individual ethnic groups may require a more individualized approach. For the Hispanic community, examine **www.hispaniconline.com**, and for the African American community, go to **www.targetmarketnews.com**. The Web site **www.planetout.com** is for the gay and lesbian community. What clues does this Web site provide about the consumer behaviors of members of this group? What evidence do you see at these Web sites of recent trends affecting consumer behaviors (see Figure 3.6)?

SUMMARY

There are five steps to the consumer buying decision-making process. Marketing experts and especially creatives must be aware of each step and prepare effective communications that will lead most directly to the decision to buy.

In step 1, the consumer recognizes a want, need, desire, or force that entices him or her to seek out purchasing alternatives. Companies must identify ways to inspire these needs and to have the product readily available for customers who are ready to start looking or to actually make the purchase.

In step 2, the consumer searches for information, internally and externally. Marketing messages must be directed to placing the product or service in the consumer's evoked set of viable purchasing prospects. The more involved the customer feels in the search, the more likely the product will have a longer-lasting impact once purchased. Those with greater needs for cognition are attracted to the process of thinking through a decision. Those with a greater degree of enthusiasm for shopping spend more time analyzing the available alternatives. Customers consider the benefits and costs of searches and make more or less rational decisions about how extensively they will seek out information.

In step 3, the consumer evaluates alternatives. Evoked sets, attitudes and values, and cognitive maps explain how an individual evaluates various choices. Evoked sets reveal which products "make the cut" and receive consideration. Attitudes and values predispose consumers toward some products and companies and away from others. Cognitive maps help the customer link what the company says about itself with other experiences. Marketing experts must identify consumer attitudes and values that affect purchase decisions and make sure they do not offend prospects with their messages. Stronger ties can be built with customers when the product or service is favorably attached to strongly held attitudes and values.

In step 4, the consumer makes the purchase. In some instances the individual ignores a decision reached because of some extenuating circumstance. It is the job of the marketing department to eliminate as many of these extenuating circumstances as possible by making the purchase itself easy to complete.

In step 5, the consumer looks for affirmation that a quality purchasing decision was reached. The less reassurance, the greater the degree of postpurchase cognitive dissonance. Marketing experts should design elements of messages and other activities to help customers feel comfortable about the purchasing decisions they have made. It is much easier to retain current customers than to continually attract new ones.

A traditional view of the consumer buying environment suggests that markets can focus on demographic groups as target markets. Factors that routinely affect purchasing decisions include heredity and the home environment; the stage in the family life cycle; life-changing events; and the cultural, social, and situational environments surrounding the consumer. People buy things to receive the utility (value) present in the product or service. They also buy to fulfill or satisfy physical, psychological, social, emotional, and epistemic needs. Marketing experts tailor messages that match their products or services with specific consumer needs.

The new millennium presents a changing buying decision-making environment to marketers. New cultural values and attitudes, time pressures, and busy lifestyles influence what people buy, how they buy, and the manner in which they can be enticed to buy. Many families try to isolate themselves from everyday pressures by cocooning. They also try to escape through indulgences and pleasure binges, by finding excitement or fantasy, and by clanning to meet social needs. An aging baby boom population is more focused on lasting values and on health issues. Marketing can address these needs and lead customers to purchases based on them.

Understanding consumer buyer behaviors within chosen target markets helps the firm construct a more complete and integrated marketing communications program. Effective advertising identi-fies and meets the various needs, attitudes, values, and goals of consumers. In the future, there will be many new challenges to conquer. Successful companies continue to know their customers and find ways to reach them so that the right product meets the right need at the right time.

REVIEW QUESTIONS

1. What are the five steps of the consumer buying decision-making process?

2. How can a marketing account manager take advantage of each step in the consumer buying decision-making process?

3. What is an evoked set? Why is it so important to the marketing department?

4. What is meant by the term *involvement* in the buying decision-making process? Why is it important to marketers?

5. What is the difference between an internal search and an external search?

6. Define attitude. What are the three main components of attitudes, and how are they related to purchasing decisions?

7. How do values differ from attitudes? Name some personal values related to purchasing decisions.

8. What is an elaboration likelihood model? What are its two main pathways, and how do they relate to consumer buyer behaviors?

9. How is the hedonic, experiential model different from the elaboration likelihood model?

10. Develop a cognitive map of your own mind about your most recent major purchase (car, stereo, computer, etc.).

11. What are the key features of the multiattribute approach to evaluating purchasing alternatives?

12. What is meant by affect referral? When is a person likely to rely on such a cognitive approach to evaluating purchasing alternatives?

13. Under what conditions might a person ignore his or her own reasoning processes when actually making a purchase?

14. What is postpurchase cognitive dissonance? Why is it so impor-tant to companies that have just sold their products or services?

15. What traditional factors, as described in this chapter, affect consumer purchasing decisions?

16. What new trends affect consumer buyer behaviors? Give an example of one that applies to your life.

17. Do time pressures affect college student purchasing decisions? If so, how?

18. Do college students cocoon? If so, how?

KEY TERMS

evoked set   consists of the set of brands a consumer considers during the information search and evaluation processes.

involvement   the extent to which a stimulus or task is relevant to a consumer's existing needs, wants, or values.

need for cognition   a personality characteristic an individual displays when he or she engages in and enjoys mental activities.

attitude   a mental position taken toward a topic, person, or event that influences the holder's feelings, perceptions, learning processes, and subsequent behaviors.

values   strongly held beliefs about various topics or concepts.

elaboration likelihood model (ELM)   a tool used in stimulat-ing consumer purchase decision-making process focusing on more rational elements of the decision.

hedonic, experiential model (HEM)   a tool used in stimulat-ing consumer purchase decisions that are spur of the moment and more irrational, based on wanting to "have fun" or to pursue a par-ticular feeling, emotion, or fantasy.

cognitive maps   simulations of the knowledge structures embedded in an individual's brain.

inept set   part of a memory set that consists of the brands that are held in a person's memory but are *not considered*, because they elicit negative feelings.

inert set   part of a memory set that holds the brands that the con-sumer has awareness of but has neither negative nor positive feel-ings about.

affect referral   a purchasing decision model in which the con-sumer chooses the brand for which he or she has the strongest lik-ing or feelings.

postpurchase cognitive dissonance   the feelings of doubt con-sumers experience after a purchase has been made.

utility   the value or expected value associated with an item.

compensatory heuristics   a purchasing decision model that assumes that no one single brand will score high on every desir-able attribute and further that individual attributes vary in terms of their importance to the consumer.

conjunctive heuristics   a purchasing decision model that estab-lishes a minimum or threshold rating that brands must meet in order to be considered.

phased heuristics   a purchasing decision model that is a combi-nation of the compensatory and conjunctive heuristics models.

CRITICAL THINKING EXERCISES

Discussion Questions

1. In a study of compulsive buying behaviors among college students, a primary influence was the family. Often one or both parents were compulsive shoppers. Families that displayed other forms of dysfunctional behaviors such as alcoholism, bulimia, extreme nervousness, or depression produced children who were more inclined to exhibit compulsive shopping behaviors. Why do dysfunctional behaviors among parents produce compulsive shopping behavior among children? Another component of compulsive buying behaviors is self-esteem. Again, self-esteem is partly inherited but also develops in the home environment.[20] How would self-esteem be related to compulsive shopping behaviors? What other influences other than family might contribute to compulsive shopping behaviors? If an individual has a tendency to be a compulsive shopper, what can (or should) be done?

2. Study the list of personal values presented in Figure 3.2. Identify the five most important to you. Rank them from first to last. Beside each value, identify at least two products or services you have purchased to satisfy those values.

   Gather in small groups of three to five students. Using the information from your list of values, discuss differences among members of the group. Identify how to design a marketing message to appeal to the top value from each person's list.

3. One recent approach used in reaching teenagers by Coca-Cola occurred in 1998. The firm distributed 55 million wallet-size "Coke cards" in various high schools and to college students at spring break parties. Individuals who purchased Coke with the card earned discounts at fast-food outlets, movie theaters, video stores, and theme parks. The real benefit to Coke was the ability to track purchasing information for 55 million teenagers and young adults. Why is this information valuable to Coke? Research has indicated that 10.3 percent of Coke's core customers account for 48.5 percent of its sales.[21] How can the information obtained from tracking Coke cards be used to convert teenagers to core customers? Why does Coke want teenagers to develop a loyalty to Coke at an early age?

4. Cultural values and norms constantly change. In groups of three to five students, discuss the cultural values and norms that have changed in the last 10 years. Are these values and norms different from those held by most parents? If so, why? What caused these changes to occur?

5. Look at the following Web sites. Would consumers tend to use the ELM or the HEM approach in processing the information at the site? Is the product or service promoted to satisfy physical, psychological, social, or emotional needs of consumers? If not, how does the site discuss the functional aspects of the product or service? Is the site designed to affect cognitive, affective, or conative elements of the consumer's attitude?

   a. Kenneth Cole (www.kennethcole.com)

   b. Starbucks (www.starbucks.com)

   c. Cadillac (www.cadillac.com)

   d. IKEA (www.ikea.com)

   e. Baby Gap (www.gap.com/onlinestore/babygap)

Inducing Consumers to Buy a Product

The products and services listed in Chapter 1 are mostly common items. For each one, some type of consumer decision-making process is involved in making a selection. To develop an effective IMC program for the product you selected to market, it is important to comprehend the manner in which a given brand is chosen as well as why one brand may be perceived as the top choice when a set of purchase alternatives appears. Go to the Prentice-Hall Web site at **www.prenhall.com/clow** or access the IMC Plan Pro disk that accompanied this textbook to complete the exercise that helps you integrate consumer purchasing activities with the other elements of the IMC program that you already have completed.

BUILDING AN
IMC
CAMPAIGN

IMC PlanPro

CASE 1

BUYING A TELEVISION? IT'S NOT THAT SIMPLE

Kelli is evaluating four console television brands. The multiattribute approach to processing information helps explain Kelli's final purchasing decision. In making this purchase, she bases her evaluation on five criteria: (1) quality of sound, (2) quality of picture, (3) style of cabinet, (4) other features, and (5) the price or value of the television. The importance ratings in Table 3.2 indicate that Kelli is most interested in the quality of the sound, because she gave it a 5 rating. Quality of picture and style of cabinet are next, with ratings of 4. Other television features and price are the least important to Kelli.

TABLE 3.2

Example of a Multiattribute Approach Evaluation of Console Televisions by Kelli

Attribute[b]	Importance[a]	Brand A	Brand B	Brand C	Brand D
Quality of sound	5	5	4	3	4
Quality of picture	4	3	4	4	5
Style of cabinet	4	4	5	2	3
Television features	3	3	3	5	4
Price of television (good value)	3	4	2	5	4
Compensatory Score[c]		74	71	69	76

[a]Ranked from 1 to 5 with 5 being highly important and 1 being unimportant.
[b]Each attribute is rated on a score from 1 to 5 with 5 being high performance and 1 being poor performance.
[c]Scores are cumulative sums of the importance rating times the brand evaluation.

The next column of numbers shows her evaluation of each attribute for each brand. In terms of quality of sound, Brand A was the best (Kelli gave it a score of 5). Brands B and D were next. The score of 4 each received indicates approximately equal sound quality. Brand C had the lowest sound quality and thus she gave it a score of 3.

After evaluating all the brands across all the criteria, Kelli will make a decision. Kelli can calculate these scores in several ways. One method is to multiply each attribute's importance rating times the corresponding evaluation for each brand. Summing these results in the scores is shown in the row labeled Compensatory Score. Using this method, she would choose Brand D because of its overall score. This method of evaluating alternatives is **compensatory heuristics**.

The compensatory heuristics method assumes that no one single brand scores high on every attribute and that individual attributes vary in importance. When considering several brands, consumers make trade-offs. Notice that, in Table 3.2, Kelli rates Brand A as having the best quality of sound, her most important product attribute. At the same time, Brand A has the worst quality picture and she ranked it lowest in terms of television features. Although Brand A had the best sound, it was not the best brand for Kelli because of the poor ratings on other attributes.

When Kelli considers Brand D, she concludes it has good sound, although the sound is not as good as in Brand A. Brand D does have the best-quality picture. In terms of price and television features, it is not the best but still good. The worst rating Kelli gives Brand D is for the cabinet style. But even there, Brand C's cabinet style rating is lower. To get the best overall

(continued)

television, Kelli has to make trade-offs and choose the best one overall of the attributes evaluated. Consumers are not likely to draw a table like Table 3.2, but they go through a similar process mentally.

A second computational form Kelli can use to make her evaluation is called **conjunctive heuristics**. In this method, Kelli establishes a minimum or threshold rating. She considers only brands that meet the threshold, even when one product ranks high in individual criteria. Going back to Table 3.2, assume Kelli has mentally established a minimum threshold of 4. She discards a brand if it scores 3 or lower on any criterion important to her. Using this method, she would eliminate all five brands because of low scores on individual attributes.

Consequently, consumers can use an *iterative approach*. Quality of sound is most important to Kelli and so she starts there. She rated Brand C a 3, and because this is below the minimum, Kelli eliminates Brand C. Next, Kelli looks closely at Brands A, B, and D. All have good or excellent sound. Therefore Kelli goes to her next most important criterion—quality of the picture. She ranks both quality of picture and style of cabinet each with a 4 in terms of importance. Before Kelli can eliminate any more brands, she has to decide which of those two criteria is more important. Assuming that quality of picture is next, she would eliminate Brand A due to its rating below the threshold. Now Kelli has narrowed her choice to two models, Brand B and Brand D. The next attribute she considers is style of cabinet. Because Brand D is below the threshold, she eliminates it. Thus, she chooses Brand B because it is the only one left.

A fourth calculation can be made using a **phased heuristic** approach. This method is a combination of the others. Going back to Table 3.2, assume that Kelli eliminates any brand with a score lower than a 3 on any criterion. Notice Brand B's rating of 2 on price and Brand C's rating of 2 on style of cabinet. Kelli immediately discards them (Brand B because it is too expensive and Brand C because she does not like its cabinet). This leaves Brands A and D. To make the decision between these two brands, she can use the compensatory heuristic approach. Consumers often use a phased approach similar to this when they have many brands to evaluate. This method easily reduces the evoked set to a smaller and more manageable subset.

Buying a television isn't easy. The same mental gymnastics are part of many purchases. Marketing experts spend a great deal of time trying to make sure that the characteristics consumers value appear in their products, services, and marketing messages.

1. Go through Table 3.2 and make sure you can explain how Kelli makes her purchase decision, whether product A, B, C, or D is chosen, using the various heuristic models.

2. Construct a similar table for one of the following products:
   a. An automobile
   b. A night out for dinner
   c. A drinking establishment
   d. A new clothing outfit
   e. A spring break vacation.

3. For each product listed in Question 2, identify a recent purchase. Explain the process you used to make the purchase decision. Which heuristic model did you use?

CASE 2

THE FOOD COURT

Chi-Hung Chien was about to begin an exciting new phase of life. Chi-Hung grew up in Taiwan but came to the United States to get his education. During his college years, Chi-Hung fell in love with a local girl, married her, and applied for a permanent visa. Even though this meant leaving his family behind, Chi-Hung believed he could get home often enough to see family and friends while building a new life in America.

For the past seven years, Chi-Hung worked at a local Chinese restaurant. He studied the moves of the owners carefully while trying to apply the many things he had learned in college from his marketing major and management minor. Finally, an opportunity presented itself. The biggest shopping mall in town had an opening for a new restaurant in its food court. The Chien family took out its life savings, applied for a small business loan, and obtained additional funding from their parents in order to open the new KA-POW! restaurant.

Chi-Hung spent a great deal of time in the mall prior to making his decision to open his business. Having studied the five steps of the buying decision-making process in college, he was interested to see how they might apply in the mall. After all, there was a considerable amount of traffic through the food court. People stopped to buy soft drinks, snacks, and full meals. Some people ate with families. Junior high and young high schoolers would "hang out" for hours. Shoppers stopped for a quick bite to eat. Even old-timers visited the food court as part of their morning "mall walking" ritual. Most wanted coffee, but the opportunity existed to sell tea to some of these patrons.

The most interesting part of the mall food-buying experience was to watch as an individual entered the food court. Some clearly had their minds made up and traveled directly to the restaurant of their choosing, whether it was McDonald's, Dairy Queen, Sbarros, or Chick-Fil-A. These national chains had steady inflows of traffic. Some of the local outlets had more trouble enticing the quick visit. Spuds Are Us, a baked potato place, and a locally owned taco place had some regular customers yet nowhere near the same number as McDonald's. Chi-Hung also knew many regulars were simply mall employees.

At the same time, Chi-Hung called numerous clients "wanderers." These shoppers would walk back and forth between shops, trying to decide what kind of food to buy. Several of the stores offered free small food samples to entice the customer to develop a stronger craving for a certain kind of food and make a purchase as a result.

The key seemed to be discovering how various consumer groups made food-buying decisions. Chi-Hung was convinced he could deliver a quality product at a competitive price, with solid service. He just wanted to make sure he knew his potential customers before they even got out of their cars in the mall parking lot.

1. Describe your buying decision-making process the last time you ate at a mall food court.

2. What decision criteria influence a family making a food court purchase? Would they be the same as those for mall rats?

3. Which group should Chi-Hung target, or should he try to sell to everyone?

4. Should KA-POW! offer takeout? Delivery? How else can the company sell additional products?

(continued)

5. Design an attractive advertisement for KA-POW! using the cognitive → affective → conative approach to influencing consumer attitudes. How can you modify the ad to use the affective → conative → cognitive approach? How can you modify the ad to use the conative → cognitive → affective approach?

6. In a group of three students, design three different advertisements, each using a distinct approach to impact consumer attitude. Compare the advertisements and discuss how each approach tries to influence consumer attitudes.

ENDNOTES

1. Len Lewis, "Coffee Culture," *Progressive Grocer,* 76, no. 11 (November 1997), pp. 20–22; "Starbucks Roasts the Competition," *Journal of Business Strategy,* 16, no. 6 (November–December), 1995; Kate Rounds, "Starbucks Coffee," *Incentive,* 167, no. 7 (July 1993), pp. 22–23; Ingrid Abramovitch, "Miracles of Marketing," *Success,* 40, no. 3 (April 1993), pp. 22–27; Jennifer Rose, "Starbucks: Inside the Coffee Cult," *Fortune,* 134, no. 11 (December 9, 1996), pp. 190–200.

2. Jeffrey B. Schmidt and Richard A. Spreng, "A Proposed Model of External Consumer Information Search," *Journal of Academy of Marketing Science,* 24, no. 3 (summer 1996), pp. 246–56.

3. Merrie Brucks, "The Effect of Product Class Knowledge on Information Search Behavior," *Journal of Consumer Research,* 12 (June 1985), pp. 1–15; Schmidt and Spreng, "A Proposed Model of External Consumer Information Search."

4. Laura M. Buchholz and Robert E. Smith, "The Role of Consumer Involvement in Determining Cognitive Responses to Broadcast Advertising," *Journal of Advertising,* 20, no. 1 (1991), pp. 4–17; Schmidt and Spreng, "A Proposed Model of External Consumer Information Search"; Jeffrey J. Inman, Leigh McAllister, and Wayne D. Hoyer, "Promotion Signal: Proxy for a Price Cut," *Journal of Consumer Research,* 17 (June 1990), pp. 74–81; Barry J. Babin, William R. Darden, and Mitch Griffin, "Work and/or Fun: Measuring Hedonic and Utilitarian Shopping Value," *Journal of Consumer Research,* 20 (March 1994), pp. 644–56.

5. Schmidt and Spreng, "A Proposed Model of External Consumer Information Search."

6. M. Fishbein and Icek Ajzen, *Belief, Attitude, Intention, and Behavior: An Introduction to Theory and Research* (Reading, MA: Addison Wesley, 1975).

7. Richard P. Bagozzi, Alice M. Tybout, C. Samuel Craig, and Brian Sternathal, "The Construct Validity of the Tripartite Classification of Attitudes," *Journal of Marketing,* 16, no. 1 (February 1979), pp. 88–95.

8. Discussion of the ELM based on Richard E. Petty and John T. Cacioppo, *Attitudes and Persuasion: Classic and Contemporary Approaches* (Dubuque, IA: William C. Brown, 1981); C. P. Haugtvedt and Richard E. Petty, "Personality and Persuasion: Need for Cognition Moderates the Persistence and Resistance of Attitude Change," *Journal of Personality and Social Psychology,* 63 (1992), pp. 308–19; Kenneth R. Lord and Myung-Soo Lee,

"The Combined Influence Hypothesis: Central and Peripheral Antecedents of Attitude Toward the Ad," *Journal of Advertising,* 24, no. 1 (spring 1995), pp. 73–85.

9. Discussion of the HEM based on Veronika Denes-Raj and Seymour Epstein, "Conflict Between Intuitive and Rational Processing: When People Behave Against Their Better Judgment," *Journal of Personality and Social Psychology,* 66, no. 5 (May 1994), pp. 819–29; Morris B. Holbrook and Elizabeth G. Hirschmann, "The Experiential Aspects of Consumption: Consumer Fantasies, Feelings and Fun," *Journal of Consumer Research,* 9 (September 1982), pp. 132–40; Elizabeth G. Hirschmann and Morris B. Holbrook, "Hedonic Consumption: Emerging Concepts, Methods and Propositions," *Journal of Marketing,* 46 (summer 1982), pp. 92–101.

10. Discussion of cognitive mapping based on Anne R. Kearny and Stephan Kaplan, "Toward a Methodology for the Measurement of Knowledge Structures of Ordinary People: The Conceptual Content Cognitive Map (3CM)," *Environment and Behavior,* 29, no. 5 (September 1997), pp. 579–617; Stephan Kaplan and R. Kaplan, *Cognition and Environment, Functioning in an Uncertain World* (Ann Arbor, MI: Ulrich's, 1982, 1989).

11. Discussion of heuristics and multiattribute model based on William L. Wilkie and Edgar A. Pessemier, "Issues in Marketing's Use of Multiattribute Models," *Journal of Marketing Research,* 10 (November 1983), pp. 428–41; Peter L. Wright, "Consumer Choice Strategies: Simplifying vs. Optimizing," *Journal of Marketing Research,* 11 (February 1975), pp. 60–67; James B. Bettman, *An Information Processing Theory of Consumer Choice* (Reading, MA: Addison-Wesley, 1979).

12. Sugato Chakravarty and Richard Feinberg, "Reasons for Their Discontent," *Bank Marketing,* 29, no. 11 (November 1997), pp. 49–53.

13. Lisa Bertagnoli, "Continental Spendthrifts," *Marketing News,* 35, issue 22 (October, 22, 2001), pp. 1–2.

14. Discussion of Second-Chancers based on Richard Halverson, "The Customer Connection: Second-Chancers," *Discount Store News,* 37, no. 20 (October 26, 1998), pp. 91–95.

15. Mark Dolliver, "Part-time Role Models," *Adweek,* Eastern Edition, 39, no. 44 (November 2, 1998), p. 20.

16. David B. Wolfe, "The Psychological Center of Gravity," *American Demographics,* 20, no. 4 (April 1998), pp. 16–19.

17. "The Devotion Cycle," *Chain Store Age,* 75, no. 1 (January 1999), pp. 52–58.

18. Hester Cooper and Ann Holway, "Consumer Behaviour: The Seven Key Trends," *New Zealand Marketing Magazine,* 18, no. 2 (March 1999), pp. 27–30.

19. Ibid.

20. Schmidt and Spreng, "A Proposed Model of External Consumer Information Search."

21. Buchholz and Smith, "The Role of Consumer Involvement in Determining Cognitive Responses to Broadcast Advertising"; Schmidt and Spreng, "A Proposed Model of External Consumer Information Search"; Inman, McAllister, and Hoyer, "Promotion Signal"; Babin, Darden, and Griffin, "Work and/or Fun: Measuring Hedonic and Utilitarian Shopping Value."

Business-to-Business Buyer Behavior

Chapter Objectives

Identify the types of business buyers in the global marketplace.

Review the buying decision-making process and apply it to business-to-business marketing.

Recognize the challenges of dual channel (retail and business-to-business) marketing programs.

Understand the new environment facing companies that sell to other businesses.

INTEL BUNNIES:

The Next Generation in Brand Awareness

Quick, name all of the companies you can think of that sell microprocessors for computers and the brand names of their products. If you are the typical consumer, you can identify one: Pentium. A few more sophisticated computer consumers may be able to recall one or two more but in the next breath would probably report that the Pentium is "the best." How did Intel reach this point?

The staggering growth and success rate of the Intel Pentium brand can be traced to an increased demand for personal computers. The original Intel 486 name could not be patented, because numbers are part of the description of the product's use. This "setback" caused Intel to develop a new brand name right at the time when everyone needed processors, but no one knew their names. The Pentium brand was advertised extensively both in the consumer retail market and in business trade publications directed toward computer manufacturers and software companies. Consumers began asking if the PCs they were about to buy had Pentium processors. At the same time, Intel formed a major alliance with Microsoft as Windows 95 was introduced. Suddenly Intel held a major advantage in the marketplace.

In 1994, a math expert discovered a flaw in one part of the Pentium processor. A second problem, named the "Wob Clobber Bug" was also revealed. What seemed like major obstacles, however, only added to name recognition of the Pentium processor. The company swiftly pointed out that the mathematical flaw would affect only a very small number of applications and just as quickly developed methods to overcome the Wob Clobber Bug problem. By the end of the year, what could have been a tremendous predicament had become an advantage because of the public admission of the problems and attempts to solve them, which bolstered consumer confidence in the company.

As the 1990s came to a close, users required newer, faster processors. Intel sought to continue its dominance in the marketplace by making sure both business customers and retail end users would ask for the Pentium part by name when purchasing computers. In 1997, Intel introduced "BunnyPeople," the workers producing the Pentium II processor. Soon, the Bunnies danced and traveled excitedly across the land in various advertisements and trade shows. These happy chip makers in shiny, colorful suits added humor and a human presence to a high-tech product. The program was so successful that the firm even authorized the manufacture of BunnyPeople dolls.

Two new issues confronted Intel following the introduction of BunnyPeople. One was an increasing insistence for privacy by some consumer groups. Intel designed the Pentium III in such a way that an ID number was easily garnered when the customer accessed the Internet. A boycott followed by a small number of customers who demanded better security from their computers. The company continues to address this issue.

Second, Intel had to move away from its "one size fits all" approach to processor design. Consequently, the company reorganized by the various types of business buyers it serves. Intel created four new business units to meet these needs: (1) the Consumer Products Group, (2) the Business Platform Group, (3) the Small Business and Networking Group, and (4) the Digital Imaging and Video Division.

The Consumer Products Group primarily targets the consumer desktop PC market. New products lines are emerging in this area, including TV set-top computing devices and PCs for automobiles. The Business Platform Group focuses on business computers, including PCs, network computers, NetPCs, workstations, and data security solutions for PCs. The Small Business and Networking Group addresses the needs of smaller companies. This group sells networking products, management software, business communications products, reseller products, and Internet services. The Digital Imaging and Video Division tries to tap a growing market in the audiovisual industry, especially related to stand-alone digital cameras.

The IMC advantage held by Intel began with a demand pull strategy, where it enticed consumers to ask for the Pentium processor by name when purchasing products. The primary message was that Intel offered the fastest and most sophisticated product. Brand recognition by both retail customers and business buyers increased through effective advertising in the early 1990s and grew when BunnyPeople added humor and personality to Intel's Pentium II and III products. By redeploying company resources at the turn of the century, Intel continued to rule the market by carefully meeting the needs of various business buyers, while maintaining its primary image and message as the Pentium IV processor reaches the market. Competitors face a major uphill battle to retake the turf currently held by BunnyPeople in colorful suits.[1]

JAVANET INTERNET CAFÉ

For many companies, the business-to-business market is a lucrative component. It is vital that the marketing department reach both traditional consumers and other businesses in a voice that is consistent and powerful. Knowing the types of companies and employees in those companies who can affect or make purchasing decisions is one ingredient. Another is developing a marketing plan that successfully reaches this group. Establishing the business-to-business component of an IMC plan is another "brick" in the foundation.

In the JavaNet Internet Café example provided on the IMC Plan Pro disk, section 3.6 is devoted to the business-to-business part of the plan. As noted in the plan, distinct groups may visit the café. Some are standard buying center members, such as executives and managers from businesses that are physically close to JavaNet locations. Others are travelers and nonexecutive local office workers looking for a place to relax, read e-mail, or surf the Internet. Customer traffic through each café will be heightened if JavaNet's marketing team develops an approach to appeal to all of these groups along with other types of customers.

---

overview

Many perceive marketing to be a glamorous profession. Students majoring in marketing think about designing various goods and services as well as creating innovative programs to move products from the manufacturer to the consumer, while making massive profits for the organization. When compared to the mundane "bean counting" tasks of accounting or the routine aspects of human resource management such as recruiting and selection, marketing indeed can appear to be more exciting than other business vocations.

Further, advertising may seem like the most glamorous aspect of marketing. Creatives designing eye-catching, funny, sexy, or humorous ads appear to work in an alluring field. Advertising design classes are often among the most popular on college campuses, both in the communications department and in the marketing field.

The reality is, of course, that very few people actually get to write ad copy and record or shoot advertisements to be released on television, radio, or through another medium. The majority of people employed in the marketing area work at some other kind of job that is often just as challenging and rewarding.

One of the most vital tasks account executives and others in the field of marketing can perform is to *identify new buyers and new markets for existing goods and services.* Many firms recognize that competition is fierce for individual consumers. As a result, it makes good sense to seek out *other companies* willing to purchase much larger quantities of a company's products. Any effective IMC program must incorporate an in-depth analysis of potential business-to-business outlets the firm can cultivate.

This chapter presents four major items. First, it defines the various types or categories of business-to-business buyers. Second, the major roles associated with making purchases, called the business buying center, are described. Third, the steps of the business purchasing processes are outlined and explained. Fourth, important new factors and issues in business-to-business sales are discussed.

Effective business-to-business sales increase a company's revenues. For some firms, sales to other businesses provide stability in sales figures by offering new markets in conjunction with retail sales efforts. For others, selling to other businesses is the company's primary or sole marketing function. In every case, effective management of communications messages begins with discovering how business buyers make decisions. Once these processes are understood, it is possible to select the proper message, media, and tools to reach these vital market segments.

TYPES OF BUSINESS CUSTOMERS

Business customers purchase both goods and services. This section describes the various types of goods companies sell as well as the various services required by companies. Many firms buy both goods and services, and many business-to-business operations involve the sale of both goods and services.

There are two ways to address business customers buying products. The first is to list the types of products that a business would sell to another business. The second is to identify the different types of customers a business would try to reach. Both approaches offer insights into the nature of business-to-business marketing.

TYPES OF PRODUCTS

Many types of goods and services are sold in the business-to-business marketplace. Goods include major equipment such as bulldozer and mainframe computers, accessories such as calculators and coffee machines, fabricated and component parts (spark plugs for cars and lawn mowers, computer processor chips), process materials such as cement and plastic, as well as maintenance, repair, and operating supplies. Each requires a distinct marketing approach.

The services that businesses sell to other businesses include operating services such as telephone and Internet services, bulk services such as health insurance policies for employees, services that accompany the sale of a product (maintenance of a copy machine), and services that are sold together, such as airline relationships with hotels and travel agencies. Table 4.1 indicates many of the products that are sold business-to-business as well as the types of customers that purchase them. Table 4.2 highlights international customers for various products. Table 4.3 summarizes many of the services that companies offer to other businesses.

The pager being advertised by Motorola is an example of accessory equipment.
Source: Courtesy of Motorola, Inc. © 1999/Personal Communications Sector.

Types of Goods and Services	Types of Customers				
	Manufacturers	**Government**	**Institutions**	**Wholesalers Distributors**	**Retail**
Major equipment	✔	✔	✔	✔	✔
Accessory equipment	✔	✔	✔	✔	✔
Component parts	✔				
Process materials	✔				
Maintenance supplies	✔	✔	✔	✔	✔
Operating supplies	✔	✔	✔	✔	✔
Raw material	✔				
Operating services	✔	✔	✔	✔	✔
Professional services	✔	✔	✔	✔	✔
Products and services for resale				✔	✔

TABLE 4.1

Business Customers and What They Buy

Importers	Firms purchasing goods from other countries, either for resale in their own retail outlets (e.g., Import Warehouse) or to other companies.
Exporters	Companies that specialize in finding international customers for goods and services. They provide shipping, billing, and other logistics, similar to domestic wholesalers.
Retail outlets	Companies that buy directly from manufacturers in other countries.
Other businesses	Firms using goods in the production of other goods, or as part of business operations.
Governments	Products and services purchased by other nations.
Institutions	Institutions (not-for-profit organizations, universities, etc.) that buy goods and services from international firms.
Individual customers	Private individuals who buy goods and services directly from firms in other countries.

TABLE 4.2

Types of International Customers

Banking and finance services	Health care services
Stock market services	Food services
Credit services	Repair and maintenance services
Insurance services	Laundry and uniform services
Educational services	Rental services
Travel services	Social services (drug and alcohol counseling)
Shipping services	Lawn and pest control services
Accounting services	Legal services
Computer services	Consulting services

TABLE 4.3

Types of Services

TYPES OF CUSTOMERS

As many successful companies have discovered, business-to-business customers offer numerous lucrative outlets for goods and services. The previous section presented various types of business products. In this section, the different types of business-to-business customers are described in order to provide a second perspective into the nature of marketing to other companies. Table 4.1 matches the products described in the previous section with the types of customers to be defined in this section. Potential customers of individual products can be placed into the following categories:

Warehousing and shipping are examples of operating services provided to business customers.
Source: Courtesy of The Image Works. Photograph by David Lassman.

- Manufacturing customers
- Governmental customers
- Institutional customers
- Wholesalers and distributor customers
- Retail customers
- International customers

An IMC program will be targeted to the type of product or service being sold as well as the type of business making the purchase. To do so requires finding and reaching the right people in the target company.

COMMUNICATION ACTION

Making Music

Manufacturers of musical instruments have experienced volatile periods of sales in the past decade. Several forces have changed the nature of the music business. One major factor is the number of children playing musical instruments. When numerous public schools began cutting back on music programs, sales to individual consumers as well as to local music stores declined. In fact, the number of small retail music stores dropped by 13 percent within a five-year period. These companies were the ones that had primarily marketed instruments to children, normally through rental or purchase agreements. Consequently, producers of musical instruments were among the first to feel the pinch of this trend.

A renewed interest in music, spurred by reports that musical training spurs intellectual growth and development, has created a stronger marketplace. Manufacturers of guitars, pianos, and other instruments noticed a resurgence in sales in the last five years. Current markets for musical instruments include:

▶ Small, independently owned music stores
▶ Grade schools, middle schools, high schools, and universities
▶ Large new music superstores, such as MARS and Guitar Center
▶ Individual buyers via the Internet and catalog sales

Instrument manufacturers must keep up with the technology of music. Computerization essentially allows for music makers of all ages to create home recording studios and to make a wide variety of sounds out of the same instrument. The one remaining major competitive threat is resale firms that market used instruments.

Future markets for instruments include aging baby boomers interested in relearning an instrument, older adults taking up new hobbies, and the next generation of children. Reaching these groups will require careful marketing efforts to schools and institutions, to retail outlets, and through direct-marketing programs.

Sources: Robert Scally, "Striking a New Chord in a Mom and Pop Industry," *Discount Store News,* 37, no. 9 (May 11, 1998), pp. 70–82; Robert Scally, "Guitar Center Acquires a Friend," *Discount Store News,* 38, no. 11 (June 7, 1999), p. 10; Nakamura Akemi, "The String's the Thing for Adults Learning Violin," *Japan Times Weekly International Edition,* 38, no. 13 (March 30–April 5, 1998), p. 16; James Mammarella, "Grow Bix: Good as New," *Discount Store News,* 36, no 9 (May 5, 1997), pp. 72, 84.

BUSINESS BUYING CENTERS

How are business-to-business purchases completed? *People* still make purchase decisions, but, within a business organization, several individuals normally become involved. Further, corporate policies provide parameters and decision rules as purchases are made. Factors such as budgets, costs, and profit considerations often influence the final choice.

Business purchases seldom are made in isolation. With so many people involved, the decision-making process becomes much more complex. The group of individuals involved in the buying decision is called the **buying center**. As illustrated in Figure 4.1, the buying center consists of five different subsets of individuals playing various roles in the process. The five roles involved in the buying center are:

▶ Users
▶ Buyers
▶ Influencers
▶ Deciders
▶ Gatekeeper

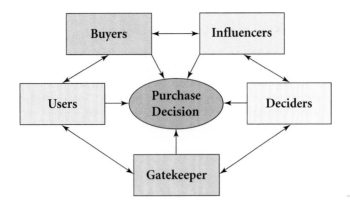

FIGURE 4.1
The Buying Center

Users are the members of the organization who actually use the good or service. When the product is office supplies, users are usually members of the secretarial staff. If the product is the tin used in the production of tin cans, users are the factory workers in the production facility. Computing staff members run mainframes and computers. In the Elekta ad on page 98, neurosurgeons are the users of the products, services, and treatment solutions offered by the company.

Buyers are the individuals given the formal responsibility of making the purchase. In larger organizations, buyers are either purchasing agents or members of the purchasing department. In smaller organizations, the buyer can be the owner or president of the company, a manager, or even a secretary.

Influencers are people who shape purchasing decisions by providing the information or criteria utilized in evaluating alternatives. Influencers often are formally appointed as part of a committee charged with selecting a vendor. In other firms, the process is more informal. For example, an engineer describes the specifications for a particular product that his or her department needs.

Deciders are the individuals who authorize decisions. They are often purchasing agents. In large organizations, a financial officer, a vice president, or even the president of the company must finalize purchase decisions. Whoever agrees to allocate funds to complete a purchase is the decider.

The **gatekeeper** controls the flow of information to members of the buying center. Gatekeepers keep people informed about potential alternatives and decision rules being used. The gatekeeper also lets members know when certain alternatives have been rejected. In some situations, it is not a specific individual who is the gatekeeper, but rather a *gatekeeping function* in which members notify each other regarding various events associated with the purchase.

Many times these five roles overlap. For example, the gatekeeper may also be the buyer. Often the purchasing department determines what information to give to members of the buying center. The department usually controls the amount of access a salesperson has to members of the buying center. Also, several individuals can occupy the same role, especially for large or critical purchases. It is not unusual for a variety of members of the organization to serve as influencers, because these roles usually are not fixed and formal. Roles change as the purchase decision changes.

The buying behavior process is unique in each organization. It varies within an organization from one purchasing decision to the next. Salespeople calling on a business must be able to locate members of the buying center and understand their roles in the process. These roles often change from one purchase situation to another, making the marketing task more difficult than one might expect.[2]

FACTORS AFFECTING MEMBERS OF BUSINESS BUYING CENTERS

The behaviors of each member in the buying center are influenced by a series of cultural, organizational, individual, and social factors.[3] These influences change the manner in which decisions are made and often affect the eventual outcome or alternative chosen. A discussion of these factors follows.

Organizational Influences

Several organizational factors affect the ways in which individuals make purchasing decisions for a company. These organizational factors include the company's goals and its operating environment (recession, growth period, lawsuits pending, etc.). Decisions are further constrained by the organization's finances, capital assets, market position, the quality of its human resources, and the country in which the firm operates.

Some organizations have highly centralized purchasing programs. In those firms, a few individuals at the corporation's headquarters make most purchase decisions. Other individuals have only minimal influence on the purchase process. Other organizations are more decentralized. These firms grant various departments and individuals autonomy in making purchase decisions and, as a result, those groups often seek advice and input from a variety of members of the company.

Studies of organizational decision making indicate that employees tend to adopt *heuristics,* which are decision rules designed to eliminate quickly as many options as possible. Company goals, rules, budgets, and other organizational factors create heuristics. One decision rule often employed is called *satisficing,* which means that when an acceptable alternative has been identified, it is taken and the search is completed. Rather than spending a great deal of time looking for an optimal solution, decision makers tend to favor expedience.[4]

Neurosurgeons who use the products, services, and treatment solutions Elekta offers are an important component of the buying center.
Source: Courtesy of Elekta Instruments Inc.

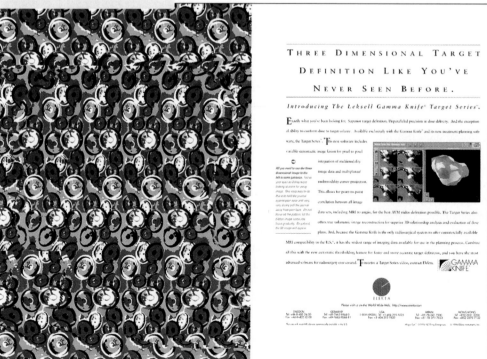

Individual Factors

At least seven factors affect each member of the business buying center: (1) personality features, (2) roles and perceived roles, (3) motivational levels, (4) levels of power, (5) attitudes toward risk, (6) levels of cognitive involvement, and (7) personal objectives.[5] (See Figure 4.2.) Each impacts how the individual interacts with other members of the center.

Regarding the issue of *personality,* a decisive person makes decisions in a manner different from one who vacillates. Confidence, extroversion, shyness, and other personality features affect both the person performing the decision-making role and others in the process. An aggressive "know it all" type affects the other members of a decision-making team, and such a personality feature does not always benefit the organization. An extrovert tends to become more involved in the buying process than a more introverted individual. The extrovert spends more time talking, and the introvert spends more time listening to sellers. The introvert might be too timid with salespeople and consequently may not ask important questions.

The *roles* people play are influenced by many of the same factors that affect consumer buyer behaviors, including the individual's age, heredity, ethnicity, gender, cultural memberships, and patterns of social interaction. These role-playing ingredients affect how the individual interacts with others in the buying center. Roles are socially constructed, which means people define how they intend to play roles as part of the negotiation process with others nearby.

It is not just the role itself that affects decisions. A person's perception of how the role fits into the buying center process and the overall organization is important. When a buying center member perceives the role as merely giving approval to decisions made by

It seems we've always been obsessed with lint.

A B-to-B advertisement directed to buyers in the apparel industry.
Source: Courtesy of Kimberly-Clark.

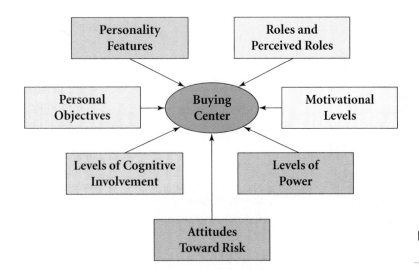

FIGURE 4.2
Factors Affecting the Behaviors of Buying Center Members

the boss (the decider), then the individual will not be an active member of the group. When members feel their inputs are important and wanted, they become more active. A person can believe his role is to provide information. Another might think she is supposed to play the devil's advocate. Someone else might perceive his role as being the person who synthesizes information provided by vendors and then relates it to the buying center to save the other members time. Roles and perceptions of roles are major factors determining how members of the buying center go about their business.

Motivation depends on how well the individual's goals match the organization's goals. If a factory foreman has a personal goal of becoming the vice president of operations, that foreman is more likely to become involved in all purchasing decisions that affect his performance and that of his department. If a purchasing agent has been charged by the CEO to cut expenses, she may take a more active role to ensure cost-cutting selections are made. Many individuals also are motivated by needs for recognition. The goal of making successful purchasing decisions is to ensure that others recognize their efforts. They believe recognition is linked to getting promotions and pay raises.

A person's *level of power* in the buying process depends on his or her role in the buying center, official position in the organization, and the impact of the purchase decision on a specific job. When a particular purchase decision directly affects an employee, that person tries to gain more power in the buying process. For instance, a factory foreman has greater power within the buying center in the purchase of raw materials, whereas the maintenance foreman has more power in the purchase of maintenance supplies. In these situations, both foremen strive to influence the decision that affects their area.

Risk is another factor that affects members of the buying center. Many vendors are chosen because buyers believe the choice has the lowest risk. Also, risk avoidance means firms tend to stay with current vendors rather than switching. In marketing to businesses, reducing risk is a major concern, especially when signing large contracts or when the purchase might affect company profits. People tend to think taking risks (especially when a failure follows) can affect performance appraisals, promotions, and other aspects of an individual's job.

A B-to-B advertisement directed to lab technicians, users of the product.
Source: Courtesy of Kimberly-Clark.

What it's doing is giving a baby who spends his first few months in an incubator a chance to bond with his parents. And, it's soothing every muscle in his little body, allowing him to tolerate his feedings and go home to his own bed sooner. The program is called skin-to-skin.

IF JUST LOOKING AT THIS HAS A PROFOUND EFFECT ON YOU, IMAGINE WHAT IT'S DOING FOR THIS THREE POUND BABY.

Kangaroo Care. It's just one of the many techniques used by the advanced team in our Level III Neonatal Intensive Care Unit. Although most of our new parents will never have to hold a baby so fragile, it's good to know we're here. Just in case.

© COLUMBIA Plantation General Hospital

We Put Women And Children First.

401 N.W. 42nd Avenue • Plantation, FL 33317 • Phone: 1•800•Columbia • Columbia's home page is http://www.columbia.net

Levels of cognitive involvement influence not only consumer buyer behaviors but also business buyers. Individuals with higher levels of cognitive capacity want more information prior to making decisions. They also ask more questions when interacting with a sales rep. These individuals spend more time deliberating prior to making a decision. Clear key message arguments are the important ingredients in persuading people with higher cognitive levels (as noted in the Chapter 3 discussion of consumer buyer behaviors).

Personal objectives are tied to motives, personality, perceptions of risk, and the other individual factors. Personal objectives can lead buyers to make purchases that help them politically in the organization, but aren't the best choice. For example, if someone knows his or her boss is friends with a particular vendor, the buyer can choose that vendor even when others offer higher quality, lower prices, or both. Personal objectives can be tied to getting promotions, making rivals look bad, "brownnosing" a boss, or the genuine desire to help the organization succeed.

Cultural Factors

Cultural patterns affect managerial styles as well as decision making processes. For many years, the Japanese management style normally included consensus-based decision making, in contrast to those of the United States and other cultures, which are often more individualistic and authoritarian. In a buying decision-making process, a key boss in a U.S. company gathers input, makes a decision, and then simply announces it. For many

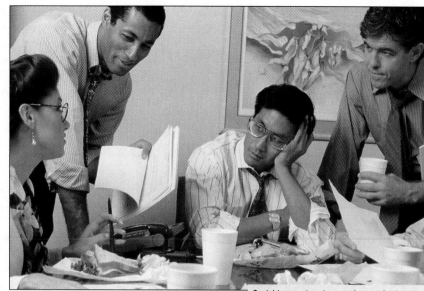

Social interactions impact the way business purchase decisions are made.
Source: Courtesy of The Image Bank. Photograph by Anne Rippy.

years, such a scenario was highly unlikely in Japanese firms, which tend to favor a more group-based approach. Therefore, marketing experts must carefully examine the culture in which the firm operates when developing a plan to reach members of the buying center.

Social Factors

The final category of items that influence business buyer behaviors is a set of social factors. Consumers are social beings. The need for social acceptance is an important element in many purchases. Each member of the buying center has certain expectations of the buying group. These expectations, combined with the individual's desire to conform to them, determine social interactions within groups.

Members of the buying center tend to adhere to group *social norms*. **Norms** are, in essence, rules of behavior regarding the proper way to behave in a group. In buying centers, one common norm is to act in a positive and friendly fashion. Another relates to understanding who is acting as the "leader" and who are the "followers" in the group. Norms affect language (cursing, use of titles, formality or informality), after-work socialization (happy hours, parties), and at-work interactions (who is invited to lunch). Norms strongly determine how problems are solved in buying centers as well as the ways in which individuals interact with one another.[6]

The buying center is a complex, interactive group of individuals. Members of the buying center serve different roles and may serve more than one role in a particular buying situation. In marketing to businesses, it is important to understand these dynamics. It is also important to recognize who is making decisions, how decisions are made, and what forces or factors may change decisions. By examining organizational, individual, and social influences, it is possible to design a communications program that will reach the key people at the right time.

TYPES OF BUSINESS-TO-BUSINESS SALES

The steps involved in the business-to-business buying process are quite similar to those individual consumers make in their purchase decisions. Before examining these steps, however, it is useful to study the types of purchase decisions. These fall into one of three categories: (1) straight rebuy, (2) modified rebuy, or (3) a new task.[7]

A **straight rebuy** occurs when the firm has previously chosen a vendor and wishes to make a reorder. This tends to be a routine process and involves only a few members of the buying center. Often the purchasing agent (buyer) and the users of the product are the only persons aware of a rebuy order. The user's role in this purchase situation is to ask the buyer to replenish the supply. The buyer than contacts the supplier and places an order. There is no evaluation of alternatives or information. Buyers often place orders electronically.

Information At The Speed Of Light

In today's business environment speed is critical. Roadway Express moves your shipment around the clock and communicates your shipment's location at the speed of light. Continuously tracked by satellite, our new sleeper tractors keep your shipment on the road and on time. You get reliable service and reliable information.

Just some of the ways we're changing to offer you exceptional service...with no exceptions.

ROADWAY
Roadway Express

This advertisement aimed at buying center members features the benefits of Roadway for shipping with improved technology.
Source: Courtesy of Roadway Corporation.

In making a **modified rebuy**, the company needs to consider and evaluate alternatives. A modified rebuy situation occurs for four different reasons. First, if a company's buyers are dissatisfied with a current vendor, they may want to look at other options. The greater the level of dissatisfaction, the greater the enticement to look for new possibilities.

Second, if a new company offers what is perceived by a member of the buying center to be a better buy, the purchase decision may be revisited. The new option may be a superior quality product or one offered at a lower price. Also, the terms of purchase may be more attractive with a different company. When the dependability of a new vendor is perceived as superior to the current vendor, the company may reconsider its previous choice.

A third reason for a modified rebuy occurs at the end of a contractual agreement. Many companies, as dictated by corporate policy, ask for bids each time a contract is written; this is true of most governmental and institutional organizations. The amount of time spent in the buying process depends on a comparison between the company's current vendor with other potential vendors.

The last modified rebuy situation takes place when a company purchases a good or service with which it has only limited or infrequent experience. For example, a company that purchases delivery trucks every five to seven years probably would make a modified rebuy, because many factors change over that amount of time. Prices, product features, and vendors (truck dealerships) change rapidly. Further, in most cases the composition of the buying group will be different.

Modified rebuys occur when someone in the buying center believes it is worth reevaluating vendors based on new information. The decision to reconsider depends on the buying center individual's ability to influence other members of the group. Company policies also dictate modified rebuy procedures. Someone seeing an advertisement for Oracle may want to look into purchasing the software to enhance his or her e-business. The buyer and influencer in the modified rebuy situation may be impressed that Oracle is the world's second largest software company. Users would evaluate the quality of the software as compared to what they currently use.

In **new task** purchasing situations, the company buys a product or service for the first time and the product involved is one with which organizational members have no experience. This type of purchase normally requires input from a number of people in the buying center, and a considerable amount of time is spent gathering information and evaluating vendors. In many cases vendors are asked to assist in identifying the required specifications.

STOP

INTEGRATED LEARNING EXPERIENCE

Access the business-to-business section of Yahoo! at **b2b.yahoo.com**. Pick one of the categories listed and work your way through the various levels to discover a specific set of products for sale. Find examples of products that would be considered modified rebuy situations for most companies and examples of new buy situations. Are any products shown ones that would be considered straight rebuy possibilities?

THE BUSINESS-TO-BUSINESS BUYING PROCESS

In new task purchasing situations, companies go through seven steps in the business-to-business buying decision process. The steps are similar to those consumers use as part of their decision-making process. The business-to-business steps are:

1. Identification of needs
2. Establishment of specifications
3. Identification of alternatives
4. Identification of vendors
5. Evaluation of vendors
6. Selection of vendor(s)
7. Negotiation of purchase terms

In new buy situations, companies go through all seven steps. In modified rebuy or straight rebuy situations, one or more of the steps are eliminated. A more in-depth examination of each of these steps follows.[8]

Identification of Needs

Just as consumers identify needs (hunger, protection, social interaction), businesses also make purchases because of their needs. Companies identify a wide variety of needs. A review of the types of products sold to various companies, as described earlier in this chapter, suggests myriad needs for everything from raw materials to complete component parts. Needs also exist for many types of services, including financial, repair, maintenance, and others. Individual buyers and members of individual firms recognize company needs on a daily basis.

Many needs in the business world are created by derived demand. **Derived demand** is based on, linked to, or derived from the production and sale of some other product or service.[9] For example, the demand for steel is largely based on the number of cars and trucks sold each year. When the demand for vehicles goes down because the economy experiences a recession or downturn, the demand for steel also declines. Steel manufacturers find it difficult to stimulate demand because of the nature of derived demand. Derived demand is often associated with the raw materials used in the production of goods and services, such as steel, aluminum, concrete, plastic, petroleum products (e.g., jet fuel for airlines), construction materials, and so forth. Derived demand also exists for services. For example, demand for mortgage money directly depends on housing sales.

Companies selling products with derived demand properties often find their sales figures are volatile. Fluctuations and swings in demand are much more common because of the **acceleration principle**. When consumer demand for a product increases or decreases, drastic changes in the derived business demand also occur.[10] For example, if the demand for a consumer product increases, it can spark the demand for new equipment and new buildings as companies expand to handle increased production. Thus, a small increase in consumer demand of 10 percent to 15 percent can cause as much as a 200 percent increase in the demand for machines, equipment, and supplies needed to supply the higher demand. Unfortunately, a small 10 percent decrease in consumer demand can cause a complete collapse in business demand for machines and equipment. Small changes in consumer demand usually have much larger impact on demand for business goods and services that support it because of its derived nature.

Another helpful concept in understanding business needs is *joint demand.* Joint demand exists when similar demand forces influence component products. The strike of suppliers of transmissions to General Motors affected demand for all of the products used to build automobiles. Suddenly, orders to the suppliers of tires, radios, car seats, batteries, and other products used in the manufacture of automobiles were cut or stopped completely. If the supply of one component used in the manufacture of a product is delayed, reduced, or stopped, it influences the demand for every component used in that product. In this case, a demand factor influencing GM also affected companies that supply GM with other component product parts.

As with consumer services, marketers can use various aspects of communication to help a firm recognize a need. For example, a Unisys advertisement could raise the question of whether a company effectively uses customer information to power its business. Seeing the ad, a company's leader may decide the firm needs more information about its customers and then contacts Unisys.

Establishment of Specifications

Once a need has been recognized, if a straight rebuy choice is made, then an order is placed with the current vendor. Occasionally specifications need to be changed, but these are normally minor alterations. In modified rebuy situations, examination of specifications makes sure they are current and meet the company's needs. In new task purchases, more complete specifications will be established.

Experts formulate specifications. Engineers specify machinery specifications. When purchasing a new computer system, the company consults a computer expert (internal or external). Sometimes the expertise of a vendor is utilized. For example, for a new telecommunications system, a firm asks various vendors to help identify the specifications, because that technology changes so rapidly. In marketing to businesses, when a company asks a vendor to assist with the development of specifications, the vendor hopes its advice and counsel will gain it an advantage in winning the contract.

A company usually writes down the specifications and distributes them internally to those in the buying center. A firm also communicates to vendors, so that each can make a case for its particular version of the product or service. Simply meeting specifications is rarely enough to win the bid—often the company must provide other incentives or reasons to be chosen.

Identification of Alternatives

In this third step, the business examines alternative ways of meeting the need identified in the first step. One primary issue is a choice about whether the product or service can be provided or created internally. Most of the time, it is necessary to go outside of the firm, though there are exceptions. Janitorial services can be provided by hiring a few employees or by a commercial service. A review of the goods and services detailed earlier in this chapter makes it clear most purchases are made from other companies. At the same time, a firm can develop an advantage or grow by creating an in-house program or through expansion into a new line of services. For instance, Sears originally provided credit cards for use solely in its own retail outlets. Over time, however, the company developed the Discover card, moving Sears into a service line retail customers and other businesses use.

The primary task involved in identifying alternatives is to consider all of the ways to meet a need. Beyond considering if the product can be provided internally, a company could identify various methods to eliminate the need. For example, when developing credit alternatives for business-to-business e-commerce customers, a firm has three choices:

▶ Use in-house credit
▶ Not offer credit to e-commerce customers
▶ Hire an external firm such as ecredit.com to provide the service

Once this decision is made, the firm is ready to move on to the next step in the buying process.

Identification of Vendors

When members of the buying center decide to pursue a supplier, potential vendors are identified and notified to see if they are interested in submitting bids. In most business situations, written, formal bids are required. A vendor's ability to write a clear proposal

BUSINESS-TO-BUSINESS BUYER BEHAVIOR

Playing Fair in B-to-B IMC Programs

When marketing to other businesses, close personal contacts are often common, both in personal sales calls and in other venues such as trade shows. Among the more serious ethical issues are gifts and bribery.

To influence sales, purchasing agents and other members of the buying company are often the recipients of gifts, meals, entertainment, and even free trips. From a personal ethics standpoint, many concerned leaders question accepting personal gifts that are designed to influence business decisions. The International Olympics Committee wrestled with this problem when Salt Lake City was chosen to host the 2002 Winter Olympics. Exorbitant gifts may have swayed the selection process.

Closely tied with the issue of receiving gifts is that of offering or accepting bribes. These can be related to gaining governmental contracts or making business contacts. Without them, permits may not be granted or are very difficult to obtain. In Germany and France, the government actually allows companies to write off bribes as tax deductions.

Marketing professionals must consider more than the U.S. perspective when dealing with the ethics of bribes and gifts. A standard business practice in one nation may be offensive or illegal in another. Each individual must consider personal feelings regarding these practices as well.

determines how successful it is in winning bids. Effective proposals spell out prices, quality levels, terms of payment, support services, and any other condition requested by the company looking to purchase goods.

One member of the buying center is normally chosen to compile files of vendors that submit proposals. The offers are circulated to all of the members of the buying center who have input into the final decision. Next, formal and informal meetings are held to discuss proposals as they arrive.

Evaluation of Vendors

Evaluations of vendors normally occur at three levels. The first level is an initial screening of proposals. This process narrows the field of vendors down to three to five competitors. Often, the purchasing department performs the initial screening. Occasionally an engineer or user of the product assists.

The number of people from the buying center involved in the initial screening depends on the dollar value of the bid and how critical the product or service is to the firm's operation. As dollar values increase and the product becomes more critical, the number of individuals involved from the buying center involved also rises. Minor choices usually are left to a single individual.

The second level of evaluation occurs as the firm undertakes a vendor audit. An audit is especially important when members of the company

One role of business-to-business advertising is to gain identification as a feasible vendor during the buying process.

When Friendlys needed to meet growing customer demand, they chose the first name in transportation:

Cindy.

Cindy Carre specializes in transportation solutions at Ryder. With our Full Service Lease, Cindy and her team work with Friendly's to keep their refrigerated trailers on the road, and their products in the hands of a hungry marketplace. Thanks to Ryder, Friendly's doesn't have to worry about breakdowns. Or meltdowns.

At Ryder, you'll find lots of people like Cindy—people who help companies like Friendly's, Hewlett Packard, and Ace Hardware become more efficient and profitable.

Want to know more? Visit us at www.ryder.com or call 1 800 RYDER OK ext. 1012. It's time you got to know us on a first-name basis.

Cindy Carre
Service Team Leader

Ryder
Ryder Transportation
Services
1 800 RYDER OK
www.ryder.com

©1999 Ryder System, Inc.
NYSE Ryder is an equal opportunity employer.

▶ **Production capability**

▶ **Quality-control mechanisms and processes**

▶ **Type and age of equipment used**

▶ **Telecommunication and EDI capabilities**

▶ **Capacity to handle fluctuations in orders**

▶ **Financial stability of the firm**

▶ **Number of competitors that purchase from the firm**

FIGURE 4.3
Typical Items Examined During a Vendor Audit

want to develop a long-term relationship with a supplier. Vendors that are the primary sources for critical components or raw materials recognize that long-term bonds benefit both the vendor and the purchasing firm.

Members of the audit team normally include an engineer, someone from operations, a quality-control specialist, and members of the purchasing department. The goal of the audit is to assess potential suppliers about a series of items (see Figure 4.3). Most audits are conducted at the supplier's business site.

The third and final level of evaluation occurs when various members of the buying center share vendor audit information. At that time, firms consider purchase procedures, and for manufacturers it may require sharing production schedules with the vendor. Sharing information, such as the production schedules with suppliers, requires a degree of trust in the vendor.

Many of the concepts described in the previous chapter regarding consumer buyer behaviors apply to this stage of the business purchasing process. Members of the buying center who believe they are performing an "official" duty when making company purchases emphasize the central route of processing (from the Elaboration Likelihood Model described in Chapter 3). The primary message arguments provided by vendors are more likely to be processed and stored in the long-term memories of buying center members.

The peripheral route, however, cannot be ignored. A shoddy brochure or a poorly dressed salesperson creates an impression that is processed peripherally. Such an unflattering message can cause a member of the buying center not to consider the primary message argument. The reverse also can occur. Peripheral cues can cause a business buyer to pay more attention to a message when it hears or sees it being repeated, or when the sales rep is dressed professionally and the materials the vendor provides are exciting and enticing.

From a marketing management perspective, the buyer may wish to employ a *procurement professional* to deal with various vendors. The goal is to reduce transaction prices and to gain more favorable terms while at the same time building the foundation for future supplier relationships. These procurement professionals examine the vendor's level of commitment to the buyer, the ability to grow, technical competence, and other dimensions of the seller's intentions and activities to see if the relationship will result in a strategic advantage for the buyer.[11]

Consequently, the vendor company must be ready and able to deal with the procurement professional. This includes taking steps to make certain the procurement professional sees the potential trading partner in the most favorable light.

It is important to remember that vendors are people and members of the buying center are people, too. Attitudes, values, opinions, and first impressions influence evaluations made about vendors. Successful marketing means carefully designing all messages, including the bids and proposals, to create favorable images in the minds of various business buyers.

Selection of Vendor(s)

Once a firm has carefully studied all of the vendors and the bids have been considered, it is time to make a final choice. At this point it is critical that marketers recall that the members of the buying center face all of the individual, social, organizational, cultural, and political pressures discussed earlier. The final decision should be made based on a comparison of dollar value of the contract to the value offered by various vendors. When selection criteria are used, the most common include quality, delivery, performance history, warranties, facilities and capacity, geographic location, and technical capability.[12] It is not likely that any one vendor will be deemed superior on all selection criteria. Therefore, the marketing team for each seller will emphasize the company's specific strengths as part of the selling process. In reality, however, politics and other forces also have a significant impact. Successful marketing requires an understanding of these forces.

A critical decision to be made at this point is whether to utilize one supplier or multiple suppliers. The advantage of using only one supplier is the ability to negotiate a lower price. Computer linkages with one company allow for continuous communication with the supplier and paperless billings. The disadvantage is that a company's entire production schedule is at the mercy of a single vendor. If the flow of a critical component is delayed or halted, the whole production process can come to a screeching halt.

Many vendor firms believe there is a method to circumvent the buying process. *Customer relationship management* (see Chapter 12) is the process of building and sustaining a relationship with a client company. By carefully tracking orders, demographics, inquiries, and other information that can be stored in a database, the vendor firm's management team can understand not only *what* the buyer wants, but also more about *why* the buyer wants those products and services. This helps build stronger bonds for the future.[13]

Once the choice is made, other items must still be completed before shipment begins, including negotiation of purchasing terms. Often, those companies not chosen are not notified until these other agreements are reached and finalized.

Negotiation of Purchase Terms

In most purchasing situations, negotiation of terms is merely a formality, because most of the conditions have already been worked out. Occasionally, however, changes are made at this point in a contract or purchase. These tend to be minor and are normally negotiated by the purchasing agent.

When the final agreement is set, goods are shipped or services provided. Assuming no further complications, the buying process is complete until the next cycle begins. At this point, firms that did not win the contract are notified. They may follow up and try to discover why they were not selected. It is in the best interests of the company to be as honest as possible, because future relationships with such companies may be possible. In the upcoming sections, two additional issues that impact business buyer behaviors are considered. The first is a review of the nature of the buying environment. The second is concerned with dual channel marketing.

INTEGRATED LEARNING EXPERIENCE

Wholesalers are a major component of the supply channel. From the Yahoo! search engine, type "wholesalers." Note the large number of organizations and the various categories of wholesalers. Pick one category and examine its wholesalers and distributors. Assume a purchase manager for a chain of grocery stores needs to locate wholesalers of vegetable and fruit produce. In Yahoo!, under "wholesalers" there is a category called "Food and Beverage" and one called "Produce." Select at least two viable vendors. Utilize the information in this section of the textbook to help the purchase manager make a buying decision.

THE BUYING ENVIRONMENT

In Chapter 3, numerous traditional and current trends were described in terms of how they affect the buying environment surrounding consumers. In a similar fashion, there are two key issues to address in the business-to-business buying environment. The first is related to the importance of the brand and branding issues. The second is understanding trends in media selection in order to reach key individuals from the buying center.

Branding Issues

Simply stated, the role of the brand has risen dramatically in the past two decades of business-to-business marketing. The Internet, brand parity, and multiple vendor choices have made it impossible to succeed simply based on price differentiation.

Brand parity exists because in most markets there are many competitors. Each forces the other to improve the quality of the good or service being offered. Over time, fewer perceived differences exist. In these circumstances, the role of the brand becomes critical, because the brand inspires recall when a purchase is about to be made. If some measure of brand equity can be built, the company has a major advantage. For example, Acme Brick is still able to charge 10 percent more than competitors due to the perception that the product is somehow superior enough that builders do not want to risk using an inferior brick, even though few real differences exist.[14]

The Internet allows business buyers to search many more possible providers. Once again, without a strong brand, it is nearly impossible to stand out in the marketplace. As Robert Duboff writes, "It is no longer sufficient to be a great company; *you must be a great brand.*"[15]

Many tactics are available to help a company build a strong brand presence. Among them are using cobranding or license tactics, ingredient branding, composite branding, sponsorships, and leveraging brand strengths in marketing messages. It is often difficult for a new, small company to be able to cobrand with a larger organization. Also, smaller companies normally will encounter resistance to ingredient branding.[16]

One small company that managed to build a strong brand presence in spite of being smaller is James Hardie Siding Products. In an industry dominated by price and delivery issues, James Hardie took another approach. The marketing agency Sawyer Riley Compton conducted market research and discovered that consumers are quite emotional about their homes. They look for products that provide safety, security, warmth, and stability. Consequently, James Hardie developed advertisements for *Southern Living, Coastal Living,* and *Sunset* magazines emphasizing strong, weather-resistant materials in the company's siding. The sales force had to be reeducated to emphasize product features rather than price and delivery. Over time, James Hardie was able to gain cobranding inroads by displaying company products on model homes and builder design centers. The net result was growth in the strength of the brand, which in turn became a 30 percent increase in annual sales.[17]

The ways to build a business-to-business brand include the following:

- Seek a clear, unified expression of the brand to both internal and external publics
- Strip away anything that might be confusing about a brand
- Find a meaningful difference that can be articulated to buyers
- Mine the customer database and gain assistance from key clients
- Embrace the future of the brand[18]

One goal of this television advertisement is to cause building contractors to believe that the Congoleum brand should be considered in the construction of new homes.
Source: Courtesy of Howard, Merrell & Partners.

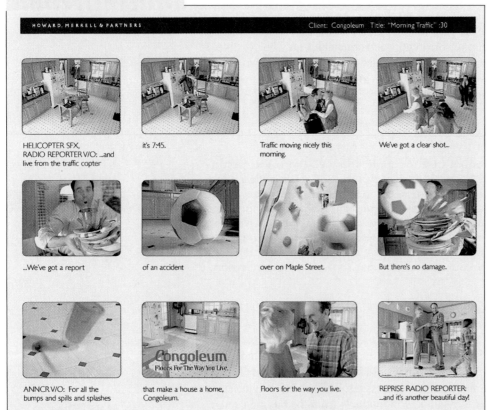

HOWARD, MERRELL & PARTNERS   Client: Congoleum   Title: "Morning Traffic" :30

HELICOPTER SFX, RADIO REPORTER V/O: ...and live from the traffic copter

it's 7:45.

Traffic moving nicely this morning.

We've got a clear shot...

...We've got a report

of an accident

over on Maple Street.

But there's no damage.

ANNCR V/O: For all the bumps and spills and splashes

that make a house a home, Congoleum.

Floors for the way you live.

REPRISE RADIO REPORTER: ...and it's another beautiful day!

Congoleum
Floors For The Way You Live.

In the case of James Hardie, the brand name "Hardiware" emphasizes the strength and quality of the product.

Many times it is not a single product, but rather the strength of the corporation's name that makes the difference. Companies with strong corporate names that have succeeded over the years include FedEx, IBM, Dell, Congoleum, and more recently Snap-on Tools. Each leverages the strength of the company's name to market individual products and services.

Trends in Media Selection

When seeking to reach members of the buying center, marketing professionals must be aware of the various ways in which individuals can be reached. At the most general level, the influence of the Internet has dramatically affected business-to-business marketing programs. Advertisers that have always used print media noticed a trend in the 1990s in which the Internet gained major inroads. More recently, however, many advertisers have returned to traditional print media, such as *The New York Times, Forbes, Fortune,* as well as television programs such as *Lou Dobbs Moneyline, Your World with Neil Cavuto,* as well as programs on CNBC and CNN. Table 4.4 features many of the most prominent places in which business-to-business ads are placed.

Many marketing experts now believe buyers go to the Internet seeking specific, targeted information. These same buyers read magazines and newspapers while enjoying leisure time. Because it is important to attract the attention of buyers *before* they are looking for more targeted information, media advertising has enjoyed a resurgence.

Who Is Buying

Another new trend in media selection is to consider the targeted individual first. Generally these individuals are divided into three categories: (1) chief executive officers, (2) top management, and (3) the C-level. Increasingly, CEOs are involved in buying decisions because of the need to integrate purchases. In this group, *The Wall Street Journal* was a key venue. Ninety-two percent of CEOs report that they read the publication. Other publications, such as *Forbes, Business Week,* and *Fortune* were not examined as regularly. Instead, CEOs tended to read Internet sites to obtain hard information about products and services.

On the other hand, the C-level group, where other members of the buying center are likely to be located, watch sports (70 percent), documentaries (65 percent), and listen to news radio (68 percent) and public radio (48 percent). Therefore, reaching members of the buying center with attention-getting information will probably be achieved in ways that are different than those used to reach the CEO ways.

When the New York-based Siemens Corporation wanted to raise brand awareness in C-level managers, the company used a unique approach. Instead of spending a great deal of funds on trade shows and industry magazines, the company placed ads in lifestyle magazines such as the *New Yorker* and sponsored various events, such as the U.S. Open golf tournament and the NCAA basketball tournament. Believing that using business-to-consumer tactics was the best way to strengthen the brand in the business-to-business area, the company took risks in potentially wasting many dollars displaying commercials to consumers who would never be interested in the company's offerings. However, by doing so Siemens raised brand awareness by staying away from the clutter that dominates typical business venues.[19]

A survey by the Omincom Group's Dormeus Advertising agency does note some common links between CEOs and members of C-level management. They provided six management psychographics that apply to both groups, including:

1. The "entrepreneurial achiever," who uses cell phones, personal digital assistant (PDA), and other technologies
2. The "Zen master" who has learned to balance work and home
3. The "career prisoner" who works late every night and is constantly overloaded
4. The "superficial sound biter" who is trendy and shallow
5. The "contented mensch" devoted to home and family who tries to get away from technology such as Palm Pilot or cell phone
6. The technophobe, who is actively resistant to and intimidated by technology

IT Magazines	General Business Publications	Internet
Baseline	Business Week	CBS MarketWatch
Business 2.0	The Economist	CNET Networks
CIO	Forbes	ebuild.com
Computerworld	Fortune	Google
Information Week	Industry Week	INT Media's
PC World		Internet.com
		New York Times.com
		Tech Target.com
		TechWeb
		ThomasRegional.com
		Wsj.com

Newspapers	Out-of-Office	Broadcast
The Wall Street Journal	Mobile billboard in Las Vegas	Academy Awards (ABC)
The New York Times	O'Hare International Airport	Bloomberg Radio
USA Today	Captivate Network, Inc.	The Masters (CBS)
Investor's Business Daily		CNBC Business Day
		Lou Dobbs Moneyline (CNN)
		ESPN NHL Telecasts
		Your World with Neil Cavuto (Fox)
		The West Wing (NBC)
		The Olympics (NBC)

TABLE 4.4

Media Power 50, B-to-B Top Venues for Advertising Messages

Trade Publications
Architectural Record
Aviation Week and Space Technology
Builder
Chemical and Engineering News
Farm Journal
Modern Machine Shop
Nation's Restaurant News
Oil & Gas Journal
Pharmaceutical Executive
Security
Utility Business

Source: "Media Power 50," B to B, 87, issue 5 (May 6, 2002), pp. 20–27.

Messages should be tailored to the recipient of the message. Each type has different buying decision-making habits. It is worth the efforts of the marketing department to develop profiles of members of the buying center to see which type of individual is involved.[20]

Internet Usage

Many CEOs spend a great deal of time examining Internet information, and many times influential IT personnel are part of the buying center. Consequently it is important to make effective use of the Internet to reach them. The Google.com network has more than 10,000 business-to-business consumer clients, and more than 150 million searches use Google each day.

The advertisements on Google are text-based. No run-of-site ads appear indiscriminately on search results pages, and traditional banners, flashing animations, and other more standard commercial Web features are not used. "Unlike traditional advertising, Google puts ads in front of people only when it's relevant. And relevancy is exactly what our advertisers want, especially our business-to-business advertisers. The more relevant an ad is to someone viewing a search page, the more likely he or she will click through," reports Google's Tim Armstrong, vice president for advertising. Google's click through rate is five times higher than the industry's average. Ads cost $200 and up.

Larger advertisers who want guaranteed fixed placement use Google's Premium Sponsorship program, which is sold on a cost-per-impression basis. Smaller advertisers use Google's auction-based self-service AdWords Select program to purchase key words at rates determined by cost-per-click performance. The ads rotate rather than being fixed.

CNet has also tailored company services to fit the business-to-business marketplace. The company has a program that makes it possible to see additional product information without forcing them to leave the site by clicking on an ad. The goals of both Google and CNet are to learn more about the natures of decision makers in the buying process, and then to adapt the site to fit those needs.[21]

In the future, the buying environment in business-to-business operations will continue to evolve. The marketing team must work to understand who is buying, how they buy, and the decision-making processes involved. Then, media selection and usage can be adapted to fit the needs of the vendor company and those in the buying center who make the purchase.

DUAL CHANNEL MARKETING

When firms sell virtually the same products or services to both consumers and businesses, it is known as **dual channel marketing**.[22] Dual marketing channels arise for several reasons. Perhaps the most common scenario occurs when a product is first sold in the business market and then adapted to the consumer market. New products often have high start-up costs including R&D expenditures, market research, and so forth. Businesses tend to be less price sensitive than are retail consumers. Thus it is logical to sell to them first.

As sales grow, economies of scale can be created. Larger purchases of raw materials combined with more standardized methods of production make it possible to attack the consumer market. The benefits of economies of scale entice manufacturers to sell products previously supplied to the business sector in the retail markets. Products such as digital cameras, calculators, computers, fax machines, and cellular phones first were marketed to businesses and then later to consumers. To make the move to the retail arena possible, prices have to come down and products need to become more user-friendly. For example, consumers can now have their photos put on a CD rather than obtain prints. The imaging technology developed by Kodak and Intel was first sold to various businesses and now is being offered to retail customers. By forming an alliance with Intel, Kodak brought the cost down and developed economies of scale needed for the consumer market.

The service sector also has used the strategy of selling the first application to business then the second to consumers. Speech-controlled telephone dialing first was developed for businesses and is now is available to consumers using mobile phones.

3M is one of many businesses that use dual channel marketing to sell their products.
Source: Courtesy of 3M.

YELLOW IS A SIGN OF IMPORTANCE.

That's why people with important business messages use our Post-it™ Notes adhesive note pads. Bright notes that stick virtually anywhere. To make sure your messages get noticed. Call 1-800-328-1684 for a free sample. Then get more Post-it Notes from a nearby stationer or retail store. And start getting the recognition you deserve.

Commercial Office Supply Division/3M

3M

Approximately 30 percent of Holiday Inn's business customers also stay with the chain on private vacations.
Source: Courtesy of PhotoEdit. Photograph by Jeff Greenberg.

Another type of dual channel marketing results from *spin-off sales.* Individuals who buy a particular product at work often have positive experiences and, as a result, purchase the product for personal use. This situation often occurs with computers and computer software. Favorable feelings about more expensive items can also result in spin-off sales. For example, a salesperson who drives a Buick LeSabre to work may like it so well that she buys one for personal use. Holiday Inn discovered that many of its private stays come from business-related spin-offs. Approximately 30 percent of Holiday Inn's business customers also stay with the chain on private vacations.[23]

Image Concerns

Image issues are major concerns for marketers vending products in dual channel situations. As noted in Chapter 2, a firm's image is an important ingredient in successful marketing programs for both business and retail customers. When a company sells virtually the same product to both markets, image transfer occurs. Marketers have to be extremely careful that the image they project in one market does not damage their image in the other market.

Any organization that sells to businesses must be wary of being considered incompetent or frivolous when it also sells consumer products. For example, Gateway may have damaged its business image by its consumer marketing communication approach. Gateway adopted a Holstein cow as its mascot to promote sales to consumers. Unfortunately, this approach created problems for the firm's business-to-business marketing program. Large corporations became leery of the company after it began to paint its computer shipping boxes with the black and white Holstein design. They also were uncomfortable with a firm that allowed employees to work in jeans and T-shirts. Gateway's image in the business-to-business market suffered further when the news stories about the company appeared showing the CEO leading a pep rally backed by rock bands and with other executives dressed as Holsteins.[24]

Differences Versus Similarities

In dual channel marketing, a primary decision to make is how to represent the product in each channel. The firm can either emphasize similarities between the two markets or focus on differences. Consumers and businesses looking for the same benefits and product features probably will see marketing messages quite similar in both channels. When consumers and business buyers value different product attributes or desire differing benefits, the marketing strategy develops more customized messages for the separate markets.

When there are substantial differences between the two channels, the typical tactics are to:

▶ Use different communication messages
▶ Create different brands
▶ Use multiple channels or different channels

In many instances the product attributes are the same, but the value or benefit of that attribute are different. Messages should focus on the benefits each segment can derive from the product. Cellular phones marketed to businesses can stress the area coverage and service options. For consumers, cell phone messages can center on the fashionable design of the product, its ease of use, or a lower price.

To avoid confusing individuals who may see both messages from the same producer, companies often utilize dual branding. For instance, when Black & Decker decided to launch a professional line of power tools, it used the DeWalt brand name. This avoided confusion with the Black & Decker name and prevented any negative image transfer from home tools to professional tools.

In most cases, business customers and consumers want the same basic benefits from products. In these situations, a single strategy for both markets is best. Tactics include:

▶ Integrating communications messages

▶ Selling the same brand in both markets

▶ Scanning both markets for dual marketing opportunities

There are two advantages to integrating consumer markets with business markets: (1) synergies and (2) economies of scale. Synergies arise from increased brand identity and equity. An image developed in the consumer market can then be used to enter a business market, or vice versa. Using one brand makes it easier to develop brand awareness and brand loyalty. A business customer who uses a company-owned American Express Card is likely to have a separate card from the same company for personal use.

Scanning both types of customers for new opportunities is an important part of dual channel marketing. For example, the firm Intuit, which sells Quicken software, discovered that individuals who use Quicken at home also are willing to use a similar version for their small businesses. Capitalizing on this need or demand, Quicken added features such as payroll and inventory control to a business software package. At the same time, Quicken maintained its easy-to-use format. By finding business needs for a consumer product, Quicken adapted a current product and captured 70 percent of the small business accounting software market.[25]

The importance of dual channel marketing should not be underestimated. A major competitive advantage can be cultivated when a producer or service vendor discovers items that can be sold in both markets. A complete IMC planning process includes the evaluation of potential business market segments as well as consumer market segments, as noted in Chapter 5. Firms that integrate messages across these markets take a major step toward reaching every potential user of the company's goods or services.

Marketing account executives must recognize differences between consumer purchases and business purchases. Although the purchasing processes are similar, those who make buying decisions vary and numerous factors may affect them. One example of the difference between consumer and business purchasing decisions is revealed by examining business buying communities.

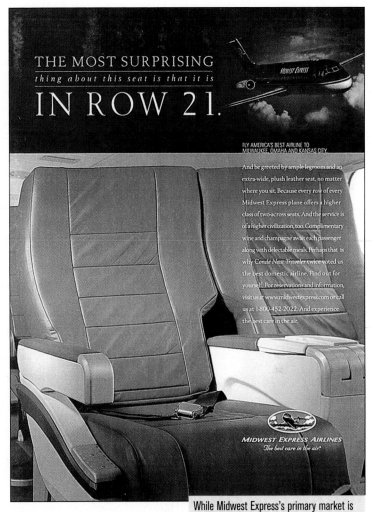

While Midwest Express's primary market is business travelers, the airline promotes the same benefits to leisure travelers.
Source: Courtesy of Midwest Express Airlines.

THE BUYING COMMUNITY

The buying community is an interlocking network of individual business owners and managers, trade organizations, social organizations, and firms that work for small and medium-size businesses. Small business owners use buying communities to obtain information pertinent to their businesses and their purchase decisions.

The buying community is an important link for small and medium-size businesses. Often these expert, reliable sources are other business owners who have made similar purchase decisions. Thus, the small business owner can go outside of his or her business to obtain information needed to make an informed decision. In these situations, the influencers of the decisions are other business owners. The buying community is normally utilized when a new task and modified rebuy decision is being made, not in straight rebuy situations.

The concept of a buying community is most important to smaller and medium-size firms. These companies tend to operate in different ways than larger organizations. Some of the primary differences are in the areas of identifying, evaluating, and selecting vendors. Decision makers in smaller organizations tend to have less expertise and experience than those in larger firms. Also, buying centers in small to medium-size companies are smaller, meaning that each member of the center must become more involved in the purchasing process. The risks associated with making purchasing decisions are often higher in smaller organizations. A bad decision can easily create a major financial crisis for the small company. Small and medium-size firms do not have the financial security to weather a poor decision that a large firm would have.[26] A buying community's expertise and advice especially helps smaller firms. A large number of companies are small to medium-size organizations. This makes the role of the buying community crucial to the economic well-being of many regions.

A recent survey demonstrates the value of the buying community. In a study of small business owners, the following sources of information were indicated as important:

▶ Members of the same business association, such as Kiwanis or Rotary (80 percent)

▶ Associates and speakers at business seminars (61 percent)

▶ Other business owners (34 percent)

▶ Business periodicals (3 percent)

▶ Local newspapers (4 percent)[27]

The problem with business periodicals and local newspapers is that they do not provide enough information to make any type of judgment. They may be important in terms of sparking an interest, but not in the evaluation stage of the buying process. Consequently, buying communities provide the information that smaller firms cannot obtain elsewhere.

The implications for business-to-business vendors are clear. First, the company needs to devote some of its IMC efforts toward key members of a buying community. Whenever possible, the firm should provide information and expertise to help smaller business owners and their purchasing departments. Communications in the form of brochures and help lines can assist smaller companies. The substantial number of small organizations currently operating makes them a viable market for many business-to-business vendors, especially those that take the time and make the effort to reach those companies directly.

INTEGRATED LEARNING EXPERIENCE

For the business community, being a member of the Chamber of Commerce presents the opportunity to network with other businesspeople. Access the U.S. Chamber of Commerce at **www.uschamber.org**. In addition to networking, what other benefits does the Chamber of Commerce provide? Access the Chamber Biz page, a resource for small businesses. Examine the information provided in the sections "Government," "Marketplace," and "BizCenter." What information is of value to small businesses? In addition to the Chamber of Commerce, memberships in organizations such as the Rotary and Kiwanis Clubs can be valuable. Access the Rotary Web site at **www.rotary.org** and the Kiwanis Web site at **www.kiwanis.org**. Which would be the best organization for a small business owner to join? Why?

> ▶ **Emphasis on accountability**
> ▶ **Importance of Web sites and Internet marketing**
> ▶ **Global branding**
> ▶ **Database mining**
> ▶ **Changes in methods of communication**
> ▶ **Focus on internal marketing communications**

FIGURE 4.4
Business-to-Business Trends

BUSINESS-TO-BUSINESS TRENDS IN THE TWENTY-FIRST CENTURY

One issue that continues to gain momentum in the marketing community is accountability (see Figure 4.4). Firms expect tangible results from the money they invest in marketing and advertising programs. As a result, account executives face growing pressures to ensure that dollars spent yield quick results. Firms expect account executives to understand their businesses as well as the many potential target markets that can be tapped. Expanding from business customers to consumers, or vice versa, is one way to respond to the increasing insistence on immediate results.

The second major trend is the expansion of e-commerce and increased Web-based marketing. One business executive recently noted that the electronic commerce revolution is probably doing more to integrate business-to-business marketing communications than any other marketing force. Engaging in Web-based commerce is no longer an option. Either firms must get involved, or it is likely that they will not stay in business.

Part of the e-commerce revolution is the creation of more effective Web sites. Web sites must be more than merely placing a catalog online. Sites need to be truly interactive, allowing business customers to gain information, product specifications, prices, and other key information. The Internet's technology saves time and money for both customers and vendors.

Another prominent trend is the development of global corporate brands. In the future, a firm's reputation and image will continue to be critical features of an IMC effort. As a result, companies must invest in brand image building projects. They should strive to convey a uniform message to business customers, retail customers, the financial community, and other publics. Part of this process includes establishing an effective global brand.

Database mining and integration in the business-to-business arena is another recent phenomenon affecting IMC programs. Firms can utilize the immense power of computers to access databases containing information about customers and prospects. Database mining searches identify buyer behavior patterns that can be matched with business communication programs. Additional analyses

In addition to print advertisements, Volvo uses a Web site to market products.
Source: Courtesy of Volvo Cars of North America.

INTRODUCING THE VOLVO 660. IT SOLVES ALL YOUR FLEET PROBLEMS. EXCEPT WHO GETS TO DRIVE.

May the best man win. We designed the new 660 to be the perfect fleet partner. Spacious and smooth handling. Efficient and easy to maintain. Built to make fleets more profitable and drivers a lot more possessive.   To find out how the Volvo 660 can help you be more successful, give us a call at 1-800-444-RSVP for a free video or visit www.volvotrucks.volvo.com.

VOLVO
Drive Smart.

can be performed to segment business customers into target groups. Then a distinct appeal can be designed to reach each group. Eventually, companies will use information to customize messages to individual consumers, based on their needs and past purchase behaviors.

Use of alternative methods in communicating with customers also continues to expand. Many firms recognize that having salespeople call on customers is expensive and time-consuming. Personal calls have given way to other methods, including contacts by mail, telephone, fax, interactive Internet sites, and e-mail. Effective IMC programs integrate all of these methods to maximize company exposure while making it extremely easy for customers to contact the firm. They also allow marketers to bypass gatekeepers in other businesses. Getting to users, deciders, and influencers in the buying center increases the firm's chances of making a sale.

The final trend emerging as the twenty-first century begins is the growing importance of internal integrated marketing communications. *Internal marketing communications* efforts include creating, packaging, and delivering the organization's IMC marketing message (including its business-to-business components) to all employees of the organization. Employees must understand and believe in the firm's image and its marketing position. Employees need to comprehend what each company brand stands for and the benefits it offers consumers. Most importantly, each employee must believe in the company and its mission. Spending more time marketing internally produces more knowledgeable and dedicated employees, who will, in turn, seek the goal of providing excellent service to customers.[28]

SUMMARY

Integrating business-to-business marketing programs into the overall IMC plan means many things. To compete both locally and globally, marketers must integrate marketing communication across all venues. This includes advertisements, public relations efforts, brand and firm image, and every other aspect of the IMC program. Rick Kean, executive director of the Business Marketing Association of Chicago said, "Integrated marketing is a term business marketers have used for years, but now it has emerged as a driving force in how companies are presenting themselves overall. There has to be a plan that puts everyone in a company on the same page; in this economy, no company can afford to have a fragmented message."[29] This includes speaking with a clear voice to both business and end user retail customers.

This chapter addresses business-to-business marketing concerns. The many potential markets available to firms desiring to sell products to other firms present a variety of opportunities to expand sales and stabilize revenues over time. The people who make purchases are members of the business buying center, which includes users, buyers, influencers, deciders, and gatekeepers. Each plays a key role in leading the firm to an eventual purchasing choice.

The types of purchases business buyers make can be divided into three types: (1) a straight rebuy, (2) a modified rebuy, and (3) a new task. The best opportunity to reach a firm is when a new task purchase is being made. A company should, however, be willing to make competitive efforts to build its sales in all three situations, because the environment changes so rapidly. Products evolve, markets grow, competitors enter and leave the marketplace, and, as a result, firms that continually seek to identify business buyers stand ready when new opportunities appear.

The steps involved in business buying processes include: (1) identification of needs, (2) establishment of specifications,

(3) identification of alternatives, (4) identification of vendors, (5) evaluations of vendors, (6) selection of vendor(s), and (7) negotiation of purchase terms. Careful understanding and input into each of the steps can improve the chances of a successful business-to-business transaction.

Dual channel marketing is vending goods and services to both consumers and businesses. Dual channels help firms develop economies of scale in production and other synergies in operations. It is important to maintain a consistent, positive image in both markets. Marketers must be careful that messages sent to one market do not present a negative image in the other. Firms must decide whether to highlight differences or similarities in products and the need requirements those products meet. When similarities are present, companies use consistent brand names and messages. When significant differences exist, firms must tailor messages to individual markets. At times, it is wise to establish separate brand names to sell in business and retail markets.

As the twenty-first century unfolds, increasing pressures for accountability may drive many companies to seek out business customers. Marketing in cyberspace makes it possible for marketing executives to reach other businesses efficiently and effectively. Global brands with consistent messages adapted to individual regions is one common approach to reaching new customers. Database mining helps vendors seeking to expand business-to-business operations. At the same time, IMC programs must communicate internally to employees and departments so that the firm can reach outward with a consistent, strong voice projecting the qualities and benefits of the firm's goods and services. Those companies that incorporate effective business-to-business components into their overall IMC plans stand a better chance of remaining successful in future years of operation.

REVIEW QUESTIONS

1. What are the two categories of items sold on a business-to-business basis?

2. Name and describe the five members of a business buying center.

3. What types of organizational influences affect business buying decisions?

4. What kinds of individual factors affect members of business buying centers?

5. How would norms affect business buying decisions?

6. Name and describe the steps of the business-to-business buying process.

7. How are the steps of the business buying process similar to the consumer buying decision-making processes described in Chapter 3?

8. What is derived demand? Why is it important to business-to-business vendors?

9. Define straight rebuy, modified rebuy, and new task. Which presents the best opportunity for a firm entering the business-to-business marketplace?

10. What is a procurement professional? What role does this individual play in the buying process?

11. Why is a strong brand so crucial in business-to-business marketing? Are there circumstances in which a strong brand is not as critical?

12. Describe the three levels of management involved in the buying process. Of the three, which is most focused on the Internet during the purchase?

13. How have Google and CNet adapted to media usage trends in buying? Which type of buyer do these networks target in business-to-business programs?

14. What is dual channel marketing? What special problems and opportunities are present in dual channel situations?

15. What is a buying community? Which types of firms does it best serve? Why?

16. What trends affect business-to-business marketing in the early part of the twenty-first century?

KEY TERMS

buying center   a group of individuals involved in a company's buying decision-making process.

users   members of the organization's buying center who actually use the product or service.

buyers   the individuals from the buying center who are given formal responsibility for making the purchase, such as purchasing agents or members of the purchasing department.

influencers   people from the buying center who influence purchasing decisions by providing the information or criteria utilized in evaluating alternatives.

deciders   individuals from the buying center who authorize decisions, including purchasing agents, financial officers, a vice president, or even the president of a company.

gatekeeper   member of the buying center who controls the flow of information to members.

norms   rules regarding the proper way to behave in a group.

straight rebuy   a purchase that occurs when the firm has previously chosen a vendor and wishes to make a reorder.

modified rebuy   a purchase that occurs when the company needs to consider and evaluate alternatives, even though the decision was made previously.

new task   a purchasing situation in which the company is buying product for the first time and the firm has no previous product experience.

derived demand   demand based on, linked to, or derived from the production and sale of some other consumer product or service.

acceleration principle   when consumer demand for a product increases or decreases, drastic changes in the derived business demand also occur.

dual channel marketing   when a firm sells virtually the same product or service to both consumers and businesses.

CRITICAL THINKING EXERCISES

Discussion Questions

1. A member of the buying center for a large shoe manufacturer tries to purchase soles for shoes from an outside vendor (or vendors). Study the list of factors affecting buying center members in Figure 4.2. Discuss the effect of each factor on the roles of members in the shoe company's buying center. How does the factory foreman's role differ from the purchasing agent's role? How do these roles differ from the company president's role?

2. A purchasing agent for a clothing manufacturer is in the process of selecting a vendor (or vendors) to supply the materials to produce about 30 pecent of its clothes. The clothing manufacturer employs about 300 people. As the audit nears completion, what factors are most important to the purchasing agent?

3. A member of the buying center has been asked to gather information about possible shipping companies for international shipments. Go to the following Internet addresses. What companies have the most appealing Web sites? Beyond Internet

materials, what additional information do they need to supply to the buying center in order to win the contract?

a. ABC India Limited (www.abcindia.com)

b. BDP International, Inc. (www.bdpint.com)

c. Falcon Transportation & Forwarding Corp. (www.falcontrans.com)

d. Global Freight Systems (www.globalfreightsystems.com)

e. NTS Transport Services (www.ntstransport.com)

4. Access the Web site www.SubmitOrder.com. Suppose you want to sell a product over the Internet. Describe how SubmitOrder.com can assist your business venture. Discuss each service offered by SubmitOrder.com and how that would fit into an Internet venture.

Developing a Business-to-Business Component of an IMC Program

All of the products and services suggested in Chapter 1 have potential business buyers or must be marketed through a distribution channel. A complete and effective IMC program identifies those buyers and channel members who would purchase the product. Utilizing the tactics described in this chapter, you can develop a plan to induce members of the buying center to consider and eventually purchase the item, in both domestic and global markets. Go to the Prentice-Hall Web site at **www.prenhall.com/clow** or access the IMC Plan Pro disk that accompanied this textbook and complete the Chapter 4 exercise for your product. Upon completing this stage of your IMC program, you have built a solid foundation from which to proceed in developing the other aspects of your marketing plan.

BUILDING AN
IMC
CAMPAIGN

IMC PlanPro!

CASE 1

STIRRING UP STEAMY SALES

Erin Snyder decided she was ready for the big move. After spending a dozen years in the publishing industry, Erin felt she had sufficient knowledge and the right kind of backing to begin her own imprint. She worked for a medium-size company that produced about 1,000 titles per year and that largely served a female target audience in both its fiction and nonfiction books. What the company did not have, however, was a list containing romance novels.

Romance books constitute a major portion of the publishing industry. By 1998, projections were that romance novels generated $800 million in annual sales, or roughly half the mass-market paperbacks sold. Romance books are staples on best-seller lists. The typical reader buys between four and 20 books *per month*. The average reader is female, near the age of 40, and lives in a household earning $40,000 per year or more. Women read such novels for escape and because these books speak in a voice that is "by women, for women," according to one romance novel scholar.

Most literary critics dismiss the books as essentially trash or soft-core porn, with tragically poor levels of writing skill. Many follow a standard 200-page formula in which the heroine first rejects the suitor and then, by page 100, discovers he was indeed Mr. Right. Early versions used no profanity, no graphic sex, no infidelity, and no interracial sex. The great majority of the books have happy endings. Sex is consensual and pleasurable, and adultery normally is not part of the story, *The Bridges of Madison County* notwithstanding. (One successful romance author noted that *Bridges* is not truly a romance novel because of the adultery, and because the couple ends up apart. As she noted, "You can tell it was written by a man.") Some feminists are angry that women in romance novels are passive and often are the victims of violence. Also, the message seems to be that a woman simply cannot get along in the world without a man.

In spite of these criticisms, the market continues to grow. Plots have become less formulaic and more complex, and topics have expanded to include alcoholism, depression, aging, and a variety of other issues. Erin felt her firm was in an excellent position to expand into the area, because her publisher had strong brand equity with female readers.

The romance novel market is stratified into a variety of customers and by several products. One method by which customers can be enticed is simply price. Wal-Mart began offering novels published by Zebra Books for $1.78 each in 1996. This approach gave these books a major advantage over the typical book, which sells for $5.99 to $7.99. Obviously the markup for such a product is low, and volume is the key.

At the other extreme in pricing are hardback or hardbound titles written by high-profile authors such as Danielle Steele. Markups are much higher, but so are "returns" of unsold books. The issue of returns is a key problem. Romance books have a shelf life of four to six weeks. Then, the company must absorb the cost of unsold books that are sent back by individual bookstores. Also, the advances paid to hardcover writers are prohibitive for smaller publishers. For example, Sandra Brown, a highly successful romance writer, received over $10 million to write three books, beginning in 1997.

There are three levels of sexuality in romance novels. "Sweet" romances have pastel covers and sketchy descriptions of sex. About one-fifth simply end with a rapturous kiss in the marital bed. One specialty area in sweet romances are the so-called Christian romances, which constitute a viable and growing market. Christian romances are sold in both regular bookstores and Christian bookstores, giving them a wider distribution. "Sensual" romances are for middle-of-the-roaders. The hero and heroine in these books have mutually satisfying sex with lots of code words used to describe body parts and the actual act. Terms like "peaks of ecstasy" dominate sensual romances. "Spicy" titles contain more graphic descriptions. Anything goes in these novels, so long as the sex is consensual and occurs in the context of a committed relationship. Even bondage and whipping make it into spicy novels.

Erin prepared her proposal to the publisher stating reasons why the imprint could succeed. She began her presentation by noting the kinds of outlets that exist for romances. Although Zebra Books and the Kensington imprint had captured Wal-Mart, many other chain discount stores might carry books, including Kmart, Target, ShopKo, and Walgreen's. Book-of-the-month clubs present a viable outlet for some customers. Also, Erin's firm was well established with the major book wholesalers and warehouses, such as Barnes & Noble and Ingram. Internet sales through **Amazon.com** represented another outlet for the titles. Erin was convinced interactive Web pages for authors and series books offered great potential to build sales and customer loyalty to her company.

Erin knew the two keys to success in starting her imprint. The first was to attract quality authors so that she could build name recognition with them. She knew Harlequin books dominated the authors' list, and that the firm "owned" the writer's pen name for seven years, even if the individual chose to move to a new publisher. Erin decided she could attract authors through writer's conventions and contests.

The second key challenge was shelf space. Because the major publishers dominated the market, Erin needed "hooks" that would encourage retailers to buy from her imprint. This meant selecting the proper niche in terms of sexuality levels and price. She would have to be able to offer a series of products or stand-alone titles different from those currently on the shelves. Erin was looking forward to the challenge.

1. Discuss the business-to-business issues present in this case.

2. Discuss the concept of the buying center and how it relates to retailers and wholesalers that Erin would contact for the romance novels.

3. What venues should Erin's imprint pursue?

(continued)

4. Is dual marketing a good option for Erin? What types of challenges would dual marketing present?

5. Would it be possible to develop romance novels for other target markets, using various demographics? If so, how?

CASE 2

TAKING THE NEXT STEP IN THE DEATH INDUSTRY

Nancy Hines was always reluctant to tell people about the business she was starting, even though she was convinced it would be a valuable service people would appreciate. It also might be quite lucrative. Still, many of her friends viewed her work as maudlin, or worse.

For the past seven years, Nancy worked as a reporter for a local newspaper. Among her duties was preparation of the daily obituary column. She made phone calls to the local mortuaries, and they would provide the basic information for each newly deceased person. Then, Nancy would rewrite or edit the materials to fit the space requirement for the paper.

During the past year, however, the paper substantially cut down her duties. The standard of eight to 12 column inches to use for an obit was reduced to one or one and one-half column inches, which would normally contain about 80 words. The paper charged a fee for the family to have a complete obituary printed. In spite of initial objections from the community, the new system was soon in place, and Nancy was relieved of her duties for that area of the paper.

A close friend of Nancy's, Margo Youker, recently completed a series of courses in the area of e-commerce. Margo saw a great opportunity for the two of them to pursue. They established a new company, **Remembrances. com**, a Web site dedicated to the mortuary industry.

The "death industry," as it is known, has peaks and valleys, which are based on how many people die in any given month or year. Fees are collected for grave sites, cremations, embalming, caskets, memorial services, and limousine services for family members and the deceased (the hearse). Margo and Nancy believed they could add to the revenues of these companies by offering an additional service: a Web site for the family of the deceased.

The Web site would contain a full-length obituary, photos, directions to the church and grave site, and requests for memorial contribution allocations. It also allowed long-distance friends to send online notes and comments. The mortuary would provide a home page directing people to the site for each individual person. It also would set up links to the newspaper (for a fee) in which the newspaper would print the Web address as part of the short obituary. The text would appear as follows:

Fred Johnson, aged 83, died on Monday, June 6, 2000, from natural causes. He was a lifelong resident of Oxnard, California. He retired from Montgomery Ward in 1981. Further information may be obtained at **Remembrances.com**.

Nancy and Margo would sell their Web site service to individual mortuaries. They would charge a fee for each person, and the cost would be passed along to the family as part of the burial price. Nancy would manage the Web site, including writing full-length obits for each person. Margo would help with additional information and make sales calls. Their intention was to build a base of operations in Southern California and to expand outward from there.

1. Describe how various morticians could use the buying decision-making process as they considered a sales pitch from **Remembrances.com**.

2. Is this a dual-channel program? Should Nancy and Margo promote this service directly to potential patrons? If so, how?

3. Will this business succeed? Why or why not?

ENDNOTES

1. Eric Hausman and Kelly Spang, "Intel Unwraps New Strategy," *Computer Reseller News,* no. 767 (December 8, 1997), pp. 45–46; Kelly Spang, "Intel: We Will Be Everywhere," *Computer Reseller News,* no. 769 (December 22, 1997), p. 104; Anya Sacharow, "Intel Power," *Mediaweek,* 8, no. 4 (January 26, 1998), pp. IQ13–IQ15; Marcia Savage, "Intel Modifies Security Feature After Outcry," *Computer Reseller News,* no. 827 (February 1, 1999), pp. 83–84; Dayna Delmonico and Joel Shore, "Pentium-Based Servers Heat Up Market," *Computer Reseller News,* no. 650 (September 24, 1995), pp. 139–142; Joshua Piven, "Can Industry Stop Microsoft–Intel Jaggernaut?" *Computer Technology Review,* 15, no. 11 (November 1995), pp. 1–20; Booke Crothers, "Pentium Pro Errata Beginning to Surface," *Infoworld,* 17, no. 50 (December 11, 1995), p. 8.

2. Discussion based on Frederick E. Webster Jr. and Yoram Wind, "A General Model for Understanding Organizational Buyer Behavior," *Marketing Management,* 4, no. 4 (winter–spring 1996), pp. 52–57. Patricia M. Doney and Gary M. Armstrong, "Effects of Accountability on Symbolic Information Search and Information Analysis by Organizational Buyers," *Journal of the Academy of Marketing Science,* 24, no. 1 (winter 1996), pp. 57–66; Rob Smith, "For Best Results, Treat Business Decision Makers as Individuals," *Advertising Age's Business Marketing,* 84, 3, (1998) p. 39.

3. Patricia M. Doney and Gary M. Armstrong, "Effects of Accountability on Symbolic Information Search and Information Analysis by Organizational Buyers," *Journal of the Academy of Marketing Science,* 24, no. 1 (winter 1996), pp. 57–66.

4. Herbert Simon, *The New Science of Management Decisions,* rev. ed. (Upper Saddle River, NJ: Prentice Hall, 1977).

5. Webster and Yoram Wind, "A General Model for Understanding Organizational Buyer Behavior"; Doney and Armstrong, "Effects of Accountability on Symbolic Information Search and Information Analysis by Organizational Buyers"; James A. Eckert and Thomas J. Goldsby, "Using the Elaboration Likelihood Model to Guide Customer Service-Based Segmentation," *International Journal of Physical Distribution & Logistics Management,* 27, no. 9–10, (1997), pp. 600–615.

6. P. F. Secord and C. W. Backman, *Social Psychology* (New York: McGraw-Hill, 1964); Marvin E. Shaw and Phillip R. Costanzo, *Theories of Social Psychology,* 2nd ed. (New York: McGraw-Hill, 1982).

7. Patrick J. Robinson, Charles W. Faris, and Yoram Wind, "Industrial Buying and Creative Marketing," *Marketing Science Institute Series* (Boston: Allyn and Bacon, 1967).

8. Adapted from Webster and Wind, "A General Model for Understanding Organizational Buyer Behavior."

9. Eugene F. Brigham and James L. Pappas, *Managerial Economics,* 2nd ed. (Hinsdale, IL: Dryden Press, 1976).

10. Ibid.

11. Bob Donath, "Purchasing Beats Marketing for Bottom Line," *Marketing News,* 35, issue 17 (August 13, 2001), pp. 9–10.

12. Charles A. Weber, John R. Current, and Desai Anand, "Vendor: A Structured Approach to Vendor Selection and Negotiation," *Journal of Business Logistics,* 21, issue 1 (2000), pp. 134–69.

13. Lawrence A. Crosby, Sheree L. Johnson, and Richard T. Quinn, "Is Survey Research Dead?" *Marketing Management,* 11, issue 3 (May/June 2002), pp. 24–30.

14. Bob Lamons, "Another Story About an Unlikely Brand," *Marketing News,* 30, issue 11 (May 27, 2002), p. 8.

15. Robert Duboff, "True Brand Strategies Do Much More Than Name," *Marketing News,* 35, issue 11 (May 21, 2001), p. 16.

16. Bob Lamons, "Another Story About an Unlikely Brand."

17. Ibid.

18. Donald Pettitt, "Five Steps to Better Brands," *Marketing News,* 36, issue 11 (May 27, 2002), p. 14.

19. Dana James, "Something in Common," *Marketing News,* 36, issue 11 (May 27, 2002), pp. 11–12.

20. Sean Callahan, "Studies Examine 'C-Level' Mindset," *B to B,* 87, issue 4 (April 8, 2002), p. 14.

21. "Media Power 50," *B to B,* 87, issue 5 (May 6, 2002), p. 20–27.

22. Discussion of dual channel marketing is based on Wim G. Biemans, "Marketing in the Twilight Zone," *Business Horizons,* 41, no. 6 (November–December 1998), pp. 69–76.

23. Ibid.

24. P. Elstrom and P. Burrows, "Can Gateway Round Up the Suits?" *Business Week* (May 26, 1997), pp. 64–68.

25. Biemans, "Marketing in the Twilight Zone."

26. Discussion of small and medium-size firms based on Karen Maru File and Russ Alan Prince, "Emerging Critical Success Factors in Marketing to the Smaller Business: Issues and Trends from the U.S. Market," *International Journal of Bank Marketing,* 10, no. 5 (1992), pp. 19–25.

27. Ibid

28. Discussion of trends based on Laurie Freeman, "Technology Influences Top Trends for 1999," *Advertising Age's Business Marketing,* 84, no. 1 (January 1999), pp. 1–2; John Obrecht, "Speculations for the Millennium," *Advertising Age's Business Marketing,* 84, no. 6 (June 1999), p. 13; Laurie Freeman, "Agencies See 37% Growth Amid B-to-B Revolution," *Advertising Age's Business Marketing,* 84, no. 7 (July 1999), pp. 1–2.

29. Richard L. Kaye, "Companies Need to Realize Internal Marketing Potential," *Advertising Age's Business Marketing,* 84, no. 7 (July 1999), p. 13.

Promotions Opportunity Analysis

THE HALLMARK DIFFERENCE:
Sending "The Very Best" to New Target Markets

Hallmark Cards has a long-standing tradition of excellence in the greeting card industry. In its early years, the firm developed and stood on the theme, "For people who only want to send the very best." The "very best" extended to the quality of cards, the types of employees who were hired, and a variety of promotional tactics, including the *Hallmark Hall of Fame* television series. Hallmark outlets, found in both freestanding locations and retail malls, are clean, well lit, and upscale, and they provide a variety of products beyond cards. Keepsakes, wedding items, and other specialty goods blend together to reinforce the theme of quality.

The greeting card business, however, has changed dramatically in the past 30 years. To keep pace, Hallmark has reanalyzed its approach to the marketplace to continue its growth pattern and record of success. As a result, Hallmark Cards, as a company, provides an excellent example of an effective integrated marketing communications program.

First, humorous cards with lighter, less sentimental messages offered the opportunity to expand sales. In response, Hallmark created the highly successful Shoebox Greetings line. Seizing the chance to be both funny and distinctive, Hallmark hired highly creative and productive writers to prepare punch lines on a daily basis. The line, launched in 1986, stresses variety and originality.

A second challenge came from specialty stores such as Factory Card Outlet and Card$mart. To meet this threat, Hallmark entered the "alternative" card market, whose cards offer offbeat humor and inspirational messages. They often result in impulse buys. To be noticed, these cards are displayed in prominent locations. Hallmark entered the business-to-business market by selling cards to other retail stores, such as drugstores and discount retailers. Hallmark used the Expressions brand to create 10 alternative card lines in 1998 alone. When particular cards work well, the verses and other artistic components

are reproduced in more conventional cards. Keeping current is one key in the alternative card market. Consequently, the Expressions brand reaches the marketplace quickly and offers cards featuring recent events.

To strengthen its position in non-Hallmark retail outlets, the firm competes with both products and prices. The company also points to the ambience in-store cards give to retail outlets, heightening the store's colors and image. Because cards carry a large markup, they retain significant retail space in many locations. Walgreen's regards Hallmark cards as a major draw to complement its drugstore, cosmetics, and photofinishing departments.

As an additional attraction for company retailers outside of Hallmark's own stores, the company offers point-of-purchase-generated information to retail outlets. By collecting information about Hallmark purchases, the company provides demographic information and other sales data to companies that agree to carry Hallmark products, making them high-tech partners in understanding consumers who shop in various places.

Recently, Hallmark began another aspect of integrating its communications program by carefully studying consumers. Company executives discovered local preferences for certain types of cards. Through data mining, Hallmark's analysis determined which cards sell best in each type of outlet. Hallmark has established databases to hold information regarding sales transactions, customers, promotions and their effectiveness levels, product profitability figures, and other information. Hallmark understands its customer base more clearly as a result. Shoppers are more satisfied with the products, and the company has been able to customize promotional activities and reduce unnecessary inventories.

Hallmark also entered the international arena, with major operations on nearly every continent. Hallmark products are sold in at least 40 other nations, including China, Germany, Brazil, Australia, Greece, and smaller countries. Besides greeting cards, the company sells calendars, gifts, gift wrap, ribbons, stationery, and party goods. Among the first to be established was business in Japan in 1966.

Finally, recognizing the influence of technology, Hallmark has developed a "Touch Screen Greeting" card, which enables customers to create individualized cards at an automated outlet. This form of card development allows consumers to express their own creative impulses on a high-markup card. It also allows Hallmark to compete with the "Create-A-Card" program of American Greetings, which made competitive inroads by starting a computerized version first. These technologically based greeting cards entice an entire new set of buyers, especially men and younger consumers in their teens and early 20s, who are more familiar with computers in general.

One goal of an IMC program is to identify opportunities and threats in the environment. By doing so, Hallmark has been able to create a competitive advantage in the marketplace. Also, company strengths and weaknesses are highlighted. Hallmark has been able to take advantage of its high-quality image to appeal to customers and retailers. Consequently, the company has been able to build on a strong past and work toward a more lucrative future, even as competitive pressures intensify.[1]

JAVANET INTERNET CAFÉ

The final element of an IMC foundation is to tie together information about the company, its brands and products, consumer groups, business buyers, and all other potential target markets into one model, which is the focus of a promotions opportunity analysis. This analysis begins with a communications market analysis, looks at opportunities, notes target markets, and identifies customers and segments. When the overall picture has formed, the marketing team is in the best position to construct a message and voice that will be clear to all of these groups.

The JavaNet Internet Café example on the IMC Plan Pro disk features an extensive Promotions Opportunity Analysis segment. It is shown in Part 2.0 along with individual elements in 2.1.1, 2.1.2, 2.1.3, 2.1.4, and in 2.2. Read these sections. Note the importance of finding ways to reach all current customers as well as potential new customers. An IMC plan is only complete when the marketing team touches every base in constructing the foundation. From the Table of Contents, notice the linkage between the elements of a Promotions Opportunity Analysis and other parts of the IMC plan, including the objectives, brand strategies, budgets, methods, media plan, and other elements. When these ingredients are consistent, the overall voice of JavaNet stands the best chance of being heard in the marketplace.

overview

ndividual customers and businesses receive myriad promotional materials every day. From pens marked with logos, to letterhead embossed with a company's mission statement, to calendars containing both advertisements and tear-off discount coupons, consumers and businesses encounter marketing materials in an increasing variety of ways. These marketing contacts do not occur by accident. At some point, a marketing official decided to distribute pens or calendars, or the printing department was asked to design letterhead. Beyond the world of advertising and personal selling, successful marketing efforts occur because *someone identified an opportunity to make a quality contact with a customer.* IMC is a program designed to help find the places to make those contacts and to present the customer with a well-defined message spoken in a clear voice by a firm.

This chapter describes the nature of a promotions opportunity analysis. The purpose of this IMC function is to identify customers and competitors in the marketplace to reveal new promotional opportunities. When these new opportunities are discovered, a company can build on its overall message by structuring it to fit the needs of various target markets. An effective promotional analysis causes the firm to specify which audiences and markets the company intends to serve. Locating key market segments helps company leaders more accurately define who they are trying to reach with their IMC programs.

In this section, target markets and promotional opportunities are linked to the processes of firm and brand image maintenance as well as consumer buyer behavior and business-to-business buyer behavior. All of these activities are key components in planning an effective IMC program.

THE MARKETING PLAN

The process of building an integrated marketing communications program begins with the construction of a quality marketing plan. That is, IMC commences with a plan to develop and coordinate the elements of the marketing mix. The four parts of the marketing mix (the prices, products, distribution methods, and promotions the company uses) should blend together to present a unified message on the firm's behalf. The purpose of the plan is to achieve a harmony in relaying messages to customers and other publics.

PROMOTIONS OPPORTUNITY ANALYSIS

Once the overall marketing plan is established, the firm is ready to seek out new promotional opportunities. A **promotions opportunity analysis** is the process by which marketers identify target audiences for the goods and services produced by the company. People are different and have unique uses for various products. The same is true for businesses. These special features are especially pronounced in global markets; therefore, communication to each group requires distinct and somewhat customized approaches. An effective promotional analysis means making quality decisions about what approach or appeal to use for each set of customers.

A promotions opportunity analysis must accomplish two objectives: (1) determine which promotional opportunities exist for the company, and (2) identify the characteristics of each target audience so a coherent advertising and marketing communications message can reach it. The more a marketer knows about an audience, the greater the chance a message will be heard, understood, and result in the desired outcome (a purchase, increased brand loyalty, etc.).

There are five steps in developing a promotions opportunity analysis, Figures 5.1 and 5.2 show the steps of planning the overall marketing program as well as the steps of planning for a promotions opportunity analysis. The upcoming sections describe the planning process in greater detail.

IMC Plan

1. **Situational analysis**
2. **Establish marketing objectives**
3. **Create marketing budget**
4. **Prepare marketing strategies**
5. **Match tactics with strategies**

FIGURE 5.1
Planning Processes

Promotions Opportunity Analysis

▶ **Conduct a communication market analysis**

▶ **Establish communication objectives**

▶ **Create communications budget**

▶ **Prepare promotional strategies**

▶ **Match tactics with strategies**

FIGURE 5.2
Promotions Opportunity Analysis

COMMUNICATION MARKET ANALYSIS

The first step of preparing a promotions opportunity analysis is to undertake a communication market analysis. A **communication market analysis** is the process of discovering the organization's strengths and weaknesses in the area of marketing communication and combining that information with an analysis of the opportunities and threats present in the firm's external environment. This process is quite similar to a managerial approach called SWOT analysis (strengths, weaknesses, opportunities, threats). The primary difference is that instead of looking at the environment from a companywide or strategic business unit (SBU) perspective, the analysis is done from a communication angle.

A communication market analysis typically has five components:

▶ Competitive analysis

▶ Opportunity analysis

▶ Target market analysis

▶ Customer analysis

▶ Positioning analysis

These five ingredients are studied together rather than sequentially. Each contributes key information to be used in evaluating the marketplace.

Competitive Analysis

A **competitive analysis** identifies major competitors. The objective is to discover who the competition is and what they are doing in the areas of advertising and communication. First, the marketing tactics being used by the competition must be identified to comprehend how they are attacking the marketplace. Consumers integrate information from a variety of sources into their knowledge structure. As a result, it is important to know what potential customers see, hear, and read about the competition.

Each company should clearly designate its competitors, both in domestic and foreign markets. After making a list of all of the competing firms, the company can continue its competitive analysis by collecting *secondary data*. The first items to look for are statements made by the competitors about themselves. Sources of secondary data about competitors can be found in:

▶ Advertisements

▶ Promotional materials

▶ Annual reports

▶ A prospectus for a publicly held corporation

▶ Web sites

The idea is to obtain as much information as possible about the competition, including what they say to their own customers.

The next task is to study what *other people* say about the competition. Marketers should read trade journals and visit vendors and suppliers who have dealt with the competition or who have read the competition's literature. The library may yield news articles and press releases about competitor activities. The importance of this step is vital to find out how other companies close to the competition view them. It also provides a sense of how they see a given company in comparison with the competition.

Another part of an analysis of the competition is *primary research.* In the retail business, it is helpful to visit competing stores to see how they display merchandise and observe their store personnel dealing with customers. For businesses other than retail, marketers can talk to salespeople in the field to obtain additional information about the competition. They also can talk to channel members such as wholesalers, distributors, and agents.

Opportunity Analysis

The next part of the communication market analysis is an **opportunity analysis**. This means watching carefully for new marketing opportunities by examining all of the available data and information about the market. Some helpful questions in conducting an opportunity analysis follow.

These ads were developed by BMW Motorcycles after an opportunity analysis revealed that females were not being targeted as important influences on purchase decisions of motorcycles.
Source: Courtesy of BMW Motorcycles.

1. Are there customers that the competition is ignoring or not serving?
2. Which markets are heavily saturated and have intense competition?
3. Are the benefits of our goods and services being clearly articulated to our customers?
4. Are there opportunities to build relationships with customers using a slightly different marketing approach?
5. Are there opportunities that are not being pursued, or is our brand positioned with a cluster of other companies in such a manner that it cannot stand out?

An opportunity analysis reveals communication opportunities that can be exploited. These opportunities exist when there are unfilled market niches, when the competition is doing a poor job of meeting the needs of some customers, or when the company has a distinct competence to offer.

Target Market Analysis

A third component of the communication market analysis is the **target market analysis**. This stage requires the marketing department to recognize the needs of various consumer and business groups. Company marketers must define the benefits customers are seeking and determine the ways in which they can be reached.

The questions asked during a target market analysis are similar to those posed in the opportunity analysis. These questions can help recognize needs of the target market that no one is fulfilling or instances in which the competition is doing a poor job. Once a company understands the general target market, it can appraise various customers within that market.

Customer Analysis

The logical extension to examining a target market is to conduct a **customer analysis**. When thinking about customers, keep in mind the three types of customers to study:

1. Current company customers
2. The competition's customers
3. Potential customers who may become interested in purchasing from a particular company

An analysis of customers reveals their interpretations of the organization's advertisements and its other marketing communications. The point is to know what works within each customer base. It is helpful to ascertain how customers perceive individual advertisements as well as what they think about the larger company. Service Metrics (see advertisement in this section) examines a firm's Web site from the customer's perspective and, more importantly, compares the Web site to the competition. This type of analysis identifies all of a firm's communication avenues.

Part of a customer analysis may include an analysis of a firm's Web site from the customer's perspective.
Source: Courtesy of Service Metrics.

Positioning Analysis

Part of a communications analysis is examining the position a firm has relative to its competition. **Positioning** is the perception created in the consumer's mind regarding the nature of a company and its products relative to the competition. The quality of products, prices charged, methods of distribution, image, communication tactics, and other factors create positioning. At this point, the marketing firm should determine the company's position to make sure it is consistent with other elements of the IMC program. A problem exists when customers view the firm's position differently than the manner in which the company sees itself.

An effective communication market analysis lays the foundation for the development of communication objectives, the next step of a promotions opportunities analysis. A poor analysis results in something similar to shooting at a target with a blindfold on. It is nearly impossible to find the target, and the chances of hitting the bull's-eye are very slim indeed.

ESTABLISHING MARKETING COMMUNICATIONS OBJECTIVES

The second step of a promotions opportunity analysis is to identify objectives. Communication objectives help account executives and advertising creatives design effective messages. Figure 5.3 lists some of the more common objectives found in profit-seeking organizations.

A communications plan is often oriented toward a single objective. It is possible, however, for a program to accomplish more than one goal at a time. For example, Dennis Max's Unique Restaurant Concepts of Boca Raton, Florida, gave a 10 percent discount to its frequent-diner members from May through October. The primary goal of this promotion was to increase customer traffic at its six restaurants during the "off" season. The catch to the discount was that it could only be used at one of the company's other restaurants, not where it issued. This encouraged customers to visit other locations in Dade and Palm Beach counties. The discounts could be accumulated, which encouraged repeat purchases.[2] This promotion reached three goals from Figure 5.3.

▶ Building customer traffic

▶ Reinforcing purchase decisions (rewarding them)

▶ Encouraging repeat purchases (at other locations)

Logical combinations of communication objectives found in Figure 5.3 and methods to accomplish them exist. For example, advertising is an excellent means of developing brand awareness and enhancing a brand's image. Further, increasing sales can be accomplished through price changes, contests, or coupons. The key is to match the objective to the medium and the message.

The process of defining and establishing communication objectives is a crucial element of promotional opportunities analysis. Without clearly specified objectives, the company can quickly drift off course or lose its focus on the overall IMC program. Objectives serve as reminders of what the firm trys to do with its communications to various customers.

ESTABLISHING A COMMUNICATIONS BUDGET

The third step of a promotions opportunity analysis is preparing a communications budget. This is a complex task. Budgets are based on various types of objectives. *Marketing objectives* are on the one hand general, because they relate to the entire

---

▶ **Develop brand awareness**

▶ **Increase good–service category demand**

▶ **Change customer beliefs or attitudes**

▶ **Enhance purchase actions**

▶ **Encourage repeat purchases**

▶ **Build customer traffic**

▶ **Enhance firm image**

▶ **Increase market share**

▶ **Increase sales**

▶ **Reinforce purchase decisions**

FIGURE 5.3
Communication Objectives

marketing plan and on the other hand specific, because they tend to be measurable. Marketing objectives include:

▶ Sales volume

▶ Increases in sales volume

▶ Market share

▶ Profits

▶ Return on investment

Communications objectives are related to various parts of the IMC program. They include reaching various target audiences, displaying product features, positioning against competitors, and generating individual responses, such as buying for the first time or increasing usage.

Many marketing professionals believe **benchmark measures** are helpful. A benchmark is a starting point that is studied in relation to the degree of change following a promotional campaign. For example, a dry cleaning company that has been in business for one year may discover, through market research, that 20 percent of the community's population is aware of the company and that the company has an 8 percent share of the city's total market. Following a campaign featuring advertisements, coupons, discounts for certain days of the week (Tuesday specials) and to senior citizens, the company could hope to achieve 40 percent awareness and a 12 percent share. This would indicate a level of success compared to the previously established benchmarks.

Budgeting Assumptions

It is important to remember that a communications budget covers more than advertising. Funds will be allocated to some or all of the items featured in Table 5.1. As shown, advertising is only a portion of the funding. In the case of business-to-business budgets, advertising represents about one-third of all monies. Other dollars are spent on direct mail, trade shows, catalogs, and even public relations programs.

Managers often make assumptions about a communications budget that confuse the process. This occurs most notably when a manager assumes there is a direct relationship between expenditures on promotions and sales, as shown in Figure 5.4. This is highly unlikely. Several factors influence the relationship between expenditures on promotions and sales, including:

▶ The goal of the promotion

▶ Threshold effects

Category	Business-to-Business	Consumer
Direct mail	27.1%	6.5%
Trade shows, exhibits	12.9	2.0
Catalogs, directories	10.7	4.1
Literature, coupons, POP	9.3	16.2
Public relations	5.3	3.1
Dealer and distributor materials	3.3	1.3
Television advertising	2.7	45.1
Radio advertising	0.8	5.6
Print advertising	27.9	14.5

TABLE 5.1

Communications Spending

Sources: Cyndee Miller, "Marketing Industry Report: Consumer Marketers Spend Most of Their Money on Communications," *Marketing News,* 30, no. 6 (March 11, 1996), pp. 1–2; Cyndee Miller, "Marketing Industry Report: Who's Spending What on Biz-to-Biz Marketing," *Marketing News,* 30, no. 1 (January 1, 1996), pp. 1–2.

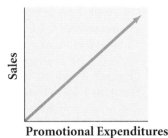

An unrealistic assumption about the relationship between promotional expenditures and sales

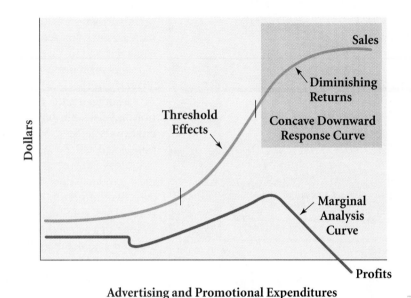

FIGURE 5.4
A Sales-Response Function Curve Combined with the Downward Response Curve and Marginal Analysis

▶ Carryover effects
▶ Wear out effects
▶ Decay effects
▶ Random events

Promotional goals differ depending on the stage in the buying process that is being addressed. For instance, in Chapter 7, a model called the *hierarchy of effects* approach will be described in detail. The model suggests many stages lead to a purchase, including: awareness, knowledge, liking, preference, conviction, and the actual purchase. A recent promotional campaign for Verizon Wireless first targeted awareness with the "Can you hear me now?" theme prominently featured. Over time, other aspects of the company's services, advantages compared to competitors, and finally financial incentives to buy the service were added. The entire campaign was designed to start at one place (awareness) and end at another (the purchase). Thus, it would not be logical to expect that early promotional expenditures would have a one-to-one relationship with sales.

Instead, what are known as **threshold effects** are present. As shown in Figure 5.4, the early effects of advertising are minimal. The same is true for all promotional expenditures. At first, there will be very little behavioral response, especially if only advertisements are featured. Over time, a consumer who is exposed enough times to a company's marketing message recalls the company and eventually is willing to make a purchase. Coupons, free samples, and other marketing tactics can help a good or service overcome the threshold. Threshold effects may be minimal in some circumstances, because the good or service is so innovative that consumers are immediately aware of its advantages and are willing to buy. In others, it is a lengthy process to capture enough attention to create sales.

Because automobiles are not purchased regularly, dealers such as Roper Pontiac rely on carryover effects to ensure a place in the consumer's evoked set.

Source: Used with permission of the *Joplin Globe*, Joplin, Missouri.

At the same time, there is a point where a promotional campaign has saturated the market, and further expenditures do not have an impact. The S-shaped curve displayed in Figure 5.4, which is known as the **Sales-Response Function Curve**, indicates the *diminishing returns* that are present. When diminishing returns are present, what is known as a **concave downward function** is present. That is, an incremental expenditures in advertising result in lower and lower increases in sales. A **marginal analysis** would show that additional expenditures on advertising and promotions at that point have an adverse effect on profits.

Another factor that influences the relationship between promotions and sales is a **carryover effect**. Many products are only purchased when needed, such as washing machines and refrigerators. Promotions for these products must be designed to generate carryover effects in which the consumer has been exposed to the company's message for so long that when the time comes to buy, the consumer remembers the key company. For example, when a washing machine breaks down and requires replacement, the goal of Maytag is for the consumer to remember the "lonely repairman" and his new assistant, so Maytag's products will be considered. These ads must carry over until the right time.

Wear out effects also complicate the budgeting process. At a certain point, a product simply becomes "old" or "boring." Creating promotions to add excitement are, at that point, difficult. Many young people consider Levi's products to be worn out and only useful for their parents. The company must spend a great deal of time trying to rejuvenate the brand in some way.

Also, **decay effects** are present. When a company stops advertising, consumers begin to forget about the company. In some instances, the degree of decay is dramatic. In others, the carryover effects are strong enough that some time can lapse before the brand drops out of the consciousness of the consumer. The promotional budget must be structured to avoid the problem of decay effects illustrated graphically in Figure 5.5.

Finally, random events affect promotions. The September 11, 2001, attacks affected a wide variety of industries and individual companies. Promotional expenditures were, in some cases, cut back as the country recovered. It would be impossible to demonstrate the

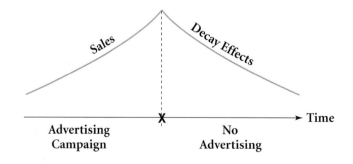

FIGURE 5.5
A Decay Effects Model

relationship between promotions and sales in such circumstances. Some new products were successfully launched almost immediately after September 11, while in other cases the advertisements simply did not result in sales.

Therefore, as the marketing team constructs the budget, the assumptions that drive the process should be considered. The newness of the product, the economy, and a wide variety of complicating factors must be part of the process of tying budgeting expenditures to marketing and communication objectives.

TYPES OF BUDGETS

There are many ways to prepare a communications budget. Companies use several methods to develop these budgets, including those listed in Figure 5.6.

The Percentage of Sales Method

One common approach to setting the communications budget is the **percentage of sales method**. Companies using this form prepare communications budgets for coming years based on either: (1) sales from the previous year or (2) anticipated sales for the next year. A major reason for using this format is its simplicity, which makes it relatively easy to prepare. Yet the percentage of sales approach also has problems. First, this type of budget tends to change in the opposite direction of what may be needed. That is, when sales go up, so does the communications budget. When sales decline, the communications budget also declines. In most cases, the communications budget should be the opposite: It should be increased during periods of declining sales to help reverse the trend. Further, during growth periods the communications budget may not need to be increased. The second major disadvantage of this method is that it does not allocate money for special needs or to combat competitive pressures. Therefore, many marketing experts believe the disadvantages of the percentage of sales method tend to outweigh its advantages.

The Meet-the-Competition Method

Some firms use the **meet-the-competition** method of budgeting. The primary goal of this form of budgeting is to prevent the loss of market share. It is often used in highly competitive markets where rivalries between competitors are intense.

The potential drawback to meet-the-competition budgeting is that marketing dollars may not be spent efficiently. Matching the competition's spending does not guarantee success, which means market share can still be lost. The concept to remember is that it is not *how much* is spent, but rather *how well* the money is allocated and how effectively the marketing campaign works at retaining customers and market share.

Arbitrary Allocation

An **arbitrary allocation** method is based on management estimates of what is needed. It is a kind of "by guess and by golly" approach in which no criteria are set and therefore no real reasoning is being used. Many small businesses use an arbitrary approach, even though it is not advisable.

> ▶ Percentage of sales
> ▶ Meet the competition
> ▶ Arbitrary allocation
> ▶ "What we can afford"
> ▶ Objective and task
> ▶ Payout planning
> ▶ Quantitative models

FIGURE 5.6
Methods of Determining the Marketing Communications Budget

The "What We Can Afford" Method

A fourth type of budgeting is the **"what we can afford" method**. This technique sets the marketing budget after all of the company's other budgets have been determined. Money is allocated based on what the company leaders feel they can afford.

This method suggests management does not really see the benefits of marketing. Instead, company leaders may view marketing expenditures as nonrevenue-generating activities. Newer and smaller companies with limited finances often use the "what we can afford" approach.

The Objective and Task Method

Another form is the **objective and task method**. To prepare this type of communications budget, management first lists all of the objectives it intends to pursue during the year, then calculates the cost of accomplishing each objective. The communications budget is the cumulative sum of the estimated costs for all objectives.

Many marketing experts deem the objective and task method the best method of budgeting because it relates dollar costs to achieving specific objectives. Unfortunately, it is the least used, primarily because it takes longer to prepare than many of the other approaches. For a company such as Procter & Gamble, which offers hundreds of products, producing a budget based on objectives for each brand and product category would take many hours; other methods are faster and simpler. Not surprisingly, in the business-to-business sector, over 60 percent of the companies set their marketing budgets using the "what we can afford" method. Less than 10 percent use the objective and task method.[3]

Payout Planning

Payout planning establishes a ratio of advertising to sales or market share based on Nielsen ratings. This method normally allocates greater amounts in early years to yield payouts in later years.[4] By allocating larger amounts at the beginning of a new product introduction, brand awareness and brand equity are built. Then, as the brand is accepted and sales build, fewer advertising dollars are needed to maintain a target growth. Unfortunately, when advertising dollars are decreased, the threshold effects shown in Figure 5.5 may occur.

Quantitative Models

In some instances, computer simulations may be developed to model the relationship between advertising or promotional expenditures with sales and profits. These models are far from perfect but do have the advantage of accounting for the type of industry and product as the model is created. Normally quantitative models are limited to larger organizations with strong computer and statistical departments.

BUDGETING EXPENDITURES

When a budget is finalized, the company has specified how much it intends to spend on each of the major communications tools. Media advertising normally accounts for 25 percent of a communications budget. Trade promotions receive about 50 percent, and consumer promotions on average about 25 percent. These percentages vary considerably from industry to industry.[4] Consumer product manufacturers

For a small business like Ozark Decorative Paving, budgeting adequate dollars to advertising is essential to build brand awareness.
Source: Used with permission of the *Joplin Globe*, Joplin, Missouri.

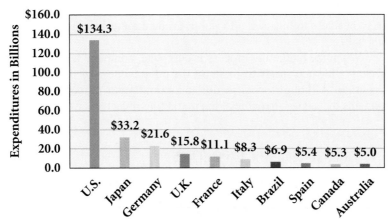

Total Advertising Expenditures

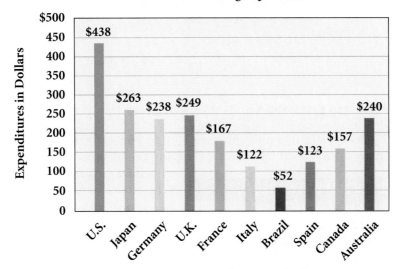

Average Expenditure per Capita

FIGURE 5.7
Global Advertising Expenditures

spend more on trade promotions directed toward retailers. Service companies tend to spend more on media advertising. Budgets also vary by product types. For example, for dolls and stuffed toys, the average expenditure on media advertising as a percentage of sales is about 15 percent, whereas for bakery products, expenditures on media advertising represent only 3 percent of sales.[5]

The United States leads the world in marketing communications expenditures. Figure 5.7 lists the top 10 countries in advertising expenditures and amounts spent per capita.

Allocations of business-to-business firms are not the same as those of consumer-oriented firms. Business-to-business expenditures also vary by industry. Marketing spending by consumer goods and services companies tends to be a higher percentage of sales revenues than in business-to-business companies.[6]

How do business-to-business advertisers allocate their budgets? Approximately 20 percent of all business-to-business ads emphasize or promote the corporate image. In contrast, 80 percent focus on specific goods or services.[7] The major goals of many business-to-business advertisements are to create awareness of new products or brands and to heighten awareness of the company. Many advertising creatives believe it is difficult to design effective business-to-business advertisements because they don't have the creative freedom possible with consumer advertisements. Also, because most business ads are print ads in trade journals, the flexibility of television and radio advertisements is not available.

Many firms have marketing programs aimed at both consumers and businesses. For example, Revlon produces television and print ads directed to consumers, but it also directs trade promotion dollars toward retailers. On average, companies spend about 30 percent of their total communications budgets marketing to other businesses. In some industries, such as services, the percentage is much higher (70 percent). In some technology-based industries, business-to-business allocations account for as little as 13 percent of the total marketing budget.[8]

When the budgeting process is complete, company leaders should believe they have wisely allocated funds to increase the effectiveness of the marketing communications program. Although specific dollar amounts and percentages vary, the overall goal remains the same—to achieve the marketing objectives as established by the plan.

INTEGRATED LEARNING EXPERIENCE

STOP

One beneficial tool that can be used to help determine an IMC advertising budget is to examine expenditures of other firms within the same industry and in other industries. The Advertising Age Web site at **www.adage.com** provides information about advertising spending levels. Access the Data Center, and review the 100 leading national advertisers. This section contains information about ad spending by brands, companies, product categories, and in the various media.

In this business-to-business advertisement, Servicesoft reinforces its corporate image while promoting its interactive e-mail system.
Source: Courtesy of Servicesoft Inc.

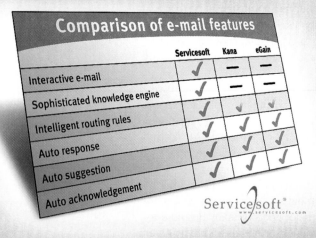

PREPARE PROMOTIONAL STRATEGIES

The fourth step of a promotions opportunity analysis program is to state the general communication strategy for the company and its products. **Strategies** are sweeping guidelines concerning the essence of the company's marketing efforts. Strategies provide the long-term direction for all marketing activities.

An excellent example of a general communications strategy is the marketing efforts of Mountain Dew. The primary market for Mountain Dew is teenagers and young adults. As a result, communications efforts are directed to that market using slogans such as "Do the Dew" to "Been There Done That" and so forth. Action-oriented commercials featuring higher-risk activities are designed to attract younger people (and the young at heart) who are more willing to take "risks" in the products they sample and adopt. The overall theme of the Mountain Dew communications program guides all other activities.

It is critical that the company's communication strategies mesh with its overall message. Both must be carefully linked to the opportunities and threats identified by a communication market analysis. Communications strategies should be directly related to established objectives and must be reachable using the allocations available in the marketing and communications budgets. Once strategies have been implemented, they are not changed unless major new events occur. Only dramatic changes in the marketplace, new competitive forces, or new promotional opportunities should cause companies to amend their strategies.

Matching Tactics with Strategies

Tactics are the things companies do to support overall promotional strategies. Tactics include promotional campaigns designed around themes based on strategic objectives. For example, the Kellogg company seeks to enhance sales of some cereals by designing unusual features for certain holidays, such as Halloween and Christmas Rice Krispies.

Tactics do not replace strategies, nor should they distract consumers from the consistent message or theme the company is trying to create. At the same time, they add excitement or interest to what the company is ordinarily doing. Holiday promotions, anniversary sales, and a wide variety of other events can be the basis for a promotional effort. Methods used in tactical campaigns include:

▶ Advertisements based on the major theme or a subtheme

▶ Personal selling enticements (bonuses and prizes for sales reps)

▶ Sales promotions (posters, point-of-purchase displays, end-of-aisle displays, free-standing displays)

▶ Special product packaging and labeling

▶ Price changes

Besides the methods of communicating with consumers and sales reps who offer the products, companies are able to add other enticements. Items that may be included in tactical efforts include:

▶ Coupons

▶ Gift certificates

▶ Purchase bonuses (a second product attached to a first)

▶ Special containers (e.g., holiday decanters or soft drink glasses)

▶ Contests and prizes

▶ Rebates

▶ Volume discounts (larger-size packages, "buy one, get one free" promotions, etc.)

The Gold Bond advertisement shown in this section uses a manufacturer's coupon to encourage people to purchase the product. The creative use of the snowy, winter scene highlights the product benefits of Gold Bond. The more creative the campaign, the better the chance the company can overcome clutter and become recognized in the marketplace.

When a promotions opportunity analysis is complete, company leaders and the marketing department should have a grasp of the organization's marketing situation, along with specific information about internal strengths and weaknesses in the promotions area. Also, they should be aware of opportunities present in the environment along with any threats to the communications program. They must study and understand the organization's competition to the greatest degree possible. Target markets must be defined and budgets set. Then, the marketing leaders of the company can

A creative message strategy is combined with the marketing tactic of a coupon to stimulate sales of Gold Bond Medicated Body Lotion.

Source: Courtesy of Chattem, Inc.

PROMOTIONS OPPORTUNITY ANALYSIS

Is Segmentation the Same as Stereotyping?

In an era in which the term "political correctness" has been tossed about by political parties and other social critics, questions remain regarding what it means to be culturally aware. This issue has emerged in the area of marketing. Consider some of the primary categories in which segments are identified: age, race, gender, social status, income. Of these, many are cultural characteristics.

Should there be a "black," "Hispanic," or "Caucasian" market? Should there be "male" and "female" markets? What about "teenagers," "Generation Y," and "baby boomers"? Are these markets distinct enough to require special advertisements and marketing promotions? Or should the general message be universal enough to reach people from all backgrounds?

Advertisements often depict teenagers in one-dimensional ways rather than reflecting the complexities of young adulthood. Rebellious, carefree, and sexually starved are common depictions. For baby boomers, the image presented is of a white, well-educated, well-off person with a spacious home and expensive cars and toys instead of the complex makeup of multiple nationalities of all income levels. From a marketing perspective, it is much easier to group people into smaller subgroups with common interests. Is it unethical, bad business, or simply a practical matter to pigeonhole consumer types in these ways?

establish strategies and tactics to guide efforts to reach specific marketing objectives and performance targets.

The next section describes in greater detail two key ingredients of the promotional opportunities analysis process. The first is the study of market segments and methods to identify viable segments for the company to target. The second is to extend promotional opportunities analysis to global or international markets.

MARKET SEGMENTATION

IMC experts use **market segmentation** to identify specific purchasing groups based on their needs, attitudes, and interests. A **market segment** is a set of businesses or group of individual consumers with distinct characteristics. Market segmentation efforts are of great value in completing a promotions opportunity analysis. These advantages include:

1. Helping marketers identify company strengths and weaknesses as well as opportunities in the marketplace
2. Working toward the goal of matching what the firm does best with the most enticing sets of customers
3. Clarifying marketing objectives associated with individual target markets
4. Focusing budgeting expenditures or consumer groups and business segments more precisely
5. Linking company strategies and tactics to select groups of customers

Thus, segmentation is an excellent example of taking a traditional marketing concept and adding an IMC approach in order to build brand loyalty and improve the odds of success for a marketing plan.

For a market segment to be considered a viable target for a specific marketing communications campaign, it should meet the following tests:

▶ The individuals or businesses within the market segment should be similar in nature, having the same needs, attitudes, interests, and opinions. This means persons or businesses *within* the segment are *homogenous.*

▶ The market segment differs from the population as a whole. Segments are distinct from other segments and the general population.

▶ The market segment must be large enough to be financially viable to target with a separate marketing campaign.

▶ The market segment must be reachable through some type of media or marketing communications method.

Marketers engaged in research spend considerable resources and amounts of time working to identify quality market segments. These groups are specified in two general areas: (1) consumer markets and (2) business-to-business markets. The following section describes each of these segments in greater detail.

MARKET SEGMENTATION BY CONSUMER GROUPS

In many instances, end users are the primary target market for a firm's offerings. Effective IMC programs help the company identify sets of consumers who are potential buyers and who have things in common, such as attitudes, interests, or needs. These consumer market segments include the seven listed in Figure 5.8.

As shown, the first method of segmentation is by demographic variables. **Demographics** are population characteristics. Typical demographic segmentation variables useful in IMC programs include gender, age, education, income, race, and ethnicity. Consumer market segmentation approaches to demographic groups are based on the idea that people with distinguishable characteristics have different needs. Companies create products and services to meet the needs of individual demographic segments.

Segments Based on Gender

The first major way to classify customers is by gender. Males and females purchase different products, buy similar products with different features (e.g., deodorants), buy the same products for dissimilar reasons (stereos, televisions), and buy the same products after being influenced by different kinds of appeals through different media.

Women constitute a major market, especially as the number of working women trying to establish successful careers continues to rise. Nearly 70 percent of the women in the workforce express concerns about balancing work and family. This worry has led to a change in how many companies market their products to women. Goods and services that offer convenience, flexibility, and independence are in demand, and marketing appeals using these hooks have been successful. At the same time, many working women do feel a certain need to reward themselves. Consequently, numerous women also are willing to indulge in purchases of CDs and other perks or seek out services including health spas and beauty salons to obtain these rewards.[9] Notice the three ways Bijan projects itself to women in their advertisement (on page 141).

Marketing to females does not stop with products oriented to women. For example, a study by Goldhaber Research Agency found that women have an enormous impact on the spending habits of men. This survey revealed that men who are sports fans will attend 57 percent more sporting events if their wives are also sports fans, compared with men who are avid sports fans but their wives are not. The number of times a man attends a professional sporting event is directly related to his spouse's attitude toward sports.

▶ **Demographics**

▶ **Psychographics**

▶ **Generations**

▶ **Geographic**

▶ **Geodemographics**

▶ **Benefits**

▶ **Usage**

FIGURE 5.8
Methods of Segmenting Consumer Markets

These four advertisements are directed to different demographic segments: mothers, fathers, renters, and seniors.
Source: Courtesy of State Farm.

Therefore, to boost attendance, many professional sports teams realize they need to market to women. This approach can have a double impact. First, more women will attend sporting events, and second, men who are zealous sports fans will attend more games.[10]

It didn't take long for BMW Motorcycles to recognize that women exert a considerable amount of influence on purchase decisions for luxury touring motorcycles. When conducting research related to the launch of a new model, the K 1200 LT (Luxury Tourer), one consumer explained that, "If mama ain't happy, nobody's happy." Couples most often use luxury touring motorcycles for long-distance touring. This became an important factor in the development of the cycle and in creating its market position. The K 1200 LT has heated seats and backrests, with separate controls for both the passenger and the rider. This was because a man tends to look at a motorcycle in terms of style, horsepower, torque, and handling. A female passenger has other concerns, notably comfort.

Consequently, BMW Motorcycles took what was learned from this research and made sure to market the motorcycle with two target audiences in mind: men as the primary purchasers and women as the decision-making influencers. Each was an important part of the promotional campaign.[11]

Some messages are directly targeted at men, because the products are masculine (aftershave) or because more men will use the product (e.g., athlete's foot remedies). Appeals aimed only at men speak in a different tone than do more general ads and messages. Notice the advertisement for milk that is directed toward men and how it differs from the one aimed at women on page 142.

Segments Based on Age

A second demographic method to segment consumers is by age. Marketing campaigns target children, young adults, middle-age grown-ups, and senior citizens. Often they combine age-related factors with other demographics such as gender. Logical combinations with other segments is a common approach. For example, older women may be primary targets for specific types of vitamins and other age-related products. Further, young working women with children are more likely to notice ads for conveniences (ready-made foods and snacks, quick lube oil change facilities, etc.). Other groups may buy vitamins, snack foods, and change their oil, yet individual segments can be targeted with messages that reach their particular sets of needs.

Children have a major impact on the purchasing decisions of their parents. Appeals to children can tie several items together, including advertisements, merchandise based on the ads, and selections from other media. For example, children attracted to Harry Potter can buy toys, see the movie, buy the books, and witness advertisements using the Harry Potter theme, such as when Burger King, KFC, and Taco Bell all combined to sponsor a campaign.

Besides children, another age-based demographic group that appeals to many firms is seniors, defined as individuals over age 55. In the past, all seniors were treated as one market and tended to be stereotyped in ads. Often they were pictured as elderly grandparents or as feeble but avid gardeners. Several firms discovered that many seniors lead active lives and many are not gardeners. Nearly 60 percent are volunteers, and many have begun dating following the loss of a spouse. More than 25 percent in the 65 to 72 age group still work and 14 million seniors care for grandchildren.[12] In segmenting seniors, at least four different groups exist (see Figure 5.9).[13] In marketing to seniors, it is important to realize that they are not one group. Ads must be targeted to more specific groups within the senior citizen category.

Segments Based on Income

Income is an important demographic segmentation variable for many goods and services. Spending is normally directed at three large categories of goods: (1) necessities, (2) sundries, and (3) luxuries. Lower levels of income mean consumers purchase mostly necessities, such as food, clothing, cleaning

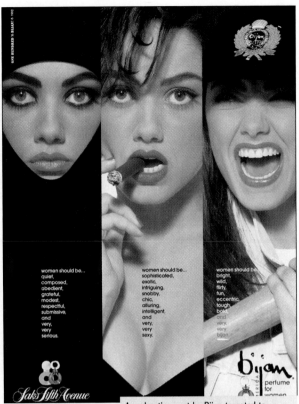

An advertisement by Bijan targeted to females.
Source: Courtesy of Bijan Fragrances, Inc.

An advertisement for milk based on nutritional benefits directed to women.
Source: Courtesy or Bozell Worldwide, Inc.

An advertisement for milk based on nutritional benefits directed to men.
Source: Courtesy of Bozell Worldwide, Inc.

supplies, and so forth. With increased income, households can buy more items categorized as sundries: those things that are "nice to own," but not necessary. Sundries include televisions, computers, CD players, and other similar goods. Vacation spending also is a sundry expenditure. Luxuries are things most people cannot afford or can afford only once in a lifetime, unless the family is a high-income household. Luxuries include yachts, expensive automobiles, extravagant vacation resorts, and other high-cost goods and services. Marketers work closely with creatives to tailor messages to various income groups and to select media that match those groups.

Segments Based on Ethnic Heritage

By the year 2010, most Americans will be nonwhite. Currently, most advertisements and marketing communications tend to be written from a white, Anglo-Saxon perspective. This represents both an opportunity and a threat: an opportunity for companies able to adapt their messages to other cultures and heritages. It may be a threat to those that do not.

Ethnic marketing is more than spending money with ethnically owned radio stations or hiring ethnically owned advertising agencies. It is more than translating an advertisement from English into Spanish. It is more than including African Americans or Asian Americans in advertisements. Successful ethnic marketing requires understanding various ethnic groups and writing marketing communications that speak to their cultures and values.

The three major ethnic groups in the United States are African Americans, Hispanics, and Asian Americans. African American economic power exceeds $400 billion annually. Hispanic sector purchases are in excess of $300 billion. In addition, a large number of

Healthy Indulgers (18% of the people over the age of 55)

This group has experienced the lowest level of traumatic life events such as retirement, death of a spouse, or chronic illness. These individuals tend to resemble their younger counterparts, the baby boomers. However, the primary difference is that the healthy indulgers are better off financially and more settled in their careers.

Healthy Hermits (36%)

These individuals have experienced at least one major life event (normally the death of a spouse). Healthy hermits have withdrawn from society and tend to isolate themselves from others.

Ailing Outgoers (29%)

These people have experienced major health problems. At the same time, they tend to maintain positive self-esteem and are active in life. They acknowledge their physical limitations but continue to live active lives.

Frail Recluses (17%)

These individuals have experienced major health problems and adjusted their lifestyles. They tend to become more spiritual and less active socially.

FIGURE 5.9
Segmentation of Senior Citizens

Sources: Rick Adler, "Stereotypes Won't Work with Seniors Anymore," *Advertising Age* (November 11, 1996), Vol. 67, Issue 46, p. 32; George P. Moschis, "Life Stages of the Mature Market," *American Demographics* (September 1996), p. 44–47; "The Ungraying of America," *American Demographics* (July 1997), pp. 12, 14–15; Faye Rice.

immigrants are arriving from India and Pakistan. Another large group is coming from the Middle East and Eastern European countries. Each ethnic group contains multiple subgroups. Within the Asian community are individuals of Korean, Japanese, Filipino, Vietnamese, and Chinese descent. The Hispanic community is made up of individuals from Latin America, Mexico, Cuba, and Puerto Rico.

Although different in many ways, several common threads exist among these ethnic groups. They all tend to be more brand loyal than their white counterparts. They value quality and are willing to pay a higher price for quality and brand identity. They value relationships with companies and are loyal to those that make the effort to establish a connection with them.

To market effectively to ethnic groups, it is important to develop new creative approaches that respect America's ethnic differences while also highlighting its similarities. Achieving this requires advertising and marketing agencies that understand the subtleties of multiculturalism. Becoming involved in sponsorships of minority and ethnic events goes a long way toward establishing ties with specific ethnic groups. Indications are strong that ethnic consumers reward companies that invest in them. In addition to sponsorships, becoming involved in ethnic community groups and civic and trade associations should prove beneficial.[14]

Ethnic marketing is similar in some ways to global marketing. It is important to present one overall message

A Skechers advertisement featuring a multiethnic approach.
Source: Courtesy of Skechers USA Inc.

COMMUNICATION ACTION

Psychographics and Technology

With the rapid development of multimedia technology, a company called Odyssey conducted pyschographic research to help the company develop a marketing program. Instead of one market, Odyssey's marketing team discovered six unique market segments with distinct attitudes about technology. Odyssey found that consumers may have identical demographic characteristics but differ greatly in how they view multimedia technology. Understanding the six different segments allowed Odyssey to create advertising and marketing themes to appeal to each segment. The six segments that Odyssey identified are:

1. **New Enthusiasts.** These households like to be on the cutting edge of technology and are eager to purchase the most recent version. This group also tends to have high incomes and higher levels of education.

2. **Hopefuls.** These households also like to be on the cutting edge of technology but lack the financial means to make extensive purchases. They are concerned that a new technology may be too difficult to use.

3. **Faithful.** These households are not eager to try new technologies but, more importantly, are not averse to trying something new.

4. **Oldliners.** These households are not interested in new technologies. Finances also concern this group.

5. **Independents.** These individuals have higher incomes and higher educational levels but do not value television or any other new form of technology. They are not eager to try new things.

6. **Surfers.** These households are ambivalent about new technologies and tend to be cynical about business and privacy issues. They have above-average incomes and are able to afford technology, but don't trust it.

Each segment clearly requires a distinct advertising appeal. In this case, similar people have differing psychological attitudes and needs for a product, even though the product itself is the same for each group.

Source: Marilyn A. Gillen, "Tracking Multimedia's Fragmented Audience," *Billboard,* 106, no. 10 (March 5, 1994), p. 60.

that is then tailored to fit the needs and values of various groups. Successfully achieving this integration of the overall message with characteristics of individual cultures should result in valuable gains in loyalty to a company and its brands, and diversify the markets the company can effectively serve.

Psychographics

Demographics are easy to identify but do not always explain why people buy particular products or specific brands, or what type of an appeal should be used to reach them. To assist in the marketing effort while building on demographic information, psychographic profiles have been developed. **Psychographics** emerge from patterns of responses that reveal a person's attitudes, interests, and opinions (AIO). AIO measures can be combined with demographic information to provide marketers with a more complete understanding of the market to be targeted.[15] The Communication Action Box "Psychographics and Technology" presents an example of marketing psychographic segmentation.

Segments Based on Generations

Beyond using gender, age, income, ethnic heritage, education, or other demographic variables for segmentation, many marketers embrace the idea of generations or cohorts. This approach does not entail obtaining psychographic information to enrich the demographics but does possess some of the richness of the psychographics. The concept behind this

Born	Cohort Name	Generation	Size (millions)	% of Population
1912–1921	Depression cohort	GI generation	13	5%
1922–1927	World War II cohort	Depression generation	11	4
1928–1945	Postwar cohort	Silent generation	41	17
1946–1954	Boomers I cohort	Woodstock generation	33	14
1955–1965	Boomers II cohort	Zoomers generation	49	21
1966–1976	Generation X cohort	Baby busters generation	41	17
1977–1994	Generation Y cohort	Echo boom generation	35	15

TABLE 5.2

Generational Marketing

Sources: Based on Berna Miller, "A Beginner's Guide to Demographics," *Marketing Tools* (October 1995), pp. 54–61; Faye Rice, "Making Generational Marketing Come of Age," *Fortune* (June 26, 1995), pp. 110–12; Geoffrey E. Meredith and Charles D. Schewe, "Marketing by Cohorts, Not Generations," *Marketing News,* 33, no. 3 (February 1, 1999), p. 22.

method of segmentation is that common experiences and events create bonds between people beyond those based merely on age.

Segmentation based on generations notes that as people experience significant external events during their late adolescence or early adulthood, these events impact their social values, attitudes, and preferences. Based on similar experiences, these cohorts of individuals develop common preferences for music, foods, and other products. They also tend to respond to the same types of marketing appeals. Based on this idea, seven cohorts or generations have been identified. Table 5.2 lists these cohorts along with the generation in which they belong, the estimated size of the segment, and the percent of the U.S. population.

A closer look at one of the groups, Generation X, illustrates generational segmentation. The aggregate income of this cohort is estimated at $1.8 trillion. From a marketing perspective, however, Generation X consists of three subgroups: (1) college and graduate students, (2) up-and-coming professionals, and (3) young married couples. All three subgroups have grown up with television and been saturated with advertising. Therefore, a more integrated approach will be necessary to reach them.

The most effective medium for Generation X is the Internet, not television. This cohort group averages 9.3 hours per week surfing the Internet, more than any other cohort group. Approximately 43 percent of this group is interested in music sites on the Web. Another 43 percent enjoys online games. An additional large segment is interested in sports sites. Integrating the Internet with television advertising can further increase the impact on this group.

Segmentation by Geographic Area

Another form of segmentation is by geographic area or region. This method is especially useful for retailers that want to limit marketing communications programs to specific areas. It also helps a company conduct a direct-mail campaign in a target area. The primary disadvantage of this approach is that everyone in a geographic area receives the marketing communication or is exposed to the advertisement, regardless of their interest in the product or service. Geographic segmentation does not allow a firm to focus in on a more specific target market containing only those most likely to make purchases.

Geographic segmentation should be reserved for more basic products (restaurants, foods) or items of specific interest to a region. For example, *Sports Illustrated* now offers "Championship Editions" in limited geographic regions when college and professional football or basketball teams win championships.

Geodemographic Segmentation

A hybrid form of geographic segmentation allows companies to enrich geographic approaches to segmentation. This new form of segmentation, called geodemographics, combines census data with psychographic information. This method is more powerful in targeting a firm's customers because it combines census demographic information, geographic information, and psychographic information into one package.

Geodemographic segmentation is especially beneficial for national firms that want to conduct a direct-mail campaign or use a sampling promotion. Normally, it is too expensive and unwise to mail a sample to every household in America. Through geodemographics, a firm can send samples to the households that match the profile of a target market. For instance, colleges and universities use geodemographics to locate zip codes of communities that match their student profiles.

One firm PRIZM (Potential Rating Index by Zip Marketing) specializes in geodemographics. PRIZM has identified 62 different market segments in the United States. The company has categorized every zip code within the United States. The concept behind PRIZM is that zip codes represent neighborhoods containing people with more uniform characteristics. Consumers tend to be attracted to neighborhoods consisting of people similar to themselves. Recognizing that more than one market segment may live within a zip code, PRIZM identifies the top market segments within each zip code.

For example, a PRIZM-coded map of downtown Jackson, Mississippi, identifies two primary clusters. The more predominant is the "Southside City" residents. This cluster is mainly young and elderly African Americans employed in low-paying blue-collar jobs. They tend to have lower levels of formal education, rent apartments, and read sports and fashion magazines. The second cluster within downtown Jackson is labeled as the "Towns and Gowns" neighborhoods. Towns and Gowns inhabitants also rent apartments, but members tend to be college graduates with better-paying white-collar jobs. This group likes to ski, reads beauty and fitness magazines, and uses ATM cards heavily.[16]

Geodemographic marketing has been expanded to the Internet. Adfinity, designed by Intelligent Interactions, allows an advertiser to direct specific ads to Web users based on user-defined demographics. Often, when users visit Web sites, they provide their names and addresses along with other demographic information to gain access. While the user is surfing a site, Adfinity's software can access the user's file in order to place a targeted ad on the page. To extend its power and effectiveness, Adfinity formed a strategic alliance with PRIZM. When a user accesses a Web site, the user is matched with data from the 62 PRIZM clusters. Based on the lifestyle and interests of that cluster, messages are sent to the user that match. For example, if the person is from the cluster "Executive Suites," then an advertisement about jazz or business books may appear, because people in the Executive Suites cluster tend to prefer those items.

A television advertisement using a benefit segmentation strategy.
Source: Courtesy of BB&T.

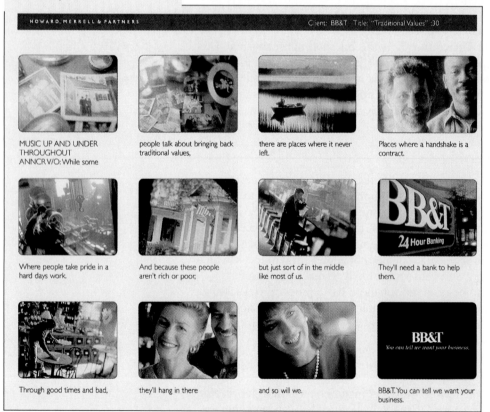

Benefit Segmentation

Benefit segmentation focuses on the advantages consumers receive from a product rather than the characteristics of consumers themselves. Demographics and psychographic information can be combined with benefit information to better identify segments. Then, the company can seek to further understand each segment's consumers.

Benefit segmentation has been used in the fitness market. Regular exercisers belong in one of three benefit segments. The first group, called "winners," do whatever it takes to stay physically fit. This segment tends to be younger, upwardly mobile, and career oriented. The second group, "dieters," exercise to maintain weight control and physical appearance. This group tends to be females over the age of 35. They are primarily interested in reliable wellness programs offered by hospitals and weight control nutritionists. The third group, "self-improvers," exercise to feel better and to control medical costs.[17] Understanding that individuals exercise for different reasons provides excellent material for a fitness center to design a marketing program.

Benefit segmentation can be very helpful in understanding what customers seek from a product. By tying these benefits to demographic and psychographic data, companies use this information to design targeted messages for each market segment.

Usage Segmentation

The final type of consumer segmentation is based on customer usage or purchases. The goal of usage segmentation is to provide the highest level of service to a firm's best customers while promoting the company to casual or light users. Usage segmentation is also designed to maximize sales to all user groups.[18]

Many companies can identify heavy users by utilizing their own databases. With bar code scanners, point-of-sale systems, and data from credit, debit, and transaction cards, in-house marketers can accumulate a wealth of information about their customers. Most companies are learning that between 10 percent and 30 percent of their customers generate 70 percent to 90 percent of their sales. Instead of using firms such as PRIZM to create customer clusters, firms develop their own customer clusters from their own databases. They place customers in clusters based on common attitudes, lifestyles, and past purchase behaviors. This technique offers a business the following advantages:[19]

1. A meaningful classification scheme to cluster customers based on a firm's actual customers.

2. The ability to reduce large volumes of customer data down to a few concise, usable clusters.

3. The ability to assign a cluster code number to each customer in the database. Each number is based on the customer's actual purchases and other characteristics (address, amount spent, credit versus cash, etc.).

4. The capacity to measure the growth and migration of customers over time and from one cluster to another, which allows for the evaluation of marketing programs.

5. The capability of using a database to develop multiple clusters based on different benefits or usages.

Not all businesses have such extensive databases. For these types of businesses, several companies sell and provide consumer databases. These consumer databases can be linked to a customer's records through a name, address, or social security number. These commercial databases contain typical information such as the household's income, the ages of household members, the length and type of residence, information about car ownership, and telephone numbers.

In summary, there are many ways to segment a consumer market. Each has advantages and disadvantages. The best methods depend on the circumstances of the company. In choosing a segmentation approach, a marketer should use the method that provides the best information and that helps in designing the best integrated marketing communications package. Remember, it is important to match the company's goods and services to its overall message and also to fit the message to the needs of various market segments, as shown in Figure 5.10. As the figure indicates, all three components must blend together and build upon one another in order to have an effectively integrated plan for the IMC program.

Goods and Services

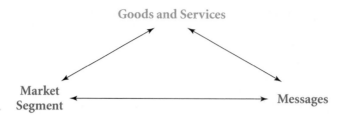

FIGURE 5.10

Market Segment ← → Messages

INTEGRATED LEARNING EXPERIENCE

For consumer markets, a leading geodemographic firm is Claritas. Go to its Web site at **www.claritas.com** and explore the various methods of segmentation. Gen-X Press at **www.genxpress.com** is a leading developer of marketing solutions for Generations X and Y consumers. Another valuable tool is American Demographics at **www.marketingtools.com**. What information and articles does American Demographics provide to assist in understanding a particular market segment?

BUSINESS-TO-BUSINESS SEGMENTATION

Some approaches to segmentation used to differentiate consumers can also be used to define business-to-business markets. There are also alternate methods. Figure 5.11 lists the various ways of segmenting business-to-business markets. Keep in mind that, as with consumer markets, the primary goals of segmentation are to provide better customer service and to group homogeneous customers into clusters to enhance the marketing effort.

Segmentation by Industry

The first method of segmentation is to decipher which industries contain potential customers. To do so, many firms use the NAICS (North American Industry Classification System) code. The NAICS code is replacing the SIC (Standard Industrial Classification) coding system. Firms can target specific industries such as construction (23) or wholesale trade (42). They also can segment within a specific category. For example, NAICS codes health care and social assistance services as 62. A company that manufactures health-related products can divide the market into four segments based on the subsections. These four market segments are:

621	Ambulatory Health Care Services
622	Hospitals
623	Nursing and Residential Care Facilities
624	Social Assistance

▶ **NAICS/SIC code**

▶ **Type of business**

▶ **Size of business**

▶ **Geographic location**

▶ **Product usage**

▶ **Purchase decision process**

▶ **Customer value**

FIGURE 5.11

Methods of Segmenting Business-to-Business Markets

If these segments are too broad, a company breaks each segment down into smaller sub-components. For example, Ambulatory Health Care Services includes physicians, dentists, chiropractors, and optometrists.

The NAICS divides the economy into 20 broad sectors instead of the 10 used by the SIC system and uses a six-digit code rather than the SIC four-digit code. The six-digit code allows greater stratification of industries and provides greater flexibility in creating classifications. The federal government records corporate information and data using the NAICS, making it a logical system to choose for identifying market segments.

Segmentation by Business

A second method of segmentation is by the type of business served in a business-to-business relationship. This approach is similar to the NAICS system. Also, it identifies various targets within a business, such as "low-end" versus "high-end" companies, in which low-end firms purchase lesser quality or reduced-price items. Business segmentation allows the marketing firm to tailor the same product or service to individual business customers.

Segmentation by Size

Another segmentation approach for businesses is by size of customers. The rationale for this method is that large firms have different needs than do smaller companies and therefore should be contacted in a different manner. For instance, the marketing effort often focuses on the other company's purchasing department when the firm is large. For smaller firms, the owner or general manager often makes the purchase decisions.

Segmentation by Geographic Location

As with consumer segmentation, geographic segmentation of businesses can be a successful tactic. This approach especially benefits businesses whose customers are concentrated in geographic pockets such as the Silicon Valley area of California. It works for other firms as well. When the Applied Microbiology firm developed a new antimicrobial agent, it needed to market it to dairy farmers. The traditional agricultural marketing and distribution channel required to launch such a new product nationally was estimated at $3 million. Such a traditional marketing plan involved national advertising in agriculture magazines plus recruiting sales agents and brokers to introduce the product.

Instead, Applied Microbiology used geodemographics, which combined geographic areas with demographic and psychographic data. Applied Microbiology used geodemographics to find areas with dairy herds consisting of 1,000 or more cows per ranch. These farmers were contacted for two reasons. First, large dairy farmers who adopted the product would buy greater quantities of it. Second, Applied Microbiology believed that the larger farmers were opinion leaders who would influence smaller farmers, thereby causing them to adopt the product.

The company mailed several separate direct-response pieces offering discounts and samples of the new product to larger farms. After sales started rising, Applied Microbiology asked farmers for testimonials. These testimonials were extremely powerful, and the company incorporated them into new direct-marketing pieces. One brochure contained three testimonials and validation of the product by Cornell University. After a dairy farmer adopted the product, direct-marketing pieces were sent to farmers in the surrounding area. Not only did this method bring excellent results, the marketing costs were one-third of the traditional approach. Using geodemographics cost only $1 million, not the traditional $3 million expenditure.[20]

Segmentation by Product Usage

Business markets can be segmented by how the product or service is used. Many services (financial, transportation, shipping, etc.) have a variety of uses for distinct customers. For example, in the hotel industry, a major source of revenue is booking business events and conferences. A hotel or resort may segment the business market based on various types of

An advertisement targeted to the large business conference segment.
Source: Courtesy of Edgewater Beach Resort.

events. Single-day seminars require only a meeting room and refreshments. A full conference may involve renting rooms for lodging, preparing banquets, furnishing meeting rooms, and planning sightseeing excursions. By segmenting the market based on the use of the hotel's facilities and staff, a manager can prepare marketing materials that address the needs of each specific type of conference. The advertisement by Edgewater Beach Resort is an example of this type of approach.

Segmentation by Purchase Decision Process

Another approach to business segmentation addresses the purchase decision process, which consists of three segments: (1) first-time prospects, (2) novices, and (3) sophisticates.[21] Each segment has specific requirements and may be convinced to purchase through different kinds of marketing tactics.

First-time prospects are companies that have never purchased a particular product or service but have started evaluating vendors. *Novices* are first-time customers who have made a recent purchase of the product or service. *Sophisticates* are companies that have already purchased the product and are ready to rebuy or have just made repeat purchases.

The key to taking advantage of this form of segmentation is understanding the needs of each segment. First-time prospects want someone to care for them. They are nervous and unsure of themselves because they have never purchased the particular good or service. They tend to rely on sales reps who know and understand their businesses. Buyers want someone they can trust. They do not want someone who talks industry jargon and cannot relate to them. Because of these needs, first-time prospects often prefer buying directly from the manufacturer. With no experience to utilize in making decisions, first-time buyers are hesitant to use catalogs or direct mail and prefer not dealing with a distributor.

Novices have recently purchased the good or service and seek different benefits as a result. They are more likely to have overcome feelings of uncertainty and a lack of trust. Novices are concerned with improving product utilization. They desire manuals and hot lines that answer questions as well as dependable service. Many novices are ready to buy from catalogs and distributors. The key for this business segment is to provide strong customer support.

Sophisticates have experience with purchasing the product so they are looking for a relationship. They evaluate the track records of vendors and are especially concerned about how quickly a vendor can react to an emergency. They are also interested in customization of a good or service and want a company that will work with them specifically and not just sell standardized components. Sophisticates are also very concerned about costs. They are willing to buy from catalogs and distributors as long as the product or service is customized to their needs.

Developing a marketing campaign using this segmentation approach requires careful attention to the appeal. For first-time prospects, the firm emphasizes trust and its long history in the marketplace. Salespeople are extremely important. Advertising and direct marketing are likely to be ineffective. For novices, the marketing appeal must switch to customer service. Salespeople are not as important with this group. The company uses advertising and direct-marketing techniques. With the last group, sophisticates, direct marketing is very successful. Price and customization are the keys to selling to this group. Although salespeople can be used, telemarketing accomplishes the same results with lower costs.

Segmentation by Customer Value

The last method of business segmentation is based on customer value. This method of segmentation is much easier for business-to-business firms to utilize than it is for consumer businesses, due to the availability of in-depth data about each business customer. A more concise value can be assigned to each individual business through sales records and other sources of data and information. This method of segmentation is illustrated by Case 1, Commercial Consolidated, at the end of the chapter.

In summary, when choosing the communication objective, it is important to decide what the desired response should be. Sometimes a company wants its customers to quickly purchase a product or service. In others, marketing managers try to persuade customers that their product is better than the competition's. For other companies, the goal is to convince a retail store to allocate more shelf space for certain products. The desired response should be based on the communication market analysis discussed in the previous section.

INTEGRATED LEARNING EXPERIENCE

The North American Industry Classification System (NAICS) developed by the federal government is available at **www.census.gov/epcd/www/naics.html**. It is also available at the Industrial Who's Who Web site at **www.industrialwhoswho. com.** This Web site does not provide the NAICS information but does offer SIC codes for comparison. It also lists the various manufacturing categories and information about companies within each one.

IMPLICATIONS FOR GIMC PROGRAMS

As first presented in Chapter 1, globally integrated marketing communications (GIMC) programs are vital for international firms. The world consists of many different languages and cultures. Brand names, marketing ideas, and advertising campaigns devised for one country do not always translate correctly to another. Consequently, understanding the international market is essential. Figure 5.12 highlights the ingredients of successful globally integrated marketing communications plans.

Recognizing the many cultural nuances throughout the world is one key. This does not mean that different marketing campaigns must be developed for each country and each cultural group within a country. Still, marketers must understand the region and its culture in order to tailor messages to individual areas.

A borderless marketing plan suggests that the firm should use the same basic marketing approach for all of its various markets. At the same time, it allows each subsidiary the freedom to determine how to implement that marketing plan. This presents the opportunity to maintain a theme while targeting the message carefully.

The same idea applies to the concept of thinking globally but acting locally. The same basic message is used throughout all markets, but how it is presented specifically within a given country may vary.

> ▶ **Understand the international market**
>
> ▶ **A borderless marketing plan**
>
> ▶ **Thinking globally but acting locally**
>
> ▶ **Local partnerships**
>
> ▶ **Communication segmentation strategies**
>
> ▶ **Market communications analysis**
>
> ▶ **Solid communication objectives**

FIGURE 5.12
Successful Globally Integrated Marketing Communications Tactics

Another key to a successful GIMC is developing local partnerships. Local partners can be marketing research firms or advertising firms that are familiar with the local language and culture. These partnerships sometimes are formed by hiring someone from a particular country with a full understanding of the market. Such a person is sometimes referred to as a **cultural assimilator.** It is also vital that the chosen individual has a clear understanding of the English language or the language of the parent firm and the parent firm's business.

As with domestic markets, segmentation is critical. The goal is to design a communications package that effectively communicates to all the market segments. Care must be given to identify target markets within other countries, using one or more of the tactics described in the consumer and business-to-business segmentation programs outlined earlier in this chapter.

A well-designed market communications analysis process is a key factor in the success of a GIMC program. Marketing managers must identify strengths and weaknesses of local competitors and places in which opportunities exist. They must also develop an understanding of how their own firms are perceived in the international marketplace.

Finally, solid communication objectives based on an effective market communication analysis greatly improve the chances that a GIMC program will be successful. Linguistics is a major hurdle to overcome. Translating an English advertisement into another language requires expertise, because exact word translations often do not exist. For example, the slogan of Ruth's Steak House, "We sell sizzle as well as steaks," could not be translated into Spanish, because there is no equivalent word for sizzle. Therefore, the translator found a Spanish idiom conveying a similar meaning in order to solve the problem.

The promotions opportunity analysis process is difficult in international settings; however, it is crucial in creating an effective GIMC. Language, culture, norms, beliefs, and laws all must be taken into consideration in the development of the GIMC program. Literal translation of a commercial's tagline may not be acceptable within a given culture. Laws concerning advertising and promotions vary by country. Further, cultures view ideas and objects differently. These differences must be considered when designing an integrated program. Also, remember that humor is especially difficult to move across cultures and languages.

Without a solid market communication analysis, international communication programs have a high chance of failing. On the other hand, one good thing about international markets is that many of the communications objectives are the same. In all countries, marketers must make consumers aware of their product or service. Marketers must break through local clutter and garner the attention of their audience. They must be able to communicate ideas effectively about their product or service. They also must present the product or service using emotions and imagery that will speak effectively to the target audience. And finally, they must somehow find a way of persuading their target audience to purchase the product or service.

SUMMARY

A promotions opportunity analysis is the process by which marketers identify target audiences for the goods and services produced by the company. It consists of five steps: conduct a communication market analysis, establish communications objectives, create a communications budget, prepare promotional strategies, and match tactics with strategies. Along the way, marketing managers must conduct a competitive analysis, an opportunity analysis, a target market analysis, a customer analysis, and a positioning analysis.

Market segmentation is identifying sets of business or consumer groups with distinct characteristics. Segments must be clearly different, large enough to support a marketing campaign, and reachable through some type of media. Consumer groups that can be segmented include those identified by demographics. These are gender, age, income, and ethnic heritage. Markets can also be segmented using psychographic, generational, and geographic delineations. Geodemographic segmentation combines demographic, psychographic, and geographic information together. Other methods to categorize consumers are by the benefits they receive from products or services and by the ways they use products.

Business-to-business segmentation can be accomplished by targeting business customers by industry, business type, size of the company, geographic location, usage, purchase decision processes, and customer value calculations. Marketing managers need to spend sufficient time specifying both consumer and business market segments, because all other promotions opportunity analysis processes are tied to the identification of key customers.

Globally integrated marketing communications efforts must also be linked to promotions opportunities analysis programs. National differences, cultural concerns, language issues, and other challenges must be viewed in light of the target markets an individual company intends to serve.

A promotions opportunity analysis program is the first step in developing a complete IMC package. Based on an overall marketing plan, company leaders gather information and generate decisions regarding target markets and marketing opportunities. They proceed to develop a further understanding of the company's image and dig deeper into the process of revealing key consumer and business buyer behaviors. They should address their message and theme to mesh with the overall IMC plan. This stage is a foundation stage in an IMC program. A solid marketing plan and promotional analysis program help the company build the rest of the IMC plan and greatly increase the chances that marketing messages will reach the right audiences. This leads to increased sales, customer loyalty, and a stronger long-term standing in the marketplace.

REVIEW QUESTIONS

1. What is a promotions opportunities analysis? Why is it a critical part of a company's marketing effort?

2. How are the components of an IMC plan comparable to the steps of a promotions opportunities analysis?

3. What are the five parts of a promotions opportunities analysis planning process?

4. What common marketing communications objectives do firms establish?

5. Name and describe the types of communications budgets. Which is best? Why?

6. What is a strategy? Give an example of a promotional strategy.

7. What are tactics? How are they related to strategies?

8. Give some examples of tactics companies can use to support promotional strategies.

9. Define demographics. How are they used to segment consumer markets?

10. How can firms take advantage of target markets by gender?

11. What generational cohorts have marketing experts identified?

12. What problems are associated with segmented markets by geographic areas?

13. What are geodemographics? Why have they been so successful in defining marketing segments?

14. Describe usage segmentation and benefit segmentation.

15. What are the common business-to-business market segmentation concepts?

16. What is a NAICS approach to segmentation? Why is it better than the old SIC format?

17. Describe a usage segmentation approach in a business-to-business setting.

18. Describe a segmentation approach based on company size.

19. How does the idea of a promotions opportunities analysis fit with a GIMC program?

KEY TERMS

promotions opportunity analysis the process by which marketers identify target audiences for the goods and services produced by the company.

communication market analysis the process of discovering the organization's strengths and weaknesses in the area of marketing communication, and combining that information with an analysis of opportunities and threats that are present in the firm's external environment.

competitive analysis the identification of competitors in the marketplace.

opportunity analysis watching carefully for new marketing opportunities.

target market analysis the examination of the target market to recognize specific needs.

customer analysis studying three distinct types of customers—current company customers, the competition's customers, and potential customers—who may become interested in purchasing from a particular company.

positioning creating a perception in the consumer's mind regarding the nature of a company and its products relative to the competition.

benchmark measures starting points that are studied in relation to the degree of change following a promotional campaign.

threshold effects for new products, initial advertisements yield little behavioral response; however, over time, a consumer who is exposed enough times to a company's marketing message will recall the company and eventually become willing to make a purchase

Sales-Response Function Curve an S-shaped curve that indicates when threshold effects are present and when diminishing returns are present.

concave downward function a model of the diminishing returns of advertisements on sales.

marginal analysis a model that shows when additional expenditures on advertising and promotions have an adverse affect on profits.

carryover effects when products are only purchased when needed, promotions for those products must be designed to generate a situation in which the consumer has been exposed to the company's message for so long that when the time comes to buy, the consumer remembers the key company.

wear out effects occur when a product simply becomes "old" or "boring" and advertising cannot easily change that perception.

decay effects occur when a company stops advertising and consumers begin to forget about the company.

percentage of sales method a form of communications budgeting in which budgeting is based on the communications budget from the previous year or anticipated sales for the coming year.

meet the competition a method of communications budgeting in which the primary rationale is to prevent the loss of market share, which occurs in highly competitive markets where rivalries between competitors are intense.

arbitrary allocation a budgeting method based on management estimates of what is needed.

the "what we can afford" method a method of communications budgeting in which the marketing budget is set after all of the company's other budgets have been determined and communications monies are allocated based on what the firm feels it can afford to spend.

objective and task method a form of communications budgeting in which management first lists all of the objectives it wants to accomplish during the year and then allocates budget to meet those objectives.

payout planning a budgeting method that establishes a ratio of advertising to sales or market share.

strategies sweeping guidelines concerning the essence of the company's marketing efforts.

tactics the things companies do to support overall promotional strategies.

market segmentation identifying specific purchasing groups based on their needs, attitudes, and interests.

market segment a set of businesses or group of individual consumers with distinct characteristics.

demographics the study of population characteristics.

psychographics the study of patterns of responses that reveal a person's attitudes, interests, and opinions (AIO).

cultural assimilator a person who is familiar with the local language and culture of a given country who can help marketing efforts in that particular country.

CRITICAL THINKING EXERCISES

Discussion Questions

1. Use a search engine to locate five companies on the Internet that sell swimwear. Do a competitive analysis of these five companies to find the type of products they sell, the type of promotional appeal they use, and the type of special offers they use to entice buyers. What type of advertising strategy would you use to sell swimwear over the Internet?

2. A promotions opportunity analysis of movie theaters reveals the primary moviegoer to be between 18 and 24 years of age. In 1986, 44 percent of the individuals in this age bracket went to movies frequently. Today, less than 34 percent are frequent moviegoers.[22] Conduct a customer analysis by interviewing five individuals between 18 and 24. Based on their responses, what suggestions would you make to movie theaters to reverse this declining trend?

3. Make a list of five consumer goods or services segmented on the basis of gender but sold to both genders. Are there any differences in the product or service attributes? Are there differences in how they are marketed? What are those differences? Do you think using a different marketing approach has worked?

4. For each of the following goods or services, identify the various benefits that consumers may derive from the product or service. Can you think of an advertisement or other marketing communication that has used the benefit as the central part of its appeal?

   a. Seafood restaurant

   b. Auto insurance

   c. Optometrist or eye care clinic

   d. Soft drink

   e. Aspirin or other pain reliever

5. Choose one of the following Internet companies. Access each company's Web site, and determine what segmentation strategy the firm uses. Describe who is the target market for the Web site. Using Figure 5.3 as a guide, what communication objective(s) do you think the company is trying to fulfill with its Web site?

   a. Sports Spectrum Greeting Cards (www.sportsgreetingcards.com)

   b. Ty Beanie Babies (www.ty.com)

   c. American Health and Beauty Aids Institute (www.proudlady.org)

   d. Advanced Hardware Architectures (www.aha.com)

   e. Dr. James R. Romano (www.jromano.com)

Conducting a Promotions Opportunity Analysis for Your Product

Each of the products listed in Chapter 1 has various kinds of competitors. In order to build a complete and solid IMC program, it is important to begin by following each of the steps of the promotions opportunity analysis. Also, to succeed, you need to identify key target markets for your item. This includes both consumer markets and business-to-business opportunities. In addition, it will be important to consider the possible international customers as you proceed. Go to the Prentice-Hall Web site at **www.prenhall.com/clow** or access the IMC Plan Pro disk that accompanied this textbook to develop a market analysis for your product by completing the exercise for Chapter 5.

BUILDING AN
IMC
CAMPAIGN

IMC PlanPro !

CASE 1

COMMERCIAL CONSOLIDATED[23]

John Mulvaney had been a marketing account manager for many years. He left a private firm to take a position at a local bank, Commercial Consolidated. Bank officials concluded that because the marketplace for financial services had become so competitive, they needed an on-staff marketing executive to continually fine-tune the bank's advertising program. The company's headquarters were in John's hometown, only 12 blocks from his house. John saw the opportunity to make a "lifestyle" move while staying active in his chosen profession.

Once he was settled in, the first issue John pursued was a promotional analysis, focusing on various customers. His research indicated that in most banks, 10 percent to 20 percent of the small business accounts yield 80 percent to 90 percent of the bank's profitability. Upon being informed of this statistic, bank officials set the goal of moving some of the small businesses within the 80 percent that was not currently profitable to become more like the 10 percent to 20 percent.

John told the bank's leaders that he wanted to pursue a customer valuation segmentation approach, assigning each business a value related to the bank's level of profitability. To illustrate how this segmentation method works, John described the ways banks could market to small businesses. He noted that the first step in customer value segmentation is to identify the drivers that impact each business customer's profitability potential. For a bank providing financial services to small businesses, the primary value drivers are:

1. Deposit balances wherein interest and other revenues exceed requirements for servicing the account

2. Consistent fee income from sundry banking and financial services

3. Efficient lending practices emphasizing underwriting, approval, and processing of profitable loans

4. Targeted customer development focusing on building relationships that would lead to profitable transactions between the bank and the small business

5. Sales and service delivery programs that match the bank's profitability goals

(continued)

John told Commercial Consolidated's management team that not all customers have the potential to be highly profitable accounts. He noted that by segmenting its small customers into customer value clusters, the bank could design different marketing programs for each segment to maximize effectiveness while minimizing marketing costs. He suggested putting a greater marketing effort into an account with high profitability potential than into one with low potential for profitability.

The marketing team decided to segment various small-business customers along several dimensions. Codes placed in each customer's data file allowed for easy clustering. The team used seven characteristics to code the bank's small-business customers. Account managers were given the following instructions for each account and its particular characteristics:

1. **Value segment.** Code the account based on how profitable it has been over the last 12 months. Codes range from highly profitable to unprofitable.

2. **Long-term value segment.** Code the account based on profitability potential for the next five years.

3. **Industry growth potential segment.** Code the growth potential of the industry in which the firm operates, from high-growth industry to negative anticipated growth.

4. **Industry position segment.** Relative to the industry, code the size of the firm from large to small within the same industry.

5. **Transaction frequency segment.** Code the business customers from high to low based on frequency of transactions with the bank over the past six months.

6. **Product propensity segment.** Code the business customers based on their propensity to purchase a 401(k) plan with the bank. This code would be based on the firm's size and growth characteristics, from high potential for a 401(k) to low potential.

7. **Creditworthiness segment.** The code indicates the businesses' relative credit risk.

This coding system allowed the bank greater flexibility in designing its marketing program. The codes identified customers with the highest profit potential based on these factors.

Commercial Consolidated's overall theme had always been focused on its "hometown" bank image. Advertisements and other promotions restated the message that dollars invested locally were more valuable to the community than those shipped to the home office of a competitor in another city or state.

Using this technique, a bank could assign customers to clusters based on loan usage. Another set of clusters could be developed for investment services. A bank could develop many different clusters with customers assigned to clusters based on their purchase behavior of that particular type of service.

From there the bank generated an aggressive marketing program including advertising, direct-mail pieces, and some personal visits to companies with high profit potential. Customers with a medium level of transaction frequency could be targeted to increase their transactions with the bank if their potential was high. The bank aimed the direct marketing program at its top 20 customers; advertising was designed to reach the next 100 customers (in terms of profit potential); and the remainder of the firm's advertising funds were spent on brand awareness commercials.

Next, individual consumers were segmented and targeted. The bank was most interested in increasing use of their highly profitable consumer credit card. To do so, it needed to understand the usage of the credit card. The bank's customer cluster analysis identified the following seven clusters:

1. **The uncommitted.**   The newest users of the credit card, these individuals tended to use the card infrequently and make relatively small purchases. This cluster primarily consisted of retired persons and individuals with low incomes.

2. **Convenience users.**   These customers used their cards frequently and normally paid off their balances at the end of each monthly billing cycle. This cluster tended to have below average assets and slightly less than average household income.

3. **Starting out.**   This cluster was predominantly young adults with lower than average incomes and low assets. They tended to have high purchases and carry moderate to high balances on their cards.

4. **Channel shoppers.**   Consists of older cardholders, these individuals had the highest income levels and were primarily females or married couples. This cluster had a low level of delinquency, low service charges, and moderate card activity.

5. **Credit addicts.**   This group had the longest tenure of cardholders in the bank. They had the highest credit limits, the greatest spending, and the highest payments due each month. This cluster was of average age with above average income.

6. **Cash driven.**   As the cash-hungry cluster, these individuals tended to pay off account balances slowly, had moderate credit limits, and used the card frequently to garner cash advances. This cluster generally included younger males and other singles with low assets.

7. **Borderline.**   The youngest of the clusters with the lowest card activity, these customers had a high delinquency rate and had low incomes.

Using the cluster information, the bank sought to expand revenues by targeting current customers. They developed specialty marketing communication pieces for each cluster. Based on the demographic and psychographic information from each cluster, marketing pieces were designed to elicit responses. This clustering information helped the bank prevent customer defections to the competition by meeting the needs of each individual segment. To maximize the success of the program, the firm's marketing team made sure that the correct services were matched with customer needs. This information was used to focus media and advertising strategies creating specific messages for specific customers.

Within a few months, bank profits had risen significantly. John received a healthy raise and concluded he had made a wise choice in moving to this particular organization.

1. Explain how the steps of a promotions opportunity analysis are present in this case.

2. Explain why John and Commercial Consolidated were so successful.

3. Based on information in this case, design a business-to-business print advertisement offering local businesses "loans" or "investment services." Where should the ad be placed? Why?

4. Choose one of the credit-card customer clusters listed in the case. Design a print advertisement to reach this group. Where should the print ad be placed? What other marketing tools could be used with the print advertisement?

CASE 2

MIKE'S REAL ESTATE

Mike Kelly, a lifelong resident of Fremont, Nebraska, had built a successful career in real estate by knowing everyone who mattered in his small community. Mike's Real Estate competed successfully against ReMax, Century 21, Realty Executives, and other firms that offered alternatives when people were ready to buy or sell a home or business.

Mike's business concept was simple. He hired only real estate agents who had been residents of Fremont for at least 10 years. He insisted on loyalty combined with an intense drive to make the real estate transaction as painless as possible for all concerned. Mike's activity in several local community events and charities gained name recognition for himself and his company.

Mike's firm developed one key advantage during the late 1980s. Prior to that time, all real estate companies had charged a fee of 6 percent of the sale price of a house to the seller. With inflation and other pressures, the larger chains raised that fee to 7 percent. Mike held the line at 6 percent. Even though Mike had experienced several unfriendly visits from local agents from other companies complaining about the price difference, he held his ground. He knew these same agencies circulated rumors about his personal life (Mike was divorced), his lack of "professionalism," and other negative comments. The same was true for the sale of businesses. Mike charged 10 percent. Several realty companies had progressed to 15 percent. As a result, even with the unethical tactics used by the competition, based on price alone, Mike's Real Estate had an advantage accentuated by the personal attention given to clients.

As the new century began, however, the field changed. One major challenge was a shift in residents. Fremont had emerged partly as a "bedroom" community serving Omaha. In other words, many people lived in Fremont but worked in the city of Omaha. This gave realtors in Omaha an advantage, because they could provide listings and a retail site in both towns. Someone living in Omaha but seeking a more quiet, smaller community would probably first call a realtor in the city, meaning Mike had lost many potential customers.

The second most significant challenge was the Internet. The larger companies were able to post their listings worldwide through Web sites. A house or business could be shown to virtually anyone, anywhere. Even though Mike added a computer specialist to build his own site, the edge he had of being "local" was lost, and the difference in fees was not enough to be able to sell a house at a lower price or to persuade a local seller to list with his company rather than a national firm with worldwide exposure.

In the previous fiscal year, Mike's listings (houses for sale registered with his company) had declined by 20 percent. He was forced to cut his staff by one person. Fortunately, one of his agents had decided to move out of the area, so he did not have to actually fire someone. Meanwhile, he was getting fewer and fewer walk-in customers. His Internet "hits" were not very substantial. Many businesses simply ignored him when he asked about being the listing agent when they decided to sell.

Mike's costs were also rising, and his agents complained that they received less per sale than those in other companies. He began to worry that he might actually lose some of his staff. It was time to take action, but he wasn't sure what to do.

1. Is Mike's situation hopeless? Why or why not?

2. What should Mike do to increase his business and revenues?

3. What, if any, market segment still exists for Mike's Real Estate?

4. Outline a communication market analysis plan for Mike's Real Estate. For each step in the communication market analysis listed in Figure 5.2, identify how Mike's Real Estate should proceed.

5. What type of segmentation strategy should Mike pursue?

ENDNOTES

1. Christy Edison, "Thinking Out of the (Shoe) Box," *Across The Board,* 36, no. 3 (March 1999), pp. 9–10; Mike Troy, "New Cards Alter Discount Convention," *Discount Store News,* 37, no. 16 (August 24, 1998), p. 35; Seth Mendelson, "Card Sharks," *Discount Merchandiser,* 38, no. 8 (August 1998), pp. 73–77; "Sell-through Is in the Details: Refined Assortments Tap Consumer Gold," *Discount Store News,* 37, no. 22 (November 23, 1998), pp. S5–S7; Mike Troy, "An Ideal Dose of Consistency," *Discount Store News,* 37, no. 23 (December 14, 1998), pp. 57, 74; Joe Dysart, "Getting the Most from Your Greeting Card Department," *Drug Topics,* 137, no. 14 (July 19, 1993), pp. 48–50; Renee Covino Rouland, "Greeting Card Boutiques, Take Two," *Discount Merchandiser,* 35, no. 6 (June 1995), pp. 68–70.

2. "Unique Adds a Twist to Frequent Dining," *Nation's Restaurant News,* 28, no. 22 (May 30, 1994), p. 12.

3. Bob Lamons, "How to Set Politically Correct Ad Budgets," *Marketing News,* 29, no. 25 (December 4, 1995), p. 6.

4. James O. Peckham, "Can We Relate Advertising Dollars to Market Share Objectives?" in *How Much to Spend for Advertising,* M. A. McNiver (ed). New York: Association of National Advertisers, 1969, p. 30.

5. "Schonfeld: Strong '98 Bodes Well for 1999," *Advertising Age's Business Marketing,* 83, no. 7 (July 1998), p. 6.

6. Cyndee Miller, "Marketing Industry Report: Consumer Marketers Spend Most of Their Money on Communications," *Marketing News,* 30, no. 6 (March 11, 1996), pp. 1–2; Cyndee Miller, "Marketing Industry Report: Who's Spending What on Biz-to-Biz Marketing," *Marketing News,* 30, no. 1 (January 1, 1996), pp. 1–2.

7. Laurie Freeman, "B-to-B Marketing Communication Budgets Grow 14.5% as Overall Spending Reaches $73 Billion," *Advertising Age's Business Marketing,* 84, no. 5 (May 1999), pp. S3–S4.

8. Matthew Martinez, "Reed Study Sees Where Ad Dollars Go," *Advertising Age's Business Marketing,* 82, no. 9 (October 1997), p. 46.

9. Cyndee Miller, "Study Dispels '80s Stereotypes of Women," *Marketing News,* 29 (May 22, 1995), p. 3.

10. Andy Bernstein, "Study: Women Vital to Pro Sports," *Denver Business Journal,* 50, no. 14 (December 4, 1998), p. 62.

11. Interview with Kerri Martin, brand manager of BMW Motorcycles, July 18, 2000.

12. Eick Adler, "Stereotypes Won't Work with Seniors Anymore," *Advertising Age,* 67, no. 46 (November 11, 1996), p. 32.

13. George P. Moschis, "Life Stages of the Mature Market," *American Demographics* (September 1996), pp. 44–47.

14. Alf Nucifora, "Ethnic Markets Are Lands of Opportunity," *Business Journal Serving Phoenix & the Valley of the Sun,* 18, no. 52 (October 16, 1998), p. 31; Steve Climons and David O'Connor, "Marketers Lose Out by Ignoring Ethnic Segments," *Advertising Age,* 70, no. 10 (May 10, 1999), p. 40.

15. Rebecca Piirto Heath, "Psychographics," *Marketing Tools* (November–December 1995), pp. 74–81.

16. Susan Mitchell, "Birds of a Feather," *American Demographics,* 17, no. 2 (February 1995), pp. 40–45.

17. Ronald L. Zallocco, "Benefit Segmentation of the Fitness Market," *Journal of Health Care Marketing,* 12, no. 4 (December 1992), p. 80.

18. "How Chains Cluster Stores and Find Sales Opportunities," *Drug Store News,* 18, no. 4 (March 4, 1996), p. 50.

19. Susan Pechman, "Custom Clusters: Finding Your True Customer Segments," *Bank Marketing,* 26, no. 7 (July 1994), pp. 33–35.

20. Gene Koprowski, "Bovine Inspiration," *Marketing Tools* (October 1996), pp. 10–11.

21. Thomas S. Robertson and Howard Barich, "A Successful Approach to Segmenting Industrial Markets," *Planning Review,* 20, no. 6 (November–December 1992), pp. 4–11, 48.

22. Shannon Dortch, "Going to the Movies," *American Demographics,* 18, no. 12 (December 1996), pp. 4–8.

23. Information for this fictional case was derived from the following articles: Sandy Berry and Kathryn Britney, "Market Segmentation," *Bank Management,* 72, no. 1 (January–February 1996), pp. 36–40; "Study Reveals Wide Use of Value-Added Cards," *America's Community Banker,* 6, no. 9 (September 1997), p. 43.

Advertising Management

Chapter Objectives

Understand the steps of an effective advertising management process.

Study the roles that the company's overall mission, its products, and its services play in advertising programs.

Recognize when to use an in-house advertising approach and when to go to an external advertising agency.

Review the steps of effective advertising campaign management programs.

Comprehend the functions performed by the advertising account manager and the advertising creative in preparing an advertising campaign.

MARKETING POWER:

Women Plus 40

Of all women buying new cars in 2001, 53 percent were over the age of 40. Of women buying computers, 54 percent were over 40, and of all women who use facial moisturizers, 60 percent were 40 plus. These statistics fly in the face of traditional marketing wisdom which suggests that the 18- to 34-year-old female demographic is the only one that matters. Young women are strong spenders, but their buying clout is smaller than those over 40. As Annette Simon of GSD&M Advertising in Austin, Texas, notes, "I make most of the buying decisions, as do my friends and my mom—let's talk to women like they have a brain." Simon, who is over 40, has created ads for Southwest Airlines, Wal-Mart, and Charles Schwab.

Art director Stuart Pittman from the Kaplan Theatre Group, Ltd. in New York, which is the agency that created the Herbal Essences "Yes, yes yes!" commercials and the AFLAC duck, states, "I like to think of 40-plus as the cocktail hour of your life. Now you're up for a good time." He believes women over 40 are "energized, terrific, and self-assured. Their humor is developed and their attitudes are out there." Jeff Weekly, from D'Arcy Los Angeles, who creates ads for both NBC and Paramount, calls this group "vibrant yet powerful."

The buying potential of women over 40 extends across other demographic divisions. For example, Louis Miguel Messianu, from the Del Rivero Messianu DDB agency in Coral Gables, Florida, suggests, "Hispanic women over 40 can be viewed as the 'chief operating officers' of the household." He believes this group is confident, in control, and discerning.

MORE magazine, which targets women over 40, recently featured a unique approach to understanding the over 40 market. Author Mary Lou Quinlan, a former ad agency CEO, noted the bias that has been a part of traditional marketing thinking. She states, "I've sat in too many casting sessions where I'd hear, 'We need one older woman to round out these models. How about so-and-so? She must be thirty-two.'"

Quinlan and *MORE* magazine arranged for five advertising agencies to create campaigns for the 40-plus group. The point of the ad had to be to change corporate decision-makers' minds about them. The advertising copy which resulted:

- "These Babies Have Boom." (The Kaplan Thaler Group, LTD, New York)
- "Spring Chickens Have Smaller Nest Eggs." (GSD&M Advertising, Austin)
- "If you want my money, stop showing me pictures of my daughter in underwear." (Dimassimo Brand Advertising, New York)
- "At 42, I still kick butt. I just do it in a more expensive shoe." (D'Arcy, Los Angeles)
- "In my house I always have the last word. . . Yes, mi vida (yes honey)." (Del Rivero Messianu, DDB, Coral Gables)

As the baby boom generation continues to age, the 40- and even 50-plus crowd grows larger. Affluence, self-indulgence, and comfort characterize typical boomer buying habits. In the future, more advertisers, who aren't getting any younger themselves, may shift toward this group in growing numbers.[1]

THE BOULDER STOP

Effective management of an advertising program involves a partnership of members of the marketing department with all of the other companies involved. In some instances, this is limited to media providers, such as television and radio stations. In others, the company first selects an advertising agency along with other groups to perform key functions associated with an advertising campaign.

Read the Executive Summary and Promotions Opportunity Analysis sections of The Boulder Stop company on the IMC Plan Pro disk. Try to gain a feeling for the nature of the company, the types of customers, and the general direction of the IMC program. Next, study the IMC Management Section (4.0) along with the Objectives (4.1), Budget (4.2), and Agency Selection process (4.3). Be sure to notice that The Boulder Stop has three different IMC Objectives. The first objective deals with the consumer market, the second with distribution channel, and the last with the business-to-business channel. In an integrated marketing plan, all must be considered simultaneously because each impacts the others. Before leaving The Boulder Stop sample plan, read sections 5.1, 6.1, and 7.1, which describe the advertising budget in greater detail.

As can be seen, the task of managing an advertising program involves careful thought, with a clear linkage between individual IMC objectives and the tactics used to reach those objectives. Advertising is just one element in the overall IMC program.

o v e r v i e w

The average person is exposed to more than 600 advertisements per day. As every marketing manager knows, people are bombarded with messages through an expanding variety of media. Television and radio have long been the staples of advertising programs, and they compete with newspaper and magazine ads, billboards, signs, direct-mail campaigns, and other traditional channels. Recently, the number of ways to contact customers has grown. Ads on the Internet, clothing lines with messages printed on them, telemarketing programs, and even messages heard while a consumer is on hold on the telephone create numerous new opportunities to contact potential customers.

This situation represents a tremendous challenge for marketers. A company simply cannot afford to prepare ads for every possible medium. Choices must be made, and messages must be of sufficient quality to give the company an advantage in a highly cluttered world, a world in which people are becoming increasingly proficient at simply tuning ads out.

To be effective, an ad first must be noticed. Next, it must be remembered. Then, the message of the advertisement should incite some kind of action, such as a purchase, a shift in brand loyalty, or at least a spot in the buyer's long-term memory.

Part 2 of this text deals with the role advertising plays in a complete integrated marketing communications program. Figure 6.1 (on page 164) is a reminder of the overall IMC approach. The upcoming three chapters describe in detail the relationship between a company's advertising program and its IMC plan.

Three ingredients must be combined to create effective advertisements: (1) development of a logical advertising management scheme for the company, (2) careful selection of media, and (3) thoughtful design of the advertisement. Selecting media and designing the actual advertisements go hand in hand: One cannot be performed without the other in mind. Actual discussions of these topics (advertising design and media selection) are presented in separate chapters. Still, it is important to remember that in reality both occur together. Only then will the ad agency or creative department be able to create consistent, effective advertisements and promotional campaigns.

Renew, Refresh, Restore, Rejuvenate, Revitalize...*Remember*

Microdermabrasion
Call today **623-7171**
$35 PER TREATMENT

A simple easy way
to have a youthful, healthy,
complexion. No chemicals,
or discomfort, just a quick
treatment to look fantastic
and feel terrific.

Call us now at **623-7171**

Two advertisements directed at 40-plus
women using middle-aged models.
Source: Used with permission of the *Joplin Glube,*
Joplin, Missouri.

Source: Courtesy of Valpak.

This chapter focuses on advertising management, which lays the groundwork for the total advertising program. Advertising campaign management is the process of preparing and integrating a specific advertising program with the overall IMC message. One key element in this process is to develop the message theme. The **message theme** is an outline of key idea(s) that the advertising program is supposed to convey. The message theme should match the company's overall marketing and IMC strategies. The message theme component of advertising is described in greater detail later.

Chapters 7 and 8 describe the advertising design process. Several primary decisions must be made at that time. They include deciding what leverage point to use, the major appeal in the advertising campaign, and the type of executional framework to use. A **leverage point** is the key element in the advertisement that taps into, or activates, a consumer's personal value system (a value, idea, or concept). The **appeal** is how to design the advertisement that attracts attention or presents information to consumers. Typical appeals include the use of humor, fear, sexual suggestiveness, logic, and emotions. The **executional framework** or theme explains how the message will be delivered. Some examples of executional frameworks include the slice-of-life approach, fantasies, dramatizations, and ads constructed using animation. Chapter 9 describes media selection.

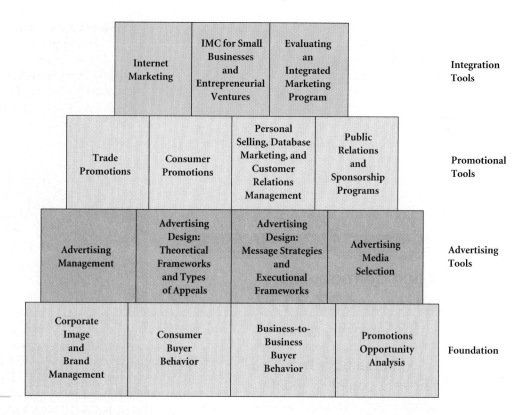

FIGURE 6.1
An IMC Plan

OVERVIEW OF ADVERTISING MANAGEMENT

An **advertising management program** is the process of preparing and integrating a company's advertising efforts with the overall IMC message that already exists. Figure 6.2 indicates how the elements of an advertising program fit together. An effective program consists of four activities, which combine to form the advertising management process. They are:

1. Review the company's activities in light of advertising management.
2. Select an in-house or external advertising agency.
3. Develop an advertising campaign management strategy.
4. Complete a creative brief.

The major principle guiding these four efforts is *consistency*. To be effective in developing successful advertisements, the company's goods or services and methods of doing business need to match the form of advertising agency chosen, the strategy of the campaign, and the work of the advertising creative. The goal is to provide a coherent message that restates the image of the overall IMC program.

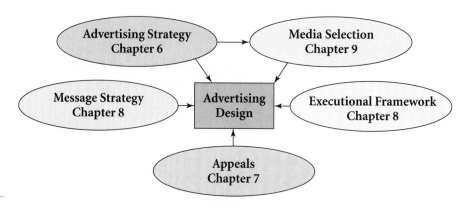

FIGURE 6.2
Advertising Overview

THE ROLE OF ADVERTISING IN THE IMC PROCESS

Advertising is one component of integrated marketing communications, as shown in Figure 6.1. It is also part of the "traditional" promotions mix of advertising, sales and trade promotions, and personal selling. These functions, along with other activities such as direct marketing and public relations efforts, form the basis for communicating with individual consumers and business customers. The role advertising plays varies by company, products, and the marketing goals established by the firm. For some products and companies, advertising is the central focus, with the other components (trade promotions, consumer promotions, and personal selling) used to support various advertising campaigns. In other situations, advertising supports a national sales force and trade promotions programs. In the business-to-business sector, advertising often supports other promotional activities, such as trade shows and personal sales calls. In the consumer sector, the reverse is often true. Advertising usually is the primary communication vehicle in reaching consumers. Other promotional tools (contests, giveaways, special packages) are then used to support the advertising function. In both business-to-business and consumer promotions, the key to using advertising effectively is to see it as one of the spokes in the "wheel" of the promotional effort with the remaining "spokes" being the other components of the IMC approach.

Lucky Brand recognizes that advertising performs a vital role in the establishment of effective communications.
Source: Courtesy of Lucky Brand Jeans.

Remember, an IMC program is more than just promotions and advertising tactics (as described in Chapter 1). Integrated communications include clear communications among departments as well as with outside customers and suppliers. IMC programs apply information technologies to develop databases that help everyone in the firm understand customer needs and characteristics, including both business customers and end user consumers. Effective integrated communications programs mean that every facet of the organization works toward the goal of reaching customers with a clear, consistent message.

Within that framework, advertising plays a *major and vital role* in establishing effective communications. Therefore, a full section of this textbook is devoted to an explanation of how to prepare advertising campaigns and work with account executives, media buyers, and advertising creatives, with the goal of incorporating advertising into the IMC program in a manner designed to effectively and efficiently use all available promotional dollars. As advertising agencies and account managers feel growing pressures to produce tangible results, developing noticeable and measurable advertising outcomes is the major challenge for the advertising agency and for the company itself.[2]

COMPANY ACTIVITIES IN ADVERTISING MANAGEMENT

Successful company leaders build their businesses by carefully tending to a few major activities. One key endeavor is to make sure the firm has a well-thought-out, clearly specified mission statement. The overall mission of an organization is a general outline of the company's direction and purpose. Many times, an IMC program is based on a similar

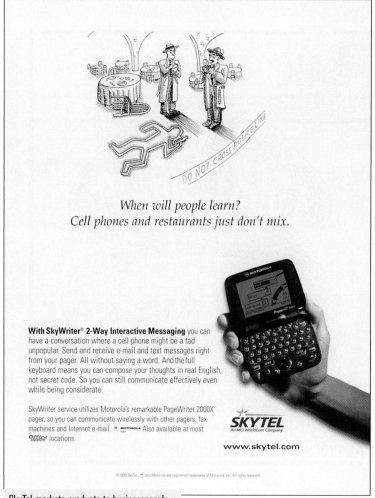

When will people learn?
Cell phones and restaurants just don't mix.

With SkyWriter® 2-Way Interactive Messaging you can have a conversation where a cell phone might be a tad unpopular. Send and receive e-mail and text messages right from your pager. All without saying a word. And the full keyboard means you can compose your thoughts in real English, not secret code. So you can still communicate effectively even while being considerate.

SkyWriter service utilizes Motorola's remarkable PageWriter 2000X pager, so you can communicate wirelessly with other pagers, fax machines and Internet e-mail. Also available at most Office locations.

SKYTEL
An MCI WorldCom Company

www.skytel.com

SkyTel markets products to businesspeople.
Source: Courtesy of SkyTel Corporation.

statement of an overall objective. From there, members of the company can complete the following tasks:

- Identify potential customers.
- Build products and services to meet customer needs.
- Match the company's IMC process with its advertising management program.

These three efforts must be coordinated in order to mesh the company's message with its desired audience while vending various goods and services. Most firms have four general categories of *potential customers:* (1) end users, (2) other businesses, (3) institutions, and (4) governmental customers. Some even argue there is a fifth, international customers. Although marketing to consumers and businesses in another country offers unique challenges, most marketers see it is an extension of these four general categories. As discussed in Chapter 5, it is important to designate which customers are being approached so that the company's messages are attractive to these target markets.

Goods and services are designed, in part, with target markets and customers in mind. For example, the minivan boom in the automobile industry is not an accidental discovery. A large segment of the car-buying community is 30- to 50-year-old parents with higher levels of disposable income who need to haul around kids, groceries, sports equipment, and other bulky items. The response to improved minivan design and heightened efforts to solicit business from well-to-do families is a phenomenal growth in sales of these vehicles, with large profit margins as a result. Similarly, in the business-to-business market, Motorola developed the PageWriter 2000X interactive communicator to meet the needs of business travelers. Motorola formed a partnership with Skytel, which also sells the device and the service. The SkyWriter advertisement featured in this section shows the product's advantage to a business person.

IMC programs and advertising campaigns are much easier to integrate with clearly specified target markets and well-designed goods and services. Thus, when the Discover Card is advertised, key customers are kept in mind as ads for this service are prepared. Effective IMC programs heavily rely on management teams defining the company's mission and aligning company activities into the same integrated, one-voice approach that speaks to all constituents. When these factors are pulled together effectively, the company can commence with more specific advertising projects.

CHOOSING AN ADVERTISING AGENCY

The first step in developing an advertising program is choosing between an in-house advertising group and an external advertising agency. Many larger-size organizations have begun to house integrated communications and advertising programs within internal departments. Part of the reasoning is that internal organization members have a better sense of the company's mission and message. By hiring a few key marketing and advertising experts, many firms can develop effective advertising programs by outsourcing some of the functions, such as the writing, filming, or recording, and editing the actual advertisement in addition to planning and purchasing media time (on television and radio) and space (in magazines, in newspapers, and on billboards). The disadvantage to this approach is that the company can go "stale" in its marketing efforts and fail to recognize other promotional or advertising opportunities. The department also may lack the expertise to carry out all of the necessary functions. Instead, the tendency may be to cut costs in developing ads rather than taking advantage of the knowledge and expertise that advertising agencies have to offer. This is especially true in the international arena, wherein a firm probably lacks the necessary understanding of language and customs, as well as key buyer behaviors in the target market.

Decision Variables

In making the decision to use an external agency or in-house department, a firm considers the following five critical issues:[3]

1. Size of the account
2. Money that can be spent on media
3. Objectivity factor
4. Complexity of the product
5. Creativity issue

Concerning the *account size,* a small account usually is not attractive to an advertising agency, because it sees little opportunity for profit. Also, with regard to *money spent on media,* smaller accounts are less economically sound for the agency, because more money must be spent on producing advertisements rather than on purchasing media time or space. A good rule of thumb is called the 75–15–10 breakdown. That is, 75 percent of the money buys media time or space, 15 percent goes to the agency for the creative work, and 10 percent is spent on the actual production of the ad. For smaller accounts, the breakdown may be more like 25–40–35, whereby 75 percent of the funds go to the creative and production work, and only 25 percent is spent on media purchases. Unless 75 percent of the company's advertising budget can be spent on media purchases, it may be wise either to do the work in-house or to develop contracts with smaller speciality firms to prepare various aspects of the advertising campaign.

An agency is likely to be more *objective* than is an in-house advertising department. The company, instead of an independent ad agency, pays creatives working for an in-house advertising department. Many times it is more difficult for in-house creatives to remain unbiased and to ignore the influences of others in the organization who may not fully understand the artistic aspects of advertising. The exception to this is advertisements for highly *complex* products. Agency members have a difficult time understanding more complicated products. To get them to understand often requires a considerable amount of time, which costs money. For complex products, in-house departments work best. For generic or more standard and simple products, ad agencies have more to offer.

The final issue to consider in choosing an agency versus performing the work in-house is *creativity.* Most agencies claim they have greater creativity than any in-house department has. Although they may, in-house departments are able to freelance with various creatives in the actual ad design process. The question, then, is how well the company's creatives or freelancers can perform as compared to an agency's creatives. For most firms, this is very difficult to judge.

Consequently, when the decision is made to utilize an external advertising agency, the company is committing substantial resources to the goal of expanding its audience

Tree Top Apple Juice is 100% pure. Naturally sweet, no sugar added. Made from crisp, delicious Washington state apples—the best on earth. Nestled in the rich, volcanic soil, our trees drink from glacier-fed rivers and bask in sunshine 300 days a year. The apples are then harvested at the peak of their flavor and turned into fresh, pure Tree Top Apple Juice. Because we care about what goes into our juice as much as you care about what goes into your kids.

Treetop's advertising success is dependent upon a clearly defined and integrated IMC plan.
Source: Courtesy of TreeTop.

through carefully designed advertising and communications programs. A brief review of the various types of agencies follows.

There is little adversity that cannot be conquered by a good plan implemented decisively.

THE SOCOH GROUP℠

An advertisement by The Socoh Group highlighting the importance of having an effective advertising team.
Source: Courtesy of the Socoh Group.

EXTERNAL ADVERTISING AGENCIES

Company leaders have a variety of options when they decide to hire an advertising agency. All sizes and types of advertising agencies exist. At one end of the spectrum are the highly specialized, boutique-type agencies that offer only one specialized service (e.g., making television ads) or that serve one particular type of client. For example, G & G Advertising of Albuquerque, New Mexico, specializes in advertising to Native Americans, a market of an estimated 10 million people.[4] At the other end of the spectrum are the full-service agencies providing all types of advertising services as well as advice and assistance in working with the other components of the IMC model, such as sales and trade promotions, direct-marketing programs, and public relations events.

Individual advertising agencies provide a number of services for companies seeking to refine their IMC programs. They may include:

▶ Consulting and giving advice about how to develop target markets

▶ Providing specialized services for business markets

▶ Providing suggestions on how to project a strong company image and theme

▶ Supplying assistance in selecting company logos and slogans

▶ Preparation of advertisements

▶ Planning and purchasing media time and space

In addition to advertising agencies, there are other closely associated types of firms. *Media service companies* negotiate and purchase media packages (called "media buys") for companies. *Direct-marketing agencies* handle every aspect of a direct-marketing campaign, either through telephone orders (800 numbers), through Internet programs, or by direct mail. Some companies focus on either *sales promotions or trade promotions* or both. These companies assist in giveaways such as pens and calendars. They also provide assistance in making posters, end-of-aisle displays, and other attention-getting mechanisms. *Public relations* firms are experts in helping companies and individuals develop positive public images and are called in for damage control when negative publicity arises. In-house members of the organization can render these activities, just as an in-house marketing department can perform advertising and IMC programs. In both instances, company leaders must decide how they can complete these key marketing activities effectively and efficiently.

A second recent trend in advertising began over two decades ago. The Young and Rubicam Advertising Agency introduced its "whole egg theory." The concept of the whole egg theory was to move from selling a client's products to helping the client achieve total success in the marketplace. Achieving success requires integrating the marketing approach by offering a fuller array of services to both business and consumer clients. Thus, as client companies began to move toward more integrated marketing approaches, agencies such as Young and Rubicam captured more accounts. Such companies continue to succeed because they work with clients on every aspect of an integrated marketing plan.[5]

The process of choosing an advertising agency is difficult. The company's leaders must decide how much involvement the agency will have and how many functions the agency should be able to perform. The next step is to develop effective selection criteria to help company leaders make wise choices in the process of hiring an advertising agency.

INTEGRATED LEARNING EXPERIENCE

A number of agencies assist business organizations with integrated marketing communications programs. Whereas some firms try to provide a wide array of services, others are more specialized. Using the Council of Public Relations Firms Web site at **www.prfirms.org**, locate some local public relations firms. What type of services do these firms offer? Access the Promotion Marketing Association, Inc. at **www.pmalink.com**. What types of information does this site contain? How would this information benefit a business, a sales promotion firm, or an advertising agency trying to outsource the sales promotions aspects of its work? For outdoor advertising, access the Outdoor Advertising Association of America at **www.oaaa.org**. What type of information does this site contain? For direct-marketing firms, check the Direct Marketing Association site at **www.the-dma.org**. What information is useful to a business organization looking for help with a direct-marketing program?

CHOOSING AN AGENCY

Choosing the advertising agency that best suits a company requires careful planning. Figure 6.3 lists the steps involved in this process. Additional information about each of these steps follows.

▶ Identify and prioritize corporate goals
▶ Develop agency selection process and criteria
▶ Initially screen firms based on credentials, size, capabilities, relevant experience, and conflict of interests
▶ Request client references
▶ Perform background checks with other firms and media agents
▶ Request written and oral presentation
▶ Meet creatives, media buyers, account executives, and other personnel who will work with account
▶ Select and draw up contract

FIGURE 6.3
Step in Selecting an Advertising Agency

Goal Setting

Before making any contact with an advertising agency, it is important to identify and prioritize various corporate goals. Goals provide a sense of direction for the company's leaders, for the agency account executive, and for the advertising creative. Each is more likely to be "on the same page" as preparation of the advertising campaign unfolds. Without clearly understood goals, it becomes virtually impossible to choose an agency, because company leaders may not have a clear idea what they want to accomplish. Unambiguous goals help ensure a good fit between the company and the agency.

Selection Criteria

The second step in selecting an agency is to finalize the process and refine the criteria that will be used. Even firms that have experience in selecting agencies must establish the process and criteria in advance. The objective is to reduce biases that may enter into the decision process. Emotions and other feelings can lead to biased decisions that are not in the company's best interests. Although good chemistry between the agency and the firm is important, this aspect of the choice comes later in the process, after the list has been narrowed down to two or three agencies.

Figure 6.4 lists some of the major issues to be considered as part of the selection process. This list is especially useful in the initial screening process, when the task is to narrow the field to the top five (or fewer) agencies.

The *size* of the agency is important, especially as it compares to the size of the company hiring the agency. If a large firm were to hire a small agency, the small agency may be overwhelmed by the account. A small firm hiring a large agency may find that the company's account might be lost or could be treated as being insignificant. A good rule of thumb to follow regarding the size of the agency is that the account should be large enough for the agency so it is important to the agency but small enough that, if lost, the agency would not be badly affected.

When Norwest Banks of Minneapolis acquired Wells Fargo of San Francisco, the company tripled in size. Norwest's agency, Carmichael Lynch, was not large enough to handle the new larger company. According to Larry Haeg, "We needed the resources and services of a larger agency."[6] In this case, it was not a matter of the firm being incompetent, but rather that the larger Norwest needed a wider variety of services and expertise.

Relevant experience in an industry is the second type of evaluation criteria that companies use. When an agency has experience in a given industry, it better understands the client firm, its customers, and the structure of the marketing channel. At the same time, it is important to be certain the agency does not have any *conflicts of interest*. An advertising firm that has been hired by one manufacturer of tires experiences a conflict of interest if the firm is hired by another tire company. Further, the agency should have relevant experience without representing a competitor. Such experience may be gained when an

▶ **Size of the agency**

▶ **Relevant experience of the agency**

▶ **Conflicts of interest**

▶ **Creative reputation and capabilities**

▶ **Production capabilities**

▶ **Media purchasing capabilities**

▶ **Other services available**

▶ **Client retention rates**

▶ **Personal chemistry**

FIGURE 6.4

Evaluation Criteria in Choosing an Ad Agency

agency sells a related product or works for a similar company that operates in a different industry. For example, if an agency has a manufacturer of automobile batteries as a client, this experience is relevant to selling automobile tires. The agency should have experience with the business-to-business side of the market, so that retailers, wholesalers, and any other channel party is considered in the marketing and advertising of the product.

All the milk advertisements in this textbook were created by Bozell Worldwide. In addition to the milk advertisements, Bozell's clients include Datek Online, Bank of America, Unisys, Lycos, Excedrin, Jergens, and the pork industry. Notice that this list does not include competing firms within the same industry. Also note that Bozell's success in promoting milk led the pork industry to believe Bozell would have the right kind of expertise to promote pork products.

The initial screening process includes an investigation into each agency's *creative reputation and capabilities.* One method of judging an agency's creativity is to ask for a list of awards the company has received. Although awards do not always translate into effective advertisements, in most cases there is a positive relationship between winning awards and writing effective ads. Most creative awards are given by peers. As a result, they are good indicators of what others think of the agency's creative efforts. Assessing creative capabilities is very important when developing advertising campaigns for a different country in which the firm has limited experience.

Production capabilities and *media purchasing capabilities* of the agencies should be examined if these services are needed as the company prepares its advertising campaign. The information is gathered to be sure the agency has the desired capabilities. A firm needing an agency to both produce the television commercial and buy media time should check on these items as part of the initial screening process. Media buying skills are important. Questions the company should ask in this area include:

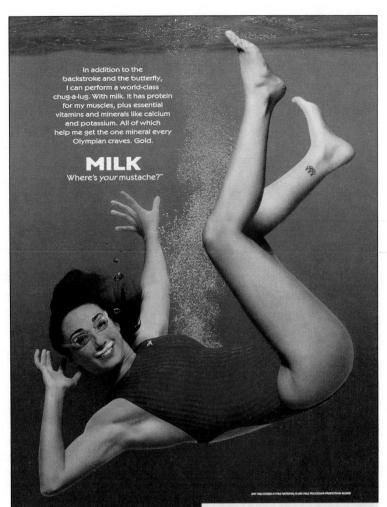

The milk industry is just one of the accounts handled by the Bozell Advertising Agency.
Source: Courtesy of Bozell Worldwide, Inc.

▶ Does the agency buy efficiently?

▶ Is the agency able to negotiate special rates and publication positions?

▶ Does the agency routinely get "bumped" by higher-paying firms, which means ads do not run at highly desirable times?

This type of information can be difficult to obtain. The company hiring the agency must be persistent and engage in thorough research. Accessing each agency's Web page, reading annual reports, and searching for news articles about individual agencies can be helpful. Most ad agencies provide prospectus sheets describing their capabilities. These reports render some information about their media buying skills.

The final three selection criteria—*other services available, client retention rates,* and *personal chemistry*—are revealed as the final steps of selection take place. These criteria help make the final determination in the selection process.

Reference Requests

Once the initial screening is complete, it is time to request references from those agencies still in the running for the contract. Most agencies willingly provide lists of their best customers to serve as references. A good strategy the company can use is to obtain references

Gillette/DuPont/Carnation/JVC/Lipton

DowBrands/Sara Lee/Pinkerton

Johnson & Johnson/Hiram Walker

Reckitt & Colman/Mead Paper

Warner Lambert/Swedish Match

Jimmy Dean Foods/Gallo/Bayer

MARKETING KNOW-HOW

THE SOCOH GROUP℠

An advertisement by The Socoh Group featuring some of the agency's major clients.
Source: Courtesy of the Socoh Group.

of firms that have similar needs. Also, when possible, it helps to obtain names of former clients of the agency. Finding out why they switched can provide valuable information. Often changes are made for legitimate reasons. Discovering an agency's *client retention rate* helps reveal how effective the firm has been in working with various clients. Poor service is not the only reason a firm switches advertising agencies. As noted in the case of Norwest Banks, the advertising agency was let go because it was too small to handle the increased size of Norwest.[7]

Background checks also provide useful information. This can be accomplished by finding firms that have dealt with each agency. Also, talking to media agents who sell media time provides insights as to how an agency buys time and deals with customers. Companies that have formed contracts with individual agencies for production facilities or other services are excellent sources of information. Background checks help the client company make sure the agency can provide quality professional services.

Oral and Written Presentations

The next step in the selection process is to request an oral and written presentation by the finalists. The agency should be willing to provide a formal presentation addressing a specific problem, situation, or set of questions. These presentations reveal how each agency would deal with specific issues that arise as a campaign is prepared. This helps client companies ascertain whether the agency uses tactics and methods that are acceptable.

Meeting Key Personnel

During the presentation phase, the opportunity exists to meet with the creatives, media buyers, account executives, and any other personnel who will be working with an account. *Chemistry* between employees of the two different firms is important. The client companies' leaders should be convinced that they will work well together and that they feel comfortable with each other.

In competing for the new Norwest–Wells Fargo account, the firm DDB was chosen over the incumbent agency, Carmichael Lynch, because Fargo executives believed DDB had greater strategic insights, a better range of services, higher-quality creatives, and offered a more thorough media plan. DDB was able to show how the agency intended to combine the strength of Wells Fargo's 150-year heritage with the excellent customer service qualities of Norwest. This presentation led to the decision to hire DDB. It came after Fargo executives listened to the presentations of both agencies and asked key questions about who would actually be working on the account.[8]

Whenever possible, a client company's leaders should visit the advertising agency's office as part of the evaluation process. Often agencies use people called "heavy hitters" to win contracts, but then turn the account over to other individuals in the agency after signing the deal. Visiting the agency's office provides an opportunity to meet every person who might work on the account. Talking with these individuals generates quality information about how the account will be handled. The visiting period also can be used to hammer out specific details, such as identifying the actual person(s) who will work on the advertisements, and either agreeing to the use of freelancers (independent contractors who provide various services) to work on the project or prohibiting the agency from using such individuals.

Selection and Contract

The final step of the process is to make the choice and to notify all finalists of the decision. A contract is drawn up with the advertising agency to specify all terms and activities, and letters are written to agencies that did not win the bid. Many times, these agencies contact the company seeking information about why they were not chosen. It is in the interests of both organizations to remain cordial and professional, even when a contract is not given, because they may do business in the future.

When the process has been completed, the agency and the company work together to prepare the advertising campaign. Along the way, the account executive plays a key role in the process, as does the advertising creative. A brief review of the activities performed by these two individuals follows later in this chapter.

INTEGRATED LEARNING EXPERIENCE

The *Advertising Age* Web site at **www.adage.com** provides considerable information about advertising agencies that helps in understanding the selection process. In the "World Brands" section, look for the list of the top 25 advertising agencies. Using the search function, enter an advertiser and see what agencies are used in the various countries in which the advertiser operates. By clicking on "Summary Chart," you can find the primary advertising agencies that various firms employ. Locate the advertising agencies Procter & Gamble, Nestlé, and Coca-Cola use. Access the Web sites of these agencies to try to discover why these particular agencies were selected. Finally, select the "Account Action" section, which contains the accounts up for renewal or open to bid. Study the various companies looking for agencies and the type of agencies being considered.

ADVERTISING PLANNING AND RESEARCH

The initial meetings between the agency that has been selected and the firm's advertising management and marketing team is when it is possible to combine all of the advertising elements together. In doing so, there remains some planning and research to conduct.

First, the agency involved should be engaged in **general pre-planning input** collection. This task involves "reading up" on the client organization in places such as books, trade publications, research reports, and the company's Web site. Also, members of the client agency should, when possible, actually use the good or service involved. By talking to members of the community, employees, and other business partners, the agency can develop a solid background of understanding about the client.

Next, **product-specific research** should be conducted. Two things should be understood at this point. One is whether there are problems associated with a given good or service. One approach is called "problem detection," in which consumers are asked to report any problems or difficulties they have encountered using a product. These issues must be addressed as part of the IMC program. The other matter to complete is discovering the **major selling idea** to be used in the ad campaign. The "got milk?" approach that is well documented in this book began with product-specific research. Customers were asked to go without milk for a week (a deprivation approach) and report back. The agency learned that the key selling point is how well milk goes with a person's lifestyle. Doing without it (deprivation) made people aware of the vital role milk plays in eating cereal, devouring cookies, and so forth. Recently, Orbitz has made "lowest fares possible" its major selling idea. In short, both the upside and the downside of a product should be clearly understood before moving forward with an advertising or IMC campaign.

Finally, **qualitative research** will assist the vendor company and its advertising agency. Focus groups are often used to bring people together to talk about a product. With a creative in attendance, it is possible to hear about the kind of person who likes a product as well as tactics which might reach that individual.

The actual collection of information can come from a variety of perspectives, including:

▶ Anthropology

▶ Sociology

▶ Psychology

The methods employed by *anthropologists* often involve direct observation. This helps the marketing team discover not only who is using a product, but also how it is being used. When Whirlpool employed anthropologists to study washing machines, it became clear that adult men and children also used the machines, not just the wife or mother. The researchers suggested making the controls on the units easier to use and understand for men and children, who may be less familiar with appropriate temperature and cycle settings for various kinds of fabrics.

Sociologists examine social class issues, trends, and analyze cohorts and family life cycles. The world of Ralph Lauren is rich, elite, and distinct. Therefore, clothes for the wealthy is the message that emerges. Trends come from media and advertising. The trend toward greater involvements with family and friends began even before September 11, 2001, but has clearly gained momentum since. Messages stressing the role a product plays in making family and home life better are on the increase. Generations that have grown up together are called "cohorts," such as the newly emerging echo boomer generation. Messages targeting this group are different than for other cohorts.

Psychology concentrates on motivation, cognition, and learning. When these come together, values emerge. The **values and life style model (VALS)** is designed to predict consumer behavior by understanding self-orientation and resources. Thus, most purchases are related to a match of lifestyle choice with funds available. A cowboy-type individual, even one who has moved to the city, will make purchases from western stores that the person can afford, because these items reflect the individual's personal self-orientation. Also, a **personal drive analysis (PDA)** helps the researcher understand psychological drives toward indulgence, ambition, or individuality, which again affect brand choices. A fine wine may be viewed as an indulgence by a consumer or as an expression of individuality. Knowing the purchasing motives of a target market can greatly enhance the effectiveness of an advertising program.

Carefully collected knowledge about the product or service and the audience for ads and advertising campaigns is crucial to success. With that knowledge in mind, the actual campaign can be developed.

One important task of the account executive is to ensure that there is a common theme among all advertisements and that the client's message is consistent with the other components of the IMC plan.
Source: Courtesy of Loeffler Ketchum Mountjoy.

THE ROLES OF ADVERTISING ACCOUNT EXECUTIVES

The **advertising account executive** is the key go-between for both the advertising agency and the client company. This individual is actively involved in soliciting the account, finalizing details of the contract, and working with the creatives who will prepare the actual advertising campaign. Many times, the account executive helps the company refine and define its major message for an overall IMC program and provides other support as needed.

Clients always want to know if they are getting a good value for their investment. Most clients believe they don't have a clue in trying to understand the relation-

ship between an agency's cost and its actual value to the company. Ron Cox, a vice president at Wrigley Jr. Company, suggests that agencies update clients regularly on the work they are doing and the results obtained. These types of reports (called *stewardship reports*) help clients understand the process and the outcome more clearly. Updating clients on what is being done for them becomes more important as the amount being spent on advertising increases.[9]

Further, periodic reviews should be held to show that the agency is doing its work. These reviews need not be confrontational. To the client company, these updates represent the opportunity to evaluate how well the agency has done and also to become better acquainted with the personnel working on the account. As part of the process, the client firm can spend time with creatives as they work on the campaign. Client companies can also talk to media buyers, public relations experts, and others working on the account. In short, the account manager oversees the process in such a way that everyone involved feels comfortable and oriented toward the goal of creating an effectively integrated advertising campaign and marketing communications program.

The traffic manager works closely with the account executive. This person's responsibility is to schedule the various aspects of the agency's work to ensure the work is completed by the target deadline. See the Communication Action Box for more information about how the traffic manager serves an important link between the account executive and the creatives.

THE ROLES OF CREATIVES

Creatives are the persons who actually develop and produce advertisements. These individuals are either members of advertising agencies or freelancers. Some smaller companies provide only creative advertising services without becoming involved in other marketing programs and activities. Creatives may appear to hold the "glamour" jobs in advertising, because they express their talents in the advertisements they produce. At the same time, creatives face long hours and work under enormous pressures to design ads that are effective and produce results that client companies and marketing account managers want. The role of the creative is discussed in the section on creative briefs later in this chapter.

Notice the consistency of this advertisement for tourism in North Carolina with the one on the previous page.
Source: Courtesy of Loeffler Ketchum Mountjoy.

For this advertisement the executive chose to utilize a new approach featuring animation.
Source: Courtesy of Loeffler Ketchum Mountjoy.

COMMUNICATION ACTION

An Interview with a Traffic Manager

One individual who plays a key role in the media scheduling process is a traffic manager. Gretchen Hoag plays this role in her agency, Publicis Technology. We asked her to describe the job. She responded

I have many responsibilities, but my main purpose is to manage the work flow and ensure that all deadlines are met. Along with managing the process, I'm also in charge of maintaining project history, creating schedules, managing resources, setting up team meetings, prioritizing projects, training new employees about agency processes, setting up new clients, routing proofs, proofreading, and whatever else is needed to get the job done. One of the best things about my job is that I work closely with every team member within the agency. Not many people have the opportunity to work with so many different types of people, as I do.

We then asked Gretchen to describe a typical day at work. She replied,

There is no such thing as a typical day in an ad agency no matter what your job is, but traffic managers probably have the least typical days of anyone. In traffic, you could spend the majority of one day creating schedules and the next routing and proofreading mechanicals, and the day after that opening up new jobs and attending kick off meetings. There are a few things that do remain constant, I always have paperwork to file, history to record in my databases, and team members to keep happy.

Usually when it comes time to schedule a project, I create a basic outline of when I think the project can be completed. This is very difficult, because the artwork has not been concepted yet. I don't know if I'm scheduling for an illustration, stock photography, a photo shoot, or a text-only ad. So I have to guess. With this client I guess the artwork will take about two weeks to complete. Once I have an outline completed, I talk with each of my team members to see if they agree with my schedule. Most importantly, I need to make sure my timing corresponds with media's timing. Once the team is in agreement on the schedule, I can create a formal estimate for the client. At this time the account team works with the client to ensure they can commit to the deadlines as well.

Of course all this guesswork changes once a concept has been chosen. Maybe we have to paint a backdrop, which will take the artist three weeks to complete before a photo shoot can happen. Or perhaps we are using stock photography, which will perhaps allow the schedule to be sped up a bit. This is where good juggling skills and flexibility come into play.

After a schedule has been approved, I evaluate all of my current projects and then work with the other

traffic managers to see what jobs they have scheduled. We reevaluate each client's needs for each team member day by day. If one person in either the creative department or the production department is overwhelmed, then we reassign work, or if everyone appears to be booked, we can try to push schedules around or perhaps bring in freelance help. Occasionally, we can predict days or weeks when we will need extra help, like the week two art directors were going to be out of the office. Basically, we do whatever is humanly possible to get the job done as efficiently and cost effectively as we can while maintaining the highest standards for our clients.

Ideally on a print project, I would like to schedule about four weeks for creative concepting, two to three weeks to simultaneously write copy and produce artwork, three to four days to build mechanical, and one week for color corrections. This will work for some of the product categories, because they have existing creative we can continue running until the new creative is completed. But there are some product categories that have media purchased and no existing creative work for. Given this information, we need to work on these jobs first and wait on the product categories we already have materials for. Before we can concentrate on the individual product categories, we have to go through a look and feel exercise.

Once the look and feel has been decided on, we can begin to produce the ads, which does not allow us much time. So, we have to crunch down what would normally take seven to nine weeks to three to four weeks. In order to do this, my creative team will present only concepts that we know we can produce in this short time frame. We also cut down on the time we can come up with ideas for the campaign and we beg for additional time from the publications to see if we can receive an extension on the material due dates. If our other clients also have jobs in the creative concepting stage, I may even need to bring in additional art directors and copywriters to work on the job.

Being a traffic manager makes her part of a larger team that also includes the account service people, clients, and creatives. Here is how Gretchen describes some of these relationships:

I work with the account service people very closely. They are the ones who are directly in front of the client representing the agency, so they play a very important role in the process. They filter through all the information from the client and pass the information on to me. I then pass the information on to the appropriate team members. I do this by meeting with all of my account service people at least once a day to be sure they are comfortable with the status of all their projects and to discuss any new information from the client.

Regarding the agency's clients, Gretchen told us:

> The account team is responsible for maintaining the relationship with the client, which includes all contact with the client. However, my number and name has been passed on to many of our clients. I have been known to serve as backup when the account teams are out of the office. I also have been pulled into meetings and conference calls to explain schedules and to give technical explanations about color and film processes.

There are also involvements with other members of the marketing team, making the job of traffic manager more complex. Here's what Gretchen told us about other people at work:

> I also have a close relationship with the creative and production teams. Let's face it, no one likes to be told what to do and how quickly it needs to be done, especially if the due date requires working on the weekend or staying past 5:00. And as a traffic manager, I am the person who has the distinct honor of relaying this kind of bad news. It is by far the hardest part of the job. But not all of our conversations are based on bad news. The creative and production departments depend on the traffic managers to help them to work uninterrupted, which is one reason why all information filters through us.

We asked her if she chooses the creatives who will work on an assignment. She replied,

> Yes and no. Since I have such a close relationship with my creatives, I do recommend to the Creative Director who I would like to see working on a particular project. I would like to think I am really in-tune with how each team member within the department likes to work, what type of projects they thrive on, and more importantly, how much work each person can handle.

Finally, we asked her to describe her role in making sure that all the communication is integrated into a common theme. She said,

> Here is another area where my role is limited. However, Publicis Technology is a real team environment. Generally speaking, we were all hired for strengths in a particular area of expertise and you would not want to overstep those bounds, but if you are lucky enough to work in the kind of team environment, those boundaries are a little less clear. Everything we produce or show the client is a reflection on the entire agency, so we all feel ownership in the projects we work on. Every client has a creative team member who is what we call a brand guardian. The brand guardian's responsibility is to maintain that particular client's standards. We also have an editor on staff who is responsible for proofing all work against the client's style sheet. The account team reviews work against the strategic and creative briefs. I review all work against my own knowledge and client notes and records that I maintain. So really all team members are looking out for the client's best interests. My main role is to point out any issues that may be found to the other team members to determine how we would like to address the issue and to make sure that all recommended changes are made.

ADVERTISING CAMPAIGN MANAGEMENT

Managing an advertising campaign is the process of preparing and integrating a specific advertising program in conjunction with the overall IMC message. An effective program consists of five steps. The steps of **advertising campaign management** are:

1. Review the communication market analysis.
2. Establish communication objectives consistent with those developed in a promotions opportunity analysis program.
3. Review the communications budget.
4. Select the media in conjunction with the advertising agency.
5. Review the information with the advertising creative in the creative brief.

The advertising program should be consistent with previous activities performed as part of the IMC program. This helps to make sure the firm presents a clear message to key target markets, and advertising efforts can then be refined to gain the maximum benefit from the promotional dollars being spent. A review of the steps involved is next.

COMMUNICATION MARKET ANALYSIS

In the first phase of planning, the account executive studies what the company's communication market analysis reveals (see Chapter 5). The *competitive analysis* identifies the firm's major competitors. The *opportunity analysis* reveals where the firm can best focus its advertising and promotional efforts by discovering company strengths along with opportunities present in the marketplace. The *target market analysis* identifies key target markets. The *customer analysis* suggests how the firm's previous marketing communications efforts have been received by the public as well as by other businesses and potential customers. A *positioning analysis* explains how the firm and its products are perceived relative to the competition. The value of reviewing the communication market analysis is in focusing the account executive, the creative, and the company itself on key markets and customers while helping them understand how the firm currently competes in the marketplace. Then the team is better able to establish and pursue specific advertising objectives.

For the purposes of advertising, two important items are outlined as part of the communication market analysis:

1. The media usage habits of the target market
2. The media utilized by the competition

When analyzing customers, knowing which media they use is vitally important. For example, teenagers watch television and listen to the radio for many hours. Only a small percentage reads newspapers and news magazines. Various market segments have differences in when and how they view various media. For example, older African Americans watch television programs in patterns quite different from older Caucasians. Males watch more sports programs than females and so forth. In the business-to-business market, knowing which trade journals or business publications the various members of the buying center most likely read is essential for the development of a print advertising campaign. Engineers, who tend to be the influencers, have different media viewing habits than do vice presidents, who may be the deciders. Discovering which media reach a target market (and which do not) is a key component in a communication market analysis and an advertising program.

Further, studying the competition reveals how other firms attempt to reach customers. Knowing how other firms contact consumers is as important as knowing what they say. An effective communication market analysis reveals this information, so that more effective messages and advertising campaigns can be designed.

INTEGRATED LEARNING EXPERIENCE

Part of a communication market analysis is understanding the media usage habits of consumers and their attitudes toward the various media. An excellent source of information in Canada is the Media Awareness Network at **www.media-awareness.ca**. Review the types of information available at this site. In the "Media Industries" section, examine the news archives. Find articles that relate to media usage to help a firm better understand its target market's media usage habits. What types of information are in the other sections such as "Media Issues" and "News"?

COMMUNICATION AND ADVERTISING OBJECTIVES

The second step of advertising planning is to establish and clarify advertising and communication objectives. Several advertising goals are central to the IMC process. Some of these goals are listed in Figure 6.5. A discussion of each individual goal area follows.[10]

Building Brand Image

One of the most important advertising goals is to build a global brand and corporate image. These, in turn, generate brand equity. As discussed in Chapter 3, brand equity is a set of characteristics that makes a brand more desirable to consumers and businesses. These benefits can be enhanced when we combine effective advertising with quality

▶ To build brand image

▶ To inform

▶ To persuade

▶ To support other marketing efforts

▶ To encourage action

FIGURE 6.5
Advertising Goals

products. Higher levels of brand equity give the company a distinct advantage as consumers move toward purchase decisions.

Advertising is a critical component in the effort to build brand equity. Successful brands have two characteristics: being (1) "top of mind" and (2) the consumers' "top choice." When consumers are asked to identify brands that quickly come to mind from a product category, one particular brand is nearly always mentioned. That name has the property of being a **top of mind brand**. For example, when asked to identify fast-food restaurants, McDonald's almost always heads the list. The same is true for Kodak film and Campbell's Soups. This is true not only in the United States but also in many other countries. The term **top choice** suggests exactly what the term implies: A top choice brand is the first or second pick when a consumer reviews his or her evoked set of possible purchasing alternatives.

Part of building brand image and brand equity is developing brand awareness, and advertising is the best method to reach that goal. Brand awareness means the consumers recognize and remember a particular brand or company name when they consider purchasing options. Brand awareness, brand image, and brand equity are vital for success.

In business-to-business marketing, brand awareness is often essential to being considered by members of the buying center. It is important for business customers to recognize the brand name(s) of the various goods or services a company sells. Brand awareness is especially important in modified rebuy situations, when a firm looks to change to a new vendor or evaluates a product or service that has not

Campbell's Soups builds on its brand name to sell a new product.
Source: Courtesy of Campbell Soup Company.

been purchased recently. In new buy situations, firms spend more time seeking prospective vendors than they do in modified rebuys. Consequently, brand equity is a major advantage for the firm with such recognition. Further, many firms have increased their importing and exporting activities. As a result, developing recognized and accepted global brands has become an increasingly important part of many marketing programs.

Providing Information

Besides building brand recognition and equity, advertising serves other goals. For example, advertising often is used to provide information to both consumers and business buyers. Typical information for consumers includes a retailer's store hours, business location, or sometimes more detailed product specifications. Information can make the purchasing process appear to be convenient and relatively simple, which can entice customers to finalize the purchasing decision and travel to the store.

ADVERTISING MANAGEMENT

Deception Versus Puffery

A deceptive advertisement gives a typical person a false impression that leads the individual to make a purchase. **Puffery** is the use of an exaggerated claim about a good or service without making an overt attempt to deceive or mislead. Typical terms associated with puffery include *best, greatest,* and *finest.* Consumers are accustomed to these claims and, therefore, they are not considered illegal.

Consider the case of herbs, supplements, and other nontested products. Claims are made regarding contributions to levels of energy, sexual stamina, and mental acuity. Others report unsubstantiated results related to weight loss.

Is it ethical, knowing that "placebo effects" exist, to claim a product will make a man better in bed, stronger, wiser, or more ambitious? After all, consumers are used to exaggerated claims. It is common for such products to offer a money-back guarantee in which the consumer may receive a full refund if not satisfied. However, most of the people who buy these products are either willing to delude themselves into believing a benefit existed when it did not or are too embarrassed to ask for a refund.

Should there be stronger policing of medical claims than for other types of claims? Should there be a stricter standard regarding puffery in these instances? Why or why not?

A Del Monte vegetable advertisement directed to senior customers by offering a price-off coupon offer.
Source: Courtesy of Del Monte Foods.

For business-to-business situations, information from some ads leads various members of the buying center to consider a particular company as they examine their options. This type of information is the most useful when members of the buying center are in the information search stage of the purchasing process. For high-involvement types of purchases, wherein members of the buying center have strong vested interests in the success of the choice, informative advertisements are the most beneficial. Low-involvement decisions usually do not require as much detail.

In marketing to both consumers and other businesses, information can help those involved reach a decision. Information is one component of persuasion, another objective of various advertising programs.

Persuasion

One of the most common goals of advertising programs is persuasion. Advertisements can convince consumers that a particular brand is superior to other brands. They can show consumers the negative consequences of failing to use a particular brand. Changing consumer attitudes and persuading them to consider a new purchasing choice is a challenging task. As described later, advertisers can utilize several methods of persuasion. Persuasive advertising is used more in consumer marketing than in business-to-business situations. Persuasion techniques are used more frequently in broadcast media such as television and radio than in print advertising.

Supporting Marketing Efforts

Another goal of advertising is to support other marketing functions. For example, manufacturers use advertising to support trade and consumer promotions, such as theme packaging or combination offers. Contests, such as the McDonald's Monopoly promotion, require extensive advertising to be effective. Retailers also use advertising to support their marketing programs. Any type of special sale (white sale, buy-one-get-one-free, pre-Christmas sale) needs vigorous advertising to attract customers to the store. Both manufacturers and retail outlets use advertising in conjunction with coupons or other special offers. Del Monte placed a 30-cent coupon in the advertisement shown in this section. The ad highlights a smaller-size container with a pull-top lid. These features match the ad's target market: senior citizens. The magazine outlet in which the ad ran was *Modern Maturity*. Manufacturer coupons are regularly redeemed at grocery stores (sometimes at double their face value), and in-store coupons are part of many retail store print advertisements. When ads are combined with other marketing efforts into a larger, more integrated effort revolving around a theme, the program is called a **promotional campaign**.

Encouraging Action

Many times firms set motivational types of goals for their advertising programs. Television commercials that encourage viewers to take action by dialing a toll-free number to make quick purchases are examples. Everything from Veg-A-Matics to CDs and cassettes are sold using action tactics. Infomercials and home shopping network programs heavily rely on immediate consumer purchasing responses.

Action-oriented advertising is heavily used in the business-to-business sector. The goal is to generate sales leads. Many business advertisements provide a Web address or telephone numbers that buyers can use to request more information or move toward a purchase more easily.

The five advertising goals of building image, providing information, being persuasive, supporting other marketing efforts, and encouraging action are not separate ideas. They work together in key ways. Image and information are part of persuasion. Thus, when Barnes & Noble announces its Internet sales program, the firm's image combines with the information provided to persuade online book buyers to consider it rather than Amazon.com. The goal of encouraging action is often part of supporting other marketing tactics. The key advertising management objective is to emphasize one goal without forgetting the others.

An advertisement by 1st Source Mortgage designed to encourage action.
Source: Courtesy of 1st Source Mortgage.

THE COMMUNICATIONS BUDGET

Once the company, account manager, and creative agree upon the major goals of the advertising campaign, a review of the communications budget is in order. In Chapter 5, various methods for establishing budgets were described. After the total dollars allocated to advertising have been established, account managers and company leaders agree to uses for the funds. This includes the media to be utilized (television versus newspaper versus billboards). Also, however, the *manner of distribution* must be arranged. Three basic tactics include:

▶ Advertising the most when sales are at peak seasons

▶ Advertising the most during low sales seasons

▶ Level amounts

Firms that advertise during peak seasons such as Christmas are emphasizing sending out the message when customers are most inclined to buy. Because consumers are on the "hot spot," this approach makes sense for some products. For example, Weight Watchers, Diet Centers, and others advertise heavily during the first two weeks of January. Many New Year's resolutions include going on a diet.

Advertising during peak seasons can be accomplished in two ways. The first is a **pulsating schedule of advertising**. This schedule involves continuous advertising with bursts of higher intensity (more ads in more media) during the course of the year, most notably during peak seasons. Companies can also utilize what is called a **flighting** approach or schedule, where ads are presented only during peak times, and not at all during off seasons.

The firms that decide to advertise the most during slow sales seasons are essentially oriented toward "drumming up business" when people do not regularly buy. In retail sales, slow seasons occur during January and February. Some companies advertise more during those periods to sell off merchandise left over from the Christmas season.

Many marketing experts believe it is best to advertise in level amounts, particularly when a product purchase is essentially a "random" event. This approach is a **continuous campaign schedule**. For example, many durable goods such as washing machines and refrigerators are purchased on an "as needed" basis. A family ordinarily buys a new washing machine only when the old one breaks down. Consequently, level advertising increases the odds that the buyer will remember a given name (Maytag, Whirlpool, General Electric). Also, there is a better chance that consumers will be exposed to ads close to the time they are ready to make purchases.

In any case, the objective should be to match the pacing of advertisements with the message, media, and the nature of the product or service. Some media make it easier to advertise for longer periods of time. For instance, billboards are normally posted for a month or a year. They can be rotated throughout a town or city to present a continuing message about the company or its products. Budgetary constraints must also be incorporated into the strategies and tactics used in the advertising program.

MEDIA SELECTION

The next step of advertising management is to develop strategies and tactics associated with media selection, refining intent of the message, and development of the actual campaign with specific ads. It is crucial to develop consistent messages that match with various media. Media buys are guided by the advertising agency or media agency, the company, and the creative. In the next chapter, the advantages and disadvantages of all relevant media are described. Also, the expanding number of usable media is described. They should complement the IMC program. When media selection is performed carefully, and messages are designed to fit with those choices, the chances for success greatly increase.

Advertising management is part of the overall IMC scheme. When effectively coordinated, a company develops a major advantage in the competitive arena. These coordination efforts are largely guided by a creative brief, which is the final step of the campaign program to accompany producing the actual advertisements.

INTEGRATED LEARNING EXPERIENCE

STOP

Media selection is an important component in a successful IMC program. A resource that contains considerable information about various media is Responservice at **www.responservice.com**. The Times-Group promotes it as the advertising, media, and marketing one-stop shop. From its menu, examine all the different sections available and the types of information within each section. How can a firm use this information in the development of an IMC plan?

> ❭ **The objective**
> ❭ **The target audience**
> ❭ **The message theme**
> ❭ **The support**
> ❭ **The constraints**

FIGURE 6.6
The Creative Brief

THE CREATIVE BRIEF

In preparing advertisements, creatives work with a document called a creative strategy or creative brief. The components of a creative brief are provided in Figure 6.6. Using this instrument, the creative takes the information provided by the account executive and is expected to produce an advertisement that conveys the desired message in a manner that will positively impact potential customers. Details about each element of the creative brief are provided next.

The Objective

The first step in preparing the creative strategy is to identify the objective of the advertisement. Possible objectives include:

❭ Increase brand awareness

❭ Build brand image

❭ Increase customer traffic

❭ Increase retailer or wholesaler orders

❭ Increase inquiries from end users and channel members

❭ Provide information

The creative must understand the main objective before designing an advertisement, because the primary objectives guide the design of the advertisement and the choice of an executional theme. An ad to increase brand awareness prominently displays the *name* of the product. An ad to build brand image can display the *actual product* more prominently as in the Soft Scrub advertisement shown in this section.

The Target Audience

A creative should know the target audience. An advertisement designed to persuade a business to inquire about new computer software will be different than a consumer advertisement from the same company. A business advertisement focuses on the type of industry and the project member of the buying center who will see it. The more detail that is known about the target audience, the easier it is for a creative to design an effective advertisement.

Target market profiles that are too general are not very helpful. Rather than specifying males, ages 20 to 35, more specific information is needed (e.g., males, 20 to 35, college educated, professionals). Other information such as hobbies, interests, opinions, and lifestyles makes targeting an advertisement even more precise. Notice that the Playtex advertisement in this section is designed for young females who enjoy

An advertisement for Soft Scrub designed to enhance the brand's image by displaying the product prominently.
Source: Courtesy of the Clorox Company.

An advertisement for Playtex using additional target market profile information to design a message directed to teenage and young adult females.
Source: Courtesy of Playtex Products, Inc.

A milk industry advertisement illustrating the importance of maintaining a consistent theme over time.
Source: Courtesy of Bozell Worldwide, Inc.

playing sports and have an active lifestyle. This additional information was needed to create an advertisement that appeals to this particular market segment of females.

The Message Theme

The message theme is an outline of key idea(s) that the advertising program is supposed to convey. The message theme is the benefit or promise the advertiser wants to use to reach consumers or businesses. The promise or unique selling point should describe the major benefit the good or service offers customers. For example, the message theme for an automobile could be oriented toward luxury, safety, fun, fuel efficiency, or driving excitement. The message theme for a hotel could focus on luxury, price, or unusual features, such as a hotel in Paris, France, noting the ease of access to all of the nearby tourist attractions. The message theme should match the medium selected, the target market, and the primary IMC message to be effective.[11]

Notice the advertisement by the milk industry featuring Sarah Michelle Gellar. The theme of milk providing the calcium needed for strong bones is consistently used in a number of "got milk?" advertisements, as is the visual display of the white mustache. Although the model and context change, the theme is consistent.

Message themes can be oriented toward either rational or emotional processes. A "left-brain" ad is oriented toward the logical, rational side, which manages information such as numbers, letters, words, and concepts. Left-brain advertising is logical and factual, and the appeals are rational. For example, there are logical features which are part of the decision to buy a car (size, price, special features). At the same time, many cars are purchased for emotional reasons. The right side of the brain deals with the emotions. It works with abstract ideas, images, and feelings. A car may be chosen for its color, sportiness, or other less rational reasons.

Most advertising is either right-brained or left-brained. Effective advertising is produced when there is a balance between the two sides. Rational, economic beings have difficulty defending the purchase of an expensive sports car such as a Porsche. Many product and service purchases are based on how a person feels about the product or service combined with rational information.[12] More complete information about the message theme is provided in Chapter 8.

The Support

The fourth component of the creative strategy is the support. **Support** takes the form of the facts that substantiate the message theme. A pain reliever advertising claim of being effective for arthritis may support this point by noting independent medical findings or testimonials from patients with arthritis. Notice the support claims Pearle Vision makes in its advertisement. The microTHINS are 30 percent thinner, 40 percent lighter, 4 times more scratch resistant, 10 times more impact resistant, antireflective, and have 99.9 percent UV protection. The creative needs these supporting facts to design effective advertisements.

The Constraints

The final step in the development of a creative strategy is identification of any **constraints**. These are the legal and mandatory restrictions placed on advertisements. They include legal protection for trademarks, logos, and copy registrations. They also include disclaimers about warranties, offers, and claims. For warranties, a disclaimer specifies the conditions under which they will be honored. For example, tire warranties often state they apply *under normal driving conditions with routine maintenance,* so that a person cannot ignore tire balancing and rotation and expect to get free new tires when the old ones wear out quickly. Disclaimer warranties notify consumers of potential hazards associated with products. For instance, tobacco advertisements must contain a statement from the Surgeon General about the dangers of smoking and chewing tobacco. Disclaimers about offers spell out the terms of financing agreements, as well as when bonuses or discounts apply. Claims identify the exact nature of the statement made in the advertisement. For example, nutritional claims must contain a statement about the size of serving or other information that makes it clear how many nutrients are actually in the product.

After these steps have been reviewed, the creative brief is complete. From this point forward, the message and the media match, and actual advertisements can be produced. Effective creative briefs focus everyone involved on both the IMC message and the current intent of an advertising campaign. This, in turn, gives companies better chances of reaching customers with messages that return measurable results and help guarantee the success of both the company and the advertising agency.[13]

When the creative brief has been completed, design of the campaign should move forward at a solid pace. Recent research suggest that campaigns designed in two months or less have the greatest likelihood of being "highly effective." Those that take longer will be only "effective" or even "ineffective." The goal is to move forward without rushing. Campaigns designed in two weeks or less are more likely to be ineffective as well.[14]

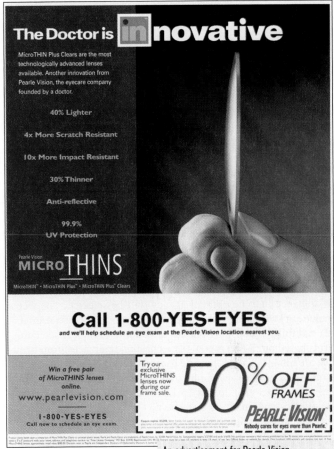

An advertisement for Pearle Vision promoting MicroTHINS lenses.
Source: Courtesy of Pearle Vision.

This Surgeon General's warning is an example of a constraint.
Source: Courtesy of Woodfin Camp & Associates. Photograph by C. Nacke.

SUMMARY

Effective advertising requires matching a noticeable message with appropriate media. Like a company's business cards, stationery, and brochures, a firm's commercials spell out the organization's identity and image. The IMC approach makes certain all of these elements speak with the same voice so that customers can understand clearly the nature of the company, its products and services, and its methods of doing business.

This chapter reviews the advertising management process. Effective advertising is more likely to occur when the firm has a well-defined mission statement and targets its energies in the direction of creating goods or services to meet the needs of a target market. Then an integrated marketing communications program can build on the central theme pursued by those in the firm.

Advertising management begins with deciding whether an in-house department or group should develop advertisements or to retain an external advertising agency. When choosing an external agency, the company's leaders establish clear steps to lead to the best chance that the optimal agency will be selected. The steps include: (1) spelling out and prioritizing organizational goals, (2) carefully establishing quality selection criteria, (3) screening firms based on those criteria, (4) requesting references from firms that are finalists, (5) performing background checks, (6) requesting written and oral presentations from the finalist agencies, (7) making an on-site visit to get to know those in the agency, and (8) offering and finalizing a contract.

Common selection criteria used in selecting agencies include: (1) the size of the agency matching the size of the company, (2) relevant experience, (3) no conflicts of interest, (4) production capabilities, (5) quality creative capabilities, (6) suitable media purchasing skills, (7) other services that can be rendered as needed, (8) client retention rates, and (9) a good chemistry between those in the company and those in the agency. Carefully utilizing these criteria increases the odds of a fit and match between the company and the agency, which heightens levels of success.

Within the advertising agency, the account manager performs the functions of soliciting accounts, finalizing contracts, and selecting creatives to prepare advertising campaigns. Account executives are go-betweens who mediate between the agency and the client company. Account executives also help client organizations refine their IMC messages and programs.

Creatives prepare advertisements and are guided by the creative brief. This document spells out: (1) the objective of the promotional campaign, (2) the target audience, (3) the message theme, (4) the support, and (5) the constraints. The message theme is an outline of the key idea(s) that the program is supposed to convey. The constraints are any warranties, disclaimers, or legal statements that are part of various advertisements.

The creative, account executive, and company should agree about which media to use in a campaign. Media are selected based on costs, types of messages, target market characteristics, and other criteria that will be discussed in detail in Chapter 9. The creatives then complete the final elements of the ad, and the campaign is prepared.

Advertising management is an important ingredient in the success of an integrated marketing communications program. Quality ads that garner the attention of the target audience, make a key memorable point, and move the buyer to action are difficult to prepare. At the same time, company officials and market account executives know that designing effective ads with tangible results is a challenging but necessary activity. It is important to go through every step of the process carefully, to help the company achieve its marketing goals in both the short and long term.

REVIEW QUESTIONS

1. What is a message theme? What role does a message theme play in an advertising campaign?

2. Define advertising management. What are the four main steps involved?

3. What is the relationship between advertising and the overall IMC process?

4. What three main company activities are part of the advertising management process? What role does the company's mission play in this process?

5. What criteria can be used to help a company decide between an in-house advertising group and hiring an external advertising agency?

6. Besides advertising agencies, what other types of organizations play roles in the communication process?

7. What steps should be taken in selecting an advertising agency?

8. What evaluation criteria should be used in selecting an advertising agency?

9. How important is interpersonal chemistry in selecting an advertising agency?

10. Describe the roles that general planning input, product-specific research, and qualitative research play in the development of an advertising campaign.

11. What three academic disciplines can play a role in advertising research? What unique contribution does each discipline make to understanding consumers and the marketplace?

12. Describe the role of an advertising agency account executive.

13. Describe the role of an advertising creative.

14. What are the steps of an advertising campaign management process? What other process in this textbook is similar in nature?

15. Describe the elements of a creative brief.

KEY TERMS

message theme an outline of key idea(s) that the advertising program is supposed to convey.

leverage point the key element in the advertisement that taps into, or activates, a consumer's personal value system (a value, idea, or concept).

appeal how that leverage point and executional theme combine to attract attention, through humor, fear, sexual suggestiveness, rational logic, or some other method.

executional framework how the message will be delivered (musically, visually, verbally, written statements, etc.).

advertising management program the process of preparing and integrating a company's advertising efforts with the overall IMC message.

general pre-planning input the task of studying a client organization by the advertising agency, from a rich set of sources, to provide understanding and background before preparing an advertising campaign.

product-specific research research that identifies whether there are problems associated with a given product or service and the major selling idea to be used in the advertising campaign.

major selling idea the primary message concerning the product or service benefits to be transmitted to consumers in an advertising campaign.

qualitative research collecting subjective information and opinions about a company, its products and services, often through the use of focus groups.

values and lifestyle model (VAL) research designed to predict consumer behavior by understanding self-orientation and resources.

personal drive analysis (PDA) a model that helps the researcher understand individual psychological drives toward indulgence, ambition, or individuality, which affect brand choices.

advertising account executive the key go-between for both the advertising agency and the client company.

creatives the persons who actually develop and produce advertisements.

advertising campaign management the process of preparing and integrating a specific advertising program in conjunction with the overall IMC message.

top of mind brand the brand that is nearly always mentioned when consumers are asked to identify brands that quickly come to mind from a product category.

top choice the first or second pick when a consumer reviews his or her evoked set of possible purchasing alternatives.

puffery the use of an exaggerated claim about a product or service without making an overt attempt to deceive or mislead.

promotional campaign combining advertisements with other marketing efforts into a larger, more integrated effort revolving around a central idea or theme.

pulsating schedule of advertising continuous advertising with bursts of higher intensity (more ads in more media) during the course of the year, most notably during peak seasons.

flighting schedule of advertising a schedule in which companies present ads only during specific times and not at all during off-seasons.

continuous campaign schedule of advertising when the company advertises in level amounts because product purchases are essentially "random" events.

support the facts that substantiate the unique selling point.

constraints the legal and mandatory restrictions placed on advertisements. They include legal protection for trademarks, logos, and copy registrations.

CRITICAL THINKING EXERCISES

Discussion Questions

Use the following Creative Brief for Questions 1 through 4.

Creative Brief for Ford Motor Company's Lincoln-Mercury Division

Product:	Mercury Cougar sports coupe.
Objective:	To reverse lagging sales.
Target audience:	25- to 35-year-old consumers, split evenly between males and females, college educated, with annual incomes of approximately $40,000.
	Psychographically, the targeted market is a group known as *individualists.* They tend not to buy mainstream products. In automobile selection, they place greater emphasis on design elements, distinctiveness, and utility.
Message theme:	An automobile is like a fashion accessory. A car is selected because of the statement it makes to others.

1. As the account executive for an advertising agency, discuss the creative brief in terms of completeness of information provided and whether the objective is realistic. What additional information should the Ford Motor Company provide before a creative can begin working on the account?

2. The media planner for the Mercury Cougar sports coupe account suggests a media plan consisting of cable television, print advertising, internet ads, and network advertising on Fox shows *Ally McBeal, The X-Files, The Simpsons,* and *King of the Hill.* Evaluate this media plan in light of the creative brief's objectives. Can these shows reach the target audience? What information does a creative and the account executive want from the media planner before starting work on actual commercials?

3. From the viewpoint of the creative assigned to this account, do the creative brief and the media plan (see Question 2) contain sufficient information to design a series of advertisements? What, if any, additional information is necessary?

4. Using the information provided in the creative brief, prepare a magazine advertisement. Which magazines might match the target audience?

5. Choose a familiar good, service, or retailer. Using the information in this chapter, prepare a creative brief.

6. Many advertisers tend to direct ads toward the right side of the brain and develop advertisements based entirely on emotions, images, and pictures. Companies often advertise auto parts and tools with a scantily clad woman to attract the attention of men. The woman has nothing to do with the product but garners attention. The rationale for using a sexy woman is that if consumers like her, they will like the product and then purchase that brand. Effective advertisements integrate elements from both the left side of the brain as well as the right. They contain elements that appeal to emotions as well as having rational arguments. A laundry detergent can be advertised as having the rational benefit of getting clothes cleaner but also contains the emotional promise that your mother-in-law will think more favorably of you. For each of the following Internet sites, discuss the balance of left-brain versus right-brain advertising appeal.

   a. Pier 1 Imports (www.pier1.com)

   b. Potbelly Pigs Online (www.potbellypigs.com)

   c. Dark Dog (www.darkdog.com)

   d. Athletic Women (www.athleticwomen.com)

   e. Discount Cheerleading.com (www.discountcheerleading.com)

   f. American Wilderness Gear (www.awigear.com)

7. You have been asked to select an advertising agency to handle an account for Red Lobster, a national restaurant chain. Your advertising budget is $30 million. Study the Web sites of the following advertising agencies. Follow the selection steps outlined in the chapter. Narrow the list down to two agencies and justify your decision. Then choose among the two agencies and justify your choice.

   a. DDB Worldwide (www.ddbn.com)

   b. Leo Burnett (www.leoburnett.com)

   c. BBDO Worldwide (www.bbdo.com)

   d. BADJAR Advertising Pty Lfg (www.badjar.com)

   e. Anderson Lucas Advertising (www.aladv.com)

   f. Grey Advertising (www.grey.com)

   g. Bozell Advertising (www.bozell.com)

8. A marketing manager has been placed in charge of a new brand of jeans to be introduced into the market. The company's corporate headquarters are in Atlanta, and the firm's management team has already decided to use one of the local advertising agencies. Two primary objectives to use to choose an agency are: (1) the agency must have the capability to develop a strong brand name, and (2) the agency must be able to help with business-to-business marketing to place the jeans into retail stores. Access Atlanta Ad Agencies at **www.AtlantaAdAgencies.com**. Follow the steps outlined in the chapter to narrow the list to three agencies. Then design a project for the agencies to prepare as part of an oral and written presentation to the company's marketing team.

Constructing an Advertising Program

You must make a key choice about advertising the product and company you selected. Is an in-house approach best or will you utilize an advertising agency? How can you make sure your advertising campaign matches the overall theme of your IMC program? How much money is budgeted for the campaign? What type of budgeting strategy will be used? These and other questions are raised in the Chapter 6 exercise for an IMC campaign. Go to the Prentice-Hall Web site at **www.prenhall.com/clow** or access the IMC Plan Pro disk that accompanied this textbook to begin the process of developing your ads. Among the items to prepare at this stage are the communication market analysis and the creative brief, which will guide the rest of your advertising program.

BUILDING AN IMC CAMPAIGN

IMC PlanPro!

CASE 1

HOW TO WIN (AND LOSE) AN ADVERTISING ACCOUNT[15]

Being selected to manage a major advertising account is a difficult but enriching process. For instance, consider the case of Atlanta-based Charter Behavioral Systems. Charter is the largest provider of alcoholism and depression treatment services in the United States. The goal was to select an agency to handle a $20 million television advertising account. Charter identified some basic goals and developed a selection process that included the criteria to use in the screening process. The six agencies identified for initial screening were McCann Erickson, BBDO, Rubin Postaer, Carat ICG, Tauche Martin, and Bates USA. The initial screening process was based on the following items:

- Size
- Capabilities
- Credentials and references
- Documented experience and past successes

Tauche Martin was dropped from the list because it was too small. Although the management team at Charter believed the staff at Tauche Martin consisted of some very bright people, the size of the account would have overwhelmed the firm. Bates USA was rejected because Bates's major client was Korean. A recent lag in the Asian economy caused the leaders of Charter to fear that Bates might be forced to close its Atlanta office if it lost its Korean client. Charter eliminated another agency based on reference checks. From television station reps to media buyers, the consistent word was "run!" At the end of the initial screening process, two agencies remained: Rubin Postaer and Carat ICG.

Rubin Postaer is a $550 million Los Angeles–based full-service agency. The firm is known primarily for work with Honda, Charles Schwab, and *Discover* magazine. Carat ICG is a $600 million agency with clients such as Ameritech, Midas, Primestar, and DHL Worldwide.

To decide between Rubin Postaer and Carat ICG, Charter asked each to make a final presentation addressing a series of 10 questions. They were further instructed to think of it as a "mock buy" in the Atlanta market. The companies were asked to provide their projected list of media buys and the rationale for the buys. The most challenging aspect of the final presentation requirement was a round table discussion with at least five of the agency's media buyers. Although each agency's management team could be present, the managers were told not to answer questions posed to the buyers.

Carat ICG included employees in the final presentation who were not going to be part of the account team. Although Charter's management team felt that it was flattering to have Carat ICG's chairman present for the three-hour presentation, Charter believed ICG's approach was more a sales presentation than a mock media buy.

ICG demonstrated a solid command of the strategies the agency believed Charter should use in the Atlanta market. Unfortunately, ICG skimped on some logistical details. Charter's leaders also thought that when ICG presented the mock buy, its representatives were quick, superficial, and had not spent a great deal of time laying out a total approach. On the positive side, ICG's senior vice president Jim Surmanek led the agency's presentation. Surmanek, the author of a media textbook, knew the media issues extremely well. In the final evaluation, Charter concluded ICG clearly was superior at developing an advertising strategy. The agency's recommendations highlighted the company's deep understanding of Charter's business.

On the other hand, Rubin Postaer made a presentation using employees who would be servicing the account. Chairman Jerry Rubin did not attend the meeting although he did meet with Charter's management briefly to

(continued)

assure them of his commitment. Charter felt Rubin Postaer made a serious mistake during the presentation. The presentation team did not bring in a buyer for the direct-response media. ICG did. At the same time, Rubin's vice president of spot buying, Cathleen Campe, grasped quickly what was most important. Campe flew in buyers from Chicago, New York, and Los Angeles to assist in the presentation. These buyers spoke often, expressing their views. Charter concluded that Rubin was more powerful in "branding" its media style with a label called *active negotiation*. Rubin's basic philosophy was that the toughest negotiations begin after buying the media time. Rubin made the claim that the agency was willing to spend more time monitoring media purchases than making the actual purchases. This advantage was substantiated by all of the references.

1. Which agency should Charter Behavioral Systems hire? Justify your answer.

2. Should Carat ICG do anything differently the next time company representatives make a presentation? Why or why not?

3. Should Rubin Postaer do anything differently the next time the firm makes a presentation? Why or why not?

4. Should "fuzzy" variables such as trust and confidence be the deciding factor in choosing an advertising agency? Why or why not?

CASE 2

MORE THAN POTS 'N PANS

Sophia Rushmore enjoyed challenges. Early in life she conquered the challenge of become a gourmet chef. She had held positions at some of the finest restaurants on the West Coast, preparing nouvelle cuisine as well as spectacular desserts. After 20 years in the business, she decided it was time to capitalize on her reputation and tackle a new aspect of the restaurant game, the equipment side.

Most people probably don't stop to consider the many items sold to restaurants. Everything from tables and chairs, booths, ovens and stoves, cooking equipment (pots and pans), silverware, cloth napkins and paper napkin dispensers, lighted menu panels, table candles, wine racks, glasses, cups, plates, and an endless variety of products are sold to both ongoing restaurants as well as new ventures.

Turnover is high in the food industry. Places come and go. It is not unusual for the same location to house four or five different types of restaurants over a 10-year period due to business failures. Each time, some of the equipment is sold to the new owner, but there is a constant demand for products to individualize the business.

Sophia raised venture capital from some of her favorite customers and former employers. She developed a kind of middle-person business that purchased all types of items from various manufacturers and then resold them to restaurants in packages. Her company created a paper catalog listing all of the products it could access and deliver and then posted the catalog on the Internet. She began by targeting new and ongoing businesses in southern California, most notably Los Angeles, San Diego, and Anaheim. Her goal was to expand the business northward over a period of five years.

Sophia personally trained the sales force. She selected an upscale name for her venture, "Accents by Sophia," hoping her new clients would respond to her reputation in the kitchen. Her company motto was "friendly, courteous, professional service to restaurants of every size and taste."

Trade shows are the staple of the food industry. Sophia established a strong presence at them. She had her life story published in a book, so she could give away free autographed copies at her display. Promotional give-aways are part of the trade show game. Sophia needed to develop her own unique set to bring attention to her business. Orders and expressions of interest at a show were followed up by phone calls, personal visits, and e-mail notes by the sales force as quickly as possible.

The final part of Sophia's new venture was to construct an advertising campaign to support her personal selling, direct mail, Internet, and promotional (trade show) efforts. Sophia had a variety of choices because she lived in a major media center, Los Angeles. Becoming established in this highly competitive marketplace was the next big step for Accents by Sophia.

1. Should Sophia hire an external agency or do the work in-house?
2. How should she spend the money for her campaign? Which media should she buy?
3. What should be the primary goal of her advertising campaign?
4. Prepare a creative brief that Sophia could provide to an advertising agency.
5. Access Los Angeles Ad Agencies at **www.LosAngelesAdAgencies. com**. Follow the steps outlined in the chapter to select an advertising agency for Sophia. Justify the selection.

ENDNOTES

1. Mary Lou Quinlan, "The *More* Ad Challenge: How to sell 40+," *More* (April 2002), pp. 53–55.
2. Based on Charles F. Frazier, "Creative Strategies: A Management Perspective," *Journal of Advertising,* 12, no. 4 (1983), pp. 36–41.
3. Al Ries, "Should Your Ads Be an Inside Job?" *Sales and Marketing Management,* 147, no. 2 (February 1995), pp. 26–27.
4. "Ad Firm's Focus: Native Americans," *Editor & Publisher,* 132, no. 28 (July 10, 1999), p. 28.
5. Beth Snyder and Laurel Wentz, "Whole Egg Theory Finally Fits the Bill for Y&R Clients," *Advertising Age,* 70, no. 4 (July 25, 1999), pp. 12–13.
6. James Zoltak and Aaron Baar, "Norwest–Wells Fargo to DDB," *Adweek,* Western Edition, 49, no. 19 (May 10, 1999), p. 50.
7. Ibid.
8. Ibid.
9. Laura Petrecca, "Agencies Urged to Show the Worth of Their Work," *Advertising Age,* 68, no. 15 (April 14, 1997), pp. 3–4.
10. Robert J. Lavidge and Gary A. Steiner, "A Model for Predictive Measurements of Advertising Effectiveness," *Journal of Marketing,* 24 (October 1961), pp. 59–62.
11. Henry A. Laskey and Richard J. Fox, "The Relationship Between Advertising Message Strategy and Television Commercial Effectiveness," *Journal of Advertising Research,* 35, no. 2 (March/April 1995), pp. 31–39.
12. Tim J. Williams, "A Whole-Brain Approach to Advertising," *Marketing News,* 29, no. 9 (April 24, 1995), p. 4.
13. Michael Alvear, "On the Spot," *Mediaweek,* 8, no. 13 (March 30, 1998), pp. 26–28.
14. "Picking up the Pace," *Marketing News,* 36, issue 7 (April 1, 2002), p. 3.
15. Michael Alvear, "On the Spot."

7

Advertising Design: Theoretical Frameworks and Types of Appeals

Chapter Objectives

Understand **how the hierarchy of effects model explains the process a creative uses to move a viewer from awareness to an eventual purchase decision.**

Reconsider **the roles attitudes and values play in developing advertising messages.**

Recognize **how visual and verbal messages are used in ads.**

Identify **times when each of the major advertising appeals will be effective and when they will not.**

Comprehend **the difficult task before the creative, as he or she begins to design the advertising message.**

IS SILENCE GOLDEN?

An interesting paradox is present in the world of advertising design. On the one hand, the advertiser has so much to say to potential customers in a world full of clutter that companies wonder how they're ever going to be heard. On the other, if the message is jammed too full with information, the message is just as easily lost. Consequently, almost every kind of ad must be framed with some type of *white space*.

White space is the absence of copy in a printed text and the absence of music or sound in a radio or television ad. White space is the area around the pictures and words on a billboard. Advertising creatives know white space is a crucial ingredient in a world cluttered with ads.

In television advertising, a space of silence, without music or some other sound, may quickly attract the viewer's attention. The contrast of sound with white space is an attention-getting factor. It may be a matter as simple as causing the viewer to turn to the television set to see if it has broken. Further, silence research indicates that ads without music often result in higher levels of attention being paid to the verbal message. The same is true for white space, or no sound at all. Viewers tend to pay more attention to the message content following the insertion of white space into the ad.

On the radio, silence is a two-edged sword. On the one hand, "dead air" is a dreaded mistake. If a listener tunes into a station with dead air, the individual quickly changes channels. Consequently, there is very little silence on the radio. On the other hand, a brief pause in a noisy commercial or song has as much attention-getting value as white space on television. The key appears to be to keep the white space so short that the viewer doesn't conclude the station has gone off the air.

Print advertisers must also incorporate white space into ads. In newspapers, ads are often "stacked" on the bottom of a page. To draw the viewer's attention, the ad must be large enough to compete visually and then must be framed enough to differentiate it from

other ads. It can be frustrating for an advertiser to pay for column inches of white newsprint, but without the spacing the ad is much less likely to be noticed. Grocery advertisements are the one obvious violation of the white space rule. Grocery ads are routinely jammed with information. Readers expect such clutter and are willing to work through the tangle of products and prices to discover food values and discounts.

Magazine ads can be, in a sense, more artistic. A full-page ad gives the creative the opportunity to arrange the banner, copy, pictures, and tag lines over the full page. White space is still used, but does not necessarily need to frame the ad because the page is already differentiated from the one next to it. The radical use of white space in the Crest advertisement illustrates the benefit of using Crest toothpaste on a regular basis.

Billboard ads also employ white space to frame the key message, which is normally just a few words. Many billboards have borders around them, often in black, which make the ad seem more like a photo. The border also distinguishes the ad from any background behind the sign.

Cluttered Internet ads are common. Many Web site managers have not yet discovered the importance of white space. Internet surfers are accustomed to flashing past the flood of ads filling the screen when a site is accessed. In the future, don't be surprised to see less screen clutter on many Web sites, unless readers begin to react to Web pages in the same way they do to grocery ads.[1]

THE BOULDER STOP

When a strong IMC foundation has been built, the marketing team has a strong sense of the company's message, individual customers, and target markets, and knows how and why various customers make purchases. This information, when combined with theoretical frameworks such as the hierarchy of effects model, means-ends theory, and visual and verbal imaging, leads to the development of the advertising approach. It is important that the company, the advertising account executive, and the creative all have a mutual understanding of how to proceed.

Sections 5.2.1, 6.2.1, and 7.21 of The Boulder Stop's IMC campaign are devoted to advertising. After reviewing the budget to be used, the campaign notes all of the parts of a creative brief that you will learn about in this chapter. This brief includes the target audience profile, message theme, the support, and the constraints. The brief is linked to the product's attributes, which in this example is high-quality climbing gear. Also, as part of the means-ends chain, the product benefit of being dependable is linked to the personal value of fun. The leverage point that emerges is suggesting Boulder Stop's products are safe by using the headline "Be sure your gear is the best." In this instance, the climber's life is at stake.

Which advertising message made the biggest impression on you in the last five years? Was Tiger Woods bouncing a golf ball in time to music? Was it something from the Super Bowl? Was it something sexy, like a Victoria's Secret model being asked to define *desire*? Or did a local commercial get your attention? Did you end up buying a product or using a service because you saw the ad, or was it just entertaining? Do you think business-to-business buyers respond to ads that differ from those oriented toward consumers?

These and other questions demonstrate how the process of designing a set of advertisements for a campaign can be one of the more challenging and interesting components in an integrated marketing communications program. The goal is not only to prepare an ad people enjoy but also to make an ad that changes their behaviors and attitudes. At the least, the goal is to have them remember the goods and services being advertised, so that the next time they consider making a purchase the company will come to mind first.

Chapter 6 described advertising from the perspective of the firm and the account executive. The account executive leads the ad agency team in making a pitch for the account, conducts media selections, and works with media planners and buyers. This chapter, which focuses on the actual message design, is largely oriented toward understanding the work of the creative.

Remember, the message design process is not performed in isolation. It is based on the creative brief, which the account executive prepares, and also takes into consideration the media that will be utilized. By combining all of these elements, the creative can design an effective advertisement.

Two major topics are covered in this chapter. The first is to describe three theoretical approaches to advertising design. They are:

▶ Hierarchy of effects model
▶ Means–ends theory
▶ Visual and verbal imaging

The second topic is to review, in detail, the major appeals advertisers use. Many of these approaches will be familiar. The goal of the account executive and the creative is to select the appeal with the best chance of leading to the desired outcome or behavior. From there, the actual message content is developed. Before beginning the process of creating the ad, it is important to remember the steps taken up to this point. These are summarized by noting the items in the creative brief.

> ▶ **The objective**
> ▶ **The target audience**
> ▶ **The message theme**
> ▶ **The support**
> ▶ **The constraints**

FIGURE 7.1
Creative Brief

THE CREATIVE BRIEF

Figure 7.1 summarizes the elements of a creative brief, introduced in Chapter 6. This outline directs the creative as he or she prepares various advertisements. Designing an effective advertising message begins with understanding the *objective* of the ad and the *target audience*. Then, the advertising group agrees on a *message theme,* an outline of the key ideas the program will convey. The account executive or client must provide the *support* for the advertising theme or claim as well as the documentation the advertisement needs. The support must match the message theme in the advertisement being designed. Finally, the creative must be aware of any *constraints* that might affect the preparation of the ad. With these key components in mind, the creative moves forward toward designing the actual message. The following section describes three theoretical approaches designed to assist in the process.

ADVERTISING THEORY

In developing an advertisement for an advertising campaign, several theoretical frameworks are useful. The first theory described is the hierarchy of effects model. The second is a means–ends chain. Both the hierarchy of effects model and a means–ends chain can be used to develop leverage points. Leverage points move the consumer from understanding a product's benefits to linking those benefits with personal values. Finally, the third theoretical perspective involves visual versus verbal framework for the ad.

Hierarchy of Effects

The **hierarchy of effects model** helps clarify the objectives of an advertising campaign as well as the objective of a particular advertisement. It also aids the marketing team in identifying the best communications strategy (see Chapter 8). The model suggests that a consumer or a business buyer moves through this series of six steps when becoming convinced to make a purchase:

1. Awareness
2. Knowledge
3. Liking
4. Preference
5. Conviction
6. The actual purchase

These steps are sequential. Consumers spend a period of time at each step before moving to the next. Thus, before a person can develop a liking for a product, he or she must first have sufficient

An advertisement by Curves for Women designed to encourage consumers to join by offering a special free "rest of summer" promotion.
Source: Used with permission of the *Joplin Globe,* Joplin, Missouri.

knowledge of the product. Once the individual has the knowledge and develops liking for the product, the advertiser can try to influence the consumer to prefer a particular brand or company more strongly.

Although the hierarchy of effects model helps creatives understand the impact of an advertisement on viewers, some of its underlying principles have been questioned. For instance, sometimes consumers first make a purchase and then later develop knowledge, liking, preference, and conviction. Shoppers sometimes purchase brands when no or little preference is involved, because coupons and impulse purchase incentives cause them to buy. At other times, someone may not even remember the name of the brand purchased. This is often the case with commodity products such as sugar and flour or even clothing purchases such as socks and shirts.

Still, the major benefit of the hierarchy of effects model is that it is one method used to identify the typical steps consumers and businesses take when making purchases. To encourage brand loyalty, all six steps must be present. A consumer or business is unlikely to be loyal to a particular brand without sufficient knowledge of the brand. Purchasers must like the brand and build a strong preference for it. Next, they must cultivate strong convictions that the particular brand is superior to the other brands on the market. None of this occurs without first becoming aware of the product. Thus, the components of the hierarchy of effects approach highlight the various responses that advertising or other marketing communications must accomplish. This is true of both consumer and business markets.

The hierarchy of effects model has many similarities with theories about attitudes and attitudinal change. Chapter 3 defined the concepts of cognitive, affective, and conative elements of attitudes. The *affective* component contains the feelings or emotions a person has about the object, topic, or idea. The *cognitive* component is the person's mental images, understanding, and interpretations of the person, object, or issue. The *conative* component is the individual's intentions, actions or behavior. The most common sequence that takes place when an attitude forms is:

$$Cognitive \rightarrow Affective \rightarrow Conative$$

It is important to remember that any combination of these components is possible. This means the structured six-step process of the hierarchy of effects model may be more rigid than is actually the case. Keep in mind that sometimes an advertisement that breaks out of the mold, or one that is different, can be very successful because it captures an individual's attention. As a general guideline, however, the cognitive strategies work best for advertising objectives of brand awareness and brand knowledge. Affective advertising strategies are superior in developing liking, preference, and conviction for a product. Conative advertising strategies are best in facilitating actual product purchases. Brand strategies are a mixture of the other three and can be used to accomplish any of the six steps in the hierarchy of effects model.

Means–End Theory

A second theoretical approach is a **means–end chain**. An advertisement contains a message or a *means* to lead the consumer to a desired end state. These *end* states include the personal values presented in Chapter 3, and listed in Figure 7.2. The purpose of the means–end chain is to cause a chain reaction in which viewing the ad leads the consumer to believe the product will achieve one of these personal values.

▶ Comfortable life	▶ Inner peace	▶ Self-fulfillment
▶ Equality	▶ Mature love	▶ Self-respect
▶ Excitement	▶ Personal accomplishment	▶ Sense of belonging
▶ Freedom	▶ Pleasure	▶ Social acceptance
▶ Fun, exciting life	▶ Salvation	▶ Wisdom
▶ Happiness	▶ Security	

FIGURE 7.2
Personal Values

Means–end theory is the basis of a model called MECCAS. **MECCAS** stands for **Means–End Conceptualization of Components for Advertising Strategy**.[2] The MECCAS model suggests using these five elements in creating ads:

▶ The product's attributes
▶ Consumer benefits
▶ Leverage points
▶ Personal values
▶ The executional framework

The MECCAS is designed to move consumers through these five elements. Thus, the attributes of the product should be linked to the specific benefits consumers can derive. These benefits, in turn, lead to the attainment of a personal value.

To illustrate the MECCAS concept, consider Figure 7.3 below and the milk advertisement shown in this section. The product attribute of calcium provides the benefits of being strong and healthy. The personal value the consumer obtains from healthy bones is feeling wise for using the product. The leverage point in this advertisement is the white mustache on each female. The white mustache and the message are designed to make the viewer believe that drinking milk is linked to preventing osteoporosis in women.

The MECCAS concept also applies to business-to-business advertisements. As discussed in Chapter 4, members of the buying center can be influenced by social, personal, and political values as well as corporate goals. Consider the advertisement for Greenfield Online in this section and the means–end chain in Figure 7.4. Each attribute is presented in

A Got Milk? advertisement illustrating the use of a means–end chain.
Source: Courtesy of Bozell Worldwide, Inc.

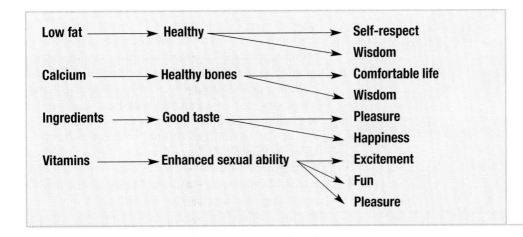

FIGURE 7.3
Means–End Chain for Milk

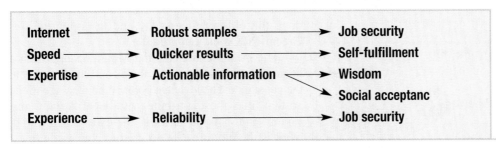

FIGURE 7.4
B-to-B Means–End Chain for Greenfield Online

terms of the benefits business customers can obtain. Although not explicitly stated, the personal values of members of the buying center choosing Greenfield Online might include job security for making good decisions, self-fulfillment, wisdom, and social acceptance by other members of the buying group.

INTEGRATED LEARNING EXPERIENCE

Means–end theory and the MECCAS model are important elements in designing advertisements. Greenfield Online is a Web-based marketing research firm. Access the company's Web site at **www.greenfieldcentral.com**. Examine the products and services it offers in the "Products and Services" section. What types of custom research help a creative develop a means–end chain similar to Figures 7.3 and 7.4? Next, access Greenfield's "Newsroom." Examine the articles and press releases under each subheading in this section. What types of information presented here would assist an advertising creative in developing a means–end chain?

Leverage Points

Both the hierarchy of effects model and the means–end chain approach are associated with leverage points. A **leverage point** is the feature of the ad that leads the viewer to transform the advertising message into a personal value. To construct a quality leverage point, the creative tries to build a pathway connecting a product benefit with the potential buyer's value system.

In terms of the hierarchy of effects model, the initial level of awareness begins the process of exposing consumers to product benefits. As the viewer moves through the six stages, he or she eventually develops the conviction to buy the product. At that point, the benefit has indeed been linked with a personal value. In the milk advertisement used to illustrate the means–end chain, the leverage point is the phrase "There's one person I won't be," which is tied with the copy message "a woman with osteoporosis." The copy goes on to explain that because of calcium (a product attribute), women can have healthy bones (product benefit). Making a conscious decision to use milk to prevent osteoporosis demonstrates the personal values of wisdom and seeking a comfortable and healthier life when a woman grows older.

In the Greenfield Online business-to-business advertisement, the leverage point is the picture of an old-fashioned woman using an old telephone sandwiched between the headline "Are you still buying marketing research done the old-fashioned way?" and the first sentence of the copy explaining that companies can "Do it better on the Internet." The picture creates an excellent mental image of marketing research done the old-fashioned way and the opportunities Greenfield Online can provide.

The means–end chain and MECCAS approaches begin with the product's attributes and the benefits to the consumer. The leverage point is the message in the ad that links these attributes and benefits with consumer values. In the ad itself, the executional framework is the plot or scenario used to convey the mes-

A Greenfield Online business advertisement illustrating the use of a means–end chain in a business ad.
Source: Courtesy of Greenfield Online Inc.

ARE YOU STILL BUYING MARKETING RESEARCH DONE THE OLD-FASHIONED WAY?

Do it better on the Internet with the company that pioneered online marketing research.

Our panel of more than one million consumers from all across the Internet is the largest of its kind. It produces robust samples of any demographic or lifestyle you choose. You'll get richer, more actionable information quicker than you can say dot com.

Join the Research Revolution!™ Contact the world's most experienced Internet marketing research company for studies online, on time, on target and on budget.

www.greenfield.com 888.291.9997

Greenfield *Online*
Leading the Research Revolution®

sage designed to complete the linkage. Chapter 8 presents executional frameworks in detail, in which dramatizations and other methods of telling the ad story help build effective leverage points.

An effective leverage point can also be associated with an attitudinal change, especially when the sequence is cognitive → affective → conative. As the attitude is formed, the individual first understands, then is moved emotionally, then takes action. A leverage point can help the viewer of an ad move through these three stages, thereby tieing cognitive knowledge of the product to more emotional and personal values.

Creatives spend considerable amounts of time designing ads with powerful leverage points. Executional frameworks and various types of appeals, as described in the upcoming pages, are the tools creatives use to help consumers make the transition from being aware of a product's benefits to incorporating them with personal value systems.

INTEGRATED LEARNING EXPERIENCE

Examine Figure 7.3, and access the following Web sites the milk industry uses to aim at different target markets.

www.got-milk.com
www.gotmilk.com
www.whymilk.com

What differences exist among these Web sites? Identify the leverage points each site uses. How does each one take the viewer from the advertising message to the personal value being stressed? What product attributes and customer benefits does it highlight? What personal values can you identify? In terms of the means–end chain, which sites are the most effective?

S T O P

Verbal and Visual Images

A third theoretical component of advertising design is the decision the creative makes to determine the degree of emphasis given to the visual element of the ad versus the verbal element. Most major forms of advertising have both visual and verbal elements, with the obvious exception of radio. A verbally biased ad places greater emphasis on words. In terms of the ELM model described in Chapter 3, a verbal ad takes the central route (most direct and easily remembered) of information processing. A visually biased ad is processed using the peripheral route.

Visual images often lead to more favorable attitudes toward both the advertisement and the brand. Visuals also tend to be more easily remembered than verbal copy. Visual elements are stored in the brain as both pictures and words. This dual processing makes it easier for people to recall the message. Further, visual images are usually stored in both the left and right sides of the brain, while verbal messages tend be stored in the left side of the brain only.

Visual images range from very concrete and realistic to highly abstract. In a concrete visual, the subject is easily recognizable as a person, place, or thing. In an abstract picture or image, the subject is more difficult to recognize. Concrete pictures have a higher level of recall than do abstract images because of the dual-coding process whereby the image is stored in the brain as both a visual and a verbal representation. For example, viewers process an ad with a picture of spaghetti used in promoting a restaurant as both a picture and a verbal representation. Ads with concrete images lead to more favorable attitudes than ads with no pictures or abstract pictures. Research offers many reasons for creatives to include visual images in their advertisements.[3]

An advertisement using a leverage point of a dog and cat snuggled together with the opening sentence "What can you possibly record in the dark?"
Source: Used by permission of Sony Electronics, Inc.

What can you possibly record in the dark? You'd be surprised. Only the Sony Handycam® camcorder offers the NightShot™ Infrared System, which allows for something we like to call "0 Lux recording." In plain English, that means you can record in complete darkness, both inside and outdoors. And, as you'll soon find out, that's when all the good stuff happens.

SONY
www.sony.com/handycam

This ASICS ad blends visual imagery with the verbal copy.
Source: Courtesy of ASICS Tiger Corporation.

A television advertisement featuring vivid visual images to create the message that BB&T knows your name and that you are important to them.
Source: Courtesy of Howard, Merrell & Partners.

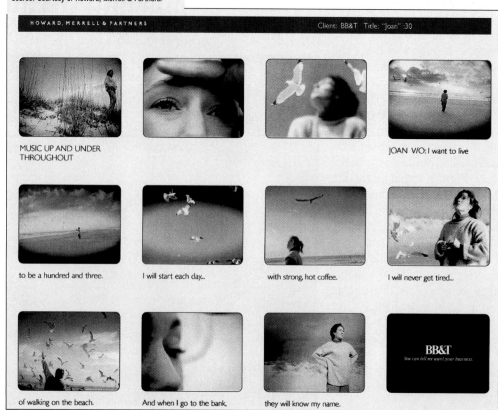

Radio does not have a visual component. As a result, radio advertisers often try to create visual images for the audience. Pepsi produced an ad in which listeners hear a can being opened, the soft drink being poured, and the sizzle of the carbonation—an excellent example of creating a visual image. If consumers can see the image in their minds, the effect is greater than actual visual portrayal. An actual visual event requires less brain activity than using one's imagination to develop the image. The secret is getting the person to think beyond the ad and picture the scene being simulated.

Visual imagery is especially important in the international arena. Global advertising agencies try to create what they call **visual esperanto**, a universal language that makes global advertising possible for any good or service. *Visual esperanto* advertising recognizes that visual images are more powerful than verbal descriptions. Visual images also transcend cultural differences.[4] To illustrate the power of a visual image over a verbal account, think of the word *exotic*. To some, exotic means a white beach in Hawaii with young people in sexy swimsuits. To others it may be a small cabin in the snow-capped mountains of Switzerland. While to others still, exotic may be a closeup of a tribal village in Africa. The verbal word can vary in meaning. At the same time, a picture of a couple holding hands in front of the Niagara Falls has practically the same meaning across all cultures. A young child smiling after eating a piece of candy also conveys an almost universal message.

The most important task in creating *visual esperanto* is to create the appropriate visual image. The creative tries to think of an image that conveys the intended meaning or message. The goal is to create a brand identity through visuals rather than words. Then the creative can use words to back up or support the visual image. For example, the creative may decide that a boy and his father at a sports event illustrates the priceless treasure of a shared family moment. In Mexico, the setting could be a soccer match instead of a baseball game in the United States. The specific copy (the words) can then be adapted to the country involved. The difficult part of obtaining a *visual esperanto* is choosing the correct image that transcends cultures. Once a universal image is created, the creatives in each of the countries represented can take the visual image and modify it to appeal to their target audience.

In the past, creatives designing business-to-business advertisements relied heavily on the verbal element rather than on visuals. The basis of this approach was the idea that business decisions are made in a rational, cognitive manner. In recent years, more business ads have incorporated strong visual elements to heighten the emotional aspects of making a purchase. In summary, all the theoretical models presented in this section provide critical ideas for the advertising creative. They suggest that some kind of sequence must be chosen as the ad is prepared. The endpoint of the ad should be a situation in which the viewer is enticed to remember the product, to think favorably about it, and to look for that product when making the purchase decision. Various kinds of advertising messages, or appeals, can be utilized to reach such key advertising objectives.

INTEGRATED LEARNING EXPERIENCE

Visual images are an important feature of any attempt to market a product globally. Access the Sun Microsystems marketing resource center at **www.sun.com/smrc**, and the "advertising" section of that center. Next, go to the "International Gallery" part of the site. Examine the advertisements for Sun that appear in various countries throughout the world. What are the similarities? What are the differences? To obtain more information, access the "Outdoor," "Radio," and "TV" sections. To view an ad agency's perspective, access Leo Burnett Agency at **www.leoburnett.com**. At the "Work" section, look at the examples of the agency's various print, television, or other media advertisements. What are the differences in the ads across the various countries?

TYPES OF ADVERTISING APPEALS

Over the years, advertisers have attempted a wide variety of advertising approaches. Seven major types of **advertising appeals** have been the most successful. Advertisers usually select from one of these types of appeals as they develop the advertisement:

- Fear
- Humor
- Sex
- Music
- Rationality
- Emotions
- Scarcity

The particular appeal to use should be based on a review of the creative brief, the objective of the advertisement, and the means–end chain to be conveyed. The actual choice depends on a number of factors, including the product being sold, the personal preferences of the advertising creative and the account executive, as well as the wishes of the client. In determining the best appeal to use, it is often a question of what appeals would be inappropriate. Advertising experts know that certain appeals are less effective at various times. For example, some research indicates that sex appeals are not effective for goods and services that are in no way related to sex.

In any case, this section provides a complete description of the types of advertising appeals that are available. Each has been successfully used and has failed in other ads. The key responsibility of the marketer is to make sure, to whatever degree is possible, that the appeal is the right choice for the brand.

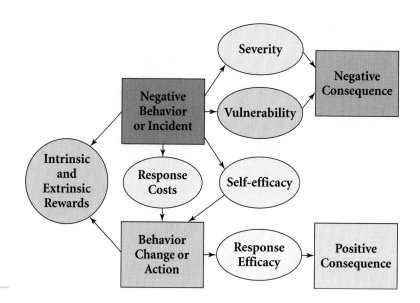

FIGURE 7.5
Behavioral Response Model

Fear

Advertisers use fear to sell a variety of products. Life insurance companies focus on the consequences of not having life insurance if a person dies. Shampoo and mouthwash ads invoke fears of dandruff and bad breath. These problems can make a person a social outcast. Fear is used more often than most casual observers realize.

Simply stated, advertisers use fear appeals because they work. Fear increases both the viewer's interest in an advertisement and the persuasiveness of that ad. Many individuals remember advertisements with fear appeals better than they do warm, upbeat messages.[5] Consumers who pay more attention to an advertisement are more likely to process the information it presents. This information processing makes it possible to accomplish the ad's main objective.

A theoretical explanation regarding the way fear works is the *behavioral response model* (see Figure 7.5).[6] As shown, various incidents can lead to negative or positive consequences, which then affect future behaviors. For an example of how to use this approach, see the Communication Action Box, "Smoking and Fear: Which Wins Out?"

In developing fear advertisements, it is important to highlight as many aspects of the behavioral response model as possible. A business-to-business advertiser offering Internet services tries to focus on the **severity** of downtime if a company's Internet server goes down. Another ad describes the firm's **vulnerability** by showing the high probability that a company's server is going to crash. The Service Metrics advertisement in this section features a picture of a blindfolded man ready to step into a manhole to illustrate the danger of e-business pitfalls. The goal of the advertisement is to make businesses realize they are more vulnerable than they think and that Service Metrics can help reveal these potential problems before they become disasters.

A business-to-business advertisement by Service Metrics using a fear appeal.
Source: Courtesy of Service Metrics.

What you **can't see** about your e-business **performance** can hurt.

How's your site?

Let Service Metrics™ remove the blindfold. We measure Web site performance from your customer's perspective, revealing potential problems before they become e-business pitfalls. With Service Metrics, you can see exactly where you stand. We don't just help you compete, we give you an unfair advantage.

SERVICE METRICS™
An Exodus Communications Company

The Best Measure of Performance™
www.servicemetrics.com

SM.UPS.AP.I/00.1

COMMUNICATION ACTION

Smoking and Fear: Which Wins Out?

For many years, the American Cancer Society has attempted to develop more effective antismoking advertisements. The behavioral response model (Figure 7.5) can be a useful guide in developing such ads. The negative behavior addressed is smoking. The goal becomes to portray negative consequences associated with smoking, such as heart problems, lung cancer, or throat cancer. The severity is the degree of possible physical or psychological harm. The severity should be quite high. Lung cancer often results in death. The vulnerability is the probability that the consequence will occur. Unfortunately, the American Cancer Society knows that many people continue smoking because they do not see themselves as being highly vulnerable.

One side of the behavioral response model includes the intrinsic and extrinsic rewards associated with various activities. Extrinsic rewards are those given by other people. Young people often begin smoking because of the social rewards they obtain such as social acceptance by peers. Intrinsic rewards are internally generated (the ones you give yourself). Teenagers gain an intrinsic psychological reward from smoking when it makes them feel like they are adults.

The fight to curb tobacco usage among teenagers is extremely difficult because of these intrinsic and extrinsic rewards. Recent antismoking ads attempted to tackle the problem by changing the nature of extrinsic rewards. These ads show teenagers who smoke as being undesirable to those of the opposite sex. The idea is that a teenager who believes his or her peers will not accept the smoking behavior is more inclined to quit or never start.

In general, smokers engage in the negative behavior because of the intrinsic and extrinsic rewards they receive and because they either minimize the severity of the consequences or do not see themselves as being vulnerable. To change their behavior requires three things. First is the response cost. In other words, what would it cost to quit smoking? Teenagers can be influenced through fear of losing social acceptance. Adults may worry that if they quit smoking, they will gain weight or become nervous and irritable. These fears must be overcome for a campaign to succeed.

Another element of the behavioral response model is self-efficacy, or a person's ability to change a behavior. Many smokers do not believe they can quit, even when they want to. In a similar fashion, some people who want to lose weight often do not even try because they feel they do not have enough willpower to stick with a diet. To convince a person to quit smoking is to build up enough self-efficacy to make it seem possible. Many recent antismoking ads use phrases such as "The *power* to quit!" to build self-efficacy in the target audience.

Another behavioral response model ingredient is response efficacy. This is the belief that the change in behavior will result in the positive consequence that is being espoused. If a person does not believe that quitting smoking results in better health or a happier life, then there is little incentive to change behaviors.

For both teenagers and adults, antismoking ads must tackle the combined problems of peer pressure, low self-efficacy, and the physical addiction to the product. Therefore, one clear goal should be to use models such as the behavioral response approach to convince young people never to start.

When using fear, one debate centers on how strong to make the appeal. Most advertisers believe a moderate level of fear is the most effective. A low level of fear may not be noticed, and the fear level may not be convincing in terms of severity or vulnerability. On the other hand, an advertisement with a high level of fear can be detrimental. A message that is too strong causes feelings of anxiety. This leads viewers to avoid watching the ad, by changing the channel or muting the sound.[7] The goal of a fear ad is to be strong enough to get a viewer's attention and to influence his or her thinking, but not so strong that the person avoids seeing the advertisement.

Fear ads match well with certain types of goods and services. Account executives, creatives, and company leaders must decide if fear is a good choice, or if some other type of appeal offers greater promise.

INTEGRATED LEARNING EXPERIENCE

To read additional articles about the use of fear in advertising, access Current Issues in Advertising at **www.yppa-currentadissues.org**. Using the search engine, type in "fear" for a list of articles on the topic. Fear appeals are more common in industries such as insurance, home and vehicle alarm systems, and pharmaceuticals. Pick an industry that is inclined to use fear approaches. Using one of the search engines, locate 10 companies within that industry. Which ones use a fear appeal on their Web page? How effective is the use of fear?

Humor

Clutter is a significant problem in every advertising medium. This makes capturing someone's attention quite difficult. Once an advertiser has the audience's attention, keeping that attention becomes even more challenging. Humor has proven to be one of the best techniques for cutting through clutter. Humor is effective in both getting attention and keeping it. Consumers, as a whole, enjoy advertisements that make them laugh. Something that is funny has intrusive value and can grab attention.

Humor is used in about 30 percent of all advertisements.[8] One reason for the success of humor in advertising may be that the population is aging. According to Abraham Maslow, people tend to develop a more comedic view of life as they mature. Also, humor helps individuals adjust to situations they cannot control and cope with life's problems. Laughing allows individuals to escape from reality. Comedy Central, improv theaters, and comedy bars have grown in popularity over the past decade. Consequently, humor is an effective approach for reaching a wide audience.[9]

The success of humor as an advertising tactic is based on three things. Humor causes consumers to: (1) watch, (2) laugh, and, most importantly, (3) remember. In recall tests, consumers most often remember humorous ads. To be successful, the humor should be connected directly to the product's benefits. It should tie together the product features, the advantage to customers, and the personal values of the means–ends chain.

Humorous ads pique viewer interest, which can lead to more careful consideration of the message in the ad. A well-done ad increases attention in such a manner that greater comprehension and recall of the message arguments and tag line result. Advertising research indicates that humor elevates people's moods. Happy consumers associate a good mood with the advertiser's products. Humor helps fix the

A Greenfield Online ad using a humor appeal.
Source: Courtesy of Greenfield Online, Inc.

Brand manager eliminates pilot costs, becomes hero

Testing new package designs online with rotating 3-D images not only saved the client expensive tooling costs but also saved time. Now manufacturers can design today and test tomorrow. Eliminating pilot costs and shortening "time to market" are just some of the many ways that Greenfield Online quantitative research beats the old-fashioned kind.

Put our expert consultants and advanced technology to work for you.
www.greenfield.com
888.291.9997

Greenfield Online
Leading the Research Revolution®

• Quantitative Studies
• Qualitative Studies
• Media Research
• Self-Directed Research
• Syndicated Studies
• Website Evaluations

HERO

company in the consumer's cognitive structure with links to positive feelings.[10]

Humor captures the viewer's attention, cuts through ad clutter, and enhances recall. Unfortunately, humorous ads can also backfire. Advertisers must be careful to avoid letting the humor overpower the advertisement. When humor fails, it is usually because the joke in the ad is remembered but the product or brand is not. In other words, the ad is so funny that the audience forgets or does not catch the sponsor's name. Although funny ads often win awards, they can fail in terms of accomplishing advertising objectives. To avoid this problem, the humor used in the ad should focus on a component of the means–ends chain. The humor should relate either to a product attribute, a customer benefit, or the personal value obtained from the product. Such ads are the most effective when humor incorporates all three elements.

Further, sarcasm and jokes made at someone's expense are often popular with younger audiences, but are not well received by baby boomer and older generations, especially among the more affluent. For example, a recent advertisement by Miller Lite of an elderly couple passionately necking on a sofa was designed to be funny to the young, male beer-drinking audience. Unfortunately, the ad was quite offensive to the older consumers. With age and maturity comes empathy. Put-downs and cruel jokes are not seen as funny by older people. Understanding these different nuances helps advertisers keep from making mistakes in the use of humor.[11]

Another potential danger of humor is offending an ethnic minority. Dinky, Taco Bell's highly visible Chihuahua, received a mixed reaction in the Hispanic community. Although some think the ads were cute, others found them offensive. Most appeared indifferent. Anytime advertisers utilize ethnicity, they must be extremely careful to avoid offending an ethnic group.

Humorous ads are fun, but difficult to design. One cynic once noted that there are only 12 funny people in the United States. Humor that doesn't work often creates a negative image for the company. Consequently, account executives must be certain the creatives they hire are truly among those who can design and execute funny and effective ads (see Figure 7.6).

Trying to make money is only half the fun.
No...that's pretty much it.

Everyone likes money, that's why you invest. And that's why E*TRADE gives you the tools you need to make better investing decisions. From market insights directly off the street to Smart Alerts that keep tabs on your investments. And at E*TRADE, you never have to spend your precious money on high commissions. Trades start as low as $4.95† with active investor rebate. For more information, visit etrade.com or call us at 1-800-ETRADE-1.

It's time for
E*TRADE

An advertisement for E-Trade using a humorous appeal.

Source: Courtesy of E-Trade Group, Inc. Photograph by Will van Overbeek. © 1999 Will van Overbeek, Photographer/Goodby, Silverstein & Partners, San Francisco, GA.

Good or Service	Hints
▶ Beer	▶ Miller Lite, Keystone, Budweiser, Heineken
▶ Restaurants	▶ Wendy's, Shoney's, Long John Silver's
▶ NBA	▶ It's Fantastic!
▶ Telephone	▶ U.S. Cellular
▶ Motels	▶ Holiday Inn, Red Roof Inn

Can you remember an advertisement for each product or service that was funny?

FIGURE 7.6
Humorous Ads Quiz

Sex

As advertisers look for ways to break through the advertising clutter, they use sexual appeals with increasing regularity. Advertisements in the United States contain more visual sexual themes than ever before. Nudity and other sexual approaches are much more common. Oddly, the actual number of verbal references to sex has decreased over the last decade. Instead, advertisements tend to be more explicitly sexual, showing contact and innuendos and suggest that sex is about to take place. For instance, several recent television ads for jewelry depict a woman wearing a nightgown in the bedroom, looking very passionate and aroused. Then, a ring and the price of the ring are shown with the company's name. Also, the amount of male–female physical contact in advertisements has tripled in the last 30 years.[12]

Sexuality has been employed in advertising in five ways, including:

- Subliminal techniques
- Nudity or partial nudity
- Sexual suggestiveness
- Overt sexuality
- Sensuality

Subliminal approaches place sexual cues or icons in advertisements to affect a viewer's subconscious mind. In an odd paradox, truly subliminal cues should not be strong enough to be noticed or create any effects. Consumers pay little attention to ads already, and a subliminal message that registers only in the subconscious mind will not be effective. If it did, there would not be the need for such strong sexual content in advertising.

The ad for Bijan perfume in this section features Bo Derek. The location of her arm, the expression on her face, and the line "Bo Derek is wearing Bijan Eau de Parfum and nothing else" provide the subliminal sexual message that she is naked.

A large number of companies use nudity or partial nudity to sell their products. Some ads are designed to solicit a sexual response. Others are not. For example, starting in 1987, underwear companies could use live models in television ads. The first commercials were modest and informational, emphasizing the design or materials used in the undergarment. Still, the first Playtex bra commercials using live models drew strong criticism from organizations such as the American Family Association. Now, advertisements for underwear go much further. Ads do much more than

A Bijan perfume advertiseing featuring a subliminal sexual message.
Source: Courtesy of Bijan Fragrances, Inc.

*Bo Derek is wearing Bijan Eau de Parfum and **nothing else!!***

bijan
perfume
Heartfelt Wishes

ADVERTISING DESIGN: THEORETICAL FRAMEWORKS AND TYPES OF APPEALS

What Is Sexually Offensive as Opposed to Effective?

A major ethical issue that has arisen in the past few decades is the use of nudity and sexuality featuring children. Critics have highly disparaged Calvin Klein for pushing the envelope for many years. The original objections arose in the 1980s, when 14-year-old Brooke Shields appeared in an advertisement saying, "Nothing comes between me and my Calvins."

Later, in an attempt to sell children's underwear, the same company decided to prepare a large billboard in Times Square to accompany a series of magazine advertisements. The photo in the ads showed two 6-year-old boys arm wrestling while two girls about the same age were jumping on a sofa. All were only wearing underwear. Only after strong objectives from numerous groups were the ads pulled.

In recent years there has been an increase in sensitivity to issues of child molestation, child pornography, and related sexual issues. Marketing professionals must carefully consider what the limits should be. Suggesting that sex sells is simply not enough, nor is making a defensive claim about freedom of speech or freedom of expression. Ethics, morals, and a clear conscience should serve as additional guides when a company pushes the limits of sexuality using young people as subjects.

show models wearing undergarments. In a recent issue of *Interview* magazine, the underwear model, Raina, is reclining on a couch, her back arched and pinkie finger tucked below her panty line. Victoria's Secret has launched a number of ads featuring girls in underwear in provocative poses, both on television and on billboards.[13]

Instead of nudity, some ads using sex appeals try sexual suggestiveness. The Clairol Herbal Essence Shampoo ads borrowed the "Yes, yes, yes!" scene from the

Two advertisements by Altoid using a sex appeal.
Source: Courtesy of Leo Burnett.

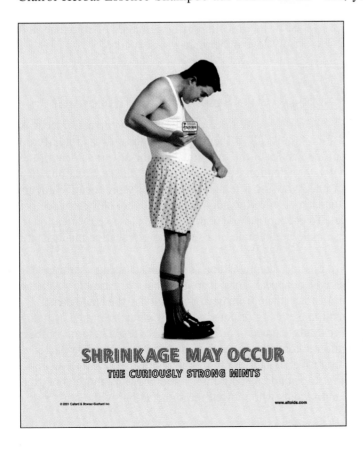

STETSON

THE ATTRACTION IS LEGENDARY

An advertisement in a woman's magazine using a partially nude male model to sell Stetson cologne.

Source: Courtesy of J. B. Stetson Company.

movie *When Harry Met Sally* to make the product seem more sensuous.

A recent trend in sexual suggestiveness is to use gay and lesbian themes. Swedish retailer IKEA was the first in the United States to use a gay theme. A television commercial showing two gay men shopping for a dining room table together first appeared in 1994. Now, a number of companies use homosexuality in advertising. New York City–based Daily Soup restaurant ran an advertisement that featured a woman meeting a blind date at a park. She sits next to an attractive man whom she thinks may be her date but instead he is met by a biker guy who grabs his butt while giving him a big kiss. Levi-Strauss, in an effort to reach younger consumers, introduced a campaign featuring interviews with real teenagers. In one ad, a young man admits to being gay while explaining that his neighbors didn't like him. Other ads, although not overtly gay, could be interpreted as such.[14]

Another recent trend in sexual appeals is the use of sensuality. These ads often target women who might respond to more of a sensual suggestion than an overt sexual approach. Instead of strong sexual images, they show an alluring glance across a crowded room. Many view sensuality as a more sophisticated sexual appeal approach because it relies on the imagination. It portrays images of romance and love rather than raw sexuality.

Are Sex Appeals Effective?

A number of studies have investigated sex appeals and nudity in advertising. Almost all of them conclude that sex and nudity do increase attention, regardless of the gender of the individuals in the advertisement or the gender of the audience. Normally, the attention is greater for opposite-sex situations than same-sex situations. That is, a male viewing a female in a sexually provocative advertisement pays more attention than a male viewing another male in a sexually provocative ad. The same is true for females. To encourage both males and females to pay attention to its ads, Guess often uses both a male and female in a sexually provocative manner in a single advertisement.

Although sexually oriented ads attract attention, brand recall for ads using a sex appeal is lower than ads using some other type of appeal. Thus, it appears that while people watch the advertisement, the sexual theme distracts them from paying attention to the brand name.[15]

In addition to gaining attention, sexually oriented advertisements are rated as being more interesting to viewers. Those ads deemed to be highly controversial in terms of their sexual content were rated as more interesting by both males and females. The paradox, however, is that although the controversial ads are more interesting, they fail to increase the transmission of information. Respondents could not remember any more about the message of the ad than could individuals who viewed the same ad but without a controversial sexual theme.[16]

Advertisements using overt sexual stimuli or containing nudity produce higher levels of physiological arousal responses. These arousal responses have been linked to the formation of both affective and cognitive responses. If the viewer is male and the sexual stimuli is female, such as a naked female in an ad for cologne, then the viewer tends to develop a strong feeling toward the ad based on the arousal response his body experiences. Female viewers of male nudity in an ad often experience the same type of response, although the arousal response tends not to be as strong. The cognitive impression made on the viewers depends on whether they felt the advertisement was pleasant or offensive. If the viewer thinks the ad is in poor taste and is demeaning, then negative feelings and beliefs about the brand result. Such was the case with a television advertisement created by Young and Rubicam, Inc. to promote radio station FM 96.9, a gay–lesbian station in Sydney, Australia, which attempted to combine humor with sexuality. The ad portrayed a singing penis dancing and singing the disco tune "Time to Party." Although the ad won a Cannes Silver Lion award for its creativity, the gay and lesbian community found the ad highly offensive. Many felt it perpetuated the stereotype that gays are more promiscuous than heterosexuals. The heterosexual community found the ad not offensive or erotic but instead extremely hilarious. The ad was well known in the Sydney area and elicited strong feelings. The trouble was that the ad offended many of the station's target audience.[17]

A Guess advertisement featuring both a male and a female model using a sexual appeal.
Source: Courtesy of Guess?, Inc.

A common sexual appeal in advertising is to use decorative models. **Decorative models** are models in an advertisement whose primary purpose is to adorn the product as a sexual or attractive stimulus. The model serves no functional purpose in the ad except to attract attention. Automobiles, tools, and beer commercials in the past often used female models dressed in bikinis to stand by their products. Figure 7.7 covers the basic conclusions of studies looking at the impact of decorative models.[18]

When researchers examined the impact of sexual visual stimuli, they found these types of stimuli affected attitudes in four ways. First, consumers tend to form inferences about the advertised brand based on the information presented in the visual part of the ad. In other words, a macho ad infers the product is manly and so forth. Second, if the visual element is evaluated positively, consumers tend to develop positive attitudes toward both the ad and the brand. If the visual element was evaluated negatively, the reverse was true. Third, in advertising with explicit visual sexual content, the sexual appeal often interferes with message comprehension. The message tends to be interpreted in terms of the ad's visual sexual image. Viewers focused more on the visual component of the ad than on the verbal or written message. Fourth, ads with explicit visual sexual components produce greater purchase intentions, which increase if the product advertised is considered sexually relevant.[19]

> ▶ The presence of female (or male) decorative models improves ad recognition, but not brand recognition.
>
> ▶ The presence of a decorative model influences emotional and objective evaluations of the product among both male and female audiences.
>
> ▶ Attractive models produce a higher level of attention to ads than do less attractive models.
>
> ▶ The presence of an attractive model produces higher purchase intentions when the product is sexually relevant than if it is not sexually relevant.

FIGURE 7.7
Factors to Consider Before Using Decorative Models

Sex Appeals in the International Arena

Although sex is found in advertising worldwide, what is appropriate in terms of sexual appeal varies across countries. Something that is acceptable in one country may not be appropriate in another. For example, in New Zealand a television ad for Rock 93 FM radio station featured a woman wearing a bikini washing a red sports car. The voice-over said, "If you think we'd stoop low enough to use beautiful women and cars to capture your attention, then you're right." The ad was accepted by the Advertising Standards Authority Complaints Board of New Zealand. On the other hand, a billboard in Wellington promoting billboard advertising showed a woman's cleavage with the caption "Exposure." The Advertising Standards Authority Complaints Board ruled this ad was unacceptable because the woman's cleavage had nothing to do with the product, billboard advertising. Other rulings of the board are more confusing. For example, one ad featured the back view of two young men, pants down around their ankles, standing in a paddock of sheep. In most countries, such advertising would not be permitted, but the ad was ruled acceptable in New Zealand.[20]

Religions, cultures, and value systems are the most important factors in determining the level of nudity, as well as sexual references and gender-specific issues. Moslem countries tend to reject any kind of nudity and any reference to sexuality and other gender-related issues. They also do not permit any type of advertising for personal goods, such as female hygiene products, contraceptives, and undergarments. Any hint of sexuality or display of the female body is strictly forbidden.

In selling swim and active wear products on the Internet, Jantzen is utilizing a sexual appeal.
Source: Courtesy of Jantzen, Inc.

Moslem countries are not the only ones with restrictive advertising for sex appeals. Many Christian countries such as Ireland, Spain, South Africa, Mexico, and the Philippines have similar standards. In Malaysia, if a man and woman are shown in the same room alone together for more than 3 seconds, it implies they had intercourse.

In other countries standards on sexually oriented advertising are quite liberal but sometimes confusing. In France sex is everywhere. Advertisers can feature seminude or completely nude models in an advertisement if it can be justified. There must be a relationship between the product and the nude model. It does not take much of a justification in France, where sex is viewed as healthy, innocent, and natural. A strange quirk in France, however, is that sex and humor cannot be mixed. The French do not see sex as silly or funny. On the other hand, Australia, which is conservative in many ways, permitted the singing penis ad used by the gay–lesbian radio station. Such an ad would be prohibited in many other countries.[21]

In many Middle East countries, sex and gender issues are taboo subjects. Sexual appeals are not used in advertising and even sexually related products are difficult to advertise. To get around this, in Egypt, Procter & Gamble hosted a call-in TV show directed toward young girls. The show's panel contained health experts, and topics ranged from marriage to menopause. The call-in show was followed up with a TV talk show called *Frankly Speaking* about feminine hygiene. The goal of the show was to tackle some of the more sensitive issues facing young Egyptian girls. Although the show discussed what happens during puberty, it was P&G's policy not to discuss sexuality. P&G sponsored the show and the primary product advertised, P&G's feminine sanitary pads, Always.[22]

A sensual appeal in an advertisement encouraging tourists to visit Helsinki, Finland.
Source: Courtesy of Sek & Grey Oy.

Disadvantages of Sex Appeals

Everyone has heard that "sex sells." Although this may be true, it may be a less powerful weapon than it used to be. How sex sells is changing. The methods for using nudity are not the same. To be effective, nudity must be an integral part of the product being sold rather than a decorative part designed to garner attention. Nudity does not have the shock value it once did. Seeing a naked person in an advertisement is much less likely to cause a viewer to pay more attention to an ad than it used to.

One major criticism of sexually based advertising is that it has perpetuated dissatisfaction with one's body. Females in print advertisements and models in television advertising are quite thin. The key to success seems to be the thinner the better. Although the models in advertisements have gotten thinner, body dissatisfaction and eating disorders among women have risen. Research indicates that women feel unhappy about their own bodies and believe they are too fat after viewing advertisements showing thin models. What is interesting is that these same ads have an impact on men, but the reverse. Men feel they are not muscular enough and are too thin or too fat. It does not make any difference if the male is viewing a male model or a female model in advertisements.[23]

In response, some firms have begun using "regular person" models in ads. Wal-Mart and Big K (Kmart) have employees pose in clothing to be sold and with other

An advertisement using a sexual appeal to promote beautiful skin.
Source: Used with permission of the *Joplin Globe*, Joplin, Missouri.

I'm here in the middle of Times Square to show off my best feature. My bones. What's my secret? Milk. It helps give bones the calcium they need to stay strong. And since they grow until about age 35, I'd say that's news worth putting on display.

got milk?

An effective use of sex to sell milk.
Source: Courtesy of Bozell Worldwide, Inc.

products. This approach has met with many positive results, which means other companies may need to rethink their positions on body image advertising.

Bijan employed an extreme approach in one series of advertisements. Instead of either a superthin model or a regular person, Bijan's advertisement featured a nude overweight female. Several magazine editors refused to carry the advertisement at first but then changed their minds. Of the more than 1,000 e-mails received by Cynthia Miller, the creative who designed the ads for Bijan, only a few were negative. The vast majority were very supportive of the move to think outside of the typical female model stereotype.

The problem with the stereotyping of females in ads takes a different twist in other countries. For example, in Saudi Arabia and Malaysia, women must be shown in family settings. They cannot be depicted as being carefree or desirable to the opposite sex. In Canada, France, and Sweden, sexism should be avoided in any advertising directed toward children. Advertisers refrain from associating toys with a particular gender, such as dolls for girls or GI figures for boys.[24]

In general, the use of sex to make products more appealing is a legitimate tactic for many companies, products, and advertising firms. The goal should be to use sex in a manner that is interesting, germane to the product, and within the ethical standards of the region. From there, taste and other more personalized standards serve as guides. The milk industry advertisement shown in this section has been very effective. Although the model is dressed in a swimsuit, it is germane to the product. It is a very effective way to persuade women that milk not only is good for healthy bones but also enhances one's appearance. By telling women that bones continue to develop until the age of 35, the ad reinforces the reasons to consume milk.

STOP

INTEGRATED LEARNING EXPERIENCE

To read additional articles about the use of sex in advertising, access Current Issues in Advertising at **www.yppa-currentadissues.org**. Using the search engine, type in "sex" to obtain a list of articles. Sex is common appeal in advertising. Choose an industry to research and locate 10 Web sites of firms in that industry. How many use a sex appeal? What type of sex appeal is used? Now choose an industry that you feel should not use sex appeals. Locate 10 Web sites. Did any of them use a sex appeal?

Musical Appeals

Music is an extremely important component in advertising. Music helps capture the attention of listeners and is linked to emotions, memories, and other experiences, especially a song or music that is known. Music can be intrusive, thereby gaining the attention of someone who previously was not listening to or watching a program. Music can be the stimulus that ties a particular musical arrangement, jingle, or song to a certain product or company. As soon as the tune begins, consumers know what product is being advertised because they have been conditioned to tie the product to the music. For example, the song "Like a Rock" is often quickly linked to Chevrolet's trucks for many people, and the Intel "tune" is readily noticed by computer buffs.

Music gains attention and increases the retention of visual information at the same time. For example, think of the McDonald's jingle, "For a good time, and a great place, try McDonald's." Most remember the song along with images of the Golden Arches or Ronald McDonald. Even when consumers do not recall the ad message argument, music can lead to a better recall of the visual and emotional aspects of an ad. Music can also increase the persuasiveness of argument. Subjects asked to compare ads with music to identical ads without music almost always rated those with music higher in terms of persuasiveness.[25]

Musical memories are often stored in long-term recall areas of the brain. Most people can remember tunes even from their childhood days. For examples, consider the musical approaches displayed in Figure 7.8.

Several decisions are made when selecting music for ads. They include answering questions such as these:

▶ What role will music play in the ad?

▶ Will a familiar song be used, or will something original be created?

▶ What emotional pitch should the music reach?

▶ How does the music fit with the message of the ad?

Before we knew it we were having Häagen~Dazs.

Fall deeply in Häagen~Dazs.

An advertisement by Häagen-Dazs utilizing a sensual appeal.
Source: Courtesy of Häagen-Dazs.

Music plays a number of roles in advertisements. Sometimes the music is incidental. In others, it is the primary theme of the ad. Occasionally, the use of music misdirects the audience so a surprise ending can be used. For instance, a Volkswagen television commercial showed people on the streets of New Orleans doing things in time to the music (sweeping, bouncing a basketball, unloading a truck) with the end line "That was interesting," and the VW logo followed. The creative must select the correct type of music, from whimsical, to dramatic, to romantic. Just as the wrong plot or wrong actors in an advertisement mean disaster, so does selecting the wrong music. Conversely, a quality match between the music and the ad theme can lead to a strong favorable reaction by the viewer or listener.

Another important decision involves the selection of a familiar tune versus creating original music for the ad. The most common method is to write a jingle or music specifically for the advertisement. Background or mood-inducing music is usually instrumental, and advertisers often pay musicians to write music that matches the scenes in the ad. Also, some companies use the same instrumental tune for each commercial, such as United Airlines, which plays "Rhapsody in Blue" in the background of its television and radio ads.

Using a well-known song in an ad has certain advantages. The primary benefit is that consumers already have developed an affinity for the song. The goal is to transfer this emotional affinity to the product. Brand awareness, brand equity, and brand loyalty are easier to develop when consumers are familiar with the music. They transfer the bond from the song to the product or company. One variation on this approach is to purchase an existing song and adapt the ad to the music.

Using popular songs is often costly. The average price for rights to an established song is $250,000. The Internet company Excite paid $7 million for the rights to Jimi Hendrix's song "Are You Experienced," and Microsoft paid about $12 million for "Start Me Up."[26]

Not all writers and musicians are willing to sell their songs for advertising. Ben McDonald rejected a $150,000 offer from Bausch & Lomb and $450,000 from Clairol for the Top 40 hit "The Future's So Bright I Gotta Wear Shades." Bruce Springsteen rejected offers in the millions for his hit song "Born in the USA." These and other songwriters feel strongly about preventing their music from becoming part of an ad. To them, it is selling out.[27]

See if you can think of the tune that matches each of the following tag lines:

▶ Like a good neighbor, State Farm is there.

▶ Feel like a woman (Revlon).

▶ Come see the softer side of Sears.

▶ The ABC News theme (also used in commercials for the news).

▶ I am stuck on Band-Aid, cause Band-Aid is stuck on me.

Now, ask your parents to sing the tune and identify the products from these jingles.

▶ You can trust your car to the man who wears the Star, the big bright **** Star!

▶ Hold the pickle, hold the lettuce, special orders don't upset us, all we ask is that you let us serve it your way.

▶ Take it off. Take it all off.

▶ My bologna has a first name, it's O S C A R . . . .

▶ **** tastes good, like a cigarette should.

▶ Plop, plop, fizz, fizz. Oh what a relief it is.

▶ It's not how long you make it, it's how you make it long.

▶ Double your pleasure, double your fun, with ****.

▶ Umm Umm good, Umm Umm good, that's **** are, umm, umm good.

▶ From the land of the sky blue waters, **** the beer refreshing.

▶ I'd like to teach the world to sing, in perfect harmony.

FIGURE 7.8
Tunes and Tag Lines

The relationship between the advertising and music industries in the United Kingdom is different than in the United States. Artists in the United Kingdom believe that if their songs are played in an advertisement, the attention leads radio programmers to play the song on the air as a single. For many artists, this can be a path to stardom. Ladysmith Black Mambazo reached the U.K. Top 30 with "The Star and the Wiseman" after the song played in a TV ad for Heinz beans. Now companies such as Virgin Records have special departments dedicated to placing songs with advertising agencies.[28]

Music is an important ingredient in ads produced for television, radio, and even for the Internet. When a company becomes associated with a popular theme or tune, recall is enhanced and often the firm is seen as delivering higher quality. Creatives must either prepare music themselves or contract for it in some form. Currently, very few organizations use long-standing musical tag lines. Instead, each ad or campaign has its own music. This makes the job of the creative more difficult. He or she must try to "hit a home run" every time a new ad is produced. Other advertising forms, most notably print and billboard, do not use music. Consequently, other appeals become a better match.

STOP

INTEGRATED LEARNING EXPERIENCE

To read additional articles about the use of music in advertising, access Current Issues in Advertising at **www.yppa-currentadissues.org**. Using the search engine, type in "music" for a list of articles. How can music be used in Internet advertising? Look for sites that use music either as a primary appeal or to support another appeal.

Rational Appeals

Rational appeals are normally based on either the ELM (elaboration likelihood model) approach (see Chapter 3) or the hierarchy of effects model. The ELM approach assumes consumers use rational thought processes when making purchase decisions. The goal of a rational appeal is to provide the information needed to help make the decision. Automobile advertisements display information about gas mileage, warranties, and other features. The U.S. Postal Service provides information about prices, delivery schedules, and access.

A rational appeal often follows the hierarchy of effects stages of awareness, knowledge, liking, preference, conviction, and purchase. Creatives design ads for one of the six steps. For example, in the knowledge stage, the advertisement transmits basic information. In the preference stage, the ad shifts to presenting logical reasons why one particular brand is superior, such as the superior gas mileage of the automobile or a better safety record. A rational ad leads to a stronger conviction about a product's benefits, so that the purchase is eventually made.

To be successful, rational appeals rely on consumers actively processing the information presented in an advertisement. In other words, the consumer must attend to the message, comprehend the message, and compare the message to knowledge embedded in a cognitive map. Messages consistent with the current concepts in the cognitive map strengthen key linkages. New messages help the person form cognitive beliefs about the brand and establish a new linkage from his or her current map to the new product. For example, a business customer who sees a Kinko's advertisement about videoconferencing services already may have the company in his cognitive structure. The business customer may have used Kinko's in the past but was not aware that the company offers videoconferencing. When Kinko's is already established in this person's cognitive map, it is only a matter of creating a new linkage to entice the customer to try its videoconferencing services.

Print media offer the best outlets for rational appeals. Print ads allow readers greater opportunities to process copy information. They can pause and take time to read the verbal content. Television and radio commercials are so short that it is difficult for viewers to process message arguments. Also, if television viewers miss the ad, they must wait until the ad is broadcast again to view it.

Business-to-business advertisers use print media extensively. These advertisers take advantage of print's ability to make rational appeals. Many advertising account executives believe trade publications are the best way to reach members of the buying center. Those in the industry read trade publications carefully. Placing an ad in a trade publication means the firm has an excellent chance of hitting its primary target market. Further, trade publications allow advertisers the opportunity to convey more details to potential buyers.

Buying center members who scan trade journals while in the information search stage of the buying process are quite likely to notice the ad, read it, and process the information. Buying center members who are not looking for information about the particular product probably will ignore the same ad. As noted in Chapter 9, magazines do not have intrusion value, and readers can easily skip or ignore an advertisement. A rational appeal usually focuses on a primary appeal, and no strong peripheral cues grab the reader's attention.

Conventional advertising wisdom states that rational appeals are well suited for high-involvement and complex products. High-involvement decisions require considerable cognitive activity, and consumers

An advertisement by Hangers Cleaners using a rational appeal.
Source: Courtesy of Howard, Merrell & Partners.

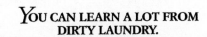

YOU CAN LEARN A LOT FROM DIRTY LAUNDRY.

spend more time evaluating the attributes of the individual brands. Thus, a rational appeal is the best approach to reach them. For some consumers, however, emotions and feelings even influence high-involvement decisions. For instance, life insurance involves both rational and emotional elements. Various insurance companies can use both in seeking to influence consumers.

In general, rational appeals are effective when consumers have high levels of involvement and are willing to pay attention to the advertisement. Message arguments and product information can be placed in the copy. Consumers then absorb this information using the central processing route of their mental functioning. Information collected in the central route is more enduring than information gathered through the peripheral route. In terms of cognitive activity, a rational appeal is superior to other appeals in developing or changing attitudes and establishing brand beliefs. This is mainly true when consumers have a particular interest in the product or brand advertised. Otherwise, consumers often ignore ads using a rational appeal. Remember, rational appeals have the lowest attraction appeal and very low intrusive capabilities.

Emotional Appeals

Emotional appeals are based on three ideas. First, consumers ignore most advertisements. Second, rational appeals go unnoticed unless the consumer is in the market for a particular product at the time it is advertised. Third, and most important, emotional advertising can capture a viewer's attention and help develop an attachment between consumer and brand.

Most creatives view emotional advertising as the key to developing brand loyalty. Creatives want customers to feel a bond with the brand. Emotional appeals reach the more creative right side of the brain. Visual cues in ads are important in emotional appeals. Notice how the visual elements in the New Balance ad contribute to a feeling or mood of serenity. Also, peripheral cues such as the music and the actor are crucial. Although individuals develop perceptions of brands based largely on visual and peripheral stimuli, it does not happen instantly. Over time and with repetition, perceptions and attitudinal changes emerge. Figure 7.9 displays some of the more common emotions presented in advertisements.

Research by the Puerto Rico Tourism Company indicated that emotions are the most important factor in the selection of a vacation destination. The emotions specifically identified included tranquility, invigoration, glamour, and enlightenment. To convey these emotional appeals to the U.S. target market, Puerto Rico used singing sensation Ricky Martin in television ads. The campaign was a departure from a more rational approach. Although factors such as price, destination, and amenities were important in choosing vacations spots, they are not as important as the emotional factors.[29]

Western Union followed a similar strategy in advertisements targeted to the U.S. Spanish-language television channels and

New Balance uses visual elements in this advertisement to create an emotional appeal of serenity and peace.

Source: Courtesy of New Balance Athletic Shoes Inc. Photographed by Paul Wakefield.

I trade sweat for strength.

I trade sleep for sunrises.

I trade doubt for belief.

I trade my walking for nothing.

achieve new balance

© 1999 New Balance Athletic Shoe, Inc.

▶ Trust   ▶ Protecting Loved Ones

▶ Reliability   ▶ Romance

▶ Friendship   ▶ Passion

▶ Happiness   ▶ Family Bonds

▶ Security   ▶ with parents

▶ Glamour–luxury   ▶ with siblings

▶ Serenity   ▶ with children

▶ Anger   ▶ with extended family members

FIGURE 7.9
Emotions Used in Advertisements

the Latin America countries. The television ads featured testimonials from people reminiscing about their relatives in Latin America whom they left behind when they came to the United States. Using scenes in kitchens, gardens, and local streets, relatives point out they all receive money from their relatives in the United States via Western Union. In one commercial, a mother and daughter make pastries in their kitchen in El Salvador. The mother talks about her son in the United States sending her money each month. Western Union's previous ads focused on product attributes. Customer focus groups in the United States revealed that many had not seen their children, parents, or cousins in Latin America for 10 years. Western Union used this emotional appeal to convey the concepts of trust and reliability, and subsequent sales grew dramatically as a result.[30]

The Effie Awards are sponsored by the New York Chapter of the American Marketing Association. In 1998, of the 34 Effie Gold Awards presented, 21 used emotional appeals. The most common approach winners used was to combine humor with emotions. The second most common approach among the emotional appeal ads focused on the consumer's life and feelings.[31] The MasterCard "priceless" campaign uses this approach.

The priceless campaign used by MasterCard was the invention of the McCann-Erickson Ad Agency. The basic tag line is "There are some things money can't buy. For everything else, there's MasterCard." One of the most popular was of a father and son going to a baseball game together. Mothers responded as favorably as men to the spot. The entire campaign was successful in creating good feelings, and it also increased both awareness and usage of the MasterCard. The agency adapted the campaign to international markets, tweaking the commercials to fit the local customs. For example, in Australia, instead of a baseball game, the father and son attend a cricket match.[32]

Business-to-business advertisers are using more emotional appeals. In the past only 5 percent to 10 percent of all business-to-business ads utilized an emotional appeal. Today, that percentage is around 25 percent. A magazine advertisement created by NKH&W Advertising Agency for a product to treat racehorses switched from a rational appeal to an emotional appeal. The target market for the ad was veterinarians.

An emotional appeal advertisement by Stihl emphasizing reliability.
Source: Courtesy of Stihl, Inc.

"About the only thing that gets in our way is gators."

Chuck's crews tackle the toughest the south Florida landscape has to offer – all day, every day. Sawgrass, Bahia grass, even the occasional water moccasin. His trimmer of choice? The STIHL FS 250. With its compact design, increased torque and high power-to-weight ratio, Chuck's crews can run longer and faster with the FS 250 than with anything else. As Chuck says, "When you're waist-deep in swamp, cutting sawgrass and snakes, your trimmer better be the best there is."

1 800 GO STIHL   www.stihlusa.com

Do you have a STIHL Story? Call 1 800 586 4717

STIHL

In the past, the ad would have opened with such ad copy as "For swelling in joints use . . . " The emotional ad has the horse thinking, "I will prove them wrong. I will run again. I will mend my spirits."[33]

The rationale for changing to more emotional business-to-business ads is the idea that emotions affect all types of purchase decisions. Members of the buying center utilize product information in making decisions but, at the same time, are just as likely to be affected by the same emotions as regular consumers. Members of the buying center do try to minimize the emotional side of a purchase, but this does not mean that they are unaffected by emotions. As individuals, the affective component of attitudes is as important as the cognitive component. In the past, business-to-business advertisers tended to ignore the affective component.

Television is one of the best media for emotional appeals. Television offers advertisers intrusion value and can utilize both sound and sight. Models in the ads can be "real people." Facial expressions can convey emotions and attitudes. Consumers learn vicariously about a particular product and develop an attitude based on these vicarious experiences. Television ads also are more vivid, more lifelike, and they can create dynamic situations that pull the viewer into the ad. Music may be incorporated to make the ad more dramatic. Such peripheral cues are important components of emotional appeals. These peripheral cues (music, background visuals, etc.) also attract a viewer's attention.

As mentioned, emotions can be tied with humor, fear, music, and other appeals to make a compelling case for a product. The same ad can influence a consumer both emotionally and rationally. The goal of the creative is to select the most appropriate emotional appeal for the product and company.

STOP

INTEGRATED LEARNING EXPERIENCE

To read additional articles about the use of emotion in advertising, access Current Issues in Advertising at **www.yppa-currentadissues.org**. Using the search engine, type in "emotion" to find articles. What type of industry uses the emotional appeal? Locate 10 Web sites from an industry of your choice. How many use emotional appeals?

Scarcity Appeals

Another appeal that is occasionally used is scarcity. When there is a limited supply of a product, the value of that product increases. Scarcity appeals urge consumers to buy a particular product because of a limitation. It can be a limited number of the products available or, more often, that the product is available for only a limited time. In 1996, General Mills introduced for a limited-time USA Olympic Crunch cereal and Betty Crocker Team USA desserts. Then, at the turn of the century, General Mills introduced a Cheerios line called Millenios as a limited-time product. Tiny "2s" were added to the familiar O-shaped cereal Cheerios.[34] McDonald's, Wendy's, and Burger King offer sandwiches (McRib, Hot N' Spicy Chicken, Dollar Whoppers) for limited time periods throughout the year. The scarcity concept is also used for musical compilations, encouraging consumers to buy the product because of its limited availability. By making sure it is not available in retail stores, marketers increase its scarcity value.

The scarcity appeal is often used with other promotional tools. For example, a manufacturer may advertise a limited price discount offer to retailers who stock up early for Christmas or some other holiday season. Contests and sweepstakes also run for limited times. The primary benefit of scarcity appeals is that they encourage consumers to take action. Creatives normally receive information about scarcity issues in the creative brief or from the account executive who has consulted with the company.

THE STRUCTURE OF AN ADVERTISEMENT

The majority of ads prepared for publication or broadcast tend to contain five elements. These ingredients create the structure of an advertisement. They include:

- The promise of a benefit, or the headline
- The spelling out of the promise, a subheadline
- Amplification
- Proof of the claim
- Action to take

In print advertising, the *headline* is crucial. A typical reader is going to look at the artwork, figure, or illustration first. Next, the reader scans the headline. To keep the potential customer interested means finding some method (rational, emotional, humor, etc.) that will move him or her to the rest of the copy. Typical features of a headline are that the words are short, simple, and limited (less than 12), inviting or interest-provoking, and action-oriented and portray enough information to let the buyer know about the product while appealing most directly to the target audience.

A headline should not be mistaken for a tag line. The **tag line** is the key phrase within the advertising copy, a television ad, or radio ad. Examples of headlines are shown in Figure 7.10.

The *subheadline*, or spelling out of the promise, accompanies the headline. In some instances, the headline is powerful enough by itself, so this step is skipped. A subheadline is similar to a second headline in a newspaper story. It delivers additional information and leads the reader to the copy. Examples of subheadlines are also shown in Figure 7.10.

The *amplification* is the text or body copy of the advertisement. The wording should be concise. The *unique selling proposition* or the *major selling idea* is portrayed in the copy. The company can be factual, imaginative, or emotional in its approach. Factual copy often is part of comparison advertising, where one product or company is directly contrasted with another. Amplification copy is especially important in business-to-business advertisements in which more complex features of a product or service must be explained or summarized.

Proof of the claim can be generated from many sources. These include seals of approval (e.g., Good Housekeeping), guarantees (money back if not fully satisfied), trial offers and samples, warranties, demonstrations, and testimonials. A company with strong brand equity is in a better position simply because of the power of the brand.

Finally, the consumer must be made aware of the *action to take*. "Buy now," "stop by for a free sample," and "tell your friends," are statements declaring the action the consumer should take. Less direct actions might be "give us a try" or "stop by for a test

STAND ALONE HEADLINES

Now you can shave your legs half as often. *(the promise of a benefit by Jergens).*

Just when you thought laundry couldn't get any more fun. *(benefit promised by Tide).*

It's so delicious you'll wish bagels didn't have holes. *(enticement, Brummel & Brown yogurt)*

Can Opener *(provocative, Maxwell House,—the opener is one finger).*

Why macaroni was invented. *(presents an existing benefit, Kraft Macaroni and Cheese Dinner Delux).*

HEADLINES WITH SUBHEADINGS

Headline: Whipped up. Fluffy. Now with better-tasting chocolate. *(presents a new benefit, 3 Musketeers).*

Subheadline: It could be better if Mr. Right fed it to you. *(targets women in Redbook, a magazine oriented to women).*

Headline: Chemo was stealing the energy I needed for my grandson. *(emotional, Procrit).*

Subheadline: Until I talked to my doctor about getting it back.

Headline: Free Face–lifts. *(creates intrigue, FTD florists).*

Subheadline: With every bouquet from your FTD florist.

FIGURE 7.10
Advertising Headlines and Subheadlines

drive." The action should mirror the stage in the hierarchy of effects model: awareness, knowledge, liking, preference, conviction, or purchase.

These five parts of the structure of an advertisement must also be contained in the use of message strategies and executional frameworks, which are presented in the following chapter. The account executive, creative, and company presenting the ad know every advertisement cannot contain every component. Instead, these factors and features should appear over time as an advertising campaign progresses.[35]

SUMMARY

Developing effective advertisements is the culmination of a series of integrated marketing communications efforts. They include knowing the objective of the ad, the target audience, the message theme used, the type of support needed, and any constraints that apply. Then, a creative must work within the context of key advertising theories in selecting the correct media and designing the leverage point and message appeal that work effectively within each medium.

Three important theoretical approaches drive the development of many advertisements. The hierarchy of effects model suggests consumers move through a series of stages as they are persuaded

to make a purchase. The steps are (1) awareness, (2) knowledge, (3) liking, (4) preference, (5) conviction, and (6) the actual purchase. Although the process probably is not a lock-step model that every buyer follows, the hierarchy of effects approach does provide important information about which mental issues to account for in various advertising campaigns. The hierarchy of effects model can be combined with the three main elements present in attitudes: (1) cognitive, (2) affective, and (3) conative components. Ads are designed to influence affective feelings, cognitive knowledge, or conative intentions to act or behave based on an attitude. A means–end chain displays the linkages between a means to achieve a desired state and the end or personal value at issue. Advertisers can select personal values that mesh with the key characteristics of the target market and then construct ads designed to provide them the means to achieve these ends by purchasing the good or service. These ideas help the creative develop a leverage point to move the buyer from understanding the product's benefits to incorporating those benefits with his or her personal values.

Visual and verbal issues should also be considered in the formation of an ad. Concrete visual images are easily recognized and recalled. Abstract images may be linked with values or emotions the product creates or the feeling the buyer should experience that may be associated with the product or company. Visual elements are key components in almost every form of advertising. Verbal elements must reach the more rational, central route of the audience's mental processing procedures.

Beyond these components, advertising creatives must form messages using one (or more) of the seven major appeals: (1) fear, (2) humor, (3) sex, (4) music, (5) rationality, (6) emotions, or (7) scarcity. Just as there are logical combinations of media, there are logical combinations of these appeals for various messages. Often, music is the backdrop for messages invoking fear, humor, sex, and emotions. Humor can be linked with sex, music, rationality (by showing how being illogical is silly or funny), and scarcity. Rationality combines with fear in many commercials. The goal of the creative is to design a message argument that takes advantage of the various characteristics of these appeals, breaks through clutter, and convinces the audience to buy the item involved. Mismatches of message tactics

are to be avoided, such as combining sex with humor in France, as mentioned in this chapter.

Business-to-business ads often appear in print, and many times include rational approaches in the copy, as the purchase decision variables are more complex. At the same time, many advertisers have recently discovered that emotional ads can be effective, which expands business-to-business advertising into other venues, such as television, radio, and the Internet.

The process of designing ads for international markets is quite similar to that for domestic ads. The major difference is careful consideration of local attitudes and customers, with due care given to the language, slang, and symbols of the area. For example, Sega recently discovered that its product's name is slang for "masturbation" in Italian, after a major advertising campaign had started. These types of mistakes should be carefully avoided.

Every marketer knows that some ad campaigns, no matter how carefully conceived, still fail. The goal is to try to reach a point where the failure of one specific ad or campaign does not have long-lasting effects on the company. To do so, a thoughtfully designed IMC program can build a firm's image in such a manner that brand and product loyalty, along with customer recognition, can reduce the ill effects of one "lead balloon" advertising campaign. In the end, advertising is only one component of an IMC program. Although it is clearly a major and important ingredient, it should be considered in the context of a long-term plan to strengthen the company, its products, and its overall image in the customer's mind.

REVIEW QUESTIONS

1. What are the five main elements of a creative brief? How do they affect the choice of advertising appeals?

2. What are the six stages of the hierarchy of effects model? Do they always occur in that order? Why or why not?

3. How are the three components of attitudes related to the hierarchy of effects model?

4. In a means–end chain, what are the means? The ends? How do they affect advertising design?

5. What is a leverage point? How are leverage points related to the hierarchy of effects model, attitudinal changes, and means–end chains?

6. Why are visual elements in advertisement important? What is the relationship between visual and verbal elements? Can there be one without the other?

7. What are the advantages and disadvantages of fear appeals in advertising?

8. When does humor work in an ad? What pitfalls should companies avoid in using humorous appeals?

9. What types of sexual appeals can advertisers use?

10. When are sexual appeals most likely to succeed? To fail?

11. What should international advertisers consider when thinking about using sexual appeals?

12. Name the different ways music can play a role in an advertisement. Explain how each role should match individual appeals, media, and the other elements in the design of the ad.

13. What are the advantages and disadvantages of rational appeals? Which media do they best match?

14. How can emotions accentuate advertisements? Why are they being used more often in business-to-business advertisements?

15. What is scarcity? How do scarcity ads lead to buyer action?

16. Name four combinations of appeals that are logical combinations for advertisers.

17. What five components make up the structure of an advertisement? Explain each one.

KEY TERMS

white space the absence of copy in a printed text and the absence of music or sound in a radio or television ad.

hierarchy of effects model a marketing approach suggesting that a consumer moves through a series of six steps when becoming convinced to make a purchase, including: (1) awareness, (2) knowledge, (3) liking, (4) preference, (5) conviction, (6) the actual purchase.

means–end chain an advertisement approach in which the message contains a means (a reasoning or mental process) to lead the consumer to a desired end state, such as a key personal value.

Means–End Conceptualization of Components for Advertising Strategy (MECCAS) an advertising approach that suggests using five elements in creating ads, including (1) the product's attributes, (2) consumer benefits, (3) leverage points, (4) personal values, and (5) the executional framework.

leverage point the feature of the ad that leads the viewer to relate the product's benefits with personal values.

visual esperanto a universal language that makes global advertising possible for any good or service by recognizing that visual images are more powerful than verbal descriptions.

advertising appeals approaches to reaching consumers with ads. The seven major appeals are: (1) fear, (2) humor, (3) sex, (4) music, (5) rationality, (6) emotions, and (7) scarcity.

severity part of the behavioral response model that leads the individual to consider how strong certain negative consequences of an action will be.

vulnerability part of the behavioral response model that leads the individual to consider the odds of being affected by the negative consequences of an action.

decorative models models in an advertisement whose primary purpose is to adorn the product as a sexual or attractive stimulus without serving a functional purpose.

tag line the final key phrase in an ad which is used to make the key point and reinforce the company's image to the consumer.

CRITICAL THINKING EXERCISES

Discussion Questions

1. Develop a means–end chain similar to the one in Figure 7.3 for each of the following branded products:
   a. Clorox bleach
   b. Durex condoms
   c. Zippo lighters
   d. Kool-Aid
   e. Sony stereos

2. Evaluate the balance of visual and verbal elements of each advertisements shown in this chapter. Which is predominant? Which images are considered appropriate for international advertising, because they have the characteristic of *visual esperanto*? Do they use white space effectively?

3. Try to recall five outstanding television commercials. Identify the appeal used in each one. Why were these five ads effective? Compare your list with those of other classmates. What was their reaction to your list? How did you feel about theirs?

4. Develop a print advertisement for vitamins using a fear appeal. Be sure to consider the means–end chain prior to starting on the advertisement. After completing the means–end chain and advertisement, to what other media could the advertisement be adapted? How?

5. Borrow a camcorder and develop a 30- or 45-second television spot for one of the following products, using the suggested appeal. Be sure to develop a means–end chain prior to creating the advertisement.
   a. Denim skirt, sex appeal
   b. Tennis racket, humor appeal

   c. Ice cream, emotional appeal
   d. Stockbroker, fear appeal
   e. Dress shoes, musical appeal

6. Record five television commercials using a VCR. Identify which appeal each advertisement uses. Discuss the quality of the advertisement and its best and worst aspects. For each ad, present another possible appeal and how it could be used. What personal values and customer benefits does each advertisement present?

7. Record five television commercials or find five print advertisements that use a sex appeal. Identify which of the five ways sexuality was used. Evaluate each ad using the seven steps presented in the Communications Action Box "Using Sex Wisely."

8. Look up each of the following Internet Web sites. Identify which type of appeal each site uses. Evaluate the quality of that appeal. What other appeals can be used to make the site more appealing? Discuss the balance of visual and verbal elements on the Web site and ad.
   a. Service Metrics (www.servicemetrics.com)
   b. Trashy Lingerie (www.trashy.com)
   c. Navison Software, U.S. (www.navison-us.com)
   d. BMW Motorcycles (www.bmwusacycles.com)
   e. Guess (www.guess.com)
   f. Wonderbra (www.wonderbrausa.com)
   g. Solomon Software (www.solomon.com)
   h. Michael Jordan cologne (www.michael-jordan-cologne.com)
   i. Sweet 'n Healthy (www.sweetnhealthy.com)

Choosing the Correct Appeal for an IMC Advertising Campaign

Three key theories should drive the development of your advertising campaign. The hierarchy of effects model, means–end theory, and visual and verbal imaging are important theoretical frameworks from which to proceed. Then, decide if you can make your product somehow sexy, or if you will use fear, scarcity, humor, rationality, or some other approach to capture the customer's attention and persuade him or her to take action and buy your product or service. These factors may vary according to the culture in which you are operating. At the Prentice-Hall Web site at **www.prenhall.com/clow**, or access the IMC Plan Pro disk that accompanied this textbook materials for Chapter 7 are designed to lead you through the process of creating the right appeal, given the firm's image and IMC theme.

BUILDING AN
IMC
CAMPAIGN
IMC PlanPro

CASE 1

SEXY CPAs[36]

Jon Johnson came from an unusual background. As an undergraduate at Southwest Missouri State University, Jon studied accounting for one year before changing his major to marketing. His musical talents plus a whimsical creative streak made him an ideal candidate to work in an advertising agency.

The most recent client Jon was asked to serve was a CPA firm called Burns, Connors, and Morris, or BCM, located in St. Louis, Missouri. The firm was quite large but was not affiliated with any of the large national accounting companies. Jon's task was to find a way to compete effectively with the services offered by the major national companies in the local market.

At his first meeting with BCM officials and Jon's account manager, they went over what is known as the AIDA methodology. AIDA stands for Attention-Interest-Desire-Action. Clearly, the ad must garner the prospective client's attention and incite interest. Desire and action are much more difficult to achieve, because a business customer must be moved to consider changing accounting firms or giving some activities to the BCM firm. Jon commented that the AIDA approach seemed quite similar to a hierarchy of effects model.

BCM officials pointed out that their business was more likely to grow by capturing new clients rather than getting long-standing large firms to change. They wanted Jon and his company to stress BCM's areas of expertise (tax accounting and advice) along with the idea that the company has a quality staff, affordable fees, excellent seminars, and the ability to handle international clients. BCM was also proud of its collaborative efforts with prominent local business leaders, politicians in St. Louis, and local law firms and insurance companies.

BCM faced the unique challenge of finding outlets to reach a target market that was smaller and growing firms in need of CPA services. The traditional approach had always been to seek out print media to present ads. Thus, BCM would reach physicians through ads in medical journals (which could be regionally, but not locally, targeted). New businesses might be enticed through ads published in local magazines and specialty journals, insurance companies could be contacted through trade journals, and small businesses through small business magazines and journals. Such an approach was costly, because of the difficulty in reaching all prospective customers in an across-the-board fashion.

In spite of these obstacles, BCM asked Jon and his firm to prepare a series of print ads for a winter campaign. This was a logical time. The key

(continued)

tax season begins in January and ends in April. Jon decided his print ad campaign must have an effective banner or headline. He knew 80 percent of readers read only that part of an ad. Most CPA firms create ads emphasizing the cost savings of using their services. The copy of these ads focused on the advantages each company held in the marketplace. Successful campaigns generally had attractive logos as well as a type of layout that make the company distinct.

Jon prepared the campaign BCM wanted, using the banner, "Small Enough to Know You, Large Enough to Serve Your Financial Needs." The print ad campaign was geared to four primary markets: (1) physicians, (2) small businesses, (3) attorneys, and (4) local restaurants. Each could be reached by magazine–trade journal advertising. The medical campaign centered on special programs and seminars for doctors and featured a photo of a physician meeting with an accountant. The small business ad showed the BCM president working in a storefront setting at a ribbon-cutting ceremony; the same ad was used for restaurants. The attorney ad photo was shot in a law library.

Jon then offered an alternative. He suggested that rather than using such a traditional approach, the company might be able to attract attention and desire with a more sexy and less rational approach. He showed BCM officials a storyboard (six stop frame pictures in sequence used to represent a television ad) for local television and cable outlets. The ad showed BCM's office and people working diligently in it, followed by several local business clients during a regular day of work. The copy featured the same advantages as the print ads. The final board displayed the same businessman from one of the local companies sitting on a beach with a phone–fax–laptop setup. He was working but also sunning himself. Behind the businessman was a woman wearing a skimpy bikini lounging with a drink. The tag line was "We take care of business, so you can take care of yours."

Jon suggested that billboards and print ads could feature the same photo as the final story-board frame and use the same, more provocative tag line. The same photo and ad could be sent by direct-mail flyer, by fax, and as the main page of BCM's Web site. Jon reported to BCM and to his company that he would be comfortable preparing either approach.

1. Did Jon meet the AIDA model with his television campaign?

2. Did Jon meet the AIDA model with his print campaign?

3. Which campaign would you run for BCM? Why?

4. What other appeal besides sex or rationality might fit BCM?

CASE 2

THE AUTO ADVANTAGE

Barry Farber has pretty much "seen it all" in his 30 years of selling used cars. His business, The Auto Advantage, had experienced a series of high and low points related to buyer whims and the nature of the industry. Barry is quick to point out that his strongest ally has always been a local advertising company in Sacramento that has helped him negotiate the troubled waters.

From the beginning, Barry has seen opportunities rise up and drift away. When he opened his modest lot in 1973, the first gas crisis was just emerging. People were dumping gas-hog cars and diligently looking for high-mileage cars and those fueled by diesel. In fact, Barry distinctly remembers offering a practically brand-new Ford LTD II, one of the most popular models of the time, at $3,000 below its "blue book" value and not being able to find a buyer for weeks due to consumer fears about oil shortages and rising gas prices.

At that time, Barry's new advertising agency manager, Wendy Mozden, pointed out an old technique that had worked wonders for years. She called it *"turning a disadvantage into an advantage."* She learned the tactic by watching old Volkswagen commercials. The original "bug" was promoted as being ugly, but economical. Many restaurants during that era bought ads pointing out that the reason they were so "slow" was due to their higher-quality food, making it "worth the wait."

Consequently, The Auto Advantage placed ads in newspapers and on the radio focusing on the "value" an individual could obtain by trading down or across. Sales reps were instructed to convey to individual buyers that a person would have to buy an awfully big amount of gas at 55 cents per gallon before a large car would actually be costly, especially when mpg (miles per gallon) differences between midsize and smaller cars were so small. The Auto Advantage managed to buy cars that other companies did not want to carry at drastically reduced prices and sell them to the customers they could educate concerning the shift from disadvantage to advantage. Within a few years, those high-priced (and hard to maintain) diesel cars disappeared, and people once again fell in love with larger gas hogs. By then Barry's company was well established in the marketplace.

Barry weathered the invasion of foreign cars into the United States by once again seeing an advantage in the disadvantage. Using patriotic themes, his company subtly pointed out that people buying foreign-made cars hurt the local economy, especially because one of the major manufacturers in the Sacramento area made replacement parts for GM cars. Sales presentations always included the question "Are you in a union?" Those who responded "yes" were easy targets for the company's "Buy American" theme during the early 1980s.

From there, Barry spent a great deal of energy making sure he understood the needs of his aging client base. Those who started families in the 1980s needed minivans in the 1990s. Those who were older and facing retirement often wanted low-maintenance cars. By carefully constructing his original message, that a person would gain an advantage by shopping at his lot, the business continued to succeed.

The next major challenge for The Auto Advantage may become the same one in which the company began. Oil prices started to rise, and the U.S. government created tighter pollution standards for almost every make and model of car. Some consumers again looked for more efficient autos, even hybrid gas–electric models as the new century began. Barry knew he would need to continue to adapt as the marketplace evolved. He continued to look for turnaround situations to find the edge to keep his clients happy with what they bought from The Auto Advantage.

1. Describe an advertisement in which the firm attempts to turn a disadvantage into an advantage.

2. If gas prices double in a one-year time period, how should The Auto Advantage respond? Design an ad to promote fuel economy using the various strategies described in this chapter.

3. Should The Auto Advantage continue to advertise to baby boomer and older clients? How can the company attract Generation X or echo boomer customers to the lot? How would the advertisements differ? Design an advertisement for the Generation X or echo boomer customer.

4. Pick one of the following appeals and use it to design a print advertisement for The Auto Advantage:

   a. Fear
   b. Humor
   c. Sex
   d. Emotional

ENDNOTES

1. G. Douglas Olsen, "Observations: The Sounds of Silence: Functions and Use of Silence in Television Advertising," *Journal of Advertising Research,* 34, no. 5 (September–October 1994), pp. 89–95.

2. Jerry Olson and Thomas J. Reynolds, "Understanding Consumers' Cognitive Structures: Implications for Advertising Strategy," *Advertising Consumer Psychology,* eds. L. Percy and A. Woodside (Lexington, MA: Lexington Books 1983), pp. 77–90; Thomas J. Reynolds and Alyce Craddock, "The Application of the MECCAS Model to Development and Assessment of Advertising Strategy," *Journal of Advertising Research,* 28, no. 2 (1988), pp. 43–54.

3. Laurie A. Babin and Alvin C. Burns, "Effects of Print Ad Pictures and Copy Containing Instructions to Imagine on Mental Imagery That Mediates Attitudes," *Journal of Advertising,* 26, no. 3 (Fall 1997), pp. 33–44.

4. Marc Bourgery and George Guimaraes, "Global Ads: Say It with Pictures," *Journal of European Business,* 4, no. 5 (May–June 1993), pp. 22–26.

5. Olson and Reynolds, "Understanding Consumers' Cognitive Structures"; Reynolds and Craddock, "The Application of the MECCAS Model to Development and Assessment of Advertising Strategy."

6. Based on Rosemary M. Murtaugh, "Designing Effective Health Promotion Messages Using Components of Protection Motivation Theory," *Proceedings of the Atlantic Marketing Association* (1999), pp. 553–57; R. W. Rogers and S. Prentice-Dunn, "Protection Motivation Theory," *Handbook of Health Behavior Research I: Personal and Social Determinants,* ed. D. Gochman (New York: Plenum Press, 1997), pp. 130–132.

7. Michael S. Latour and Robin L. Snipes, "Don't Be Afraid to Use Fear Appeals: An Experimental Study," *Journal of Advertising Research,* 36, no. 2 (March–April 1996), pp. 59–68.

8. Harlan E. Spotts and Marc G. Weinberger, "Assessing the Use and Impact of Humor on Advertising Effectiveness," *Journal of Advertising,* 26, no. 3 (fall 1997), pp. 17–32.

9. David B. Wolfe, "Boomer Humor," *American Demographics,* 20, no. 7 (July 1998), pp. 22–23.

10. Hillary Chura and Mercedes M. Cardona, "Online Broker Datek Stakes 'Serious Turf' with $80 Mil," *Advertising Age,* 70, no. 10 (October 18, 1999), pp. 1–2.

11. Wolfe, "Boomer Humor."

12. Jessica Severn and George E. Belch, "The Effects of Sexual and Non-Sexual Advertising Appeals and Information Level on Cognitive Processing and Communication Effectiveness," *Journal of Advertising,* 19, no. 1 (1990), pp. 14–22.

13. Pat Sloan and Carol Krol, "Underwear Ads Caught in Bind Over Sex Appeal," *Advertising Age,* 67, no. 28 (July 8, 1996), p. 27.

14. Laurel Wentz, "Global Village," *Advertising Age,* 68, no. 10 (March 10, 1997), p. 3; Michael Wilke, "A Kiss Before Buying," *Advocate* (April 27, 1999), pp. 34–35.

15. Severn and Belch, "The Effects of Sexual and Non-Sexual Advertising Appeals and Information Level on Cognitive Processing and Communication Effectiveness."

16. D. C. Bello, R. E. Pitts, and M. J. Etzel, "The Communication Effects of Controversial Sexual Content in Television Programs and Commercials," *Journal of Advertising,* 3, no. 12 (1983), pp. 32–42.

17. Based on M. S. LaTour and R. E. Pitts, "Female Nudity, Arousal and Ad Response: An Experimental Investigation," *Journal of Advertising,* 9, no. 4 (1990), pp. 51–63; Bob Garfield, "Pushing the Envelope: The Performing Penis," *Advertising Age International* (July 12, 1999), p. 4.

18. Based on G. Smith and R. Engel, "Influence of a Female Model on Perceived Characteristics of an Automobile," *Proceedings of the 76th Annual Convention of the American Psychological Association,* 15, no. 3 (1968), pp. 46–54; Leonard Reid and Lawrence C. Soley, "Decorative Models and the Readership of Magazine Ads," *Journal of Advertising Research,* 23, (April–May 1983), pp. 27–32; R. Chestnut, C. LaChance, and A. Lubitz, "The Decorative Female Model: Sexual Stimuli and the Recognition of Advertisements," *Journal of Advertising,* 6 (fall 1977), pp. 11–14.

19. Andrew A. Mitchell, "The Effect of Verbal and Visual Components of Advertisements on Brand Attitude and Attitude Toward the Advertisement," *Journal of Consumer Research,* 13 (June 1986), pp. 12–24; Severn and Belch, "The Effects of Sexual and Non-Sexual Advertising Appeals and Information Level on Cognitive Processing and Communication Effectiveness."

20. Kevin Lawrence, "Sex and Marketing," *New Zealand Marketing Magazine,* 18, no. 5 (June 1999), pp. 10–17.

21. Gerard Stamp and Mark Stockdale, "Sex in Advertising," *Advertising Age's Creativity,* 7, no. 6 (July–August 1999), pp. 35–36; Garfield, "Pushing the Envelope: The Performing Penis," Jean J. Boddewyn, "Sex and Decency Issues in Advertising: General and International Dimensions," *Business Horizons,* 34, no. 5 (September–October 1991), pp. 13–20.

22. Elizabeth Bryant, "P&G Pushes the Envelope in Egypt with TV Show on Feminine Hygiene," *Advertising Age International* (December 14, 1998), p. 2.

23. Howard Levine, Donna Sweeney, and Stephen H. Wagner, "Depicting Women as Sex Objects in Television Advertising," *Personality and Social Psychology Bulletin,* 25, no. 8 (August 1999), pp. 1049–58.

24. Boddewyn, "Sex and Decency Issues in Advertising: General and International Dimensions."

25. G. Douglas Olsen, "Observations: The Sounds of Silence: Functions and Use of Silence in Television Advertising," *Journal of Advertising Research,* 34, no. 5 (September–October 1994), pp. 89–95.

26. Michael Miller, "Even Out of Context, the Beat Goes On (and On)," *Pittsburgh Business Times,* 18, no. 18 (November 27, 1998), p. 12.

27. John Marks, "Shake, Rattle, and Please Buy My Product," *U.S. News and World Report,* 124, no. 20 (May 25, 1998), p. 51.

28. Paul Sexton, "This is How They Do It in the U.K.," Adweek, Eastern Edition, 39, no. 43 (October 26, 1998), pp. SPS14–SPS15.

29. Gay Nagle Myers, "Puerto Rico Targets Emotions in New Ad Campaign," *Travel Weekly,* 58, no. 82 (October 14, 1999), p. C4.

30. Joy Dietrich, "Western Union Retraces Roots: The Emotions of Money Transfers," *Advertising Age International* (October 1999), pp. 24–25.

31. Scott Rockwood, "For Better Ad Success, Try Getting Emotional," *Marketing News,* 30, no. 22 (October 21, 1996), p. 4.

32. Hank Kim, "MasterCard Moments," *Adweek,* 40, no. 15 (April 12, 1999), pp. 30–32.

33. Karalynn Ott, "B-to-B Marketers Display Their Creative Side," *Advertising Age's Business Marketing,* 84, no. 1 (January 1999), pp. 3–4.

34. Stephanie Thompson, "Big Deal," *MediaWeek,* 7, no. 44 (November 24, 1997), p. 36; Judann Pollack, "Big G Has Special Cheerios for Big '00'," *Advertising Age,* (June 14, 1999), pp. 1–2.

35. J. Thomas Russell and W. Ronald Lane, *Kleppner's Advertising Procedure,* 15th edition. (Upper Saddle River, NJ: Prentice Hall), pp. 423–437.

36. Some of the case information came from the following article: Jay P. Granat, "How to Create an Effective Advertisement," *CPA Journal,* 61, no. 1 (January 1991), pp. 68–80.

Advertising Design: Message Strategies and Executional Frameworks

Chapter Objectives

Develop **awareness of the four types of message strategies (cognitive, affective, conative, and brand), and match them with the media chosen for an advertising campaign.**

Study **the roles message strategies play in designing effective leverage points and executional frameworks.**

Know **how all of the executional frameworks described in this chapter operate and when to use them.**

Learn **the value of an effective source or spokesperson, plus the criteria to use in selecting the individual for the ad campaign.**

Utilize **the principles of effective advertising to be certain the message has the best chance of reaching and affecting the audience.**

VIAGRA ADVERTISING:
(Place Your Own Joke Here)

When Pfizer first introduced the drug *sildenafil citrate* under the brand name Viagra, a wave of interest swept across the nation, from talk shows to an entire episode of the TV sitcom *Mad About You.* Jokes were everywhere. On the other hand, sales of the prescription drug reached more than $180 million in the first two months following the product's launch.

The initial Viagra television ad featured politician Bob Dole and did not name the product nor its manufacturer. Instead, Dole talked about the courage needed to face the problem of erectile dysfunction. Many viewers believed it was simply a public service announcement and didn't know that Dole was compensated by Pfizer for appearing in the spots. Dole did not name the product. No disclaimers about side effects or the ingredients were necessary as a result.

Following Viagra's release, several incidents generated negative publicity. For openers, at least 30 men died from heart attacks or strokes. These men had taken the pill, and the strain of having sex was the primary cause of death. Further, some women complained that their husbands, who had given up womanizing with advanced age and less interest in sex, had returned to their old habits. The company scrambled to offset these negative images by producing the second wave of ads showing happy couples who had benefited from the product.

Pfizer's success largely depended on a $35 million first-year advertising budget. In that first year, over 2 million men took the prescription. This generated expected sales of over $1 billion by the second year.

Continuing issues haunted the product. First, Canadian buyers were not able to obtain the drug. Next, online purchases made its availability seem far too easy, and fears emerged that unregulated purchases would have a further adverse effect. Also, counter-

feiters seized the opportunity to sell fake Viagra pills online. Internet problems gave the company a major headache. Also, the high price of the medicine deterred many buyers.

Many HMOs refuse to cover the cost of Viagra, pointing out that it would take away at least $100 million from coverage of other prescriptions, most notably antiviral drugs. Other health care providers expressed concerns about its safety.

The executives selling Viagra remained unfazed. The next generation of ads featured seven reasons to "feel good" about the product, including how it works, when it works, research results, and assurances that most men tolerate the product well. The tag line "Love life again" is now associated with Viagra ads.

In the upcoming years, Pfizer seeks to maintain steady sales and fend off competing products. Time will tell if the product has longlasting users. In the meantime, constructing persuasive, tasteful, and informative ads remains the company's goal. Many approaches, including sensuality, romance, and information, can be used. Which would work for you? For your parents? For your grandparents?

THE BOULDER STOP

"Only One Stop. The Boulder Stop." This is the tag line for the print ads for The Boulder Stop retail operation. Based on the creative brief described in Section 5.2.1 of the IMC Plan Pro example, the visual and verbal components of the advertising campaign can be prepared.

An advertising message strategy is chosen after considering options from cognitive to conative, to affective, to various brand strategies. In the case of The Boulder Stop, the brand image is the key. Consumers must believe the company offers products related to personal safety that may be purchased in a pleasant atmosphere.

Using a dramatization approach, The Boulder Stop's advertisements are designed to convince the consumer that The Boulder Stop can literally "come to the rescue" in a dangerous climbing situation. An effective advertising campaign must combine the firm's overall image with the distinct message a single ad is supposed to convey. Reread sections 5.2.1, and study sections 6.2.1 and 7.2.1 of the IMC Plan Pro disk. Consider other message strategies and executional frameworks that might portray the same information.

overview

The essence of an integrated marketing communications program is designing a message that effectively reaches a target audience. These messages must be, in a very real sense, quite personal. They are designed to change or shape attitudes. They must be remembered. They should lead to some kind of action, in either the short or long term.

In the most general sense, messages can travel in two ways. First, a personal message can be delivered through a personal medium. Thus, a sales rep closing the deal, shaking the hand of the buyer, giving a reassuring tap on the shoulder, smiling, and talking communicates in an intimate, warm, human fashion. Clearly, personal media (sales reps, repair department personnel, customer services representatives, etc.) must be included as part of the overall IMC program and approach.

At the same time, the various forms of advertising media are impersonal. Television sets are indifferent as to what appears on the screen. Radios deliver any sound that can be transmitted. Computer screens are nothing more than high-tech television screens. The challenge to the marketing account executive, the company, and especially the creative is to design a message that will seem personal, even as it is delivered through an impersonal medium.

Account executives are acutely aware of the importance of effectively reaching a target audience. It is not simply a matter of reach, frequency, and continuity. The message must engage the targeted buyer and influence the individual to the point that he or she will recall and use the advertised or promoted product.

Beyond the goal of making a message personal, many marketers are interested in tangible, measurable results that can be reported to clients and to prospective new customers. Therefore, the relationship between the executive and the creative reaches a critical point at the stage in which an advertisement is designed.

This chapter focuses on several major topics. First, four types of message strategies are described. Each may be used to help convince the consumer to make a purchase, either through reason, emotion, action, or belief in a firm or brand's image. Second, the major types of executional frameworks are noted. These forms of advertising presentation help the creative prepare original, convincing, and memorable ads. Third, four types of sources or spokespersons who appear in various advertisements are described, and the criteria used to select them are reviewed. Fourth and finally, the principles of effective advertising campaigns are noted. When advertisements are combined with other elements of the promotions mix in an integrated fashion, the net result is a stronger company image and a clear IMC theme that will entice consumers to remember the company and take action when they are ready to buy.

Cognitive Strategies	Conative Strategies
▶ Generic	▶ Action-inducing
▶ Preemptive	▶ Promotional support
▶ Unique selling proposition	**Brand Strategies**
▶ Hyberbole	▶ Brand user
▶ Comparative	▶ Brand image
Affective Strategies	▶ Brand usage
▶ Resonance	▶ Corporate
▶ Emotional	

FIGURE 8.1
Message Strategies

MESSAGE STRATEGIES

As noted in Chapter 6, the **message theme**, or the outline of the key ideas in the ad, is a central part of the creative brief. The message theme can be created using a number of message strategies. A **message strategy** is the primary tactic used to deliver the message theme. There are four broad categories of message strategies:

1. Cognitive strategies
2. Affective strategies
3. Conative strategies
4. Brand strategies[1]

The first three represent the components of attitudes as described earlier. All four of the message strategies are described in this section. Figure 8.1 lists the four brand strategies along with various forms or approaches from each category.

COGNITIVE STRATEGIES

A **cognitive message strategy** is the presentation of rational arguments or pieces of information to consumers. The advertisement's key message focuses on the product's attributes or the benefits customers obtain from using the product. The product's attributes include a huge range of benefits. Foods may be described as healthful, pleasant tasting, low calorie, and so forth. A tool can be shown as durable, convenient, or handy to use. A drill press machine used in a manufacturing operation may be depicted as reliable or faster than comparable machines on the market. Cognitive message strategies should make these benefits clear to potential customers. There are five major forms of cognitive strategies:

1. Generic messages
2. Preemptive messages
3. Unique selling proposition
4. Hyperbole
5. Comparative advertisements

Generic messages are direct promotions of product or service attributes or benefits without any claim of superiority. This type of strategy works best for a firm that is clearly the brand leader and dominant in its industry. The goal of the generic message is to make the brand synonymous

An advertisement using a generic cognitive message strategy.
Source: Used with permission of the *Joplin Globe,* Joplin, Missouri.

An advertisement using a preemptive message strategy.
Source: Courtesy of the Chrysler Corporation.

An advertisement for Bonne Bell featuring a unique selling proposition.
Source: Courtesy of Bonne Bell.

with the product category. Thus, Campbell's Soups can declare "soup is good food" without any claim to superiority because the company so strongly dominates the industry. When most consumers think of soup, they think of Campbell's. Nintendo uses similar strategies because the company dominates the video game market with over 70 percent of the market share. Generic message strategies are seldom found in the business-to-business market because few firms dominate an industry to the extent of Campbell's or Nintendo. One major exception is Intel, which controls 75 percent of the microprocessor market. The generic message "Intel inside" has been used for years to convey to both businesses and end users that the processor inside practically any PC is made by Intel. Because the Intel name became synonymous with quality, IBM was forced to display the Intel inside logo to assure buyers that IBM computers contain Intel microprocessors. IBM had always used Intel microprocessors. For several years IBM tried to discontinue displaying the Intel logo, because the IBM marketing team thought it distracted from IBM's name. The return to displaying the Intel inside logo illustrates the power a generic message can have when the firm dominates the market.[2]

Preemptive messages are claims of superiority based on a specific attribute or benefit of a product. Once made, the claim normally preempts the competition from making such a statement. For example, Crest toothpaste is so well-known as "the cavity fighter" that the brand has preempted other companies from making similar claims, even though all toothpastes fight cavities. Thus, when using a preemptive strategy, the key is to be the first company to state the advantage, thereby preempting the competition from saying it. Those that do are viewed as "me-too" brands or copycats.

A **unique selling proposition** is an explicit, testable claim of uniqueness or superiority that can be supported or substantiated in some manner. Brand parity makes a unique selling proposition more difficult to establish. Reebok claims it is the only shoe that uses DMX technology, which provides for a better fit. Because of patents, Reebok can claim this unique selling proposition. In the Bonne Bell advertisement aimed at teenagers, the company proposes the unique selling proposition that a Bonne Bell Lipshade is the "One and only, one-handed, sleek sweep flipstick."

The **hyperbole** approach makes an untestable claim based upon some attribute or benefit. When NBC claims that its Thursday night lineup is "America's favorite night of television," the claim is a hyperbole. These claims do not have to be substantiated, which makes this cognitive strategy quite popular.

The final cognitive message strategy is a **comparative advertisement**. When an advertiser directly or indirectly compares a good or service to the competition, it is the comparative method. The advertisement may or may not mention the competitor by name. Sometimes, an advertiser simply presents a "make-believe" competitor, giving it a name like product X. This approach, however, is not as effective as comparative advertising that states the actual competitor's name. To provide protection from lawsuits, companies must be sure they can substantiate any claims made concerning the competition.

AT&T and MCI compare rates. VISA brags that many merchants using the card will not accept American Express. Burger King explains the advantages of flame broiling as opposed to frying, which McDonald's and Wendy's use. In the business-to-business sector, shipping companies compare their delivery times and accuracy rates.

The major advantage of comparative ads is that they often capture the attention of consumers. When comparisons are made, both brand awareness and message awareness increase. Consumers tend to remember more of what the ad says about a brand than when the same information is in a noncomparative ad format.

The negative side of using comparative ads deals with believability and consumer attitudes toward them. Many consumers think comparative ads are less believable. They view the information about the sponsor brand as exaggerated and conclude that the information about the comparison brand probably is misstated to make the sponsor brand appear superior.

Another danger of comparative ads is the negative attitudes consumers may develop toward the ad. If viewers acquire negative attitudes toward the advertisement, these negative attitudes can transfer to the sponsor's product. This is especially true when the sponsor runs a *negative comparative ad.* The form of advertisement portrays the competition's product in a negative light, such as when Pringles shows someone creating a greasy mess eating regular potato chips. Although the Pringles ad does not create a problem, other negative comparisons may not be as effective.

A Tylenol advertisement featuring a comparative cognitive message strategy.
Source: Courtesy of Johnson & Johnson.

In psychology, the concept of *spontaneous trait transference* suggests that when someone calls another person dishonest, other people tend to remember the speaker as also being less than honest. When a comparative ad criticizes the comparison brand based upon some particular attribute, viewers of the ad may attribute that deficiency to the sponsor brand as well. This is most likely to occur when the consumer uses the comparative brand, not the sponsored brand.[3] Companies must be careful in choosing an appropriate comparison firm.

Comparison ads are less common in other countries due to both social and cultural differences as well as legal restrictions. Therefore, it is important to be cognizant of cultural and legal issues. For example, many countries in Europe classify comparative advertising as illegal. In Japan, it is not illegal, but it runs against the society's cultural preferences. In Brazil, the advertising industry is so powerful that any attempt to create a comparative advertisement has been challenged and stopped. Many times, international consumers not only dislike the advertisements but often transfer that dislike to the company sponsoring the ad.[4]

The comparative message strategy is beneficial if used with caution. The comparison brand must be picked carefully to ensure consumers see it is a viable comparable brand. Actual product attributes and customer benefits must be used, without stretching the information or providing misleading information. If there are actual differences to compare, then comparative advertising works well. If the comparisons are all hype and opinion, with no substantial differences, comparative advertising does not work as well. Of course, if the comparison is misleading, the FTC can step in to investigate. The largest category of complaints that the FTC deals with is comparative advertising.

ADVERTISING DESIGN: MESSAGE STRATEGIES AND EXECUTIONAL FRAMEWORKS

Medical Advertising and Ethical Practices

Is it ethical to advertise physician's services and new drugs? For many years, attorneys, dentists, and physicians did not advertise for fear of being viewed as "ambulance chasers." Recently the trend has gone in the opposite direction. In some instances, a dermatologist will advertise a "skin rejuvenation" practice with only a bare mention that it is also part of a medical practice. Critics argue this takes medicine into the area of merchandising and suggest that it is deceptive to do so.

Pharmaceutical companies now spend millions advertising new drugs. A recent television news report noted that anti-inflammatory and nonsteroidal pain killers such as Celebrex and Vioxx have benefitted from massive advertising campaigns, yet there is some medical evidence that they are no more effective than much cheaper alternatives, such as Advil or Alève.

When consumers are in pain and simply want the best relief possible, should he or she be subjected to marketing programs that include free samples and gifts to physicians, along with extensive advertising programs, or should there be some way to know which medicine is clinically proven to be the most effective? Congressional regulators are now looking into this issue. In addition, individuals within the marketing field are debating the role of advertising in promoting medical practices and drugs, and whether the advertising profession should adopt guidelines. Other marketers, however, contend that medical practices and drug companies have the right to market their services or goods as much as Nike has the right to promote their products. In the meantime, advertising companies and marketing teams are being asked to convince consumers to purchase drugs such as Celebrex and Vioxx.

Source: ABC Nightly News (May 30, 2002).

In general, comparing a lesser known brand to the market leader seems to work well. On the other hand, comparing a new brand with the established brand is often not effective. Many times, a wise strategy is to simply make the comparison without naming the competitor. This strategy worked well for Avis, which usually does not mention Hertz in ads, yet comparisons are made and consumers know which competitor Avis refers to.[5]

All five of these cognitive message strategies are based on some type of rational logic. They generally are oriented toward the central processing component of the ELM (elaboration likelihood model). In terms of attitudes, the sequence of cognitive → affective → conative is the plan of attack in developing a rational approach. The intention of a cognitive message strategy is first to present consumers with rational information about a product, service, or company, and then to help them develop positive feelings about the same product or company.

Affective Strategies

Affective message strategies invoke feelings and emotions and match them with the product, service, or company. They try to enhance the likability of the product, recall of the appeal, or comprehension of the advertisement. Affective strategies elicit emotions that, in turn, affect the consumer's reasoning process and finally lead to action. For example, an emotion such as love can help convince a consumer that a safer but more expensive car is worth the money. Affective strategies fall into two categories: (1) resonance and (2) emotional.

Resonance advertising attempts to connect a product with a consumer's experiences to develop stronger ties between the product and the consumer. For example, use of music from the 1960s takes baby boomers back to that time and the experiences they had growing up. Any strongly held memory or emotional attachment is a candidate for resonance advertising. Take a look at the advertisement for Cheerios in this section. This resonance

A Cheerios advertisement utilizing a resonance affective message strategy.
Source: Courtesy of General Mills.

This Cable One Digital ad utilizes a conative message approach.
Source: Used with permission of the *Joplin Globe*, Joplin, Missouri.

approach shows three generations of a family in the picture combined with the words "Your heart has better things to do than deal with heart disease." Family memories and emotions combine with the product feature of being a heart-smart (low-cholesterol) cereal.

Emotional advertising attempts to elicit powerful emotions that eventually lead to product recall and choice. As described in Chapter 7, many emotions can be connected to products, including trust, reliability, friendship, happiness, security, glamour, luxury, serenity, pleasure, romance, and passion.

As noted in Chapter 7, emotional appeals are not used only in consumer advertisements. They can also be used in business-to-business ads, because members of the buying center are human beings who do not always make decisions based on only rational thought processes. Emotions and feelings also affect decisions. If the product's benefits can be presented within an emotional framework, the advertisement is normally more effective, even in business-to-business ads.[6] When neither reason (cognitive) nor emotional (affective) pitches are the best, an action-based approach or a brand appeal is utilized.

Conative Strategies

Conative message strategies are designed to lead more directly to some type of consumer behavior. They can be used to support other promotional efforts, such as coupon redemption programs, Internet "hits" and orders, and in-store offers such as buy-one-get-one-free.

These "Big Sale" signs are a conative strategy designed to encourage customers to make a purchase.
Source: Courtesy of PhotoEdit. Photograph by David Young-Wolff.

The goal of a conative advertisement is to elicit behavior. A conative strategy is present in television advertisements for music CDs or cassettes that seek to persuade viewers to call a toll-free number to purchase the music. They further encourage the action by stating the CD cannot be purchased at stores and is available for only a limited time.

Action-inducing conative advertisements create situations in which cognitive knowledge of the product or affective liking of the product may come later (after the actual purchase) or during product usage. For instance, a point-of-purchase display is designed (sometimes through advertising tie-ins) to cause people to make *impulse buys*. The goal is to make the sale, with affective feelings and cognitive knowledge forming as the product is used.

Promotional support conative advertisements are designed to support other promotional efforts. Besides coupons and phone-in promotions, a company may advertise a sweepstakes that a consumer enters by filling out the form on the advertisement or by going to a particular retailer.

Brand Strategies

The final category of message strategy is not as directly oriented to consumer attitudes. Instead, **brand message strategies** build or enhance the brand or corporate name in some way. Brand strategies can be placed into four categories:

1. Brand user strategies
2. Brand image strategies
3. Brand usage strategies
4. Corporate advertising

Brand user strategies focus on the type of individuals that use a particular brand. One example of a brand user strategy involves celebrity endorsements. When celebrities are present in advertisements, the ad tends to show the user of the brand more than the brand itself. The idea is that consumers who like the celebrity will transfer that liking to the brand itself. Thus, golfers who like Tiger Woods will use the Nike brand, baseball fans who like Nolan Ryan will buy Advil, and so forth. The endorsers who use the product help consumers recall the brand's name and develop a preference for that brand.

Apple Computers used a more common brand user strategy in the company's early years of focusing on educational users. This strategy was so successful that in later years when Apple tried to convince businesses to use Apple's Macintosh computers, business buyers had difficultly perceiving Apple in the business environment. The public still perceives the Apple brand as a computer designed for educational users, not business users.

A **brand image strategy** works toward the development of a brand "personality" (e.g., Mountain Dew). In brand image advertising, the focus is on the brand rather than the user. It generally does not use celebrities in the ads. Often the ad may not even feature a person at all. If a spokesperson appears in the advertisement, it is a typical person rather than a celebrity. The advertisement for Skechers Sport Footwear in this section is an example of a brand image strategy. Often no verbal copy other than the brand name appears in the advertisement except for the Internet address and toll-free number for a catalog.

The importance of a strong brand in the global business environment has led many businesses to devote more money to brand image advertising. In addition to developing the brand image in trade journals, business advertisers use broadcast media such as television and radio and print media such as magazines. Business advertisers realize that having a strong brand name such as AT&T or Microsoft gives the company a better opportunity to bid on business contracts and to be considered in modified and new buy situations.

Brand usage messages stress the different uses for a particular brand. A classic example of this approach is the Arm & Hammer baking soda commercials that suggest new uses of the product. When home baking declined, to spur the sales of their baking soda, the company advertised that the baking soda could be used to reduce odors in the refrigerator. Later the company's marketing team promoted the idea that it will freshen carpets and reduce odors in cat litter boxes. Then, building on the brand name, Arm & Hammer developed its own line of toothpaste and another of deodorants.

Corporate advertising promotes the corporate name and image rather than the individual brand. As companies continue to face pressure from the public to be socially responsible, corporate advertising becomes an increasingly important advertising strategy. This is especially true when consumer trust is a key issue. Therefore, banks and financial institutions engage in a great deal of corporate ads.

An advertisement for Skechers Sport Footwear using a brand image message strategy.
Source: Courtesy of Skechers USA Inc.

Companies selling chemical products are also likely to commission corporate advertising to build consumer trust. For instance, many years ago DuPont Chemical realized that corporate advertising was essential. Marketing research indicated a strong distrust of chemical companies because of environmental pollution and chemical spills. DuPont's public efforts were necessary despite the fact that almost all chemical companies sell products to other companies rather than to individuals.[7]

The primary goal of each of these brand strategy approaches is to develop the brand, including its image, awareness of the brand, and positive reactions to the brand. Whether it is the user, the image, product usage, or corporate image, the nature of a message strategy should be to incorporate the advertising messages conveyed with the overall IMC theme.

Cognitive, affective, conative, and brand strategies can be matched with the hierarchy of effects approach described in the previous chapter. In that model, consumers pass through a series of stages, from awareness to knowledge, liking, preference, conviction, and finally purchase. As shown in Figure 8.2, each strategy can highlight different stages of the hierarchy of effects model and components of an advertisement.

The message strategy is a key component of every advertising program. To be effective, the message strategy must be matched carefully with the media used, the leverage point, and the executional framework. The creative and the account executive must remain in constant contact throughout the process to be certain all the advertising ingredients remain consistent. In the following section, the next element, the executional framework, is described.

INTEGRATED LEARNING EXPERIENCE

To observe a large collection of print advertisements, access **www.adsGallery. com**. Go the "Agencies" section and the "Browse Collection" menu. Pick at least 10 advertisements and see if you can determine the types of message strategy used. Which message strategies are the most common? Look for the type of appeal each ad uses (see Chapter 7). Notice that the site provides information about the ad, the ad campaign, and the agency for each advertisement. You can view additional ads from the same campaign or ads from the same agency. The site also provides Web addresses for each agency so you can explore more ads.

S T O P

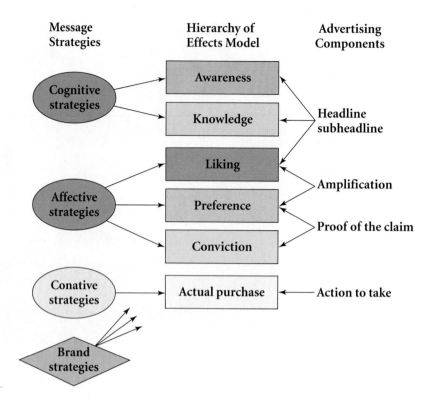

FIGURE 8.2
The Hierarchy of Effects Model,
Message Strategies, and
Advertising Components

EXECUTIONAL FRAMEWORKS

An **executional framework** is the manner in which an ad appeal is presented. The ad appeal is like the script in a movie (e.g., comedy, drama, action film). The ad appeal spells out the overriding format to be used. In Chapter 7, the types of appeals described included: (1) fear, (2) humor, (3) sex, (4) music, (5) rationality, (6) emotions, and (7) scarcity.

If the ad appeal is the script, then the plot of the movie is the actual executional framework. The creative normally decides which executional framework to utilize; however, the media buyer and the account executive also influence the choice. For example, a radio advertisement program as chosen by the executive and purchased by the buyer probably would not feature animation, because it is very difficult to create. Only well-known voices such as Donald Duck or Bugs Bunny would be useful (and probably expensive).

Figure 8.3 displays the various styles of executional frameworks. This chapter describes each framework in detail. Almost any of them can be used within the format of one of the various appeals. For example, a slice-of-life can depict fear, as can a dramatization. Informative ads can be humorous, but so can animations. Testimonials or demonstrations are rational or emotional, and so forth.

> ▶ Animation
> ▶ Slice-of-life
> ▶ Dramatization
> ▶ Testimonial
> ▶ Authoritative
> ▶ Demonstration
> ▶ Fantasy
> ▶ Informative

FIGURE 8.3
Executional Frameworks

Animation

Animation is one useful type of executional framework. In recent years animation in advertising has increased, due primarily to the greater sophistication of computer graphics programs. The technology now available to advertising creatives is far superior to the cartoon type previously used. Currently, a technique called *rotoscoping* is accessible to many creatives. Rotoscoping is the process of placing hand-drawn characters digitally into live sequences. At a result, it is possible to present both live actors and animated characters in the same frame. One well-known live action television spot using cell animation featured Michael Jordan and Bugs Bunny (and other cartoon characters) in MCI commercials.

Animated characters can be human, animal, or product personifications. Animation was originally a last resort technique for advertisers who did not have money to do a live commercial. Most agencies did not hold it in high regard. In contrast, animation has become the preferred technique for many advertisers. Popular Disney films such as *The Little Mermaid* and *The Lion King* have continued the interest in animation advertising.

Besides cartoons, another method of animation, made popular by the California Raisins commercials, is clay animation. Although expensive to create, clay animation has been successful. Another popular product personification is the Pillsbury Doughboy. Computer graphics technology now allows production companies to superimpose these personifications in live scenes.

Animation is used mostly in television spots, although it can also be produced for movie trailers and Internet ads. Single shots of animated characters, such as Tony the Tiger, can also be placed into print ads. Animation was a rarity in business-to-business advertising primarily because of the negative view most advertising agencies held about it. Many firms believed animation was appealing to children but was not for businesspeople. These conclusions have changed. More business ads are placed on television because of the availability of high-quality graphics technologies that allow various businesses to illustrate the uses of their products through animated graphics.

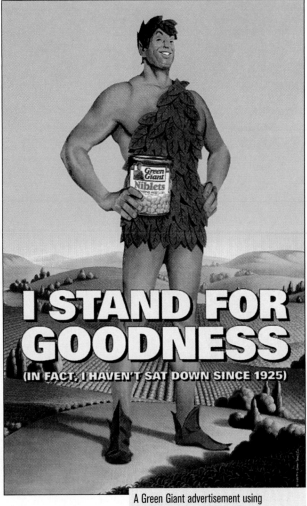

A Green Giant advertisement using animation.
Source: Courtesy of the Pillsbury Company.

INTEGRATED LEARNING EXPERIENCE

The use of animation in advertisements has increased in popularity because of computer technology sophistication. Even the Green Giant and the Pillsbury Doughboy are still popular. Each has a Web site. The Green Giant is available at **www.greengiant.com**. Be sure to check out "The Green Giant Around the World." The Doughboy is at **www.doughboy.com**. Notice that Pillsbury created both animations. To get an insight into the mind of an animation creative, read Vince Backeberg's 3D Site at **www.teleport.com/~v3d/index.html**. If you are interested in adding animation to your Web site, or when a business wants to add animation, Animation Factory at **www.camelotdesign.com** contains several thousand free animations. Free animation also is available at the Animation Library at **www.animationlibrary.com**.

STOP

Slice-of-Life

In slice-of-life commercials, advertisers attempt to provide solutions to the everyday problems consumers or businesses face. These advertisements normally show common things people experience, especially problems they encounter. Then, the good or service is made available to solve the problem.

If...

the average *single female*
BREAKS UP with 4.3 **men**,
avoids 237 phone calls and *ignores*
approximately **79 RED LIGHTS** per year –
What are the *c h a n c e s* she'll read
your e-mail message?
...Say something specific.

Contact us for e-messaging
campaigns that *get results.*

messagemedia
e-mail • e-customers • e-business
www.messagemedia.com
888.440.7550

A business-to-business advertisement for
Messagemedia.com containing a slice-of-life
executional framework.
Source: Courtesy of MessageMedia.

The most common slice-of-life format has four components:

1. Encounter
2. Problem
3. Interaction
4. Solution

Actors portray the dilemma or problem and sometimes solve the problems themselves. In others, a voice-over explains the benefits or solution to the problem that the product, service, or company provides.

A typical slice-of-life commercial starts with a child playing soccer and her parents cheering her on (the encounter). Her dirty uniform is then shown with comments by the child that it will never come clean for the championship game or a voice-over stating the same message (the problem). Another parent or the announcer in some form of interaction then introduces the benefits of the new laundry detergent (the interaction). Then the commercial ends with a proud parent taking her daughter to a championship game in a clean uniform (the solution). This commercial can be shot in several ways. The actors can talk to each other in the scenario, making the audience the third party who essentially is "eavesdropping" on the conversation. Or, the commercial can be shot with voice-overs that highlight the problem and solution portions of the commercial, with the announcer speaking directly to the audience. The slice-of-life approach was introduced and made popular by Procter & Gamble.

In print advertisements, slice-of-life frameworks are more difficult to prepare. In a business-to-business advertisement for Messagemedia in this section, the encounter is the potential female customer. The problem is that the "average single female breaks up with 4.3 men, avoids 237 phone calls, and ignores approximately 79 red lights per year." The interaction occurs through the copy "What are the chances she'll read your e-mail message?" The solution to this problem is Messagemedia's "e-messaging campaign."

The slice-of-life executional framework has become popular in Japan in recent years. The slice-of-life style is easily adapted to Japan's more soft-sell approach compared to the more hard-sell approach of the United States. Japanese advertising tends to be more indirect, and the slice-of-life approach allows advertisers to present a product in a typical everyday situation. Benefits can be presented in a positive light without making brazen or harsh claims and without directly disparaging the competition.[8]

Business-to-business advertisements also use slice-of-life commercials heavily. This executional framework is popular because it allows the advertiser to highlight how a product can meet business needs. For example, a typical business-to-business ad begins with a routine business experience, such as a sales manager making a presentation to the board of directors. Then, the projector used does not have a clear picture at the distance the presenter wants to use. Then the ad offers the solution: a projector from Sony. The presentation is made with great clarity, and the board of directors accepts the customer's bid for the account. As with all slice-of-life commercials, disaster is avoided and, by using the advertised brand, a happy ending results.

Slice-of-life executional frameworks are possible in most media, including magazines or billboards, because a single picture can depict a normal, everyday situation or problem. The secret is to let one image tell the entire story, with the product being the solution.

Dramatization

A dramatization is similar to slice-of-life executional framework. It uses the same format of presenting a problem, then a solution. The difference lies in the intensity and story format. Dramatization uses a higher level of excitement and suspense to tell the story. A dramatization story normally builds to a crisis point.

An example of a dramatization is a recent Maytag commercial, which appeared after the company abandoned the "lonely repairman" theme the company had used for decades. The commercial was designed for the launch of the Gemini range. Thirty- and 60-second spots featured children carrying pizzas yelling and rushing toward a throng of adults carrying casserole dishes. The groups run toward each other on a battlefield. The two groups are ready to break into battle when the Maytag representative intervenes with the dual-oven range that will accommodate the needs of both groups.[9] This Maytag commercial has all of the critical components of a drama executional framework. It tells a story in a dramatic way leading up to a suspenseful climax wherein the teenagers and adults are just about ready to go to war. Suddenly, from nowhere appears the Maytag product that provides a solution to the crisis.

An effective and dramatic advertisement is difficult to pull off, because it must be completed in either 30 or 60 seconds. Building a story to a climatic moment is challenging, given such a short time period. Not all dramatic executional styles accomplish the high level of suspense required to make them successful. It is often much easier to simply produce a slice-of-life framework.

Testimonials

The testimonial type of executional framework has been successful for many years, especially in the business-to-business and service sectors. When a customer in an advertisement tells about a positive experience with a product, this is a testimonial. In the business-to-business sector, testimonies from current customers add credibility to the claims being made. In many business buying situations, prospective vendors are asked for references. Testimonials provide references in advance. Further, most buyers believe what others say about a company more than they do what a company says about itself. Thus, testimonials by someone else offer greater credibility than self-proclamations.

Testimonials also are an effective method for promoting services. Services are intangible; they cannot be seen or touched. Consumers cannot examine the service before making decisions. A testimony from a current customer is an effective method of describing the benefits or attributes of the service. This matches the method most consumers use in selecting a service. When choosing a dentist, an attorney, or an automobile repair shop, consumers often ask friends, relatives, or coworkers. A testimonial ad for a service simulates this type of word-of-mouth recommendation.

One major reason companies choose testimonials is that they enhance company credibility. Endorsers and famous individuals do not always have high levels of credibility because consumers know they are being paid for their endorsements. In testimonials, everyday people, often actual customers, are the main characters. Other times they are paid actors who look like everyday consumers, not models.

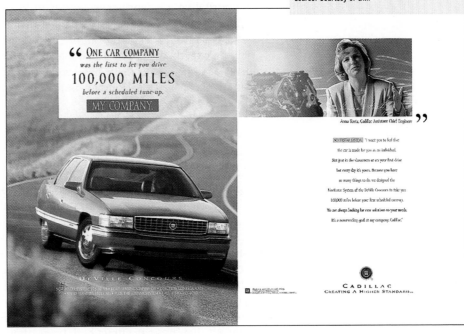

Cadillac uses a testimonial execution strategy in this advertisement.
Source: Courtesy of GM.

When more dramatic or slice-of-life types of venues are not the best, the creative considers the use of testimonials. He or she can present them in practically every advertising medium, and they can focus on both the product itself and the overall image of the brand or firm.

Authoritative

In using the authoritative executional framework, an advertiser seeks to convince viewers that a given product is superior to other brands. One form is **expert authority.** These ads employ a physician, dentist, engineer, or chemist to state the product's advantages over other products. Lance Armstrong and Bob Vila are celebrities with authoritative voices. Firms also can feature less recognized experts such as automobile mechanics, professional house painters, nurses, or even aerobics instructors. Advertising presents each of these as an expert or authority in a particular field. These experts also talk about the brand attributes that make the product superior.

Many authoritative advertisements include some type of scientific or survey evidence. Independent organizations such as the American Medical Association undertake a variety of product studies. Quoting their results gives an ad greater credibility. Survey results are less credible. Stating that four out of five dentists recommend a particular toothbrush or toothpaste is less effective, because consumers do not have details about how the survey was conducted. On the other hand, when the American Medical Association states that an aspirin a day reduces the risk of a second heart attack, it is highly credible, and a company such as Bayer can take advantage of the finding by including it in its ads. The same is true when a magazine such as *Consumer Reports* ranks a particular brand as the best. Any scientific and independent source not paid by the advertising company can make an ad claim more powerful.

Authoritative advertisements have been widely incorporated into business-to-business sector ads, especially when available scientific findings provide support for a company's products. Independent test results are likely to have a more profound influence on members of the buying center. Members actively look for rational information to help them make decisions. A recent TWA advertisement states that J.D. Power rates TWA as "#1 in frequent traveler satisfaction [for] short flights."

The authoritative approach assumes consumers and business decision makers rely on the central processing route from the ELM (elaboration likelihood model) approach. When they do, the authoritative approach works most effectively in print ads when buyers take the time to read the claim or findings the advertisement provides.

Authoritative ads work especially well in specialty magazines. For example, in a hunting magazine, having an expert hunter discuss the superiority of a particular gun is effective, because readers have an interest in hunting. Brides observe the endorsements of wedding experts in special bridal magazines. Readers notice these specialized advertisements, and the claims made have greater credibility. The same is true in business-to-business magazines. Trade journals in the business world are similar to specialty magazines in the consumer world.

Demonstration

Advertisements using the demonstration executional framework show how a product works. A demonstration is an effective way to communicate the attributes of a product to viewers. Other product benefits can be described as the product is exhibited. For example, one recent advertisement showed how a new form of dust cloth could be attached to a handle or used separately. The demonstration highlighted the product's multiple uses by cleaning a television screen, a wooden floor, a saxophone, and light fixtures on the ceiling. Thus, consumers were shown how to use the product and were able to observe its advantages at the same time.

Business-to-business ads often present demonstrations. They allow a business to show how a product can meet the specific needs of another business. Amway relies heavily on demonstrations to entice retail customers to buy products and to convince individuals to begin selling to company's merchandise. When coupled with magazine and brochure ads, the firm can attract both types of customers.

Demonstration ads are especially well suited to television. To a limited extent, the print media can feature demonstrations, especially when a series of photos shows the sequence of product usage.

Fantasy

Some products lend themselves to the fantasy type of executional framework. Fantasy executions are designed to lift the audience beyond the real world to a make-believe experience. Some fantasies are meant to be realistic. Others are completely irrational. Often, the more irrational and illogical ads are, more clearly consumers recall them. Fantasies can deal with anything from a dream vacation spot or cruise ships to a juicy hamburger or an enticing Digiorno pizza. The Jantzen ad in this section encourages consumers to fantasize about what the world would be like if they ruled. People are even encouraged to share their fantasies by accessing Jantzen at **www.jantzen.com**.

The most common fantasy themes, however, are still sex, love, and romance. According to some marketing experts, raw sex and nudity in advertisements are losing their impact. In their place, advertisers show a softer, more subtle presentation of sex. Fantasy fits nicely with preferences for a tamer sexuality, which primarily is found in older members of the population. For some senior citizens, raw sex and nudity simply are offensive. Fantasy is an excellent way to approach older individuals by taking them into a world of romantic make-believe rather than hard-driving sexuality.[10]

One product category that uses fantasy is the perfume and cologne industry. In the past, the most common theme was that splashing on a certain cologne causes women to flock to you. For women, the reverse was suggested. Although used extensively, these ads were not particularly effective because few people believed them. Currently, perfume advertisers tend to portray the product as enhancing the love life of a couple or even making a man or woman feel more sensuous, rather than turning a man into a "babe magnet" or a woman into a "diva."

Television fantasy ads for cruise lines show couples enjoying romantic, sensuous vacations together, swimming, jet skiing, and necking. The goal is to make the cruise into more than just a vacation—it should become a romantic fantasy trip. Fantasy ads also can show people experiencing the thrill of winning a major sports event or sharing a common product (beer, pizza) with a beautiful model. Effective fantasies can inspire both recall and action.

The business-to-business advertising field has not used fantasy a great deal primarily because of fear that members of a buying center would not take a fantasy approach seriously. However, as with the other executional frameworks, creatives are using more fantasy in business-to-business ads.

Informative

A common advertising executional framework is an informative ad. Informative ads present information to the audience in a straightforward matter. Agencies prepare informative ads extensively for radio advertisements, because only verbal communication is possible. Informative ads are less common in television and print because consumers tend to ignore them. With so many ads bombarding the consumer, it takes more than just the presentation of information to grab someone's attention.

A Jantzen ad utilizing a fantasy executional framework.
Source: Courtesy of Jantzen Inc.

The most common fantasy themes are sex, love, and romance.
Source: Courtesy of Corbis/Stock Market. Photograph by Ariel S. Kelley.

Finally. A sophisticated weapon in the war against plaque.

These days, it seems like every product from mouthwash to toothpaste wants to help you fight plaque. And for very good reason. Plaque buildup is a leading cause of gum disease which can have a number of very serious complications.

But among the so-called "plaque attackers," the INTERPLAK Home Plaque Removal Instrument stands out as a true technological breakthrough.

The INTERPLAK Home Plaque Removal Instrument cleans teeth virtually plaque-free.

If plaque is not removed daily, its bacterial film can lead to gingivitis, an early stage of gum disease, and tooth decay. But clinical studies have shown that manual brushing removes only some of the plaque buildup. Those same studies, on the other hand, show the INTERPLAK instrument cleans teeth and gums virtually plaque-free.

How the INTERPLAK instrument cleans circles around ordinary brushing.

With manual or even electric toothbrushes, you move the bristles up and down or back and forth. But with the INTERPLAK instrument's patented design, the brush remains still while the bristles rotate. Ten tufts of bristles rotate 4,200 times a minute, reversing direction 46 times a second. They literally scour off plaque and stimulate your gums. And at the precise moment they reverse direction, the tufts fully extend to clean deep between teeth and under gums. Yet because the bristles are four times softer than the softest toothbrush, the INTERPLAK device is no more abrasive than manual brushing with toothpaste.

Dental professionals approve.

The INTERPLAK Home Plaque Removal Instrument has received rave reviews from dentists and periodontists across the country.

"I am recommending the INTERPLAK Home Plaque Removal Instrument to all my patients."—Dr. L. K. Yorn. Cedar Grove, NJ

"At last, my patients enjoy using a product which we recommend."—Dr. J.W. Blackman, III, Winston-Salem, NC

"Since my patients have been using the INTERPLAK instrument, I have seen a dramatic improvement in the health of their teeth and gums."—Dr. S.G. Newhart, Orthodontist, Beverly Hills, CA

"The INTERPLAK Home Plaque Removal Instrument is a technical breakthrough in home dental care."—Dr. Alan Kushner, Chicago, Il.

Ask your own dentist about the benefits of using the INTERPLAK instrument.

Serious plaque removal for the whole family.

Each INTERPLAK Home Plaque Removal Instrument comes with two interchangeable brush heads. You can purchase additional brush heads so every family member can benefit from cleaner teeth and gums. The INTERPLAK instrument is also cordless, recharging between uses in its own stand.

For more information or the name of a retailer near you, call toll-free **1-800-537-1600**, and ask for **Operator 188**.

Do it soon. Because if you are really serious about fighting the war against plaque, you couldn't have a stronger ally.

Bristles rotating 4,200 times a minute literally scour plaque off your teeth

INTERPLAK®
HOME PLAQUE REMOVAL INSTRUMENT

An Interplak advertisement featuring an informative execution strategy.
Source: Courtesy of Bausch & Lomb, Inc.

Consumers highly involved in a particular product category pay more attention to an informational ad. Such is often the case when business buyers are in the process of gathering information for either a new buy or modified rebuy. On the other hand, if the business is not in the market for a particular product, buying center members do not pay much attention to informative ads. Thus, informative ads work well only in high-involvement situations. Many advertisers believe that business buyers need detailed information to make intelligent buying decisions. As a result, the informative framework continues to be a popular approach for business-to-business advertisers.

One of the keys to informative advertising is the placement of the ad. An informative advertisement about a restaurant placed on a radio station just before noon is listened to more carefully than if it runs at 3:00 in the afternoon. An informative ad about a diet product in an issue of _Glamour_ that has a special article on weight control or exercising will be noticed more than if it is placed in the fashion section of the magazine. An informative business ad about lathes works well next to an article about capital cost of equipment. Consequently, informative ads have limited uses but can be effective when placed properly.

Beyond these types of executional frameworks, the creative decides about all of the other ingredients, including music, copy, color, motion, light, and size (see the cases at the end of this chapter). Finally, one element remains.

STOP

INTEGRATED LEARNING EXPERIENCE

For producing television commercials, access **www.commercialtelevision.com** to review a three-step approach for developing an advertising campaign. Be sure to look at the "Creative Ideas," "Hollywood Productions," and "Media Planning" sections. For information about Super Bowl ads, access **www.superbowl-ads.com**. What makes a Super Bowl ad affective?

SOURCES AND SPOKESPERSONS

One other major issue remains for the creative, the company, and the account executive. Selecting **sources and spokespersons** to use in advertisements is a critical decision. Four types of sources are available to advertisers:

1. Celebrities
2. CEOs
3. Experts
4. Typical persons

Approximately 20 percent of all advertisements use some type of _celebrity spokesperson._ Payments to celebrities account for around 10 percent of all advertising dollars spent.[11] Celebrity endorsers are used because their stamp of approval on a product can enhance the product's brand equity. Celebrities also help create emotional bonds with the products. The

COMMUNICATION ACTION

The Changing World of the Creative

The advertising landscape is changing. New pressures have affected the role of the creative. For some, the most dramatic shift is in the center of power of the entire industry. For many decades Madison Avenue agencies were viewed as being on the cutting edge of innovation in advertising. Currently, if you believe renowned creatives Bob Kuperman and Roy Grace, the shift has most of the "action" to the west.

Kuperman states that: "The Madison Avenue label may play to middle America. But any client or marketing head knows he doesn't have to go to New York to get what he wants in terms of creativity." Grace is more blunt. He states that too many creative decisions fall within a safety zone of familiar styles, concepts, and sales techniques, especially in the Big Apple.

One of the reasons for the change is the shift to market research–driven advertising development. Focus groups and other forms of testing have made it so that, according to Grace, "There's too much testing and too much research. Advertising is too much of a science and not as much of an art." This frustration appears to be growing throughout the industry. Winston Fletcher notes that every major creative decision is subjected to research. When things get modified, creatives can scream themselves hoarse, but don't win out over the focus group.

To regain control, some creatives have moved into the role of director, splitting their time between commercial development and commercial production. In this new role, creatives limit themselves to one company per industry. For example, one creative noted that he had just prepared a $50 million campaign for Jack in the Box and therefore would not film for clients such as McDonald's or Burger King. The Chicago-based Fusion Idea Lab, which creates a number of Bud Light spots, will not film ads for other breweries.

Taking over the new role of director also puts the creative more directly in the line of fire, in terms of reporting tangible results. Unfortunately, "Creatives are probably the worst judges of their own work," states Don Williams, creative director at the PI Design agency. The new accountability may force some creatives away from directing and back into simple development.

Creative Stuart Burnett concludes that the best route to take is to find a marketing communications firm rather than a simple ad agency. He states that "marketing communications agencies are best responding to the [new] challenges. Their media-neutral, integrated approach is winning more and more fans and is getting them sexier work, bigger budgets, and meatier problems to solve."

No matter who employs the creative, the goal is to keep things original. According to Jeff Goodby, a major creative in San Francisco, "Advertising very quickly turns into formulas, and the real enemy of the creative organization is the formulaic feeling." Consequently, the firm Goodby, Silverstein & Partners is working to make sure the agency's creatives take risks and work to sell themselves to clients.

If you are looking for a dynamic, interesting, and evolving career, the job of creative offers many challenges and opportunities. As the next generation of creatives moves forward, the nature of the advertising game will continue to shift with the times, making things exciting for everyone involved.

Sources: Alice Z. Cuneo, "Goody Grows Up," *Advertising Age,* Crain Communications (2000), at **www.webinfo@adage.com**; Winston Fletcher, "Drop in Creative Tension May Kill Off Imagination," *Marketing,* Haymarket Publishing, Ltd. (August 27, 1998); Stuart Burnett, "Comment," *Marketing,* Haymarket Publishing, Ltd. (December 16, 1999); Kathy Desalvo, "Two-timers," *SHOOT,* BPI Communications (March 26, 1999); Justin Elias, "Now and Then," *SHOOT,* BPI Communications (September 10, 1999); Robert Mcluhand, "Creatives Can Sharpen Focus," *Marketing,* Haymarket Publishing Ltd. (April 20, 2000).

idea is to transfer the bond that exists between the celebrity and his or her audience to the product being endorsed. This bond transfer often is more profound for younger consumers. Older consumers are not as susceptible to celebrity endorsements. Still, many advertisers believe they are effective. Figure 8.4 lists some major brands and their endorsers.

Agencies also utilize celebrities to help establish a "personality" for a brand. The trick is to the tie the brand's characteristics to those of the spokesperson, such as Elizabeth Taylor's love of the finer things in life being attached to her line of scents and perfumes as well as other products. In developing a brand personality, the brand must already be established. The celebrity just helps define the brand more clearly. Using celebrities for new products does not always work as well as for already established brands.

There are three variations of celebrity endorsements: (1) unpaid spokespersons, (2) celebrity voice-overs, and (3) what may be called *dead-person endorsements*. Unpaid spokespersons are those celebrities who support a charity or cause by appearing in an ad. These types of endorsements are highly credible and can entice significant contributions to a cause. Politicians, actors, and musicians all appear in these ads. VH1's "Save the Music" ads are a recent campaign of this type.

Many celebrities also provide voice-overs for television and radio ads without being shown or identified. Listeners often respond to the ads and try to figure out who is reading the copy. This adds interest to the ad but may also serve as a distraction, when the individual does not hear the message while trying to identify the speaker.

A dead-person endorsement occurs when a sponsor uses an image, or past video or film, featuring an actor or personality who has died. Because dead persons do not have legal rights, many companies use them in ads without paying high fees. Dead-person endorsements are somewhat controversial but are becoming more common. John Wayne, Fred Astaire, Will Rogers, John Belushi, Elvis Presley, and many others have appeared in ads and even become spokespersons for products after dying. Colonel Sanders has become a spokesperson in animation for KFC.

Instead of celebrities, advertisers can use a CEO as the spokesperson or source. Dave Thomas of Wendy's was possibly the most famous CEO in commercials in the 1990s. For many years, Lee Iacocca was the spokesperson for Chrysler, and Michael Eisner served as the main voice for Disney. A highly visible and personable CEO can become a major asset for the firm and its products. Many local companies succeed, in part, because their owners are out front in small market television commercials. They then begin to take on the status of local celebrities.

Expert sources include physicians, lawyers, accountants, and financial planners. These experts tend not to be famous celebrities or CEOs. Experts provide backing for testimonials, serve as authoritative figures, demonstrate products, and enhance the credibility of informative advertisements.

- **Ace Hardware: John Madden**
- **Adidas: Steffi Graf**
- **American Express: Jerry Seinfeld**
- **Amway: Shaquille O'Neal**
- **AT&T: Whitney Houston**
- **Campbell Soup: Wayne Gretzky**
- **Converse: Larry Bird, Larry Johnson, Lattrell Sprewell**
- **Danskin: Nadia Comaneci**
- **Fila: Naomi Campbell, Grant Hill, Kathy Ireland, Vendela**
- **GMC Trucks: Grant Hill**
- **Hanes Hosiery: Fran Drescher**
- **Hanes Underwear: Michael Jordan**
- **KFC: Barry Bonds**
- **L'eggs: Jamie Lee Curtis**
- **MasterCard: Tom Watson**
- **Nintendo: Ken Griffey Jr.**
- **Outback Steakhouse: Rachel Hunter**
- **Revlon: Cindy Crawford**
- **Subaru: Paul Hogan**
- **Sprite: Kobe Bryant**
- **Taco Bell: Spike Lee, Shaquille O'Neal, Hakeem Olajuwon**

FIGURE 8.4
Celebrity Endorsers

The final category of spokesperson are *typical-person sources.* Typical persons are one of two different types. The first category consists of paid actors or models who portray or resemble everyday people. The second is actual, typical, everyday people used in advertisements. Wal-Mart, as already mentioned, features its own store employees in freestanding insert advertisements. Agencies also create many "man-on-the-street" types of advertisements. For example, PERT shampoo recently prepared ads showing an individual asking people if they would like their hair washed. Dr. Scholl's interviews people about problems with their feet that might be resolved with cushioned shoe inserts.

Real people sources are becoming more common. One reason for this is the overuse of celebrities. Many experts believe that consumers have become saturated with celebrity endorsers and that the positive impact today is not as strong as it was in the past. One study conducted in Great Britain indicated that 55 percent of the consumers surveyed reported that a famous face was not enough to grab their attention. Celebrities held a greater appeal for the 15- to 24-year-old age bracket. Sixty-two percent of that group stated that a famous person in an ad would get their attention.[12]

Source Characteristics

In evaluating sources, most account executives and companies consider five major characteristics. The effectiveness of an advertisement may depend on the degree to which a spokesperson has one or more of the five characteristics, which are:

1. Attractiveness
2. Likability
3. Trustworthiness
4. Expertise
5. Credibility

An advertisement for the U.S. Marines using a typical person spokesperson.
Source: Courtesy of the U.S. Marine Corps.

One reason for using celebrities is that they are more likely to possess at least an element of all five characteristics. A CEO, expert, or typical person probably lacks one or more of them.

Attractiveness has two ingredients: (1) physical characteristics and (2) personality characteristics. Physical attractiveness is usually an important asset for an endorser. Bijan used Bo Derek's physical attractiveness to promote its line of menswear, perfume, and jewelry. Advertisements with physically attractive spokespersons fare better than advertisements with less attractive people. This is true for both male and female audiences. At the same time, the attractiveness of the spokesperson's personality is also important to many consumers. This personality component helps viewers form emotional bonds with the spokesperson. If the spokesperson is seen as having a sour personality, even if physically beautiful, consumers are less likely to develop an emotional bond with the individual and the product.

Closely related to attractiveness is the concept of **similarity**. Consumers are more inclined to be influenced by a message delivered by a person who is somehow similar. For example, a "stay at home" mom is more likely to be influenced by an advertisement that starts out with a woman saying, "Since I made the decision to stop working and care for my family full-time. . . " Both similarity and attractiveness can create **identification**, in which the receiver is able, in some manner, to identify with the source. At times this

A Bijan perfume advertisement featuring Bo Derek.

Source: Courtesy of Bijan Fragrances, Inc.

may involve the fantasy of identifying with a rich person buying a BMW. At others, identification is based on believing the source has similar beliefs, attitudes, preferences, behaviors, or is in the same or a similar situation as the customer.

Closely related to the personality component of attractiveness is *likability*. Consumers respond more positively to spokespersons they like. This liking arises from various sources, including situations in which they like either the actor or the character played by the actor in a movie. An athlete gains likability if he or she plays on the consumer's favorite team. Other individuals are likable because they support the favorite charities of consumers. Even though they may never actually meet the spokesperson, consumers can develop a liking or disliking for them based on their exposure to them. As noted earlier in this text, many people knew Dennis Rodman as a talented basketball player but dislike his flamboyant personality and fashion choices. When Monica Lewinsky began endorsing Jenny Craig, several local companies pulled the ads over fears of negative consumer reactions. If consumers do not like a particular spokesperson, they are likely to transfer that dislike to the product the celebrity endorses. This is not an automatic transfer, because consumers recognize that endorsers are paid spokespersons. Still, there is almost always a negative impact on brand attitude.

A celebrity may be likable or attractive, but he or she may not be viewed as *trustworthy*. Trustworthiness is the degree of confidence or the level of acceptance consumers place in the spokesperson's message. A trustworthy spokesperson helps consumers believe the message. Two of the most trusted celebrities are Michael Jordan and Bill Cosby. Likability and trustworthiness are highly related. People who are liked tend to be trusted and people who are disliked tend not to be trusted.

The fourth characteristic advertisers look for when examining sources is *expertise*. Spokespersons with higher levels of expertise are more believable than sources with low expertise. Richard Petty and Jeff Gordon are seen as experts when automobile products and lubricants are advertised. Often when expertise is desired in an ad, the ad agency opts for the CEO or a trained or educated expert in the field. American Express features Maria Barraza, a small business owner and designer, to promote its Small Business Services.

A potential negative side to using a CEO as the spokesperson may be present: Although he or she has a high degree of expertise, the individual may lack some of the other key characteristics (attractiveness, likability, or trustworthiness). Expertise can be valuable in persuasive advertisements designed to change opinions or attitudes. Spokespersons with high levels of expertise are more capable of persuading an audience than someone with zero or low expertise.[13]

The final source selection characteristic is *credibility*, which is the sum of the other characteristics. It is a composite of attractiveness, trustworthiness, likability, and expertise. Credibility affects a receiver's acceptance of the spokesperson and message. A credible source is believable. Most sources do not score highly on all four attributes, yet they need to score highly on at least two in order to be perceived as credible.

Matching Source Types and Characteristics

The account executive, ad agency, and corporate sponsor, individually or jointly, may choose the type of spokesperson. They can choose a celebrity, CEO, expert, or typical person, and the specific individual must have the key characteristics. This section matches source types with various characteristics.

Celebrities normally score well in terms of trustworthiness, believability, persuasiveness, and likability. These virtues increase if the match between the product and celebrity is a logical and proper fit. For example, Gabriela Satatini endorsing Head Sportswear is a good fit. An athlete endorsing any type of athletic product fits well. Companies can be creative but also use common sense in making quality matches. For instance, the match of boxer George Foreman to his Lean Mean Grilling Machine is a great success. On the other hand, convincing consumers that celebrities such as Charles Barkley, Sammy Sosa, Dan Marino, and Emmitt Smith eat at McDonald's is more challenging.

Several dangers exist in using celebrities. The first is negative publicity about the celebrity caused by inappropriate conduct. In the early 1990s, Pepsi discovered that actions by celebrities such as Mike Tyson, Madonna, and Michael Jackson became a liability. This potential for negative publicity has lead some advertisers to use deceased celebrities, because what was essentially *negative likability* became attached to the company and its products. Many companies concluded that there was no need to risk bringing embarrassment or injury to themselves or the brand. It is also a reason that more ads use cartoon characters. Practically everyone likes cartoons.

The second danger of using celebrities is that their endorsement of so many products tarnishes their credibility. For example, after Sammy Sosa's historic home run chase with Mark McGwire, Sosa signed endorsement contracts with McDonald's, Spanish-language TV network Telemundo, Fila, Fuji Photo Film USA, Chicago clothier Bigsby & Kruthers, a comic book company, Total Sports Concepts, a cereal called Slammin'
Sammies from Famous Fixins', and sunglass marketer Native Eyewear.[14] Only a few exceptional celebrities such as Michael Jordan and Bill Cosby can get away with endorsing so many products. Advertisers hope Sammy Sosa's personality, likability, and high level of trustworthiness put him in the same class with Cosby and Jordan.

Another problem associated with celebrity endorsements is credibility. Consumers know celebrities are paid, which detracts from their believability. If the celebrity endorses a number of products, consumer evaluations of that person's credibility declines further. Some advertising research indicates that when a celebrity endorses multiple products, it tends to reduce his or her credibility and likability as well as consumers' attitudes toward the ad.[15]

As a result, careful consideration must be given to the choice of a celebrity. The individual cannot simply be famous. The person should possess as many of the characteristics as possible, match the product or service being advertised, not be "spread too thin" or overexposed, and promote a positive image that can be transferred to the product, service, or company.

A *CEO* or other prominent corporate official may or may not possess the characteristics of attractiveness and likability. CEOs should, however, appear to be trustworthy, have expertise, and maintain a degree of credibility. A CEO is not a professional actor or model. Coming across well in a commercial may be difficult.

Companies must be aware of the trustworthiness issue. For example, many times the owner of a local auto dealership represents it as the spokesperson. The primary problem is that many consumers view used car salespeople as those who cannot be trusted. Other local business owners may be highly trustworthy, such as restaurant owners, physicians, eye care professionals, and so forth.

Advertising creatives and account executives should be careful about asking a CEO or business owner to serve as a source. They first must be convinced that the individual has

Bijan • menswear • jewelry • fragrances • 420 north rodeo drive beverly hills, ca • 699 fifth avenue new york, ny

Michael Jordan is one of only a few celebrities who can endorse a number of products and maintain a high level of credibility.

Source: Courtesy of Bijan Fragrances, Inc.

"Jockey For Her is the best fitting underwear I've ever worn. It's so comfortable. And now my favorite granddaughters wear Jockey For Girls®. Just Jockey."

Catherine Councell Moll
Grandmother/Banker
Sheboygan, Wisconsin

So Comfortable JOCKEY For Her

For Pantyhose That Fit . . . Wear Jockey For Her Pantyhose with Lycra®

This Jockey advertisement features an older typical person model.
Source: Courtesy of Jockey International.

enough key characteristics to promote the product and gain the consumer's interest and trust.

Experts, first and foremost, should be credible. The ad agency should seek out an expert who is also attractive, likable, and trustworthy. Experts are helpful in promoting health care products and complicated products that require explanations. In other situations, consumers will place a degree of trust in the company when purchasing the product or service recommended by an expert. An expert who is unattractive and dislikable cannot convince consumers that he or she can be trusted, and credibility drops as a result. Business-to-business ads often feature experts. The agency should be certain that an expert spokesperson has valid credentials and will be able to clearly explain a product or service's benefits. Then the source's trustworthiness and credibility rise.

Typical person ads are sometimes difficult to prepare, especially when they use real persons. First, typical-person sources do not have the name recognition of celebrities. Consequently, advertisers often use multiple sources within one advertisement to build credibility. Increasing the number of sources in the ad makes the ad more effective. Hearing three people talk about a good dentist is more believable than hearing it from only one person. By using multiple sources, viewers are motivated to pay attention to the ad and to process its arguments.[16]

Real person ads are a kind of two-edged sword. On the one hand, trustworthiness and credibility rise when the source is bald, overweight, or has some other physical imperfections. This can be especially valuable when the bald person promotes a hair replacement program or the overweight source talks about a diet pill. On the other hand, attractiveness and likability may be lower.

Using customers in ads can be difficult, because they will flub lines and look less natural on the screen. These difficulties with actual customers and employees lead many ad agencies to turn to professional models and actors portraying ordinary people. Professional actors make filming and photographing much easier. Also, the agency is in the position to choose a likable but plain person. The desired effects (trustworthiness and credibility) are often easier to create using professional actors and models.

In general, the ad agency should seek to be certain that the source or spokesperson has the major characteristics the ad needs. When the appeal is humor, likability is very important. In a rational or informational ad, expertise and credibility are crucial, especially in business-to-business ads. In each case, the goal is to try to find as many of the characteristics as possible when retaining a spokesperson.

CREATING AN ADVERTISEMENT

Figure 8.5 illustrates the process a typical creative uses in preparing an advertisement. The process begins with the creative brief, which outlines the message theme of the advertisement as well as other pertinent information. Using the creative brief as the blueprint, the creative develops a means–ends chain, starting with an attribute of the product that generates a specific customer benefit and eventually produces a desirable end state. This means–end chain is the foundation on which all of the decisions will be made.

Following the development of the means–end chain, the creative chooses a message strategy, the appeal, and the executional framework. He or she also decides about a source or spokesperson at this point, because the choice usually affects other creative decisions. Selection of the leverage point is usually done after the creative begins work

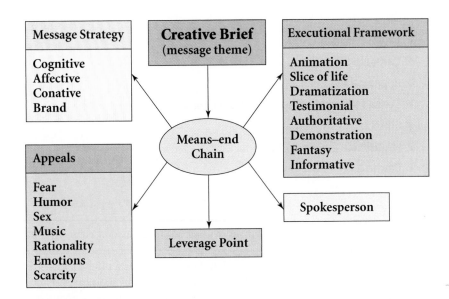

FIGURE 8.5
Creating an Advertisement

on the advertisement. The leverage point takes the consumer from the product attribute or customer benefit to the desired end state. The type of leverage point used depends on the message strategy, appeal, and executional framework.

Although certain combinations tend to work well together, the creative has an almost infinite number of ways of preparing an advertisement or campaign. For example, if the creative wants to use a cognitive message strategy, the most logical appeal is rationality. The creative, however, can use fear, humor, sex, music, or scarcity. The one appeal that would not work as well is emotions. It can be used, but the emotional part of the advertisement can overpower the cognitive message the creative is trying to send to the viewer. If the creative decides to use a humor approach with a cognitive strategy, other logical and illogical combinations emerge. In terms of the executional framework, dramatization and authoritative tend not to work as well with humor. Any of the other executional frameworks are suitable. This flexibility allows an almost infinite number of advertisements to be possible from a single means–end chain. The combination to use depends on the creative's expertise and experience as well as the creative's opinion about the best way to accomplish the client's advertising objectives.

INTEGRATED LEARNING EXPERIENCE

Creating an award-winning advertisement requires skill and knowledge about both advertising and the marketplace. Access DDB Needham Agency at **www.ddbn.com**, and find the "Work" section. Examine its winning works under "Recognition," along with other advertisements it has produced. Pay close attention to the "State of the Art" section concerning the methods used to create advertisements.

ADVERTISING EFFECTIVENESS

Producing effective ads requires the joint efforts of the account executive, creative, media planner, and media buyer. Working independently can produce some award-winning ads, but often they will not be effective ads that meet a client's objectives. One major problem ad agencies face is producing a commercial to stand out among the thousands of existing ads. If an agency can break through the clutter, half the battle is won. All that remains is for consumers or businesses to react to the ad in the appropriate manner.

To be effective means creating an ad that accomplishes the objectives desired by clients. The task of making sure the ad meets the IMC objectives requires that creatives

▶ **Visual consistency**

▶ **Campaign duration**

▶ **Repeated tag lines**

▶ **Consistent positioning - avoid ambiguity**

▶ **Simplicity**

▶ **Identifiable selling point**

▶ **Create an effective flow**

FIGURE 8.6
Principles of Effective Advertising

and account executives follow the seven basic principles described in greater detail next (see Figure 8.6).

The first principle is to maintain **visual consistency**. Seeing a specific image or visual display over and over again helps embed it in long-term memory. Visual consistency is important because consumers, whether individual consumers or members of a business buying center, spend very little time viewing or listening to an advertisement. In most cases, it is just a casual glance at a print advertisement or a cursory glimpse at a television ad. Visual consistency causes the viewer to move the advertising message from short-term memory to long-term memory. Consistently used logos and other long-standing images help fix the brand or company in the consumer's mind. For example, people remember Frosted Flakes because of the visually consistent use of Tony the Tiger. They know Green Giant products by their cartoon spokesperson. Logos such as the Nike swoosh and the Prudential Rock emblem are well established in the minds of many consumers.

The second principle of effective advertising is concerned with *campaign duration.* Consumers do not pay attention to advertisements. This means the length or duration of a campaign is important. Using the same advertisement over an appropriate period of time helps embed the message in long-term memory. Account executives should give careful thought to how long to use an advertisement. The ad should be changed before it becomes stale and viewers become bored with it; however, changing ads too frequently impedes the retention process. Reach and frequency affect the duration of a campaign. Higher frequency usually leads to a shorter duration. Low reach may be associated with a longer duration. In any case, typical campaigns last one to two months, but there are exceptions. Marlboro and Camel still use the same visual imagery and have never changed their basic advertisements, but these are rare cases.

The third method used to build effective advertising campaigns is *repeated tag lines.* Visual consistency combined with consistent tag lines can be a more powerful approach. The advertisement can change, but either the visual imagery or the tag line remains the same. The U.S. Army has promoted the tag line "Be all that you can be" for many years, and the Marines are known as "The few. The proud. The Marines." Tag lines help consumers tie the advertisement into current knowledge structure nodes already in their minds. Figure 8.7 contains some of the more common tag lines. See how many you can identify.

A fourth advertising principle is *consistent positioning.* Maintaining consistent positioning throughout a product's life makes it easier for consumers to place the product in a cognitive map. When the firm emphasizes quality in every ad, it becomes easier to tie the product into the consumer's cognitive map than if the firm stresses quality in some ads, price in others, and convenience in a third campaign. This inconsistency in positioning makes the brand and company appear more confused

Visual consistency is maintained in this Wal-Mart ad through the rollback visuals and the tagline "Always low prices. Always."
Source: Courtesy of Wal-Mart.

◗ It's everywhere you want to be.

◗ Are you feeling it?

◗ Just do it.

◗ You're in good hands.

◗ The brushing that works between brushings.

◗ Driving excitement.

◗ A different kind of company. A different kind of car.

◗ When you care enough to send the very best.

◗ The ultimate driving machine.

◗ It takes a licking and keep on ticking.

FIGURE 8.7
Which Tag Lines Can You Identify?

Answers: VISA, Reebok, Nike, Allstate, Colgate, Pontiac, Saturn, Hallmark, BMW, Timex.

and harder to remember. Consistent positioning avoids ambiguity, and the message stays clear and understandable.

Simplicity is the fifth principle of effective advertising. Simple advertisements are easier to comprehend than are complex ads. A print ad with a simple tag line and limited copy is much easier to read than an overloaded or complex one. Consequently, advertisers must resist the temptation to relate all of a product's attributes in a single advertisement. This practice is more prevalent in business-to-business print advertisements and should be avoided there as well. Further, consumer ads on radio or television spots often are so verbally overloaded that the announcer is forced to talk faster. This is usually ineffective, because the listener has too much information to grasp in such a short time period.

The principle of simplicity should be applied more carefully to Internet advertising. The primary reason for simplicity with the Internet is load time. Individuals surfing the Internet will not wait more than a few seconds for something to load; if it doesn't load quickly, they move on to another site.

The next principle of effective advertising is the concept of an *identifiable selling point*. The emphasis should be placed on all three of the words: (1) identifiable, (2) selling, and (3) point. The advertisement should have a selling point (price, quality, convenience, luxury, etc.) that is easily identifiable to the viewer of the ad. It is important to remember that an advertisement should sell a product's *benefits* as much as the product itself. Also, the concept is a selling point, not selling *points*. The best advertisements are those that emphasize one major point and do not confuse the viewer by trying to present too many ideas. An advertisement's primary goal is to fix the product into the cognitive map of the viewer through establishing new linkages or strengthening current linkages. An identifiable selling point helps reach that goal.

The final principle is to *create an effective flow*. In a print ad, the reader's eye should move easily to all of the key points in the ad. In a television ad, the points to be made should flow in a manner that leads the consumer to the appropriate action or conclusion. Ads without flow confuse the consumer or are simply tuned out.

This advertisement illustrates the concept of simplicity and consistent positioning by noting that Hershey's has been unchanged since 1899.
Source: Courtesy of Hershey's.

Beating Ad Clutter

As noted earlier, overcoming clutter is the first step in creating an effective advertising campaign. The presence of a competitor's ad within the same medium or time spot makes the ad clutter problem worse. A recent survey of television advertising revealed that during prime-time programming, 42 percent of the ads shown had one or more of their competitors also advertising during the same hour. Research suggests that the effectiveness of an advertisement is significantly reduced when a competitor advertisement was also shown during the same time slot.[17]

One method advertisers use to overcome this brand interference is repetition. Repeating an ad can increase brand and ad recall. In advertising studies, this repetition is effective in increasing recall if no competitor ads are present. When competitor ads are present, repetition does not help the competitive ad interference problem and does not stimulate greater recall.

Because mere repetition of an ad does not always work, advertisers have begun to take advantage of the principles found in **variability theory**.[18] In this theory, variable encoding occurs when a consumer sees the same advertisement in different environments. These varied environments increase an ad's recall and effectiveness, by encoding it into the brain through various methods. Creatives can generate this effect by varying the situational context of a particular ad. For example, the MasterCard campaign noted previously uses various settings to convey the same basic message, "There are some things money can't buy. For everything else, there's MasterCard." Varying the context of the ad increases recall. This is a very effective method to overcome competitive ad interference.[19]

Another method designed to decrease the negative impact of competing ads is to use a second medium. Using two media to convey a message generally is more effective than repeating an advertisement within the same medium. Using more than one medium also

These two advertisements for Absolut Vodka beat ad clutter through repetition and through the use of variability theory in using more than one message.
Source: Under permission by V&S Vin & Spirit AB. Absolut Country of Sweden Vodka & Logo, Absolut, Absolut Bottle Design and Absolut Calligraphy are trademarks owned by V&S Vin Spirit AB © 2002 V&S Vin & Spirit AB.

reduces competing ad interference. An ad that appears on television and in magazines works better than one that appears only on television. Consumers seeing an advertisement in a different medium are more likely to encode the ad than if it is always seen in only one medium.

Clutter remains a difficult problem in advertising. Creatives who are able to capture the attention of the audience and transmit messages successfully are in great demand. Companies constantly experiment with various approaches to reach the audience. When the program works, the advertising firm and its client have a great deal to celebrate.

INTEGRATED LEARNING EXPERIENCE

At **www.zeldman.com** is the "Ad Graveyard." This site contains real ads that did not run. Go to this site. Based on the principles you learned in Chapters 7 and 8, identify what is wrong with the ads. What could be done to turn the buried ad into a usable one? Compare these ads to those you observed at **www.adsGallery.com**.

SUMMARY

Advertising is the process of transmitting a personal message across one or more impersonal media. The message should reflect the image that occurs throughout an IMC program. Four types of message strategies are present in advertisements. Cognitive strategies emphasize rational and logical arguments to compel consumers to make purchases. Affective strategies are oriented toward buyer emotions and feelings. Conative strategies are linked to more direct responses, behaviors, and actions. Brand strategies are designed to strengthen the image of the firm or brand. These strategies should be integrated with various types of appeals through the media selected for the campaign.

Executional frameworks tell the story in the ad. Animation has become more sophisticated and provides many new creative approaches in the design of ads. The slice-of-life approach and dramatizations are problem-solving types of ads, leading the consumer to something better by using the product. Testimonials are rendered by individuals who have realized the benefits of a product. An authoritative expert can build consumer confidence in a product or company. Demonstrations show how products can be used. A fantasy takes people away from the real world to a make-believe place. This makes the product more exotic and desirable. Informative ads render basic information about the product. Each can be used effectively to persuade consumers and business-to-business buyers to consider a company's offerings.

Celebrities, CEOs, experts, and typical persons can be chosen to be "out front" in the advertisement. Each has advantages and disadvantages. The marketing team selects sources or spokespersons based on the individual's attractiveness, likability, trustworthiness, expertise, or credibility. The more of these characteristics that are present, the better off the advertiser will be.

Effective ad campaigns are based on the six principles of visual consistency, a sufficient campaign duration, repeated tag lines, consistent positioning, simplicity, and presentation of an identifiable selling point. Creatives and account executives must incorporate these principles into the advertising campaign to enhance the odds of success. Also, clutter must be overcome by repeating ads and showing them in various media, or in some other way.

Designing ads is often considered the most glamorous part of the advertising industry, and it is in many ways. Remember, however, that the other side of the glamour coin is hard work and the constant pressure to perform. Many people think being a creative is a burnout-type of job. At the same time, those who have proven track records of success are well rewarded for their efforts. Utilizing the principles presented in this chapter can be key to success in the highly competitive and exciting business of advertising design.

REVIEW QUESTIONS

1. Name the four types of message strategies creatives can use. How are message strategies related to the message theme?

2. What types of products or services best match cognitive message strategies? Name the five types of cognitive approaches.

3. When will an affective message strategy be most effective? What two types of affective messages can creatives design? Give an example of each.

4. What is the primary goal of a conative message strategy?

5. What does a brand message strategy emphasize? Describe the four forms of brand strategies.

6. How is an executional framework different from an ad appeal? How are they related?

7. List as many uses of animation-based advertisements as possible. What forms of animation are possible with the available technology?

8. How are slice-of-life and dramatization executional frameworks similar? How are they different?

9. How are authoritative and informational executional frameworks similar? How are they different?

10. What types of testimonials can advertisers use? Give an example of each.

11. Which media are best for demonstration-type ads?

12. What kinds of products or services are best suited to fantasy-based executional frameworks? What products or services are poor candidates for fantasies?

13. Name the four main types of sources or spokespersons. What are the advantages and disadvantages of each?

14. Name the five key criteria used when selecting a spokesperson. Which four build to the fifth?

15. Name the tactics available to overcome clutter. How does variability theory assist in this process?

KEY TERMS

message theme the outline of the key idea(s) that the advertising program is supposed to convey.

message strategy the primary tactic used to deliver the message theme.

cognitive message strategy the presentation of rational arguments or pieces of information to consumers.

generic messages direct promotions of product or service attributes or benefits without any claim of superiority.

preemptive messages claims of superiority based on a specific attribute or benefit of a product that preempts the competition from making the same claim.

unique selling proposition an explicit, testable claim of uniqueness or superiority that can be supported or substantiated in some manner.

hyperbole making an untestable claim based upon some attribute or benefit.

comparative advertisement the direct or indirect comparison of a product or service to the competition.

affective message strategies ads designed to invoke feelings and emotions and match them with the product, service, or company.

resonance advertising attempting to connect a product with a consumer's experiences to develop stronger ties between the product and the consumer.

emotional advertising attempting to elicit powerful emotions that eventually lead to product recall and choice.

action-inducing conative ads advertisements that create situations in which cognitive knowledge of the product or affective liking of the product follow the actual purchase or arise during usage of the product.

promotional support conative advertisements ads designed to support other promotional efforts.

brand message strategies ad messages designed to build or enhance the brand or corporate name in some way.

brand user strategy focus on the type of individuals who use a particular brand.

brand image strategy working toward the development of a brand "personality."

brand usage messages stressing the different uses for a particular brand.

corporate advertising promoting the corporate name and image rather than the individual brand.

executional framework the manner in which an ad appeal is presented.

expert authority when an advertiser seeks to convince viewers that a given product is superior to other brands.

sources and spokespersons persons in the advertisement who make the actual presentation.

similarity consumers are more inclined to be influenced by a message delivered by a person who is somehow similar.

identification occurs when the receiver is able, in some manner, to identify with the source, either through a fantasy or by similar beliefs, attitudes, preferences, behaviors, or by being in the same or a similar situation.

visual consistency occurs when consumers see a specific image or visual display over and over again.

variability theory a theory stating that when a consumer sees the same advertisement in different environments, the ad will be more effective.

CRITICAL THINKING EXERCISES

Discussion Questions

1. Mark 10 advertisements in a magazine. Identify the message strategy, appeal, and executional framework each uses. Did the creative select the right combination for the advertisement? What other message strategies or executional frameworks could have been used?

2. Record 10 television advertisements on videotape. Identify the message strategy, appeal, and executional framework each uses. Did the creative select the right combination for the advertisement? What other message strategies or executional frameworks could have been used?

3. Studies involving comparative advertisements as compared to noncomparative ads produced the following findings.[20] Discuss why you think each statement is true. Try to think of comparative ads you have seen that substantiate these claims.

   a. Message awareness was higher for comparative ads than for noncomparative ads if the brands are already established brands.

   b. Brand recall was higher for comparative ads than for noncomparative ads.

   c. Comparative ads were viewed as less believable than noncomparative ads.

   d. Attitudes toward comparative ads were more negative than toward noncomparative ads.

4. Suppose Charles Schwab wants to develop an advertisement with the message theme that Charles Schwab understands the needs of individual consumers and can design an investment strategy to meet each person's particular needs. Which type of message strategy should Schwab choose? Why? Based on the message strategy chosen, which executional framework should the company use? Why? What type of source or spokesperson should Schwab use? Why? Would the type of media being used for the advertisement affect the message strategy choice? Explain your answer.

5. A resort in Florida wants to develop an advertisement highlighting scuba diving classes. Pick one of the following combinations of message strategy, appeal, and executional framework. Then design an advertisement using those components.

   a. Hyperbole cognitive message strategy, humor appeal, and demonstration.

   b. Emotional message strategy, emotional appeal, and slice-of-life.

   c. Conative message strategy, scarcity appeal, and informative.

   d. Emotional or resonance message strategy, sex appeal, and fantasy.

   e. Comparative message strategy, fear appeal, and a testimonial.

6. For each of the following executional frameworks, identify a commercial that uses it. Evaluate the advertisement in terms of how well it is executed. Also, did the appeal and message strategy fit well with the executional framework? Discuss why you remember the advertisement. What makes it memorable?

   a. Animation

   b. Slice-of-life

   c. Dramatization

   d. Testimonial

   e. Authoritative

   f. Demonstration

   g. Fantasy

   h. Informative

7. Name three influential commercial spokespersons. For each one, discuss the five characteristics to use to evaluate spokespersons. Next, make a list of three individuals who are poor spokespersons. Discuss each of the five evaluation characteristics for each of these individuals. What differences exist between an effective and a poor spokesperson?

8. Find a copy of a business journal such as *Business Week* or *Fortune,* or a trade journal. Also locate a copy of a consumer journal such as *Glamour, Time, Sports Illustrated,* or a specialty magazine. Look through an entire issue. What differences between the advertisements in the business journal and consumer journals are readily noticeable? For each of the concepts that follow, discuss specific differences you noted between the two types of magazines. Explain why the differences exist.

   a. Message strategies

   b. Executional frameworks

   c. Sources and spokespersons

9. Access the following Web sites. For each one, identify the primary message strategy it uses. What executional framework does it use? Does it use any sources or spokespersons? What type of appeal does it use? For each Web site, suggest how the site could be improved by changing either the message strategy or the executional framework or both. Be specific. Explain how the change would improve the site.

   a. Georgia Pacific (www.gp.com)

   b. Playland International (www.playland-inc.com)

   c. MGM Grand (www.mgmgrand.com)

   d. The Exotic Body (www.exoticbody.com)

   e. Cover Girl (www.covergirl.com)

   f. American Supercamps (www.americansupercamp.com)

   g. Windmill Hill Place (www.windmillhill.co.uk)

Selecting an Executional Framework for an IMC Advertising Campaign

Finally, you are ready to prepare the actual ad. To complete the task, think about the various message strategies to employ, including cognitive, affective, conative, and brand strategies. You also need to decide on an executional framework format, such as animation, slice-of-life, testimonial, dramatization, or one of the others. Another significant ingredient in your campaign's success level is your choice of a spokesperson. Visit the Prentice-Hall Web site at **www.prenhall.com/clow** or access the IMC Plan Pro disk that accompanied this textbook to complete this stage of your IMC plan. The exercise for this chapter leads you through these decisions. At the end, you need to design and execute the ad for your product. If this is done correctly, the ad will reflect the IMC theme and all of the other components of the IMC program you have completed up to this point.

BUILDING AN
IMC
CAMPAIGN
IMC PlanPro!

CASE 1

CHARITABLE COMPETITION

John Mulvaney was placed in charge of his company's newest account, the United Way Charities of Savannah, Georgia. This branch of the United Way had never retained the services of an advertising agency but had gotten caught in the crush of competitive problems in the past decade. Consequently, the organization decided it was necessary to prepare more professional advertisements in order to succeed in the new millennium.

At the first meeting with the organization's leaders, John discovered a world of competition he had never envisioned. First of all, the number of charities competing for contributions had grown exponentially in the past decade. Churches, illnesses, women's shelters, homeless shelters, performing arts facilities (art galleries and community theaters), veterans groups, colleges and universities, minority organizations, Girl Scouts, Boy Scouts, and dozens of other charities were in the marketplace for charitable dollars. Illnesses alone included heart disease, lung disease, AIDS, MD (Jerry Lewis telethon), blindness, and many others. Organizations representing these causes contact small and large donors alike.

Second, bad publicity had tainted the entire industry. Church scams combined with spending abuses by leaders of other charities created a negative impact. Many people believe charities simply fund themselves, with very few of the dollars actually reaching people in need. As a result, contributions declined.

Third, a booming economy had created an odd effect. On the one hand, the number of extremely rich people had grown, especially those associated with Silicon Valley. Many of these individuals were actually trying to be effective altruists. Unfortunately, far too many of these givers wanted to see their names on buildings rather than simply making contributions to operating budgets. Also, prosperity (lower unemployment, fewer people in poverty) has created a kind of complacency in which many regular givers have begun to assume there was simply less need for charity.

The United Way received major support from the NFL for over two decades. Visibility was high, and the organization had a solid base of donations. The goal was to build on this base and combat the problems that had grown. John contacted his best creative, Tom Prasch, to see what could be done.

Tom argued that the primary problem with United Way ads was that they were boring. They typically showed a football player visiting a sick child or shaking hands with some community leader. Viewers could tune them out easily. Tom said the United Way needed something that would recapture the attention of John Q. Public. Tom told John and the United Way that he believed strongly in the use of seven attention-getting factors:

1. Intensity
2. Size
3. Contrast
4. Repetition
5. Motion
6. Novelty
7. Familiarity

Intensity means that bright, loud, strong stimuli capture the attention of the audience. A large-size billboard or full-page newspaper ad is more likely to be noticed than something normal or small. Contrast is the difference between dark and light or loud and soft. Repetition means something repeated has attention-getting value. Motion captures attention, even in print ads where the illusion of movement can be created. Novelty occurs when someone encounters a novel stimulus in a familiar setting (a new piece of furniture in a living room will be immediately noticed). Familiarity means finding something familiar in an unfamiliar setting such as seeing the Golden Arches in a foreign country.

Tom suggested that United Way had only one solid attention-getting factor: its logo. It was highly recognizable from being repeated for so many years. None of the other factors was featured in the ads.

John gave the United Way a major discount in billing for services. He also constructed a very conservative budget. The group agreed that any endorser must volunteer his or her time in order to serve. Then, they turned Tom loose to create a new local campaign.

1. Design a campaign for the United Way of Savannah. Use Tom's attention-getting factors to create the ads.
2. Which media should the United Way use? Why?
3. What kind of message strategy would be best? Why?
4. What kind of executional framework should be used? Why?
5. What kind of source or spokesperson is best for this campaign? Defend your choice.

CASE 2

KID'S PALACE

Pam Burns loved kids. She had raised three of her own and now had two grandchildren. With an "empty nest," Pam decided it was time to put the two main loves of her life, kids and free enterprise, into one package. With the help of her husband and investment capital from her personal savings and the adventuresome spirit of a few friends, Pam purchased an old building near the largest outdoor mall in Memphis, Tennessee. There she created her new business, Kid's Palace.

Kid's Palace provided a variety of fun activities. Playrooms filled with plastic balls, tunnels, jungle gyms, a video arcade, plus other toys and games were inside. Also, tables and chairs were set up in a crafts area. At one end of the building a snack bar carried not only traditional junk food but also healthier treats such as milk, orange juice, fruit bars, cheese, and crackers.

(continued)

Pam designed Kid's Palace to be a place children could go to play while under the supervision of several college-age students. Parents could leave older children, and younger children had areas with tables, chairs, and age-appropriate activities, so that parents could watch them in a comfortable setting and socialize with other adults at the same time.

Pam's snack bar area had a section dedicated especially to birthday parties. Parents could bring their own cakes, and Kid's Palace provided plates and plastic forks. The student helpers assisted at the parties. Video screens in the snack bar area ran cartoons and other children's programs continuously. Music played in the rest of Kid's Palace at a low volume.

Repeat business was Pam's primary marketing goal. She hoped to entice adults to bring kids to her indoor park and conclude it was a great alternative form of entertainment. Troublemakers and other problem children were quickly escorted out of the building, given a refund, and told they could come back only if they behaved.

Pam went to a local advertising agency seeking advice on the kinds of ads she could run for her new business. She had budgeted enough to support a fairly strong television and radio campaign. She also considered mailing coupons to parents or giving them away at PTA meetings.

The remaining questions were:

▶ Should she advertise to parents or to children?

▶ What kind of message should Kid's Palace send?

After a long visit with the agency, the campaign was ready. Pam hoped to have a long and prosperous run providing an alternative form of fun, so that young people could do more than stay home, watch television, and play video games.

1. What kind of message strategy, leverage point, and executional framework should the ads for Kid's Palace provide?

2. What kind of spokesperson or source should Kid's Palace use in its advertisement?

3. Apply the principles of effective advertising to ads for Kid's Palace.

4. Design a print or television advertisement for Kid's Palace.

ENDNOTES

1. David Aaker and Donald Norris, "Characteristics of TV Commercials Perceived as Informative," *Journal of Advertising Research,* 22, no. 2 (1982), pp. 61–70; Henry A. Laskey, Ellen Day, and Melvin R. Crask, "Typology of Main Message Strategies for Television Commercials," *Journal of Advertising,* 18, no. 1 (1989), pp. 36–41.

2. Bradley Johnson, "IBM Moves Back to Intel Co-op Deal," *Advertising Age* 68, no. 10 (March 10, 1997), p. 4.

3. Dhruv Grewal and Sukumar Kavanoor, "Comparative Versus Noncomparative Advertising: A Meta-Analysis," *Journal of Marketing,* 61, no. 4 (October 1997), pp. 1–15; Mark Dolliver, "So, If You Can't Say Something Nice. . . ," *Adweek, Eastern Edition,* 39, no. 14 (April 6, 1998), p. 21.

4. Naveen Donthu, "A Cross-Country Investigation of Recall of and Attitudes Toward Comparative Advertising," *Journal of Advertising,* 27, no. 2 (summer 1998), pp. 111–21.

5. Grewal and Kavanoor, "Comparative Versus Noncomparative Advertising: A Meta-Analysis"; "Bring Back Brand X," *Advertising Age,* 70, no. 46 (November 8, 1999), p. 60.

6. Karalynn Ott, "B-to-B Marketers Display Their Creative Side," *Advertising Age's Business Marketing,* 84, no. 1 (January 1999), pp. 3–4.

7. Karen Heller, "Responsible Care—Public Outreach: The Stakes Are High," *Chemical Week,* 148, no. 26 (July 17, 1991), pp. 81–84.

8. Michael L. Maynard, "Slice-of-Life: A Persuasive Mini Drama in Japanese Television Advertising," *Journal of Popular Culture,* 31, no. 2 (fall 1997), pp. 131–42.

9. Hillary Chura, "Maytag Airs Epic Drama for $35 Mil Range Intro," *Advertising Age,* 70, no. 28 (July 5, 1999), p. 4.

10. J. Levine, "Fantasy, Not Flesh," *Forbes,* 145, no. 2 (January 22, 1990), pp. 3–5.

11. Sam Bradley, "Marketers Are Always Looking for Good Pitchers," *Brandweek,* 37, no. 9 (February 26, 1996), pp. 36–37.

12. Claire Murphy, "Stars Brought Down to Earth in TV Ads Research," *Marketing* (January 22, 1998), p. 1.

13. Roobina Ohanian, "Construction and Validation of a Scale to Measure Celebrity Endorsers' Perceived Expertise," *Journal of Advertising,* 19, no. 3 (1990), pp. 39–52.

14. Wayne Friedman, "Home Runs Kings Still, But Not with Ad Deals," *Advertising Age,* 70, no. 28 (July 5, 1999), pp. 3–4.

15. Carolyn Tripp, Thomas D. Jensen, and Les Carlson, "The Effects of Multiple Product Endorsements by Celebrities on Consumers' Attitudes and Intentions," *Journal of Consumer Research,* 20 (March 1994), pp. 535–47.

16. David J. Moore and John C. Mowen, "Multiple Sources in Advertising Appeals: When Product Endorsers Are Paid by the Advertising Sponsor," *Journal of Academy of Marketing Science,* 22, no. 3 (summer 1994), pp. 234–43.

17. Raymond R. Burke and Thomas K. Srull, "Competitive Interference and Consumer Memory for Advertising," *Journal of Consumer Research,* 15 (June 1988), pp. 55–68.

18. A. W. Melton, "The Situation with Respect to the Spacing of Repetitions and Memory," *Journal of Verbal Learning and Verbal Behavior,* 9 (1970), pp. 596–606.

19. H. Rao Unnava and Deepak Sirdeshmukh, "Reducing Competitive Ad Interference," *Journal of Marketing Research,* 31, no. 3 (August 1994), pp. 403–11.

20. Grewal and Kavanoor, "Comparative Versus Noncomparative Advertising: A Meta-Analysis."

Advertising Media Selection

Chapter Objectives

Master **the process of creating a media strategy.**

Understand **the roles media planners and media buyers play in an advertising program.**

Utilize **reach, frequency, continuity, impressions, and other advertising objectives in the preparation of an advertising program.**

Study **and incorporate the advantages of various media in developing an ad program.**

Recognize **the value of an effective mix of media in an advertising campaign.**

THE AFLAC DUCK MAKES A BIG SPLASH

Just a few years ago, AFLAC advertised the company's insurance in a manner similar to practically every other insurer. Images of happy families looking lovingly at each other and having warm, fuzzy interactions with an insurance agent were common. After all, supplemental health insurance is supposed to provide peace of mind, so matching the message to the theme with soothing music seemed the most logical choice.

In 1999, the marketing team working with AFLAC took a bold step. They noticed that AFLAC ads were competing for viewers' attention in a barrage of television advertisements, some of which were stacked 10 to 15 deep during a commercial break. Many of these competing images were funny and smart.

Enter the duck.

Linda Kaplan Thaler, CEO of the Kaplan Thaler Group Ltd., a New York-based agency, had a track record of developing innovative and attention-grabbing advertising approaches. Her organization created the Clairol Herbal Essences "Yes, Yes, YES!" campaign. Kaplan Thaler said that the biggest challenge was trying to find some way to build the AFLAC brand, which is an acronym, not a word. Finally, when an employee said the name sounds like the squawking of a duck, the team was off and running.

In addition to buying time on national television, the media buyer suggested buying spots on CNN Airport news and on in-flight television shown on American Airlines, Delta, United, and Continental. The target market for the company's product is employees who work in businesses with fewer than 500 employees. A number of these individuals are underinsured or not insured with health coverage. AFLAC's supplemental policies cover loss of income, deductibles, and nonmedical expenses that are sometimes not covered by standard health, life, and disability policies. Many of these employees and leaders of those companies spend time in airports and on airplanes.

The white Pekin duck, which appears in key spots of commercials, shouts out the company's name in response to a problem. For example, an early spot features a passenger in an airport tripping over a piece of luggage. The flight attendants standing nearby discuss a friend who was hurt on the job and did not have supplemental insurance. At the end of the spot, the duck is flying alongside the plane, still trying to get the attention of the people involved. In another, the duck rides a roller coaster trying to get the message to a couple taking a thrill ride.

"He's the underduck," Linda Kaplan Thaler reports. "We can rant and rave against policies and institutions, but as one person, we never feel as if we're heard. That's the role of the duck. He'll even go on a roller coaster to tell the world about supplemental insurance."

To make sure every ingredient of the plan was in place, the company featured the duck in its annual report, including footprints and feathers on every page. The theme presented to the company was, "If it ain't broke . . . fix it anyway!" The duck image was shown throughout the organization before the campaign even began.

The campaign has been a major success. Sales have risen by 27 percent since the ads began running. The company's name shows up on late-night talk shows as well as a list of ads that have made an impact on popular culture, prepared by the *Wall Street Journal.* Lewis Lazre, a writer for the *Chicago Sun-Times,* notes, "The duck does stick in the mind, and you can remember it and the name of the company."

Currently, AFLAC now sells a stuffed toy duck and other duck-related merchandise on its Web site. This process, known as *merchandising the advertising,* features another twist: The profits from the sales of the merchandise support the AFLAC Cancer and Blood Disorder Center at the Children's Healthcare of Atlanta hospital.

The advertising team continues to look for new ways to feature the duck, including ads with Olympic-like skaters during the 2002 Olympics and another starring Yogi Berra during the baseball season. AFLAC's media budget was over $40 million in 2002. With creativity, careful media selection, and a strong "spokesperson," AFLAC has built a stronger brand in a market where differentiation is difficult to achieve. "He has very long legs," reports one AFLAC employee. It would be hard to argue with that.[1]

THE BOULDER STOP

In the development of an advertising campaign two critical issues are the selection of an advertising agency and the selection of the media. Sometimes the same agency handles both responsibilities, while at other times a different agency is used to purchase media time and space. The decision about who will buy the media time and who will plan the media buys should be based on a variety of factors, including the media agency's internal capabilities, the characteristics of the advertising agencies to be considered, and the nature of the media to be involved in the campaign. All of these issues should be reviewed in light of the company's overall strategies, IMC message, and other marketing concerns.

The Boulder Stop example on the IMC Plan Pro disk includes the choice of The Ralston Group as the advertising agency. The rationale for this choice is made in section 4.3 of the plan. The breakdown of funding for all marketing efforts is shown in section 4.2 with a breakdown for each of the three primary IMC objectives. Subsequent individual IMC objectives are shown in sections 5.1, 6.1, and 7.1.

Study sections 5.2.1, 6.2.1., and 7.2.1 in terms of the budget for various media. For the consumer market, the heaviest advertising budget is for TV advertising with additional advertising on the radio, newspaper, and the Internet. For the channel objective (6.2.1), the entire advertising budget is spent on print ads, while for the b-to-b objective The Boulder Stop uses mostly print ads with limited TV and radio ads.

o v e r v i e w

If a tree falls in the forest, and no one is present, does it make a sound? This philosophical question has been around for many years. In the world of advertising, one common problem is that many "trees" fall as unheard and unseen advertisements. Successful marketing account executives help a firm identify target markets and then find media that reach the members of those markets, in both retail situations and business-to-business marketing efforts. Once they identify the right media, creatives design clever, memorable, exciting, and persuasive advertisements to help convince customers to purchase products.

This chapter is devoted to helping you become a more savvy marketing expert by explaining the nature of advertising media selection. The topics include:

- The nature of a media strategy
- Media planning processes and the roles of the media planner and buyer
- Advertising objectives
- Media choices based on the advantages and disadvantages of each medium
- Media selection in business-to-business and international settings

Development of an advertising campaign within the framework of an integrated marketing communications program is the most important function an advertising agency can provide. Client companies depend on cost-effective ads to attract customers and entice them into purchasing various goods and services. The goal is to build a firm's image and to reach a larger consumer base. Advertising media selection is an important element in the success of any advertising program. A review of the elements of selection process follows.

MEDIA STRATEGY

One of the most important ingredients in matching an advertising campaign with the overall integrated marketing communications program is to prepare an effective media strategy. A **media strategy** is the process of analyzing and choosing media for an advertising and promotions campaign.

The average consumer reads or looks over only nine of the more than two hundred consumer magazines on the market. A radio listener usually tunes in to only three of the stations available in a given area. Television viewers watch fewer than eight of the 30-plus stations available by cable or satellite, and average network prime-time ratings have declined by more than 30 percent over the last decade. Simply finding the right places to speak to potential customers is an increasingly challenging task (see the Communication Action Box "Out with the Old: In with the New").

Also, to make the account executive and media buyer's jobs more difficult, prices for advertisements have not gone down and often have risen. Client budgets for advertising have not kept up with inflation, yet they have increased their demands for results and accountability. The marketing team faces many difficulties as they seek to provide the right media outlets for the company.

Once the media strategy is in place, other aspects of media selection can proceed. The first step is to prepare a thorough media planning program using the general advertising methods and objectives.

MEDIA PLANNING

Media planning begins with a careful analysis of the target market. One method of addressing media planning is to approach it from the customer's viewpoint. The idea is to plot the choices in media that a specific, defined target market might experience through the course of a typical day.[2] For example, this list can include the examples in Figure 9.1.

Specific details of this type can be extremely valuable in developing the media strategy. Demographics such as age, sex, income, and education are not enough to determine the media habits of a person in a target market. Discovering viewing patterns of customers means companies can design messages to appeal to key consumers and make them available at the times and locations for key consumers to receive them.

No two media plans are alike. Each plan should, however, integrate the overall IMC strategy with specific marketing tactics. The typical components of a media plan includes the following elements:

▶ A marketing analysis
▶ An advertising analysis
▶ A media strategy
▶ Media scheduling
▶ Justification and summary

The media strategy guides companies such as A.G. Edwards in the selection of appropriate media outlets for their advertisements.
Source: Courtesy of A.G. Edwards.

▶ A favorite wake-up radio station or one listened to during the commute to work

▶ A favorite morning news show or newspaper

▶ Trade or business journals examined while at work

▶ A radio station played during office hours at work

▶ Favorite computer sites accessed during work

▶ Favorite magazines read during the evening hours

▶ Favorite television shows watched during the evening hours

▶ Internet sites accessed during leisure time

▶ Shopping, dining, and entertainment venues frequented

FIGURE 9.1
Examples of Times Workers Are Exposed to Advertisements

COMMUNICATION ACTION

Out with the Old: In with the New

To be successful in advertising in today's global market, many firms must change their view of advertising. The old advertising model had three distinct components. The first was the idea that a "mass-market" exists and can be reached through effective broadcast advertising. Second, the old model suggests that segmentation based on demographic factors such as age, income, gender, and education is sufficient to create effective ads. Third, with enough repetition and reach to the mass-markets, favorable impressions can be made. An analysis of the typical advertising budget using the old model shows the majority of advertising dollars spent on network television aimed at a mass audience with the goal of building brand equity, whereby the consumer believes a given product or company has a distinct advantage in the marketplace. This perspective concludes that increased brand awareness is the key, because it eventually leads to a high level of brand equity. Therefore, advertisers felt regional and local advertising was not necessary and they were not interested in other media channels.

A revised view of advertising suggests a mass-appeal type ad is not likely to be effective. Further, merely knowing a target market's demographic makeup is not sufficient, and using only network television does not automatically result in brand awareness, brand equity, and brand loyalty. The new method of advertising campaign development is based on the idea that it takes a more integrated approach based on an in-depth understanding of the target market. In addition to demographics, it is essential to know the members of a target market's lifestyles, how these consumers think, and what their opinions are and to have a solid grasp on the nature of their media habits.

This new approach emerged when consumers became more sophisticated as they gained access to more outlets. More clutter creates a highly refined ability to tune out ads and messages. To counter this tendency, the advertising agency chooses spots, magazine placements, newspaper sections, Internet links, and billboard locations based on the customer's strongest interests. In those situations, the individual is more likely to listen to, watch, or read an ad and actually process the information. The old method is simply "zapped" too easily, as consumers become increasingly better at ignoring mass-appeal approaches.

Source: Gary Blake, "Tune In to the New Face of Advertising," *Franchising World*, 26, no. 5 (September–October 1994), pp. 8–10.

A *marketing analysis* is a comprehensive review of the fundamental marketing program. This includes a statement of current sales, current market share, and prime prospects to be solicited (by demographics, lifestyle, geographic location, or product usage). These elements should reflect a compatible pricing strategy based on the product, its benefits and distinguishing characteristics, and the competitive environment involved.

An *advertising analysis* states the fundamental advertising strategy and budget to be used in meeting advertising objectives. The *media strategy* reflects which media will be used and the creative considerations. The *media schedule* states when ads will appear in individual vehicles. The *justification and summary* states the measures of goal achievement. Each of the elements of a media plan is discussed in greater detail in the upcoming sections.[3]

Several individuals are involved in media planning. In addition to account executives and creatives, most agencies utilize **media planners** and **media buyers**.[4] In smaller agencies, the media planner and media buyer can be the same person. In larger companies, they usually are different individuals. A discussion of the main tasks performed in these positions follows.

Media Planners

Media planners provide extremely valuable functions. The primary job of the media planner is to formulate a program stating where and when to place advertisements. Media planners work closely with creatives and account executives. It is important for the creative to know which media will be used, because the choices have such a large impact on how advertisements are designed. Thus, television ads are designed differently than are radio or newspaper ads.

One of the primary tasks of the media planner is to conduct research to match the product with the market and media. If a product's target market is 18- to 25-year-old males with college degrees who love the outdoors, then the media must have a high percentage of its audience in the 18- to 25-year-old, male, college-educated, outdoor category. Thus, it is no accident that a fishing magazine contains advertisements for a bass boat and fishing gear next to articles about the summer feeding habits of bass and other fish. A successful media planner identifies these ideal

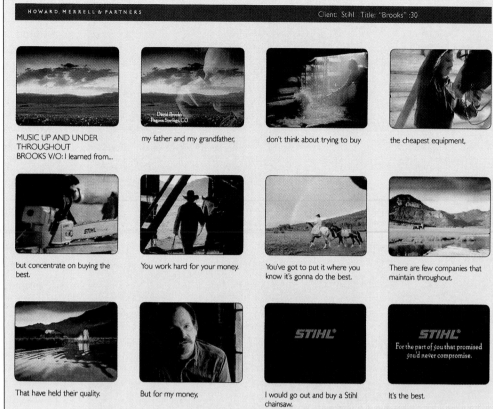

The primary task of the media planner is to match the product's target market with the correct media and programs within the chosen media.

Source: Courtesy of Howard, Merrell & Partners.

locations for the client's advertisements. For example, the New Balance running shoe ad on page 268 was placed in *Runner's World* near an article about running. The media planner formulates a media plan spelling out the best way to reach the client's customers.

Part of the media planner's research is devoted to gathering facts about various media, such as the circulation rates and demographic groups each medium reaches. Besides demographic information, media planners want to know something about the lifestyles, opinions, and habits of each medium's audience. For instance, the audience for television shows may be quite different than those of radio stations and magazines. Careful research improves the chances of selecting appropriate media for the campaign.[5]

Media Buyers

After the media are chosen, someone must buy the space and negotiate rates, times, and schedules for the ads. This is the work of the media buyer. Media buyers stay in constant contact with media sales representatives. They should have a great deal of knowledge about rates and schedules. Media buyers also look for special deals and tie-ins between different media outlets (e.g., radio with television, magazines with the same owner, etc.).

To ensure promotional dollars are spent wisely, it is best to involve the media planner and the media buyer with the creative and the account executive in the design of an advertising campaign. Each plays a critical role in the development of an integrated marketing communications program. The challenge of coordinating the efforts of these individuals intensifies when they are from different companies.

The size of the advertising agency or media buying firm alone does not ensure effective media purchases. Although it would seem logical to assume that larger agencies have the clout to dictate lower prices from media outlets, this is not true. There is little connection between the size of an advertising firm and the prices it can negotiate. In fact, in one study the differences in media costs were based on the time the actual purchase was made (closer to the day the ad was to run) rather than the size of the agency.[6] Other major factors in cost differences are knowledge of the marketplace and the ability to negotiate package deals. Spot television media plans vary by as much as 45 percent in

When does a jogger become a runner?

On a day like this.

achieve new balance

An advertisement featuring New Balance shoes that was placed in *Runner's World* magazine.
Source: Courtesy of New Balance Athletic Shoes Inc. Photograph by Paul Wakefield.

the price of the spot. A spot ad is one that is placed on a local television station. Rates are negotiated individually by the times ads appear with individual stations. For example, a media plan costing one firm $10 million can cost another firm $15.3 million. Radio time slots vary by as much as 42 percent and national print ads by as much as 24 percent.[7]

More importantly, differences in effectiveness of advertising are often related to:

- ▶ Quality media choices (the right ones) made by each agency
- ▶ Creativity
- ▶ Financial stewardship ("bang" for your advertising buck)
- ▶ Agency culture and track record
- ▶ Computer systems to analyze data
- ▶ Relationships between the agency and the medium's sales representative

Thus, the negotiated price is only one element in the success of an advertising program. Effectiveness in advertising is also determined by quality of the selections made by the marketing team and the content of the ad itself. Media should be selected and purchased with specific advertising objectives in mind. These goals assist marketing team members in choosing the right media and combining them effectively to achieve the desired results.

ADVERTISING OBJECTIVES

In selecting media, it is important to review the communications objectives established during the development of the IMC program. These objectives guide media selection decisions as well as the message design (see Chapter 8). Several concepts or technical terms are used in media objectives including:[8]

- ▶ Reach
- ▶ Frequency
- ▶ Gross rating points
- ▶ Effective rating points
- ▶ Cost
- ▶ Continuity
- ▶ Impressions

These ingredients are the key features of an advertising program. **Reach** is the number of people, households, or businesses in a target audience exposed to a media vehicle or message schedule at least once during a given time period. A time period is normally four weeks. In other words, how many targeted buyers did the ad reach? A country and western radio station is more likely to reach someone wanting to buy a cowboy hat. An ad in *Business Week* is more likely to reach a member of the buying center seeking financial services for a business.

Frequency is the average number of times an individual, household, or business within a particular target market is exposed to a particular advertisement within a specified time period, again, usually over four weeks. Or, how many times did the person see the ad during the campaign? A regular viewer sees the same ad shown each day on *Hollywood Squares* more frequently than an ad shown once on *Fear Factor,* even though the program has a far greater reach.

Gross rating points (GRP) is a measure of the impact or intensity of a media plan. Gross rating points are calculated by multiplying a vehicle's rating by the frequency or number of insertions of an advertisement. GRP give the advertiser an idea about the odds of the target audience actually viewing the ad. By increasing the frequency of an advertisement, the chances of a magazine reader seeing the advertisement will increase. It makes sense that an advertisement in each issue of *Time* over a four-week period is more likely to be seen than an advertisement that appears only once during that time period.

Cost is a measure of overall expenditures associated with an advertising program or campaign. Another useful number that can be calculated to measure a program's costs is its **cost per thousand (CPM)**. CPM is the dollar cost of reaching 1,000 members of the media vehicle's audience. The cost per thousand is calculated by using the following formula:

CPM = (Cost of media buy / Total audience) × 1,000

Table 9.1 shows some basic cost and readership information. The first three columns of the table provide the name of the magazine, the cost of a four-color full-page advertisement, and the magazine's total readership. The fourth column contains a measure of the CPM of each magazine. Thus, the cost per thousand (CPM) for *National Geographic* is $16.44. This means that it takes $16.44 to reach 1,000 *National Geographic* readers. Notice the CPM for *Sports Illustrated* is $71.11 and for *Travel & Leisure,* $83.09. The readership of *Travel & Leisure* is the lowest, and its CPM is the highest of all eight magazines. In terms of cost per thousand readers, the best buy is *Southern Living,* at only $1.98 per thousand.

Reach, frequency, and gross rating points are important considerations in choosing the appropriate media outlet for a Nivea advertisement.
Source: Courtesy of Nivea, a division of Beirsdorf, Inc.

Magazine	Cost for Four-Color Full Page Ad	Total Readership (000s)	CPM Total	Target Market (20M)	
				Rating (Reach)	Cost per Rating Point (CPRP)
National Geographic	$ 346,080	21,051	$16.44	16.1	$21,496
Newsweek	780,180	15,594	50.03	12.2	63,949
People	605,880	21,824	27.76	9.4	64,455
Southern Living	11,370	5,733	1.98	2.4	4,738
Sports Illustrated	965,940	13,583	71.11	10.5	91,994
Time	1,324,282	21,468	61.69	15.9	83,288
Travel & Leisure	183,216	2,205	83.09	2.3	79,659
U.S. News and World Report	100,740	8,929	11.28	8.3	12,137

TABLE 9.1

Hypothetical Media Plan Information for Select Magazines

Another cost calculation can be made besides CPM. One critical concern is the cost of reaching a firm's target audience. Therefore, a measure called the **cost per rating point (CPRP)** was developed. The cost per rating point is a relative measure of the efficiency of a media vehicle relative to a firm's target market. **Ratings** measure the percentage of a firm's target market that is exposed to a show on television or an article in a print medium. To calculate the cost per rating point, the formula is

$$CPRP = Cost\ of\ media\ buy\ /\ Vehicle's\ rating$$

Table 9.1 ratings were generated for potential buyers of a 35 mm camera (see the case at the end of this chapter). The table shows the CPRP for *National Geographic* is $21,496. This is the average cost for each rating point or of each 1 percent of the firm's target audience (35 mm camera buyers). Not all readers of a magazine are part of the firm's target market. The CPRP more accurately measures an advertising campaign's efficiency than does CPM. Notice that the CPRP is the lowest for *National Geographic, Southern Living,* and *U.S. News and World Report.*

CPRP provide a relative measure of reach exposure in terms of cost. For example, it costs $21,496 to reach 1 percent, or 200,000, of the 20 million in this firm's target market using *National Geographic.* To reach 1 percent, or 200,000, using *Sports Illustrated* costs $91,994. To reach 1 percent, or 200,000, using *Southern Living* costs only $4,738. Because *Southern Living* is so efficient, why wouldn't a media planner just do all of the advertising in that magazine? The answer lies in the rating for *Southern Living.* Advertising in only that magazine reaches just 2.4 percent of the target audience, meaning 97.6 percent of the target market does not read *Southern Living.* Thus, another magazine or media outlet is necessary to reach them. This example explains why diversity in media is essential to reach a large portion of a firm's target market.

To further study whether or not an ad has reached the target market effectively, a **weighted (or demographic) CPM** figure may be calculated, as follows:

$$Weighted\ CPM = \frac{advertisement\ cost \times 1000}{actual\ audience\ reached}$$

For example, if the cost of an advertisement in *Sports Illustrated* is $115,000, and the magazine reaches 4,200,000 readers, the standard CPM would be $27.38. If the ad targets parents of Little League baseball players, and research indicates that 600,000 of *Sports Illustrated*'s readers are Little League parents, the result would be:

$$Weighted\ CPM = \frac{\$115,000 \times 1000}{600,000} = \$191.66.$$

This figure could be compared to figures for the *Sporting News, ESPN Magazine,* and other sports magazines.

Continuity is the exposure pattern or schedule used in the ad campaign. The three types of patterns used are continuous, pulsating, and discontinuous. A **continuous campaign** buys media time in a steady stream. For instance the Skechers ad shown in this section uses a continuous schedule if the company buys ad space in specific magazines over a period of one to two years. By rotating the advertisement, readers do not become bored with one particular ad. A firm that uses a **pulsating schedule** always maintains some minimal level of advertising but increases advertising at periodic intervals. For instance, a retailer such as JC Penney may advertise some throughout the whole year but will increase advertising in small, short bursts around holidays such as Christmas, the day after Thanksgiving, Memorial Day, Labor Day, Mother's or Father's Day, and Easter. The goal of pulsating advertising is to take advantage of consumer interests in making more purchases or buying special merchandise during holidays. For instance, the Blockbuster advertisement just prior to Christmas encouraged consumers to purchase a Blockbuster gift card. A **discontinuous campaign schedule** places advertisements at special intervals with no advertising between. For example, a ski resort can use discontinuous advertising by running ads during the fall and winter seasons with none during the spring and summer.

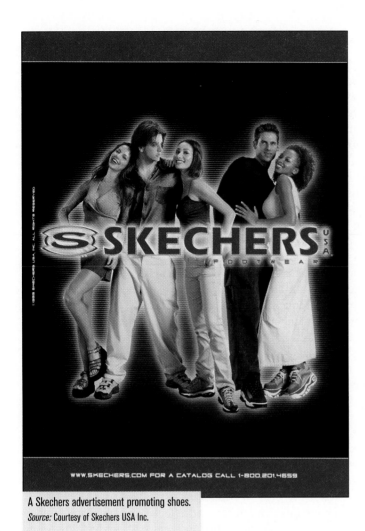

A Skechers advertisement promoting shoes.
Source: Courtesy of Skechers USA Inc.

A Christmas advertisement by Blockbuster promoting a gift card as the "perfect holiday gift."
Source: Courtesy of Blockbuster Entertainment Group.

The final objective advertisers consider is the concept of *impressions.* The number of **gross impressions** is the total exposures of the audience to an advertisement. It does not take into consideration what percentage of the total audience may or may not see the advertisement. Table 9.1 indicates the total readership of *National Geographic* is 21,051,000. If six insertions were placed in *National Geographic,* multiplying the insertions by the readership would yield a total of 126 million impressions.

INTEGRATED LEARNING EXPERIENCE

A major supplier of media research information is Nielsen Media Research. Access its Web site at **www.nielsenmedia.com**. Go to the "Who We Are and What We Do" section. After reading this, go to "Ratings 101" to learn about the terms Nielsen uses and how it determines ratings. The "What TV Ratings Really Means" section provides information about what ratings mean. The "Services" section presents information about the services Nielsen's offers. Why would this data be important in media planning? For the Internet, the Nielsen organization provides current information about top banner ads, top advertisers, and Web usage. Access this information from the main page under the heading "Hot Off the Net." In Canada, a valuable source of information about radio and television markets is BBM Bureau of Measurement at **www.bbm.ca**. Study the statistical tidbits presented (in the "Get Data" section) about Canadian radio and television markets.

STOP

ACHIEVING ADVERTISING OBJECTIVES

One basic issue facing advertisers is how many times a person must be exposed to an ad before it has an impact on that consumer. Most agree that a single exposure is not enough. Deciding on what is the actual number inspires a great deal of debate. Some argue it takes three exposures whereas others say as many as 10. The basic rule, developed by Herbert Krugman, states it takes a minimum of three exposures for an advertisement to be effective. This is the *three-exposure hypothesis.* Most media planners have followed it for quite a while.[9]

Many advertisers believe three exposures are not enough to create an impression in the consumer's mind, because of the amount of clutter that exists. Clutter also can affect the types of objectives firms try to accomplish. For instance, increasing brand awareness may be easier than building brand image, because attention getting is easier than capturing someone's interest long enough to make a point about the firm's image. Also, a well-known brand that is the first choice of the majority of consumers can accomplish its objective with fewer ad exposures than a less well-known brand.

Seeking to discover the minimum number of exposures needed to be effective is based on two concepts: effective frequency and effective reach. **Effective frequency** refers to the *number of times* a target audience must be exposed to a message to achieve a particular objective. **Effective reach** is *the percentage of an audience* that must be exposed to a particular message to achieve a specific objective. Implied in the concept of effective reach is that some minimum number of exposures exists.

Both effective frequency and effective reach are crucial factors. Too few exposures means the advertiser will fail to attain its intended objectives. On the other hand, too many exposures wastes resources. The goal is to discover the optimal reach and frequency mix to accomplish the intended objectives without experiencing diminishing returns from extra ads. The challenge appears when consumer differences are considered. It may take three exposures to an advertisement to impact one consumer but 10 for another. Differences in interests, personalities, and exposures to the chosen media outlets all influence individual consumers.

Other elements can enhance effective frequency and effective reach. They include the size and placement of ads. A small magazine advertisement will not have the same impact as a larger ad. In television advertising, a spot in the middle of an ad sequence usually does not have the same impact as those at the beginning and end of the series. If a firm is using 15-second television ads, effective frequency may require six exposures compared to only four if they use longer 45-second spots.

Another important factor that affects these objectives is the number of different media a particular advertising campaign uses. Generally, a campaign involving two types of media, such as television and magazines, has greater effective reach than a campaign using only one medium, such as magazines only. Media mixes will be described in detail later in this chapter.

In recent years, numerous media companies have

The size and placement of this Palm-Aire magazine advertisement will have an impact on its effective frequency and effective reach.
Source: Courtesy of Howard, Merrell & Partners.

developed computer models designed to make certain reach and frequency are optimized. One of the more popular include *Nielsen SAVIE,* which examines cable TV alternatives and calculates the value of each using criteria such as Nielsen TV audience data (ratings), product purchasing information, customer preference cluster data, and specific systems data. The *ADplus* software combines reach and frequency information with media mix information, budgeting data, and customized information for the individual advertiser. *Adware* provides Arbitron and Nielsen rating information, calculates media costs, and is designed to project GRP.

These and other computer models are designed to help evaluate effective reach and frequency using probability theory as a basis. They help firms allocate advertising dollars and may also show where interaction effects are present. An interaction of an attention-getting television ad with a magazine ad with copy that explains the product's feature may have a synergistic effect, in which the two together are much more potent than the impact of either alone.

Recency Theory

A new theory concerning reach and frequency challenges the traditional three-exposure hypothesis. This approach, called recency theory, suggests that a consumer's attention is selective and focused on his or her individual needs and wants.[10] The traditional three-exposure hypothesis is based on the *intrusion value* of advertisements and the idea that advertisements can make an impact on an audience regardless of individual needs or wants. **Intrusion value** is the ability of media or an advertisement to intrude upon a viewer without his or her voluntary attention.

Recency theory states that consumers use selective attention processes as they consider advertisements. They give attention to messages that might meet their needs or wants. The closer, or more recent, an ad is to a purchase, the more powerful the ad will be. Also, when a consumer contemplates a future purchase of the product being advertised, it becomes more likely that the consumer will pay attention to and react favorably toward the ad. For example, a member of a buying center from a business that is in the market for a new copier notices advertisements about copiers. Someone not in the market for a copier ignores the same ad. The same is true in consumer markets: An individual needing a new pair of jeans notices clothing ads, especially ones that deal with jeans.

Recency theory notes that advertising is a waste of money when ads reach individuals who are not in the market for a particular product and who do not need the product. Advertisers must give careful attention to targeting ads to individuals who want or need a firm's goods and services. In other words, advertising life insurance to teenagers wastes promotional funds. At the same time, advertising supplemental health insurance to the elderly on social security is highly likely to be noticed and have a profound impact on that target market.

For an individual in the market for ski boots, one exposure to this advertisement may be enough to get her attention.
Source: Courtesy of Lange USA.

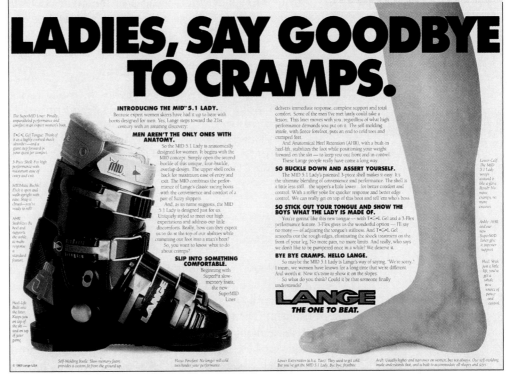

MAYBE THE BEST WAY TO HANDLE RISK IS TO AVOID IT ALTOGETHER.

That's why Minolta created the No-Risk Guarantee. It takes you out of harm's way by letting you

decide whether you're happy with the copier's performance.

Even better, it covers our EP 9760 Pro Series Copier, which was recently voted first overall in productivity in the high-volume class.*

Here's how it works. If you're not completely satisfied with our copier within the first three years of normal operation, we will replace it with an identical or comparably equipped model, free of charge. In other

words, it works or it walks. An award-winning copier combined with an iron-clad guarantee? The only risk involved is passing this opportunity up.

For more information, call 1-800-9-MINOLTA.

*Source: Thomas A. Stevens editor, The Copier Productivity Index

NO-RISK COPIERS
ONLY FROM THE MIND OF MINOLTA

MINOLTA

For a business needing a copier, one exposure may be enough for the Minolta brand to be considered as a viable option by a member of the buying center.
Source: Courtesy of Minolta.

One difference in recency theory is the idea that one ad exposure is enough to affect an audience when that person or business needs the product being promoted. Additional exposures actually may be a waste of money. The advertising strategy that matches recency theory spreads the message around using a variety of media, each one providing only one exposure per week or time period. In the case of selling supplemental health insurance to the elderly, magazines such as *Senior Living,* televisions spots on local news and weather programs, and newspaper ads close to the obituary section can quickly reach the target audience in a cost-effective manner. Such an approach, which maximizes reach, accomplishes more than increasing frequency.

In the business-to-business arena, application of recency theory means ads should appear in a number of outlets rather than running a series of ads in one trade journal. Many times, a number of individuals are members of the buying center. Each has different interests and training. To make sure each one sees the ad, placing ads in all of the journals that might contact a given buying center member is important. To facilitate the purchasing process for a company seeking to buy an audioconferencing system, the media buyer purchases space in trade journals, human resource journals, sales journals, and business journals to effectively reach various members of the buying center. Recency theory suggests that one exposure might be enough for each member, because the member is looking for information and ready to help make a purchase decision. To reach business personnel while traveling, Polycom recently placed an advertisement in the Delta Airline's *Sky* magazine, because of the higher odds that more than one buying center member might see the ad while flying with Delta.

INTEGRATED LEARNING EXPERIENCE

Achieving advertising objectives normally requires blending various media in an advertising plan. Access Benchmark Communications at **www.bmcommunications.com**. Examine the information provided about traditional media, including newspapers, radio, and television. After examining each of the major media, look at the "Web Site Creation and Design" section. How can Benchmark Communications tie a firm's Web site into the traditional advertising media (newspapers, radio, and television)?

GATHERING EVIDENCE OF SUCCESS

Technology has made it easier to define effective reach and effective frequency. For instance, a business placing an advertisement in a business journal such as *Inc.* or *Business Week* can gain access to research tallying the number of responses to the advertisement. Then the business can track the impact of the message. If the objective were to increase inquiries about a product by 10 percent, the business can see how many direct inquiries were made before and after the ad runs. If the ad appears in successive issues of a magazine, it can be relatively easy to track increases in inquiries associated with each successive issue.

A business also can hire professional media research firms to track the reach of the advertisement. The research firm develops measures of how other businesses responded. Such firms provide information about whether the ad affected the buying decision and if members of the buying center remembered seeing the ad. Although these methods are not foolproof, they do provide better information than an educated guess or past experience. Actual records kept over time can become valuable assets in determining effective frequency and effective reach.

Once the media buyer, media planner, account executive, and company leaders agree about basic objectives of the advertising campaign, they can select the actual media. Marketing experts consider each medium's distinct pros and cons. They also consider logical (and illogical) combinations of media. The next section examines media that an advertising program can use, leading to the final selection of media for the company's campaign.

MEDIA SELECTION

In this section, various forms of advertising media are described. As noted earlier, effectively mixing media is an important part of designing quality advertising. In order to do so, the advantages and disadvantages of each individual medium must be understood so that an advertising campaign uses successful combinations.

A business advertisement for Polycom.
Source: Courtesy of Polycom Inc.

Television

Choosing appropriate television advertising outlets is not easy because there are so many options. Companies must carefully select those programs and channels most likely to reach their target audiences. Table 9.2 lists the advantages and disadvantages of television advertising. As shown, television offers advertisers the most extensive coverage and highest reach of any of the media. A solitary advertisement can reach millions of viewers simultaneously. Even though ads are quite expensive, the cost per contact is relatively low. This low cost per contact justifies spending $2 million for a 30-second spot on the Super Bowl, which continues to be the television program that charges the most for advertising. Television has the advantage of intrusion value, which as noted earlier, is the ability of a media or advertisement to intrude upon a viewer without his or her voluntary attention. Television ads with a catchy musical tune, sexy content, or motion can grab the viewer's attention.

Advantages	Disadvantages
1. High reach	1. Greater clutter
2. High frequency potential	2. Low recall due to clutter
3. Low cost per contact	3. Channel surfing during commercials
4. High intrusion value (motion, sound)	4. Short amount of copy
5. Quality creative opportunities	5. High cost per ad
6. Segmentation possibilities through cable outlets	

TABLE 9.2

Television Advertising

egg beaters. *Fleischmann's*

"WAITRESS/HEN" TV :30

NABISCO FOODS COMPANY RNEB-3033

ANNCR: (VO)
The only difference between these eggs

and our eggs is...

um, er,....uh....hmmmm...

Oh yeah, ours don't have any fat or cholesterol.

WAITRESS:
Mmmm.

ANNCR: (VO)
Eggbeaters. We're good eggs.

ANNCR: (VO)
Where do you find new Eggbeaters?

Same place you find eggs.

In the egg section.

Of course, you'll still find us in the freezer section too.

Eggbeaters.

We're good eggs.

FCB/LEBER KATZ PARTNERS EB0884-B

A storyboard of a television advertisement for Egg Beaters.

Source: Courtesy of Fleischmann's Co., Division of Nabisco Foods.

Television provides many opportunities for creativity in advertising design. Visual images and sounds can be incorporated together to gain the attention of viewers as well as to persuade them. Products and services can be demonstrated on television in a manner not possible in print or using radio advertisements.

It is advisable to match a firm's target audience (market segment) with specific shows. Each television network and each television show tends to attract a specific type of audience. Cable television programming often provides a well-defined, homogeneous audience that matches more narrowly defined target markets.

Clutter remains the primary problem with television advertising, especially on network programs. One episode of NBC's *Law and Order* contained a commercial break lasting more than five minutes. Similar breaks occur on ABC, CBS, and Fox, and they are often packed with eight to 15 commercials. Many viewers simply switch channels during long commercial breaks. Thus, messages at the beginning or near the end of the break have the best recall. Those in the middle often have virtually no impact. Therefore, clutter makes it difficult for a single message to have any influence.[11]

Television commercials have short life spans. Most ads last 15 or 30 seconds. Occasionally an advertiser purchases a 45- or 60-second ad, but those are rare. Another disadvantage of television is the high cost per ad not only for the media time but also in terms of production costs. Outstanding commercials often are expensive to produce. At the same time, because television ads are shown so frequently, they quickly lose the ability to attract the viewer's interest. Companies are forced to replace the ads with something new before consumers get tired of them and tune them out, while at the same time firms try to air them long enough to recover some of the production costs involved.

To gain a quick sense of how well an advertisement fared in terms of reaching an audience, a given program's *rating* can be calculated. The typical ratings formula is:

$$\text{Rating} = \frac{\text{number of household turned to a program}}{\text{total number of households in a market}}$$

In the United States, the total number of households with television sets is approximately 100 million. To calculate the rating of an episode of *Survivor,* if the number of households tuned to the season finale was 24 million, then the rating would be:

$$\text{Rating} = \frac{24{,}000{,}000}{100{,}000{,}000} = 24.0$$

Next, if the advertiser were interested in the percentage of households that actually were watching television at that hour, the program's share could be calculated. If 50 million of the 100 million households had a television turned on during the hour in which the *Survivor* finale aired, the share would be:

$$\text{Share} = \frac{\text{number of households tuned to } Survivor}{\text{number of households with a television turned on}} = \frac{24{,}000{,}000}{50{,}000{,}000} = 48$$

A 24 rating would mean 24 percent of all televisions in the U.S. were tuned to *Survivor.* A 48 share means 48 percent of the households with a television actually turned on were watching the program.

Of course, there is no guarantee that the viewers saw the commercial. Ratings and share are only indicators of how well the program fared against the competition. They are used to establish rates for advertisements. Cable and satellite television programs have lowered the rating and shares of the major networks dramatically in the past decade. The primary organization that calculates and reports rating and share is the A. C. Nielsen Company. The company also provides local channel information regarding shares of stations in local markets known as *designated marketing areas (DMAs)*. Data gathering techniques used by Nielsen include diaries written by viewers who report what they watched, audience meters that record what is being watched automatically, and people meters in which viewing habits of individual members of families can be tracked.

These numbers can be further refined to help advertisers understand whether an advertisement reached a target market. Within rating and share categories, the viewers can be subdivided by certain demographics, such as:

- Age
- Income
- Gender
- Educational level
- Race or ethnic heritage

Organizations that prepare this kind of information include the Nielsen Media Research, Starch INRA Hooper, Inc., Mediamark Research, Inc., Burke Marketing Research, and Simmons Market Research Bureau. For instance, it would be helpful to an advertising team to know that viewers of *The West Wing* tend to be college-educated, over 40, and with incomes over $50,000. If psychographic information can be added in, such as the show is mostly watched by people who voted for Democrats in the previous election, then the advertiser has a good sense of whether this is the best audience for a given advertisement or campaign.

For local advertisers, syndicated programs such as *Wheel of Fortune* and *Oprah Winfrey* offer the opportunity to buy spots on shows with consistent audiences. It is also possible to advertise on the same program five days per week to increase frequency and to allow the media buyer the opportunity to negotiate better rates.

Television remains a "glamour" medium. Its wide audience continues to hold a great appeal for companies vending goods and services with more general target markets. This includes most durable goods (washers, dryers, cars, etc.), many staple items (detergent, soap, deodorant), general appeal products (snack foods, beers, soft drinks, and Internet sites), and various luxuries marketed to larger groups (cruise ships, theme parks, credit cards).

Business-to-business advertisers use television for several reasons. First, it is becoming more difficult to reach members of the business buying center, and they do watch television. Second, increased ad clutter in trade journals and traditional business outlets makes televisions spots a more desirable alternative. Third, business advertisements now use more emotional appeals, and television can portray emotions effectively. Fourth, because the importance of a strong brand identity is a growing factor in the business-to-business sector, television ads can be a source of brand identity. Finally, television is an excellent medium to reach members of the buying center when they are not preoccupied with other business concerns. Consequently, they may be more open to advertising messages.

Radio

Radio may not be considered as glamorous as television. This makes it more difficult to attract talented creatives to prepare ads. At the same time, a well-placed, clever ad is a one-on-one message (announcer to driver in a car stuck in traffic). Many smaller local companies still heavily rely on radio advertising, and most radio ads are produced locally and with small budgets. Table 9.3 summarizes the advantages and disadvantages of radio advertising.

Advantages	Disadvantages
1. Recall promoted	1. Short exposure time
2. Narrower target markets	2. Low attention
3. Ad music can match station's programming	3. Few chances to reach national audience
4. High segmentation potential	4. Target duplication when several stations use the same format
5. Flexibility in making new ads	5. Overload
6. Able to modify ads to fit local conditions	
7. Intimacy (with DJs and radio personalities)	
8. Mobile—people carry radios everywhere	
9. Creative opportunities with music and other sounds	

TABLE 9.3

Radio Advertising

Radio offers several advantages to advertisers. Skillful radio advertisers help the listener remember the message by creating a powerful image to visualize or by repetition. It is important to help the consumer move the ad from short-term to long-term memory. Various sound effects and lively memorable tunes assist in this process. Through repetition a person hears an advertisement often enough to assist in recall; just like repeating a phone number or e-mail address, helps you remember numbers or letters.

Radio stations tend to have definable target markets based on their formats. Certain formats (talk radio, lite mix, oldies, etc.) attract similar audiences throughout the United States. This means a firm that wants to advertise on pop stations in the East can find similar stations across the country. Campbell's Soup found radio spots were an effective way to promote its Chunky Soup and its tie-in with the National Football League. The company advertised on radio stations with primarily male audiences and strong sports programming using professional football players praising Chunky Soup.[12]

Radio advertisers can also examine the rating and share of a program as well as the estimated number of people listening to a program. The primary organization that calculates these numbers is Arbitron on a local level, and the *Radio's All-Dimension Audience Research,* or RADAR, for national radio networks.

Radio stations offer considerable flexibility and a short lead time. Commercials can be recorded and placed on the air within a few days and sometimes within hours. Ads can be changed quickly. This is especially helpful in volatile markets or in the retail sector wherein companies want to change the items featured on sale. Radio also helps a national company that wants to modify each advertisement to fit local conditions. In other words, a manufacturer can develop one national advertisement and change it for each dealer or retailer that carries the manufacturer's merchandise. The modification can be as simple as providing an address, phone number, or Web address for each local outlet.

One major advantage of radio is *intimacy.* Listeners can develop a closeness to the DJs and other radio personalities. This closeness grows over time. Listening to the same individual becomes somewhat personalized, especially if the listener has a conversation with the DJ during a contest or when requesting a song. The bond or intimacy level gives the radio personality a higher level of credibility and an edge to products and services the radio celebrity endorses. No other medium offers this advantage.

Besides intimacy, radio is *mobile.* People carry radios to the beach, the ballpark, work, and picnics. They listen at home, at work, and on the road in between. No other medium stays with the audience quite like radio.

Radio also has disadvantages. One is the short exposure time of an ad. Like television, most radio advertisements last only 15 or 30 seconds. Listeners involved in other activities, such as driving or working on a computer, may not pay attention to the radio. Further, people often use radio as a background to drown out other distractions, especially at work.

For national advertisers, covering a large area with radio advertisements is challenging. To place a national advertisement requires contacting a large number of companies. Few large radio conglomerates means contacts must be made with multiple stations. Because of this independence, negotiating lower rates with individual stations based on volume or because it will be a national advertisement does not occur. In fact, local businesses can negotiate better rates than a national advertiser because of the relationships the radio stations develop with local firms over time.

There are four national radio networks: Westwood One, ABC, CBS, and Unistar along with a few other strong networks such as ESPN radio and the CNN News Network. Nationally syndicated programs such as the Paul Harvey news and Rush Limbaugh's program do offer some opportunities to national advertisers.

In large metropolitan areas, another problem is target duplication. Several radio stations may try to reach the same target market. For instance, Chicago has several rock stations. Advertising on every station is not financially feasible, yet reaching everyone in that target market is not possible unless all rock stations are used. The rock music audience is divided among those stations, with each having its own subset of loyal listeners.

Finally, because many ads are locally produced, a common problem with radio ads is putting too much information into one ad. It overloads the consumer and very little is retained.

Radio advertising is a low-cost option for a local firm. Ads can be placed at ideal times and adapted to local conditions. The key to radio is careful selection of stations, times, and construction of the ad. Tests can be created to see if ads effectively reach customers. Immediate response techniques, contest entries, and other devices provide evidence about whether customers heard and responded to ads. Radio *remotes* occur when the station broadcasts from a business location. Remotes are a popular method of attracting attention to a new business (restaurants, taverns, small retail shops, etc.) or to a company trying to make a major push for immediate customers. Effective ratio promotions can be combined with other media (local television, newspapers, etc.) to send out a more integrated message.

For business-to-business advertisers, radio provides the opportunity to reach businesses during working hours, because many employees listen to the radio during office hours. More importantly, radio can reach businesspeople while in transit to or from work. Both radio and television usage has increased for business-to-business marketing.

INTEGRATED LEARNING EXPERIENCE

One of the problems with radio advertising is choosing from the large number of stations on the air. Selecting the right ones can be difficult. Access **www.100topradiosites.com** for a list of the top hundred radio stations, and examine three of these. Why were they selected as top stations? For additional information on radio advertising, access the Radio Advertising Bureau at **www.rab.com**. Review the menu items to get an idea of how much information this site offers. Go to "Media Facts" for information about choosing the various media. Information is listed about each medium type's advantages and disadvantages. Notice how the benefits change when the medium is combined with radio.

S T O P

Outdoor

Billboards along major roads are the most common form of outdoor advertising. Billboards, however, are only one form of outdoor advertising. Signs on cabs, buses, park benches, and fences of sports arenas also are types of outdoor advertising. Some would argue that even a blimp flying over a major sporting event is a form of outdoor advertising.

Outdoor advertising has changed its image from "booze and (cigarette) butts" advertising to a legitimate medium over the past few decades. In 1979, tobacco ads accounted

Outdoor advertising in Times Square.
Source: Courtesy of Liaison Agency, Inc. Photograph by Frederick Charles.

for 39 percent of outdoor advertising revenues. Alcohol accounted for another 11 percent. Today those numbers have dwindled to 11 percent for tobacco and only 2 percent for alcohol.

Currently, retailers account for approximately 10 percent of outdoor advertising and media outlets for another 8 percent. Other ads feature upcoming movies, video stores, broadcast television networks, newspapers, and radio stations. Other fast-growing outdoor ad programs are from the fashion industry. The Gap, Calvin Klein, Ralph Lauren, and DKNY regularly buy outdoor space. In Times Square in New York and on Sunset Boulevard in Los Angeles, large outdoor billboards cost as much as $100,000 per month.[13] Table 9.4 lists the basic advantages and disadvantages of outdoor ads.

One primary advantage of billboard advertising is its long life. For local companies, billboards are an excellent advertising medium because the message is seen only by local audiences. Local services such as restaurants, hotels, resorts, service stations, and amusement parks are heavy users of billboards. Billboards provide an effective way to communicate a firm's location to travelers. Individuals who want to eat at a particular restaurant (Wendy's, Shoney's, Burger King) while on the road can normally spot a billboard for that restaurant.

In terms of cost per impression, outdoor advertising is a low-cost media outlet. Outdoor advertising also offers a broad reach and a high level of frequency if multiple billboards are purchased. Every person who travels past a billboard has the potential of being exposed to the message. Many billboard companies provide "rotation" packages in which an ad moves to different locations throughout a town during the course of the year, thereby increasing the reach of the ad.

Billboard ads can be large and spectacular, making them major attention-getting devices. A billboard's large size creates the impression that the product and message are important. Movement and lighting can add to the attention-capturing qualities of billboards.

A major drawback of outdoor advertising is the short exposure time. Drivers must pay attention to the traffic as they speed by an outdoor ad. Most either ignore billboards or give them just a brief glance. Ironically, in large cities along major arteries the cost of billboard spots is increasing. The reason: traffic jams. People stuck in slow-moving traffic spend more time looking at billboards. If this space is not available, a firm can seek billboard locations where traffic stops for signals or at stop signs.

Billboards provide limited opportunities for creativity. The short exposure time means the message must be extremely brief. People usually ignore a complicated or detailed message. Further, billboards offer limited segmentation opportunities because a

Advantages	Disadvantages
1. Able to select key geographic areas	1. Short exposure time
2. Accessible for local ads	2. Brief messages
3. Low cost per impression	3. Little segmentation possible
4. Broad reach	4. Cluttered travel routes
5. High frequency on major commuter routes	
6. Large, spectacular ads possible	

TABLE 9.4

Outdoor Advertising

wide variety of people may view the billboard's message. To help overcome this problem, some companies use geodemographic software technologies to identify the profile of individuals who will pass by a billboard in a specific neighborhood. Such an approach works well on local streets of cities and towns but is not very effective along major interstates, with local and long-distance traffic.

Procter & Gamble uses the most current technology to place billboard advertising for Luvs diapers, by identifying geodemographic segments. P&G uses billboards placed near day care centers and hospitals and in areas with a high number of young marrieds with no children or young marrieds with very young children.[14]

In the past, outdoor advertising was seldom considered in the planning of an integrated marketing communications program or the development of the media plan. Now outdoor advertising is an additional tool to reach consumers. To illustrate, Procter & Gamble as late as 1994 spent virtually no money on outdoor advertising; today, this budget is almost $10 million. Billboard ads can be combined with other advertising media to repeat and reinforce messages for audiences.

INTEGRATED LEARNING EXPERIENCE

One of the leading outdoor advertising companies is the Lamar Advertising Company at **www.lamar.com**. Under "Rates and Markets," find your home state and local area. What are the company's published rates for outdoor advertising? Compare these rates with those of nearby areas as well as of other states. To understand the different products, access the "Products and Services" section of Lamar's Web site. Finally, access "Why Lamar?" What are the benefits of using outdoor advertising? Why should Lamar be chosen?

Internet

Forty years ago, the newest medium was television. About 15 years ago, it was cable television. Currently, it is the Internet.[15] There is some evidence that television audiences are migrating to the Internet. A study by Forrester Research indicates that 24 percent of Internet users give up time spent eating or sleeping to be on the Web. The vast majority (75 percent) reported that they gave up time watching television to surf the Web instead. A report by the A. C. Neilsen company states that the number of U.S. households watching prime-time television declined by one million viewers in just one year. During that same year, the number of North Americans with online Internet services had almost doubled. It is highly likely that the million fewer viewers of prime-time television have shifted some of their attention to the Internet. Table 9.5 presents a brief review of the major advantages and disadvantages of Internet advertising.

As shown, a major benefit of Internet marketing is the creative opportunities available and the short lead time. Creativity is possible because banners can be composed using many different types of graphics. Animation and streaming videos can be incorporated into banner ads. Short lead time is possible because an advertisement can be changed and posted on the Internet immediately, even when ads are placed on other sites.

Advantages	Disadvantages
1. Creative possibilities	1. Clutter on each site
2. Short lead time to send ad	2. Difficult procedures to place ads and buy time
3. Simplicity of segmentation	3. Only for computer owners
4. High audience interest on each Web site	4. Short life span
5. Easier to measure responses directly	5. Low intrusion value
	6. Hard to retain interest of surfers

TABLE 9.5

Internet Advertising

Segmentation is easy to accomplish with the Internet. The company can track who is clicking on an advertisement and viewing various pages. Engage Technologies records the paths individuals use as they move from site to site. The company uses these data to create a profile of the person and then match it to profiles in a database. Based on the person's profile, appropriate advertisements are then sent. Web surfers are not even aware this tracking takes place and often are amazed that products they like suddenly appear on the screen.[16]

The demographic characteristics of users are fairly well defined. Web surfers are young, well educated, and have relatively high incomes. Women represent about 42 percent of Internet users and men 58 percent. The average age is 34.9 years old. Over 65 percent of Internet users have household incomes of $50,000 or more, compared with 35 percent of the U.S. population as a whole. In terms of education, 75 percent of the Internet users have attended college compared to 46 percent of the U.S. population. These demographics are beginning to change as more senior citizens get on the Internet to communicate with children and grandchildren. Targeting a specific audience is not too difficult with the Internet, because most companies selling advertising space have a good idea of their audience characteristics.

Audience interest is another advantage of the Internet. Internet browsers normally go to Web sites that attract them. Advertising on these pages is efficient because the audience is already curious about the site. For example, two lucrative places to advertise are on sports-related sites and music sites. Each draws a large number of hits per day, although demographics vary. Sports sites tend to attract males. Music sites tend to attract females. Both have high levels of interest.

The use of the Internet as an advertising medium for business-to-business marketing has increased substantially. Placing ads on business sites is an excellent method of targeting ads to interested buyers. When employees search for information about a particular product, they often will click on Internet ads to see what is offered. Business buyers look for information and consequently pay more attention to ads they see during the search. Internet ads allow individual companies to advertise their own services. For example, an employee gathering information on a vendor's site may see an advertisement for other products the company sells or products from the firm's subsidiary. As more businesses install the Internet for their employees, reaching buying center members through advertising on the Internet should become increasingly productive.

As for disadvantages, Internet clutter is one problem. The explosion of Internet advertising means many sites show numerous ads several layers thick. Web surfers quickly bypass these ads. In addition, a Web site filled with advertisements that delay its loading causes many surfers to become impatient and move on to other sites.

Another major problem for national companies is buying procedures. Almost all advertising spots must be purchased individually from each site. No national buyers that sell Internet space on a set of sites exists yet. As Internet advertising matures, it seems likely that entrepreneurs will seize the opportunity to meet this need.

At this time, the Internet is still limited to those who can afford a computer and Internet services. The Internet is a new medium that many computer use owners only for e-mail or other relatively simple services.

Another problem is that Internet ads have short life spans. The wear-out time for Internet ads seems to be even shorter than that of other media.[17] This means advertisers must spend more time updating the advertisements if they hope to gain audience attention.

Unlike television, the Internet tends not to have intrusion value. Web surfers do not have to pause on an advertisement as one would have to do when looking at a magazine or newspaper. To get surfers to stop (i.e., to intrude upon individuals), ad banners feature streaming videos and flashing displays. This approach worked for a while when it was new, but soon became old. To correct this disadvantage, some advertisers have developed what is called *interstitial advertising,* which interrupts a person on the Internet without warning. These type of ads have to be clicked off to remove them from the screen and are extremely controversial. Although they have intrusion value, they also are annoying. Interstitial ads can come onto a person's computer even after logging off of the Internet or come on the screen when the next time the person logs on.[18] Although untested at this time, interstitial advertising could prove extremely valuable to business-to-business marketers. Targeted ads could be sent to members of the buying center even after they log off of the computer. The chances of capturing some level of attention increase because these ads must be clicked off. Also, if the business buyer has been searching for information about a product and an advertisement for that product pops onto the screen, the individual will likely study the ad to see what is being offered.

The Internet is the fastest-growing medium in history. It took television 13 years to reach 50 million viewers. It took radio 38 years to reach 50 million. Experts estimate it took only 5 years for the Internet to reach 50 million users.

It is too early to know for sure the full impact of Internet advertising. If it is measured by the number of *click-throughs*, whereby the ad is quickly zapped, Internet advertising appears not to be as successful as advertisers first thought. Studies have shown that Web users tend to ignore banners, and most Internet users can't even remember the last banner they clicked on. Some studies indicate that Internet advertising is ineffective. Other studies reveal the Internet as a successful method of advertising. A study by Millward Brown International concluded that brand awareness using Internet brand banners increased between 12 percent and 200 percent. Compared to brand awareness studies of television and radio ads, Internet banners generated greater ad awareness with a single exposure than did either television or radio.[19]

Internet advertising programs are certain to grow in the future. Chapter 14 is devoted to Internet marketing and e-commerce.

Magazines allow a brand such as Tree Top to develop ads targeted to a highly segmented audience, such as this ad targeted to mothers of infants.
Source: Courtesy of Tree Top Apple Juice.

Magazines

The glamour of television has overshadowed magazines for a long time. For many advertisers, magazines have always been a second choice. Recent research, however, indicates that in some cases magazines are actually a better option. A study by the A. C. Neilsen Company revealed that people who viewed ads in magazines were from 2 percent to 37 percent more likely to purchase the product. Also, a study by Millward Brown examining the cost effectiveness of magazine advertising revealed promising information for magazines. The study suggested that magazine advertising is three times more cost effective than television.[20] Naturally, the validity of these results have been staunchly debated by television executives. In any case, evidence exists that magazine advertising can be effective. Table 9.6 displays the pros and cons of magazine advertising.

Advantages	Disadvantages
1. High market segmentation	1. Declining readership (some magazines)
2. Targeted audience interest by magazine	2. High level of clutter
3. Direct-response techniques (e.g. coupons, Web addresses, toll-free numbers)	3. Long lead time to ad showing
4. High color quality	4. Little flexibility
5. Availability of special features (e.g., scratch and sniff)	5. High cost
6. Long life	
7. Read during leisure time (longer attention to ad)	

TABLE 9.6

Magazine Advertising

A major advantage of magazines is the high level of market segmentation available. Magazines are highly segmented by topic area. Specialized magazines are much more common than general magazines with broad readerships. Even within certain market segments, such as automobiles, a number of magazines exist. Magazines are so highly differentiated that high audience interest becomes another advantage. An individual who subscribes to *Modern Bride* has some kind of strong attraction to weddings. People reading magazines also tend to view and pay attention to advertisements related to their needs and wants. Often, readers linger over an ad for a longer period of time, because they read magazines in waiting situations (e.g., doctor's office) or during leisure time. This high level of interest, segmentation, and differentiation are ideal for products with precisely defined target markets.

Magazines, both trade and business journals, are a major medium for business-to-business marketing. Businesses can target their advertisements. The copy provides a greater level of detail about products. Readers, if interested, take time to read the information in the ad. Ads can provide toll-free telephone numbers and Web addresses so interested parties can obtain further information.

Magazines offer high-quality color and more sophisticated production processes, providing the creative with the opportunity to produce intriguing and enticing advertisements. Motion, color, and unusual images can be used to attract attention. Magazines such as *Glamour, Elle,* and *Cosmopolitan* use scratch and sniff ads to entice women to notice the fragrance of a perfume or cologne. Even car manufacturers have ventured into this type of advertising by producing the smell of leather in certain ads.

Magazines have a long advertising life, lasting beyond the immediate issue because subscribers read and reread them. This means the same advertisement is often read by more than one person. It is not unusual for an avid magazine reader to examine a particular issue several times and spend a considerable amount of time with each issue. This appeal is attractive to advertisers because they know the reader will be exposed more than once and likely pay more attention to the ad. In addition, magazine ads last beyond the current issue. Weeks and even months later, other individuals may look at the magazine. In the business-to-business sector, trade journals are often passed around to several individuals or members of the buying center. As long as the magazine lasts, the advertisement is still there to be viewed.

One major disadvantage facing magazine advertisers is a decline in readers. The culprit is the Internet. The Leo Burnett Company's *Starcom Report* states that magazines lost 61 million readers from the 18- to 49-year-old age bracket in just one year. Most moved to the Internet. Mediamark Research Inc. recently reported that magazine readerships declined by 5.9 percent for the same year. Of the 200 magazines examined, 56 gained readers while 144 lost readers. The largest gains were in *Vibe, Men's Fitness, Men's Health,* and *Inc.* magazine. The largest losers were *The National Enquirer, Sports Illustrated, TV Guide, Consumer Reports, Field & Stream, People,* and *Newsweek.*[21] To combat this trend, many of the magazines losing readers have combined with television networks, such as *People* with NBC's *Dateline* program.

Clutter is another big problem for magazine advertisers. For example, a recent 318-page issue of *Glamour* contained 195 pages of advertising and only 123 pages of content. Ads can be easily lost in those situations. To be noticed, the advertisement must be unique or stand out in some way.

Long lead times are a major disadvantage of magazines, because advertisements must be submitted as much as six months in advance of the issue. Consequently, making changes in ads after submission is very difficult. Also, because of the long life of magazines, images or messages created through magazine advertising have long lives. This is good for stable goods or services, but not for volatile markets or highly competitive markets wherein the appeal, price, or some other aspect of the marketing mix changes more frequently.

Cost is also a major factor with magazines. Because of its high-quality production and long shelf life, magazine advertising tends to be expensive. Ads can run over a million dollars for a single four-color page.

Magazines continue to proliferate even with the problems of declining readership. The wide variety of special interests makes it possible to develop and sell them. Many advertisers still can target audiences and take advantage of various magazine features, such as direct-response Internet addresses and coupon offers. This is especially true in the business market. Although business-to-business marketers increasingly use other media, trade journals and business magazines remain an effective method of reaching their target markets. As a result, the nature of advertising in magazines may change, but individual companies still will find effective uses for the outlets.

INTEGRATED LEARNING EXPERIENCE

The primary professional organization for magazines is the Magazine Publishers of America at **www.magazine.org**. Browse the various sections of the Web site to see what information is available. Examine a few of the articles in the "What's New" section. Review the recent advertising revenues for magazines. To get the feel for one of the many specialty magazines on the market, access the Web site of *Divorce Magazine* at **www.divorcemag.com**. Scan the various articles in the magazine and current advertisers. Access the "Advertise with Us" section to obtain information about rates and the reasons why a company might wish to advertise in *Divorce Magazine*.

Newspapers

When *USA Today* was launched, few believed a national daily newspaper could succeed. Obviously it has. The nature of news reporting has changed, many small local papers no longer exist, and conglomerates such as Gannett own most major city newspaper chains. Still, daily readership continues.

For many smaller local firms, newspaper ads, billboards, and local radio programs are the only viable advertising options, especially if television ads are too cost prohibitive. Newspapers can be distributed daily, weekly, or in partial form as the advertising supplements found in the front sections of many grocery stores and retail outlets. Table 9.7 on page 286 displays the basic advantages and disadvantages of newspaper advertising.

Retailers still rely heavily on newspaper ads because they offer geographic selectivity (local market access). Promoting sales, retail hours, and store locations is easy to accomplish in a newspaper ad. Short lead time allows retailers to change ads and promotions quickly. This flexibility is a strong advantage. It allows advertisers the ability to keep their ads current. They can modify ads to meet competitive offers or to focus on recent events.

Newspapers have a high level of credibility. Readers rely on newspapers for factual information in stories, giving newspapers greater credibility. Newspaper readers hold high interest levels in the articles they read. They tend to pay more attention to advertisements as well as news stories. This increased audience interest allows advertisers to pro-

Newspapers are an ideal medium for local companies such as Ozark Memorial Park.
Source: Used with permission of the *Joplin Globe*, Joplin, Missouri.

vide more copy detail in their ads. Newspaper readers take more time to read copy, unless simply too much information is jammed into a small space.

Newspaper advertisers receive volume discounts for buying larger *column inches* of advertising space. Many newspapers grant these volume discounts, called *cumulative discounts,* over one-month, three-month, or even year-long time periods. This potentially makes the cost-per-exposure even lower, because larger and repeated ads are more likely to garner the reader's attention.

Advantages	Disadvantages
1. Priority for local ads	1. Poor buying procedures
2. High flexibility	2. Short life span
3. High credibility	3. Major clutter (especially holidays)
4. Strong audience interest	4. Poor quality reproduction (especially color)
5. Longer copy–message possible	5. Internet classified competition
6. Cumulative volume discounts	
7. Coupons and special-response features	

TABLE 9.7

Newspaper Advertising

Newspaper reach is reported by the Audit Bureau of Circulations (ABC). The organization details the number of households in a given community that receive the newspaper.

Many local consumers rely heavily on newspaper advertising for information about grocery specials and other similar price discounts. Many local merchants use newspaper coupons. Newspapers also provide other special-response features ("Mention our ad in today's paper, and receive 10% off").

At the same time, there are limitations and disadvantages to newspaper advertising. First, newspapers cannot be targeted as easily to specific market segments (although sports pages carry sports ads, entertainment pages contain movie and restaurant ads, and so forth). Newspapers also have a short life. Once read, a newspaper normally is cast to the side, recycled, or destroyed. If a reader does not see an advertisement during the first pass through a newspaper, it probably will go unnoticed. Readers rarely pick up papers a second time. When they do, it is to continue reading, not to reread or rescan a section that has already been viewed.

Newspaper advertising suffers from two clutter problems. First, Wednesday papers containing grocery ads are usually larger and more cluttered. Second, holiday season newspapers, especially between Thanksgiving and Christmas, hold the most ads of the year. Thus, clutter is at the highest during peak selling seasons.

Newspaper ads often have poor production quality. Few companies buy color ads because they are much more expensive. Photos and copy tend to be harder to read and see clearly compared to other print media, especially magazines. Newspaper ads tend not to be wild or highly creative. Newspapers editors normally avoid and turn down anything that may be controversial, such as Calvin Klein ads featuring more-or-less naked models. Newspapers are very careful about offending their readers.

Newspapers suffer poor national buying procedures. Many newspapers in small towns are independent, or small holding companies own them. For a national advertiser, this means contacting numerous companies. Also, newspapers tend to favor local companies over national firms. Local businesses generally receive better advertising rates than do national advertisers, because local companies advertise on a more regular basis and receive volume discounts.

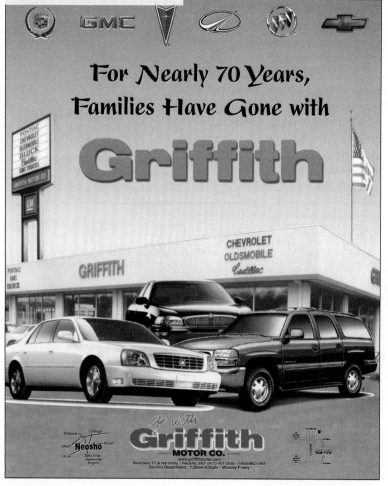

This award-winning advertisement was prepared by the staff of the *Joplin Globe*.
Source: Used with permission of the *Joplin Globe*, Joplin, Missouri.

Also, newspapers want to have a strong local appeal. By favoring local companies in ad rates, they can meet this goal and seem more desirable to local patrons.

A new threat to newspapers is the Internet, not a decline in newspaper readership due to movement to the Internet, but rather a shift by advertisers from classified newspaper ads to classified Internet ads. Two large electronic competitors are Microsoft's Sidewalk and CarPoint. Newspapers experience a decline in newspaper ads as retailers move into e-commerce, because retailers are the major advertisers in newspapers. Retail sales via e-commerce is over $8 billion annually.[22] As more households acquire computers and hook to the Internet and consumers become more accustomed to e-commerce, more advertising will shift from newspapers to the Internet.

Newspapers are used by many food manufacturers to promote their products.
Source: Used with permission of the *Joplin Globe*, Joplin, Missouri.

It is ironic that as newspapers lose advertising, especially classifieds, to the Internet, it is being replaced by advertising for Internet companies. As with the other media, the largest growth category are the dot.com advertisements, especially in the financial and telecommunication industries.

Newspapers counter the trend of classified advertisements moving to the Internet by establishing their own Internet classified sites. Various newspapers own AdOne, CareerPath, Classified Ventures, and PowerAdz. The major obstacle is that the competition is growing faster. Microsoft, America Online, and Yahoo! all have established strong classified ad sections. In one year, the number of classified ad sites increased by 269 percent.[23]

There is even competition in the area of want ads. Monster.com provides help wanted ads on a national scale, which may reduce purchases of local want ad space from newspapers. Thus, newspapers face significant challenges in retaining their advertising revenues.

There is some hope, however. Procter & Gamble now uses newspapers for the first time to promote its Tide detergent. Other national advertisers moving to newspapers include Johnson & Johnson, Kraft, Nestlé, and General Motors.[24] In this uncertain future, newspaper owners must become more creative and resourceful to entice larger companies to advertise locally on a regular basis.

Newspapers have not been a major medium for business-to-business marketers primarily because of their local nature. Most vendors and suppliers seeking the business of local companies do not reside in the same local area. Local companies can use newspapers in efforts to get business from other local companies. Often this approach is not cost effective because of the inability to target the ad to any given business target market.

Direct Mail

Another major advertising medium is direct mail. Many companies send ads directly to target markets of customers through mailing lists or blanket a region for more general products. Wal-Mart, Big K (Kmart), Target, Sears, and other national retail chains often send advertisements to consumers through the mail. Credit card companies are notorious for sending out enticements to apply for their cards, especially to lower-income families and college students. National restaurant chains (KFC, Pizza Hut) also mail directly to potential buyers. These firms mail free samples, coupons, and other special features to potential customers on a daily basis.

The major advantage of direct mail is that it normally lands in the hands of the person who opens the mail, who usually makes a significant amount of family purchasing decisions. Many mail offers include direct-response programs, so results are quickly measured. Direct mail also can be targeted to geographic market segments.

The primary disadvantages of direct mail include costs, clutter, and the "nuisance" factor. To be noticed, direct-mail advertising usually requires a color brochure, making the mailings more expensive to produce. As postage rates continue to rise, so do the costs of direct mail. Mailings tend to clutter post office boxes and become more prevalent during key seasons, such as Christmas. Many people are genuinely annoyed by "junk mail" and actively seek to have their names taken off mailing lists, especially for catalog-type operations.

Some people find direct mailing to be the least "reputable" form of advertising, because many mail-fraud scams have arisen in the past few decades. Direct mail best suits well-known local or national firms seeking a more immediate response (e.g., coupon redemption) or when the company wants to reinforce ads presented in other media. Direct mail reaches some customers who do not buy newspapers. Record clubs, book clubs, and others have used direct mail effectively over the years. It is likely many firms will continue to use direct mail in the future.

Direct mail remains a favorite marketing tool for business-to-business marketers. It provides a method of bypassing gatekeepers when the names of actual members of the buying center can be obtained. Direct mail can be one method of reaching businesses when they are in a rebuy situation and not open to calls by salespeople. Even if the direct mail is ignored when it is received, many people often file it away for future use. Although the cost per contact is high for direct mail, so is the response rate as compared to other media. The key to success for businesses is to make sure that the direct-mail piece gets into the hands of the right person in the buying center and that it is attractive enough to grab attention.

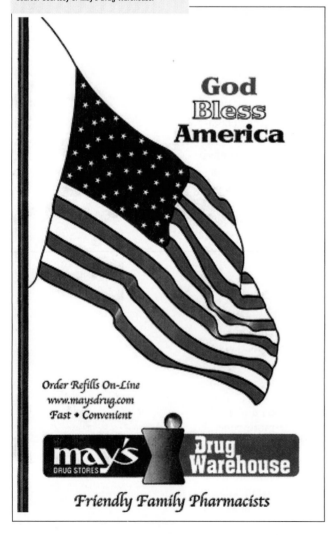

May's Drug Stores placed this patriotic advertisement on all of the company's pharmacy bags to enhance the brand name.
Source: Courtesy of May's Drug Warehouse.

Alternative Media

Besides all of the "traditional" and new (Internet) media discussed, numerous new ways are available for companies sending out advertisements. The key, as always, is to make certain the ads reach the right target market with the proper message. Some examples of additional forms of advertising—some that are new and some that have existed for many years—include:

▶ Leaflets, brochures, and carry-home menus

▶ Ads on carry-home bags from stores (grocery stores and retail outlets)

▶ Ads on T-shirts and caps (promotional giveaways and products sold)

▶ Ads on movie trailers both in theaters and on home video rental products

▶ Small, freestanding road signs

▶ Self-run ads in motel rooms on television, towels, ice chests, and so on

▶ Yellow pages and phone book advertisements

▶ Mall kiosk ads

▶ Ads sent by fax

▶ Ads shown on video replay scoreboards at major sports events

▶ In-house advertising magazines placed by airlines in seats

▶ Ads on the walls of airports, subway terminals, bus terminals, and inside cabs and buses or transit advertising

Each of these has additional benefits and problems. For example, small, free-standing road signs effectively gain attention, but many local governments and community citizens consider them eyesores. Yellow page advertising has become more difficult as additional firms enter into the phone book preparation market. Mall kiosk ads are placed in high traffic areas, but are easily defaced by vandals. Ads sent by fax are low cost and can be highly targeted (luncheon specials faxed to local companies just before noon). Still, many business owners become angry when their fax machines are tied up receiving ads. Ads on replay scoreboards have high intrusion values, yet can be ignored or even "booed" by those attending the game. Nonetheless, advertisers must consider all of the possibilities as they prepare advertising campaigns. The goals of reach, frequency, cost, and continuity must all be considered as individual media are selected and groups of media formulated into a campaign mix.

One of the more widely used alternative media programs is called **guerrilla marketing**, which is a focus on low-cost, creative strategies to reach the right people. Guerrilla marketing means the marketing team looks for ways to reach individuals and small groups in a unique way that will cause them to take notice. Creativity is the key to guerrilla marketing. For example, a booth at a golf tournament may be set up to allow customers to hit a t-shot and have a computer estimate the distance and accuracy of the drive. When the customer is handed a small piece of paper with the information, the paper contains not only the golf shot information, but also the advertiser's brand, tag line, and logo. This piece of paper will be kept and shown to others, thereby increasing awareness of the advertiser at a low cost, plus those shown the paper will be interested golfers, which is the target market.

Many small businesses do not have the money to send marketing messages in the ways they would like. Consequently, the owner must look for ways to make an impression, and marketing dollars should be spent on methods that have the strong potential for locating potential customers. Additional information about guerilla marketing and a program known as *lifestyle marketing* is provided in Chapter 15.

Many national products are also displayed as part of a television program or movie. These are called *product placements*. The most recent James Bond film featured a switch

---

ADVERTISING MEDIA SELECTION

Selecting the Right Medium for Adult Products

In 2002, NBC began accepting money to run advertisements for liquor products with alcohol contents that were stronger than beer or wine. Almost immediately a host of critics argued that it would be unwise to subject minors to such ads. Eventually the network decided against running the ads. The debate once again raises questions about free speech and free enterprise and why the tobacco and alcohol industries are banned from advertising on specific media when other product categories do not face this media restriction.

Since television tobacco advertising has been banned by the government, marketers have utilized a series of tactics to make certain company products are mentioned on the air. Sponsorship of the Virginia Slims tennis tournament and Marlboro cup racing have come under congressional scrutiny, because sportscasters must state the names of the products while reporting scores and results. Is this ethical?

Many adult products require tasteful advertising and marketing programs, even when they are free to be shown through any medium. Feminine hygiene, jock itch remedies, condoms, and other personal adult products may be featured in practically any medium. It is the responsibility of the marketing professional to select media that are appropriate as well as create ads that will not be offensive.

In the international arena, this responsibility becomes even greater. In many Islamic countries advertisements for personal hygiene or sexually related products would be highly offensive. It is important the company leaders explore these cultural differences before undertaking any kind of marketing campaign.

to a BMW as the car used by Bond, rather than the longstanding Austin Healy. The increase in product placements was spoofed in the film *Wayne's World II.* Placements are relatively low-cost methods of achieving additional product exposures during a television program or film. Typical fees charged by film companies are $20,000 for showing the product, $40,000 for mentioning it, and $60,000 for the actor to actually use the product.

Another form of placement is the purchase of advertising space in what will be key camera shots during sporting events. For instance, many Major League Baseball teams now allow ads to be displayed behind home plate, so that a center field camera shot of the pitcher and the batter will also reveal the advertisement. Professional golfers, not to be outdone, are paid fees for wearing caps carrying the names of various companies. Tiger Woods wears a cap featuring the Nike swoosh, and Phil Mickelsen wore one for KPMG Consulting for several years.

One of the more creative approaches to establishing an alternate method of reaching customers involves using what is essentially "flip card" technology in subways. Instead of riders seeing barren walls, 20- to 30-second commercial messages appear through the windows. Target was among the first advertisers to utilize this unique new method for reaching customers.

The use of alternative media has risen dramatically in the past 20 years. Clutter and consumer disinterest in traditional advertising methods have driven marketing teams to look for new, distinctive ways to reach customers. They may be tied to traditional advertisements or stand alone. They must, however, match the company's brand, image, and theme to be successful.

MEDIA MIX

Selecting the proper blend of media outlets for advertisements is a crucial activity. As campaigns are prepared, decisions must be made concerning the appropriate mix of media. Media planners and media buyers are both excellent sources of information on the most effective type of mix for a particular advertising campaign. It is the challenge of the creative to design ads for each medium that speaks to the audience yet ties in with the overall theme of the integrated advertising campaign. A survey of Table 9.8 shows considerable differences in media mixes that different consumer industries use. Notice that retailers spend more on newspaper advertising (61.1 percent) than they do on any other media. At the same time, all of the other categories spend more on television advertising. Choosing the appropriate advertising channels and then effectively combining outlets requires the expertise of a media planner who can study each outlet and match it with the product and overall message.

Recent studies by Millward Brown and A. C. Neilsen highlight the benefits of combining different media.[25] Using a telephone survey, Millward Brown found that ad awareness was 65 percent when consumers viewed the ad both on television and in a magazine. It was 19 percent for those who saw only the magazine ad and 16 percent for those who saw only the television ad. The increased impact of using two or more media is termed the **media multiplier effect**, which means the combined impact of using two or more media is stronger than using either medium alone. Business-to-business firms

TABLE 9.8

Advertising Expenditures by Categories

Category	Magazines	Newspapers	Outdoor	Television	Radio
Retail	4.2%	61.1%	2.0%	27.8%	5.0%
Automotive	14.0	32.7	0.7	50.8	1.8
Services	12.6	36.8	1.6	44.3	4.6
Entertainment	2.3	17.2	1.8	75.8	2.9
Foods	14.9	0.7	0.3	80.5	3.6
Cosmetics	32.5	0.5	0.07	66.2	0.7
Total	11.4	32.7	1.2	51.3	3.3

Source: Jack Nott, "Media Buying and Planning," *Advertising Age,* Vol. 70, no. 32, pp. 1–2.

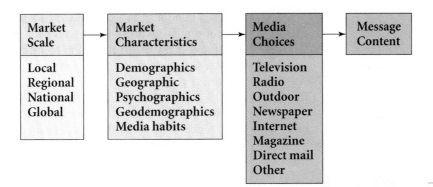

FIGURE 9.2
Developing Logical
Combinations of Media

are just now applying this concept as they use more than traditional trade journals for their advertising dollars. The key is to find effective combinations of media when designing a media mix.

Figure 9.2 shows possible linkages between various media. Consider the many possible options and combinations. Media experts work continually to decide which go together for individual target markets, goods and services, and advertising messages.

MEDIA SELECTION IN BUSINESS-TO-BUSINESS MARKETS

Identifying differences between consumer ads and business-to-business ads is becoming more difficult, especially in television, outdoor, and Internet ads. In the past, it was easy to spot business-to-business ads: The content was clearly aimed toward another company, and television, outdoor, and the Internet were seldom used. Currently, about 64 percent of all business advertising dollars are spent in nonbusiness environments.[26]

Several items explain this shift to more nonbusiness media. First, business decision makers are also consumers of goods and services. The same psychological techniques used to influence and gain consumer attention can also be used for business decision makers.

Second, and probably the most important, business decision makers are very difficult to reach at work. Gatekeepers (secretaries, voice mail systems, etc.) often prevent information flow to users, influencers, and decision makers. This is especially true for straight rebuy situations whereby orders are given to the current vendor. If a company is not the

To increase the impact of their advertisements, Defend ran both television ads and print ads simultaneously.
Source: Courtesy Howard, Merrell & Partners.

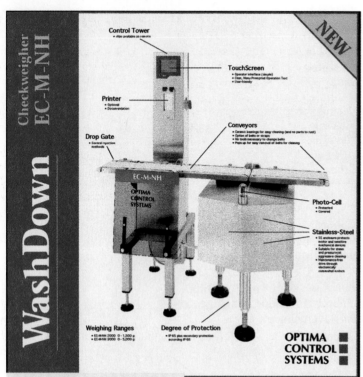

A business-to-business advertisement by Optima Control Systems.

Source: Courtesy of Bevil Advertising.

chosen vendor, it is extremely difficult to get anyone's attention. To avoid various gatekeepers, business-to-business firms try to reach the members of the buying center at their homes, in their cars, or in some other non-business venue.

A third reason for this shift to nonbusiness media is that the clutter among the traditional business media has made it more difficult to get a company noticed. Business advertisers realize that to have a chance for a sale, they must have a recognizable brand name. Taking lessons from brand giants such as Nike, Campbell's Soups, Wal-Mart, and Tide, business marketers now know they must establish a strong brand name. A strong brand name helps the company gain the attention of members of the buying center.

W. W. Grainger Company sells industrial maintenance supplies such as motors, tools, lights, sanitary supplies, heating, and air-conditioning equipment to other businesses. Believing that purchasing agents are likely to watch football, Grainger decided to enhance the company's brand name via television rather than use cluttered trade journals. Research conducted by Grainger indicated that the users and influencers for its products, maintenance and repair foremen, are likely to watch sports. Consequently, Grainger purchased advertising space on *Monday Night Football* and other sporting events such as NCAA basketball.[27]

In the past, business ads were fairly dull, but now they look much more like consumer ads. Creative appeals and the use of music, humor, sex, and fear, similar to consumer ads, are used. The boldest business ads sometimes include nudity or other more risqué material. In fact, many consumers cannot tell the difference. These firms hope that few business decision makers will notice they are seeing a business ad. When they don't, the business advertiser has succeeded.

Figure 9.3 identifies how business-to-business advertising expenditures are divided among the various media. Figure 9.4 lists the top six business-to-business advertisers. As shown, trade journals remain the number-one media used in business settings. Almost one-third of all advertising dollars are spent here. Trade journals offer a highly targeted audience.

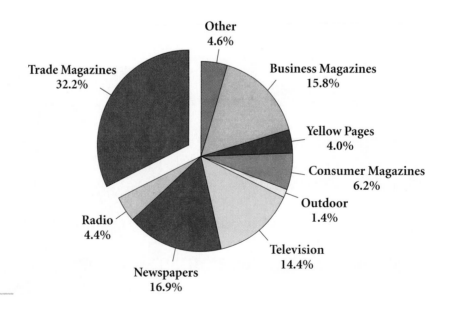

FIGURE 9.3
Business-to-Business Advertising Expenditure

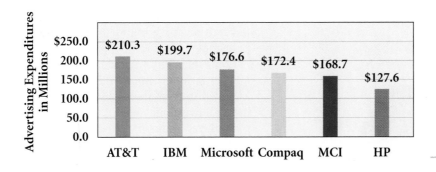

FIGURE 9.4
Top Six B-to-B Advertisers

Trade journals provide an opportunity to reach members of the buying center whom salespeople cannot reach. Gatekeepers cannot prevent trade journals from reaching different members of the buying center. Unfortunately, if the firm is in a straight rebuy situation, it is doubtful the ad will be noticed. If the firm is in a modified rebuy and the buying center is in the information search stage, then the ad has a better chance of success.

Clutter is a major problem in trade journals. Also, business advertisers often fill their adds with too much information. Therefore, ads should be designed to gain the reader's attention, and the copy must be manageable.

In addition to trade journals, business-to-business advertisers also use business magazines such as *Business Week* and consumer magazines. A total of 54.2 percent of the advertising budget goes for magazines. When newspapers and yellow pages are added to this list, print media accounts for about 75 percent of all business-to-business dollars spent. The primary reasons for these high levels of expenditures in print media are because they have highly selective audiences and the ads have longer life spans in print. Business decision makers and members of the buying center spend more working time examining print media than any other medium. Business will notice the advertisement by WingspanBank.com on page 294 more if it is located in a trade journal than in a general magazine such as *Time* because the former's readers are more likely to notice and read the advertisement, especially if they have been working or thinking about banking or financial services within their company.

Many goals in business-to-business advertisements are the same as those devoted to consumers. It remains important to identify key target markets, to select the proper media, and to prepare creative, enticing ads resulting in some kind of action, such as a change in attitude toward the company or movement toward a purchase decision. Many of the variables shown in Figure 9.2 apply equally well to business advertising.

INTEGRATED LEARNING EXPERIENCE

One of the best sources for business-to-business advertising information is Advertising Age's Net B2B.com. Access this Web site at **www.netb2b.com**. Under special features, notice "The BtoB 100," which lists the top 100 business-to-business advertisers. Under "BtoB's Best and Brightest" are profiles of the leading media buyers and strategists. The "NetMarketing 200" section ranks the best business-to-business Web sites. What other information is available at this Web site to assist business-to-business advertisers in selecting the right media?

MEDIA SELECTION IN INTERNATIONAL MARKETS

Understanding media viewing habits in international markets is important for successful advertising programs. In the United States, network television has been the primary advertising tool; in other countries, it is not as dominant. For instance, in Europe the best way to reach elite consumers is through magazines. Television and newspapers are second and third, respectively. The most popular magazines in Europe are *Reader's Digest, National Geographic, Cosmopolitan, Marie Clarie, Elle, Vogue, L'Express,* and *Paris Match.* The most watched European television stations are Eurosport, CNN International, Euronews, and Kabel Eins.[28]

It works because
it was built from the Internet up.
Not from a bureaucracy down.

Checking
Credit Cards
Loans
CDs
Bill Pay
Mortgage Finder
Investing
Planning Tools

WINGSPAN
BANK.COM

While traditional banks trundle online with the same old thinking, we're harnessing the power of the
Internet to give you new financial power. Like loan answers in 51 seconds. Electronic bill pay. Even a credit card
that saves 5% at leading web merchants. Someone has to lead banking in a new direction. Why not you?

www.WingspanBank.com ©1999. Bank products by FCC National Bank. Member FDIC. Investments through Wingspan Investment Services, Inc. Member NASD/SIPC.
INVESTMENTS NOT FDIC INSURED. MAY LOSE VALUE. NO BANK GUARANTEE.

An advertisement for Internet banking.

Source: Courtesy of WingspanBank.com.

In Asia and Latin America, cable television and satellite are growing in popularity as more homes become hooked to cable or satellite. As a result, more companies buy regional time rather than national and international time. Both Pepsi and Coke have redirected some of their international advertising dollars to smaller regional and local television cable and satellite markets. Companies find this is more effective because of the differences in consumer needs and media habits across the European countries. MTV split its programming into three subregions: (1) the United Kingdom and Ireland; (2) the German-speaking countries of Germany, Switzerland, and Austria; and (3) the Scandinavian countries.[29]

Just as media viewing differs, media buying in other countries often differs. For example, the trend in France is to farm media buying out to international media specialists. France's largest advertiser, PSA Peugeot Citroen, turned over its media buying to Euro RSCG's Mediapolis. Another advertising agency, the Danone Group, chose Carat Media Services France to handle its media buying. Several international companies operating in France follow this trend. Nestlé used to have its own internal company, Societe Publi Edition Distribution Courtage, to purchase media. Now it uses Optimedia, a media specialist firm.[30]

In other countries, the reverse may be true. For example, the top advertising agencies in Brazil fiercely oppose all independent media buying groups. The plan is to push for a change in the law that prohibits the payment of agency commissions and discounts from media buying to any firm that is not a full-service advertising agency. In India, the Advertising Agencies Association passed a stern resolution requiring members to stop handling media-only accounts or risk expulsion from the association. The Advertising Agencies Association of India believes it is critical for the full-service agency to be involved in all aspects of a brand's advertising, including media buying. The resolution and opposition of the Advertising Agencies Association to media buying independents is aimed at Carat Media Services India—India's first independent media buying service. Carat successfully persuaded Charagh Dink, India's largest shirt maker, to move its entire media buying account to Carat while hiring a freelancer to do the creative work. Carat also captured business from BBC World, Cadbury India, and Virgin Music. To prevent expulsion from the Advertising Agencies Association of India, agencies such as Madison DMB&B, which handles media buying for firms such as Coca-Cola, have added small creative assignments.[31]

In Brazil, purchasing media means turning an advertising account over to a full-service agency that also provides creative work. In France, creative work and media buying are seldom done by the same firm. Thus, media purchase varies from country to country.

In international settings, it is important to understand the media habits of consumers as well as their daily lifestyles. McCann-Erickson Worldwide launched a multinational media research effort called Media In Mind in Europe. The goals of this research were to: (1) improve media effectiveness by matching a firm's advertising to the time of day the audience will be most receptive, and (2) select the correct medium. Such firms as Motorola, Johnson & Johnson, General Motors, Coca-Cola, and Boots Healthcare International use Media In Mind. They report their media effectiveness has increased as much as 20 percent over those firms that have not used Media In Mind.

Part of the Media In Mind research in Europe has focused on consumer moods throughout the day. Boots Healthcare International used this research in advertising of cures for headaches. The research found that in Poland the people classified in the "headache" category were more likely to have the headache from the time they woke up until around noon. Thus, Boots Healthcare advertises on billboards that people see on their way to work or at lunch. The company also advertises on radio during the morning hours.[32]

Although outdoor advertising in most countries is primarily billboards, travelers near Riyadh and Jeddah, Saudi Arabia, see unique outdoor advertising. Publi-Graphics transformed two water towers into replicas of Nestlé's Nido brand powdered-milk cans. These two Nestlé powdered-milk can replicas are the largest outdoor advertising of its kind in the region and can be seen for miles around.[33]

In general, many tactics used to develop advertising campaigns in the United States apply to international advertising. What differs is the nature of the target markets, consumer media preferences, and the processes used to buy media. Also, companies must carefully attend to cultural mores to make sure the buying process does not offend the cultural and religious attitudes prevalent in any given region. A cultural assimilator must carefully screen clothing, gestures, words, symbols, and other ingredients as a company purchases advertising time or space and prepares ads.

INTEGRATED LEARNING EXPERIENCE

Advertising expenditures across the various media vary widely throughout the world. To see the difference, access the "Top Global Ad Markets" segment through the "Ad Age Dataplace" at **www.adage.com**. Compare ad spending by medium for the United States and the other countries listed. What differences are there in spending on television, radio, and magazines among the various countries listed? Notice the Web site also lists the top advertising companies, the top ad categories, the largest newspapers and magazines (based on circulation figures), and the ad rates for these particular publications.

SUMMARY

The traditional view of advertising has been to design a message that will accomplish the intended IMC objective, then find the best media channel. This view is slowly being replaced as the roles of media planners and media buyers have grown in importance. According to Bob Brennan, chief operating officer of Chicago-based Leo Burnett Starcom USA, in the past "95 percent of your success was great creative and 5 percent was great media. Now it's much closer to 50–50."[34]

This chapter reviews the media selection process. A media strategy is the process of analyzing and choosing media for an advertising and promotions campaign. Media planners and buyers complete much of this work. The media planner's primary job is to formulate a program stating where and when to place advertisements. Media planners work closely with creatives and account executives. Media buyers purchase the space, and they negotiate rates, times, and schedules for the ads.

The goals of reach, frequency, gross rating points, effective rating points, cost, continuity, and impressions drive the media selection process. Reach is the number of people, households, or businesses in a target audience exposed to media vehicle or message schedule at least once during a given time period. Frequency is the average number of times an individual, household, or business within a particular target market is exposed to a particular advertisement within a specified time period. Gross rating points (GRP) measure the impact or intensity of a media plan. Cost per thousand (CPM) is one method of finding the cost of the campaign by assessing the dollar cost of reaching 1,000 members of the media vehicle's audience. Cost per rating point (CPRP) is a second cost measure, which assesses the efficiency of media vehicle relative to a firm's target market. Ratings measure the percentage of a firm's target market that is exposed to a show on television or an article in a print medium. Continuity is the schedule or pattern of advertisement placements within an advertising campaign period. Gross impressions are the number of total exposures of the audience to an advertisement.

In addition to these basic concepts, advertising experts often utilized the concepts of effective frequency and effective reach. Effective frequency is the number of times a target audience must be exposed to a message to achieve a particular objective. Effective reach is the percentage of an audience that must be exposed to a particular message to achieve a specific objective.

In seeking advertising goals, marketing experts, account executives, and others must assess the relative advantages and disadvantages of each individual advertising medium. Thus, television, radio, outdoor billboards, the Internet, magazines, newspapers, and direct mail should all be considered as potential ingredients in a campaign. Other new media can be used to complement and supplement the more traditional media outlets. Logical combinations of media must be chosen to make sure the intended audience is exposed to the message. The three-exposure hypothesis suggests that a consumer must be exposed to an ad at least three times before it has the desired impact; other experts believe even more exposures are necessary. In contrast, recency theory suggests that ads truly reach only those wanting or needing a product, and therefore only one exposure is necessary when someone is "on the hot spot" and ready to buy.

In business-to-business settings, companies can combine consumer media outlets with trade journals and other business venues (trade shows, conventions, etc.) to attempt to reach members of the buying center. In many cases, enticing ads using consumer appeals such as sex, fear, and humor have replaced dry, dull, boring ads with an abundance of copy.

When designing business advertising, remember that advertising is just one component of the integrated marketing communications plan. It must be integrated with the sales force, sales promotions, trade promotions, and public relations. Business-to-business advertising using traditional consumer media cannot accomplish all of the communications objectives a business needs to accomplish. They help develop brand awareness and build brand equity, but are usually not the best for providing information the buying center needs.

International advertising media selection is different in some ways from that which takes place in the United States, because media buying processes differ as do media preferences of locals in various countries. At the same time, the process of media selection is quite similar: Marketing experts choose media they believe will reach the target audience in an effective manner.

Media selection takes place in conjunction with the message design and within the framework of the overall IMC approach. Effective media selection means the company spends enough money to find the target audience and does not waste funds by overwhelming them with the same message. Account executives, creatives, media planners, media buyers, and the company's representative must all work together to make certain the process moves as effectively and efficiently as possible.

REVIEW QUESTIONS

1. What is a media strategy? How does it relate to the creative brief and overall IMC program?

2. What does a media planner do?

3. Describe the role of media buyer in an advertising program.

4. What is reach? Give examples of reach in various advertising media.

5. What is frequency? How can an advertiser increase frequency in a campaign?

6. What are gross rating points? What do they measure?

7. What is the difference between CPM and CPRP? What costs do they measure?

8. What is continuity?

9. Describe the three-exposure hypothesis.

10. How is recency theory different from the three-exposure hypothesis?

11. What is effective frequency? Effective reach?

12. What are the major advantages and disadvantages of television advertising?

13. What are the major advantages and disadvantages of radio advertising?

14. What are the major advantages and disadvantages of Internet advertising?

15. What are the major advantages and disadvantages of magazine advertising?

16. What are the major advantages and disadvantages of newspaper advertising?

17. Is the strong intrusion value of television an advantage? Why or why not?

18. Name a product and three media that would mix well together to advertise that product. Defend your media mix choices.

19. What special challenges does media selection present for businesses? What roles do gatekeepers play in creating those challenges?

20. What special challenges does media selection present for international advertising campaigns? What differences and similarities exist with U.S. media selection processes?

KEY TERMS

media strategy the process of analyzing and choosing media for an advertising and promotions campaign.

media planner the individual who formulates the program stating where and when to place advertisements.

media buyer the person who buys the space and negotiates rates, times, and schedules for the ads.

reach the number of people, households, or businesses in a target audience exposed to media vehicle or message schedule at least once during a given time period.

frequency the average number of times an individual, household, or business within a particular target market is exposed to a particular advertisement within a specified time period.

gross rating points (GRP) a measure of the impact or intensity of a media plan.

cost per thousand (CPM) the dollar cost of reaching 1,000 members of the media vehicle's audience.

cost per rating point (CPRP) a measure of the efficiency of media vehicle relative to a firm's target market.

ratings a measure of the percentage of a firm's target market that is exposed to a show on television or an article in a print medium.

weighted or demographic CPM a measure used to calculate whether or not an advertisement has reached the target market effectively.

continuity the schedule or pattern of advertisement placements within an advertising campaign period.

continuous campaign media buys that result in a steady stream of advertisements over time.

pulsating schedule a minimal level of advertising punctuated by increases at periodic times.

discontinuous campaign placing ads at special intervals with no advertisements shown between those intervals.

gross impressions the number of total exposures of the audience to an advertisement.

effective frequency the *number of times* a target audience must be exposed to a message to achieve a particular objective.

effective reach the *percentage of an audience* that must be exposed to a particular message to achieve a specific objective.

intrusion value the ability of media or an advertisement to intrude upon a viewer without his or her voluntary attention.

guerrilla marketing focusing on low-cost, creative strategies to reach the right people in a market area.

media multiplier effect the combined impact of using two or more media is stronger than using either medium alone.

CRITICAL THINKING EXERCISES

Discussion Questions

1. To be effective, multiple media should be chosen and integrated carefully. Individuals exposed to an advertisement on combinations of channels selected from television, radio, the Internet, and billboards are more inclined to process the information than if only a solitary media is used. Fill in the following chart by putting in the probability of you being exposed to an advertisement if it were put into each medium. The percentages across each row should add up to 100 percent.

Product	Television	Radio	Newspaper	Magazine	Outdoor	Internet	Direct Mail
Movie							
Restaurant							
Clothing							
Jewelry							
Dry cleaner							

2. Billboard advertising in Times Square is so popular that space has already been sold for 10 years. Coca-Cola, General Motors, Samsung, Prudential, NBC, Budweiser, and the *New York Times* pay rates in excess of $100,000 a month to hold these spaces for the next 10 years. Inter City is building a 50-story hotel at Broadway and 47th Street to accommodate 75,000 square feet of advertising. Even before the completion of the hotel or tower, such companies as Federal Express, Apple Computers, AT&T, HBO, Levi-Strauss, Morgan Stanley, and the U.S. Postal Service have purchased space.[35] Why would companies pay so much for outdoor advertising? What are the advantages and disadvantages of purchasing billboards at Times Square?

3. Repetition and a short, catchy name are the keys for an effective radio spot. Sports equipment retailer Fogdog.com has been very successful with its radio spots. The URL is easy to remember and is reinforced with the sound of a howling dog. People don't have to fumble with finding a pencil to write it down. After a few repetitions, they remember it.[36] Another Web company, Sandbox.com—a fantasy sports game site—wants to develop a radio and billboard campaign. Develop both a radio and a billboard advertisement that will catch people's attention and be easy to remember. What are the advantages of combining a radio campaign with billboards?

4. Xerox has a color printer that sells for $1,200 which it wants to market to businesses. What media mix would you suggest Xerox consider for its $20 million advertising campaign? Justify your answer.

5. Pick either the table of cosmetics companies or the table of clothing companies listed on the next page. Access each firm's Web site. Indicate how many advertisements you have seen in each of the media listed within the last month. Then discuss each company's media plan. Does the company project an integrated message? What target market does the Web site attract? Does the Web site convey the same message broadcast in the other media?

Cosmetics Companies

Company (Web address)	TV	Radio	Newspaper	Magazine	Outdoor	Internet
Estee Lauder (www.esteelauder.com)						
Maybelline (www.maybelline.com)						
Eve (www.eve.com)						
Clinique (www.clinique.com)						
Revlon (www.revlon.com)						

Clothing Companies

Company (Web address)	TV	Radio	Newspaper	Magazine	Outdoor	Internet
Polo (www.polojeansco.com)						
Pepe (www.pepejeans.com)						
Squeeze (www.sqz.com)						
Guess (www.guess.com)						
Lee (www.leejeans.com)						
Wrangler (www.wrangler.com)						

6. The table to the right provides the population of the top 10 Demographic Marketing Areas (DMAs). The target market for a particular company is yuppie boomers, or those 35 to 54 years old who are professionals or managers. Based on the percentage of adults in each DMA that fits the target market profile, calculate the size of the target market in each DMA. Washington has been completed for you. If you had funds to advertise in only 5 of the 10 DMAs, which 5 would you choose? Why?

7. A business-to-business firm has decided to expand into Brazil. The company decided to conduct a print advertising campaign and follow it later with a direct-mail campaign. The primary goal of this print campaign is to build brand awareness. The print budget is $250,000. Access the Brazmedia Web site at www.brazmedia.com. Develop a print media campaign based on the information provided. Select the print magazines or newspapers you would use. Also, describe the size of the ad and the frequency of the campaign. Justify your media plan.

DMA	Population	DMA Percent	Number in Target Market
Washington	3,965,200	18.4%	729,600
San Francisco–Oakland	4,824,600	14.2	
Boston	4,495,600	13.6	
Dallas–Ft. Worth	3,669,900	13.3	
Houston	3,251,100	13.1	
New York	14,432,500	12.0	
Chicago	6,483,800	11.7	
Philadelphia	5,655,800	11.6	
Los Angeles	11,391,200	11.3	
Detroit	3,549,600	11.1	

Selecting Media for an IMC Advertising Campaign

Following your decision about choosing an in-house approach or an external advertising agency, you must make another set of choices. The media you select to advertise your product need to match the budget, the theme of the IMC program, the specific message, and the product itself. Therefore, carefully consider both traditional media as well as creative ways your company can develop to get your product's message out. Visit the Prentice-Hall Web site at www.prenhall.com/clow or access the IMC Plan Pro disk that accompanied this textbook and complete the exercise for this chapter. You will be asked to describe both the media you've selected and the ones that were rejected. Also, the reasoning process used to include or exclude media should be identified. Remember that your choices may be affected by local conditions and international considerations.

BUILDING AN
IMC
CAMPAIGN
IMC PlanPro!

CASE 1

CREATING A PHOTO OP

Manuel Ortega was placed in charge of an advertising campaign for a new 35 mm camera. His company was going to compete directly with Nikon and Yashica. As the account manager, Manuel was given a $12 million budget for the first phase of the campaign, which was to run for one month.

The objective of the campaign is to explain the firm's version of disk technology. Images recorded on computer disks rather than film are sharper and easier to use. The complexity in conveying the details of the new technology and the benefits to consumers makes the campaign more difficult. Manuel consulted carefully with his media planner, media buyer, and creative after receiving the contract from the company. They agreed to use magazine ads to be followed up with television spots.

Part of their reasoning for choosing magazines was the profile of the target market for this particular type of camera. The company's research indicated that the target buyer is between 18 and 44 years of age, has completed at least two years of college, and has a family income in excess of $30,000. These individuals read magazines at home and subscribe to most of the magazines they read. Manuel knew that individuals who subscribe to a magazine pay more attention to advertisements than do those who purchase the same magazine from a store. The other major characteristic of this group is that they have purchased a 35 mm camera in the past. The company believed those who had not purchased a 35 mm camera in the past were unlikely to buy into this new technology.

The company believed that 20 million individuals in the United States fit the target market profile for the 35 mm camera, and 3.22 million of those individuals read *National Geographic.* Manuel explained to the company's leaders that by dividing the percentage of the total target market by those who read *National Geographic,* the yield is 16.1 percent. In other words, 16.1 percent of the target market for this camera reads *National Geographic* and would be exposed to an advertisement placed in the magazine. As shown in Table 9.9, the percent sign is dropped and the reach for *National Geographic* is listed simply as 16.1. In the advertising industry, this number is the rating for that particular vehicle and can be obtained from commercial sources.

Table 9.9 indicates that *National Geographic* and *Time* magazines have the largest ratings. *Travel & Leisure* and *Southern Living* have the smallest ratings. Two things explain the difference in ratings: (1) The size of the circulation of the various magazines. For example, the total circulation for *National*

TABLE 9.9

Creating a Photo Op Case Study

Magazine	Cost for Four-Color Full Page Ad	Total Readership (000s)	CPM Total	Target Market (20 M) Rating (Reach)	Cost per Rating Point (CPRP)
National Geographic	$ 346,080	21,051	$16.44	16.1	$21,496
Newsweek	780,180	15,594	50.03	12.2	63,949
People	605,880	21,824	27.76	9.4	64,455
Southern Living	11,370	5,733	1.98	2.4	4,738
Sports Illustrated	965,940	13,583	71.11	10.5	91,994
Time	1,324,282	21,468	61.69	15.9	83,288
Travel & Leisure	183,216	2,205	83.09	2.3	79,659
U.S. News and World Report	100,740	8,929	11.28	8.3	12,137

(continued)

Geographic is 21,051,000 readers compared to only 2,205,000 for *Travel & Leisure;* (2) the percentage of the readers who fit the target audience. Not all readers of *National Geographic* fit the target profile for this 35 mm camera. In fact, only 15.3 percent of *National Geographic's* readers fit this profile compared to 20.8 percent of *Travel & Leisure's* readership. (Manuel calculated these percentages by multiplying the rating times 20, then dividing by the readership of the magazine in millions.)

The advertising team decided two primary factors would determine the reach of the campaign. First was the number and diversity of media being used. A media plan using the eight magazines would have a greater reach than a media plan using only five magazines. Notice that the total reach for the eight magazines is 77.1. Thus, 77.1 percent of the target market for this 35 mm camera would be exposed at least once during the next four-week time period to an advertisement. In addition to the quantity, the diversity of media will have an impact. Magazines that are different from each other tend to overlap less than magazines that are not different. Advertising only in sports magazines, for example, would overlap considerably because the same individuals probably read the various sports magazines. Reach measures the unduplicated percentage of a firm's target market exposed to an advertisement. Ads in media with nearly identical target markets do not reach as many people as advertising in vehicles with different target markets.

1. Use the information provided in the case and Table 9.9 to develop the magazine media selection plan for the print advertising campaign for Manuel Ortega. Each magazine must have at least one advertisement insertion but no more than eight insertions.

   Use Table 9.10 to calculate the gross rating points for the magazine campaign and the total cost. As noted in the case, Manuel has a $12 million budget to work with. To illustrate how to calculate the gross rating points and total cost, the first magazine, *National Geographic,* has already been completed. The goal is to maximize the gross rating points while staying within the constraints of the $12 million budget. (Those familiar with linear programming can solve this problem using a linear program to maximize the gross rating points. It also can be solved using a spreadsheet and what-if analysis.)

TABLE 9.10

Media Plan for Case Study Creating a Photo Op

Magazine	Cost for Four-Color Full-Page Ad	Rating	Number of Insertions	GRPs	Total Cost
National Geographic	$ 346,080	16.1	8	128.8	$2,768,640
Newsweek	780,180	12.2			
People	605,880	9.4			
Southern Living	11,370	2.4			
Sports Illustrated	965,940	10.5			
Time	1,324,282	15.9			
Travel & Leisure	183,216	2.3			
U.S. News and World Report	100,740	8.3			
		Total			

Note: The goal is to maximize the GRPs within the $12 million budget. There is a minimum of one insertion per magazine and a maximum of eight per magazine. Based on a linear programming solution, the optimal number of *National Geographic* insertions is eight. *National Geographic's* information has already been completed.

2. Justify the solution, especially in terms of frequencies chosen.

3. Is television a logical medium for the next phase of the campaign? Why or why not? If not television, which medium would be best?

4. If the client wanted to have a fully integrated communications media package, what package of media would be most likely to succeed? Explain the choices.

5. For a long-term project, investigate similar costs for television and radio advertising in your local area. Construct a budget and develop a media buying plan for each medium.

CASE 2

BASS ATTACKS

Rusty Johnson has had a lifelong love for fishing of all types. He has been on the ocean and on numerous lakes and streams, and occasionally he has made trips to small ponds in the area just to catch small catfish. Having made a fairly significant amount of money in his real estate career, Rusty is looking for a new challenge. He decided to manufacture and sell bass fishing boats in the Lake Ponchartrain area of Louisiana.

Fishing in southern Louisiana takes two forms. First, some anglers like going into the swamps and bayous to get near underwater foliage, where some kinds of bass and crappie hide. Others enjoy getting out on the larger lake, using radar equipment to identify bigger fish resting in the deeper and cooler areas of water in the summertime.

The swamp fisherman requires a maneuverable boat with a small hull, so it does not get hung or scratched in the shallow waters. The large lake fisherman wants more stability and a larger boat to negotiate waves in the deeper open areas. Both wanted a boat that made it easy to pull fish in, with a live well holding tank. Other accessories could then be added depending on the tastes of the fisherman.

Rusty created two kinds of boats in response to the marketplace. He designed the first, the Bass Attack Prowler, for smaller spaces. He named the larger boat the Bass Attack Mastercraft, figuring Bass Attack sounded quite a bit like Bass Tracker, the leader in the field. He also believed the name was unique enough for the seasoned fisherman who would know the difference.

As the company completed the development of a manufacturing site and production of the initial run of boats, it was time to advertise. Rusty knew the real estate advertising market quite well, but he did not feel as confident about reaching fishermen. He faced the problem of geographic dispersion. Beyond the locals in the area, bass fishermen were spread out through the entire state of Louisiana and across the country. They came from a wide variety of backgrounds, some wealthy, some quite poor. Rusty's goal was to get some of the locals to consider his boat instead of the higher-priced, better-known models offered by Bass Tracker.

In the first year of operation, Rusty's company budgeted $200,000 for local advertising and more for "want ads" in some larger outlets, such as Internet sites, fishing magazines, and possibly some travel magazines or newspapers. He also considered billboards and other lower-cost possibilities. He knew he had a quality product; now the goal was to get the word out and generate some sales.

1. Describe the difficulties Bass Attack boats will encounter in its integrated marketing program.

(continued)

2. Which media should Bass Attack use? Which should the company eliminate? Why?

3. For each of the following media, identify four specific outlets that Bass Attack could use for advertising. For instance, for magazines, a logical outlet would be *Field and Stream*; for television, ESPN fishing shows.

a. Magazines
b. Radio
c. Television
d. Internet

4. What kind of ad do you think will be successful for this company? Defend your answer.

ENDNOTES

1. Much of the information in this vignette may be found in Lisa Bertagnoli, "Duck Campaign is Firm's Extra Insurance," *Marketing News,* 35, issue 18 (August 27, 2001), pp. 5–6.

2. Liz Davis Smith, "90s Require Integrated Marketing Programs," *Birmingham Business Journal,* 12 (March 27, 1995), p. 12.

3. Mickey Marks, "Millennial Satiation," *Advertising Age,* 14 (February 2000), p. S16. J. Thomas Russell and W. Ronald Lane, *Kleppner's Advertising Procedure,* 15th edition (Upper Saddle River, NJ: Prentice Hall), 2002, pp. 174–175.

4. Discussion of media planners and media buyers based on Angela M. Manueal, "Media Planners Rarely Seen, but Play Key Role in Projects," *Business First—Louisville,* 11, no. 42 (May 22, 1995), pp. 42–44.

5. Jack Neff, "Media Buying & Planning," *Advertising Age,* 70, no. 32 (August 2, 1999), pp. 1–2.

6. Arthur A. Andersen, "Clout Only a Part of Media Buyer's Value," *Advertising Age,* 70, no. 15 (April 5, 1999), p. 26.

7. Ibid.

8. R. F. Dyer and E. H. Foreman, "Decision Support for Media Selection Using the Analytic Hierarchy Process," *Journal of Advertising,* 21, no. 1 (March 1992), pp. 59–62.

9. Herbert E. Krugman, "Why Three Exposures May Be Enough," *Journal of Advertising Research,* 12, no. 6 (1972), pp. 11–14.

10. Betsy Tabor, "Is Your Advertising Strategy Obsolete?" *Mississippi Business Journal,* 20, no. 34 (August 24, 1998), p. 28.

11. Chuck Ross, "Now, Many Words from Our Sponsors," *Advertising Age,* 70, no. 40 (September 27, 1999), pp. 3–4.

12. Stephanie Thompson, "Food Marketers Stir Up the Media," *Advertising Age,* 70, no. 42 (September 11, 1999), p. 18.

13. Katy Bachman, "The Big Time," *Adweek, Western Edition,* 49, no. 38 (September 20, 1999), pp. 50–51.

14. Carol Krol, "Look Up! Seeing Is Believing," *Advertising Age,* 70, no. 32 (August 2, 1999), p. 2.

15. "Why Internet Advertising?" *Adweek, Eastern Edition,* 38, no. 18 (May 5, 1997), pp. 8–12.

16. Richard A. Shaffer, "Listen Up! Pay Attention! New Web Startups Want Ads That Grab You," *Fortune,* 140, no. 8 (October 25, 1999), pp. 348–349.

17. Kathy Sharpe, "Web Punctures the Idea That Advertising Works," *Advertising Age,* 70, no. 38 (September 13, 1999), p. 44; Shaffer, "Listen Up! Pay Attention! New Web Startups Want Ads That Grab You."

18. Ibid.

19. "Why Internet Advertising?"

20. Rachel X. Weissman, "Just Paging Through," *American Demographics,* 21, no. 4 (April 1999), pp. 28–29; "The Scoop on Magazine Advertising," *Florist,* 33, no. 5 (October 1999), p. 16.

21. Ann Marie Kerwin, "Magazine Blast Study Showing Reader Falloff," *Advertising Age,* 70, no. 10 (March 8, 1999), pp. 3–4.

22. John Morton, "A Looming Threat to Newspaper Advertising," *American Journalism Review* (May 1999), p. 88.

23. Tony Case, "Reading the Numbers," *Brandweek,* 40, no. 35 (September 20, 1999), Media Outlook, p. 64.

24. Ibid.

25. Lindsay Morris, "Studies Give 'Thumbs Up' to Mags for Ad Awareness," *Advertising Age,* 70, no. 32 (August 2, 1999), pp. 16–17; Rachel X. Weissman, "Broadcasters Mine the Gold," *American Demographics,* 21, no. 6 (June 1999), pp. 35–37.

26. Adrienne W. Fawcett, "Creativity in Other Media Is Raising the Bar in Print," *Advertising Age's Business Marketing,* 82, no. 8 (September 1997), p. 32.

27. Laurie Freeman, "Internet Shows Rapid Growth as Communications Tool, Helping to Change Marketers' Use of Traditional Media," *Advertising Age's Business Marketing,* 84, no. 5 (May 1999), p. S6.

28. Julia Korantang, "European Survey Uncovers the Best Ad Vehicles," *Advertising Age International* (August 9, 1999), pp. 15–16.

29. Joy Dietrich and Normandy Madden, "Multichannel Ad Revenues Up 23% in 98," *Advertising Age International* (June 14, 1999), pp. 21–22.

30. Larry Speer, "Nestlé Joins Trend of Farming Out Media Buys in France," Advertising Age International (October 1999), p. 1.

31. Laurel Wentz and Mir Maqbool Alan Khan, "The Backlash Against Indies in Brazil," *Advertising Age International* (October 5, 1998), p. 14.

32. Suzanne Bidlake, "Consumers Under Microscope," *Advertising Age International* (February 8, 1999), p. 21.

33. Korantang, "European Survey Uncovers the Best Ad Vehicles."

34. Neff, "Media Buying & Planning."

35. Bachman, "The Big Time."

36. Noah Liberman, "Web Marketers Use Radio to Net Audience Members," *Atlanta Business Chronicle,* 22, no. 16 (September 24, 1999), p. 73A.

10

Trade Promotions

Chapter Objectives

Recognize **the important relationship between advertising programs and the other parts of the promotions mix.**

Understand **the difference between trade promotions and consumer or sales promotions, and when to use each tool.**

Become **aware of how trade promotions tools build strong ties with other members of the marketing channel (retailers, wholesalers, distributors, etc.).**

Know **when and how to use each of the major trade promotions tools.**

Overcome **the barriers and obstacles to effective use of trade promotions.**

WHAT'S GOOD FOR WAL-MART, IS GOOD FOR AMERICA?

It wasn't that many years ago when a prominent citizen proclaimed, "What's good for General Motors is good for America." The quote inspired considerable debate as to what constitutes "good." The domination of the Big Three (Ford, Chrysler, General Motors) in the auto industry was viewed as beneficial by some and essentially an unfair oligopoly by others.

Currently, Wal-Mart and Target are dominant forces in the retail industry. These and other megafirms have changed the structures of many marketing programs. Previously, a series of mom-and-pop operations created opportunities for small manufacturers to gain an entryway into retail markets. Now, with so many customers using one-stop shopping, the entire retail game has changed.

First, in many small communities, a number of retail stores have simply been pushed out of business. Many small bookstores, drugstores, and other local entrepreneurial operations simply cannot compete with megastores. As a result, manufacturers and distributors direct less attention to those that remain, instead seeking to capture the "big prize" of a megastore's account.

Second, megastores offer megadiscounts. Manufacturers are being forced to grant major discounts to these large chains to keep their items on the shelves. Among other things, this creates huge barriers to entry for smaller companies trying to sell to the megagiants, because they simply cannot afford the same price cuts.

Capturing key shelf space on a megastore's main aisle is a major victory for a manufacturer. Each season the process begins again as various companies try to garner favor from large retail outlets. For example, one major new campaign program is found in the back-to-school season (August and September). Everyone from lunch box manufacturers to food suppliers has been forced to adjust to the needs of the megastore.

In one recent back-to-school season, the Kellogg company created Snack Pack cereals, Kraft made Stove Top meal kits for kids, Quaker prepared Instant Oatmeal Dinosaur Eggs, and Nabisco introduced its Tiger Toys and Snacks line. Each was trying to maintain shelf space in the larger retail operations. Contests, promotions, cooperative advertising programs (shared ad costs between the manufacturer and the retailer), and other incentives were a major part of the plan.

Besides these new products, other companies tried to keep favor with the Big Three through different programs. Dannon Natural Spring Water tried a tie-in with the National PTA program. Campbell's created a Labels for Education Program, and Kraft created a Nickel-O-Zone promotion as a tie-in with Nickelodeon's programming. Each company sought to create attention for its products that would drive the retailers to display its products prominently in key areas of the store.

At the same time, retailers continue to flex their marketing muscles, asking mostly for price discounts rather than other gimmicks. Stores set up in-house displays featuring their own favored products, and the manufacturer can do little to change this policy.

Whether or not megaretailers are good for the nation's economy remains a major debate. Many smaller community leaders have become frustrated by the negative effects a Wal-Mart can cause, because entrepreneurial jobs are lost in favor of shelf stocker/checkout counter positions with lower pay. Regardless of how the trend plays out, it is clear that manufacturers, wholesalers, and distributors must pay careful attention to the role megastores play in the futures of these companies. Incentives and promotions will remain one key element in the process.[1]

WILLAMETTE FURNITURE COMPANY

An IMC program is much more than mere advertising. It is the consistent message and voice that the company uses across advertising campaigns over time, meshed with all other marketing activities. A tie-in between advertising and trade promotion sends the message to other businesses in the marketing channel in a powerful manner. Financial incentives and other methods help build bonds that ensure a given company's products will be well supported by various vendors.

Read the Executive Summary, Promotions Opportunity Analysis (section 2.0), Communications Market Analysis (2.1), along with any other information that will help you understand the nature of the Willamette Furniture Company featured on the IMC Plan Pro disk. Then, study the IMC Budget for the company (section 6.1) and Willamette's use of trade promotions (section 6.2.2). Reading the distribution strategy found in Section 3.4 might also be helpful. In this company, expenditures for trade promotions are greater than those for advertising in the business-to-business market. This is relatively common. Still, the plan will only be successful if the message is consistent and distinct in all of Willamette's marketing communications.

overview

Marketing goods and services can seem like a bold and exciting process at times. Creating television advertisements, Internet Web sites, radio spots, and other marketing efforts is attractive to many people interested in highly visible marketing careers. At the same time, however, it is important to remember that effective integrated advertising and *marketing* communications programs include both visible and subtle ingredients. And sometimes, those more subtle elements actually end up enticing the customer to make the purchase. In fact, about 75 percent of all promotional dollars are spent on things other than advertising.

This section explores the other parts of an IMC program. As shown in Figure 10.1, these critical components add significantly to the impact of any IMC effort, especially when they are executed correctly. When the marketing team fails to incorporate the other parts of the promotions mix into the IMC plan, it is incomplete and the odds of success are diminished.

A successful IMC program builds on the foundations established earlier. Consumer markets are defined, business-to-business customers are identified, and various buyer behaviors are studied. Next, advertising campaigns are formulated to reach all key customers. Then, trade promotions and the others parts of the promotions mix can be structured to enhance the IMC message and lead to the final purchase decision.

Many marketing account executives recognize the major role the promotions mix plays in portraying the firm's clear voice and message. As noted in Chapter 1, there are four components to the promotions mix:

1. Advertising
2. Trade promotions
3. Sales promotions
4. Personal selling and sales management

The previous part of this text dealt with the first component in the mix: advertising. This part is devoted to the final three. First, in this chapter, trade promotions are described, with the other elements presented in Chapters 11 and 12.

When the promotions mix is truly integrated, the company's internal and external publics both speak with the same voice. Employees know what the organization tries to achieve with its marketing program, the advertising agency designs messages that por-

Internet Marketing	IMC for Small Businesses and Entrepreneurial Ventures	Evaluating an Integrated Marketing Program	Integration Tools
Trade Promotions	Consumer Promotions	Personal Selling, Database Marketing, and Customer Relations Management / Public Relations and Sponsorship Programs	Promotional Tools
Advertising Management	Advertising Design: Theoretical Frameworks and Types of Appeals	Advertising Design: Message Strategies and Executional Frameworks / Advertising Media Selection	Advertising Tools
Corporate Image and Brand Management	Consumer Buyer Behavior	Business-to-Business Buyer Behavior / Promotions Opportunity Analysis	Foundation

FIGURE 10.1
An IMC Plan

tray the company speaking with one clear voice, and individual customers as well as business buyers are aware of the company's products and services. This, in turn, bodes well for the future of the firm.

THE NATURE OF TRADE PROMOTIONS

Trade promotions are the expenditures or incentives used by manufacturers and other members of the marketing channel to help push their products through to retailers. The best way to understand trade promotions is to note that they are incentives that members of the trade channel use to entice another member to *purchase goods for eventual resale.* In other words, trade promotions are aimed at retailers, distributors, wholesalers, brokers, or agents. A manufacturer can use trade promotions to convince another member of the trade channel to carry its goods. Wholesalers, distributors, brokers, and agents can use trade promotions to entice retailers to purchase products for eventual resale.

The difference between trade promotions and consumer or sales promotions is that the latter involves a sale to an *end user or customer.* When a manufacturer sells products to another business for end use, the enticements involved are consumer or sales promotions tools. On the other hand, when a manufacturer sells to another business for the purpose of having the goods resold, then trade promotions tools are being used.

The role played by trade promotions is to build strong relations with other members in the channel. When a retailer stocks the merchandise a manufacturer promotes, consumers have the opportunity to buy the product. The same is true for distributors, wholesalers, brokers, or agents. If they carry the product, they help push it down to retailers.

According to Ernst & Young, between 7 percent and 10 percent of sales revenues received from all branded goods are spent on trade promotions. In other words, for every dollar of sales, 7 to 10 cents has been spent on trade promotions.[2]

In marketing consumer goods, the same survey indicates that the amount spent on trade promotions has grown from 38 percent of total promotional expenditures in the

> ▶ **Trade allowances**
> ▶ **Trade contests**
> ▶ **Trade incentives**
> ▶ **Training programs**
> ▶ **Vendor support programs**
> ▶ **Trade shows**
> ▶ **Specialty advertising**
> ▶ **Point-of-purchase advertising**

FIGURE 10.2
Trade Promotional Tools

1980s to approximately 50 percent today. Although it is difficult to estimate the exact amount spent on trade promotions, there is no doubt manufacturers devote more money to trade promotions than to any other promotional tool. Many manufacturers would like to reduce these expenditures or cut them out entirely. What they find, however, is a situation in which they can do neither because of resistance from retailers, directions from their own sales managers, the effects on profits, and pressures from competitors that still offer trade promotions.

To be effective, trade promotions should be an integral part of the IMC program. Unfortunately, in most companies, the individual handling trade promotions is not involved in the IMC planning process. These companies often view trade promotions as being merely a means for getting products onto retail shelves or satisfying some channel member's request. To satisfy the administration's demand to increase sales, trade managers often feel greater and greater pressure to use trade promotions to push their products. Little consideration is given to the other components of the IMC program when trade promotions programs are developed.

To solve this problem, the marketing executive must explain the benefits of a systematic approach to all parts of the marketing mix to company leaders. Tie-ins between ad campaigns and trade promotions programs can help companies achieve more "bang" for their marketing bucks. The account executive also has a vested interest in bringing the trade promotions program in line with the other parts of the IMC plan, because the goal is to generate tangible sales and other measurable outcomes.

A variety of trade promotional tools exists. These items are used by manufacturers as well as other members of the trade channel. Figure 10.2 lists the most common promotional tools.

TYPES OF TRADE PROMOTIONS

Individual companies select trade promotions techniques based on a variety of factors. These include the nature of the business (manufacturer versus distributor), the type of customer to be influenced (e.g., selling to a retailer versus selling to a wholesaler), company preferences, and the objectives of IMC plan being used. Each type of trade promotion offers various benefits. A review of the major categories follows.

Trade Allowances

The first major type of trade promotion manufacturers and others use in the channel is a trade allowance. **Trade allowances** can be packaged into a variety of forms, including the four described in Figure 10.3. The purpose of a trade allowance is to offer financial incentives to other channel members in order to motivate them to make a purchase. The channel member then is in a better position to offer discounts or other deals to their customers.

> ▶ **Off-invoice allowance:**   A per-case rebate paid to retailers for an order
> ▶ **Drop-ship allowance:**   Money paid to retailers who bypass wholesalers or brokers for preplanned orders
> ▶ **Slotting fees:**   Money paid to retailers to stock a new product
> ▶ **Exit fees:**   Money paid to retailers to remove an item from their SKU inventory

FIGURE 10.3
Trade Allowances

An **off-invoice allowance** encourages channel members to place orders, because they receive a financial discount on each case ordered. Companies often use these types of allowances during holiday seasons to encourage retailers to purchase large quantities of various items. Orders must be placed by a specific date to receive a holiday off-invoice allowance. Manufacturers also can place a minimum order size as a further condition. Off-invoice allowances are a common trade promotion and are used extensively because they help accomplish many IMC objectives.

A second type of trade allowance is called a **drop-ship allowance**. As defined in Figure 10.3, a drop-ship allowance is money paid to retailers who are willing to bypass wholesalers, brokers, agents, or distributors when making preplanned orders. Passing the middle members of the channel benefits both the manufacturer and retailer. Profit margins can increase for both the manufacturer and the retailer. Instead of keeping the larger margin a drop-ship allowance offers, retailers can pass along the savings to consumers by lowering prices.

Drop-ship allowances have other advantages. For instance, by shipping merchandise directly to the retailer, a stronger relationship with the retailer results. Also, the manufacturer does not have to rely on the middle person to handle various transactions. The manufacturer also does not need to give additional effort, trying to make sure the middle person will push the manufacturer's brand. When wholesalers represent several manufacturers, they either push all equally or, more likely, push the brand that makes them the most money.

The primary disadvantage of bypassing a wholesaler or distributor is that a wholesaler who handles other products for the manufacturer may retaliate by either dropping the manufacturer or not pushing its other products. Manufacturers must try to avoid damaging relationships with wholesalers when using drop-ship allowances.

Perhaps the most controversial form of trade allowance is a slotting fee. **Slotting fees** are funds paid to retailers to stock new products. Retailers justify charging slotting fees in several ways. First, retailers must spend money to add new products to their inventories and to stock the merchandise. If the product is not successful, the investment in initial inventory represents a loss, especially when the retailer has stocked a large number of stores.

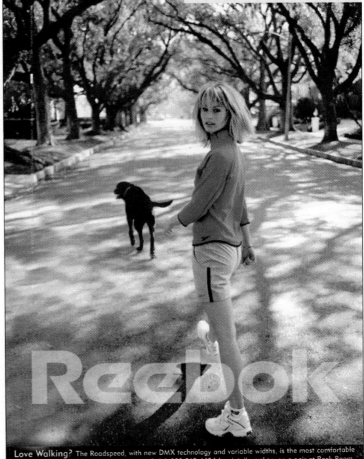

Trade allowances are an important component of Reebok's integrated marketing plan.
Source: Courtesy of Reebok.

Get Carried Away... with Ott's

New products, such as a new salad dressing (even from an existing line such as that offered by Ott's) are charged slotting fees.

Source: Used with permission of the *Joplin Globe*, Joplin, Missouri.

Second, adding a new product in the retail store means allocating shelf space to it. Because most shelves are already filled with products, adding a new product means either deleting another brand or product or reducing the amount of shelf space allocated to other products. Regardless of the method used, the retailer has both time and money invested when making the adjustment for the new product.

Third, slotting fees make it easier for retailers to finalize decisions about new products. The typical supermarket, which carries 40,000 SKU (stock-keeping units), must evaluate at least 10,000 new products per year. The amount of money a manufacturer is willing to pay to get a product on the shelf indicates the manufacturer's faith in that new product. For some stores, slotting fees are as much as $25,000 per item. Some national chains charge slotting fees in the millions. A manufacturer that does not believe the product will succeed is reluctant to invest millions of dollars in slotting fees. Consequently, retailers contend that slotting fees force manufacturers to conduct careful test marketing on products before introducing them.

The other issues lead to the fourth reason for charging slotting fees. Retailers support slotting fees because they reduce the number of products introduced each year. This, in turn, drastically reduces the number of new-product failures. Fifth, and finally, slotting fees add to the bottom line. Many products have low margins or markups. Slotting fees provide additional monies to support retail operations. It has been estimated that 20 percent to 40 percent of the net profits earned by retailers come from trade promotion monies.[3]

The other side of the argument comes from manufacturers, which claim slotting fees are practically a form of extortion. Many manufacturers believe slotting fees are too high and are unfair in the first place. These fees force manufacturers to pay millions of dollars to retailers that could be used for advertising, sales promotions, or other marketing efforts. Slotting fees virtually prohibit small manufacturers from getting their products on store shelves because they cannot afford them. Although some large retail operations have small vendor policies, getting merchandise on their shelves still is extremely challenging. For example, one small manufacturer experienced a drop in sales from $500 per day to only $50 per day when its shelf space was reduced. A large national manufacturer paid the store a large slotting fee, which took space away from the smaller firm.[4] In addition to keeping small manufacturers out of the market, slotting fees favor incumbent suppliers. New entrants into the market face tremendous investment of up-front money already, and then they must add on slotting fees. Unless they are absolutely sure their brand will compete, a new competitor may decide not to enter a market simply because of slotting fees.

A fourth approach to granting a trade allowance is called an exit fee. **Exit fees** are monies paid to remove an item from a retailer's inventory. This approach is often used when a manufacturer wants to introduce a new size of a product or a new version, such as a 3-liter bottle of Pepsi or Pepsi One. PepsiCo already has products on the retailer's shelves. Adding a new version of the product involves lower risk and is not the same as adding a new product. Rather than charging an up-front fee such as a slotting allowance, retailers ask for exit fees if the new version of the product fails or if one of the current versions must be removed from the inventory.

Disadvantages of Trade Allowances

Although trade allowances are key incentives used to build relationships with retailers, there are some disadvantages. These include:

1. Failing to pass along allowances to retail customers
2. Forward buying
3. Diversion

First, in extending trade allowances to retailers, manufacturers assume that a portion of the price reduction will be passed on to consumers. This occurs less than 50 percent of the time. In the majority of cases, retailers charge consumers the same price and pocket the allowance.[5] When a portion of the price allowance is passed on to consumers, retailers often schedule competing brands, so they can have at least one deal going at all times. It is not an accident that one week Pepsi offers a reduced price and the next Coke offers a discount. The two products are rarely promoted **on-deal** (passing along trade allowance discounts) at the same time. By offering only one on-deal at a time, the retailer always has a reduced price competitor for the price-sensitive consumer. The retailer also can charge the brand-loyal consumer full price 50 percent of the time. While accomplishing these goals, the retailer receives special trade allowances from both Pepsi and Coke.

Another problem trade allowances create is the practice of forward buying. **Forward buying** occurs when a retailer purchases excess inventory of a product while it is on-deal. The retailer then sells the on-deal merchandise after the deal period is over, saving the cost of purchasing the product at the manufacturer's full price. Forward buying provides two options to the retailer. First the retailer can choose to extend price savings to customers by selling the product cheaper than its competitors. The second option is to charge full price for the product. This increases the retailer's margin of profit on the product, because the company purchased the merchandise at a reduced price. The disadvantage of forward buying to retailers is the additional costs of holding inventory, which are known as the *carrying charges* associated with the merchandise. The decision to forward buy and

Trade allowances are common in the apparel industry.
Source: Courtesy of Diesel Jeans.

TRADE PROMOTIONS

Ethical Issues and Trade Promotions

When creating trade promotions programs, the marketing professional encounters numerous ethical concerns. Slotting fees are a controversial form of trade allowance. These fees, which are paid to entice retailers to stock new products, may be viewed as a standard and acceptable business practice or as almost a form of extortion.

At the same time, forward buying and diverting are used by retailers to enhance their profit margins. Both practices defeat the purpose of trade allowances provided by manufacturers. In addition, most trade allowances given to retailers are never passed onto consumers. Instead, they are pocketed by the retailer. As long as the retailer holds the balance of power in the distribution channel, these types of questionable behavior will continue unless manufacturers band together. That type of action, however, is considered collusion and is illegal.

In the 1950s and 1960s, manufacturers controlled the distribution channel. They controlled what retailers sold, how they sold it and what price they sold it for. Retailers who dared violate a manufacturer's policy were removed from the manufacturer's list of customers. For a large manufacturer, this could spell doom for the small retailer.

Because of the intense competition in the distribution channel, ethical behavior is often dictated by the need to earn a profit and for some, the need to survive. While legal, are retail actions such as slotting fees, forward buying, and diverting ethical?

how much to forward buy depends on the potential additional profit that can be earned compared to the additional costs and carrying charges for inventory.

Another practice retailers engage in is diversion. **Diversion** occurs when a retailer purchases a product on-deal in one location and ships it to another location where it is off-deal. For example, a manufacturer may offer an off-invoice allowance of $5 per case for the product in Texas. Diversion tactics mean the retailer purchases an excess quantity in Texas and has it shipped to stores in other states. As with forward buying, retailers have to examine the potential profits they can earn compared to the cost of shipping the product to other locations. Shipping costs tend to be relatively high compared to trade allowances offered. Consequently, retailers do not use diversion nearly as much as forward buying.

Although these three disadvantages are important considerations, many manufacturers still conclude that they must grant trade allowances in order to succeed. As a result, they remain a major part of the retail distribution process.

Trade Contests

To achieve sales targets and other objectives, manufacturers sometimes use trade contests. Rewards are given as contest prizes to brokers, retail salespeople, retail stores, wholesalers, or agents. These funds are known as **spiff money**. The rewards can be items such as luggage, a stereo, a television, or a trip to an exotic place such as Hawaii. Contests can be held at various levels, such as:

1. Brokers versus brokers
2. Wholesalers versus wholesalers
3. Retail stores within a chain versus one another
4. Retailer store chains versus other retail chains
5. Individual salespersons within retail stores versus one another

In other words, the contest can be between brokers or agents who handle the manufacturer's goods. It can be for wholesalers, or it can be a sales volume contest among individual retail stores. Although contests can be designed between retail organizations (e.g., Target versus Wal-Mart), they are seldom used because of conflict of interest policies in many large organizations. Buyers in large organizations are often prohibited from participating in vendor contests because they create conflicts of interest and unfairly influence their buying decisions. Although this is exactly what a contest is designed to accomplish, many large retail organizations do not want buyers participating, because they may make purchase decisions for 500 to 2,500 stores. This places undue pressure on the buyer.

When conducting a contest at the individual store level, most channel members agree that these contests work best when restricted to a specific region. Many times, they are also limited to exclusive dealerships, such as auto, truck, or boat dealers that sell a particular brand.

The final type of trade contest is among salespeople in various retail outlets. The goal of this type of trade contest is to encourage salespeople to push the manufacturer's brand over competing brands. These types of contests are quite popular among salespeople and are common in many industries such as those producing durable goods (refrigerators, boats, dishwashers, etc.).

Trade Incentives

Trade incentives are similar to trade allowances. The difference is that trade incentives involve the retailer performing a function in order to receive the allowance. Figure 10.4 lists various trade incentives and their definitions. The goals of trade incentives vary. Therefore, the primary purpose for most plans is to encourage retailers either to push the manufacturer's brand or to increase retailer purchases of that brand.

The most comprehensive trade incentive is the **cooperative merchandising agreement (CMA)**, which is a formal agreement between the retailer and manufacturer to undertake a cooperative effort. The agreement can involve a certain number of advertisements by the retailer that also mentions the manufacturer's brand. Another approach is to feature the manufacturer's brand as a price leader. Also, a cooperative agreement can be made to emphasize the manufacturer's brand in an in-house offer made by the retail store or a special shelf display featuring a price incentive. The advantage of the CMA agreement in featuring various price breaks is that the manufacturer knows that the retailer passes the price allowance on to the customer. One final form of CMA is a special in-store display that the retailer agrees to use on certain dates or for a specific time period. For example, when Coors beer features a display featuring supermodel Heidi Klum at

---

▶ **Cooperative merchandising agreement (CMA):** An annual incentive contract to pay retailers for advertisements, special displays, or price features for the manufacturer's brand over a period of time

▶ **Corporate sales program (CSP):** A promotion across a manufacturer's total brand portfolio with products usually shipped directly from the factory in ready-to-display pallets

▶ **Producing plant allowance (PPA):** An incentive to a retailer to purchase full or half truckloads directly from the factory

▶ **Back haul allowance (BHA):** Monies paid to retailers that send their own trucks to the manufacturer to pick up merchandise

▶ **Cross-dock or pedal run allowance:** Monies paid to retailers for placing full truck orders for multiple stores that can be distributed by a single truck from the manufacturer

▶ **Premium or bonus pack:** Free cases of merchandise for placing an order within a specified time period or for ordering a specific quantity

FIGURE 10.4
Trade Incentives

Halloween, a special cooperative merchandising agreement may be reached with individual liquor stores to get them to set up the displays.

CMAs are popular with manufacturers because the retailer must perform a function in order to receive money. Consequently, the manufacturer retains control over the functions performed. Also, if price allowances are made as part of the CMA, the manufacturer knows that the retailer passes a certain percentage of the price discount on to the consumer. Further, CMAs allow manufacturers to create annual contracts with retailers. These longer-term commitments reduce the need for last-minute trade incentives or trade allowances.

Possibly the most important benefit of a CMA to a manufacturer is that it creates trade incentives designed to support specific marketing objectives and also can be incorporated into an overall IMC plan. Cooperative merchandising agreements allow the manufacturer to plan the trade promotional component of the integrated marketing communications program rather than relying heavily on trade promotions to accomplish short-term, last-minute goals.

CMAs also benefit retailers. The primary benefit of a CMA from the retailer's perspective is that it allows them to develop calendar promotions. **Calendar promotions** are promotional campaigns the retailer plans for customers through manufacturer trade incentives. By signing a CMA, a retailer can schedule the weeks a particular brand will be on sale and offset the other weeks with other brands. By using calendar promotions, the retailer will always have one brand on sale while the others are off-deal. Calendar promotions allow the retailer to rotate the brands on sale. This arrangement is attractive for price-sensitive customers, because one brand is always on sale. For the brand-loyal consumer, the retailer carries the preferred brand at the regular price sometimes and on sale at others. By arranging sales through trade incentives, the margins for the retailer are approximately the same for all brands, both on-deal and off-deal, because they rotate. Retailers can effectively move price reductions given to the customer to the manufacturer rather than absorbing it themselves. A store may feature Budweiser on-deal one week and Heineken the next. Loyal beer drinkers stay with their preferred brand, while price-sensitive consumers can choose the on-deal brand, and the liquor store retains a reasonable markup on all beers sold.

A **corporate sales program (CSP)** is another form of trade incentive. CSPs are offered primarily by highly specialized manufacturers. The CSP is a promotion across a manufacturer's total brand portfolio. The manufacturer ships individual products to the retailer in ready-to-display pallets. As a result, the retailer does not have to prepare the merchandise for display, because it is already on a pallet. These display pallets work well for warehouse stores or retailers such as automobile parts stores in which decor is not a critical issue. By offering the incentive on all of the manufacturer's brand, the manufacturer encourages the retailer to carry all of its brands and not just some of them.

When a manufacturer offers a retailer an incentive called **producing plant allowance (PPA)**, the retailer purchases a full or half truckload of merchandise in order to receive a major discount. The high cost of shipping means manufacturers always look for ways to reduce these costs. Making stops at a dozen retail stores costs more than stopping at only one or two. Smaller manufacturers or highly specialized manufacturers that typically sell through a distributor or some other type of middle person use PPAs. For these manufacturers, in addition to saving money on transportation, the retailer and manufacturer can save money that would normally have gone to the distributor. The only time a large manufacturer such as Procter & Gamble uses PPAs is for small retailers that typically purchase small quantities. Grocery stores, furniture outlets, and sporting goods stores may hold "truckload clearance" sales occasionally to raise volume and increase interest in the retail outlet.

Another form of trade incentive is called a **back haul allowance (BHA)**. A BHA is granted when the retailer pays the cost of shipping. The primary difference between a PPA and a BHA is that the retailer, instead of the manufacturer, furnishes delivery trucks. With the back haul allowance, the retailer gets a much greater incentive allowance but also absorbs the cost of shipping.

For small retailers with multiple stores, a **cross-dock or pedal run allowance** can be obtained. These allowances are paid to retailers for placing a full truck order, which is then divided among several stores within the same geographic region. For example, if a small grocery chain has eight stores within a 50-mile radius, the company can order a full truckload of merchandise from a manufacturer and divide the groceries among the stores. One of the keys to the cross-dock allowance is that each store accepts a full pallet. No pallets have to be broken, making it faster to load and unload goods.

The final type of trade incentive is a **premium or bonus pack**. Instead of offering the retailer a discount on the price, the manufacturer offers free merchandise. For example, a manufacturer may offer a bonus pack of one carton for each 20 purchased within the next 60 days. The bonus packs are free to the retailer and are awarded either for placing the order by a certain date or for agreeing to a minimum-size order. Often, to receive the free merchandise, the retailer must meet both stipulations, a specified date, and a minimum order size.

Trade incentives are often tied in with consumer sales promotions. For example, to generate interest in the Chrome Visa card developed by Harley-Davidson motorcycles, Harley-Davidson launched the Harley Dream Sweepstakes for consumers and a trade incentive program for retailers. At the consumer level, a new Big Twin motorcycle was awarded each week for 52 weeks. Chrome Visa cardholders received one entry into the sweepstake for each dollar spent, and H-D raised the amount to two entries per dollar spent in participating Harley retail stores. To encourage Harley retailers to push the Chrome Visa credit card and place the display on their counters, Harley-Davidson created a trade incentive. For each customer who filled out the Chrome Visa card application and was subsequently approved, the retailer received a $20 credit toward Harley-Davidson merchandise for the store.[6]

Harley-Davidson launched the Harley Dream Sweepstakes using both trade and consumer promotions.
Source: Courtesy of Corbis/SABA Press Photos, Inc. Photograph by Laura Kleinhenz.

Training Programs

Another type of trade promotions program involves providing training. Manufacturers often provide training programs to the members of the sales staff at a retailer location or to wholesalers. Manufacturers are willing to provide training to these salespeople, because they learn more about the manufacturer's brand. This makes it more likely that the retail or wholesale sales force will push the manufacturer's brand instead of a competitor's product. Having additional knowledge about one brand over other brands biases salespeople toward that brand.

To compete in the highly competitive software market, Microsoft launched a training program aimed at value-added resellers. The training program was entitled "Helping Clients Succeed." The three-day workshop was designed to help resellers better understand Microsoft software. Traditionally, Microsoft's field representatives concentrated on technology. Resellers tended to focus on providing solutions to customer problems. The primary goal of the training program was to encourage resellers to utilize Microsoft's factory representatives in consultative selling.[7] While SBLI focused on training at the retail level, Microsoft focused on training at the reseller or wholesaler level.

Vendor Support Programs

Vendor support programs are trade promotions manufacturers offer to support a retailer, wholesaler, or agent's programs. Naturally, vendor support programs are designed to support the vendor's activities that most favor the manufacturer. The two most frequently used vendor support programs are billbacks and co-op advertising. In a **billback** program, the manufacturer pays the retailer for special product displays, advertisements, or price cuts. In this case, the retailer or wholesaler initially pays for the display, advertisement, or price cut. Then the retailer or wholesaler bills the manufacturer for the activity, thus the term *billback*. The primary advantage of the billback to the manufacturer is that the retailer is willing to perform a function on behalf of the manufacturer in order to receive the trade incentive. The second advantage is that the retailer or wholesaler pays full price for the merchandise sold and bills the manufacturer only for the support program.

The more common vendor support program is co-op advertising. In a **cooperative advertising program**, the manufacturer agrees to reimburse the retailer a certain percentage of the advertising costs associated with advertising the manufacturer's products in the retailer's ad. To receive the reimbursement, the retailer follows specific guidelines concerning the placement of the ad and its content. In almost all cases, no competing products can be advertised. In most cases, to receive the reimbursement, the manufacturer's product must be displayed prominently. There may be other restrictions on how the product is advertised as well as specific photos or copy that must be used.

In most cooperative advertising programs, retailers accrue co-op monies based on purchases. This is normally a certain percentage of sales. For example, B.F. Goodrich, a manufacturer of automobile tires, offers a 4.5 percent co-op advertising fund on all purchases. This money can be accrued for one year, then it starts over again. B.F. Goodrich pays 70 percent of the cost of an approved advertisement. Any of the media can be used for the advertisement such as radio, newspaper, magazines, television, and outdoor. This unlimited media choice does not hold true for all manufacturers. For example, Dayton, another tire manufacturer, does not allow magazine advertisements to be used for co-op advertising dollars. B.F. Goodrich allows group ads for co-op monies; Dayton does not. Further, Dayton requires preapproval for some of the media buys and advertisements while Goodyear does not require any preapprovals. Thus, each manufacturer has its own set of restrictions that must be followed if the retailer wants to qualify for co-op monies.[8]

Each year manufacturers offer an estimated $25 billion in co-op money to retailers, of which only about two-thirds is claimed. Why does almost $8 million go unclaimed? Some of the more common reasons include:

1. The manufacturer rejects co-op claims because of errors in filing.
2. Purchase accruals are tracked inaccurately.
3. Retailers are unaware of a co-op program.
4. Restrictions placed by the manufacturer are not followed correctly.[9]

Although errors do occur in the filing of claims, the more common reasons for not collecting are that purchase accrual records were not kept accurately or that retailers simply were not aware that a cooperative program was in place. Figure 10.5 provides examples of common co-op types of situations.

Cooperative advertising programs are used heavily by automobile manufacturers such as Volkswagen.

Source: Courtesy of West & Vaughan, Inc.

Volkswagain.

Remember everything you heard about the new Volkswagen Beetle in the '50's?

This time it's even better. See for yourself at Southern States Volkswagen. 2421 Wake Forest Road. (919)828-0901.

Remember everything you heard about the new Volkswagen Beetle in the '60's?

This time it's even better. See for yourself at Southern States Volkswagen. 2421 Wake Forest Road. (919)828-0901.

Remember everything you heard about the new Volkswagen Beetle in the '70's?

This time it's even better. See for yourself at Southern States Volkswagen. 2421 Wake Forest Road. (919)828-0901.

▶ **Best Buy and Hewlett Packard**

▶ **Goody's and Dockers**

▶ **Ace Hardware and Tru-Test Products**

▶ **Intel and IBM**

▶ **Toshiba and HP**

▶ **Motorola and Skytel**

▶ **JC Penney and Reebok**

▶ **Sprint and Radio Shack**

▶ **Radisson Hotels and TGI Fridays**

FIGURE 10.5
Cooperative Advertising

Many cooperative advertising programs allow accrual of co-op monies over a year; however, some manufacturers restrict when the times co-op dollars can be spent. For example, a firm that produces snowblowers probably would provide co-op dollars only during the fall and winter. The rest of the year people rarely buy snowblowers, so the funds would not be spent wisely.

Keeping track of co-op dollars is difficult. One firm, the Archer–Malmo Advertising company, uses the Internet to track co-op dollars for companies such as Samsung Electronics, Pennzoil Corporation, General Electric, and RCA. Each firm reports co-op expenditures online. Retailers can then access these statements and view how much money is available in co-op funds along with the deadline (usually annual) by which the remainder must be spent. To make it more user friendly, the firm now makes it possible for retailers to submit claims online. Retailers can also download manufacturer's graphics and logos for various ads. This use of the Internet is likely to increase in the future. Using the Internet simplifies the co-op process for both the retailer and the manufacturer.[10]

The Intel Corporation provides probably the largest co-op advertising program in the world. Intel spends about $750 million a year to promote the "Intel inside" theme. Intel offers a 6 percent co-op fund to all PC makers that place the Intel logo on their computers. Further, Intel allows a 4 percent fund accrual on the cost of print ads featuring the Intel inside logo and provides 2 percent for television and radio ads featuring the Intel video or audio tag. This accrued co-op money can be used to pay up to 66 percent of the cost of a print advertisement or 50 percent of the cost of a broadcast ad. Intel cuts any payment in half for any advertisement that features a third-party logo of any type to ensure it is the only co-op brand featured in an ad. Approximately 1,400 PC makers worldwide as well as the top 10 PC makers take advantage of the Intel co-op advertising program.[11]

Co-op advertising programs benefit most retailers because retailers are able to use manufacturer dollars to expand advertising programs. In a co-op ad, the retailer gains additional ad coverage at minimal cost. Retailers also benefit from the image of a national brand, which can attract new or additional customers to the store. From the retailer's perspective, there is little to lose in co-op programs. The only negative side is that the retailer is reimbursed following the placement of the ad.

Manufacturers also benefit from co-op ads. Manufacturers gain additional exposure at reduced costs, by sharing ad costs with retailers. More importantly, almost all co-op advertising programs are tied to sales. The retailer accrues co-op advertising dollars based on a certain percentage of sales. Thus, to get the co-op money, the retailer must not only promote the brand prominently but also purchase the product for resale. As a result, it is not surprising to see the wide variety of cooperative advertisements appearing so regularly in all media, for both consumer products and business-to-business ads.

Over $12 billion are spent on trade shows each year.

Source: Courtesy of Liaison Agency, Inc. Photograph by Jeff Scheid.

Trade Shows

In business-to-business marketing, total expenditures on trade shows ranks third, with only advertising and sales promotions receiving greater funding. Over $12 billion are spent on trade shows each year. Manufacturers spend between $70,000 and $100,000 to attend a major trade show; this includes airline fees, hotels, entertainment costs, booth fees, and equipment. Retailers pay about $600 per person for those who attend trade shows.[12]

From a manufacturer's standpoint, a trade show offers the opportunity to discover potential customers and sell new products. Also, relationships with current customers can be strengthened at the show. A trade show often provides the chance to find out what the competition is doing. Many times, trade shows present a situation in which the manufacturer's sales team can meet directly with decision makers and buyers from business-to-business clients. A trade show can be used to strengthen the brand name of a product as well as the company's image.

From the retailer's perspective, a trade show allows buyers to compare merchandise and to make contact with several prospective vendors in a short period of time. In some cases the retailer can negotiate special deals. Trade shows are an ideal place for buyers and sellers to meet in an informal, low-pressure situation to discuss how to work together effectively.

Some national and international trade shows are attended by thousands of buyers. To be sure the trade show is successful, manufacturers seek out key buyers and try to avoid spending too much time with nonbuyers. Narrowing down the large number of contacts to those most promising is called *prospecting*. Figure 10.6 identifies five categories of buyers who attend trade shows. It is important to weed out the education seekers who are not interested in buying. Manufacturers should concentrate their efforts on three groups: solution seekers, buying teams, and power buyers. Asking the right questions identifies solution seekers and buying teams. The power buyers are more difficult to identify because they don't want to be identified. They often do not wear badges at trade shows so vendors do not know who they are. The Communication Action box in this section provides more information about how to make the most of a trade show.

In the United States, few deals are finalized during trade shows. Buyers and sellers meet, discuss, and maybe even negotiate, but seldom are buys completed. Instead, manu-

> ▶ **Education seekers:** Buyers who want to browse, look, and learn but are not in the buying mode
>
> ▶ **Reinforcement seekers:** Buyers who want reassurance they made the right decision in past purchases
>
> ▶ **Solution seekers:** Buyers seeking solutions to specific problems and are in the buying mode
>
> ▶ **Buying teams:** A team of buyers seeking vendors for their business; usually are in the buying mode
>
> ▶ **Power buyers:** Members of upper management or key purchasing agents with the authority to buy

FIGURE 10.6
Five Categories of Buyers Attending Trade Shows

COMMUNICATION ACTION

Making the Most of a Trade Show

Trade shows require a substantial investment of time, money, and personnel. To make sure these funds are spent wisely, one well-known writer recommends several key tasks and ideas to complete and implement.

1. Ask the right questions. Among other things, this means asking open-ended questions to help you find out if the buyer is serious or browsing. Avoid pat questions such as "May I help you?" which usually draws a response of "No, just looking."

2. Spend time with the right attendees. The MAN profile works best, whereby money, authority, and need (in the budget) direct the booth worker to the correct prospect. Make sure the person in the booth can actually afford the products he or she is viewing.

3. Be a careful listener. Keep notes because most sales do not take place at the actual show, but rather months later. Identify the customer's needs and special circumstances to effectively close the deal in a later follow-up contact.

4. Know the difference between a person who is an actual prospect and someone who is just a "name" on a business card. Instead of spending too much time "pitching" the product, invest your energy in finding out what customers are looking for, and then make sure to follow up later to fill those needs.

5. Do not bombard potential clients with literature. They will probably throw it away anyway. Instead, give a small fact sheet, and send major mailings to their office later, where they are much more likely to actually review the materials you send, especially if they contain a well-written cover letter.

6. Avoid overcrowding a booth with materials. In one 1999 small appliance trade show, a company displaying only seven products sold more merchandise than the company in the next booth, which offered over 50 items. Keep it simple, so the potential customer can handle the goods and become more interested as a result.

7. Pay attention to matters such as "booth etiquette" and body language. Do not stand with your arms folded, and do not eat, drink, or make phone calls while on duty. Keep the booth area clean and not crowded with briefcases and empty coffee cups. Dress appropriately for the show.

Effective booth management also should tie in with the firm's image and IMC program. The goal is to build sales and long-term relationships as various companies spend the time and energy needed to attend trade shows.

Source: Dale English, "On Displays," *Business First, Western New York,* 16, no. 9 (November 29, 1999), p. 31.

facturers collect business cards as leads to be followed up later; however, the procedure varies for international customers.

Several differences exist when international companies attend trade shows.[13] The first major difference is that international attendees tend to be senior executives with the authority to make purchases. They fit into the power buyer category listed in Figure 10.6. American manufacturers must understand that the international attendee often wishes to conduct business during the trade show, not afterward. The second contrast is that international attendees spend more time at each manufacturer's booth. They stay longer in order to gather and study information in greater detail. Because of the travel expense involved, the international guest wants more in-depth information than an American counterpart usually needs. The increase in international participants has caused trade show centers to set up more meeting spaces, conference centers, and even places to eat where buyers and sellers can meet to discuss buys.[14] The number of international trade show visitors has increased dramatically in the past decade.

NAME THAT WEED

Signalgrass is just one of many weeds that Pennant® prevents. So now you can choke out your worst weeds without beating up on ornamentals and warm-season turf.

P E N N A N T

©1992 CIBA-GEIGY Corporation. Always read and follow label directions.

Many pesticides are featured in agricultural trade shows.

Source: Courtesy of Howard, Merrell & Partners.

Trade shows have changed in other ways. Large national and international shows are being replaced by niche shows. For example, in the 1990s, many mega-sports trade shows were attended by everybody in the sporting goods business. For instance, the National Sporting Goods Association World Sports Expo in Chicago attracted over 90,000 attendees during the mid-1900s. The number has dwindled to fewer than 40,000 today. Now manufacturers and retailers attend specialty trade shows that focus on only one sport. Smaller shows are cheaper to set up, and individual companies believe they are much more effective in making viable customer contacts. Many have concluded that it is too easy to be lost in the crowd at the bigger shows.[15]

The decision on whether to attend a general national show or a specialty show depends on the objective the firm wishes to accomplish. When the goal is to enhance the firm's brand or corporate name, generally large national shows are the best. When the goal is to expand a market base beyond the regional or current customers, a national show works well. On the other hand, specialty shows are better in three situations, most notably when the goal is to:

1. Establish a client base quickly
2. Establish a new brand
3. Promote a new product

Manufacturers should look beyond the numbers when choosing trade shows. Large trade shows may have a greater number of attendees, but if the attendees do not fit the profile of a manufacturer's customers the show will not be profitable. One easy method of finding out if the attendees match a manufacturer's customer profile is to talk to customers and competitors to discover which trade shows they attend. Before spending thousands of dollars on a show, a manufacturer should find out who attends and how well the show fits with the firm's goals and target market. Trade shows should match with the objectives of the overall IMC program as well as other marketing tools that are being used.

STOP

INTEGRATED LEARNING EXPERIENCE

The best resource for trade shows can be found at **www.tsnn.com**. Information about the overall trade show industry is available as well as articles about trade shows in specific industries. Explore the Web site for items that would benefit manufacturers attending trade shows. What information is available to retailers or other attendees of trade shows? Next, look for trade shows that will be held in your area during the next few months. Another valuable source of information is the *TradeShow Week Magazine* at **www.tradeshowweek.com**. What additional information is at this site? Read about trade show trends and the article archives available at this site.

Specialty Advertising

Specialty advertising, also known as *giveaways,* can be integrated into an IMC program to provide an additional feature designed to impress customers. These gifts, such as pens, coffee mugs, calendars, key chains, and many others, have the name of the firm

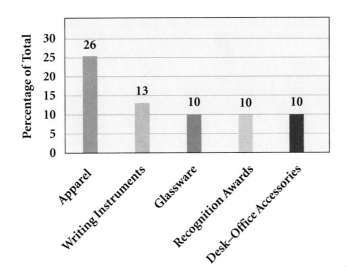

FIGURE 10.7
Top Categories in Specialties Advertising

imprinted on them. The items sometimes include a message, logo, or tag line. These messages are tied in with the advertising theme.

A promotional gift provides the customer with a constant reminder of the company. No other IMC tool can remain with a customer over such a potentially long period of time. A coffee mug with the firm's name and logo might be used every day. A shirt imprinted with the company's logo will be seen by dozens of people. Figure 10.7 displays the top five types of gifts given to customers.

Specialty advertising gifts are often distributed at trade shows, by salespeople, or via direct-mail campaigns. Companies spend almost $12 billion annually on promotional items.[16] The concept behind specialty gifts is **reciprocation**. Whenever someone receives a gift, the human desire is to return a gift or favor. In business, this psychological advantage can be used in a number of ways. At a trade show, promotional gifts create a positive impression of the business. Care must be taken, however, to ensure the gift conveys the intended message. For example, if one booth hands out a plastic mug to trade show attendees, while the next one gives a porcelain mug, attendees get different impressions of the two vendors. The tendency would be to view the business giving the plastic cup more negatively, meaning the gift actually worked against the company that gave it.

One of the best strategies in selecting advertising specialties is to make sure the item is unique and conveys the company's message. For example, at one trade show a cotton gin company gave away miniature bales of cotton with its logo printed on the bale. The item was not really useful, but it was unique. In another setting, a florist gave a rose to each woman attending a Latino businesswomen's conference. Both times the gift served its purpose by being unique enough to gain attention but also by focusing on the company's product.[17]

Specialty gifts can help reinforce buying decisions. In other words, they can make a customer feel that he or she made a good choice. Gifts can strengthen business relationships and also help stimulate interest from a new potential prospect. In general, specialty gifts can be an important means of strengthening communications with all types of customers.

Point-of-Purchase Advertising

Point-of-purchase (POP) advertising is any form of special display that advertises merchandise. POP displays are often located near cash registers in retail stores, at the end of an aisle, in a store's entryway, or any other place where they will be noticed. Point-of-purchase advertising includes displays, signs, structures, and devices used to identify, advertise, or merchandise an outlet, service, or product. POP displays should serve as an important aid to retail selling.

POP displays are very helpful when selling products such as cosmetics, perfume, or cologne.
Source: Courtesy of Bijan Fragrances, Inc.

The store shelf and point-of-purchase display represent the last chance for the manufacturer to reach the consumer.[18] They can be used to make an impression just before a purchase is made or to leave an impression when the buyer exits the store. More than 55 percent of mass-merchandisers and 60 percent of supermarket shoppers remember seeing a point-of-purchase display immediately following a trip to a retail outlet.

POP displays are highly effective tools for increasing sales. About 50 percent of the money spent at mass-merchandisers and supermarkets is unplanned. Often these purchases are *impulse buys.* When consumers make purchases, they often do not decide on the particular brand until the last minute. For food purchases, 88 percent of the decisions about brands are made in the store at the time of the purchase. For all products, 70 percent of brand choices are made in the store. In many instances, point-of-purchase materials influenced the decision.

Coca-Cola reports that only 50 percent of soft drink sales are made from the regular store shelf. The other 50 percent result from product displays in other parts of the store. American Express found that 30 percent of purchases charged on the American Express card came from impulse decisions by customers seeing the "American Express Cards Welcome" sign. Other research indicates that an average increase in sales of 10 percent occurs when one POP display is used and 22 percent when there are two. Consequently, POP advertising is very attractive to manufacturers.[19]

Currently, manufacturers spend more than $13 billion each year on point-of-purchase advertising materials. The largest users of POP advertising are restaurants, food services, apparel stores, and footwear retailers. The fastest-growing categories are fresh, frozen, or refrigerated foods, and professional services.[20]

Manufacturers view POP displays as an attractive method of getting a brand more prominently displayed before customers. Many retailers have a different perspective. Retailers believe POP materials should either boost sales for the store or draw customers into the store. Retailers are not interested in the sales of one particular brand, but instead want to improve overall sales and store profits. Retailers prefer displays that educate consumers and provide information. As a result, retailers are most inclined to set up POP displays to match their objectives. Several factors cause retailers to leave POP materials unused. Some of these problems are shown in Figure 10.8.

The most common reason retailers do not use displays furnished by manufacturers is that they are inappropriate for the channel. In other words, a display that works well in a discount store may not be appropriate for a supermarket or a specialty store. Various retailers and channel members have different needs in terms of what they want in a POP display design. Manufacturers should consult with each type of channel member to ensure the display meets these needs.

The size of a display is important to retailers. Store space is limited, and customers do not respond well when freestanding displays at the end of aisles block traffic through the store. Consequently, individual retailers normally will use only POP displays that fit the allocated space. Retailers prefer easy to assemble, easy to stock, and adaptable dis-

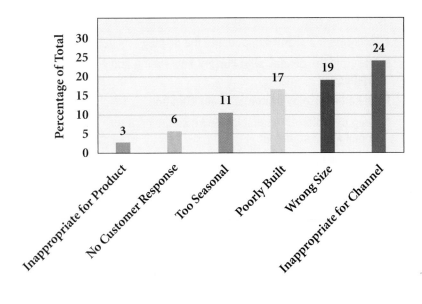

FIGURE 10.8
**Top Weaknesses of Manufacturer-
Supplied POP Displays**

plays. Consequently, manufacturers must remember that if a retailer does not like a display, it won't be used, no matter how great it looks.

Retailers want displays to be durable. Corrugated cardboard (which is often used) tends to wear out and tear. Poorly built displays are often thrown away. Retailers do not have time to repair displays. They also take down worn, shabby-looking exhibits. Retailers give preference to manufacturers offering customized displays for individual stores.

To be effective, POP displays must communicate the product's attributes clearly. Pricing and other promotional information is also useful. The display should encourage the customer to stop and look, pick up the product, and examine it. A customer who stops to examine a product on display is more likely to buy it. The best POP displays are those integrated with other marketing messages. Logos and message themes used in advertisements should appear on the POP. The POP display should reflect any form of special sales promotion. Customers more quickly recognize tie-ins with current advertising and promotional themes as they view displays.

Recent research indicates that POP displays increase sales when they have the following ingredients:

▶ Brand signs

▶ Base wrap under the display

▶ Standee (base of support)

▶ An inflatable component or mobile above the POP display

▶ A tie-in to a sport, movie, or charity shown on the display

Of these, the tie-in adds most significantly to sales.[21]

The POP display should make a clear, succinct offer that customers immediately understand. Many times the POP display only has three-tenths of a second to capture the customer's attention. If it fails, the customer simply moves on to other merchandise. Colors, designs, merchandise arrangements, and tie-ins with other marketing messages are critical elements of effective POP displays.[22] Figure 10.9 lists some additional pointers for point-of-purchase advertising.

Three new trends are present in the use of POP displays:

1. Integration with Web site programs

2. Displays that routinely change messages

3. Better tracking of POP results

> ▶ **Integrate the brand's image into the display**
>
> ▶ **Integrate the display with current advertising and promotions**
>
> ▶ **Make the display dramatic to get attention**
>
> ▶ **Keep the color of the display down so the product and signage stand out**
>
> ▶ **Make the display versatile so it can be easily adapted by retailers**
>
> ▶ **Make the display reusable and easy to assemble**
>
> ▶ **Make the display easy to stock**
>
> ▶ **Customize the display to fit the retailer's store**

FIGURE 10.9
Effective POP Displays

Each of these items represents key changes in POP programs. A review of these issues follows.

The first new trend is integrating POP displays with the Internet site and Web address of the company. For example, Tucker Federal Bank distributed POP materials to its 14 branch banks encouraging people to sign up for a free checking service. The display encouraged people to go to the bank's Web site. The URL, **www.justrightbank.com**, was integrated with the advertising tag line "Not too big. Not too small. Just right." Customers who visited the bank's Web site could complete and submit the application for free online checking. Effective integration of e-messages involves more than just printing a Web address on the POP display. The company should encourage customers to go there for a specific reason, such as was the case with Tucker Federal.[23]

The second trend in POP advertising is developing displays with the capability of changing the message. Messages are changed daily, weekly, or, in some extreme cases, several times per day. One method manufacturers use to accomplish these changes is by featuring LED electronic signs, which can be changed via computer. This allows the manufacturer or retailer to offer new messages more frequently to keep the POP fresh to consumers. To the retailer, the big advantage is that messages can be localized and designed to meet changing local needs. To the manufacturer, it offers an opportunity to partner with retailers in looking for ways to maximize sales.[24]

The third issue is accountability. Both retailers and manufacturers look for methods to measure the effectiveness of POP displays. Retailers have limited space and can set up only a fraction of the displays sent to them. They want to use the most effective displays. Manufacturers invest money into building, shipping, and promoting POP displays. The manufacturer wants its display to be utilized and not set in a storeroom or simply thrown away. Thus, it is in the best interests of both parties to develop methods for measuring effectiveness.

One method to measure results is tying the POP display into a point-of-sale (POS) cash register. Items on the display are coded so that the POS system picks them up. Then individual stores measure sales before and during a POP display program by using cash register data. The data also help the retailer decide when to withdraw or change a POP display due to slumping sales. This technology allows retailers to identify the POP displays with the largest impact on sales. A retailer even could use this method to test-market different types of POP displays in various stores. The most effective displays can then be rolled out nationally.

From the manufacturer's viewpoint, using POS data can help it improve POP displays. It also provides the opportunity to strengthen a partnership with the retailer. This bond helps the manufacturer weather poor POP showings, because the retailer may stay with a manufacturer that tries to develop displays of benefit to both parties.

Internet trading may have reduced some retail store traffic. Still, many customers shop and window-shop frequently. A POP advertising program remains an important ingredient in selling to the end user and in strengthening bonds with retailers as part of a larger trade promotions effort.

INTEGRATED LEARNING EXPERIENCE

Point-of-purchase displays should be an important component of a firm's IMC program. Research indicates that effective POP displays have a positive impact on sales. Access the following firms that produce POP displays.

Melrose Display Inc. (www.melrosedisplays.com)
Visy Displays (www.visydisplays.com)
Vulcan Industries (www.vulcanind.com)
Display Design & Sales (www.displays4pop.com)
Acrylic Designs, Inc. (www.acrylicdesigns.com)

Which firm's site is the most attractive? Which firm would be the best from the standpoint of developing displays for manufacturers? For retailers?

OBJECTIVES OF TRADE PROMOTIONS

The trade promotions manager should be included in the planning stages of the IMC program. This increases the chances that trade promotions and incentives will be effectively coordinated with the other components of the IMC process. Regrettably, the process is more difficult than it appears, because manufacturers and retailers have objectives that differ from each other and from those of distributors.

For manufacturing operations, the primary goal is to increase sales of their brands. Retailers, on the other hand, try to increase the market shares of their stores. Retailers may be less concerned with which brand sells the most. Instead, they promote the brands that have the highest sales or contribute the most to profits. Often retailers play one manufacturer against another to see which one will offer the best deal. Therefore, manufacturers are limited in which trade promotions they can or cannot use by the retailers who sell their products. This problem becomes even more complicated when a wholesaler or distributor is involved. These organizations also have specific goals related to volume and profit.

Figure 10.10 lists the major objectives of trade promotions from the manufacturer's perspective. At times one takes precedence over another, but each one may be a key goal for a given trade promotions effort. These objectives are described next.

> ▸ **Obtain initial distribution**
> ▸ **Obtain prime retail shelf space or location**
> ▸ **Support established brands**
> ▸ **Counter competitive actions**
> ▸ **Increase order size**
> ▸ **Build retail inventories**
> ▸ **Reduce excess manufacturer inventories**
> ▸ **Enhance channel relationships**
> ▸ **Enhance the IMC program**

FIGURE 10.10
Objectives of Trade Promotions

Obtaining Initial Distribution

When a firm begins operations, enters a new territory, or seeks to expand into global markets, one primary concern is finding retail outlets to carry the product. The company must be able to develop a distribution network through either a "pull" or a "push" strategy. *Demand pull* occurs when advertising and publicity causes consumers to become aware of a product's availability. These individuals then ask retailers if they carry the product, which leads the retailer to become more interested in it. A *push strategy* is the result of aggressive marketing efforts by the manufacturer to entice retailers to consider placing the product on its shelves. One goal of a trade promotions effort is to assist in this form of push strategy. Trade shows, slotting fees, vendor support programs, specialty advertising, and point-of-purchase displays help a manufacturer gain a wider audience for a new product.

Obtaining Prime Retail Shelf Space or Location

Retail shelf space is critical in selling merchandise. Simply stated, a manufacturer that cannot get its products onto retailer shelves will not sell merchandise. Quality spots of shelf space mean higher sales. A manufacturer who has 24 inches of prime shelf space is likely to do better than a company given only 10 inches of shelf space. To get quality space and more space means manufacturers must be willing to provide incentives to retailers in the form of trade promotions in addition to providing products with high consumer demand. Trade allowances, contests, training programs, and trade incentives can assist in capturing and maintaining quality shelf space.

Companies such as Keebler often use trade promotions in conjunction with consumer promotions such as coupons.
Source: Courtesy of Keebler Company.

Supporting Established Brands

Trade promotions efforts often are used to increase shelf space for current, well-established products. Even in situations where the manufacturer merely tries to maintain current shelf space, trade promotions are needed to keep competitors from taking retail space. More often than not, the competition continually tries to find ways to offer retailers a better deal. This forces manufacturers to make sure they stay on top of what is happening in order to maintain quality shelf space and lead the retailer to support established brands. For instance, if a new competitor were to enter the potato chip market, that manufacturer would logically spend considerable funds seeking to push out more established brands, such as Lays and Frito-Lay. These chip suppliers would be interested in maintaining superior locations on grocery store and convenience store shelves. Every trade promotions tool can be used to support established brands.

Countering Competitive Actions

Manufacturers often use trade promotions to counter a competitive action. The competitive action may be a trade promotion deal being offered by the competition to retailers, a consumer promotion, an aggressive advertising campaign designed to increase demand pull, or some other promotional effort. To ensure channel members do not emphasize the competition instead of their products, manufacturers offer some type of trade promotion that matches the competition's effort or that is attractive to the channel member. This can become a vicious spiral in which manufacturers pump more and more dollars into trade promotions just to keep up with one another.

On the other hand, failing to fend off competitive threats has even greater consequences. A firm helps its own cause by taking care of other parts of the business relationship, such as by meeting delivery deadlines, providing support services to retailers, accepting returns without problems in crediting retailer accounts, entering into cooperative advertising agreements, and other activities designed to build strong ties between the two organizations. Each time the competition acts, the manufacturer chooses to use either the same trade promotions tactic or another form designed to counteract the competition's efforts.

Increasing Order Sizes

Another goal of trade promotions programs is to push an individual brand through the channel of distribution in such a way that order sizes increase. Manufacturers primarily use trade allowances and sales contests to increase order sizes. The objective may be to increase the order size from either the retailer or the distributor. Occasionally, a POP will induce a larger order from the retailer, if the display features a major advertising campaign or a key season for the product, such as starter fluid for barbecue grills featured in the summer.

Building Retail Inventories

Another marketing goal can be to build retail inventories, thus preempting the competition. A large retail inventory of a particular brand should result in the retailer pushing that particular brand over competing brands. Trade allowances that lead to forward buying or diversions may actually help reach the goal of larger retail inventories. Other parts of the IMC plan, such as advertising and consumer sales promotions, also drive the retailer to hold larger inventories in anticipation of increased retail sales.

Reducing Excess Manufacturer Inventories

Trade promotions help manufacturers reduce inventory levels. This often occurs near the end of a fiscal year or near the end of an evaluation period when sales have not met forecasts. To ensure a quota is met, a manufacturer offers retailers an especially attractive trade promotion deal. This in turn helps reduce excess manufacturer inventories.

Enhancing Channel Relationships

Manufacturers also utilize trade promotions to enhance relationships with other channel members. Contests, allowances, incentives, giveaways, and training all make the relationship between the manufacturer's sales rep and the company's buyers more personal and intimate. Maintaining positive relationships is especially important if the competition also is heavily involved in granting trade promotions.

Trade promotions are important in developing international markets.
Source: Courtesy of Electrolux.

Enhancing the IMC Program

Finally, trade promotions should be used to enhance other IMC efforts. If a manufacturer plans a massive consumer promotion campaign, it makes sense to support the consumer sales promotion effort with trade promotions. The same is true for a major advertising campaign. Manufacturers spending large amounts of money on advertising campaigns want to be sure their products are available in stores. Manufacturers also try to be sure certain retailers promote the product with desirable shelf space or end-of-aisle displays. To obtain these more desirable locations normally requires a more concerted trade promotions effort. It is important to remember that the company's image and theme should be enhanced not only through clever advertisements but also through the other elements of the promotions mix, including trade promotions incentives.

INTEGRATED LEARNING EXPERIENCE

Trade promotions are an important element in accomplishing IMC objectives. Many firms turn to speciality agencies or full-service agencies to handle trade promotions programs. The same agency often handles the sales promotion component and manages trade promotions in order to ensure the two mesh together. Look up the following firms to see what type of trade promotion services they offer. What appears to be each agency's strengths? While reviewing the various trade promotions objectives discussed in this chapter, which agency appears to be the best selection, given those objectives?

C-E Communications (www.cecom.com)
Co-op Communications, Inc. (www.coopcom.com)
TradeOne Marketing (www.tradeonemktg.com)
Sable Advertising Systems (www.sableadvertising.com)

CONCERNS IN USING TRADE PROMOTIONS

Beyond manufacturers, every other member of the marketing channel should also work to incorporate trade promotions into overall IMC efforts. This occurs only if top management buys into the integrated marketing communications concept and insists on including the trade promotion manager on the marketing team. The manager must also make sure all the team members work together with a common marketing agenda.

In most organizations, employee pay structures encourage the use of trade promotions irrespective of the IMC plan. Sales managers face quotas, and if sales fall behind, the easiest way to boost them is to offer retailers a trade deal. Further, companies often evaluate brand managers based on the sales growth of a brand. The easiest way to ensure continuing sales growth is to offer trade deals. The pattern of using trade deals to reach short-term quotas rather than long-term image and theme building will not change until top management adopts a new style. The IMC approach will only succeed when a long-term horizon is considered and compensation structures change to accommodate this long-term view of success.

To illustrate why a change in management philosophy is necessary, consider the following situation. A sales manager or brand manager has one month left in the fiscal year and is 12 percent behind on a sales quota. To ensure the quota is reached, the sales manager requests a trade deal to encourage retailers to buy excess merchandise. In the short term, the goal has been achieved. In the long run, however, the brand's image may have eroded. It takes a long-term perspective for management to say that increasing trade promotions to meet the quota is not part of the IMC plan and should not be done. Eroding brand image to meet short-term goals is not in the company's best long-term interest. If a strong brand image can be developed, retailers will stock the brand with fewer trade deals because it pulls customers into their stores.

Meanwhile, as company leaders consider ways to include trade promotions into an overall IMC plan, they need to be aware of potential problems associated with trade promotions programs. These include:

1. Costs
2. The impact on small manufacturers
3. Overreliance on trade promotions to move merchandise
4. The potential erosion of brand image

The first major concern is the cost of trade promotions. Manufacturers spend billions of dollars per year on trade promotions. In turn, these costs are often passed on to consumers in the form of higher prices. It is estimated that 13 cents out of every dollar spent for frozen food items goes directly for the cost of trade promotions. Seven to 10 percent of the price for all brands pays for trade promotions.[25] Therefore, management must try to keep these costs at a reasonable level and make sure the money is spent wisely. Rather than simply getting into "bidding wars" with competitors, the company should use trade promotions dollars to build relationships and achieve key IMC goals.

The second major concern with trade promotions is their impact on small manufacturers. When the cost to get an item initially stocked in a store ranges anywhere from $1,000 to $20,000, large manufacturers have the advantage. They can afford to invest more heavily in trade allowances. Only eight of the top 15 retailers in the United States have programs that allow small vendors opportunities to stock their merchandise. Figure 10.11 displays both types of retailers. Although these retailers have special programs for small manufacturers, there is no guarantee they will get shelf space when a large manufacturer such as General Mills offers millions of dollars in trade incentives such as slotting fees and cooperative advertising programs (including coupon redemption programs).[26] Small-scale manufacturers must discover creative ways to gain shelf space, both in major retail chains and through smaller vendors. It is clearly a challenging part of the process, but one that must be addressed in order to achieve long-term success.

The third major concern is that the use of trade promotions has led to a situation in which merchandise does not move until a trade promotions incentive is offered. In the grocery industry, an estimated 70 percent to 90 percent of all purchases made by retailers are on-deal with some type of trade incentive in place. The constant use of deals has trimmed manufacturer margins on products and created competitive pressures to conform. If a manufacturer tries to quit or cut back on trade promotions, retailers replace the manufacturer's products with other brands or trim their shelf space to allow more room for manufacturers offering better deals. For example, Procter & Gamble cut back on trade promotions in an effort to sell more products off-deal to boost profit margins. In a retaliatory action, Safeway cut some of the less popular P&G sizes and brands from its stores. Curbing trade promotional expenditures is extremely difficult because trade promotions

Retailers with Small Vendor Programs	Retailers with No Small Vendor Programs
▶ Wal-Mart	▶ Circuit City
▶ Sears	▶ Consumer-Electronic
▶ Sam's Warehouse	▶ Office Depot
▶ Price Costco	▶ Service Merchandise
▶ Target	▶ Wal-Mart Supercenter
▶ Home Depot	
▶ Toys "R" Us	

FIGURE 10.11
Retailers and Small Vendor Programs

are a critical part of moving goods from manufacturers to retailers. Manufacturers will have to use trade promotions more wisely, to ensure they accomplish the intended IMC objectives.[27]

The fourth major concern with trade promotions is that they can cause the erosion of a brand's image. As more and more money is pumped into trade promotions, less money is spent on advertising. As discussed in Chapter 2, brand image is built through intensive advertising and high product quality. When advertising expenditures are cut, consumers no longer seek out specific brands in their purchase decisions. Instead, they choose from brands viewed as being equal in quality (called brand parity). The situation worsens when trade promotions discounts are passed on to consumers. At that point, brands already seen as being equal are selected only on the price or discount being offered. Instead of choosing a specific brand with superior attributes, consumers make the purchase decision based on price, and brand image no longer has any meaning.

The best way to correct these problems is to spend more on advertising focused on rebuilding a brand's image. Also, it is important to be certain promotions fit the brand's image. "If it doesn't fit," writes Brian Sullivan in *Marketing News,* "don't use it."[28] Unfortunately, to spend more on advertising means cutting trade promotions incentives. The risk becomes that other competitors will move in by offering trade promotions to retailers, and shelf space will be lost as a result. Then, the vicious cycle begins again.

The management of trade promotions programs is a challenging part of the marketing planning process. Effective IMC programs achieve a balance between all elements of the promotions mix and identify clear goals and targets for trade promotions programs. Only then is the company able to compete on all levels and not just through a cycle of trade promotions bidding wars.

SUMMARY

The marketing mix consists of four basic components: (1) advertising, (2) trade promotions, (3) consumer promotions, and (4) personal selling. Trade promotions are the primary tool members of the marketing channel use to push products onto retailer shelves. Any time a product is being promoted for resale, a trade promotions program is being utilized.

A wide variety of trade promotions programs exists, including trade allowances, trade contests, trade incentives, training programs, vendor support programs, trade shows, specialty advertising, and point-of-purchase displays. Several major factors affect the choice of promotional tool, most notably:

- Standard practice in the industry
- Competitive pressures
- Company preferences
- Marketing goals and objectives

Common objectives for trade promotions programs include obtaining distribution for new products, gaining prime retail space, supporting established brands, countering the competition, increasing order sizes, enlarging retailer inventories or reducing manufacturer inventories, enhancing channel relationships, and building on other parts of the IMC program. Various trade promotions tools match with these goals.

The major issue facing marketers who work with promotional programs is making sure the promotions match overall IMC goals. They should be coordinated with advertising expenditures and campaigns and balanced with other parts of the promotions mix. Trade promotions are costly and place enormous pressures on small manufacturers. Many wholesale and retail firms simply will not place orders for merchandise until a trade promotions incentive is offered. Company leaders must work diligently to build and maintain brand image and not fall into the trap of simply engaging in competitive trade promotions bargaining to retain retail space. Instead, brand image and strong relationships with various vendors can counterbalance competitor attempts to steal space merely by offering a short-term price discount.

As with all of the other ingredients of an IMC plan, the primary task is to develop a coordinated and balanced plan of attack to reach the marketplace with one clear message. Trade promotions must be included in the process and not dominate marketing expenditures to the point that other aspects of the marketing mix are neglected. When this balance is achieved, the company can compete in the long term for better position with other members of the channel as well as retail customers. Maintaining the vision to see long-range goals is one key element in managing trade promotions.

REVIEW QUESTIONS

1. What is a trade promotions program? How is it related to other elements of the marketing mix?

2. What is the difference between trade promotions and consumer sales promotions?

3. Describe the four main types of trade allowances and the goals they are mostly likely to achieve. Which is the most controversial? Why?

4. What is forward buying? Why is it a problem for manufacturers?

5. What is a diversion tactic? Why are diversions used less frequently than forward buying?

6. What is spiff money?

7. Name and briefly describe the various forms of trade contests. Which is the least likely to be used?

8. Name and briefly describe the major forms of trade incentives. Which ones involve retailers paying some of the costs first, before receiving compensation?

9. Why are training programs considered to be a form of trade promotion? What objectives will a quality training program be most likely to achieve?

10. What is a billback?

11. What advantages do cooperative advertising programs hold for manufacturers? For retailers?

12. Why have smaller specialty trade shows begun to replace larger, more general shows?

13. How are international attendees different from local attendees at a trade show? What should a manufacturer do to meet these differences?

14. What are the five top giveaways associated with specialty advertising? How are they related to the concept of reciprocation?

15. What are the characteristics of a high-quality, effective POP display?

16. What are the major objectives manufacturers try to achieve with trade promotions programs? Are these objectives different than those of wholesalers or distributors? Why or why not?

17. What problems are associated with trade promotions programs? How can manufacturers overcome these problems?

18. How should a retailer respond to trade promotions incentives? Should retailers try to get manufacturers involved in bidding wars? Why or why not?

19. What role should trade promotions play in the overall IMC plan?

KEY TERMS

trade promotions the expenditures or incentives used by manufacturers and other members of the marketing channel to help push their products through to retailers.

trade allowances financial incentives offered to another channel member to motivate it to make a purchase.

off-invoice allowance a financial incentive offered to a channel member to place an order and receive a discount on each case ordered.

drop-ship allowance money paid to retailers who are willing to bypass wholesalers, brokers, agents, or distributors when making preplanned orders.

slotting fees funds paid to retailers to stock new products.

exit fees monies paid to remove an item from a retailer's inventory.

on-deal when a price allowance is being given as part of a trade promotions program.

forward buying when a retailer purchases excess inventory of a product while it is on-deal.

diversion when a retailer purchases a product on-deal in one location and ships it to another location where it is off-deal.

spiff money rewards given as contest prizes to brokers, retail salespeople, retail stores, wholesalers, or agents.

trade incentives given when the retailer performs a function in order to receive the discount or allowance.

cooperative merchandising agreement (CMA) a formal agreement between the retailer and manufacturer to undertake a cooperative effort.

calendar promotions promotional campaigns retailers plan for their customers through manufacturer trade incentives.

corporate sales program (CSP) a form of trade incentive offered by highly specialized manufacturers.

producing plant allowance (PPA) a trade incentive in which the retailer purchases a full or half truckload of merchandise in order to receive a major discount.

back haul allowance (BHA) a trade incentive whereby the retailer pays the cost of shipping and the retailer, instead of the manufacturer, furnishes delivery trucks.

cross-dock or pedal run allowance monies paid to retailers for placing a full truck order that is then divided among several stores within the same geographic region.

premium or bonus pack given by offering the retailer free merchandise rather than a discount on the price.

billback the manufacturer pays the retailer for special product displays, advertisements, or price cuts.

cooperative advertising program the manufacturer agrees to reimburse the retailer a certain percentage of the advertising costs associated with advertising the manufacturer's products in the retailer's ad.

reciprocation a psychological concept that whenever someone receives a gift, the human desire is to return a gift or favor.

point of purchase (POP) any form of special display that advertises merchandise.

CRITICAL THINKING EXERCISES

Discussion Questions

1. One type of trade show that has received considerable publicity recently is the gun show. While some gun trade shows are restricted to only retailers, others allow anyone to attend. What is your evaluation of gun shows? Should they all be restricted to only retailers?

2. AgrEvo Environmental Health held a trade contest to launch a new line of DeltaGard low-dose formulations. DeltaGard is an insecticide sold to pest control companies and retailers. To encourage pest control companies to purchase DeltaGard, AgrEvo teamed up with Harley-Davidson and developed the DeltaGard Win-a-Harley Sweepstakes. Entry forms were available only to licensed pest control companies and were featured at the annual National Pest Control Association trade show, at official AgrEvo DeltaGard distributors, on the AgrEvo Web site, and in a series of advertisements that ran during the trade contest. First place was a Harley-Davidson motorcycle valued at over $12,000. Second place was a Harley-Davidson leather jacket. Third place was a Harley-Davidson wristwatch.[29] Was this trade contest a good idea? Would every pest control company be motivated by the prizes offered? Could this trade contest be improved to create greater participation?

3. Debate has continued for many years about the use of slotting fees by retailers. Recently, the U.S. Congress examined the practice when it considered them to potentially restrict free trade. Using an academic search engine, locate some recent articles about slotting fees. Should they be permitted, or should laws be passed restricting or even eliminating them?

4. Study a recent Sunday or Wednesday newspaper. How many cooperative advertisements are present? What brands does the retailer's advertisement promote? Are these advertisements effective from the viewpoint of the manufacturer? How effective are they for the retailer?

5. Go to a nearby retail store. How many POP displays are present? Which ones are the most impressive? Why? Which ones did not succeed in gaining your interest? Why? Return to the same store a week later. How many new POP displays are there? Which ones are still up?

6. Interview a retail store manager about trade promotions used at his or her store. Especially discuss POP displays and trade allowances. Find out what percentage of the POP displays received are not used. Why are others not used? What criteria does the store manager use in deciding?

7. From the list of stores in Figure 10.11, pick one that is close by. Interview the manager about the store's small vendor program or lack of a small vendor program. Report the findings to your class.

8. Access the Trade Show News Network at www.tsnn.com. Pick one trade show from each of the following categories:

   a. Apparel
   b. Boating and yachting
   c. Gender specific
   d. Photography
   e. Physical fitness and health

   Find out the following information about each trade show. Evaluate it as being potentially successful or a waste of time for the exhibitor and the attendee.

   f. Type of show
   g. Location of show
   h. Show date
   i. Number of exhibitors
   j. Number of attendees
   k. Names of exhibitors
   l. Names of the attendees

9. Access the Trade Show News Network at www.tsnn.com. Pick one category of trade shows from the list in Exercise 8. Assume you are a small manufacturer in that industry. Locate five trade shows that would be feasible to attend as an exhibitor. Evaluate each one. If you could afford to attend only one, which show would you choose? Why?

10. Access the Trade Show News Network at www.tsnn.com. Pick one category of trade shows from the list in Exercise 8. Assume you are a buyer for a retail outlet. Locate five trade shows that would be feasible to attend as a buyer. Evaluate each one from the viewpoint of a buyer.

Matching Trade Promotions Tactics with an IMC Advertising Campaign

With an integrated approach, there will be a tie-in between the advertising campaign you employ and the trade promotions offered. These include all the kinds of discounts that are passed along to retailers as well as other items. Does your product lend itself to a point-of-purchase display? What other incentives can you offer to the retailer to lead the company to prominently display and emphasize the product you are selling? If a wholesaler distributes your product, what incentives should you offer to encourage the wholesaler to push your product through the channel? What kinds of trade promotions can be used for services, if that was the thing you decided to promote? To help you work out these issues, both in domestic markets and internationally, complete the exercise for Chapter 10 by accessing the IMC Plan Pro software included with this textbook or by accessing the Web site at www.prenhall.com/clow.

BUILDING AN IMC CAMPAIGN

IMC PlanPro

CASE 1

WATERBED WORLD

Bernice Kepford prepared for an important staff meeting with her clients at Waterbed World, knowing that the next year or two would be crucial in that company's life. Bernice's advertising agency had long served Waterbed World in a fairly simple fashion, preparing print ads for trade journal advertising campaigns. Now, however, the company needed a strong boost to sales.

Waterbed World began as a small "head shop" operation in the early 1970s. At that time, the owner sold posters, black lights, subversive literature, and drug paraphernalia. As a side product, the local company (in Fort Myers, Florida) also carried waterbeds. At the time, the quality of the product was low and it was not the store's main feature. Later, as waterbed quality improved, the owner decided an upscale clientele would be more profitable. He relocated Waterbed World to a freestanding store near a major mall. Salespeople began to wear dresses and suits, and the store sold waterbeds along with quality furniture and other higher-markup items.

In the early 1980s, Waterbed World acquired a mattress manufacturer, and the seamless waterbed mattress became the company's most visible product. Waterbed World expanded to sell its mattresses and frames on a national level. Traveling sales reps visited waterbed stores throughout the country and the firm grew quickly to a major scale. Three primary promotional tools were used: (1) trade shows for furniture and waterbeds, (2) trade journal advertisements, and (3) personal selling techniques of the traveling reps.

As the millennium ended, interest in waterbeds had begun to diminish. The beds had a loyal set of consumers, but the increased quality of regular mattress and air mattresses provided substantial competition. The owner of Waterbed World believed the company needed to move the product into other, more mainstream, markets in order to survive. Specialty waterbed stores were not the answer.

The company asked Bernice to create a trade promotions campaign to go along with consumer ads for Waterbed World's products. The goal was to expand the sales of mattresses and frames into furniture stores, and even into places such as Wal-Mart's Supercenters and Sam's Club outlets. No distributors or wholesalers would be involved. Waterbed World wanted to sell directly to an entirely new set of retailers.

Consumer ads would promote two features: (1) better sleep and (2) healthy rest. They would portray other mattresses as less comfortable and harder on the joints and back as the person sleeps. Ads also would emphasize product quality and customer support.

One of Bernice's primary concerns was how the company could convince various retailers that waterbeds would bring in potential customers and generate profits for the stores. She knew retail space was limited, especially for such large items.

1. What trade promotions tools should Bernice recommend? Which ones would not work?

2. How can Waterbed World integrate this new emphasis on retail accounts with consumer sales promotions and advertising?

3. What obstacles will Waterbed World encounter as the firm makes this move into new markets?

THE CHRISTMAS RUSH

Musa Pinar, the promotions trade manager for Galactic Toys, knows his firm is in for a new experience. Galactic Toys is a highly successful company in its home country, Turkey. In that region, the toy business is not as strongly dictated by the successes and failures of films and is not quite as dominated by the Christmas season. In an effort to build sales and "test the waters," Musa has been asked to study the U.S. toy market to see if the firm's biggest-selling line, Galaxy Conquest toys, could compete effectively.

In the United States, each year over half of all toy purchases are made at the retail level during November and December. The summer movie schedule provides some clues as to which "fad" toys are most likely to succeed. Any new *Star Wars* film boosts sales of its figures, and the same is true for *Star Trek, Toy Story,* and many others. A second set of toys has a more annual and traditional base, including Barbie, GI Joe, as well as standard board games and more generic products such as Lincoln Logs and Legos. These products are updated to keep them more current and are staples for several manufacturers in the industry.

Seasonal toys are featured in major trade shows every summer. Major companies set up booths and hold extravagant release campaigns for new products and other innovations. The media are invited and a feature story can become the lifeblood of a new fad product. Cabbage Patch Dolls, Teenage Mutant Ninja Turtles, Tickle Me Elmo, and Furby toys have created near riotous conditions in various retail outlets following successful media campaigns in the pre-Christmas publicity season. Toys tied to movies enjoy the additional benefits of the Halloween costume season ahead of actual toy sales.

Toy buyers can be distributed roughly into four categories. First, those who buy for small children tend to rely on major name brands, such as Fisher-Price and Playskool. At a slightly older age, Tonka toys are big sellers. Second, grade-school-age children constitute the primary market for fad and trendy toys. Parents view many of these products as "status symbols" as much as they are playthings for kids. Thus, owning a Furby represents not only a fun toy, but a major one-upmanship factor for parents who want their kids to have everything. The third set of buyers tends to purchase more staple toys. These shoppers are often lower-income families who cannot afford the more extravagant prices paid for the season's hottest item or parents who simply withdraw from the "keeping up with the Joneses" mentality associated with high-status toys. Fourth, junior-high-age kids now buy more sophisticated technology-based toys, especially Nintendo products.

Galactic Toys would normally be placed in the GI Joe–*Star Wars* section of toy store shelves. Individual products are high-quality, but reasonably priced for more staple buyers who are less driven by trends and more inclined to seek out items that do not break easily. The problems Musa believes the company will experience are:

▶ Gaining attractive booths at major trade shows

▶ Breaking through the publicity campaigns of major fad toys, to build interest by various stores

▶ Convincing retailers that Galactic Toys are more year-round, and less seasonal, products (e.g., toys for birthday gifts and other minor celebrations or occasions)

To succeed, Musa thinks he should start with the trade shows themselves. He attended a few shows and noticed glamorous women dressed in attractive fashions showing off dominos and checkerboards. He watched the video presentations, saw giveaways, and examined other attention-seeking devices. Next, Musa subscribed to all key trade journals and solicited information about prices, locations in magazines, and other information about ads. Third, Musa has been looking for tie-ins with other products, such as breakfast cereals, T-shirts, and others. Still, in his report to company leaders, Musa wrote that making headway in such a tough marketplace is going to be a challenge, even with the company's best efforts.

1. Assess Musa's report.
2. Design a trade promotions campaign and integrate it with a larger IMC program and theme for Galaxy products.
3. Besides trade shows, are there any other trade promotions tools Galactic Toys can use to increase sales?
4. Are there any other special challenges a Turkish toy company will encounter when trying to compete in the United States? What are they?

ENDNOTES

1. Stephanie Thompson, "Red Letter School Days," *Brandweek,* 39, no. 29 (July 20, 1998), pp. 22–25; Susan Greco, "Selling the Superstores," *Inc.,* 17, no. 10 (July 1995) p. 54.

2. Jack J. Kasulis, "Managing Trade Promotions in the Context of Market Power," *Journal of the Academy of Marketing Science,* 27, no. 3 (summer 1999), pp. 320–32; Anthony Lucas, "In-Store Trade Promotions," *Journal of Consumer Marketing,* 13, no. 2 (1996), pp. 48–50.

3. Kasulis, "Managing Trade Promotions in the Context of Market Power."

4. Martin Hoover, "Supermarket 'Slotting' Leaves Small Firms Out," *Business Courier: Serving the Cincinnati-Northern Kentucky Region,* 16, no. 25 (October 8, 1999), pp. 3–4.

5. Philip Zerillo and Dawn Iacobucci, "Trade Promotions: A Call for a More Rational Approach," *Business Horizons,* 38, no. 4 (July–August 1995), pp. 69–76; Jack Mohr and George S. Low, "Escaping the Catch-22 of Trade Promotion Spending," *Marketing Management,* 2, no. 2 (1993), pp. 30–39.

6. Laurie Watanabe, "Duel at Dawn," *Dealernews,* 33, no. 12 (November 1997), p. 59.

7. Michele Marchetti and Andy Cohen, "In Search of Microsoft's Softer Side," *Sales and Marketing Management,* 151, no. 12 (December 1999), p. 20.

8. Roger A. Slavens, "Getting a Grip on Co-op," *Modern Tire Dealer,* 75, no. 3 (March 1994), pp. 34–37.

9. Ibid.

10. Dana Blankenhorn, "Memphis Company Solves Co-op Ad Accounting Problem Online," *Advertising Age's Business Marketing,* 83, no. 12 (December 1998), pp. 3–4.

11. Bradley Johnson, "IBM Moves Back to Intel Co-op Deal," *Advertising Age,* 68, no. 10 (March 10, 1997), p. 4.

12. Jim Martyka, "Sports Trade Shows Shrink, Specialize," *City Business: The Business Journal of the Twin Cities,* 17, no. 13 (August 27, 1999), p. 10; Laurie Freeman, "B-to-B Marketing Communications Budgets Grow 14.5% as Overall Spending Reaches $73 Billion," *Advertising Age's Business Marketing,* 84, no. 5 (May 1999), pp. S3–S4.

13. Matthew Flamm, "Alien Influences," *Crain's New York Business,* 15, no. 46 (November 15, 1999), pp. 35–36.

14. Ibid.

15. Martyka, "Sports Trade Shows Shrink, Specialize."

16. Alastair Goldfisher, "Firms Give Away Everything to Capture Trade-Show Traffic," *Pacific Business News,* 37, no. 3 (April 2, 1999), p. 21.

17. Polyack, "Creativity Is Key to Successful Giveaway Marketing Campaigns," *Business Journal Serving Fresno and the Central San Joaquin Valley,* no. 322532 (November 1, 1999), p. 4.

18. Hilary S. Miller, "P-O-P Has High Recall, Survey Shows," *Beverage Industry,* 85, no. 12 (December 1994), pp. 15–16; Matthew Martinez and Mercedes M. Cardona, "Study Shows POP Gaining Ground as Medium," *Advertising Age,* 68, no. 47 (November 24, 1997), p. 43.

19. David Tossman, "The Final Push—POP Boom," *New Zealand Marketing Magazine,* 18, no. 8 (September 1999), pp. 45–51.

20. Ibid.; Martinez and Cardona, "Study Shows POP Gaining Ground as Medium."

21. "Signposts: The Power of Point-of-Purchase," *Marketing News,* 35, issue 1 (May 21, 2001), p. 3.

22. Alf Nucifora, "Point-of-Purchase Advertising Now a Marketing VIP," *Business Journal [Phoenix],* 19, no. 49 (September 17, 1999), p. 32.

23. Dana James, "Seeing Green," *Marketing News,* 33, no. 24, (November 22, 1999), p. 19.

24. Scott Flom and Mark Mitchell, "New Age of P-O-P Indicates Alliances Make for Good Marketing," *Marketing News,* 33, no. 24 (November 22, 1999), p. 22.

25. Richard Merli, "Retailers and Suppliers Agree: Trade Promo Stinks," *Frozen Food Age,* 48, no. 2 (September 1999), p. 51; Anthony Lucas, "In-Store Trade Promotions," *Journal of Consumer Marketing,* 13, no. 2 (1996), pp. 48–50.

26. Greco, "Selling the Superstores," pp. 55–61.

27. Kasulis, "Managing Trade Promotions in the Context of Market Power."

28. Brian Sullivan, "Make Sure Promotional Items Fit Brand Perfectly," *Marketing News,* 35, issue 19 (September 10, 2001), p. 15.

29. "Harley Sweepstakes Kicks Off AgrEvo's DeltaGard Promotion," *Pest Control,* 65, no. 9 (September 1997), pp. 28–29.

11

Consumer Promotions

Chapter Objectives

Be aware of the goals, advantages, and disadvantages for each promotions program that can be used in marketing a company or product.

Tie consumer promotions with trade promotions and other elements of the promotions mix and then match them to the overall IMC program.

Seek out quality uses of consumer promotions for sales to business-to-business buyers.

Understand the limitations that are present when consumer promotions programs are developed for international customers.

TIME-SHARE VACATION PROPERTIES:
Half-Product–Half-Service Promotions

Leisure time activities and recreation generate major revenues for the economies of various regions, states, and even nations. Many types of organizations attempt to lure tourists into their areas, through hotels, restaurants, theme parks, and other activities. One of the more lucrative parts of tourism is that vacationers spend money in different ways while on trips. Items ordinarily considered too expensive are more readily purchased.

One set of companies that has taken advantage of the desire for quality leisure time is the time-share industry. Basically, time-share property holders own blocks of time for condominiums, apartments, townhouses, or motel rooms in resort towns. Normally a block is one week long. Time-shares are "goods" in the sense that a person buys ownership of the location for the specified time period. A deed is prepared, and usually the ownership can be resold or passed along to heirs when the original owner dies.

Time-shares also are services. The typical time-share agreement includes a clause stating that the owner will pay a "maintenance" fee each year. The fee covers housekeeping, lawn care, and other services the time-share company provides. More importantly, other aspects of time-shares make them truly unique. These time allocations can be traded across nationwide networks of time-share locations. A person can exchange a week in Santa Cruz, California, for a week in Branson, Missouri. The trade involves paying a fee for the swap to the company running the network.

Various weeks of time have more or less "value" depending on the season. For instance, a time-share week in New England during the autumn, when the leaves are changing to their spectacular colors, has more value than a week in the winter. A week in New Orleans during the Mardi Gras season has more value than a week in the middle of summer. Most firms declare weeks of ownership to have one of three levels: (1) peak, (2) regular, or (3) off-season.

Peak season weeks may be traded for all three types, and off-season can usually be exchanged only for off-season times.

Promotion of time-shares involves a variety of tactics. First, the firms advertise heavily in tourist magazines and magazines devoted exclusively to time-share properties. Second, the typical time-share program includes granting a prospective buyer a small period of time (usually one night to a full weekend) to stay free at a time-share property. The prospect must agree to tour the facility and hear the sales pitch in order to receive the free night(s) of lodging. Often, small gifts are given. Meals, fruit baskets, bottles of wine, and other small tokens such as T-shirts and lawn chairs are part of the package.

The tour involves showing the client the property in detail, plus a presentation of all the additional benefits of time-sharing, including the exchange network. Then, at the close of the sale, the prospect is usually offered a one-time, must-buy-today discount to purchase a week of time.

To beef up prospect lists, members of the time-share community are given gifts for bringing in potential buyers. A member may receive extra days or weekends of time for finding prospects. Some are even given "upgrades" for their weeks (e.g., from off-season to regular) for identifying someone who might visit the area.

The exchange program also offers vacations to non-time-share areas, along with coupons and discounts for tours and other activities in tourist areas, such as coupons for meal discounts and reduced-price boat rides at lake resorts.

There is even an after market for time-shares. Many can be resold. Firms that resell time-shares can work either separately from or in conjunction with the time-share management team. These properties normally do not offer the free visits and gifts used to entice first-time buyers of the property.

Competition in the time-share market is intense. Locations that do not fill up the time slots for each room quickly face cash flow problems. Some critics argue the free visits are simply "bait and switch" techniques that cause people who cannot afford to make purchases to spread themselves too thin. Those who enjoy time-share privileges argue the programs are among the best investments in leisure time. As the baby boom generation continues to age and accumulate additional disposable income, the odds are high that time-share companies will continue to prosper. At some point, you may find yourself tempted by a free vacation, a few goodies, and a very polished sales rep seeking to lure you into the exciting world of vacation property ownership.

WILLAMETTE FURNITURE COMPANY

Of the many ways to reach customers beyond advertising programs, consumer promotions are often the most effective. This is because they directly entice customers to make purchases using various kinds of incentives, including coupons, samples, contests, sweepstakes, bonus packs, and price-off deals. These methods should be carefully selected based on the message theme of the company featured in the overall IMC program.

In the Willamette Furniture Company example provided on the IMC Plan Pro disk, consumer promotions are an important feature. The overall budget for consumer objectives is shown in section 5.1. While consumer promotions are not major expenditures, they remain as crucial ingredients in an overall IMC plan. Section 5.2.2 presents the consumer promotions to be used. Notice the emphasis on high quality. Since Willamette is a high-end furniture store, only high-quality premiums should be offered. They must be carefully tied in to personal selling (5.2.3) and other marketing efforts.

o v e r v i e w

Many methods are available to entice consumers to take the final step and make a purchase. Advertising creates interest and excitement and can be used to offer the deal that brings the consumer into the store. At the same time, marketers use other tactics in conjunction with advertising programs. Besides trade promotion incentives offered to retailers, consumer promotions programs can be highly effective in generating sales and building traffic.

Consumer promotions (sometimes called *sales promotions*) are the incentives aimed at a firm's customers. These customers can be end users of the good or service, or they may be other businesses. As noted in Chapter 10, the difference between consumer promotions and trade promotions is that trade promotions are directed at firms that resell the manufacturer's or firm's products. Consumer promotions are directed toward individuals or firms that use the product and do not resell it to another business. Thus, consumer promotions can be used in both consumer markets and business-to-business markets.

The two most general categories of promotions are: (1) *consumer franchise-building promotions* and (2) *consumer sales-building promotions*. Consumer franchise-building promotions are designed to increase awareness of and loyalty to a brand. The goal is to build a favorable image by pointing out unique features and selling points, with the goal being reduced reliance on discounts to entice sales. Sales-building promotions focus on immediate sales, rather than brand equity or loyalty, through discounts, prizes, or other enticements.

Marketing managers must carefully design promotional programs to meet the various IMC goals. In the early stages of a product's life cycle, promotions should match advertising and other efforts designed to achieve brand awareness, create opportunities for trial purchases, and stimulate additional purchases. Later, the goal may shift to strengthening a brand, increasing consumption, fending off competition, or finding new markets. Also, there may be tie-ins with other products designed to build brand equity in both products (e.g., a coupon for a free two-liter bottle of 7-Up in association with the purchase of Seagram's is design to build equity in both "7 and 7" companies).

> ❱ **Coupons**
> ❱ **Premiums**
> ❱ **Contests and sweepstakes**
> ❱ **Refunds and rebates**
> ❱ **Sampling**
> ❱ **Bonus packs**
> ❱ **Price-offs**

FIGURE 11.1
Types of Consumer Promotions

As with other parts of the promotions mix, consumer promotions should be tied into the integrated marketing communications plan. Figure 11.1 lists the most common consumer promotions. A review of each type follows.

COUPONS

A coupon is a price reduction offer to a consumer. It may be a percentage off the retail price such as 25 percent or 40 percent, or an absolute amount ($.50 or $1.00). In the United States, 300 billion coupons were distributed and 4.8 billion redeemed in 1999. This 2 percent redemption rate represents approximately $3.6 billion in savings for consumers, or about 70.2 cents per coupon. Approximately 78 percent of all U.S. households use coupons, and 64 percent are willing to switch brands with coupons.[1]

Nearly 80 percent of all coupons are distributed by manufacturers. Figure 11.2 lists the various forms of coupon distribution. Eighty-eight percent of all coupons are sent out through print media, with 80 percent distributed through **free standing inserts (FSI)**. FSI are sheets of coupons distributed in newspapers, primarily on Sunday. Another 4 percent of coupons are distributed through direct mail, and 3.5 percent more are distributed either on or in a product's package. The remaining 5 percent are delivered in other ways.[2]

Most companies prefer using FSI and print media to distribute coupons for several reasons. First, consumers must make a conscious effort to clip or save the coupon. Second, coupons create brand awareness because consumers see the brand name on the coupon even if they do not actually use the coupon. Third, FSI encourage consumers to purchase brands on the next trip to the store. Manufacturers believe that consumers are more likely to purchase a couponed brand and remember the name when they redeem a coupon. This moves the brand to the consumer's long-term memory. Hopefully, consumers will recall the brand and buy it the next time the need arises, even when they do not have coupons. The S.C. Johnson advertisement on page 340 encourages consumers to buy Windex Multi-Surface using the coupon in the advertisement.

A consumer promotion by Folks Southern Kitchen offering lunch combos for only $5.99.
Source: Courtesy of Sheri Bevil, Bevil Advertising.

> ▶ Print media
> ▶ Direct mail
> ▶ On or in package
> ▶ In store
> ▶ Sampling
> ▶ Scanner delivered
> ▶ Cross ruffing
> ▶ Response offer
> ▶ Internet
> ▶ Fax
> ▶ Sales staff

FIGURE 11.2
Methods of Distributing Coupons

Types of Coupons

Coupons are often distributed in retail stores and placed on or in packages. The consumer immediately can redeem the coupon while making the purchase. This type of coupon is called an **instant redemption coupon**. These coupons often lead to trial purchases and purchases of additional packages of a product. Some coupons are given out along with free samples of a product to encourage consumers to try a new brand. Many grocery stores allow a company to cook a new food product and offer free samples of it along with coupon giveaways. Coupons also are placed in dispensers near various products, which provide convenient access for customers. All of these are forms of instant redemption coupons, because customers can use them immediately.

A manufacturer's coupon from SC Johnson encouraging consumers to purchase Windex Vinegar.

Source: Courtesy of SC Johnson & Son, Inc.

Coupons also can be placed inside packages so that customers cannot redeem them quite as quickly. This approach encourages repeat purchases, and the coupons are called **bounce-back coupons**.

Firms can issue coupons at the cash register. They are called **scanner-delivered coupons**, because they are triggered by an item being scanned. The item being scanned is normally a competitor's product. Firms use this approach to encourage brand switching.

Another way to distribute coupons is cross-ruffing. **Cross-ruffing** is the placement of a coupon for one product on another product. For example, a coupon for a French onion dip placed on a package of potato chips is a cross-ruffing coupon. To be successful, cross-ruff coupons must be on products that fit together logically and usually are purchased and consumed simultaneously. Occasionally, a manufacturer uses cross-ruffing to encourage consumers to purchase another one of its products. For example, the Kellogg company may place a coupon on a Rice Krispies box for another cereal, such as Frosted Flakes or an oatmeal product. This type of couponing tactic encourages consumers to purchase within the same brand or family of products.

Coupons also stimulate trial purchases of new products. Manufacturers send coupons in advance to consumers, making it more likely a trial purchase will follow. Prior to a shopping trip, a consumer may not have decided upon a specific brand to purchase. This means the consumer is more willing to purchase the brand with an introductory coupon mailed to his or her home than if the coupon is available only in the store, where the consumer is less likely to take the time to examine it.

Response offer coupons are issued following requests by consumers. Requests may be via a toll-free number or the Internet. Coupons then are mailed to the consumer or sent by Internet to be printed by the consumer. The coupon can also be faxed. In the business-to-business sector, a fax is the most common method of distributing response offer coupons. Office supply companies and other vendors use response offer coupons to invite business customers to make purchases or place orders. Firms also distribute coupons through their sales representatives, which allows for instant redemptions, because the salesperson also takes the order.

Another form of coupon is one that is *electronically delivered*. The first retailer to offer "U-pons" (paperless, Internet-delivered) was Dick's Supermarkets, which used San Francisco–based Planet U to send out coupons to 50,000 Savings Club members in Wisconsin and Illinois. In that program, redemption rates for baby products averaged 36 percent, cheese and peanut butter 30 percent, bread 24 percent, prepared frozen foods 22 percent, and cookies 20 percent in the first year. U-pons can be sent electronically to the retailer's point-of-sales system. The coupon also has a code printed on it to trace it back to the house where it was used. Consumers using this electronic distribution method click on the coupons they want on their computers while at home. The amount of the coupon discount is automatically deducted from the purchase price through the use of a frequent-shopper card presented at the store.[3]

Coupon Responses

The typical response rate for a coupon distribution is less than 2 percent. Coupon distribution has increased since 1998; however, redemption rates are down. The most common coupons to be distributed are for household cleaners, breakfast cereals, condiments, medications, and prepared foods.[4] Redemption rates for Internet-delivered coupons average more than 20 percent. Research into coupon redemptions helps retailers understand how consumers respond. For example, coupons are not used equally among various ethnic groups. African Americans and Hispanics tend to redeem coupons less than does the population as a whole, because there is a lower distribution rate to certain ethnic groups. Freestanding inserts in Sunday papers account for 80 percent of the distribution of coupons. Minority groups tend to read ethnically oriented newspapers and magazines and are less inclined to subscribe to publications aimed at the general population. Consequently, the FSI do not reach them. Magazines and newspapers targeting individual ethnic groups contain fewer coupon offers than do more general-appeal print media. Lower redemption rates can make ethnic groups appear to be less attractive and, therefore, they receive fewer direct-mail coupons. To correct this cycle, manufacturers and other distributors of coupons can improve their targeting approaches by sending out offers through ethnic publications.[5]

Problems with Coupons

There are drawbacks to the use of coupons as a promotional tactic. They include:

▶ Reduced revenues

▶ Mass-cutting

▶ Counterfeiting

▶ Misredemptions

The first disadvantage is that current brand users who are already brand loyal simply redeem the coupon with their next purchase, thereby reducing full-price revenues. Brand-loyal customers redeem approximately 80 percent of all coupons.[6] Some argue that offering them a price discount when they would be willing to pay full price does not make sense. Manufacturers, however, point out that these consumers may be willing to stock up on the item, which means they won't use the competition's coupons. Consequently, manufacturers recognize that brand-loyal customer redemptions are a "necessary evil" if mass-distribution is used. Some firms use direct mail to distribute the coupon primarily to nonloyal customers. They try to target nonusers and the competitor's customers. The primary disadvantage of this method is the high cost of direct mail, especially in light of the low response rate associated with direct-mail coupons.

The second problem associated with coupons is that, of the $3.6 billion in coupons that are used, between 10 percent and 30 percent are illegally reimbursed. One common form of coupon fraud is called *mass-cutting*.[7] This occurs when coupons are "redeemed" through a fraudulent retail outlet that does not exist, except at a mailbox set up by an illegal "coupon ring." At $.50 to $3.00 per coupon, mass-cutting of coupons is highly lucrative. Many times these rings take advantage of charitable organizations and religious groups that think they are helping a worthy cause by sending in coupons to the mailbox to receive a percentage of the proceeds. Instead, they actually are aiding an illegal activity.

Counterfeiting occurs when coupons are copied and then sent back to the manufacturer for reimbursement. The manufacturer pays for phony coupons. Newspaper-generated black-and-white coupons are the easiest to counterfeit. Color copiers have made other forms of counterfeiting easier to pursue.

Retailers usually are not involved in mass-cutting or counterfeiting of coupons. They can, however, engage in the *misredemption* of coupons. For instance, a coupon for soup often states the size of can for which the discount applies. If the discount is used for another size, such as a 12-ounce can instead of the 24-ounce can, then a misredemption occurs. This may be due to an error on the part of the clerk who did not check the coupon carefully. Or, the clerk might have known it was the wrong-size can but did not want to bother finding the correct size or risk making the customer mad by denying the coupon. Other times, clerks honor coupons for merchandise that was not purchased when they take the coupon and subtract it from the customer's total without matching it to the actual product.

Some misredemptions are performed by retail "clearinghouses" that collect money for coupons even when they were not actually redeemed by customers. Other retailers submit coupons for reimbursement rather than placing them on the shelf or some other location in the store. The typical supermarket redeems more than 1,000 coupons per day. As a result, there is ample opportunity for errors, mistakes, and fraud.[8]

STOP

INTEGRATED LEARNING EXPERIENCE

One method of reducing coupon fraud is to use electronic coupon distribution and redemption. Access In Store Media Systems, Inc. at **www.ismsi.net** to learn about its patented electronic Coupon Exchange Center. What would be the advantage of such a system to manufacturers? To retailers? To consumers? What potential disadvantages are there to this system of distributing and redeeming coupons?

Tactics to Improve Coupon Effectiveness

Three factors influence how attractive a particular coupon appears to consumers. First is the face value of the coupon. The higher the face value, the more attractive the coupon becomes and the more likely it will be redeemed.

Second is the distribution method. Research indicates that FSI are the most attractive to consumers because they can choose coupons in the privacy of their homes. In-store coupons are less attractive because consumers do not want to take time to process information while in the store.

The third attractiveness factor is whether the coupon is for a preferred brand or at least for a brand that is already in the consumer's evoked set (readily recalled brands). Coupons for the preferred brand or one from the evoked set tend to be more attractive than those for unknown or unrecognized brand names.

STOP

PREMIUMS

A second form of consumer promotion is the offer of a premium. Premiums are prizes, gifts, or other special offers consumers receive when purchasing products. When a company offers a premium, the consumer pays full price for the good or service, in contrast to coupons, which are price reductions. Some marketing experts believe the overuse of coupons damages a brand's image. Conversely, premiums actually can enhance brand image. The key is to pick the right type of premium. Premiums can be used in the attempt to boost sales; however, they usually are not as successful as coupon sales. Nevertheless, premiums remain a valuable consumer promotional tool with over $4.5 billion per year being spent on them in the United States alone.[9]

There are four major types of premiums:

1. Free-in-the-mail premiums
2. In- or on-package premiums
3. Store or manufacturer premiums
4. Self-liquidating premiums

Free-in-the-mail premiums are gifts individuals receive for purchasing products. To receive the gift, the customer must mail in a proof of purchase to the manufacturer, who then mails the gift back to the consumer. Sometimes more than one purchase is required to receive the gift. Review the premiums being offered by The Fisher Boy advertisement in this section. Consumers collect points from the front of Fisher Boy packages to be redeemed for "cool" prizes. To further encourage sales, the advertisement has a coupon attached.

Credit card companies use premiums to entice individuals to sign up for credit cards. Instead of providing a proof of purchase, the consumer needs only to activate the card.[10]

In- or on-package premiums are usually small gifts, such as toys in cereal boxes. Often the gift is disguised or packaged so the consumer must buy the product to find out which premium it contains. The most famous of these may be Cracker Jack's prizes. At other times the gift is attached to the package, such as package of blades with the purchase of a razor.

Store or manufacturer premiums are gifts given by either the retail store or the manufacturer when the customer purchases a product. Fast-food restaurants offer children a toy with the purchase of a child's meal. To entice luxury-car purchases and leases, Cadillac dealers developed a unique premium. They offered a personalized video golf lesson featuring Greg Norman to consumers who test-drove Cadillacs. To receive the tape, however,

A free-in-the-mail premium offer by Fisher Boy.
Source: Courtesy of Fisher Boy.

In addition to coupons, this advertisement makes a premium offer of "Buy one, get Chicken or Country Fried Steak Free."
Source: Courtesy of Bevil Advertising.

the customer had to come back a second time, which increased the chances of a purchase. During the first visit to the showroom, the customer's golf swing was videotaped. It was then mixed with footage from Greg Norman's golf swing. Customers who came back for the second visit were presented with the videotape.[11]

The last major type of premium is called the **self-liquidating premium**, because the consumer must pay an amount of money for it. For example, the premium may be offered for only $4.99 plus shipping and handling and two proofs of purchase from boxes of Cheerios. The premium is called self-liquidating because the $4.99 covers the cost of the premium. The manufacturer also receives money for shipping and handling so consumers pay most or all of its actual cost.

Problems with Premiums

The two major problems associated with premium programs are: (1) the time factor and (2) the cost.

Premiums tend to have short life spans. Many companies try to find items that are hot and adopt them as premiums. The problem is that by the time the marketing material is developed and the merchandise arrives, the item no longer is popular. Many companies have warehouses full of premiums that turned out to be busts because either they waited too long to order the merchandise or the product they thought would be a great premium turned out to be ignored by customers. Such was the case with KFC. Knowing of the popularity of Pokemon and seeing Burger King's success led KFC to promote Pokemon bean bags. The program turned out to be a disaster. Most KFC stores still had huge stocks of the bean bags six weeks after the end of the promotion.[12]

The second problem connected to premiums is the cost. A premium exclusively offered often increases the demand for the item. For example, numerous Disney tie-ins with fast-food restaurants are exclusive contracts. In these arrangements Disney promises not to sell the premium to any other vendor or restaurant. Yet it may offer the merchandise to other types of businesses or to retail outlets. This type of deal normally raises the price of the item and cost to the firm. Consequently, a rising scale seems to exist. Lower-cost premiums generate less interest and probably fewer sales. Higher-cost premiums create more sales, but cost more to provide.

Building Successful Premium Programs

Figure 11.3 highlights the primary keys to building successful premium programs.[13] First, and probably most important, is to match the premium to the target market. For a target market such as older, high-income individuals, the premium may be china or fine crystal. If the market is children, a cartoon figure or a character from Disney or Sesame Street would be attractive. The premium should match the desires and interests of target market members.

Next, the best premiums are those that reinforce the firm's image in some way. They should not be cheap trinkets. Offering cheap merchandise insults customers and can damage the image of a firm.

Premiums are more likely to succeed when they are tied into the firm's products. These items can enhance the image of the product as well as the image of the firm. For instance, Sears offered a 20-piece Pfaltzgraff dinnerware set to everyone who purchased a Kenmore microwave. Customers had a choice of four different patterns. In just six

- ▶ Match the premium to the target market
- ▶ Carefully select the premiums (avoid fads, try for exclusivity)
- ▶ Pick a premium that reinforces the firm's product and image
- ▶ Integrate the premium with other IMC tools (especially advertising and POP displays)
- ▶ Don't expect premiums to increase short-term profits

FIGURE 11.3
Keys to Successful Premiums

Source: Based on Bon Jagoda, "The Seven Habits of Highly Successful Premiums," *Incentive* (August 1999), Vol. 173, Issue 8, pp. 104–105.

weeks, 4,000 premiums were redeemed. Offering the dinnerware dishes with the purchase of a microwave reinforced Sears products while the high quality of the dishes reinforced the Kenmore brand image.[14]

As with coupons, it is important to integrate premiums with the other components of the IMC program. Premiums are an excellent means of adding value to a product instead of slashing prices or using coupons. They can reinforce the brand's image. Premiums can serve as a "thank you" to current customers or to attract new customers. *Sports Illustrated* has a rich history of premium programs, from videos to watches to phones, which are presented for either renewing a subscription to the magazine or ordering one for the first time.

There are three principles to remember when using premiums. First, premiums should build rational involvement in some fact about the good or service. A moving company giving out tote bags that say, "No job too large or small" communicates the point that the mover can help any size household. Second, premiums should build emotional involvement, such as feeling more warm and secure or simply happy about the item given. Third, the premium must build involvement with the product, not just the premium.[15]

CONSUMER PROMOTIONS

Ethics and Promotions

One of the fastest-growing problems in the United States is addiction to gambling by young people. Access to gaming facilities and gambling opportunities has never been greater, as individual states set up lotteries, dog tracks, and other operations. Many college students gamble regularly.

In this environment, does a marketing team worsen the problem by offering contests and sweepstakes? Currently, many consumers do not recognize that gambling can be a problem. Offering a contest may cause an individual to buy more product simply to obtain the chance to win a big prize. Is the marketing team comfortable with this possibility?

Another ethical concern in the area of promotions is coupon redemptions. Should stores honor coupons that have been created fraudulently, thereby risking alienating the stores' customer base? Retailers also face the issue of honoring coupons for the wrong size of a product, such as one aimed at a 10-ounce size rather than a 15-ounce. Once again, the retail store's customer is happy, but the coupon provider loses money.

Manufacturers trust retail stores to accurately and honestly follow the rules of consumer promotions such as contest, sweepstake, premium, coupon, or bonus pack. The difficulty is that manufacturers have no way of ensuring the rules are followed, and with so many retailers being involved, it is impossible for them to police all of the activity. In this type of environment, it becomes tempting for a retailer to violate rules if it will increase the retailer's profit or satisfaction levels of customers.

Although premiums are an excellent method of adding value or enhancing a brand, they are not as effective at increasing profits. Therefore, a clear relationship between the premium's intention and IMC goals should be established. Logically the goal should be more about image than profit.

CONTESTS AND SWEEPSTAKES

Contests and sweepstakes are popular forms of consumer sales promotions. Both are used in consumer markets as well as business markets. A primary factor in the success of this type of appeal is the prize list. Members of the target market for the contest or sweepstakes must believe the prizes are desirable enough to entice them to participate. Prizes perceived to be of low or no value do not work.

The words *contest* and *sweepstakes* tend to be used interchangeably, yet there are some differences, primarily legal. *Contests* normally require the participant to perform some type of activity. The winner is selected based on who performs best or provides the most correct answers. Often, contests require a participant to make a purchase to enter. In some states, however, it is illegal to force a consumer to make a purchase to enter a contest. It is important in developing contests to know the different state and federal laws that apply.

Contests range from the controversial bikini or suntan contests at local nightclubs to popular television shows such as *Jeopardy* or *Survivor* in which contestants must answer questions correctly to win prizes. While some contests are mostly chance (e.g., *Wheel of Fortune*), others require skill. For example, a Woodcraft store held a contest for its customers to demonstrate their woodworking skills. Woodcraft gave a prize of $100 to the person who demonstrated the greatest skill in making his or her first piece of furniture with wood purchased from the company.[16]

No purchase can be required to enter a *sweepstakes*. Consumers enter as many times as they wish. It is permissible for firms to restrict customers to one entry per visit to the store or some other location. The chances of winning a sweepstakes are based on a probability factor. The probability of winning must clearly be stated on all point-of-purchase (POP) displays and advertising materials. In a sweepstakes, the probability of winning each prize must be published in advance. This means the firm must know how many winning tickets, as compared to total tickets, have been prepared.

People enter contests and sweepstakes that they perceive as being worth their time and attention. Consumers do not enter every contest or sweepstakes they encounter. Instead, they selectively choose. The decision is often based on the perceived value of the contest or sweepstakes prize combined with the odds of winning. The greater the perceived odds of winning, the more likely a person will play the contest or enter the sweepstakes.

The perceived value of a prize has two components: (1) extrinsic value and (2) intrinsic value. The extrinsic value is the actual attractiveness of the item (a car versus an all-expense-paid vacation). The greater the perceived value, the more likely the person will participate. Intrinsic values are those associated with playing or participating. A contest requiring the use of a skill, such as the one with Woodcraft or an essay contest, entices entry by individuals who enjoy demonstrating a skill. In that case, extrinsic rewards become secondary. Instead, participants enjoy competing and demonstrating their abilities, which in part explains the popularity of fantasy football and baseball leagues and "pick the winner" sports contests.

The impact of a contest and sweepstakes can be enhanced when it is marketed with other elements of the IMC plan. For an example, see the Communication Action Box in this section.

A new media trend for contests and sweepstakes is offering them over the Internet.
Source: Courtesy of LuckySurf.com.

Problems with Contests and Sweepstakes

The problems associated with contests and sweepstakes are:

▶ Costs
▶ Consumer indifference
▶ Clutter

Company leaders must seek to overcome these issues in order to create successful promotional programs.

Contests and sweepstakes require companies to provide prizes, entry forms, legal statements, supportive advertising and other promotional activities, and often enticements to retailers to set up POP displays and other contest-related materials. Failure to support a contest fully means the odds of success diminish. Companies must be prepared to undertake all of the necessary expenditures associated with the program.

Consumers are increasingly indifferent to many contests and sweepstakes because of the rising availability of gambling opportunities. State lotteries, casinos, riverboat gambling, and Internet gambling make it possible to play games of chance and skill frequently. As a result, a contest offering a prize of a free dinner or $100 may not seem very exciting.

Clutter results from the number of firms promoting contests at any given time. With so many legal and illegal places to play games of chance, the idea of making a purchase or trip to the store to enter one more contest is less appealing.

Creating Successful Contests and Sweepstakes

One factor in the success level of a contest is finding the right prize. Firms can be creative in trying to reach this goal. For example, instead of money, Lever Brothers' Sunlight dishwasher soap developed a tie-in with Molly Maids to offer housecleaning for a year to 25 prize winners. In a similar contest, Molly Maids teamed up with Maxwell House coffee to offer 30 house cleanings. More than 500,000 people entered these contests.

COMMUNICATION ACTION

Racing to Sell Cereal

Recently, General Mills developed a $10 million IMC Cheerios promotion with a NASCAR tie-in. The NASCAR sweepstakes theme was featured on POP displays in retail outlets as well as on special Cheerios cereal boxes. Although the primary brand for the promotion was Cheerios, General Mills supported the sweepstakes on other brands such as Trix, Lucky Charms, Cinnamon Toast Crunch, Hamburger Helper, SuperMoist cake mixes, Rich & Creamy frosting, and Gold Medal flour.

General Mills used trade promotions to encourage retailers to display the Cheerios POP materials. The sweepstakes was promoted using print advertisements, FSI, and radio advertisements. Consumers could win tickets to the Daytona 500, go-carts, and other merchandise featuring Cheerios car driver Johnny Benson. Thirty-eight percent of NASCAR's fans are females. In the majority of families, the female does the grocery shopping. Consequently, General Mills wanted to make sure female fans would see the in-store displays. To encourage retailers to use the displays, General Mills awarded special VIP treatment at the Daytona 500 for any retailer that increased the volume of Cheerios sold during the promotion by 20 pallets.

The innovative tie-in between two seemingly unrelated products was a great success. Other firms, including Pepsi, have followed with NASCAR promotions. Thus, it has become clear that car races can be used to sell more than just motor oil.

Source: Stephanie Thompson, "General Mills to Pump $10M into 10-Brand Daytona Promo," *Brandweek,* 39, no. 39 (October 9, 1998), p. 6.

A second factor in generating a more successful contest is to be able to take advantage of a special event, such as a sports contest or some other celebration.

The Internet provides several opportunities for individuals who play contests and sweepstakes for their intrinsic value. The Internet allows for interactive games that can challenge the contestant's ability. Yoyodyne Entertainment has designed over 100 contests and games for companies such as H&R Block, MCI, American Express, Fox TV, and *Rolling Stone* magazine. H&R Block's contest called "We'll Pay Your Taxes" was designed to drive traffic to and through the H&R Block Web site. Through a series of weekly e-mail messages, players were directed to H&R Block's Web site for the answers. Each e-mail message contained brief product messages from H&R Block. The game ran just two months but averaged 46,000 hits per week, more than H&R Block had the entire previous year.[17]

To encourage consumers to continue playing a contest, the extrinsic values of prizes can be increased by allowing small, incremental rewards. A consumer who wins a soft drink or a sandwich in a sweepstakes at Subway is more likely to continue playing. Scratch-and-win cards tend to be effective because the reward is instant. As with coupons, instantly redeemed prizes are more popular with consumers than are delayed rewards. Using special Java technology, scratch-and-win cards can even be used on the Internet so that consumers can win instant prizes.

To fully ensure the success of the contest or sweepstakes, it is important to coordinate the promotion with the advertising, POP displays, and other marketing tools. All of these elements must be directed toward the same target audience and convey a united message. These features add to the cost of the contest; however, such integration is a crucial ingredient in achieving the desired goals.

When the contest or sweepstakes program features a tie-in with another company, the two firms should carefully coordinate their activities. It is a daunting task to include all creatives, trade promotion managers, consumer promotion managers, media buyers, and media planners, but it is also necessary in order to create a successful program.

The primary goals of contests and sweepstakes are to encourage customer traffic and boost sales. There is no doubt that a contest or sweepstakes increases customer traffic. The question is if they actually boost sales. Some do, others do not. Marketers are beginning to realize that intrinsic rewards tend to draw consumers back. This means many Internet games are exciting prospects, because they can be structured to create intrinsic rewards.

Marketing research has demonstrated that brand awareness increases with multiple exposures to an advertisement or contest. Therefore, although contests and sweepstakes may not boost sales in the short run, they can be a driving force behind brand awareness and brand image development over longer periods of time. As a result, they remain another weapon in the marketing arsenals of many organizations.

INTEGRATED LEARNING EXPERIENCE

Sweepstakes and contests are excellent methods for building customer traffic for a retail outlet. Certain firms can assist in the development of sweepstakes and contests. This becomes more important in the case of sweepstakes and contests due to the legal restrictions imposed by various states. Access the following companies to see what types of services they can offer. How could they assist a firm in developing a contest or sweepstakes?

Sweepstakes Builder (www.sweepstakesbuilder.com)
Promotions Activators, Inc. (www.promotionactivators.com)
ADPAC Corporation (www.adpaccorp.com)

What other consumer promotional services can these firms offer? What are the advantages and disadvantages of using one firm for all of a firm's consumer promotions?

STOP

REFUNDS AND REBATES

Refunds and rebates are cash returns offered to consumers or businesses following the purchase of a product. Consumers pay full price for the product but can mail in some type of proof of purchase, and then the manufacturer refunds a portion of the purchase price. A *refund* is a cash return on what are called "soft goods," such as food or clothing. *Rebates* are cash returns on "hard goods," which are major ticket items such as automobiles. Normally refunds are small and rebates are larger. For example, the typical refund offered on a food item may be $1 while the typical rebate on a car may be $500, $1,000, or more, depending on the price and size of the car.

Rebates can be given on services. In an effort to drive traffic to their Web sites, 12 banks developed a tie-in rebate program with Amazon.com. Students and parents could receive the rebate by purchasing books from Amazon.com through each bank's Web site. For each purchase made, a 3 percent rebate was offered to whichever local school the customer designated. The tie-in increased traffic to the banks' Web sites and also provided money for the local schools to purchase books from Amazon.com. The plan turned out to be a great community service project for the banks.[18]

Sometimes rebates from several sources are packaged together. Circuit City advertised a personal computer system valued at $980 for only $300. The $680 savings were in the form of four different rebates. The first rebate was a mail-in rebate to Hewlett-Packard, the computer manufacturer. The second rebate was from Canon for the printer. The third was from Circuit City, and the fourth from CompuServe. To get the CompuServe rebate, the customer had to sign a three-year Internet contract at a cost of $21.95 per month.[19]

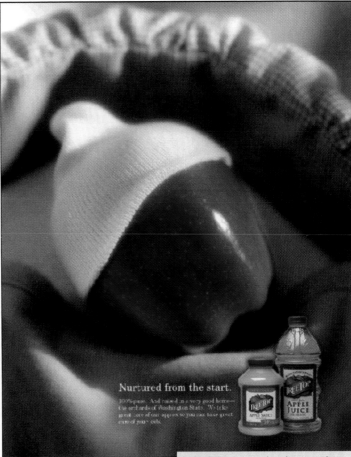

In developing a strong brand name such as Tree Top, it is important to choose the right consumer promotion.
Source: Courtesy of Tree Top Apple Juice.

Problems with Refunds and Rebates

The problems associated with refunds and rebates include their costs, the paperwork involved, and diminished effectiveness. The retail outlet must carefully document manufacturer rebates so that the customer is reimbursed. To hold down the paperwork, many automobile dealerships have the rebate assigned to the dealer and deduct the amount from the sales price. This often lessens the "impact" of the rebate, because no check is ever delivered to the customer.

The cost of a refund or rebate is the lost revenue from the sale price combined with the mailing and record-keeping costs involved. Further, a promotional or advertising campaign emphasizing the offer must be developed, or the program goes unnoticed. These extra promotional expenditures further add to the costs of the plan.

Many rebate programs suffer from diminished effectiveness, because consumers have come to expect them. For example, many car dealers find their customers won't buy until rebates are offered. As a result, there is no new purchase activity associated with the rebate, but rather a delay in the purchase as consumers "wait out" auto manufacturers.

Creating Effective Refund–Rebate Programs

To generate an effective refund or rebate program, the offer must have:

1. Visibility
2. Perceived newness
3. An impact

An advertisement by Tropical Tan offering consumers a free visit to use the company's new aqua massage bed or a premium of two free tanning sessions with a purchase of a 10-pack.

Source: Used with permission of the *Joplin Globe,* Joplin, Missouri.

The refund should be visible. Customers must find out about the program before they can take advantage of it. Refunds and rebates have their greatest successes when they are perceived as being new or original. When they are an entrenched part of doing business, they have simply become an expected discount. Rebates and refunds must have the impact of changing the buyer's behavior, either by leading to more immediate purchases or by causing the customer to change brands.

Retailers tend to like refunds and rebates, because the retailer maintains its margin or markup on the product which means the item or service is sold at full price. Recently, Iomega offered a $50 rebate on its Zip drive that sold for $199. Retailers responded favorably to the Iomega rebate because it was easy for consumers to understand, the display materials were attractive, and implementing the rebate was easy for retailers. Also, the rebate was large enough to stimulate sales and encourage consumers to choose the Iomega brand.[20] Consequently, effective rebate programs are an option for various companies seeking to heighten the buying excitement levels associated with their products.

SAMPLING

One method of encouraging consumers to try new product is sampling. Sampling is the actual delivery of a product to consumers for their use or consumption. Normally, samples are provided free of charge. Often a coupon or price-off incentive then is used to persuade the consumer to make a purchase of a larger version of the product, such as a full-size package.

In business-to-business markets, companies often provide samples of products to potential clients. Sampling also can be used in the service sector. For example, a tanning salon may offer an initial visit free to encourage new customers to try its facilities. Dentists and lawyers use sampling when they offer an initial consultation free of charge.

Figure 11.4 lists various ways samples are distributed. The most common consumer method is *in-store distribution,* such as when food product companies have personnel cooking the food and passing it out to individuals in the store. *Direct sampling* is a program in which samples are mailed or delivered door to door to consumers. Various demographic target markets can be identified for free samples. In the business-to-business sector, salespeople often deliver direct samples. *Response samples* are made available to

▶ **In-store distribution**

▶ **Direct sampling**

▶ **Response sampling**

▶ **Cross-ruff sampling**

▶ **Media sampling**

▶ **Professional sampling**

▶ **Selective sampling**

FIGURE 11.4
Types of Sampling

individuals or businesses responding to a media offer on television, on the Internet, from a magazine, or by some other source. *Cross-ruff sampling* plans provide samples of one product on another. A laundry detergent with a free dryer sheet attached to the package is a cross-ruff sample. *Media sampling* means the sample is included in the media outlet. For example, a small sample of perfume can be included in a magazine advertisement. *Professional samples* are delivered by professionals, such as when doctors provide patients with free drug samples. First, the doctor received a package of samples from the drug company. *Selective samples* are distributed at a site such as a state fair, parade, hospital, restaurant, or sporting event. For instance, many times Power Bars are given to people attending football or basketball games. There is a tie-in between the product (nutrition) and the event (athletics).

Sampling is an effective method to entice consumers to try a product.
Source: Courtesy of PhotoEdit. Photograph by Bill Aron.

The target audience determines the best method of sampling to use. Direct sampling is generally the ideal for business-to-business situations. Other methods tend to work better for consumers. For example, women tend to prefer mail samples they can examine at home. Men prefer samples given to them at a store or an event. The advantage of passing out samples at an event is that the person receiving the sample receives the personal touch. A smile, a greeting, and even information can be conveyed along with the sample. Also, if the consumer liked the event, then he or she may transfer the good feelings toward the event to the sampled product.[21]

Internet-based response sampling programs have become popular with both consumers and manufacturers. Bristol-Myers/Squibb was one of the first companies to utilize the Internet for product sampling. The company offered a free sample of Excedrin to individuals who requested the sample and were willing to provide their name, address, and e-mail information. In addition to the 12-pack sample of Excedrin, consumers received coupons for additional Excedrin purchases along with the quarterly Excedrin Headache Relief Update Newsletter.[22] The advantage of this form of response sampling is that only consumers who request the product receive it. By using the Internet, a company gathers additional information to be added to a database.

Problems with Sampling

Product sampling is an effective method to introduce a new product and generate interest in that product. The primary disadvantage of this form of promotion is the cost. A special sample-size package must be developed. The package must be very similar to the regular-size pack, so consumers will be able to identify the product after using up the sample. Many times samples are mailed, adding to the expense of the program. Even samples given out in stores require either an individual to distribute them or some kind of permission from the store.

To fully cover an area with samples requires careful planning of the distribution. Many times people simply discard the sample without even trying the product. Therefore, careful market research must be employed before undertaking a sampling program.

Effective Use of Samples

As with the other consumer promotions, sampling must be a central part of the IMC plan. The primary purpose of sampling is to encourage trial use by a consumer or a business. Sampling is most effective when it introduces a new product or a new version

WAITING
ISN'T WORKING.

Videoconferencing never looked so good.

| | With today's reduced budgets and increased travel times, now more than ever Polycom's award-winning videoconferencing products are essential, must-have tools for getting business done. With the only end-to-end solutions that efficiently integrate video, voice, data and web collaboration, Polycom lets you be there without going there. As the industry leader, we can show | you how our state-of-the-art video and audio quality redefines the concept of face-to-face meetings. And how our solutions can be tailored to fit any room and any budget. So isn't it time you got Polycom and stopped waiting in line? | RISK-FREE TRIAL! TRY ANY POLYCOM VIDEOCONFERENCING SYSTEM FREE FOR 30 DAYS.* |

Call today 1-877-POLYCOM
Go to www.polycom.com/see

* 100% Financing available on all Polycom systems

☗ POLYCOM

Sampling is important in the business-to-business market to encourage trial usage of a product. Polycom offers companies a free 30-day, risk-free trial.
Source: Courtesy of Polycom.

of a product to a market. Samples also help promote a current product to a new target market or to new prospects.

In one survey, 71 percent of a set of consumers said they would try a new product if they liked a sample. An amazing 70 percent reported that they would be willing to switch brands if the trial use of the product was a positive experience. Many companies have achieved high success levels with sampling programs. For instance, the market share of Colgate-Palmolive's Nourishing Shower Gel doubled after its sampling campaign. Sales for Avon's True Color eyeshadow increased 38 percent after a sampling venture. Thus, sampling can be a successful way to stimulate trials and increase sales.[23]

BONUS PACKS

When an additional or extra number of items is placed in a special product package, it is called a bonus pack. For example, instead of the regular number of bars of soap in a package, the consumer buys four bars for the price of three in a bonus pack promotion. Recently, Rayovac offered three free AA batteries in a bonus pack containing nine batteries. Bonuses range from 20 percent to 100 percent with a 30 percent bonus being the most typical.

Figure 11.5 identifies the major objectives of bonus packs. Increasing the size or quantity of the package can lead to greater product use. For example, if a cereal box is increased in size by 25 percent, the consumer is likely to eat more cereal, because it is readily available. This is not true for products that have a constant rate of consumption. For instance, if Colgate increases the size of a toothpaste container by 25 percent, consumers will not use more toothpaste. In effect, what this does is delay the customer's next purchase. Still, manufacturers do offer these types of bonus packs, because they may help preempt the competition. A consumer with a large quantity of the merchandise on hand is less likely to switch to another brand, even when offered some type of deal, such as a coupon.

A firm's current customers often take advantage of a bonus pack offer. When customers stockpile a quantity of a particular brand it discourages purchasing from a competitor. Bonus packs reward customer loyalty by offering them, in effect, free merchandise.

Bonus packs rarely attract new customers, because the consumer has never purchased the brand before. Obtaining an extra quantity does not reduce the purchase risk. In fact, it adds to the risk, especially when the customer does not like to waste a product by throwing it away if dissatisfied with the product.

Bonus packs can lead to brand switching if the consumer has used the brand previously. Facing purchase decisions, consumers may opt for brands that offer a bonus pack at the regular price. These products hold an advantage over competitive brands that do not offer bonus packs.

▶ **Increase usage of the product**

▶ **Match or preempt competitive actions**

▶ **Stockpile the product**

▶ **Develop customer loyalty**

▶ **Attract new users**

▶ **Encourage brand switching**

FIGURE 11.5
Reasons for Using Bonus Packs

Problems with Bonus Packs

Some marketing research indicates that consumers are skeptical of bonus pack offers. When the bonus is small (20 percent to 40 percent), consumers often believe the price has not truly changed. Unfortunately, when the bonus is large, such as two-for-the-price-of-one sale, consumers tend to believe that the price was first increased to compensate for the additional quantity. Even though increasing the size of a bonus catches the consumer's attention, it may not convey the desired message.[24]

Bonus packs are costly because additional amounts of product sell for the same or a similar price. Also, they may incur new packaging and shipping costs. Cash flows may slow down, because customers buy larger quantities and therefore purchase the item less often.

Using Bonus Packs Effectively

Bonus packs tend to be popular with manufacturers, retailers, and customers. A retailer can build a good relationship with a manufacturer that uses a bonus pack to increase brand switching and stockpiling. Retailers gain an advantage because the bonus pack is a "bargain" or "value" offered through the retail outlet.[25] Customers like bonus packs because they get additional product at the same price. For ongoing products with high competition, the bonus pack approach is one way to maintain brand loyalty and reduce brand switching at a minimal cost.

PRICE-OFFS

A price-off is a temporary reduction in the price of a product to the consumer. A price-off can be physically marked on the product, such as when a bottle of aspirin shows the regular retail price marked out and replaced by a special retail price (e.g., $4.99 marked out and replaced by $3.99). Producing a label with the price reduction premarked forces the retailer to sell the item at the reduced price. This ensures the price-off incentive provided to the retailer through the trade promotion is actually passed on to the consumer. At other times, the price-off is not on the actual item, but on a POP display, sign, or shelf.

Price-offs usually stimulate sales of an existing product. They work well in the business-to-business area. They also can entice customers to try new products, because they reduce the financial risk of making the purchase. Companies often tie price-off offers with samples of new products.

The retailer can initiate a price-off promotion. Retailers usually offer price-off discounts to draw traffic into the store. The idea is for customers to purchase additional items other than those on sale. During the holidays and other times of the year, price-off sales are very common. Retailers advertise major price-off sales at Christmas, Thanksgiving, and Presidents' Day. Many use Presidents' Day sales to reduce inventories of winter clothes and unsold Christmas merchandise.

Problems with Price-Off Promotions

Price-offs are easy to implement and can have a sudden impact on sales; however, they also can cause problems. While a price-off offer may have a large impact on sales, it can be devastating for profit margins because it normally takes at least a 20 percent increase in sales to offset each 5 percent price reduction.

A bonus pack offer for two packages of Lean Slices by Carl Buddig.
Source: Courtesy of Carl Buddig & Company.

A special price-off offer by Papa John's.
Source: Courtesy of Papa John's International.

Perhaps even a greater danger is that price-off programs encourage consumers to become more price sensitive. In the same way that customers respond to rebates, they can either wait for a price-off promotion or choose another brand that happens to be on sale. An estimated 25 percent of consumers base their purchase decisions on price. Price-offs are often necessary because of competitive and trade pressures. Individual firms must be careful not to overrely on price-offs.[26] Remember, however, that too many price-off offers can create a detrimental impact on the firm's image.

Using Price-Off Offers Effectively

Price-off programs can be used to increase store traffic and generate sales. They work better with higher markup items and for goods or services that normally do not offer discounts. The goal should be to create new interest in the product to entice buyers to take a second look. Loyal customers may be attracted to a price-off discount and buy to stock up, but they should not be the primary targets for price-off programs. Instead, new users or customers who have drifted away to other products should be the target market.

Price-offs have proven to be successful consumer promotions for two reasons. First, the price-off has the appeal of a monetary savings to consumers. Second, the reward is immediate. Unlike rebates, refunds, contests, sweepstakes, and other promotional incentives, consumers do not have to wait for the reward. As always, price-off programs should be incorporated into the firm's overall IMC program.

INTEGRATED LEARNING EXPERIENCE

Many companies offer special consumer promotions on their Web sites. Examine the following company Web sites for consumer promotions.

Taco Bell (**www.tacobell.com**)
Hershey's (**www.hersheys.com**, look under consumer info)
Quaker State (**www.quakerstate.com**)

What types of promotions are available? What are the objectives of the various consumer promotions? Do the promotions on the Web sites mesh with their advertising and consumer promotions at retail outlets?

OTHER ISSUES IN PROMOTIONS PROGRAMS

The major forms of consumer sales promotions programs are coupons, premiums, contests, refunds, sampling, bonus packs, and price-off offers. Each has distinct advantages and problems. The marketing account executive's goal should be to help the company select a consumer sales promotion approach that matches its trade promotions efforts, advertisements, and personal selling tactics. The entire promotions mix can then be structured to mesh with a more integrated IMC plan.

At times companies combine two or more consumer promotions activities into a single campaign, called an *overlay.* For example, to attract Chinese consumers in Canada, Tropicana combined sampling with coupons. Free samples (50,000 cups of orange juice) were given out along with 30,000 coupons at a Chinese New Year's celebration in

Vancouver. Asians who live in the United States and Canada are not typically large users of coupons; however, Tropicana Canada's research showed that the Chinese consider oranges to be harbingers of good luck. A few weeks after the promotion, 40 percent of the coupons were redeemed, and sales of Tropicana orange juice among the Chinese community in Canada increased considerably.[27]

Another common strategy is to develop a consumer promotion with another product or company such as the ad featuring General Mills Betty Crocker brand and Tyson in this section. This is called a tie-in. *Intracompany tie-ins* are the promotion of two different products within one company using one consumer promotion. The more common tie-in is with another company, such as General Mills and Tyson, which is an *intercompany tie-in.* When the Spice Girls reached the peak of their popularity, Pepsi promoted a tie-in offering Spice Girl prizes across nine countries in Europe. Fast-food restaurants often use tie-ins with movies and toys to attract children.[28] Whether a promotion is a stand-alone, overlay, or tie-in program, careful attention must be given to planning the event to maximize its effect.

PLANNING FOR CONSUMER PROMOTIONS

In planning the consumer promotions component of the IMC, it is vital that the promotions support the brand image and the brand positioning strategy. To ensure this occurs, it is first necessary to bear in mind the target audience of the program. Then research must be conducted to identify the core values present in the target audience as well as opinion regarding the firm's products, especially as they relate to the competition. Once this information is gathered, the firm is ready to finalize the consumer promotions plan. In terms of sales promotions, consumers can be divided into three general categories:

1. Promotion prone consumers
2. Brand-loyal consumers
3. Price-sensitive consumers

Promotion prone consumers regularly respond to coupons, price-off plans, or premiums. They are not brand loyal and purchase items that are on-deal. A **brand-loyal consumer** purchases only one particular brand and does not substitute regardless of any deal being offered. Few consumers are completely promotion prone or brand loyal. Instead, buying is more like a continuum anchored at its ends by promotional proneness and brand loyalty. People tend toward one approach or the other, but sometimes lapse into the other approach. The tendency toward being promotion prone or brand loyal may depend on the product being purchased. A beer drinker may be extremely promotion prone, while a wine drinker may be quite brand loyal. The same beer drinker may be extremely loyal to a pizza brand, and the same wine drinker may be quite promotion prone when it comes to buying potato chips.

For the **price-sensitive consumer**, price is the primary if not the only criterion used in making a purchase decision. Brand names are not important and these individuals will not pay more for a brand name. They take advantage of any type of promotion that reduces the price. It is important to identify the set of promotion prone or price-sensitive consumers who will be targeted by a consumer promotions program.

For brand-loyal consumers, sales promotions can be crafted to boost sales and reinforce the firm's image. For example, one small

An intercompany tie-in by Betty Crocker with Tyson.
Source: Courtesy of Betty Crocker and Tyson.

Southwest Airlines is promoting their swavacations.com Web site with tie-ins for hotels, car rentals, and other vacation activities.
Source: Courtesy of Southwest Airlines.

local restaurant has a monthly drawing for a free meal for two. To enter, patrons put a cash register receipt from the last meal at the restaurant in a box upon leaving. Each month the restaurant draws five names. The more often a person dines at the restaurant, the greater the chance of winning. A simple promotion such as this can boost sales for the restaurant by tying chances of winning with additional meals. The additional cost to the restaurant to run this promotion is minimal and can result in excellent goodwill from its customers.[29]

In any event, planning promotions programs should always tie together the theme of the IMC plan with more specific goals associated with the product and the target market being attacked. Building brand image is more of a long-term goal, and generating sales is more short range. Price-based offers normally are designed to: (1) attract new customers or (2) build sales. Other consumer promotions such as high-value premiums can be used to enhance a firm's image.

INTEGRATED LEARNING EXPERIENCE

Planning consumer promotions requires considerable expertise. Most firms lack the skills to design cost-effective consumer promotions. The same is true of many advertising agencies that specialize in advertising, not consumer promotions. At the same time, to be effective, a consumer promotions program must be integrated with advertising and all of the other forms of marketing communications. Use a search engine to locate some consumer promotion firms in your area. In addition, examine the following Web sites.

www.gravesgroup.com
www.salespromo.com

A Valpak advertisement soliciting other businesses to offer consumer promotions within the Valpak mailer.
Source: Courtesy of Valpak.

She loves her home
(saved 20% on painting supplies)

fresh flowers
(saved $5 on a mixed bouquet)

family pictures
(saved 50% on enlargements)

and the blue envelope.

There's something in it for you.®
Discover great savings like these inside the envelope and online at www.valpak.com.
To advertise, call 800-355-9642, today.

BUSINESS-TO-BUSINESS PROGRAMS

Sales promotions are used extensively in the business-to-business area. In fact, 18.7 percent of business-to-business marketing budgets are spent on sales promotions. Manufacturers are the most inclined to offer some type of sales promotion to their customers.[30]

Sales promotions are not monies offered to retailers, wholesalers, distributors, or agents who stock the manufacturer's products for resale. Those funds are trade promotions monies. Instead, manufacturers offering some type of special promotion to their customers (another business) are involved in business-to-business sales promotions. For example, a manufacturer needing paper for copy machines may be enticed to buy from a paper company offering a sales promotion incentive. The paper itself is necessary for the company, but is not used in making products and is not resold.

Finance, insurance, and real estate services are the second largest business-to-business users of sales promotions. Although many finance, insurance, and real estate companies service consumers, a large portion of their revenues comes from business-to-business customers. A bank offering a premium or sweepstakes to small businesses uses a sales promotion. The same would be true for insurance companies and real estate companies that use sales promotions aimed at business customers.

Coupons often are used in the business-to-business sector. For example, an office supply company may fax or mail coupon offers to its business customers. A pest control business may offer an introductory coupon to encourage businesses to sign up for its services. Microsoft offered a $99 off coupon on its one-day training session about installing and supporting BackOffice SBS, which is designed for small- to medium-size businesses. The coupon was made available only to CPAs who were official members of the American Institute of Certified Public Accountants (AICPA).[31]

While FSI and print media work well for consumer promotions aimed at end users, direct mail, fax, or coupons distributed by sales staff work best for business markets. In business-to-business promotions, companies need to be more focused on targeting. Few business buyers would see or use a FSI coupon. To be effective, the coupon must reach the hands of the purchasing agent or someone who has the authority to make the purchase decision or can influence the purchase decision.

Premiums also can be offered in business-to-business markets. They can be additional merchandise given to the firm for making a purchase. For example, a company such as Quaker State can offer a free case of motor oil for placing an order within a specified time period or for a specific size of order. John Deere used Christmas ornaments and John Deere trading cards as premiums with its dealers. Gifts such as these should be aligned with the products being sold.

Contests and sweepstakes can be used to attract purchases in much the same way as they are used in consumer markets. Business buyers are just as interested in winning prizes as are customers in other situations.

Sampling is an excellent method to encourage a business to try a product. For example, an office supply store offers a company the use of a copier for a month in an effort to land a contract to supply all of the firm's copiers. The types of products that lend themselves well to sampling in the business arena include:

▶ Fabricated and component parts
▶ Maintenance and repair parts
▶ Process materials
▶ Operating supplies
▶ Raw materials

For example, providing a sample in the area of process materials has the advantage of giving the engineers an opportunity to analyze the materials to see if it meets their standards. Through analysis, they may find that the material is actually superior to the product they currently use. Sampling is an effective method of getting a company's products into the hands of the individuals who are the influencers in business purchase decisions.

Bonus packs also can be part of business-to-business marketing. Offering a prospective business a bonus pack may attract new users. The lure of additional merchandise at no additional cost appeals to cost-conscious business buyers.

Price is often a negotiated item in the business-to-business sector. Consequently, *price-off programs* are not used as often. Many business relationships are formalized by a contractual agreement, and the price is fixed by that contract. Price-off discounts can be offered by vendors seeking to obtain a new business contract by enticing the business customer to at least consider the firm making the offer. Also, a vendor can offer a price-off program to tempt customers to purchase additional merchandise. Price-offs can be used to preempt competitive deals. The latter situations occur when there is no formal contract between the firm and the vendor. Firms furnishing operating supplies normally operate without contracts and use price-offs as part of their marketing programs.

As a result, the importance of business-to-business consumer promotions programs will continue. Marketing managers should integrate these efforts into all other parts of the promotions mix, for both business buyers and other customers.

INTERNATIONAL CONSUMER PROMOTIONS PROGRAMS

As first discussed in Chapter 1, to fully integrate marketing communications means the firm must develop an overall, global IMC program. Each country or each region requires some flexibility in order to adapt marketing activities, including consumer promotions, to fit local needs.

Although the desire may be to centralize global consumer promotions programs, this process can be difficult. Customs, laws, and views toward various types of sales promotions differ throughout the world. Even within Europe, the laws governing consumer promotions are not consistent. For example, in France and England, contests offering free prizes are legal; however, in Germany, the Netherlands, and Belgium, they are illegal. Coupons, which are common in the United States, are legal in all European countries except Germany. At the same time, German laws allow on-pack price reductions and gifts inside of a package.

In Japan, the maximum value of a premium is either 10 percent of the selling price or 100 yen (80 cents). Thus, it would not make sense to use a premium in Japan. Although companies would like to utilize the same sales promotional tactic throughout the world in order to gain economies of scale, it is not always possible.[32]

Coupons are not as prevalent in the United Kingdom as they are in the United States. Culturally, coupon redemption is associated with being underprivileged in England. Customers fear that using coupons will cause the cashier to judge them to be poor and needy.[33] Still, coupon redemption rates are higher in Europe than they are in the United States. Table 11.1 compares redemption rates and distribution methods of the United States with three European countries: England, Italy, and Spain. As shown, the overall redemption rates are 14.3 percent in Italy and 16 percent in Spain as compared to only 2 percent in the United States.

A primary explanation for the difference in redemption rates is distribution. In the United Kingdom, 5.4 billion coupons were distributed. Newspapers were the predominant means of distribution, but magazines, door-to-door, in- or on-pack, and in-store distribution methods were also heavily used. In Italy, in- or on-pack distribution accounted for 63.2 percent of the 621 million coupons distributed. When the coupon is already in or on the package, it is easily redeemed, thus creating the highest rate. In Spain, door-to-door and in- or on-pack distribution are the primary methods. A total of 106 million were distributed.[34]

In Japan, restrictions on print media carrying coupons were not lifted until 1990. Retailers and consumers are still reluctant to use coupons. In 1991, Japanese newspapers were allowed to carry freestanding inserts, but the average redemption rate still is only 1.2 percent. To encourage retailers to redeem coupons, Japanese supermarkets are offer-

TABLE 11.1

Couponing in Selected Countries

Media	Redemption Rate				Distribution Method			
	England	Italy	Spain	U.S.	England	Italy	Spain	U.S.
Newspaper	1.9%	–	1.4%	0.8.%	26%	–	10.0%	1.9%
Magazine	2.8	1.4	1.4	0.3	13	5.7	14.7	4.2
Door to door	11.0	13.7	12.9	–	18	2.0	43.0	–
In/on pack	25.1	20.3	30.7	9.2	15	63.2	25.2	2.5
In store	27.7	32.3	28.2	6.8	19	22.1	5.5	1.9
FSI	12.0	–	–	1.4	1	–	–	85.4
Mailing	–	6.6	–	3.6	–	6.5	–	1.1
Overall average	6.8	14.3	16.0	2.0				

Sources: "International Coupon Trends," *Direct Marketing,* 56, no. 4 (August 1993), pp. 47–49; "FSI Coupon Redemption Rate for Frozen Foods," *Frozen Food Age,* 47, no. 3 (October 1998), p. 70.

ing checkout coupons. Checkout coupons issued for competing products have had some success.[35]

Contests and sweepstakes are successful in many countries. Marketers must be careful to research the laws, regulations and, most importantly, consumer attitudes toward contests and sweepstakes. A cultural assimilator helps the company assess the potential impact of local attitudes toward the contest.

In order to manage the consumer promotion function within a global market successfully, a company needs an experienced international sales promotion coordinator or manager. Some of the major responsibilities of this coordinator are:[36]

1. Promoting the transfer of successful consumer promotion ideas among the company's brands from one country to another

2. Proposing and soliciting ideas for consumer promotions within and across each region or country

3. Developing and presenting training on consumer promotions planning to each local region that is responsible for developing them

4. Gathering performance data on each sales promotion program and making the information available to each regional sales promotion manager

5. Developing methods for measuring the effectiveness and efficiency of the various consumer promotions

6. Coordinating relationships with all sales promotion agencies that are being used

7. Coordinating efforts among advertising agencies, media buying agencies, and any other agencies or firms that are working with sales promotions in a region or country

8. Making sure all consumer promotions fit into the firm's overall IMC program

Effective management of a global IMC program is one of the keys to long-term success. Using sales promotions tactics wisely is one ingredient in the formula. A truly integrated marketing communications program pulls together all elements of the marketing mix so that the firm's voice is heard clearly in all areas in which it competes.

INTEGRATED LEARNING EXPERIENCE

One widely read journal featuring promotional marketing is called *PROMO*. Access its Web site at www.promomagazine.com. Examine the table of contents. Who is the Agency of the Year? What other agencies are listed in the top 25? Read at least two articles from the current issue of *PROMO*. How would *PROMO* be of assistance to a firm designing promotional materials? How would *PROMO* be valuable to promotional and advertising agencies?

SUMMARY

An IMC program highlights all four elements of the promotions mix. In the previous section of this textbook, advertising was carefully considered, because it is often the main "voice" of the IMC message. At the same time, other parts of the mix (trade promotions, consumer promotions, and personal selling) play a crucial role in the success or failure of the overall marketing program.

This chapter reviews the techniques available to attract consumers to the company by using consumer sales promotions. These tactics include coupons, premiums, contests and sweepstakes, refunds, rebates, samples, bonus packs, and price-off deals. These items should be combined with specific promotional goals to have the right impact on customers.

Consumer promotions are often used to boost sales. They can be an excellent short-term method to increase sales or a firm's market share. They can also be an excellent means of introducing new products. Often a consumer promotion prompts consumers to at least try the product where selling it at the regular price will not. Coupons and contests have been successful tactics for attracting new customers. Consumer promotions can boost sales of a particular brand, and evidence suggests that they increase sales of the overall product category rather than just take sales away from competitors.

Sales promotions also can be used to increase the household inventory of the item being promoted. Consumers with more of a particular product in their house experience fewer home "stock-outs" and often increase their usage of the product. In other words, having more potato chips on hand means people in the home might consume them at a faster rate.[37]

In many large companies, a consumer or sales promotion manager handles the planning and execution of all of the consumer promotions. In smaller companies, this person may handle both trade and consumer promotions. The same is true for agencies. Full-service agencies often have specialists in the fields of trade and consumer promotions, or they employ subsidiary firms to handle the sales promotions.

The New York–based advertising agency DDB Needham handles advertising for brands such as Budweiser, Volkswagen, American Airlines, and Sony. Louis London, a sales promotion subsidiary agency of DDB Needham, handles the sales promotion aspect of these accounts. The large advertising agencies seldom actually do consumer promotions within the agency. Companies that do not have relationships with subsidiary consumer promotions agencies often have a separate internal division to handle consumer promotions. The recent push toward more fully integrated marketing communications programs has led some clients to seek out firms that can manage every aspect of the communications program, including consumer sales promotions.

Just as large advertising firms are branching out into consumer promotions, specialty consumer promotion firms are adding additional services. To be able to meet the advertising needs of their clients, they often utilize freelance creatives. Regardless of which type of agency is used, full-service or specialty, the trend for both is to expand offerings to allow for a greater degree of integration of the consumer promotion component with the other elements of the IMC plan.[38]

Unfortunately, many sales promotions still are not part of the integrated marketing communications plan. They start out being part of the IMC program and may be carefully designed to support the IMC plan and firm's desired brand image. As long as sales increase and the goals of the firm are being met, all is fine. If, however, sales slump and target goals are not met, marketers often turn to additional sales promotion tactics, seeking a quick remedy. Printing and distributing 50-cent coupons yields results much faster than does increasing advertising. Yet, as was discussed in Chapter 10, money spent on promotions and taken away from advertising often dilutes the brand's image. When the brand image is tarnished, consumers then base purchase decisions on criteria such as price or a promotional offer rather than brand name or perceived brand quality. While increased use of sales promotions techniques often provides a short-term solution to slumping sales, their overuse can damage the brand's image in the long run.[39]

The most crucial step in planning an integrated consumer promotions program is to match the firm's target market, specific marketing goals, and promotional tactics together. Goals range from quick boosts to sales, to increased brand awareness, to improved brand image, and establishing solid relationships between manufacturers and members of the marketing channel, specifically retailers. Consumer promotions programs also can expand the reach of the company into the business-to-business market. Again, carefully set goals combined with well-chosen tactics are the key.

Internationally, consumer promotions programs can be used when they are chosen based on the characteristics, attitudes, laws, regulations, and cultural nuances of a given geographic region. The primary objective of any promotions program must always be to enhance the message sent forth in other aspects of the IMC program in a manner that helps the company reach its long-term marketing objectives in a cost-effective and positive fashion.

REVIEW QUESTIONS

1. What is a consumer sales promotion? How is it different from a trade promotion?

2. What is an FSI? What kind of sales promotion is distributed through FSI?

3. Name and describe five types of coupons. Which is the most popular with manufacturers? Which has the highest redemption rate?

4. What is a U-pon?

5. What problems are associated with coupon programs?

6. How can companies most successfully utilize coupons?

7. What is a premium? What four types of premium programs can companies use?

8. What are the disadvantages of premium programs?

9. How can companies enhance the odds of success of a premium program?

10. What is the difference between a contest and a sweepstakes?

11. What problems are associated with contests and sweepstakes?

12. What tactics can be used to improve the success rates of contests and sweepstakes? What role might the Internet play in this process?

13. How is a refund different from a rebate?

14. What problems are associated with refunds and rebates?

15. What can be done to make rebate programs more successful?

16. Name and describe six types of sample programs that manufacturers can employ.

17. What disadvantages are there to sampling programs?

18. What can be done to enhance the odds of success of a sampling program?

19. What is a bonus pack? How is it different from samples?

20. What problems are associated with bonus pack programs?

21. What bonus pack plans are most effective?

22. What is a price-off sales promotion?

23. What are the disadvantages of price-off programs?

24. How can manufacturers most successfully employ price-off discounts? How can retailers most successfully use price-off discounts?

25. Describe sales promotion tactics in business-to-business settings.

26. What problems must be overcome when developing international sales promotions programs?

KEY TERMS

consumer promotions (sometimes called *sales promotions*) incentives designed for a firm's customers.

free standing inserts (FSI) sheets of coupons distributed in newspapers, primarily on Sunday.

instant redemption coupon coupon that customers can redeem immediately when making a purchase.

bounce-back coupons coupons that customers cannot redeem instantly but instead must be used at a later purchase.

scanner-delivered coupons coupons issued at the cash register, which are triggered by an item being scanned.

cross-ruffing the placement of a coupon for one product on another product.

response offer coupons coupons are issued (or mailed) following requests by consumers.

free-in-the-mail premiums gifts given to individuals for purchasing products; however, the customer must mail in a proof of purchase to the manufacturer to receive the gift.

in- or on-package premiums small gifts, such as toys in cereal boxes, in which the gift is often disguised or packaged so the consumer must buy the product to find what it is.

store or manufacturer premiums gifts given by either the retail store or the manufacturer when the customer purchases a product.

self-liquidating premiums gifts that accompany purchases whereby consumers must pay an amount of money for them.

promotion prone consumers individuals who are not brand loyal and regularly respond to coupons, price-off plans, or premiums, only purchasing items that are on-deal.

brand-loyal consumer someone who purchases only one particular brand and does not substitute regardless of any deal being offered.

price-sensitive consumer a consumer for whom price is the primary, if not the only, criterion used in making a purchase decision.

CRITICAL THINKING EXERCISES

Discussion Questions

1. According to Kim James, sales promotion manager for Eckerd Drug, "The teen and preteen segments are important because they (teens) are developing buying habits and loyalties during these ages and are our future loyal consumers." In addition to established brands such as Cover Girl and Maybelline, Eckerd Drug now stocks brands such as Bonne Bell, Jane, and Naturistics.[40] Which consumer promotions would be the best to attract teens and preteens to the cosmetics in Eckerd Drug? What tie-ins or overlays would you recommend?

2. Many manufacturers believe the best method for differentiating their brands from competitors is advertising. It is true that consumer and trade promotions cannot replace advertising in brand development. At the same time, well-chosen promotional tactics can support brand differentiation. Discuss which consumer promotions manufacturers should and should not use to develop their brands. Justify your answer.

3. As with the other consumer promotions, international expansion requires understanding the laws and customs of each country and culture. For example, in Saudi Arabia and other Muslim countries, Clinique had to modify its sampling techniques. In the United States and Western cultures, Clinique provides cosmetic samples in retail outlets for customers to try. In the United States, females normally sell retail cosmetics, while in Saudi Arabia males do. At the same time, Muslim custom prohibits a male from touching a female, so female customers must either apply the cosmetics themselves or bring their husbands to the store with them.

    Asking a female customer "What color are your eyes?" constitutes a grave offense in Saudi Arabia, because the eyes are believed to be the gateway to the soul. Asking her about skin tone does not make sense, because females keep their faces covered after they reach the age of 14. Sampling is very important for Clinique in Saudi Arabia.[41] How would you organize a sampling program in light of these cultural factors? What other consumer promotions could be used? If you have someone in your class from a Muslim country, ask your classmate to discuss the use of consumer promotions in his or her home country.

4. Design a magazine advertisement with a detachable coupon or premium for one of the following products. Compare your offer with those of other students in your class. Discuss the differences between the offers.

    a. SunBright Tanning Salon

    b. Dixie Printing

    c. Hamburger Haven

    d. Blue Bell Ice Cream

5. Suppose the Rawlings Sports Equipment Company tries to increase sales of baseball gloves this season. The company intends to use consumer coupons. Discuss the pros and cons of each method of distributing coupons for Rawlings listed in Figure 11.2. Which methods should it use? Why?

6. To maintain its strong brand image, suppose Revlon's marketing team decides to use a premium for each of its lipstick products. What type of premium would you suggest for Revlon for each of the target markets listed below? Which premium would you use? Justify your answers.

    a. Caucasian females over the age of 50

    b. African American females, ages 14 to 19

    c. Hispanic females, ages 25 to 40

    d. Professional females, ages 30 to 50

7. Meet in groups of four to six students. Ask each group member to identify the last contest and the last sweepstakes he or

she entered. What was the enticement to enter? What was the extrinsic reward? What was the intrinsic reward?

8. Video games generate huge revenues for many companies. One manufacturer decided to use sampling as a method to reach the primary target market, males between ages 15 and 30. The sampling could have been distributed in one of two ways. First, the actual game could be loaded on a computer for targeted individuals. Second, potential customers could be sent an abbreviated version of the game. Which sampling method would be the best? Using Figure 11.4, discuss the pros and cons of each sampling method in terms of this new video game. Which type and method of sampling would you recommend? Why?

9. Consumers can be divided into three broad categories in terms of how they respond to consumer promotions: (1) promotion prone, (2) brand loyal, and (3) price sensitive. Identify two services or goods that would fit into each category for you personally. For example, you may be promotion prone when you buy soft drinks (your favorite brand is "What's on Sale!") but be very brand loyal when you buy shoes (Nike, Reebok). Compare your completed list with those of other students. Discuss the differences you observe.

10. Interview three people who have lived in another country about the use of consumer promotions in their countries. Make a list of those promotions heavily used and those not used. Present your findings to the class.

Creating Consumer Promotions for an IMC Advertising Campaign

Besides all of the offers your company might make to retailers, other offers go directly to consumers. Coupons, premiums, sweepstakes, and contests and other sales promotions can spice up your IMC approach by appealing to various individuals. When these promotional materials are tied in with the firm's theme, image, and advertisements, the result can be a positive impact on how people view the product and the company. This chapter's exercise is designed to cause you to consider the relationship between consumer promotions and trade promotions for individual purchasers, international customers, channel members, and other businesses. Access this information from your IMC Plan Pro disk or at **www.prenhall.com/clow**.

BUILDING AN
IMC
CAMPAIGN

IMC PlanPro!

CASE 1

SUNNY SUCCESS

Jessica Corgiat faced a difficult challenge as she took over the Sun Products, Inc. account. As a relatively new account executive, Jessica knew it was important to establish measurable results when conducting various advertising campaigns. Sun Products sells items primarily oriented toward beach-related activities, the most successful of which is the company's line of sunscreen products.

The tanning industry faces a unique set of challenges as a new generation of consumers emerge. First, more than ever consumers are aware of the dangerous long-term effects of tanning. These include more wrinkles along with vastly increased chances of developing skin cancer in later life. In Australia, where the ozone layer is the most depleted, exposure to the sun is even more hazardous. More importantly, however, is a potential shift in cultural values regarding appearance.

A few generations ago in Europe, completely white skin was a sign of affluence. Those who were forced to work outside developed tans. Those who lived as royalty or as the wealthy class could show their high social standing by simply keeping out of the sun.

As the new millennium commences, it is possible that a certain set of consumers will begin to believe that tanning is equal to foolishness. Or at least, that a suntan is no longer as "sexy" as it has been for many years. Beach bums and bunnies continue to run counter to this trend. The question remains, however, whether a national obsession with being browner continues in the general population.

One method to counter this problem is by developing new products designed to screen out the sun rather than enhancing the sun's tanning properties. Lotions with higher SPF (sun protection factor) values generally sell at higher prices. Higher-quality sunscreens do not wash off in a pool or while swimming. Further, items containing herbal ingredients and new aromas are designed to entice new interest. Sun Products with aloe vera and vitamin E may help reduce the pain and heal a sunburn more quickly. Products that "tan" without exposure to the sun are being developed for those who want the beach look without doing time in the sand.

At the same time, to promote more "traditional" products to college students on spring break and others who still enjoy a deep, dark tan requires careful promotion. Advertisements often stress the "fun" aspects of being outdoors.

Hawaiian Tropics, one of the chief competitors in the tanning industry, has taken a unique approach to the promotion of its products. The company holds an annual contest in which the Tropics team of beach girls is chosen to represent the firm. Contestants are female, beautiful, and have good tans. Those who win the contest tour the country promoting Hawaiian Tropics products and appear on television programs such as *Wild On* on the E! channel.

At individual events held at beaches across the United States and in other locations, free samples of Hawaiian Tropics may be given out, along with coupons and other purchase incentives. Giveaways of beach towels and other beach equipment are used to heighten interest in the product at various stores.

Jessica is considering how to respond to this quickly changing marketplace. Besides product development, she needs to describe a "theme" the company can use, either oriented toward "safety" or "sexy" or "safety with sexy." She is considering the entire range of promotional possibilities, from coupons for new products, to premiums as giveaways for existing products, to contests, sampling, bonus packs (with various ranges of SPF values in the same pack), to refunds for higher-priced lotions. She knows the key is to maintain a message and theme for this company, which will help it stand out in the crowd of Coppertone, Bain de Soleil, and Hawaiian Tropics. She realizes to succeed she needs Sun Products' POP displays placed prominently in as many places as possible, from drugstores to swimming specialty stores.

1. Which consumer sales promotions items will be least helpful to Jessica and Sun Products?

2. Which consumer sales promotions items will be most helpful to them?

3. Design an IMC program for Sun Products, Inc., focusing on advertising themes, trade promotions, and consumer sales promotions. Explain how it will differentiate the company from other suntan product companies.

CASE 2

A STICKY EUROPEAN MESS

Irene Freitas knew she faced an uphill battle. Irene has been the marketing director for the highly successful Phil's Fabulous Pastries for the past seven years. Phil's is well known across the East Coast for cinnamon rolls, turnovers, twists, and a variety of fruit-laden pastries. Many of its customers are highly brand loyal, and many smaller cafés and coffee shops (although not Starbucks) feature Phil's pastries.

Phil Diamond, CEO of the company, decided that the firm had saturated the marketplace. Expansion to the Midwest invites competition from many

(continued)

highly successful Chicago and Kansas City–based pastry companies. The idea of moving farther west was not inviting, because Phil was concerned that his company could not compete well there either.

Phil decided to consider the possibility of expanding into Europe. Phil loved to travel to France, Spain, and Germany. He has seen many small bakeries that were thriving, but believed no real major pastry competitor existed in many countries in the European community. He asked Irene to travel there to investigate the opportunity to "go global."

What Irene was afraid to tell Phil was that, most Europeans tended to highly resent U.S. companies. She had seen some recent surveys indicating that the majority of Europeans from many countries believed companies from the United States were driven by profits and nothing more. They also resented the exportation of U.S. "culture" through its films and Internet sites, which many considered to be destructive to the well-being of the youth. Europeans think Americans carry and use too many guns, are racist, and are too materialistic.[42] Irene also hated to think that she would need to tell Phil that he might be a prime example of what Europeans tend to dislike. He was a "bottom line" kind of guy, gruff, and not exactly versed in the ways of other cultures.

Phil's pastries always entered a new local market in the same way. The company would set up a series of sampling sites, where free pastries were given out with coffee or other beverages at restaurants, coffee shops, and grocery stores. Quickly, two-for-one coupons were distributed to those who would fill out free-drawing entries for prizes at the giveaway locations.

Later, Phil's followed up with local newspaper coupons and cooperative television advertising for any location that would carry its pastries. Phil's never set up freestanding retail outlets, instead focusing on simply shipping product to other stores. The net result was low overhead, with a high markup on each item. Phil's shared the costs of coupon redemptions and other giveaways with local stores. Irene was dubious as to whether these tactics would work in the European community.

1. Assess the odds of success for Phil's Fabulous Pastries.

2. Would Phil's do well in France, where pastries are quite popular? Why or why not?

3. What kinds of consumer promotions programs have the best chances of working when selling pastries in the United States and in other countries?

ENDNOTES

1. Kapil Bawa and Srini S. Srinivasan, "Coupon Attractiveness and Coupon Proneness: A Framework for Modeling Coupon Redemption," *Journal of Marketing Research,* 34, no. 4 (November 1997), pp. 517–25; "Coupon Use Seen Growing," *Editor and Publisher,* 129, no. 47 (November 23, 1996), pp. 16–17; "DSN Charts: Coupons," *Discount Store News,* 38, no. 9 (May 3, 1999), p. 4.

2. Corliss L. Green, "Media Exposure's Impact on Perceived Availability and Redemption of Coupons by Ethnic Consumers," *Journal of Advertising Research,* 35, no. 2 (March–April 1995), pp. 56–64.

3. "Net Coupons Deliver High Redemption Rate," *Frozen Food Age,* 47, no. 3 (October 1998), p. 63; "Replace Coupon Clipping with Clicking," *Chain Store Age,* 74, no. 12 (December 1998), p. 226.

4. "Are Coupons Still Cutting it with Customers?" *Marketing News,* 34, issue 22 (October 23, 2000), p. 6.

5. Green, "Media Exposure's Impact on Perceived Availability and Redemption of Coupons by Ethnic Consumers."

6. Elizabeth Gardener and Minakshi Trivedi, "A Communication Framework to Evaluate Sales Promotion Strategies," *Journal of Advertising Research,* 38, no. 3 (May–June 1998), pp. 67–71.

7. "Coupon Rooks, Sybil Gets a Sole, Just Imitate It, etc.," Adweek, Western Edition, 45, no. 24 (June 12, 1995), p. 24.

8. "DSN Charts: Coupons."

9. Don Jagoda, "The Seven Habits of Highly Successful Promotions," *Incentive,* 173, no. 8 (August 1999), pp. 104–5.

10. Rachel McLaughlin, "Freebies: From the Financial Side," *Target Marketing,* 21, no. 7 (July 1998), pp. 67–68.

11. Kate Bertrand, "Premiums Prime the Market," *Advertising Age's Business Marketing,* 83, no. 5 (May 1998), p. S6.

12. Theresa Howard and Terry Lefton, "KFC Units Buried in Bean Bags," *Brandweek,* 40, no. 4 (January 25, 1999), pp. 4–5.

13. Jagoda, "The Seven Habits of Highly Successful Promotions."

14. Bertrand, "Premiums Prime the Market."

15. Alexander Haim, "Match Premiums to Marketing Strategies," *Marketing News,* 34, issue 20 (October 25, 2000), p. 12.

16. Allen Fishman, "Sales Promotions Easy Way to Plug Business," *Denver Business Journal,* 49, no. 3 (September 26, 1997), p. 28A.

17. Rodney J. Moore, "Games Without Frontiers," *Marketing Tools* (September 1997), pp. 38–42.

18. Matt Andrejczak, "12 Banks Help Schools Get Rebates on Books Through Marketing Pact with Amazon.com," *American Banker,* 164, no. 205 (October 25, 1999), p. 18.

19. "Doin' the Rebate Rumba," *Consumer Reports,* 64, no. 11 (November 1999), pp. 62–63.

20. Aaron Ricadela, "Rebates Bundles Promote Margins," *Computer Retail Week,* 167 (April 21, 1997), pp. 41–42.

21. Alison Wellner, "Try It—You'll Like It!" *American Demographics,* 20, no. 8 (August 1998), pp. 42–43.

22. Jennifer Kulpa, "Bristol-Myers Squibb Breaks Ground with Direct Response Product Sampling Website," *Drug Store News,* 19, no. 7 (April 7, 1997), p. 19.

23. Claire Mahoney, "Because It's Worth It," *Soap, Perfumery and Cosmetics,* 72, no. 7 (July 1999), pp. 61–64; Wellner, "Try It—You'll Like It!"

24. Beng Soo Ong and Foo Nin Ho, "Consumer Perceptions of Bonus Packs: An Exploratory Analysis," *Journal of Consumer Marketing,* 14, no. 2–3 (1997), pp. 102–12.

25. Larry J. Seibert, "Are Bonus Packs Profitable for Retailers?" *Chain Store Age,* 72, no. 12 (December 1996), pp. 116–18.

26. Mike Ogden, "Price-Based Promotions May Hurt Your Bottom Line," *Washington Business Journal,* 18, no. 6 (June 18, 1999), p. 54.

27. Showwei Chu, "Welcome to Canada, Please Buy Something," *Canadian Business,* 71, no. 9 (May 29, 1998), pp. 72–73.

28. Allyson L. Stewart-Allen, "Cross-Border Conflicts on European Sales Promotions," *Marketing News,* 33, no. 9 (April 26, 1999), p. 10; Chu, "Welcome to Canada, Please Buy Something"; Howard and Lefton, "KFC Units Buried in Bean Bags."

29. Fishman, "Sales Promotions Easy Way to Plug Business."

30. Christine Bunish, "Expanded Use of Collateral Material, Catalogs Boost Sales Promotions," *Advertising Age's Business Marketing,* 84, no. 5 (May 1999), p. S11.

31. "Microsoft, CPAs Unite on Market," *Computer Reseller News,* no. 766 (December 1, 1997), p. 66.

32. Stewart-Allen, "Cross-Border Conflicts on European Sales Promotions."

33. Allyson L. Stewart-Allen, "Below-the Line Promotions Are Below Expectations," *Marketing News,* 29, no. 19 (September 11, 1995), p. 9.

34. "International Coupon Trends," *Direct Marketing,* 56, no. 4 (August 1993), pp. 47–49

35. "Targeting Supermarket Shoppers," *Target Marketing,* 19, no. 10 (October 1996), p. 44; "International Coupon Trends."

36. Kamran Kashani and John A. Quelch, "Can Sales Promotion Go Global?" *Business Horizons,* 33, no. 3 (May–June 1990), pp. 37–43.

37. Kusum L. Ailawadi and Scott A. Neslin, "The Effect of Promotion on Consumption: Buying More and Consuming It Faster," *Journal of Marketing Research,* 35, no. 3 (August 1998), pp. 390–98.

38. Kenneth Hein, "The New Players," *Incentive,* 173, no. 6 (June 1999), pp. 21–24.

39. Mike Mohammad, "Making All Strands Lead Back to Brand," *Brandweek,* 39, no. 43 (November 16, 1998), pp. 28–29.

40. Liz Parks, "Chains See Today's Wealthy Teens as Tomorrow's Loyal Customers," *Drug Store News,* 21, no. 15 (September 27, 1999), p. 84.

41. Vanessa Friedman, "Planet Clinique," *Elle,* 13, no. 9 (May 1998), pp. 218–19.

42. *Joplin Globe,* "Many Europeans Hostile Toward U.S. Companies." (May 10, 2000), p. B-4.

Personal Selling, Database Marketing, and Customer Relationship Management

12

Chapter Objectives

Understand the role personal selling plays in the success of both retail outlets and manufacturing operations.

Recognize the critical function of personal selling in business-to-business IMC programs.

Examine the role of personal selling in buying decision-making processes of retail customers, other businesses, and international customers.

Learn how to match a database program with an IMC program.

Use a database to improve direct-marketing, permission marketing, and frequency programs.

Apply the database to customer relationship management (CRM).

HAIR CARE:

The Personal Selling of Personalized Services

A salon treatment is more than just a cut or a perm. For men, the trend is moving toward exfoliating pores, smoothing skin with moisturizers, and using hair colors, especially in Europe. Even so, sales of men's toiletries exceeded $2.8 billion in the United States in 1998. For women, hair coloring, shampoos, lighteners, treatments, and permanents still are the staples.

Those who dispense beauty products for men and women have unique roles. Customers expect the hair care professional to deliver a high-quality style or coloring treatment and also to function as a fashion adviser. While women often are interested in the cosmetic benefits of products, men tend to focus on the functional performance benefits of a scent or look. The personal service person working in a salon must know how to complete the technical tasks of cutting and shaping hair, and have the interpersonal sales skills needed to vend the outlet's other goods and services.

The second half of the twentieth century witnessed a shift in the nature of personal services. Previously, men went to barber shops and women patronized beauty salons. Unisex trends have changed the traditional structure of hair care, and chains such as Prime Cuts, Master Cuts, and others grew in response to demands for places where Mom, Dad, and the kids could all be served at the same time. Freestanding hair care locations compete with style salons in malls and with those that operate as parts of other retail stores, such as JC Penney. Small individual shops face rugged competition from companies specializing in not only cutting and styling but also other personal care features.

Individual stylists know the keys to personal success include repeat business and good tips. Therefore, while delivering a shampoo or style, the stylist often tries to personalize the contact enough so that a new customer will ask to be served by the same employee on the next visit.

One trend many firms utilize to increase store revenues is to become the sole provider of a supplier's hair care products within a given territory. One shop may feature Nexus conditioners and shampoos, while another sells Wella products. The Wella cosmetic supplier, featuring pro-ducts such as Koleston Perfect, Viva Color, High Hair, and Wellaflex, became well established in Germany in the 1990s. Since then, the company has become strong in Europe, Asia, and South America. Wella currently is trying to strengthen its hold on Japan and Malaysia. Many male customers enjoy Wella's mousse and styling gel products.

Salon employees may or may not be happy with the idea that they must sell various products in addition to rendering services. Although a stylist gains commissions and incentives for selling the goods, the same individual does not want to risk alienating a client by "pushing" a given set of products onto the customer. This creates a balancing act between the goals of the job (repeat customers and tips) and the goals of the organization (increased revenues based on product sales). Management must carefully monitor both, with the ultimate goal remaining: to serve a happy and satisfied customer base.

The U.S. trend toward megastores may continue to change not only the selling of personal products but also the venues in which those products are delivered. A full-service boutique offers not only hairstyling and care but also massage, manicure–pedicure, and facial treatment services. Specialists in each area will be expected to continue to provide quality personal care but also to sell store tie-ins with individualized suppliers.

The ultimate winners in this environment may be customers, who can shop around for quality and price in the personal services area. The losers may be the small, old-time barbershops and beauty salons, which must upgrade and add services in order to compete in this new, dynamic, and complex environment.[1]

WILLAMETTE FURNITURE COMPANY

Personal selling is another key component of an IMC plan. The relationships a company builds with customers often begin with a sales call or contact by an in-store salesperson. These individuals must speak with the same voice that is being used throughout the rest of the company. The message must stay clear and consistent in order to support advertisements, consumer and trade promotions, and other marketing activities. To accommodate these efforts, the marketing team must work diligently to develop and maintain a solid database.

In the Willamette Furniture Company example provided on the IMC Plan Pro disk, personal selling is described in sections 5.2.3 and 6.2.3. In this type of environment, long-term relationships with customers are especially crucial. The database program is described in section 5.2.5. Willamette's marketing team needs a strong handle on who buys the furniture, what causes them to buy, and the types of information they need. Managing the entire customer relationship process helps the firm present its message in a clear and consistent manner, designed for the long haul.

overview

An integrated marketing communications program relies heavily on the skills of those who have the most interaction with customers. These individuals become the "face" of the company. Quality relationships between representatives of the company and buyers are crucial ingredients in the entire marketing program. Intimate, trusting, and friendly interactions create long-term bonds that help a firm build and maintain a strong share of the market. A positive purchasing experience often causes the buyer to provide word-of-mouth-recommendations to as many as six other people, such as family members or friends. A complaining customer is likely to tell as many as 11 other people when something bad happens.[2] Therefore, personal selling is a major factor in the success or failure of an IMC program, and of the company itself.

In this chapter, three closely related topics are examined. First, personal selling is described both in terms of consumer programs and business-to-business selling activities. Second, database marketing programs are examined. Third, customer relationship management (CRM) is described. The primary goals of all three of these activities are: (1) to make certain they match with other IMC efforts, and (2) to make sure they mix well with each other. When this occurs, the company's message reaches the customer through both personal (sales rep) and impersonal (media) channels.

PERSONAL SELLING

Personal selling is sometimes called the "last 3 feet" of the marketing function, because 3 feet is the approximate distance between the salesperson and the customer on the retail sales floor as well as the distance across the desk from the sales rep to a prospective business customer. A bond or partnership between a sales representative and his or her clients can be one of the most valuable assets a company holds in the marketplace. Personal selling can be divided into two major categories: (1) retail sales and (2) business-to-business selling.

RETAIL SALES

Sales to consumers are finalized by retail salespeople. Transactions occur on the sales floor, in checkout lines, on the telephone, and in other places. The most common thread tying these selling activities together is that the salesperson "is" the company as far as the customer is concerned. Retail selling and its ties to the overall IMC program are vitally important to marketing success.[3] It can be divided into four general categories:

1. Selling in shops and stores
2. Personal selling and services
3. Telemarketing
4. Other retail sales activities

Selling in Shops and Stores

The most common form of retail selling is the **single transaction** type, in which a salesperson meets with the customer and works with that individual until the sale is finalized or the person decides to shop elsewhere. Most specialty stores (e.g., jewelry, fashion boutiques, antique stores) feature single transaction sales, as do automobile dealerships and other bigger-ticket item stores.

The type of selling that is rapidly replacing single transactions in shops and stores is the **order taker** type of sale. Order takers are individuals who perform tasks as simple as filling an order at Burger King to more involved orders in hardware or lumber stores. Many times order-taking in a retail situation overlaps with serving as the *cashier.* Large operations such as Lowe's, Target, and Wal-Mart separate cashier work from order-taking; however, in a smaller setting such as a bookstore one person provides both functions.

Personal Selling and Services

Services can be divided into two categories. First, some services are simply sold by the sales rep, and that is the fundamental activity driving the relationship. Insurance sales are an example of this kind of selling. The insurance agent writes the contract. The insurance company is responsible for processing claims and other aspects of the relationship with the customer. This type of selling is often a single transaction, but also can be a **repeat transaction** type of relationship, when customers routinely return to the same company and salesperson. Often this form of selling involves some aspect of *problem-solving,* in which individual customers solve problems by making purchases.

The second type of service is one in which the person doing the selling also performs the service. Many individuals sell or perform services for retail customers. Lube and oil shops sell oil and provide oil change services at the same time. Many people sell the services they render, including the personal services of hair care, massage therapy, lawn mowing, gardening, and so forth. These service providers need *repeat business* to succeed. Loyalty and trust are key parts of the relationship. These individuals must be skilled at providing the services and work well with the public.

Telemarketing

Another type of retail selling takes place using telemarketers. These individuals use the telephone to make sales calls and presentations. **Inbound telemarketing** occurs when employees only handle inbound calls. They do not make initial contacts. Instead, they respond to telephone orders or inquiries. Many foll-free numbers are designed to attract inbound calls.

Outbound telemarketing means sales representatives call prospective customers or clients. Typical consumer products sold in this manner include long-distance service, credit cards, service contracts for appliances previously purchased, and an endless variety of aluminum siding to college fund-raising campaigns. Many people consider these calls invasive and annoying. Many states have now developed "no-call list" programs, in which registered citizens can insist on not being called.

GE PROFILE ARCTICA™
The Ultimate in Refrigeration

- **Express Chill™**
  Chill Beverages in Minutes, Not Hours.
- **Express Thaw™**
  Defrost Food in Half the Time
- **Quick Ice™**
  Provides Ice Up to 40 Percent Faster Than Normal for Parties and Social Gatherings

All While Using Up To 40 Percent Less Energy!

FREE AREA DELIVERY!

FREE INSTALLATION!

GREEN ⟨GE⟩ YATES

35 YEARS OF SERVING THE JOPLIN AREA   **1821 Main   623-5125**   WE SERVICE WHAT WE SELL

Understanding the consumer buying process is very important for sales staff at Green-Yates when selling large ticket items such as refrigerators.

Source: Used with permission of the *Joplin Globe*, Joplin, Missouri.

Other Retail Sales Activities

Other retail selling activities are used to enhance profits. For example, restaurants sometimes employee individuals whose sole job is to display an attractive array of desserts or serve as a wine steward. Many bookstores such as Borders offer coffee and small snacks to customers. Video stores employ individuals to stock shelves and make sales by offering movie-renting advice to regulars who frequent the shop.

These activities, including providing small repair services, advice, and help filling out credit applications are crucial ingredients in building profitability for smaller retail outlets and chain stores. A well-integrated IMC plan notes the importance of these additional functions that make customers happy and keep them coming back.

RETAIL SALES PRESENTATIONS

The typical retail sales presentation involves more than just trying to close a deal. Objectives include gathering information and developing a relationship for the future. A well-managed IMC program stresses the important of quality contacts between salespeople and customers on the retail floor. As a customer interacts with a company, there are five steps in the consumer buying process, which are shown in Figure 12.1. Chapter 3 described those steps in detail.

From a *selling* perspective, the salesperson must effectively respond to each stage. In the problem recognition stage, the sales rep must be aware that the customer has not completely come to grips with the need and should react by helping the customer clarify that need. Thus, a person buying a refrigerator should consider the size, freezer space needed, ice maker option, cold water feature, and color before thinking about a particular brand.

The sales rep may also assist in an information search by providing facts about several models, designs, or options. This occurs while favoring his or her company's brand. As the customer evaluates the alternatives, the salesperson can discuss the benefits of all brands and show how his or her company's option is superior. When the purchase decision is made, the rep stops selling the product and starts selling other related items, such as service contracts. It is important to make sure the customer is assured the product was a great choice.

Unfortunately, many salespeople in single transaction settings use high-pressure tactics to make sales. They also fail to recognize the importance of the first three steps of the buying decision-making process. Doing so costs the company repeat business and causes

> ▶ **Problem recognition**
>
> ▶ **Information search**
>
> ▶ **Evaluation of alternatives**
>
> ▶ **Purchase decision**
>
> ▶ **Postpurchase evaluation**

FIGURE 12.1
Consumer Buying Process

more shoppers to walk out before a purchase because they are confused and frustrated by not having sufficient information.

A retail sales presentation is primarily made to end users. Courtesy, attentiveness, and a pleasant demeanor are the main ingredients needed to become a successful retail salesperson. Marketing executives should emphasize to all members of the organization that personal selling is a key element of the IMC program. Salespeople execute the final phase of a successful IMC program—completing the sale.

INTEGRATED LEARNING EXPERIENCE

Retail sales are important for both retailers and manufacturers. Just as manufacturers want a retailer to push their products, retailers want their salesclerks to encourage customers to purchase from them rather than another retail outlet. Retailers are not concerned about which brand customers buy as long as they buy it from them. Articles about retail selling are available at "Retailer News" in the Archive section at **www.retailernews.com**. To get a feel for companies that offer training to retail salespeople, access Sales Train in Ontario, Canada, at **www.retailsalestrain.com**. For the United States, Accelerated Performance Training offers a number of products and services for retail sales. Examine the services available under "Programs" and "Products" at its Web site, **www.aptretail.com**.

The Manufacturer's Dilemma in Retail Selling

From the manufacturer's perspective, one problem remains: More than half the time, a customer finalizes a purchase decision while *in the store.* The retail salesperson has a tremendous impact on that decision, yet the manufacturer has little or no influence over that retail employee. For example, a retail salesperson who prefers Amana refrigerators steers customers toward those models, even when General Electric, Coldspot and others are available.

To combat this problem, manufacturers rely on three strategies. First, the manufacturer can provide training to retail salespeople emphasizing the manufacturer's products. Second, advertising may be used to gain the attention of both customers and retail salespeople. And third, contests and incentives may be used to emphasize the manufacturer's products. Also, many manufacturers utilize **missionary salespeople**, who try to develop goodwill, stimulate demand, and provide training incentives to enhance the manufacturer in the retailer's mind. Missionary salespeople are also known as *merchandisers* and *detailers.*

Cross-Selling

Cross-selling involves the marketing of other items following the purchase of a good or service. For example, banks offer insurance, loans, and other financial services in addition to checking and savings accounts. Inbound telemarketing calls are a good time to cross-sell goods and services.[4] Customers are not defensive because they have initiated the call. Resolving the problem or answering the question that prompted the call makes the customer feel better. The inbound telemarketer often has access to customer information as the call takes place.

While advertising can develop a strong brand name like Peerless, salespeople at a hardware store often influence which brands are finally purchased.
Source: Courtesy of Delta Faucet Company. Photograph by John Welzenbach.

Now that you've stopped playing the field, maybe it's time to think about another kind of diamond.

Congratulations. You've decided to pop the question. Now it's time to select that special ring. Make sure it's a Keepsake.

The name Keepsake engraved on the inside of your ring is your assurance of superior quality and lasting value. It tells you that your center diamond has been laser inscribed and authenticated by a certificate to meet the standards known as the 4Cs. Your diamond is Cut to proper proportions, its Clarity is brilliant, its Color is dazzling, its Carat weight is genuine.

It also assures you of a 5th C, Confidence. Confidence that your Keepsake ring has been mounted by master artisans. Confidence that its quality is warranted for a lifetime. Confidence that whichever classic design you choose, she will love it. And love you for it.

Only a Keepsake says, *Love always.*
For information about Keepsake 1-888-iKEEPSAKE

KEEPSAKE
DIAMOND JEWELRY *since* 1930

When consumers evaluate alternatives, salespeople have the opportunity to discuss the benefits of brands such as Keepsake.
Source: Courtesy of Keepsake.

Successful cross-selling involves collecting quality customer data, integrated information technology, specialized software, computerized decision models, training, and the right type of salespeople. These individuals must be able to recognize when a customer is too angry or frustrated, or simply in a hurry and therefore not open to cross-selling tactics. Cross-selling may be part of both a retail and business-to-business marketing operation. An example of a business-to-business cross-selling program is present when a janitorial service company offers to provide pest-control protection to an ongoing client.

BUSINESS-TO-BUSINESS PERSONAL SELLING

Personal selling is the vital link between a vendor and a client. Effective presentations to business customers can build sales and create positive long-term relationships for the vendor. The three primary forms of business-to-business selling are: (1) field sales, (2) in-house sales, and (3) telemarketing, Internet, and technology-based programs.

Field sales involve the salesperson visiting the customer's place of business. Presentations are made to develop new customers or to encourage repeat business from ongoing customers. **Order getters** are salespeople who actively seek out new customers and sales.

In-house sales mean salespeople work from the company's office. They handle phone-in orders, faxes, and Internet accounts. Occasionally the rep makes the initial contact with the customer; however, normally these reps merely respond to or take orders from ongoing customers.

Telemarketing, Internet, and technology-based programs include both inbound and outbound calls. Internet programs and Web sites help firms develop more sophisticated linkages with various customers. Database programs and customer relations management are described later in this chapter.

Buyer-Seller Relationships

Personal selling can play a major role in creating a successful business-to-business marketing effort. Figure 12.2 illustrates various forms of buyer-seller relationships. The degree of interaction and length of the relationship vary dramatically depending on the form involved.

Single transaction sales are made in new-buy situations. Depending on the complexity of the purchase, it may be one rep (such as a real estate agent helping a company buy or sell a building) or a team of marketing professionals. If the potential contract is long and involved, more individuals will be involved in the single transaction sale.

Occasional transactions are often modified rebuy situations. Computers, telecommunications equipment, and manufacturing equipment are examples of occasional transac-

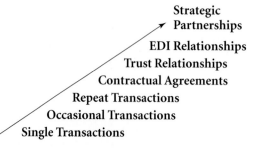

Strategic
Partnerships
EDI Relationships
Trust Relationships
Contractual Agreements
Repeat Transactions
Occasional Transactions
Single Transactions

FIGURE 12.2
Types of Selling Relationships

tions and modified rebuys. The buyer examines several vendors before making a purchase.

Repeat transactions occur when buyers purchase on a regular basis. Raw materials and component parts for machines are often repeated transactions in the business sector. They are similar to straight rebuy purchase decisions.

Contractual agreements are used to guarantee that the price and delivery of the good or service will remain stable over the length of the contract. With a contractual relationship, the seller does not need to worry about competitors until the next contract. It is important to create as much mutual trust as possible in these relationships.

Trust relationships move beyond contracts. The two parties have interacted and worked together so well that both parties believe they benefit from the relationship, and each party trusts the other.

An *electronic data interchange (EDI) relationship* expands the levels of trust to include the sharing of data. EDI relationships occur when one company provides full access to another in order to manage orders, purchases, shipping information, production data, and other relevant materials. EDI relationships are much more exclusive than other forms.

A *strategic partnership* is the most intimate. The goal is to collaborate on plans to benefit both parties and their customers. The seller looks for ways to modify or engineer products to improve the other company's position in the marketplace.

Each of these forms represents a different selling perspective. The potential value of each customer is evaluated as the firm develops relationships. Those with low potential do not evolve into more trusting situations. Figure 12.3 displays the steps involved in developing a strategic partnership.

An advertisement by Ceco Building Systems encouraging business customers to contact them to discuss their needs.
Source: Courtesy of Robinson & Associates, Tupelo.

▶ **Awareness:** The customer becomes aware of a vendor's capabilities.

▶ **Exploration:** The initial trial period at the transaction level with no or limited commitments by both parties.

▶ **Expansion:** The expansion of the interactions, commitments, and profits of both parties. A contractual arrangement may be reached.

▶ **Commitment:** The agreement by both parties on an exclusive trust relationship that may involve EDI interchanges.

▶ **Partnership:** The sharing of people, resources, data, and mission to accomplish a unified goal that benefits both parties.

FIGURE 12.3
Steps in Developing a Strategic Partnership

Source: Based on James C. Anderson, "Relationships in Business Markets: Exchange Episodes, Value Creation, and their Empirical Assessment," *Journal of the Academy of Marketing Science*, Vol. 23 (1996), pp. 346–350.

FIGURE 12.4
Personal Selling Process

- Identifying prospects
- Qualifying prospects
- Knowledge acquisition
- Sales approaches
- Sales presentation
- Follow-up

MANAGING THE BUSINESS-TO-BUSINESS SELLING PROCESS

Chapter 4 described the steps involved in business buying behavior as well as the individuals involved (members of the buying center). Understanding the process and reaching these individuals is best managed through the personal selling process displayed in Figure 12.4. No matter which type of salesperson is involved (field sales, in-house, or telemarketing), the steps involved are quite similar.

Identifying Prospects

Prospects are potential customers. It is important to quickly narrow prospects down to the most viable. First, however, the pool must be created. Figure 12.5 lists some of the most common places companies go to find prospects. Customer referrals are one of the best sources for leads, because the buyer already has some level of satisfaction with the seller. Databases, as described in the next section, help fine-tune prospects for individual products or services. Trade shows are places to gather names because attendees are potential buyers. Advertising and Internet inquiries mean the buyer has a higher level of interest and is making contact. Sales and trade promotions, such as a contest or sweepstakes, foster interest in companies that have some level of familiarity with the seller. Channel leads are similar to customer referrals, because there is a degree of confidence in the seller. Networking through professional, social, and business organizations may also provide new names. Cold calls are going to be the least productive, because nothing is known about the prospective buyer before making contact.

Qualifying Prospects

Qualifying prospects is the process of choosing individuals or companies holding the highest potential. This is a vital step, because sales calls are very expensive. Prospects may be grouped as low, medium, or high potential based on the questions shown in Figure 12.6. Every individual responsible for qualifying prospects should be thoroughly familiar with the firm's IMC plan. Advertisements and other messages should effectively reach prospects with the highest potential.

FIGURE 12.5
Methods of Prospecting

- Customer leads
- Databases
- Trade shows
- Advertising inquiries
- Internet inquiries
- Sales promotions
- Vendor leads
- Channel leads
- Networking
- Cold calls

▶ **What is the sales volume potential?**

▶ **Is the prospect dissatisfied with its current vendor?**

▶ **Does the prospect use single or multiple sourcing?**

▶ **Is the prospect a good fit with current customers?**

▶ **Does the prospect fit with the firm's IMC plan?**

▶ **How difficult will it be to get past the gatekeeper(s)?**

FIGURE 12.6
**Questions for
Qualifying Prospects**

INTEGRATED LEARNING EXPERIENCE

The high cost of making personal sales calls requires companies to narrow prospect lists down to the most attractive potential customers. To get a feel for qualifying prospects, assume you are a supplier of fiberglass that is used to manufacture surfboards. Listed below are manufacturers of surfboards. Look at each company's Web site. Then reduce the list to the best four prospects. Write down the criteria you used to qualify them using the information provided in this textbook as a guide.

Becker Surf Sport (www.beckersurf.com)
Aloha Surf Boards (www.alohasurfboards.com)
Bamboo Surfboards of Australia (www.bamboosurfboards.com.au)
Bruce Jones Surfboards (www.brucejones.com)
Stickman LLC (www.stickmansurf.com)
Schroedel Surfboards and Clothing (www.schroedel.com)
Gordon & Smith (www.gordonsmith.com)

Knowledge Acquisition

The goal of knowledge acquisition is to provide the information needed to make an effective sales presentation. Figure 12.7 lists the typical information that a salesperson obtains about a prospect prior to a call. The information can be used to either disqualify, downgrade, or upgrade a prospect. The sales rep's time will be used most efficiently when attention is given to the first three steps of the process. Many salespeople tend to skip these steps, moving forward to making sales pitches because sales are what generate commissions. Doing so, however, may cause the rep to waste time on nonproductive clients.

The salesperson should have a good sense of who might buy, the nature of the competition, potential buyers of the prospect's goods and services, and other factors that will affect the purchase decision. It is especially important to know if the prospect believes

▶ **Identify current vendor(s)**

▶ **Identify prospect's customers**

▶ **Assess customer needs**

▶ **Determine roles of price, service, and product attributes in the purchase decision**

▶ **Determine roles of trade and sales promotions in the purchase decision**

▶ **Determine critical customer benefits or product attributes**

▶ **Identify risk factors in switching vendors**

▶ **Identify buyer's personality type**

FIGURE 12.7
Knowledge Acquisition

there is risk involved in switching vendors. This information can help the salesperson and company structure the presentation as well as trade and sales promotions that may make the vendor look more attractive and less risky.

There are three personality types when it comes to buying. These reflect the *value orientation of the buyer*. They include: (1) intrinsic value buyers, (2) extrinsic value buyers, and (3) strategic value buyers.[5]

Intrinsic value buyers understand the product, know how to use it, and view the product as a commodity, making price the most important element. Often order takers can be used in finalizing intrinsic value purchases.

Extrinsic value buyers focus more on product attributes and the solution a particular product can provide. These buyers prefer a consultative sales approach in which the seller understands the problem and helps the buyer discover solutions.

Strategic value buyers usually seek out partnerships with suppliers. They want vendors who are willing to be partners in satisfying customer needs. These relationships normally involve cross-functional teams, such as when IBM sent a group to help Monsanto explore gene-mapping issues, a collaboration that became worth several hundred million dollars.[6]

Sales Approaches

Many sales approaches are used, and they may be classified into four main categories: (1) stimulus-response, (2) need-satisfaction, (3) problem-solution, and (4) mission-sharing. Each may be used effectively in the proper context.[7]

A **stimulus-response sales approach** uses specific statements (stimuli) to solicit specific responses from customers, similar to what is called a "canned" sales pitch. Often the salesperson memorizes the stimulus statement (the pitch). Telemarketers, retail sales clerks, and new field sales reps often use this method.

The goal of the **need-satisfaction sales approach** is to discover a customer's needs and then provide solutions that satisfy those needs. The salesperson must be skillful at asking the right questions. Quality relationships with customers make it easier to discover their needs.

The **problem-solution sales approach** requires the selling organization to analyze the buyer's operations. A team including engineers, salespeople, and other experts is normally required to understand a company's operations, its problems, and to offer feasible solutions. This approach matches well with complex new-buy situations.

In a **mission-sharing sales approach**, two organizations develop a common mission. They then share resources to accomplish that mission. This partnership resembles a joint venture as much as a selling relationship.

The biggest determinant of which sales approach will be used is the form of buyer-seller relationship present. The goals of the sales presentation and the nature of the product being offered also affect the sales approach that will be chosen.

Sales Presentations

There are similarities and differences between selling to other businesses as opposed to retail customers. Both go through a purchasing process that involves identifying needs and comparing alternatives (see Figure 12.8 for the business process). The primary dif-

▶ **Identification of need**

▶ **Establishment of specifications**

▶ **Identification of alternatives**

▶ **Identification of vendors**

▶ **Evaluation of vendors**

▶ **Selection of vendor(s)**

▶ **Negotiation of purchase terms**

FIGURE 12.8

The Business-to-Business Buying Processes

ference is that a retail customer is in a store and is, in essence, a "captive audience." In contrast, when selling to other businesses, the buyer can consider several companies at the same time. Therefore, the sales rep must take advantage of opportunities in which the rep has the buyer's full attention.

In new-buy situations, the salesperson can improve his or her chances by helping the customer establish product specifications. This allows the sales rep to display his or her concern and expertise, and also makes it possible to structure specifications to promote the rep's company.

In rebuy situations, most vendors experience difficulties getting past company gatekeepers when trying to reach members of the buying center. Often every rep is excluded in early stages of the buying process (Figure 12.8) except the current vendor. To succeed, other vendors must find creative ways to make contact and offer products and advantages that the current vendor does not have. When presented with the opportunity, the sales presentation must effectively and clearly establish the reasons why a new vendor should be considered.[8]

Follow-Up

The follow-up is as crucial as the sales presentation to the selling firm when a sales has been made. Keeping customers happy after they buy results in repeat business and brand loyalty. It is much more cost effective to retain customers than to continually find new ones. Unfortunately, successful follow-ups are hard to create. The salesperson will often not want to spend time on the customer, because commissions come from new sales, not following up on old ones.

The best method to create the proper environment so that follow-up calls will be made by the sales force starts with educating them about the value of brand loyalty, which is the quickest path to sales in the future. Next, they must be properly motivated. Retaining part of a commission until a follow-up call has been documented is one approach. It is also possible to simply pay or grant other credits for follow-up calls. It also helps to have experienced reps show new employees the value of long-term repeat business, both monetarily in terms of commissions and in reducing the stress of continually trying to find new customers.

Managing the business-to-business selling process is a crucial part of the IMC program. The sales manager and key sales reps should be included in the IMC planning process. Their inputs and advice can be valuable assets to the overall marketing program.

THE EVOLUTION OF MORE EFFECTIVE INCENTIVES FOR BUSINESS.

For rewards that drive business results, American Express Incentive Services has some of the most innovative ideas you'll find anywhere. Cash and retail gift certificates only go so far compared with high-tech rewards like Persona℠ Select – an electronically prepaid reward card that frees recipients to purchase what they want most. Do more for your associates. Do more for your business. Persona℠ Select. Only from American Express.

1.800.700.7610, ext. 900 | www.aeis.com

In an effort to help corporations motivate salespeople to drive business results, American Express Incentive Services offers a broad range of incentive reward solutions.
Source: Courtesy of American Express Incentive Services.

Videoconferencing never looked so good.

With today's reduced budgets and increased travel times, now more than ever Polycom's award-winning videoconferencing products are essential, must-have tools for getting business done. With the only end-to-end solutions that efficiently integrate video, voice, data and web collaboration, Polycom lets you be there without going there. As the industry leader, we can show you how our state-of-the-art video and audio quality redefines the concept of face-to-face meetings. And how our solutions can be tailored to fit any room and any budget. So isn't it time you got Polycom and stopped waiting in line?

RISK-FREE TRIAL!
TRY ANY POLYCOM
VIDEOCONFERENCING
SYSTEM FREE FOR
30 DAYS.*

Call today 1-877-POLYCOM
Go to www.polycom.com/see

* 100% Financing available on all Polycom systems

POLYCOM

In addition to a sales call, potential customers of Polycom's Videoconferencing System can contact Polycom through the Internet or by calling 1-877-POLYCOM.
Source: Courtesy of Polycom.

NEW TRENDS IN BUSINESS-TO-BUSINESS PERSONAL SELLING

Many recent trends in marketing have affected personal selling. As product parity becomes the norm, where there are fewer distinguishable differences between brands, it is important to understand how to create loyalty and a strong brand name as the company encounters these new selling trends, which are summarized in Figure 12.9.

Decline in the Number of Salespeople

Some sources estimate that the number of sales positions present in the United States will decline by as much as 50 percent in the next decade.[9] Technology makes it possible to use fewer people. As a result, sales managers must adapt by making sure the reps who remain have both the technical and selling skills necessary to meet consumer needs.

Expansion of Sales Channels

In today's market, many buyers purchase products or make orders without ever contacting a salesperson. The Internet and EDI technology make it possible to place and take orders electronically. Special selling enticements can also be delivered in new ways, such as through faxes and e-mails. Customers contact the company in numerous ways, such as by phone, in person, and through e-mail. All of these contact points should stress the same IMC message and theme. It is also important to track customer contacts to make sure customer needs are being met. Accounts should be regularly reviewed to make sure no client is left without service and follow-up attention.[10]

Long-Term Relationships and Strategic Partnerships

New technologies have led many companies to reduce the number of vendors with which they deal. In exchange, these buyers seek stronger relationships. Utilizing fewer vendors increases order sizes, allows for more quantity discounts, and establishes a better flow of materials from the seller to the buyer. When a company deals with a single vendor, that company must make certain the buyer receives all purchases in a timely fashion. A manufacturer missing one component part due to a later delivery must stop production. Therefore, logistics management becomes a crucial element of a strategic partnership or any other long-term, more exclusive relationship.[11]

Team Selling

The movement toward seeking out few vendors and stronger long-term commitments means more companies utilize teams rather than individuals to sell. Teams often include engineers as well as salespeople. The team's goal should be to provide better service to

FIGURE 12.9
Trends in Personal Selling

▶ **Decline in the number of salespeople**

▶ **Expansion of selling channels**

▶ **Long-term relationships and strategic partnerships**

▶ **Team selling**

ETHICS AND IMC PROGRAMS

Deceptive Sales Practices

For many consumers, the statement "salespeople cannot be trusted" applies to more than just car salespeople. From a business-to-business perspective, many buyers believe that salespeople will say or promise anything and everything to close a deal. Often this creates an adversarial situation where cooperation should exist. Here are some of the reasons why salespeople should avoid deceptive practices:

1. Repeat business is important to the salesperson and the company.
2. Word-of-mouth is a key part of creating new clients and customers.
3. Complaints may be filed with the Better Business Bureau.

There are also times when a salesperson would be less concerned about being deceptive. These include:

1. Situations in which it will be a one-time sale.
2. The salesperson and/or company believes there is an unending supply of new customers available.
3. The salesperson is about to leave the job or company.

In response to these concerns, many laws have been enacted. For example, in real estate transactions, new "disclosure" forms must be completed indicating that the seller is willing to reveal known problems associated with a house or property before making the sale and is financially responsible when known defects are not disclosed. Consider other industries and sales situations. Are "disclosures" possible in places other than housing sales? Which ones?

---

the buyer. It is essential that salespeople and engineers are trained to work together. Both should view their roles as problem solvers and consultants. The selling process should follow what has been described previously, starting with carefully identifying the buyer's needs. Then, the vending company can offer its best solution to the problem. Finally, careful follow-up is important.[12]

PERSONAL SELLING IN INTERNATIONAL MARKETS

Personal selling in international markets is difficult. A series of issues must be overcome in order to succeed. There are language problems, regional differences in culture, customs, and mores, and often suspicion, doubt, and mistrust are present. It takes time to build long-term, trusting relationships in many international settings.[13]

There is always a choice to be made when setting up an international personal selling system. The firm can hire and manage local members of the community to make sales calls, or company leaders can elect to send their own sales force overseas. Figure 12.10 lists some tips for training an international sales force. The salesperson must understand the vendor company while at the same time taking advantage of any expertise in working with the local culture.

One key individual is the *cultural assimilator,* as mentioned in earlier chapters. This individual helps screen company messages and methods of operation in order to avoid offending clients in other nations and cultures.

International competition has forced many companies to examine selling functions closely. Cold calls are difficult to justify because of the high cost. Marketing teams are willing to spend more time and money qualifying prospects in order to increase success rates of the sales force. Free-lancers, specialists, and other firms are available to provide assistance to companies seeking prospects in new regions.

> ▶ Provide information about culture, morés, customs, and traditions
>
> ▶ Ensure instructors have credibility
>
> ▶ Use instructors with experience in international sales
>
> ▶ Include in the training individuals native to the countries or regions
>
> ▶ Encourage salespeople to consider the positive experiences they are about to have
>
> ▶ Provide benefits that people in international markets seek from products being sold
>
> ▶ Present, discuss, and rehearse sales presentations and closings within cultural context
>
> ▶ As much as possible, provide language training instead of relying on translators

FIGURE 12.10
Tips for Training International Salespeople

The secret to managing personal selling in international settings is to carefully plan out the approach, account for the culture, and follow up when difficulties arise. As the world becomes smaller, more and more experts are available to help deal with the various nuances present in individual countries.[14]

DATABASE MARKETING

An extension of the selling activities a company performs is its database development and marketing program.[15] Developing an IMC database is not the same thing as database marketing. **Database development** is the creation of a database to support the overall company, IMC program, and total marketing effort. The steps involved in developing a database are described in Figure 12.11.

Determining Objectives

The objectives and role of the database in the marketing program determine much of what will take place as the data is generated. They typical questions posed concerning the data include:

- ▶ Who will use this information?
- ▶ What kinds of data are available?
- ▶ When (or how often) will information be collected and used?
- ▶ Where will the data be located or stored?
- ▶ Why do we need certain data and not other types?
- ▶ How will the data be used?

> ▶ Determine obectives
>
> ▶ Collect data
>
> ▶ Build data warehouse
>
> ▶ Mine data for information
>
> ▶ Develop marketing programs
>
> ▶ Evaluate marketing programs and data warehouses

FIGURE 12.11
Steps in Developing a Database

> ▶ **Internal customer data**
> ▶ **Commercial database services**
> ▶ **Survey data of customers**
> ▶ **Channel members**
> ▶ **Governmental data sources**

FIGURE 12.12
Sources of Data

Answers to these questions allow the marketing department to design the system. It is important to make sure the information helps the company maintain a successful IMC program.[16] Typical objectives for an IMC database include:

▶ Provide useful information about a firm's customers

▶ Create information about why customers purchase the products they do

▶ Share information with creatives as they prepare advertisements and promotional materials

▶ Reveal contact points to be used in direct-marketing programs

▶ Yield information about members of various buying centers in business-to-business operations

▶ Track changes in purchasing behaviors and purchasing criteria used by customers

These objectives may change or be modified over time. The essential information, however, remains relatively consistent.

Collecting Data

After the objectives of the IMC database have been determined, the firm is ready to seek out potential sources of data. Most firms use both internal and external sources. Customers are an internal source. Other sources are called secondary or external data. Figure 12.12 lists the major sources of data.

Internal customer data can be a rich source of information. Modern information technology makes it possible to collect more than just names and addresses. Through scanning technology, the purchasing behaviors of buyers can be examined. This information helps the marketing team identify and profile the company's best customers, cross-sell goods and services to key customers, and create profiles of consumers who might be enticed to become new company customers. Internal customer data should answer the questions posed in Figure 12.13. If they do not, the firm's marketing team should look for ways to expand the database and data collection techniques.

> ▶ **Where are the customers located?**
> ▶ **What have they purchased?**
> ▶ **How often have they purchased?**
> ▶ **How did they initially make contact?**
> ▶ **How do they order or purchase (in person, Web, mail, phone, etc.)?**
> ▶ **What is known about their families, occupations, payment histories, interests, attitudes, and so forth?**
> ▶ **In business-to-business situations, who are the influencers, users, deciders, and purchasers?**
> ▶ **In business-to-business, is it a corporate office or branch offices?**

FIGURE 12.13
Internal Data Information

Dialog is an online database service that can be used by companies in the development of a database.
Source: Courtesy of Dialog.

Internal customer data is not sufficient to meet all the needs of an IMC program. *External data* are also required. Psychographic, lifestyle, and attitudinal information can be valuable external data that are used to supplement what was collected from regular customers. The sources of secondary data include *commercial database services.* These services offer demographic information, such as data regarding income, age, race, marital status, and household type for various groups. Profiles such as a *neighborhood lifestyle cluster* are offered by commercial database services.

Another source is *survey data* collected from customers. To prevent bias in the surveys, it is often advisable to hire an external marketing research firm to conduct the interviews. A major advantage to hiring an external firm is that the company can supplement current customer data with noncustomer data. Then, the two groups can be compared.

Information obtained from *channel members* is helpful because channel members are often customers. Wholesalers and retailers are the manufacturer's primary customers and should be able to provide useful information about end users.

Finally, there are times in which the organization can collect information from *governmental data sources.* The government makes economic information available. Also, the Bureau of Vital Statistics and the Census Bureau offer information about various individuals.

Simply collecting data does not place them into useful form. The next step is to construct a system that makes the information helpful to the marketing team and others involved in the company's operations.

Building a Data Warehouse

Constructing a useful data warehouse requires an understanding of all the various ways members of the organization might use data. Some of the more common uses are:

- Targeting customers for a direct-marketing program
- Developing a system so that field salespeople have access to important customer information while making sales calls
- Making it possible for internal salespeople to be able to access the database when a customer calls to place an order
- Giving the service department and customer relations department access to customer data as they deal with inquiries and complaints

In building a data warehouse, internal information is combined with external data. One common method of enhancing internal information is through **geocoding**, which is the process of adding geographic codes to each customer record so the addresses of customers can be plotted on a map. Geocoding is especially helpful when decisions are made about placements of retail outlets. It is also useful when combining demographic information with lifestyle data. This helps the marketing team select media where ads will be most likely noticed (e.g., newspapers, radio stations, television programs).

One version of geocoding software is called CACI Coder/Plus. The software identifies a cluster in which an address belongs. A group such as Enterprising Young Singles in the CACI system would contain certain characteristics, such as enjoying dining, spending money on videos and personal computers, and reading certain magazines. A retailer could then target this group with mailings and special offers.[17]

Once the data warehouse has been built, other activities can begin. Convenient and accessible data make it possible to conduct quality data mining programs.

INTEGRATED LEARNING EXPERIENCE

Many companies turn to professional firms for assistance when developing a data warehouse. A company in New Zealand called Brains (**www.brains. co.nz**) has developed a customer relationship management system that allows companies to develop a sophisticated database. U.S. firms that provide similar services are Sagent Technology at **www.qmsoft.com** and Centrus at **www.centrus.com**. Access these Web sites to see what types of services they offer. What information can they add to a firm's database that would turn the database into a data warehouse? A major source of commercial data that can be added to a firm's database is provided by Donnelly Marketing at **www. donnellymarketing.com**. From its "Products and Services" menu, find the types of data a firm can purchase that would help supplement a database.

Data Mining

Data mining normally involves one of two approaches: (1) building profiles of customer groups, or (2) preparing models that predict future purchase behaviors based on past purchases. Data mining is used to develop a profile of the company's best customers. The profile, in turn, helps identify prospective customers. It may also be used to examine "good" customers to see if they are candidates for sales calls to move them from "good" to a higher value. Companies offering different types of goods and services will develop multiple profiles. These profiles are used to target sales calls and to look for situations in which cross-selling is possible.

The second approach to data mining is to develop models that predict future sales based on past sales activities. For example, Staples, Inc. used modeling to examine the company's catalog customers. The model allowed the marketing team to identify the names of the most frequent buyers and then target customized mailings to them.[18]

The method used to mine data is determined by specific informational needs. A direct-mail program to current customers is different than one designed to attract new customers. Profiles and models assist in designing the database best suited for each purpose or program.

This advertisement for men's clothes was placed in several women's magazines after analysis of the data indicated that many women are the ones who are actually choosing or purchasing the men's clothes.
Source: Courtesy of Haggar.

Developing Marketing Programs

Once the data have been mined for information, individual marketing programs can be designed. The data provide clues about the best approach for each group of customers. A quality database helps the marketing team decide

on types of sales promotions to be used, advertising media to be selected, and the type of information that will spark the interest of a particular group of customers. Thus, a group of high-end shoppers for apparel can be targeted when a new fall line of clothes is in stock.

Marketing programs may also enhance customer loyalty. For example, if a hotel chain knew in advance that a particular business traveler prefers a nonsmoking room, a queen-size bed, and reads *USA Today,* these items could be made available as the business person arrives. Training hotel clerks and other employees to use the database will lead them to providing better service, thereby building loyalty from regular customers.[19]

In the modern marketplace, account executives are increasingly interested in making sure someone from the client's database department is part of any project team. By supplying creatives with information such as psychographics, attitudes, purchase behaviors, lifestyles, and trends, the advertising agency is able to prepare messages with the best appeal to the most valuable customers.

COMMUNICATION ACTION

Levi-Strauss & Company: Building Relationships Through Database Management

To be effective, a company's database must be much more than a collection of names and addresses. Levi-Strauss & Company, when threatened by a combination of market forces and image problems, was able to respond by developing a strong database marketing program. Old Navy, Calvin Klein, and other brands had made inroads into the marketplace, just as Levi's had become associated with the older generation, possibly not hip enough to suit the younger consumer.

Levi's reacted by emphasizing the concept of *relationship marketing.* This meant trying to understand what consumers want and then giving them a voice to be heard by company leaders. To meet these objectives, the firm identified five consumer groups for a pilot program using a major survey. Using the database that was already in place, the company contacted various shoppers and enticed them to fill out questionnaires. In total, nearly 100,000 consumers completed questionnaires, which were distributed at stores, colleges, the Lilith Fair, and via customer service lines. Levi's carefully recorded the "doorway" each respondent used and tied it to other information, which eventually yielded the five major groups of shoppers. Each of the five groups expressed differing needs when it came to jeans.

Next, Levi's targeted the groups individually. Promotions were structured to match the nature of the customer profile that emerged. For example, one group known as Valuable Shoppers were individuals willing to spend $60 or more on a pair of pants. These patrons were sent thank you gifts following purchases of custom-fit jeans. The gift was a planter with flower bulbs and a card signed by the clerk who took the fitting. Responses from this group were impressive. A Valuable Shopper who received a gift purchased, on average, 2.3 more pairs of jeans within the next few weeks.

Online shoppers, who largely came from a group identified as Echo Boomers, or persons ages 15 to 25, were not sent this type of premium. Instead, this group was enticed with fashion messages. The goal was to match the promotional approach with the buyer group's characteristics.

By contacting consumers through questionnaires, gifts, promotions, and service lines, Levi's believed it was able to establish a two-way, more intimate form of communication with its clientele. This, in turn, helped the company combat declining interest in its products. The keys to success started with having a fairly well-established database to begin the program, enhancing the database, and listening to what consumers had to say. Any organization that is willing to utilize the talents and programs made available from an effective database management team may be in the position to reap similar rewards.

Source: Betsy Spethmann, "Can We Talk?" *American Demographics,* 21, no. 3 (1999), pp. 42–45.

Other marketing programs can result from database analysis. Internet programs, trade promotions, consumer promotions, and other marketing tactics can be facilitated by carefully using the database.

Evaluating Marketing Programs and the Data Warehouse

A high-quality data warehouse contains information about as many customers as possible. Each transaction is recorded. This allows for the analysis of various purchasing trends among customer groups and even of individual customers. Continually collecting information makes it possible to evaluate the overall IMC program. Questions to be answered can be as general or as specific as the ones that follow.

▶ Do our customers know our overall theme and image?

▶ Have we moved toward greater brand equity in the past year?

▶ Which items are our customers most inclined to buy? Which are not selling well? Do we know why?

▶ Is our customer base changing? Is this because we changed, or because a new group is better suited to our products?

▶ What should be done to improve our position?

This evaluation is necessary to determine which programs work and which do not. Then, the marketing program can be modified to better meet customer needs. One application of this database is to market directly to consumers or businesses that purchase the product.

INTEGRATED LEARNING EXPERIENCE

One of the major advantages of maintaining a database is the opportunity to mine it for information about current customers and prospective customers. AIM Marketing at **www.aim-mktg.com** offers predictive modeling and analysis. DB-Marketing at **www.db-marketing.com** offers both data mining services as well as geomarketing services. From the DB-Marketing Web site, examine what is said about database marketing and geomarketing. A third company you may want to access for information about data mining is Database Marketing Solutions at **www.database-marketing.com**.

DIRECT MARKETING

One program that is closely tied to database marketing is direct marketing. **Direct marketing** is vending products to customers without the use of other channel members. Figure 12.14 identifies the most typical forms of direct marketing. Regardless of the type chosen, it is important to display a toll-free number and Web site address frequently so that consumers are able to contact the company for additional information.

▶ **Mail**

▶ **Catalogs**

▶ **Telemarketing**

▶ **Mass-media**

▶ **Alternative media**

▶ **The Internet**

▶ **E-mail**

FIGURE 12.14
Methods of Direct Marketing

Mail

The most common form of direct marketing is through the mail. Direct-mail can be easily targeted to various consumer groups. Also, the impact is easily measurable by comparing the number of mailings to the number of responses. Marketing teams can test every component of a direct-mail campaign, including the type of offer, the copy in the ad, graphics used, color, and the size of the mail packet.

Direct-mail is used for consumer programs and in business-to-business operations. The company's database can be used to limit the total number of pieces sent by identifying the best possible prospects. The disadvantage of direct-mail is clutter. Most consumers are bombarded with direct-mail ads on a daily basis. Therefore, one key aspect of direct marketing is to make certain only viable prospects receive mailings.

Cysive, a developer of e-business systems for businesses, developed a very successful direct-mail marketing program. Their marketing approach was based on how they actually develop e-business systems.

Cysive's e-systems are designed by engineers with input from their clients. While looking for a way to market Cysive, John Saaty, the company's vice president of marketing, compared the building of an e-system to that of constructing a building. A firm that wants a state-of-the-art facility would hire professional contractors to do the work. The same should be true for building an e-system. It should be constructed by expert engineers. According to Mr. Saaty, "70 percent of all e-commerce projects fail because of lack of expertise of those constructing the Web site."

Using the concept of building an e-system, Cysive advertisements were designed that featured a hammer hitting an e-nail, or a message in the shape of a nail. The slogan "E-business systems built like nobody's e-business" is supported by ad copy that highlights how the system would be built by senior engineers and would be scalable, expandable, and secure.

Prior to the direct-mail campaign, Cysive ran the advertisements in the *Wall Street Journal, Business Week,* and *Fortune.* The two main objectives of the print ad campaign, according to Saaty, were to "develop brand awareness and produce leads."

The second part of the campaign was a direct-mailer. According to Saaty, "The first step is to understand your target market, and you must have a specific target market in mind when developing a direct-mailer." Using the concept of building an e-business system, Cysive developed a direct-mailer aimed at CEOs from large companies, especially Fortune 500 companies. CEOs were targeted for two reasons. First, the type of system that Cysive builds cost in the millions of dollars. Therefore, it is likely that the CEO would be involved in the decision as well as in negotiations. Second, if the CEO's attention could be garnered, even if he or she is not involved in the decision process, the CEO may be willing to ask someone in the office to contact Cysive for further information.

Because the target market was Fortune 500 CEOs, Saaty knew the typical direct-mail piece would not work. It had to be something special. Using the concept of building, Cysive developed a direct-mailer that included a box with a real hammer. Cysive's logo was placed on the hammer. On the outside of the box were the words, "Some e-business systems are held together with bubble gum and spit." Inside was the hammer with the phrase, "We take a different approach." The initial survey of CEOs indicated the hammer was well received.

When asked why an actual hammer that costs the firm much more than a traditional direct-mail piece, Saaty replied, "These were going to CEOs. The traditional approach would not work. We needed something different, something symbolic of building an e-business system. We also wanted something the CEO would not throw away but would be useful. While mailing the actual hammer was 10 times more expensive than the traditional approach, it got the CEO's attention."

Approximately 500 hammers were mailed to CEOs. The response rate was 2 percent to 3 percent. Cysive eventually signed a multimillion dollar contract. According to Saaty, "Just the one contract covered the cost of the direct-mail program." Salespeople followed up every lead generated from the direct mailing. In addition, salespeople contacted those who did not respond. In almost all cases, the hammer opened the door to talk to the CEO or some other high-ranking official.[20]

The technology of direct marketing has greatly improved. It is now possible to create mailings that are customized to the individual recipient, through the use of **digital direct-to-press**, which is a software that instructs the computer to send a tailor-made message. Digital direct-to-press is popular in the business-to-business sector, because the pitch can be designed and customized for each customer. The program is costly, which limits its use in consumer mailings.[21]

Catalogs

Many consumers have favorable responses to catalogs, because they are viewed at one's leisure. Catalogs have a longer time impact as they are kept and shared. They are a low-pressure direct-marketing tactic that allows consumers time to consider goods and prices.

Successful cataloging requires an enhanced database. Many catalog companies such as L.L. Bean, Spiegel, and JC Penney create specialty catalogs geared to specific market segments. The items have a lower cost and a higher yield, because they find individual groups.

Catalogs are essential selling tools for many business-to-business marketing programs. They provide more complete information to members of the buying center as well as prices for the purchasing agent. When combined with the Internet, a catalog program can provide a strong linkage to individual customers.

Mass Media

The most common forms of mass media used in direct marketing are television, radio, magazines, and newspapers. Television ads can be targeted to various programs or cable channels. Infomercials may also be designed to entice an immediate "call now" response. Radio does not have the reach of television, but can be targeted by the type of station format. Radio ads must repeat the response number frequently so consumers can make contact. Print media can be sent to various market segments with quick-response messages regarding Web site information and toll-free numbers.[22]

Alternative Media

Direct-marketing programs using alternative media represent new ways to reach consumers. **Package insert programs (PIPs)** are materials placed in order fulfillment packages, such as when a record club includes direct response order forms for jewelry, customized checks, or CD players in a package of CDs or tapes. **Ride alongs** are materials that are placed with another company's catalog or direct-mail piece, such as the additional marketing materials packaged with a record club's catalog. A **card pack** is a deck of 20 to 50 business reply cards, normal 3½ inches by 5 inches, placed in a plastic pack. These can be sent to consumers or as part of a business-to-business program.[23]

The Internet

The Internet provides another channel for direct marketing. With growing consumer confidence about security, many individuals and businesses are willing to make purchases online. Internet direct-marketing programs are

Valpak offers businesses an effective way to direct market products to customers who are more likely to purchase.
Source: Courtesy of Valpak.

fast, and the goods and services can be suggested to consumers based on past purchasing or click-stream behaviors.

E-mail

In addition to Web sites, many companies are developing e-mail direct-marketing campaigns. One recent success story was generated by Williams-Sonoma Inc., a retailer of cookware and household goods. E-mail was used to promote an online bridal registry. Approximately 5 percent of the customers contacted by e-mail visited the store. This total was considerably higher than any previously used direct-mail campaign.[24]

INTERNATIONAL CONCERNS IN DIRECT MARKETING

Direct marketing across international borders provides several unique challenges. There are language differences, different postal systems, and various forms of currency. Most larger companies translate direct-marketing materials and catalogs into the native language of the local population. Operators who speak the language must be hired to handle inbound calls and answer questions.

For smaller companies, preparing marketing materials and catalogs in English works well. Many residents of Europe speak English as a second language. At the same time, it is important to keep the language simple.[25]

STOP

INTEGRATED LEARNING EXPERIENCE

Permission marketing has gained considerable popularity on the Internet. Access the following firms with permission marketing services to see what types of services each offers. Compare and contrast the firms. Which firms do you like and which ones do you not like?

E@symail. (**www.easymailinteractive.com**)
United Marketing Group, Inc. (**www.united-marketinggroup.com**)
Focalex, Inc. (**www.focalex.com**)
Targetmails, Inc. (**www.targetmails.com**)

PERMISSION MARKETING

A new form of direct marketing is called **permission marketing**, in which a company sends promotional information only to consumers who give the company permission to do so. Permission marketing can be created over the Internet, by telephone, and through direct-mail. Response rates are often higher in permissions programs, because consumers are only receiving marketing materials they have asked for. The steps of permission marketing are:

1. Obtain permission from the customer
2. Offer the consumer a curriculum over time
3. Reinforce the incentive to continue the relationship
4. Increase the level of permission
5. Leverage the permission to benefit both parties

Permission is normally obtained by providing an incentive for volunteering. Information, entertainment, a gift, cash, or sweepstakes are common incentives. The curriculum of information is more educational and less advertising-oriented. Reinforcing the incentive involves an additional new incentive beyond the original gift. Permission levels are increased by obtaining more in-depth information about a consumer, such as hobbies, interests, attitudes, and opinions. Information is leveraged into additional purchases in which the participant gets a special deal, which creates a win-win situation for both parties.

Three large auto manufacturers—General Motors, Ford Motor Company, and DaimlerChrysler—have utilized permission marketing programs. The incentives include auto repairs, insurance offers, and eventually are designed to lead to auto purchases.[26]

Permission marketing programs have several advantages, including the potential to build a strong relationship with a customer over time. They also reduce the typical disadvantages of direct marketing programs: clutter, competition, brand parity, and short time periods for programs.

FREQUENCY PROGRAMS

A **frequency program** is an incentive plan designed to cause customers to make repeat purchases. When brand parity exists, such as in the airline industry, a frequent flyer program is one method to encourage repeat business. Figure 12.15 lists various reasons for developing frequency programs. Frequency programs were first developed to differentiate one brand from its competition; however, now they tend to be common across all competitors in an industry (airline, hotel, etc.).

Companies develop frequency programs for two reasons. The first is to develop loyalty from customers. The second is to match or preempt the competition. Keeping customers creates repeat purchases and makes it possible to cross-sell other goods and services.

An advertisement for Southwest Airlines Rapid Rewards frequent flier program.
Source: Courtesy of Southwest Airlines.

Three principles are used in building a loyalty program. The first is to *design the program to enhance the value of the product.* It should add to what the product offers or provide a unique new feature. When frequent flyer miles are given for using a credit card, the feature is unique, just as the cash back feature is for the Discover card. Second, *calculate the full cost of the program.* Make sure all record keeping is considered as part of the cost. Many times the cost of maintaining a frequency account is greater than the profits earned. Third, *design a program that maximizes the customer's motive to make the next purchase.* Moderate users of a product are most likely to be enticed by a frequency program. The added incentive encourages loyalty to a particular company or brand.

 ▶ **Maintain sales, margins, or profits**

 ▶ **Increase loyalty of existing customers**

 ▶ **Preempt or match a competitor's frequency program**

 ▶ **Induce cross-selling to existing customers**

 ▶ **Differentiate a parity brand**

 ▶ **Preempt the entry of a new brand**

FIGURE 12.15
Frequency Program Objectives

Source: Grahame R. Dowling and Mark Uncles, "Do Customer Loyalty Programs Really Work?" *Sloan Management Review* (Summer 1997), Vol. 38, No. 4, pp. 71–82.

When You Use Your Free Ticket To Fly To Any One Of Our Great Destinations, You'll Have Plenty Of Money For Other Things.

With Southwest Airlines' Rapid Rewards, it only takes eight roundtrips within 12 consecutive months to earn a free ticket. That means there's no counting miles or waiting forever to get your free trip. And with 52 cities to choose from, including some of the most popular vacation spots you want to visit, it also means your souvenir collection should grow pretty fast.

SOUTHWEST AIRLINES RAPID REWARDS A SYMBOL OF FREEDOM

An advertisement by Southwest Airlines highlighting the benefit of being a member of their Rapid Rewards program.
Source: Courtesy of Southwest Airlines.

In Japan, frequency programs are just beginning. One successful program was created by Oura Oil, a gasoline retailer. To combat hypermarts and other competitors, Oura developed a program called the "Five-Up Club." Those who signed up were given "welcome" gifts such as coffee mugs in exchange for providing personal information as well as information about their car. Gasoline purchases earn award certificate points that can be redeemed for gift certificates or merchandise. To make the program more complete, Oura sends out special offers to members and also sends a birthday present each year. A newsletter is also mailed and has expanded to include a mail-order operation for imported merchandise.[27]

Frequency programs are also used in the business-to-business sector. For example, the Philadelphia-based Bell Atlantic company developed a frequency program for corporate customers called "Business Link." Members saved approximately 15 percent on direct-dial calls when their monthly usage exceeded a minimum amount. Customers also earned points that were redeemed for various items such as gift certificates to restaurants and tickets to shows. This helped Bell Atlantic's marketing team identify buying center members in various corporate customers.[28]

Successful frequency programs rely on the company's database to collect and store purchasing information. New "swipe" technology using a magnetic card is helpful to many companies. The goals of frequency programs are highly compatible with the elements of most IMC plans.

CUSTOMER RELATIONSHIP MANAGEMENT

One of the newest trends in the application of data to the selling process is called **customer relationship management (CRM)**. These programs are designed to build long-term loyalty and bonds with customers through the use of a personal touch facilitated by technology. CRM programs go beyond the development of a database and traditional selling tactics. They include product modification to meet the needs of individual customers.

Typically, creating a CRM program has four steps.[29] First, *identify the company's customers.* This may be accomplished using standard data collection techniques and the firm's database.

Second, *differentiate customers in terms of their needs and their value to the selling company.* There are two CRM metrics involved: (1) the lifetime value of the customer, and (2) share of customer. The **lifetime value** is based on the average number of visits per year times the average amount of money spent per visit times the average life span of a customer. From this number, deduct the costs of acquiring and servicing the customer, then add in the value of accounts this customer refers to the company. The resulting figure should then be discounted over the time the customer would stay with the firm.

The underlying principle of CRM is that some customers are more valuable than what they spend in any one given year, and some customers are much more valuable to the firm than others. **Share of customer** means the potential value that could be added to a given customer's lifetime value. In other words, if more is invested in developing this relationship, what will the yield be over time? A CRM program involves understanding what various kinds of customers will contribute to profits over time.[30]

Third, *interact with customers in ways that improve the cost efficiency and the effectiveness of your interaction.* This means the company is able to provide what the customer wants in a timely fashion so that neither the company nor the customer wastes time.

Fourth, *customize some aspect of the goods or services being offered to the customer.* These offerings better meet the needs of the customer, who in turn rewards the company with long-term loyalty. For example, Barnes & Noble has a database program in which book buyers' long-term purchasing habits are recorded. The sales force will receive a prompt when, for example, a customer has purchased all books written by one author except for one title. In that case, the customer is contacted and offered the outstanding book at a discounted price. In the future, the customer is contacted when the author publishes any new title. Seth Godin, author of *Permission Marketing* writes that, "Instead of trying to find new customers for the products you've got, you find new products for the customers you've already got."[31]

CRM works best when customers have highly differentiated needs, highly differentiated valuations, or both. CRM has three technological underpinnings:

1. Database technology, including the ability to analyze and map data

2. Interactivity through Web sites, call centers, and other means of contacting customers

3. Mass customization technology, or the ability to customize a good or service to better meet a customer's needs[32]

American Airlines' customization technology is used in the firm's A-Advantage program. Frequent flyers are able to create personalized travel profiles and customized travel packages based on those profiles. The key is to know what the customer wants and then to tailor a good or service to meet those needs using mass customization technology.[33]

CRM programs do not work in every instance. The Gartner Group, a research and advisory firm, notes that 55 percent of all CRM projects do not produce results. Failures are normally attributed to four factors. First, the program is often implemented before creating a solid customer strategy. Market segments must be identified so that customization programs can proceed. Failing to understand the segments creates a kind of "ready, fire, aim" situation.[34]

As part of its CRM program, Glaxo has pharmaceutical professionals available to provide information about company products.
Source: Courtesy West & Vaughan, Inc.

Second, rolling out a CRM program before changing the organization to match it will create problems. Because a CRM program changes the entire view of how to treat not only customers but also the delivery of goods and services, a changed management program is essential. Neglecting to educate the entire staff about this new perspective and approach will quickly lead to problems.

Third, becoming technology-driven rather than customer-driven causes the failure of some CRM programs. Technology can only assist in record keeping and some aspects of order fulfillment. The rest is the responsibility of the employees, who must understand the customer and develop customized approaches.

Fourth, CRM programs fail when customers feel like they are being "stalked" rather than "wooed." Trying to build a relationship with a disinterested customer will be more annoying than helpful. For example, the *Dallas Morning News* discovered that its telemarketing program to gain subscribers was annoying people rather than winning them over. Moving to direct-mail was costly, but yielded better results. The marketing team must identify those customers who wish to become partners and then reach them in ways that adds value.

A CRM program relies on quality service. Overreliance on technology such as a Web site turns service into self-service. Many marketing teams are learning that delays such as voice menus, reams of Web click-throughs, and slow lines at check-in counters lowers perceptions of service quality. Empowering employees to actually provide service adds greatly to the value of a relationship with a company in the eyes of the consumer. Personalized service is a great asset. For example, a woman at a resort hotel lost her engagement ring on the beach nearby. The hotel staff tried to help her find the ring, but was unsuccessful. Later that night, one employee rented a metal detector, went back to the beach, and found the ring. It would be difficult to estimate how much value was added in terms of return business to the hotel chain and referrals to family, coworkers, and friends.

Mitchell's of Westport is a high-end clothing store that has made effective use of a CRM program. The company has data available to the sales staff regarding customer preferences, sizes, previous purchases, and other data. Purchases are followed up with thank you notes, and customers are notified of sales and given invitations to special events when specific products are available. Loyalty to the store is very high. Even customers who have moved to new cities return to the store to buy clothing.[35]

CRM programs must be customized to fit each company's needs. When the possibility of building relationships is low and there is little difference in valuations of customers, the program is less likely to succeed. Each marketing team should assess the company's profile before investing in a CRM plan. [36]

SUMMARY

Personal selling takes place in several major and important ways. First, manufacturers as well as small companies put products into the hands of end users and customers. Second, many relationships exist between salespeople and clients in other businesses.

Retail clerks interact directly with customers. These relationships ordinarily take place on a transactional level; however, effective store employees can influence customer attitudes toward the retail outlet. Competent, friendly, and helpful store clerks encourage customers to return in the future.

In business settings, it is important to identify key needs and then to sell products that fulfill those needs. Relationships that are strengthened over time move from single or occasional transactions toward more strategic alliances with business customers. A sales force must adjust to international settings by understanding the natures of international customers and by working within the norms, customs, and laws of a foreign country.

Personal selling is enhanced by the effective use of the company's database. Managing a database begins with establishing clear goals for the program. Data sources, both internal and external, must be evaluated so that those offering the most vital information are used. Then a data warehouse can be built, and data mining can begin.

One of the most important applications of a database program is direct marketing. These efforts may be made by mail, catalog, phone, fax, mass media, the Internet, or e-mail. Geocoding identifies individuals with the right attributes by zip code. Others may identify themselves when they contact the firm by telephone or through the company's Web site.

Permission marketing is a selling approach in which the customer agrees to receive promotional materials in exchange for various incentives. Frequency programs are incentives customers receive for repeat business. Both are designed to create customer loyalty over time.

Customer relationship management is a program designed to build long-term loyalty and bonds with customers through the use of a personal touch facilitated by technology. CRM programs go beyond the development of a database and traditional selling tactics. They include product modification to meet the needs of individual customers.

As the role of personal selling evolves, the use of technology to facilitate marketing efforts is likely to rise. An effective IMC program incorporates people skills, understanding of customer needs and wants, and technology into a seamless program designed to differentiate the company and build customer loyalty over time.

REVIEW QUESTIONS

1. What is a single transaction sale? What mistakes do sales reps make when finalizing this type of sale?

2. Describe the personal selling aspect of marketing services.

3. How is a retail sales presentation related to the steps of the consumer buying decision-making process? What is the manufacturer's dilemma in this process? How can a missionary salesperson help?

4. What is cross-selling? How is it related to inbound telemarketing calls?

5. What are the three basic forms of business-to-business personal selling? How do they relate to the various types of buyer-seller relationships?

6. What are the steps involved in managing the business-to-business selling process? How do intrinsic value buyers differ

from extrinsic value buyers and strategic value buyers when going through these steps?

7. Name and briefly describe the four selling approaches. Which is the most intense and interpersonal? Why?

8. What trends are present in personal selling? How should marketing managers respond to those trends?

9. What issues, problems, and opportunities exist in international selling?

10. Describe database development and its relationship to an IMC program.

11. What is the primary source of internal database information? How can this data be collected?

12. What is geocoding? What role does it play in database programs?

13. Describe the various methods that can be used to facilitate direct-marketing programs.

14. Describe a permission marketing program. What are the key benefits of this approach?

15. What are the steps involved in an effective permission marketing program?

16. Describe a frequency program. Which type of user pays off the best in a frequency program—light, medium, or heavy users?

17. What is customer relationship management? What are the four steps involved?

18. What is the lifetime value of a customer? Why is the concept crucial to a CRM program?

19. When is a CRM program most likely to be effective? What problems can cause the program to fail?

KEY TERMS

single transaction occur when the buyer and seller interact for the purpose of only one solitary purchase.

order takers salespersons whose primary tasks are to take orders.

repeat transactions occur when buyers purchase on a regular basis.

inbound telemarketing selling in response to inbound telephone calls.

outbound telemarketing selling by making outbound calls to retail customers or other businesses.

missionary salespeople members of the sales force who try to develop goodwill, stimulate demand, and provide the training and incentives needed to enhance the manufacturer in the retailer's mind.

cross selling the marketing of another item following the purchase of a good or service.

field sales occur when a salesperson travels to the customer's place of business or home.

order getters salespeople who go out and solicit orders.

intrinsic value buyers buyers who understand the product, know how to use it, and view the product as a commodity-type item.

extrinsic value buyers buyers who focus more on product attributes and the solution a particular product can provide.

strategic value buyers buyers who seek out partnerships with suppliers.

stimulus-response sales approach using specific statements (stimuli) to solicit specific responses from customers (sometimes called a "canned" sales pitch).

need-satisfaction sales approach discovering a customer's needs and then providing solutions that satisfy those needs.

problem-solution sales approach the selling organization uses a team to analyze the buyer's operation and offer solutions through various products and services.

mission-sharing sales approach when two organizations develop a common mission and then share resources to accomplish that mission.

database development the creation of a database to support the overall company, IMC program, and total marketing effort.

geocoding adding geographic codes to each customer record to make it possible to plot the addresses of customers on a map.

data mining developing a process to sift through information to help the firm better understand customers.

direct marketing vending products to customers without the use of other channel members.

digital direct-to-press software that instructs the computer to create a tailor-made message for a customer.

package insert programs (PIPS) materials placed in order fulfillment packages.

ride alongs materials that are placed with another company's catalog or direct-mail piece.

card pack a deck of 20 to 50 business reply cards, normally 3½ by 5 inches, placed in a plastic mail pack.

permission marketing a form of database marketing in which the company sends promotional materials only to customers who give the company permission to do so.

frequency program a marketing plan designed to cause customers to make repeat purchases by offering them incentives.

customer relationship management (CRM) programs designed to build long-term loyalty and bonds with customers through the use of a personal touch facilitated by technology.

lifetime value the contribution of a customer over the lifetime of a relationship.

share of customer the potential value that could be added to a given customer's lifetime value if more were invested in that customer.

CRITICAL THINKING EXERCISES

Discussion Questions

1. Personal selling in retail stores varies greatly depending on the type of retail outlet. Discuss the differences in selling approaches between a retail salesperson in a discount store (Wal-Mart) versus a retail salesperson at a high-end department store (Macy's or Saks Fifth Avenue).

2. Visit a nearby local retail store. Ask the manager to describe the tactics that manufacturers use to encourage retail store salespeople and clerks to push a specific manufacturer's brand. Ask individual salespeople to specify the brands they encourage customers to purchase. Based on your conversations, discuss the challenges manufacturers have in encouraging sales in the retail store.

3. In relationship marketing, the company concentrates more on one individual potential customer than on trying to gain a large market share within an industry. Relationship marketing focuses on selectivity, whereby firms concentrate their resources on just a few customers, rather than trying to sell to every customer in the industry. Consequently, preferential treatment is given to the valued customers who offer the highest potential for long-term relationships and long-term profits.

   Unlike the typical transactional buyer–seller relationship, which tends to be antagonistic, relationship marketing focuses on loyalty and commitment between the buyer and seller. Using this philosophy means that firms concentrate their efforts on fewer firms, but strive to be more heavily involved with those firms. The goal is to be the only vendor for a smaller number of customers rather than one of several vendors for a large number of companies. What are the advantages to this type of strategy? What are the disadvantages? What dangers are there in concentrating too much of a firm's sales with a few firms? Are there dangers in trying to serve too many customers?

4. For classes that have international students, ask these individuals to discuss retailing in their home countries. Do store clerks sell in the same way as in the United States? Discuss mores or cultural traditions in each country, and try to explain how they would affect personal selling. If any students have experience as a field salesperson or know of someone in their home country who is a field salesperson, ask them to discuss how it is different than field selling in the United States.

5. Assume you are the account executive at a database marketing agency. A music retailer has asked you to develop a database for the company. How would you go about building a data warehouse? What type of data mining would you do for the music retailer?

6. Examine the methods of direct marketing highlighted in Figure 12.4. Evaluate each method for the following types of businesses. Which ones would be the best? Which ones would not work as well? Justify your answers.

   a. Shoe store

   b. Printing service

   c. Internet hosiery retailer (sells only by the Internet)

   d. Manufacturer of tin cans for food processing companies

   e. Tractor parts dealer

7. Form a group of four to five classmates. Ask each person to list the catalogs that came into his or her home during the last two weeks. Have each person discuss why he or she receives certain catalogs. Next, discuss how often each of you order something out of a catalog and how the order was placed. Is anyone in the group accessing the Internet for information given in a catalog or ordering from a catalog after accessing a Web site? Discuss how important the catalog market is to you and what you see as the future of catalog marketing.

8. Almost all hotels have some type of frequency or loyalty program. Look at the loyalty programs of the following hotels. Critique each one. Which ones are best? Why?

   a. Best Western (www.bestwestern.com)

   b. Days Inn (www.daysinn.com)

   c. Doubletree Inn (www.hilton.com/doubletree/index.html)

   d. Holiday Inn (www.basshotels.com/holiday-inn)

   e. Marriott (www.marriott.com)

   f. Radisson (www.radisson.com)

   g. Wyndham Hotels & Resorts (www.wyndham.com)

9. Discuss how a customer relationship management (CRM) program could be developed for a local retail clothing store. How would a CRM program be developed for a national retail clothing store? What are the similarities and differences? What about manufacturers such as Guess that sell to clothing stores? How would they develop a CRM program?

Developing Your Sales and Database Programs

Which personal selling theories, approaches, and tactics best match the good or service you are offering? Are they the same in retail markets, the distribution channel, and in business-to-business sales? What kind of sales presentation should be made? The answers to these and other questions should help you more effectively manage the sales force that will be marketing your product. It is important to remember that most of the other promotional items are delivered through some kind of "impersonal" media (a television, radio, or point-of-purchase display). This is one chance you have to deliver your IMC message personally to those who might buy the product.

In addressing your database needs, what kinds of customers are most likely to buy your product? Who may use it heavily? Which ones are light or moderate users? Where can your key customers be contacted? How will your database be used? By answering these key questions, you will be able to develop your database marketing programs.

The Web site exercise for Chapter 12 is designed to lead you through three major issues: (1) developing a personal sales program, (2) managing a database program, and (3) examining a direct-marketing program. You will be asked to consider whether a direct-marketing program will work for your product, service, or organization, how your database should be organized, and what type of personal selling strategy you should develop.

BUILDING AN
IMC
CAMPAIGN

IMC PlanPro

CASE 1

TRAVEL TROUBLE

Jerry Rogers was angry, frustrated, and ready to quit his job. Jerry had been specially trained to become a travel agent. All his adult life he felt as if that were the one position that would fit him best. He believed that he would get the best travel discounts and see the world as part of the job. He found a school that focused on helping people prepare for entry-level travel agency positions.

Upon completing the program, Jerry took his first job with World-Wide Travel, a small but growing enterprise in northwest Arkansas. Many told Jerry the company was in an ideal place, because there were so many retirees close by in Bella Vista, a senior citizen community.

World-Wide Travel consisted of 13 operating locations in a four-state region (Missouri, Oklahoma, Arkansas, and Kansas). Michelle Dutton owned all of the outlets. She believed agents should be hardworking, commission-oriented, customer-centered employees. She also thought setting up goals and incentives would help lead them to higher sales.

Two weeks after taking the job, Jerry was informed about a major contest in which all of the operating locations would be given quotas to meet. Those who exceeded their quotas by the greatest amount (in dollars and by percent of the quota) would receive free airline tickets to be used whenever they wanted. Also, first prize included $3,000 to be divided among all of the winning outlet's agents.

Jerry was immediately in a difficult situation. He just had begun to learn the computer system, even though he was pretty well-versed in booking tickets of all kinds. He still was uncomfortable with World-Wide's paperwork. In addition, Jerry quickly discovered that the older retiree residents in his area were quite loyal to their agents. He was left with "walk-in" traffic to serve on a rotating basis with all of the experienced employees. Walk-ins were much less likely to book something on the spot, instead asking to "think about it" before actually making the purchase.

(continued)

Unfortunately, they would often phone in to make reservations later without specifically asking for Jerry, who had done all of the groundwork on the sale.

It wasn't long before Jerry was receiving snide comments from other agents about "pulling your weight" when it came to sales. His outlet was in fourth place in the contest, and he was nearly last in individual sales.

Michelle Dutton traveled to the northwest Arkansas location three weeks into the two-month-long contest. She sat down with Jerry and asked him how he felt about the job. He told her he loved the work, but he felt the contest was putting him in a bad situation. First, the unit had the highest (and he believed most difficult) quota to reach of all the units, making winning the contest almost impossible. Second, his "failure" to contribute was making it difficult to make friends with people in the location. He had always figured the job consisted of teamwork, not rivalries. Michelle responded that she was certain she could find somebody who would like the job and the pressure if he felt he couldn't hack it.

When the contest ended, Jerry's unit had moved into second place. He was clearly the scapegoat for not winning, although his sales had improved to the point that he was eligible for several company bonuses based on sales. He tried to point out to his office manager the unfairness of the quota system and how he had been forced into the contest before fully learning the job. The officer manager, Marty, was more sympathetic than Michelle had been, because he knew how his particular area worked and the type of clientele Jerry had to attract in order to gain their trust. Marty complained that Michelle was just a "money-hungry boss" who just made people miserable.

The Friday night after the contest ended, Marty invited Jerry to the "Friday afternoon staff meeting," a code phrase for "happy hour." Jerry received the invitation with mixed emotions, hoping it would turn out to be a morale-enhancing, team-building experience but fearing he would just end up catching flak from his colleagues.

Jerry's fears were realized. After about three drinks, the leading representative from the unit announced that Jerry was the guy that cost them their bonus. Jerry was not a confrontational type of person, so he just left.

The next day Jerry received a call at home from Marty. Marty suggested that the two of them start their own agency. They discussed how they could raise the start-up capital needed. Marty figured with his contacts in the community, the Small Business Institute nearby, and luck, they could create the kind of company where cooperation would replace the cutthroat atmosphere at World-Wide.

Michelle soon became aware of their plan. She called a meeting with them both (who had not yet quit at World-Wide), fired them, and showed them their employment contracts where they had signed a "noncompetition agreement" as a condition of employment. She threatened them with a lawsuit if they started a firm in town.

For the first time in his life, Jerry became confrontational. He told Michelle to "shove it" and marched out. Marty and Jerry soon opened their business in southwest Missouri, just a few miles across the border. They quickly stole many of Michelle's customers. It wasn't long before Jerry was completely content, figuring he'd finally gotten the job he wanted in the first place.

1. What kind of selling takes place at the travel agency?

2. How did Michelle's goal-setting program go wrong? Or, do you believe Michelle's program was fine and Jerry and Marty simply did not "fit" with the World-Wide company?

3. What kinds of contests could Michelle create that would encourage competition but less conflict?

CASE 2

LINCOLN MEDICAL SUPPLY

Sara Holmes has just taken on a unique dual role in her job at Lincoln Medical Supply. She was to be in charge of the marketing database for the company and also would serve as liaison with the advertising firm and marketing group that provided promotions for the organization. Sara was told her input would be heavily counted on to help with key decisions to build the size and scope of the company in the next several years.

Lincoln Medical Supply was located in Lincoln, Nebraska. The company served both retail and business-to-business markets by selling and servicing various types of medical equipment, from items as basic as ankle braces to those as sophisticated as fetal monitors. The company had achieved a great deal of success simply through the sheer demand for various products, but the management team was concerned that no coherent marketing plan had ever been developed.

Sara was told that the company had three basic customer groups:

1. Retail walk-in buyers
2. Physicians' offices
3. Hospitals

Retail customers purchased the lower-cost, less intricate items such as braces, bandages, and cold packs. Physicians bought more elaborate equipment and also provided referrals for patients. Hospitals ordered the big-ticket items. Each customer type generated a solid source of revenue for the organization.

Sara's first challenge was to develop a database for each type of customer. Her potential sources for retail customers were insurance forms (many filed for insurance to pay for the items involved) and sales ticket information requested from each person. Doctors' offices could be sources of a great deal of information, but the company often had to "push" the staff to provide statistics on numbers of patients, types of expenditures, and other key facts. Hospitals could be assessed through internal company reports and as well by accessing data from external sources.

Following the simple generation of data, Sara would need to decide if all this information should be compiled into one overall data warehouse, or if it should be separated by customer type. Clearly the needs of each group were different, and therefore it seemed plausible that the marketing tactics used for each customer type would also vary. At the same time, Sara wanted a consistent message sent out that Lincoln Medical Supply stood for consistent, high-quality, and excellent service advantages. She knew the name "Lincoln" didn't help, because so many companies in the city also used the name (e.g., Lincoln Electric Supply, Lincoln Party Favors, and so forth).

Sara held a meeting with the marketing team. The group told her the primary goal was to build greater brand equity in the name, as a new medical supply house had just opened near one of Lincoln's biggest hospitals. Next, the company's leaders wanted to know how to get walk-in buyers to purchase more items, and how to expand purchases from the other two segments of the business at the same time. The leaders discussed the use of catalogs and an Internet site to widen the scope of product offerings. They also considered the possibility of opening satellite locations in Omaha (50 miles away), Grand Island (90 miles west), and North Platte (400 miles away). They wanted to develop an understanding of the type of individual who would venture into a medical supply store, what the person might buy, and what the person would not buy. They also needed to know if they were meeting the needs of physicians and hospitals. With all of these challenges in mind, Sara took a deep breath and started working.

(continued)

1. Name the sources of internal and external data for all three types of customers.
2. What types of data should Sara collect from each type of customer?
3. How can Sara meet the goals imposed on her by the marketing group?
4. What kinds of marketing programs could be developed from the data Sara generates? Should the data be separated by customer type or combined into one major database? Why or why not?
5. Is Lincoln Medical Supply a candidate for a CRM program? Why or why not?

ENDNOTES

1. Tara Rummel, "Enduring in a Sea of Instability," *Global Cosmetic Industry,* 166, no. 1 (January 2000), pp. 16–21; Dana Butcher, "More Than a Shave and a Hair Cut," *Global Cosmetic Industry,* 166, no. 1 (January 2000) pp. 45–48.

2. C. W. L. Hart, J. L. Heskett, and E. W. Sasser, "The Profitable Art of Service Recovery," *Harvard Business Review,* 68, (July–August 1999), pp. 148–56.

3. E. Jerome McCarthy, *Basic Marketing,* 7th ed. (Homewood, IL: Richard D. Irwin, 1981).

4. David Howe, "The Cross-Sell Connection," *Banking Strategies,* 74, no. 6 (November–December 1998), pp. 120–24.

5. Alf Nucifora, "Traditional Sales Thinking Doesn't Work Any Longer," *Business Journal: Serving Greater Tampa Bay,* 19, no. 29 (July 16, 1999), p. 37.

6. Ibid.

7. Patricia R. Lysak, "Changing Times Demand Front-End Model," *Marketing News,* 28, no. 9 (April 25, 1994), p. 9.

8. *The Wall Street Journal* (December 28, 1999), p. C9.

9. Dana Blankenhorn, "E-mail Use Shifts from Prospects to Closures," *Advertising Age's Business Marketing,* 85, no. 1 (January–February 2000), pp. 29–30.

10. Ibid.

11. Tim Stevens, "A Bird in the Hand," *Industry Week,* 247, no. 5 (March 2, 1998), pp. 39–47.

12. Eric R. Baron, "Adding Engineer to Sales Can Improve Outcome," *Electronic Engineering Times,* no. 1088 (November 22, 1999), p. 65; Tricia Campbell and Geoffrey Brewer, "Getting Top Executives to Sell," *Sales and Marketing Management,* 150, no. 10 (October 1998), p. 39.

13. Bill Bregar, "When in Rome . . . Execs Detail Global Trade," *Plastic News,* 11, no. 33 (October 4, 1999), p. 33.

14. Charlene Marmer Soloman, "Managing An Overseas Sales Force," *World Trade,* 12, no. 4 (April 1999), pp. 4–6.

15. Rodgers L. Harper, "Sorting Business Customers to Enhance Return on Equity," *American Banker,* 164, no. 159 (August 19, 1999), p. 4.

16. Steve Del Zotto, "Personal Selling Gives Companies an Edge," *Computer Dealer News,* 14, no. 15 (April 20, 1998), p. 27.

17. Leo Rabinovitch, "America's 'First' Department Stores Mines Customer Data," *Direct Marketing,* 62, no. 8 (December 1999), pp. 42–45.

18. Eric Cohen, "Database Marketing," *Target Marketing,* 22, no. 4 (April 1999), p. 50.

19. Rabinovitch, "America's 'First' Department Store Mines Customer Data."

20. Interview with John Saaty, Vice President of Marketing, Cysive, May 15, 2000.

21. Patrick Totty, "Direct Mail Gets a New Lease on Life," *Credit Union Magazine,* 66 no. 4 (April 2000), pp. 36–37.

22. Based on Jay Kiltsch, "Making Your Message Hit Home: Some Basics to Consider When . . . ," *Direct Marketing,* 61, no. 2 (June 1998), pp. 32–34.

23. John Ahern and Rachel McLaughlin, "What You May Not Have Known, But Were Afraid To Ask," *Target Marketing,* 21, no. 9 (September 1998), pp. 14–15.

24. Jeff Sweat and Rick Whiting, "Instant Marketing," *Information Week,* no. 746 (August 2, 1999), pp.18–20.

25. Rolf Rykken, "List Serve in the Real World," *Export Today's Global Business,* 15, no. 11 (November 1999), pp. 34–37.

26. Based on David Sedgwick and Mary Connelly, "GM Sees Dollars in Its Mountain of Buyer Data," *Automotive News,* 73, no. 5819 (May 17, 1999), pp. 3–4.

27. Richard Cross, "High-Octane Loyalty," *Marketing Tools* (April 1997), pp. 4–6.

28. Sarah Lorge and Chad Kaydo, "How to Build a B-to-B Frequency Program," *Sales and Marketing Management,* 151, no. 4 (April 1999), p. 80.

29. "A Crash Course in Customer Relationship Management," *Harvard Management Update,* 5, issue 3 (March 2000), pp. 3–4.

30. "CRM Metrics," *Harvard Management Update,* 5, issue 3 (March 2000), pp. 3–4.

31. "A Crash Course in Customer Relationship Management," *Harvard Management Update.*

32. "The Technological Underpinnings of CRM," *Harvard Management Update,* 5, issue 3 (March 2000), pp. 3–4.

33. Horst Schulze, "Where Has All the Service Gone?" *Strategy & Leadership,* 28, issue 5 (2000), p. 21.

34. Darrell K. Rigby, Frederick F. Reichheld, and Phil Schefter, "Avoid the Four Perils of CRM," *Harvard Business Review,* 80, issue 2 (February 2002), pp. 101–108.

35. Brian Sullivan, "Winners Focus on Customers" *Computerworld,* 35, issue 24 (June 11, 2001), pp. 50–51.

36. Mary McCaig, "A Small Retailer Uses CRM to Make a Big Splash," *Apparel Industry,* 31, issue 10 (October 2000), pp. 30–34.

13

Public Relations, Regulations, and Sponsorship Programs

HOW DO THEY DO IT?
The WWF Crashes to the Top

In an all-too-cynical world, it may at first seem odd that a contrived, theatrical performance such as that provided by the World Wrestling Federation is able to flourish at such a high level. Yet, no one can deny the dramatic rise in popularity of the WWF. One recent direct competition resulted in the WWF capturing a 4.2 share on cable when starting at 11:00 P.M., as compared to a 1.0 share for tennis that was aired during prime time on the same station.

How can this be? Cries of "fake," "phony," "contrived," and "violent" have been aimed at pro 'rassling for years. The sport had to overcome concerns about steroid use in the Hulk Hogan era, criticism from family groups opposed to violence on television, and even the death of a major star in a fall during a stunt at a pay-per-view event. In spite of these difficulties, major WWF personalities are now as well known as many television stars.

The WWF's primary audience is from 6- to 17-year-old boys, especially those ages 11 to 15. Other strong groups are 18- to 24-year-old women and 18- to 44-year-old men. High-tech shows and increased theatrics attracted an even wider audience as the new century began. The WWF extends its reach through numerous tactics, each designed to "spin" positive publicity at the general public.

For example, the WWF sponsored a commercial at the end of the 2000 Super Bowl, in which the spokesman notes that wrestling is "a wholesome form of entertainment," while execs smash each other with chairs and trash conference rooms. In the next scene, a couple necks while a buxom woman purrs, "We never use sex to enhance our image." Finally, a man flies out of a window to the tag line, "WWF attitude. Get it?" For people who "get it," says Jim Byrne, the senior vice president for marketing, being aware of the irony of the sport is one key.

WWF celebrities have ventured into the publishing world, with a book by "The Rock" making the best-seller list. Personal appearances, autographs, and other events designed to keep fans up close and personal with wrestling celebrities have been used to broaden the appeal.

Two magazines also promote various extravaganzas, *WWF Raw* and *WWF for Kids*. Clothes carrying WWF trademarks are sold by JC Penney and Wal-Mart. The Undertaker, Shawn Michaels, and Steve Austin are three hot property names, somewhat replacing Hulk Hogan and former Minnesota Governor Jesse "The Body" Ventura.

The single biggest obstacle to overcome may be "overmarketing." Too many shows and too many pay-per-view events may dilute the market. The WWC, owned by Turner Sports, offers an alternative set of characters and television programs. Those in charge seek to maintain a balance between interest and overexposure.

The WWF "soap opera" is a nonstop series of episodes and events. Key characters move through a series of ups and downs, and enthusiastic fans follow via television, Internet, magazine, and personal appearance venues. The popularity of the WWF extends to other products, including those sold by Daily Juice Products of Verona, Pennsylvania, which offers Piledriver Punch, Backbreaker Blue, and Drop Kick Orange, each with a photo and action shot of a wrestler on the package. Tie-ins with individual wrestling events build recognition for both the WWF and for firms that serve as sponsors for special "cards" featuring more famous wrestling personalities.

Building a manageable public image while keeping a crowd interested in sex, violence, and carnage is a major juggling act. As long as the WWF succeeds, a number of muscle-bound men and women, and their marketing partners, will keep making money-laden trips to the bank.[1]

WILLAMETTE FURNITURE COMPANY

Public relations programs have two major elements. The first is to present the firm in the most positive light possible. The second is to take strong action when negative events or bad publicity affect the firm. As with advertising, public relations programs can be designed internally, or they can be passed along to an agency that specializes in this type of work. In both instances, the firm should tie in public relations with sponsorship programs. Sponsorships should be chosen based on their compatibility with the firm's overall IMC message theme.

In the Willamette Furniture Company plan featured on the IMC Plan Pro disk, sponsorship programs are present in section 5.2.4, and the public relations strategy is described in section 3.6. Willamette chose to sponsor the Habitat for Humanity because of a logical tie-in between lumber and furniture. Also, symphonies are supported because many of Willamette's potential customers would attend such musical events. Because Willamette is strongly interested in brand awareness and image, these methods for reaching the public are in tune with the message of being a high-quality producer of furniture.

o v e r v i e w

The traditional marketing mix consists of advertising, sales promotions, personal selling, and public relations efforts. At this point in the textbook, the first three elements in the mix have been presented. This chapter is devoted to the fourth element, public relations. Closely related are the topics of IMC regulations and sponsorships.

In Hollywood, one well-worn phrase is, "There's no such thing as bad publicity." While this may be true for a bad-boy actor trying to get his name before the public, in the world of marketing and communications, bad publicity is *worse* than no publicity. Many business organizations spend countless hours fending off negative news while trying to develop positive and noticeable messages and themes.

Public relations efforts, government regulations, and sponsorships should be part of the overall integrating marketing communications approach. The same unified message should appear in every marketing endeavor, from the appearance of the company's letterhead and stationary, to advertisements, promotional items, and any sponsorship program. The goal of an IMC plan is to make sure that each component of a firm's communication plan speaks with one voice. Extending this goal to the public relations function can be difficult but remains an important challenge for the marketing team.

This chapter is devoted to understanding the nature of a public relations function within an integrated marketing plan. Second, organizational stakeholders are described, because they constitute the major publics that interact with the public relations department. Methods used to reach stakeholders are also noted. Third, government and industry regulations are discussed because any lawsuits or accusations of violating government regulations would be handled by the public relations staff. Fourth, sponsorship programs and event marketing tactics are outlined to show how the company can make quality contacts with existing customers, new prospects, vendors, and other key publics. The goal of these activities must be to reach the general public with the same clear voice that has been developed in other marketing approaches, such as advertising and personal selling. When this goal is reached, the firm's image is enhanced and its brands are better known and perceived more favorably in the marketplace.

THE PUBLIC RELATIONS DEPARTMENT AND ITS FUNCTIONS

The **public relations (PR) department** is a unit in the firm that manages items such as publicity and other communications with all of the groups that make contact with the company. Some of the functions performed by the public relations department are similar to those provided by the marketing department. Others are largely different. Moving public relations under the IMC umbrella begins with a major problem: Often the public relations department is separate from the marketing department. The two may cooperate with and consult each other, yet each has a separate role to perform. Bringing the two together can result in "turf wars," with each trying to protect its own area.

Some marketing experts argue that public relations should be part of the marketing department, just as advertising, trade promotions, and sales promotions are under the jurisdiction of the marketing manager. Others suggest that public relations is a different function and cannot operate effectively within a marketing department. Instead, a member of the public relations department should serve as a consultant to the marketing department. Still others contend that a new division, called the department of communications, should be created to oversee both marketing and public relations activities.

In any case, many public relations functions should not be considered typical marketing functions. This is because the marketing department tends to concentrate on customers and the channel members en route to those customers, such as wholesalers and retail outlets. On the other hand, the public relations department focuses on a variety of internal and external stakeholders including employees, stockholders, public interest groups, the government, and society as a whole.

The three key public relations functions are displayed in Figure 13.1. Each represents the tasks given to public relations personnel, whether they are internal employees or members of a public relations company hired to perform those functions.

As a result, one major decision firms must make concerning public relations is who will handle these activities. Most firms have an internal public relations officer or department. Others hire public relations firms to handle either special projects or all of their public relations functions. Still, even when a public relations agency is retained, a firm normally places someone in charge of internal public relations, because most public relations firms deal only with external publics.

The decision criteria used in selecting advertising agencies can be applied to selecting a public relations firm. It is important to develop a relationship with the public relations agency and to carefully spell out what the firm expects from the agency. In some cases, the goal of a public relations firm is simply to get hits. A **hit** is the mention of a company's name in a news story. Hits can be positive, negative, or even neutral in terms of their impact on a firm. The concept behind getting hits in the news is that the more a consumer sees the name of a company in a news-related context, the higher the brand awareness will become. This may be true, but it is important to consider the type of image that is being developed. It may be a wiser strategy to seek fewer hits and to make sure that those hits project the company in a positive light that also reinforces the firm's IMC theme.

Consequently, when a public relations firm is used, the agency's personnel must be familiar with their client's IMC plan. Then, the public relations firm is able to work on

> ▶ **Monitor internal and external publics**
>
> ▶ **Provide positive information to each public that reinforces the IMC plan**
>
> ▶ **React quickly to any shift by any of the publics from the desired position**

FIGURE 13.1
Public Relations Functions

We are a company of Americans.

32,000 men and women who grieve
with our nation.

32,000 men and women who are proud of our
country and our company.

32,000 men and women with a mission:
to keep America flying.

Nothing can keep our country or Southwest Airlines
from moving ahead.

SOUTHWEST AIRLINES ♡

The Public Relations Department placed this advertisement in *USA Today* immediately after the terrorist attacks of September 11th, 2001.

Source: Courtesy of Southwest Airlines.

ideas that reinforce the plan. Special events, activities, and news releases can be developed to strengthen the "one voice" concept needed to build a successful IMC program. The following sections describe the targets of various company communications and define the natures of the messages sent out.

TYPES OF STAKEHOLDERS

All the recipients of company communications are important. Any constituent who makes contact with a company should receive the same unified message. In this section, the stakeholders who are targets of publics relations efforts are described. A **stakeholder** is a person or group that has a vested interest in the organization's well-being.[2] A vested interest can be a variety of items, including:

▶ Profits paid as common stock dividends
▶ Loan repayments that a lending institution seeks to receive
▶ Sales to the company or purchases made from the company
▶ Community well-being
▶ A special-interest topic

In other words, any number of items can give a person or another company a stake in the firm's well-being.

To understand the nature of public relations programs, it is helpful to begin by identifying the publics that make contact with various companies. Figure 13.2 identifies the primary internal and external stakeholders that the public relations department should monitor.

In addition to sending communications to each of the stakeholders, the public relations department must closely monitor the actions and opinions of each group. When changes in attitudes, new views, or serious concerns develop, the public relations department should be ready to address the problem. Most importantly, it is the responsibility of the public relations department to be certain that all forms of communications to each of these publics remain consistent with the firm's IMC plan and the image the firm seeks to project.

Stakeholders may be divided into two sets of groups: (1) internal publics and (2) external publics. Both sets of constituents seek out information from the organization regarding various issues, from pay, to ethical concerns, to details about company profitability.

Internal Stakeholders

The primary internal stakeholders are the employees of the organization, unions, and corporate shareholders. A brief presentation regarding each follows.

Employees should receive a constant stream of information from the company. Many employees are quite distant from the marketing department, yet they should still be aware of what the company is trying to achieve with its IMC program, even if this means only basic knowledge. Those closest to the marketing department are going to be more acutely aware of the nature of the IMC plan, including how the company's message theme is being sent to all other constituents.

▶ Employees	▶ Media
▶ Unions	▶ Local community
▶ Shareholders	▶ Financial community
▶ Channel members	▶ Government
▶ Customers	▶ Special-interest groups

FIGURE 13.2
Stakeholders

The Motorola advertisement in this section states that the company's "Wireless Communications Centers help you stay connected." Employees who are aware of Motorola's theme can communicate the same message when dealing with customers, vendors, and other publics.

To work effectively in communicating with employees, the public relations department must keep in close contact with the human resource (HR) department. Publications and communications aimed at employees must be consistent with the image and message that the firm is espousing to customers and other groups. For example, any firm that uses advertising to suggest that employees are always ready to assist customers should make sure those employees are aware of the message. Employee behaviors should then be consistent with the advertising theme that is being conveyed to customers. The HR department should try to hire the kind of worker who is attracted to such an approach and structure performance appraisals and rewards to favor those who "buy into" the company's overall IMC approach. The emphasis on providing information about company activities must logically extend to every public relations event and sponsorship program.

The company's intended message and theme should also be conveyed to *unions*. Even though the union may represent employees from a number of organizations, the same unified sense of direction applies. A public relations program aimed at, for example, the hard-core unemployed, should be communicated carefully to the union, which may be interested in cosponsoring any such effort. Creating a partnership with the union for public relations ventures is likely to build a stronger bond with that organization, which may bode well in future negotiations.

Shareholders also have strong vested interests in company success. Therefore, all communications that go out to them (profit statements, publicity, proxy vote notices) should reflect the company's main strategy and the central idea that guides the organization. Again, a public relations campaign should cause stockholders to "feel better" about the company, which will be helpful in the future.

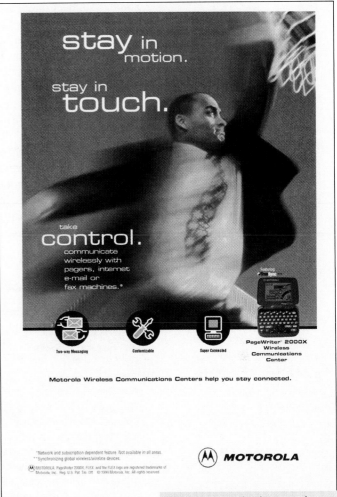

Motorola's theme is that the company's "Wireless communications centers help you stay connected." The theme should be used by employees in all communications.
Source: Courtesy of Motorola, Inc./Personal Communications Sector. © 1999.

External Stakeholders

Most of the time, the public relations department is able to access internal stakeholders fairly easily. Management can call meetings, send memos and letters, and use numerous other available venues to make contact with these constituents. On the other hand, communications with external publics are more difficult to oversee. In this section, a brief review of the importance of the external stakeholders that company leaders encounter is presented.

Channel members, including wholesalers and retailers, have a direct effect on the success of a firm. Beyond influencing these members with trade promotions and advertising, the company makes contact with them in many other ways. Salespeople can inform the channel member about public relations and sponsorship programs while pitching products and services. The goal is to make sure all marketing efforts present a unified message to these critical links with customers.

Customers may be strongly influenced by promotional campaigns. In some instances, the influence is quite positive. At other times, publicity may seem more like a ruse than a genuine attempt to do something altruistic. Consider, for example, the information provided in the Communication Action Box in this section regarding the Philip Morris company.

Some customers may believe the firm is truly concerned about the community, yet others might be much more cynical.

Overseeing external communications is a daunting task, because the company has little or no influence on how these publics perceive organizational activities. Publicity may or may not be reported by the *media*. The company has little power over how the media report any public relations effort it makes. It is wise to remember that most reporters are looking more for a "story" than to be shills for a company's publicity machine. Therefore, great care must be given to the release of information to newspapers, magazines, and television and radio stations.

The *local community* may be directly and indirectly influenced by public relations efforts. For example, when McDonald's sends employees out with trash bags to clean up the neighborhoods surrounding a local unit, the city may notice. Customers may or may not buy more Big Macs, but those who live nearby are going to feel much more favorably about having the company in the neighborhood. A grocery store that allows recycling bins

COMMUNICATION ACTION

Building Positive Publicity Can Be a Tough Sell

Philip Morris began as a tobacco company. Many of its products remain in that industry. In addition, the company has acquired the Miller Brewing Company and 7-Up over the years. Because many of Philip Morris's products are considered "vices," the company has a strong vested interest in creating as many positive contact points as possible.

One program devised to generate goodwill is the "We Card" campaign. In conjunction with the Coalition for Responsible Tobacco Retailing, Philip Morris sends out placards to retailers suggesting that they ID any customer who looks to be 27 years old or less. All 50 states have a minimum purchase age of 18, except Alabama, Alaska, and Utah, which require customers to be 19. Philip Morris has heavily advertised its involvement with the We Card effort. This may be, in part, due to complaints that the tobacco industry targets young people to attract new business.

The We Card program also allows Philip Morris to build more positive ties with retail outlets along with local police officers. Combating underage purchases is easier with the We Card kits. In addition, the company provides training to retailers regarding crime prevention.

Another major thrust developed by the public relations team is the food program for the elderly. This venture combines Philip Morris with the National Meals on Wheels Foundation. Again, substantial positive publicity results from this type of effort.

In the area of disaster relief, Philip Morris employees volunteered their time on several occasions to help provide food and water to those who had been flooded or struck by hurricanes or ice storms. Miller Brewing used its facilities to provide fresh water to those whose systems had been contaminated during storms. Advertisements showing Miller beer trucks rushing to deliver fresh water emphasized the company's involvement in helping people during times of personal crisis.

Beyond these efforts, the Marlboro team is linked with programs to reduce domestic violence, as well as disaster relief, hunger, and youth access to tobacco. These may seem like conflicting messages, yet the company, which also relies on humor in its ads, may be able to convince consumers that the company is not out just to push products on unsuspecting members of the public. Doing so may be one of the keys to success in the future, as tobacco suit settlement agreements drive up cigarette prices and continuous negative press bombards the organization.

Sources: "Philip Morris to Provide More Than 1 Million Meals to the Elderly in All 50 States," *Fund Raising Management,* 30, no. 6 (August 1999) p. 1, Philip Morris press releases, December 19, 1995, March 23, 2000; Philip Morris Web site; and Mike Bierne and Aaron Baar, "Burnett Supports New Marlboro Entry," *Adweek,* 40, no. 2 (October 18, 1999), p. 1.

to be placed in the parking lot may receive additional business from those who stop by to discard old phone books and make a quick purchase at the same time.

Another key stakeholder is the *financial community,* which lends money to the company. This group is most interested in the firm's financial well-being, but also is interested in any goodwill the company can generate.

Finally, both the *government* and various *special-interest groups* will carefully monitor and watch company activities, especially in the negative areas of pollution, discrimination, harassment, and unfair treatment of employees. A concerted public relations effort may be developed to fend off investigations of anything negative, while at the same time building on the positive elements of the organization's activities.

In general, a totally integrated communications program accounts for all types of messages that an organization delivers to both internal and external stakeholders. Every contact point provides the opportunity for a message to be sent. The marketing department tends to create contact points with customers and potential customers. To complement this effort, the public relations department deals with the myriad contact points that are not created or planned, yet are just as critical as those that are planned. An unplanned contact point such as a news story or an individual talking to an employee of the firm at a social gathering allows the firm to build a positive image or reduce any negative messages that are being passed along. Naturally, it is more difficult to deal with unplanned contact points, because they cannot always be anticipated. The key is constantly to monitor what is going on around the firm in order to keep constituents as happy and satisfied as possible.

An advertisement by Wal-Mart directed to its employees, local communities, and other stakeholders.
Source: Courtesy of Wal-Mart.

INTEGRATED LEARNING EXPERIENCE

Public relations are normally handled within an organization. Still, a number of organizations and publications exist to assist public relations personnel. Although individual companies may hire public relations firms to handle specific issues, almost all companies maintain public relations departments. The Public Relations Society of America (PRSA) at **www.prsa.org** is one of the major associations that creates PR for individuals. The PSRA produces two publications: *Public Relations Tactics* and *The Strategist.* In Canada, the primary PR association is the Canadian Public Relations Society (**www.cprs.ca**). For those involved in international corporations, an excellent publication is the *PR Week Magazine* found at **www.prweek.net**. For organizations wanting to hire a PR firm, the Council of Pubic Relations Firms is an excellent source.

PUBLIC RELATIONS EVENTS

There are various ways in which a firm seeks to change the views of consumers and other stakeholders directly. The first is through altruistic activities, the second is cause-related marketing, and the third is green marketing. These *planned events* are designed to draw positive attention to the organization.

Altruistic Activities

Altruistic activities are things provided to employees and other internal stakeholders. Examples include sending flowers to employee families who have lost loved ones or have family members in the hospital. Enlightened companies work to build loyalty and commitment from employees, through programs such as drug or alcohol counseling, child care for workers' children, purchase discounts, and numerous other benefits and programs. Beyond simply providing these services, it is helpful for the public relations department to communicate carefully that the department is available to both internal constituents and external publics, when appropriate.

Cause-Related Marketing

A second form of a planned public relations event is **cause-related marketing**. When a firm ties a marketing program into some type of charity work or program, goodwill can be generated. American businesses spend over $600 million each year to buy the rights to use a not-for-profit organization's name or logo in company advertising and marketing programs. This type of partnership agreement between a not-for-profit and a for-profit business is based on the belief that consumers will purchase from companies willing to help a good cause.

As has been noted many times in this text, brand parity has become the norm for many goods and services. In other words, customers perceive that there are few notable differences between products and the companies that sell them. Many marketers use cause-related marketing to help develop stronger brand ties and to move consumers as well as businesses toward brand loyalty. A recent survey revealed that 66 percent of those who responded said they would be willing to switch brands and 62 percent said they would be willing to switch retailers to a firm associated with a good cause.[3] One difficulty businesses can encounter is that what is a "good" cause to one customer may be disliked by another. For example, Dayton Hudson found a large number of picketers outside company stores objecting to contributions made to Planned Parenthood, even as others praised Dayton Hudson's involvement.[4]

In the past, some companies donated to causes with little thought to the impact or benefit of such gifts. These philanthropic efforts were expected of big business. Currently, most companies want to know what the benefit will be. Although company leaders may be concerned about the environment, supporting environmental causes must, in some way, result in tangible benefits for the company. Otherwise the company will not be able to give support. "Benefits" include:

▶ Additional customers

▶ Increased profits

▶ Consumer goodwill for the future

▶ Better relations with governmental agencies

▶ Reduced chances of facing lawsuits

These and other potential benefits lead companies to get involved. Relationships that do not yield positive benefits to the business sponsor do not last long. Figure 13.3

▶ Improve public schools	52%
▶ Dropout prevention	34%
▶ Scholarships	28%
▶ Cleanup of environment	27%
▶ Community health education	25%

FIGURE 13.3
Causes Consumers Prefer

Source: Bevolyn Williams-Harold and Eric L. Smith, "Spending With Heart," *Black Enterprise* (July 1998), Vol. 28, No. 12, p. 26.

highlights the top five areas consumers want businesses to consider as they seek out causes to support.

In choosing a cause, a company must focus on issues that relate to its specific business. Supporting such efforts is received more positively by consumers. When the company supports an unrelated cause, consumers may feel the business simply is trying to benefit from the not-for-profit's reputation. This may lead some consumers to stop buying the company's products. Consumers are becoming skeptical about the motives behind the increased emphasis given to various charities. Even though most people understand that a business must benefit from the relationship, they still tend to develop negative views when they believe that the business is exploiting a relationship with a not-for-profit.

When a good fit exists, much more positive reactions emerge. For example, a good fit exists between Calphalon, a maker of gourmet cookware, and Share Our Strength (SOS), an antihunger organization. Calphalon raises millions of dollars to help feed hungry people throughout the United States. Twice a year, Calphalon selects one size of pan to feature the SOS logo. The sale of each pan carrying the SOS logo results in a $5 donation by Calphalon to SOS. Sales of pans displaying the SOS logo have averaged 10 times more than sales of pans without the SOS logo. Thus, SOS is a good fit for Calphalon, because Calphalon benefits through additional sales and an enhanced public image.[5]

Cause-related marketing is also important for not-for-profit organizations. Competition has increased in both the business world and the not-for-profit world. An increasing number of not-for-profit organizations currently compete for contributions and gifts. Strategic relationships with businesses can boost contributions for a not-for-profit organization considerably. For example, the American Cancer Society sold its logo to the Florida Department of Citrus for $1 million per year. The American Cancer Society also endorses the Nicoderm nicotine patch produced by SmithKline Beecham for $1 million per year.

The American Lung Association received $1.25 million per year in a deal with Nicotrol, a patch produced by McNeil Consumer Products that competes with Nicoderm. The American Heart Association receives $2,500 per product the organization certifies as healthy. Each year the Association receives $650 for recertification of the product.[6] These relationships with businesses result not only in direct increases in revenues but also in greater publicity for the not-for-profit organization.

Green Marketing

Green marketing is the development and promotion of products that are environmentally safe. When asked, consumers strongly favor the idea of green marketing. They indicate support for companies selling biodegradable products such as laundry detergents and trash bags and endorse the recycling of paper, aluminum cans, and other materials. Normally, green marketing programs generate positive publicity and word of mouth for a company. In fact, a firm may actively advertise green products, such as when Ray O Vac utilized Michael Jordan to promote a new line of rechargeable batteries.

To increase the size of the green market requires firms to produce levels of quality in their environmentally safe products at prices comparable to their non-green counterparts. Many company leaders believe it

A Wal-Mart advertisement highlighting a social cause.
Source: Courtesy of Wal-Mart.

will be well worth the effort. When supported by the government and other social leaders, green marketing may become a strong positive force in the business world.

One bright spot for green marketing is the U.S. federal government, which spends over $200 billion annually for goods and services. In 1993, President Clinton signed an executive order directing the EPA to develop guidelines for federal agencies to help them seek out and purchase environmentally safe products.

A company may not need to develop green products to be socially conscious. Those who render services can do so in a professional and ethical manner and seek to help the community in some other way. The key to becoming an effective and socially responsible company is to look at "both sides of the coin" and make a concerted effort to reduce negative practices while emphasizing positive outcomes.

INTEGRATED LEARNING EXPERIENCE

Cause-related marketing is as important in other countries as it is in the United States. Not-for-profit organizations and social agencies can use this tool to address social issues with the help of corporate funds and resources. Contributing companies benefit from the publicity and patronage of customers who support a particular cause. Access the Cause Related Marketing (CRM) Web site of the United Kingdom at **www.crm.org.uk**. Notice the companies that have received awards for their CRM work as well as the benefits they received. Examine the case study information as well as the press releases. What role do you see cause-related marketing playing in a company's integrated marketing communications plan? For a different perspective, access the National Charities Information Bureau (NCIB) Web site at **give.org**. The mission of NCIB is to promote informed giving by corporations to charities.

DAMAGE CONTROL

One of the most important public relations functions is damage control. Corporate and brand images can be easily damaged by negative publicity. Strong images, which took years to build, may be destroyed in just a few months or even weeks. Not all negative press is generated by the media. Sometimes negative publicity comes from word-of-mouth communication from one customer to another.

Damage control in defense of an organization's image takes place in two ways: (1) reactive strategies and (2) proactive strategies (see Figure 13.4). Firms must react in two potential areas. The first occurs when the firm has made an error or caused legitimate consumer grievances. The second takes place when unjustified or exaggerated negative press appears.

Reactive Strategies

Company leaders often must react to unforeseen events, because they cannot anticipate every possible contingency. In these instances, managers must work diligently to blunt the effects

Reactive Strategies	Proactive Strategies
1. Crisis Management	1. Entitling
2. Apology	2. Enhancements
3. Defense of innocence	3. Inernet interventions
4. Excuses	
5. Justifications	
6. Other explanations	

FIGURE 13.4
Damage Control Strategies

of unwanted bad publicity by every means possible. Crisis management and other techniques should be designed to help the firm cope with circumstances that threaten its image.

Crisis Management

A crisis may be viewed as either a problem or an opportunity. Many times a crisis contains the potential to improve the firm's position and image. For example, when PepsiCo encountered a series of charges of hypodermic needles being found in its products, the management team quickly responded with photographs and video demonstrating that such an occurrence was practically impossible, because the bottles and cans are turned upside down while empty before being filled with any soft drink. Next, footage of a con artist slipping a needle into a can was shown. This fast and powerful answer eliminated the negative publicity, and Pepsi was able, at the same time, to make a strong statement about the safety of its products. Pepsi's reaction was quite effective in dealing with this particular crisis. Unfortunately, company leaders sometimes manage only to make matters worse. The problem with tires made for the Ford Explorer is an example of a serious safety problem. Time will tell whether the recall of 6.5 million tires was sufficient to resolve the crisis and the damage done to Bridgestone's image.

Crisis management involves either accepting the blame for an event and offering an apology, or refuting those making the charges in a forceful manner. Typically, the steps of crisis management are:

1. Advance preparation for any crisis (a crisis management team should be in place).
2. Recognize the crisis.
3. Contain the crisis.
4. Resolve the crisis.
5. Build an advantage from the crisis.

Apology Strategies

Using **an apology strategy** is a reactive form of crisis management and damage control. If the end result of the investigation is the revelation that the firm is at fault, an apology should be offered quickly. A full apology contains five elements:[7]

1. An expression of guilt, embarrassment, or regret
2. A statement recognizing the appropriate behavior and acceptance of sanctions because of wrong behavior
3. A rejection of the inappropriate behavior
4. Approval of the appropriate behavior and a promise not to engage in the inappropriate behavior again
5. An offer of compensation or penance to correct the wrong

Apologies are most often used either in situations in which the violation is minor or ones in which the firm or person cannot escape being found guilty.

Responding to Negative Publicity

Negative press causes leaders of companies to behave in the same ways as any person would to protect his or her own personal image. The tendency to protect one's self-image is called **impression management**, or "the conscious or unconscious attempt to control images that are projected in real or imagined social interactions."[8] In order to maintain or enhance self-image, individuals and corporations attempt to influence the identities they display to others. The goal is to project themselves in such a manner as to maximize access to and the visibility of positive characteristics while minimizing any negative elements.

Any event that threatens a person's self-image or desired identity is viewed as a predicament. When faced with such predicaments, individuals make concerted efforts to reduce or minimize the negative consequences. If the predicament cannot be avoided or concealed, then an individual engages in any type of remedial activity that reduces the potentially harmful consequences. Remedial tactics include the following:[9]

▶ Expressions of innocence

▶ Excuses

▶ Justifications

▶ Other explanations

An *expression of innocence* approach means company leaders provide information designed to convince others (clients, the media, government) that they were not associated with the event that caused the predicament. In other words, they say, "We didn't cause this to happen. Someone (or something) else did."

Excuses are explanations designed to convince the public that the firm and its leaders are not responsible for the predicament or that it could not have been foreseen. Thus, they should not be held accountable for the event that created the predicament (e.g., "It was an act of God. It was totally unavoidable.").

Justifications involve using logic designed to reduce the degree of negativity associated with the predicament. Making the event seem minor or trivial is one method. Making the argument that the firm had to proceed in the way it did (e.g., "We pollute because if we don't we'll be out of business, and our employees will lose their jobs") is another form of justification.

Other explanations may be created to persuade individuals that the cause of the predicament is not a fair representation of what the firm or individual is really like. In other words, the case was the exception rather than the rule, and customers should not judge the firm too harshly as a result. (You will hear comments such as "This was a singular incident, and not indicative of the way we do business.")

A few years before the Bridgestone problem, Firestone used the defense of innocence approach when charges were leveled that its tires tended to blow up, or explode. Firestone's leaders made the charge that a small segment of consumers was simply putting too much air in the tires, and that this was the cause of the problem. Although the tactic worked in terms of eliminating governmental and class-action suits against the firm, many customers switched their brand loyalties to other manufacturers. In essence, Firestone did not complete the task of managing the crisis and lost an opportunity. Had company leaders developed a different tactic, such as a tire pressure gauge giveaway to instruct consumers on proper tire maintenance, it may have been possible to eliminate the negative effects of its defective products completely and turn the situation into something more positive.[10]

INTEGRATED LEARNING EXPERIENCE

Because of the potential damage bad press can cause a firm, a number of consulting firms have been created to offer crisis management expertise. Public Image Corporation at **www.publicimagecorp.com** is a full-service public relations agency. Lexicon Communications Corporation at **www.lexiconcommunications.com** is one of the leading crisis management firms. Access these two firms to see what they say about crisis management as well as what services they offer.

Proactive Strategies

Rather than waiting until harmful publicity occurs and then reacting, many firms utilize proactive strategies to minimize the effects of any bad press. Such approaches may prevent negative publicity from starting in the first place. One method of avoiding negative publicity comes from using a proactive form of impression management. Two positive impression management techniques are called entitlings and enhancements.[11] **Entitlings** are attempts to claim responsibility for positive outcomes of events. **Enhancements** are attempts to increase the desirable outcome of an event in the eyes of the public.

Entitling occurs when a firm associates its name with a positive event. For example, being the official sponsor of a U.S. Olympic team that wins a gold medal attaches the company's name to the athletic achievements of people who don't even work for the firm, yet the firm can claim responsibility for some aspect of the success.

Enhancements occur when a bigger deal is made out of something that is relatively small. For instance, many products now claim to be *fat free,* which makes it sound like they are diet foods. In fact, many fat-free products have just as many calories as do products that contain fat. At the same time, the fat-free label helps convince customers that the company tries to help them eat a more healthy diet and watch their weight at the same time.

Another method of proactive management is for companies to become involved in their local communities by participating in special events and supporting social causes. The rationale for this type of involvement is to build a "good neighbor" image. If a company constantly pushes the image of being a solid social citizen and neighbor, the public tends to view it in a more positive fashion and is less affected by any negative reports. Also, the media are not as quick to investigate any single consumer complaint they hear. Although these strategies will not overcome bad decisions, poor customer service, illegal or unethical behavior, they do help in some situations.

Internet interventions are another method of combating negative word of mouth communication. With the rise of the popularity of the Internet, a new forum for sharing negative word of mouth and spreading bad experiences has arisen: the chat room. Chat rooms provide an environment in which consumers from every part of the world can share horror stories. Because of freedom of speech and First Amendment rights, individuals even can put up Web sites that blast certain industries, companies, or brands.

In an effort to manage proactively what is being said about companies in chat rooms, many companies hire individuals to monitor them. When they see messages criticizing their company or proclaiming untruths, company representatives log into the chat room. They immediately identify themselves as company representatives and attempt to explain the company's viewpoint and correct misconceptions.

SOCIAL RESPONSIBILITY

Social responsibility is the obligation an organization has to be ethical, accountable, and reactive to the needs of society. This definition suggests that socially responsible firms undertake two things: (1) eliminating negatives and (2) doing positives. Figure 13.5 outlines some of the general areas in which firms can become more ethical and reactive to society's needs. It is the task of the public relations department to manage both of these activities.

In general, business experts agree that socially responsible firms are more likely to thrive and survive in the long-term. Companies engaged in positive activities generate quality publicity and customer loyalty. Firms that work strongly toward reductions in unfair practices, pollution, harassment, and other negative activities are more likely to stay out of court, and they suffer fewer negative word-of-mouth comments by dissatisfied consumers.

Image-Destroying Activities	Image-Building Activities
‣ Discrimination	‣ Empowerment of employees
‣ Harassment	‣ Charitable contributions
‣ Pollution	‣ Sponsoring local events
‣ Misleading communications	‣ Selling environmentally safe products
‣ Deceptive communications	‣ Outplacement programs
‣ Offensive communications	‣ Support community events

FIGURE 13.5

Examples of Socially Responsible Activities

PUBLIC RELATIONS TOOLS

The public relations department has several tools available to make people aware of various public relations programs. Figure 13.6 lists these tools. Each represents the opportunity to make a planned contact with various constituencies, thereby enhancing the image of the firm while providing other information. A review of each of these tools follows.

Most public relations departments produce some type of *corporate newsletter* for the organization's employees, which is an excellent means of communicating important internal information, such as results of sales contests and other company activities. Newsletters also transmit "soft" information, including articles about company picnics, notes about employees who have had babies, and so forth. The concepts developed in the IMC program can be reinforced in a newsletter, both directly and indirectly. Articles about the firm's IMC program and its marketing goals are direct approaches. Other, more indirect stories that note the spirit and concepts of the IMC can also appear. For example, if part of the IMC effort is emphasis on customer service, then articles about customer service in the newsletter support this aspect of the IMC plan. Further, if each newsletter featured an employee who had demonstrated superior customer service, employees would realize that management does recognize good customer service.

Newsletter articles can emphasize the communications program directly and indirectly at the same time. For instance, a plaque or reward given to an employee may be featured in a newsletter article. In that story, employees learn that management emphasizes quality customer service and that rewards are available for employees who excel in that area. The article may also have an impact on various managers. Department heads and other managers recognized for superior service serve as examples both to other managers and to subordinates. The newsletter can be an extremely valuable tool for mentioning the firm's IMC concept and making the case to support the effort.

In addition to official newsletters, public relations may employ other types of *internal communications,* including bulletin boards, e-mail list server groups, letters, and memos. These venues routinely reach internal publics and are utilized to make sure employees remain informed about events and happenings both within and outside of the organization. When company leaders are about to make a public announcement, it is best for employees to hear the message first. A company that is the target of bad press or criticism by a consumer special-interest group should alert and inform employees so that they respond in an appropriate fashion, even if it means simply discussing the problem with friends and neighbors while not at work.

A *bulletin board* is another method used to communicate internally. Although the public relations department should not be responsible for everything that appears on a bulletin board, the department's staff must work to make sure all messages sent out match with what the firm wishes to communicate. This is especially true for items targeted to various employee groups. For example, if the company wants to communicate to all its target markets that quality is number one, then bulletin board messages sent out by the PR department should convey and support this theme. A memo encouraging employees to increase output or cut costs might send the wrong message.

> ▶ **Corporate newsletters**
> ▶ **Internal communications**
> ▶ **Media news releases**
> ▶ **Stockholder correspondence**
> ▶ **Annual reports**
> ▶ **Special events**
> ▶ **Collaboration with internal publics**

FIGURE 13.6
Public Relations Tools

PUBLIC RELATIONS, REGULATIONS, AND SPONSORSHIPS

Alcohol and Minors: Ethics, IMC, and the Brewing Industry

By the age of 18, the average American teen has viewed over one hundred thousand beer commercials. Critics of the brewing industry and marketing agree: Many beer commercials are designed to encourage underage drinking and build brand loyalty or brand switching in a population that is not even supposed to use a product. This group can develop an addiction within a few months, because they are less developed mentally, physically, and emotionally.

Young males are often the targets of ads prepared for baseball, football, basketball, and auto racing telecasts. Use of sexuality and social acceptance are common themes, along with humor. Recent reviews by Congress and the Federal Trade Commission suggest the brewing industry is walking a fine line.

The question becomes: Do a few public relations ads, such as the "Know When To Say When" campaign authorized by Budweiser and the "21 Means 21" advertisements sponsored by Coors represent a real response, or are they simply designed to placate the government and the public?

Drunken driving, diminished performance in school, health problems, and even death by binge drinking are all a part of the underage drinking problem. In the alcohol industry, as in many other circumstances, the role of public relations should be real and genuine, not simply designed to keep the government away. Marketing professionals will continue to confront this issue in the years to come.

Other public relations tools are more oriented to external stakeholders, even though internal groups may also read them. For instance, media **news releases** are messages issued by the company regarding a wide variety of topics, including the release of a new product, a change in corporate leadership, or any other newsworthy item that generates a positive public image. Even though public relations people are anxious to send out news releases, they need to remember that members of the media are selective in what they consider newsworthy. A company or agency that bombards the media with releases eventually may find even the firm's most important news releases will be ignored. Therefore, PR department managers must carefully select the releases that go out. Sending only key releases builds credibility with members of the media. The goals of a news release are to build goodwill with the public and use the news media to gain exposure to the public. Information printed or broadcast by the news media has a higher level of credibility with the public than does advertising.

In most companies, the public relations department prepares the annual report and other *stockholder correspondence*. These documents should speak with the one clear voice found in all other materials. In other words, the IMC theme present in advertising, promotions, and the other IMC components must also be prominently displayed in the *annual report*, proxy vote statements, and other mailings.

Another venue available to develop positive publicity is a company-sponsored *special event*. One example of this type of approach is Saturn's annual "homecoming," initiated in 1994, in which Saturn owners are invited to a picnic in Spring Hill, Tennessee.

REGULATING MARKETING COMMUNICATIONS

Over the years, the federal government of the United States has passed a great deal of legislation designed to keep companies from taking advantage of consumers. These laws pertain to food quality, fair interest rates and collateral arrangements, the legal rights of workers, protection of minors, and a variety of additional measures. Various states also regulate matters such as cleanliness in restaurants and provide assistance to individuals who are injured by products or company operations. Many of these statutes also create regulatory agencies to oversee enforcement. In this section, governmental actions are reviewed in the areas of legislation and regulation of company marketing practices.

Unfair and Deceptive Marketing Practices

Federal laws have been enacted and the courts have worked in conjunction with various regulatory agencies to guard consumers from unfair and deceptive marketing communication practices. These laws also protect businesses from unfair and deceptive marketing communications by other businesses.

Deceptive or false advertising liability can stem from many types of marketing communications including advertising on billboards, in mailings, in corporate literature, on labels, on packaging, through oral and written communications by salespeople or salesclerks, and on Internet Web site materials. Numerous ordinances have been enacted to defend consumers from wrongful practices. Other laws have established regulatory agencies for enforcement.

At the federal level the *Wheeler-Lea Amendment* (1938) to Section 5 of the Federal Trade Commission Act, prohibits false and misleading advertising. A firm can violate the act even when the company did not expressly intend to deceive. An advertisement or communication is deemed to be deceptive or misleading when:

1. A substantial number of people or the "typical person" is left with a false impression or misrepresentation that relates to the product.

2. The misrepresentation induces people or the "typical person" to make a purchase.

These conditions lead to the conclusion that a violation has occurred. Both individuals and businesses can sue. In the case of a business versus business lawsuit, the competing firm must show either infringement of a trademark or false advertising.[12]

A recent court case demonstrates the extent of the Wheeler-Lea Amendment's reach. Patrick Fish sued the Wendy's hamburger chain for $30 million in U.S. District Court in Syracuse, New York, for false advertising and misleading marketing practices. Fish claimed Wendy's had misrepresented its veggie pitas as vegetarian food in statements by employees and in its nutritional guide. Specifically, Fish, who was a vegetarian, purchased a veggie pita only after workers in a Wendy's restaurant assured him it contained no meat or animal products of any kind. Later he discovered that the dressing used in the pita contained gelatin made from animal products. As a result of the court action, Wendy's has taken gelatin out of the recipe for the veggie pita and recalled all of the company's nutritional guides.[13]

Deception Versus "Puffery"

Before going any further into a discussion about misleading advertising, it is important to point out that firms can use what is called "puffery" in their advertisements and messages. **Puffery** exists when a firm makes an exaggerated claim about its products or services, without making an overt attempt to deceive or mislead. Terms normally associated with puffery include words such as *best, greatest,* and *finest.* Therefore, it is acceptable to state that a company's tacos are the

An advertisement by Cruex using puffery.
Source: Courtesy of Novartus Consumer Health Inc.

best in town. Courts and the regulatory agencies view these statements as puffery and believe that consumers expect firms to use them routinely in their advertisements. The ad becomes false or deceptive if it states the company's tacos contain more meat than the competitor's when they do not. Such a statement would be difficult to prove and would probably lead to objections by the competition. Notice the Tree Top advertisement. Saying Tree Top apple juice is "twice as good" is considered puffery and would be acceptable.

Obviously quite a bit of gray area exists when a claim about a false or misleading statement is made. Consequently, lawsuits are filed and governmental agencies are forced to address complaints and violations of the law. These agencies strongly affect individual marketing practices as well as other company actions.

Governmental Regulatory Agencies

Numerous governmental agencies serve as watchdogs to monitor for potential violations of the law, some of which are only partially related to marketing. For example, the Food and Drug Administration (FDA) regulates and oversees the packaging and labeling of products. The FDA also monitors advertising on food packages and advertisements for drugs, yet its primary responsibilities are ensuring food quality and drug safety.

The Federal Communications Commission (FCC) has authority over television, radio, and the telephone industry. The primary responsibility of the FCC is to grant (and revoke) operating licenses for radio and television stations. The FCC also has jurisdiction over telephone companies. The FCC does not have authority over the content of advertisements transmitted by mass media. Further, the FCC does not control which products may be advertised. The organization is, however, responsible for monitoring advertising directed toward children. Under FCC rules, TV stations are limited to 12 minutes per hour of children's advertisements during weekdays and 10 minutes per hour on weekends.[14]

The U.S. Postal Service (USPS) watches over all mail-type marketing materials. The USPS also investigates mail fraud schemes and other fraudulent marketing practices. The Bureau of Alcohol, Tobacco and Firearms (ATF) rules when the sale, distribution, and advertising of alcohol and tobacco are at issue. Ordinarily, the governmental agency that examines incidents involving deceptive or misleading marketing tactics is the Federal Trade Commission (FTC). These agencies are listed in Figure 13.7. The next section examines the FTC in greater detail.

Twice as Good

Tree Top puts 2 apples in every glass. And nothing else.

Every delicious glass of Tree Top apple juice is made from the juice of two fresh, Washington state apples. Nothing added (not a single granule of sugar). And nothing taken away. It's simply pure apple juice. Pasteurized. And naturally sweetened by the sun.

An advertisement for Tree Top apple juice with the claim that it is "Twice as Good."
Source: Courtesy of Tree Top Inc.

▶ **Food and Drug Administration (FDA)**

▶ **Federal Communications Commission (FCC)**

▶ **U.S. Postal Service (USPS)**

▶ **Bureau of Alcohol, Tobacco and Firearms (BATF)**

▶ **Federal Trade Commission (FTC)**

FIGURE 13.7
Governmental Regulatory Agencies

THE FEDERAL TRADE COMMISSION

The most powerful federal agency with jurisdiction over marketing communications is the **Federal Trade Commission**, or FTC, which was created in 1914 by the passage of the Federal Trade Commission Act. The act's original intent was to create an agency to enforce antitrust laws and protect businesses from one another. It had little authority over advertising and marketing communications except when an advertisement would be considered unfair to the competition and therefore restrict free trade.

In 1938, Congress passed the Wheeler-Lea Amendment to increase and expand the authority of the FTC. The agency then had the ability to stop unfair or deceptive advertising practices and to levy fines when necessary. The law also granted the FTC access to the courts to enforce the law and ensure that violators abide by FTC rulings.

How Investigations Begin

Various types of complaints can trigger an FTC investigation. These include problems noticed by:

- Consumers
- Businesses
- Congress
- The media

Each can raise questions about what appears to be an unfair or deceptive practice. Most investigations by the FTC are confidential at first, which protects the agency and the company being investigated. If the FTC believes a law has been violated, a **consent order** is issued. If company leaders sign the consent order, they have agreed to stop the disputed practice without admitting guilt. Most FTC investigations end with the signing of a consent order.

An example of this process involves the Automotive Breakthrough Services (ABS) company. The FTC issued ABS a consent order, requesting that the company discontinue advertisements for its ABS/Trax system brakes. The ads claimed the brakes were as effective as factory-installed antilock brakes. While investigating the complaint, the FTC concluded that the advertiser's claims about the brakes were not supported by competent and reliable scientific evidence. The FTC was especially insistent that ABS neither claim nor even vaguely suggest that its brakes provided the same benefit as factory-installed antilock brakes.[15]

If a consent agreement cannot be reached, the FTC issues an **administrative complaint**. At that point a formal proceeding similar to a court trial is held before an administrative law judge. Both sides submit evidence and render testimony. At the end of the administrative hearing, the judge makes a ruling. If the judge feels a violation of the law has occurred, a *cease and desist order* is prepared. The order requires the company to stop the disputed practice immediately and refrain from similar practices in the future. If the company is not satisfied with the initial decision of the administrative law judge, the case can be appealed to the full FTC commission.

The *full commission* holds hearings similar to those before administrative law judges. Rulings are made after hearing evidence and testimony. Companies not satisfied with the ruling of the full FTC commission can appeal the case to the U.S. Court of Appeals and further to the highest level, the U.S. Supreme Court. The danger for companies that appeal cases is that consumer redress can be sought at that point. This means companies found guilty of violating laws can be ordered to pay civil penalties.

Court Actions

Occasionally, the FTC uses the court system to stop unfair and deceptive advertising and communications practices when a company violates FTC cease and desist orders. For example, an ongoing case began in 1974 involving the National Talent Associates (NTA) organization. The FTC issued a complaint against National Talent Associates (NTA) claiming the company misrepresented its ability to place children as models and entertainers with professional acting jobs. In 1975, the company agreed to a consent order, which prohibited NTA from misrepresenting NTA's services. NTA agreed in the consent order to disclose specific information to customers about NTA's placement rates and to allow customers a three-day cooling-off period after signing their contracts. In 1979, NTA agreed to pay $25,000 in civil penalties for violation of the consent order. Again in 1985, the FTC found National Talent Associates in violation of the consent order and the company agreed to pay $150,000 in civil penalties.

In 1999, National Talent Associates was in court once again for violations of the consent agreement and was ordered to pay $160,000 in civil penalties. More importantly, the court has permanently prohibited NTA from making the claim to customers about any expertise to judge people's suitability as models, actors, and entertainers or to provide them with job placement. The FTC also prohibited NTA from making any in-home or in-office sales presentations until it satisfactorily instituted reforms of sales presentations made by company members that would prevent future violations of the FTC's ruling.[16]

In a more drastic step, members of the Federal Trade Commission immediately went to court to stop the practices of the company Screen Test USA. The FTC viewed Screen Test USA as a bogus front used to sell expensive modeling services. The FCC believed that Screen Test USA promised individuals easy access to professional modeling and acting jobs. Screen Test USA then persuaded consumers to purchase an assortment of products and services by representing itself as run by experts and professionals, when in fact they were not.[17] The FTC obtained a temporary injunction order from a federal judge in New Jersey. The injunction effectively stopped Screen Test USA's operation by freezing assets and appointing a receiver pending the final hearing. In that instance, the FTC believed the violations to be so serious that a consent decree was not sufficient and immediately took the case to the courts instead.

Corrective Advertising

In more severe instances of deceptive or misleading advertising, the FTC can order a firm to prepare **corrective advertisements**. These rare situations occur only when the FTC feels that discontinuing a false advertisement will not be a sufficient remedy. When the FTC concludes that consumers believed the false advertisement, it can require the firm to produce corrective ads to bring consumers back to a neutral state. The goal is for consumers to once again hold beliefs they had prior to the false or misleading advertisement.

The FTC utilized corrective advertising following an advertisement presented by Volvo Cars of North America. This television ad showed cars placed in a row being destroyed by a monster truck as it ran over them, except for a Volvo. Upon investigation, the FTC learned that the Volvo car had been altered with steel bars to prevent it from being crushed. The FTC concluded that the ad would cause consumers to believe that Volvo was a safer automobile than it actually was. As a result, the FTC deemed it necessary for Volvo not only to discontinue the advertisement, but also to run a series of new ads explaining how the car had been altered to obtain the effect in the advertisement.[18]

Trade Regulation Rulings

The final type of action the FTC takes is called a **trade regulation ruling**. These findings implicate an entire industry in a case of unfair or deceptive practices. Normally the commission holds a public hearing and accepts both oral and written arguments. The commission then makes a ruling that applies to every firm within an industry. As with other FTC rulings, decisions can be challenged in the U.S. Court of Appeals.

In 1984 and again in 1994, the FTC investigated pricing practices within the funeral home industry and subsequently issued a trade regulation ruling. The ruling requires funeral homes to provide an itemized list of funeral goods and services that state both the price and a detailed description of the good or service. As part of the itemization, the ruling requires all funeral homes to disclose the following four statements to consumers: (1) Consumers have the right to select only the goods and services they desire. (2) Embalming is not always required by law. (3) Individuals desiring cremation of a

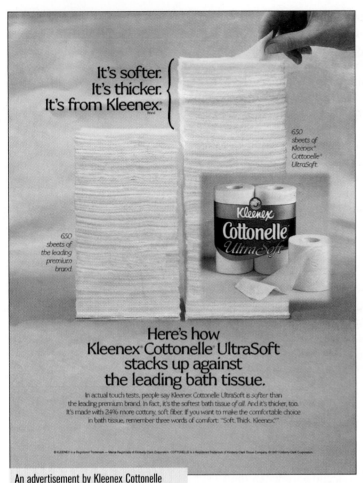

It's softer.
It's thicker.
It's from Kleenex.

650
sheets of
the leading
premium
brand.

650
sheets of
Kleenex
Cottonelle
UltraSoft.

Here's how
Kleenex Cottonelle UltraSoft
stacks up against
the leading bath tissue.

In actual touch tests, people say Kleenex Cottonelle UltraSoft is softer than
the leading premium brand. In fact, it's the softest bath tissue of all. And it's thicker, too.
It's made with 24% more cottony, soft fiber. If you want to make the comfortable choice
in bath tissue, remember three words of comfort: "Soft. Thick. Kleenex."

An advertisement by Kleenex Cottonelle
using a substantiated claim.

Source: Courtesy of Kimberly-Clark Corporation. The
illustrated advertisement, all copyrights thereto and
rights to the trademarks appearing therein are the
property of Kimberly Clark Corporation and used with
its permission.

loved one can use alternative containers for the remains. (4) The only fee a consumer can be required to pay is the nondeclinable basic service fee.[19] A trade regulation ruling is designed to keep firms in industries from conspiring or colluding to become involved in the kinds of misleading or deceptive practices that also occur in individual companies.

Substantiation of Marketing Claims

FTC rules cover every aspect of marketing communications. Regardless of the type of communication, the FTC prohibits unfair or deceptive marketing communications. Marketers must be able to substantiate claims through competent and reliable evidence. If companies use endorsers, these statements must be truthful and represent their experiences or opinions. If they use expert endorsements, these statements must be based on legitimate tests performed by experts in the field. All claims must reflect the typical experience that a customer would expect to encounter from the use of a good or service, unless the advertisement clearly and prominently states otherwise.[20] Kleenex used actual touch tests by consumers as evidence that its brand was softer. The company then used engineering or lab tests to show that Kleenex tissue is made with 24 percent more cottony, soft fiber.

One of the keys to FTC evaluations of advertisements and marketing communications is the idea of **substantiation**. Firms such as Kleenex must be able to substantiate (e.g., prove or "back up") any claims made. Failure to do so can result in some form of FTC action.

For example, the FTC issued a consent order to Fitness Quest, Inc. because of the company's failure to substantiate claims of weight loss made regarding their exercise gliders and abdominal devices. Fitness Quest suggested that its exercise gliders would burn calories at the rate of 1,000 per hour, burn three times more calories than walking, and burn nearly twice the calories of cross-country skiing. The FTC ruled the company could not substantiate any of those claims. The rationale for the decision against Fitness Quest was partially based on the test that the claim must reflect the typical experience that a customer would expect. Fitness Quest used testimonials of consumers in its advertisement; these testimonials demonstrated how effective the gliders and abdominal exercise devices were in helping a person lose weight. The FTC, however, ruled that the testimonials did not reflect what the typical or ordinary person could expect from the use of the equipment.[21]

INDUSTRY REGULATION OF NEGATIVE MARKETING PRACTICES

It is clear federal regulatory agencies cannot oversee all industry activities. Although various industry regulatory agencies have no legal power, they can reduce the load on the FTC and the legal system. Many allegations or complaints about unfair and deceptive advertising and marketing communication are handled and settled within the industry system. Although each industry has its own system of regulating marketing communications, the three most common are: (1) the Better Business Bureau, (2) the National Advertising Division, and (3) the National Advertising Review Board (Figure 13.8).

The Better Business Bureau is a resource available to both consumers and businesses. Consumers and firms can file complaints with the bureau about unethical busi-

▶ **Better Business Bureau**

▶ **National Advertising Division (NAD)**

▶ **National Advertising Review Board (NARB)**

FIGURE 13.8
Industry Regulation

ness practices or unfair treatment. The bureau compiles a summary of all charges leveled against individual firms. Customers seeking information about the legitimacy of a company or its operations can contact the bureau. The bureau gives them a carefully worded report that will raise cautionary flags when a firm has received a great number of complaints and reveals the general nature of customer concerns. The Better Business Bureau is helpful to individuals and businesses that want to make sure they are dealing with a firm that has a low record of problems.

Complaints about advertising or some aspect of marketing communications are referred to the National Advertising Division (NAD) of the Better Business Bureau for review. The role of the NAD is to discover the real issue. The NAD collects information and evaluates data concerning the complaint to determine whether the advertiser's claim is substantiated. If it is not, the NAD negotiates with the business to modify or discontinue the advertisement. If the firm's marketing claim is substantiated, then the complaint is dismissed.

Individuals and companies both can file complaints about unfair ads. Sometimes, however, they do not receive the ruling they are seeking. For example, General Motors filed a complaint with the NAD challenging a set of TV, print, and Internet advertisements by Ford Motor Company. In these comparative ads, Ford claimed that the Ford Expedition was the "best in class." GM claimed these ads were deceptive because in their conclusions, Ford had not compared the Explorer to GM's Chevrolet Suburban. GM claimed the Suburban was in the same sport utility class as the Ford Explorer. In its investigation, the NAD found Ford's advertisements to be substantiated and ruled against GM. The rationale was based on GM's own advertisement, which positioned the Suburban in a different class than the smaller Yukon and Tahoe. It was the Yukon and Tahoe that Ford used as comparison vehicles (the class).[22]

When a complaint is not resolved by the NAD or the advertiser appeals the NAD's decision, it goes to the National Advertising Review Board (NARB). The NARB is composed of advertising professionals and prominent civic individuals. If the NARB rules that the firm's advertisements are not substantiated, it then orders the firm to discontinue the advertisements. This is very similar to the consent order by the FTC, but is issued by this private advertising board. If the business firm being accused refuses to accept the NARB ruling, then the matter is turned over to the FTC or an appropriate federal regulatory agency.

The NARB has been involved in numerous business versus business disputes. For instance, Minute Maid orange juice was ordered to modify its ads because the ad copy claimed that consumers preferred Minute Maid to Tropicana by a 2–1 margin. Tropicana originally lodged the complaint about the ad and won when it was heard by the NAD. Minute Maid disagreed with the NAD ruling and appealed to the NARB. Minute Maid complained that the decision by the NAD placed an unnecessary and unfair burden on comparative advertising because all claims relative to a competitor must be substantiated. The NARB supported the NAD decision and forced Minute Maid to comply with the ruling.[23]

The NARB does not always rule in favor of the firm or consumer making the complaint. For example, MCI objected to AT&T's advertising claim that calling 1-800-CALL-ATT always costs less than MCI's 1-800-COLLECT. MCI filed a complaint with the NAD that was referred on to the NARB. Unfortunately for MCI, the NARB ruled that AT&T did not need to modify its advertisement because the pricing claim was substantiated.[24]

Occasionally the NARB will reverse a ruling by the NAD. FedEx lodged a complaint about the U.S. Postal Service's advertisements. FedEx wanted the U.S. Post Office to disclose in its comparative advertisements that Priority Mail neither tracks nor guaranteed its packages as do both FedEx and UPS. The NAD had originally ruled that the U.S. Postal Service did have to make such a disclosure in ads comparing Priority Mail to shipments by UPS and FedEx. The NARB reversed the NAD ruling, saying the U.S. Postal Service did not have to make such disclosures.[25]

The NARB seldom refers a case to the Federal Trade Commission. In fact, such an action has been taken only four times in the last 25 years. The last was a case dealing with Winn-Dixie, which made direct price comparisons with competitors. The NARB found that Winn-Dixie was using prices that were sometimes up to 90 days old. The NARB ruled that any price comparisons made in an advertisement by Winn-Dixie must use prices that are no more than 7 days old. The decision to forward the case to the FTC was made when Winn-Dixie refused to modify its ads and accept the NARB ruling.[26]

These industry-based actions are designed to control the marketing communications environment and prevent legal actions by either the courts or a regulatory agency. Effective management, however, should become proactive rather than reactive. Company leaders should work to create an image of a socially responsible firm rather than a firm that must constantly be watched by consumers and regulatory agencies. The next section looks at proactive methods firms can use to create a positive image.

SPONSORSHIP MARKETING

Sponsorship marketing means that the company pays money to sponsor someone or some group that is participating in an activity. A firm can sponsor a practically unending list of groups and individuals. For years, local firms sponsored everything from little league baseball and soccer teams to adult bowling teams. Other organizations sponsor college scholarship programs, participate in special "days" (such as Labor Day festivals), as well as individuals who enter various contests. Many local car racetracks feature drivers who are sponsored by various companies. On a national scale, Nike purchases sponsor "exemptions" for golf tournaments. In Tiger Woods's first year on the PGA tour, this meant he could enter a professional tournament without being "qualified" (a top money winner or winner of a tournament in the previous year). A company can sponsor boxers, players, and occasions (a "home run giveaway" at a baseball game).

Sponsorships are used to accomplish many different objectives for organizations. For example, sponsorships can:

▶ Enhance a company's image

▶ Increase a firm's visibility

▶ Differentiate a company from its competitors

▶ Showcase specific goods and services

▶ Help a firm develop closer relationships with current and prospective customers

▶ Unload excess inventory

In choosing a sponsorship, it is important to match the audience profile with the company's target market. Thus, a firm may choose to sponsor a participant at an event attended primarily by females if a company's main market is female. Marketing executives also consider the image of the individual participant or group and how it relates to the firm's image. For instance, a contestant in an "upscale" competition, such as a beauty contest, should be sponsored by a tuxedo or formal gown company. Sponsorships are designed to help the company present a unified message to all audiences, which projects a positive corporate image. If possible, the firm should be the exclusive sponsor of the person or team. It is much easier to be remembered if the firm is the only sponsor rather than one of many sponsors.

Many sponsorships are related to sports. Sporting events are highly popular and often attract large crowds. In addition to the audience attending the game or competition, many more watch on television. Athletes tend to be idolized by fans and can be effective spokespersons for various products.

The same is true for music concerts. Several companies sponsor bands at rock and pop concerts as a means of reaching loyal listeners and fans. The idea is to take the loyalty associated with the musical entertainer and transfer part of it to the product or company serving as the sponsor of the concert.

Some organizations have moved away from sports sponsorships toward more cultural events, such as classical music groups and jazz bands, visual art exhibits by noted painters, dance troupes, and actors for various theater performances. Cultural sponsorships are not a good match for every firm. They are effective for those products sold to the more affluent members of society. Consequently, financial institutions are the primary sponsors of these types of performers. In the past, many institutions provided funds without receiving much recognition. Now these philanthropic efforts are being leveraged by having the name of the company strongly associated with the cultural activity. This includes printing the name of the firm on programs and regularly mentioning the brand or corporate name as being responsible for arranging for the artist to be present at the cultural event. Also, sponsors usually receive choice seats at performances that can be given to key clients. For example, Credit Suisse sponsors the U.S. Equestrian Team and the individual performers for the Lincoln Center Theater. The company uses these cultural activities to help them establish long-term relationships and build goodwill with key clients, who get good seats at horse shows and theatrical performances.[27]

TNN uses a different type of sponsorship approach when the network sponsors groups or performers at music concerts, rodeo cowboys, and car race drivers. TNN sends network celebrities to these occasions in a specialized mobile van. By creating a physical presence at an event being broadcast on TNN, the network believes it can build stronger relationships with viewers. The 30-foot truck is equipped with several entertainment devices including auto racing video games, prizes, T-shirts, hats, and music premiums. The type of merchandise carried on the truck is geared to the event featuring the sponsored person or group. CMT (Country Music Television) has been using the same approach for a number of years and visits over 1,000 sites each summer.[28]

It may be hard to measure the impact of a sponsorship program directly. This can make such a program seem like a dangerous approach for a small, struggling company. For example, some marketing experts viewed Rachel's Gourmet Snacks' three-year, multimillion-dollar sponsorship of two Indianapolis 500 race cars as a dangerous strategy. At the time, the company was struggling financially. Even though it may indeed have been a risky tactic, it worked out exceptionally well for Rachel's. Eddie Cheever, one of the drivers sponsored by Rachel's, overcame 30-to-1 odds and won the Indianapolis 500. Rachel's name was prominently displayed on the car, on Eddie Cheever's uniform, and on the uniforms worn by his pit crew. The name was seen by 300,000 fans at the raceway and by millions on television. The company was immediately flooded with phone calls from customers. Soon, Rachel's opened distribution outlets throughout the United States. Therefore, even though the sponsorship program seemed risky, the return was overwhelming.[29]

In addition to milk, notice all of the corporate sponsors listed on Jeff Gordon's uniform.
Source: Courtesy of Bozell Worldwide, Inc.

To maximize the benefits of a sponsorship effort, it is important to define the primary goals of the program. As with the other marketing tools, the goals of the sponsorships should be integrated with the firm's overall IMC theme. The public should easily recognize the link between the person or group being sponsored, the activity, and the company involved.

To achieve the maximum impact for the sponsorship, the message should be combined with other advertising and promotional efforts, such as the TNN van program mentioned earlier. Normally a company spending $100,000 on a sponsorship should also spend $200,000 to $400,000 leveraging that sponsorship. Advertising the sponsorship prior to the event is essential. Most marketing experts recommend that no more than 10 percent of a firm's marketing budget be allocated to sponsorships. Rachel's Gourmet Snacks gambled on the firm's sponsorship of Eddie Cheever by spending substantially more than 10 percent of its budget, which is partly what made the approach such a risky strategy for the firm.

Finally, when conducting a sponsorship program, the marketing team should try to incorporate other trade and consumer promotions. At the event itself, sampling is an effective method to encourage people to try a product. Unless a sponsorship is surrounded by some kind of supporting marketing effort, the money invested may not accomplish as much.

INTEGRATED LEARNING EXPERIENCE

Sponsorships are big business both for the not-for-profit organizations holding events and for the companies providing the support. In Canada, the *Sponsorship Report* is a publication dedicated to fostering successful partnerships between corporations and not-for-profit groups. Access the Sponsorship Report at **www.sponsorship.ca** to see what services it offers. To assist firms in selecting the best sponsorships that will integrate well with their IMC plans, a number of agencies are available. Examine the following Web sites to see what types of services are being offered to companies to assist them in their sponsorship activities.

Performance Research (www.performanceresearch.com)
IEG Sponsorship (www.sponsorship.com)
BDS Sponsorships Ltd (www.sponsorship.co.uk)

EVENT MARKETING

Event marketing is quite similar to sponsorship marketing. The major difference is that sponsorship marketing involves a person, group, or team. Event marketing occurs when the company supports a specific event. Event marketing is closely related to *lifestyle marketing*, which is described in Chapter 15. Both often include setting up a booth or display and having some type of physical presence at an event. Almost $8 billion is spent annually on event marketing, with General Motors and Philip Morris as the top two spenders in the past several years.[30]

Many events are sports related. A rodeo sponsored by Lee Jeans or a music concert put on by a radio station are marketing events. In addition, many more segmented events are held. For instance, a Hispanic fiesta funded by a food company or a health fair conducted by a local hospital (e.g., "An Affair of the Heart" wellness program sponsored by Freeman Medical Hospital) is event marketing.

Sponsoring the right event can provide the sponsoring organization with greater brand-name recognition and help develop closer ties with vendors and customers. Also, events can help boost morale for the employees who participate or attend. Sponsoring local events provides a company with the potential to generate free publicity. These events may also be used to enhance the company's image in the local community.

There are several key steps to take when preparing an event. Therefore, to ensure the maximum benefit from event sponsorships, companies should[31]:

1. Determine the objective(s) of sponsoring events
2. Match each event with customers, vendors, or employees
3. Cross-promote the event
4. Make sure the company is included in all event advertising and brochures
5. Track results
6. Evaluate the investment following the event

The company should determine the key *marketing objectives* to accomplish before becoming involved in a particular event. When the objective is to reward customers, it is crucial to find an event major customers would be interested in attending. Objectives that are more internally oriented, especially those designed to get employees involved and boost morale, should be met by finding events internal members will enjoy. Many times, the goals of sponsoring an event are to:

1. Help the firm maintain its market share
2. Build strong brand presence in the marketplace
3. Enhance the product or firm's image

To meet these goals means carefully selecting a program to sponsor that matches the firm's *customers, vendors,* or *employees.*

Matching the event with a segment of the firm's target market helps the company keep in contact with customers and vendors. For 40 years, General Motors has been involved in golfing events, especially the PGA Tour. Buick is the title sponsor at four or five PGA Tour locations each year and also is present at other tournaments. The model emphasized by Buick varies depending on the projected audience for the event. Golf is attractive for GM due to the match between the target audience (golfers and golf fans) and Buick's target market. Golf attracts an upscale, primarily male audience similar to the profile of a typical Buick owner. To support the company's involvement in golf tournament events, Buick offers free tickets to attend through in-store promotions at Buick dealers, sweepstakes, and test-driving campaigns.[32]

Cross-promotions boost the impact of an event marketing program. General Motors developed a tie-in promotion between its Oldsmobile Intrigue sedan and the first *X-Files* movie. The objective of the event marketing program was to attract young, married adults with children to test-drive the Intrigue. Produced by event marketing agency Frankel & Company of Chicago, "*X-Files* Expo" events were held in several major cities. They offered attendees free movie tickets, prizes, and photo opportunities with the stars of the film. The *X-Files* Expo events resulted in 8,554 consumer test-drives for the Intrigue and 10,000 requests for information about the car.[33]

Sponsoring participants in an event should insist on *placement of the company name,* logo, and other product information in every advertisement and brochure for the event. Many attendees of special events keep the program as a souvenir or as something to show others. Placing the sponsor's name and message on the program generates an ad with a long life span. The sponsoring business must work to maximize brand-name exposure by connecting the firm's name with the event's marketing program. Working closely with the event management team is vital to seeing that the sponsor's name receives prominent attention in all materials associated with the event.

Some events turn out better than others for the sponsor. To determine the best events, firms need to *track results.* In addition to sales, the company can monitor how many pieces of literature were given to attendees, the number of samples distributed, and the number of visitors to the sponsor's display booth. Further, marketing research can be conducted to measure brand awareness before and after the event to discover if any new brand recall or brand awareness developed.

Results and marketing information allow the business to *evaluate the investment* in the event. Company leaders and marketing managers then can decide if sponsoring a particular event was beneficial and whether to sponsor the event in coming years or similar events in the future. Event marketing has increased in popularity during the past decade due to its potential to reach consumers on a one-to-one basis. In the future, event marketing tie-ins with other media, especially the Internet, will rise. Events including rock concerts, boat shows, and other more specialized programs will continue to see an increased interest by marketing firms trying to make contact with customers in personalized ways that do not directly involve a sales call. Event marketing and sponsorship programs make these contacts easier to generate.

INTEGRATED LEARNING EXPERIENCE

Event marketing used wisely can enhance the image of a corporation. The key is to choose the right kinds of events. Each one should match the firm's goals and IMC plans. As with other forms of promotions, certain companies specialize in event marketing, and others offer event marketing services as part of a wider portfolio of services. Examine the following firms. Study the types of events they offer and the types of services they render in relation to events marketing.

Advantage International, LLC (**www.advantage-intl.com**)
Pierce Promotions and Event Management, Inc. (**www.ppem.com**)
Trojan Sports and Event Marketing (**www.trojansports.com**)
Event Marketing Concepts, Inc. (**www.emconcepts.com**)
Woolf Associates (**www.woolfassociates.com**)
RPMC Event Marketing and Promotion Agency (**www.rpmc.com**)

SUMMARY

The public relations department should play a major role in an integrated marketing communications program, whether the department is separate from marketing or combined as part of a communications division. Public relations efforts are primarily oriented to making sure that every possible contact point delivers a positive and unified message on behalf of the company.

There are many stakeholders inside and surrounding a company. Any person or group that has a vested interest in the organization's activities is a stakeholder. Internal stakeholders include employees, unions, and stockholders. External publics include members of the marketing channel, customers, the media, the local community, financial institutions, the government, and special-interest groups.

To enforce fair standards in the areas of advertising and marketing communications, a number of governmental agencies are ready to take action when needed. These include the Federal Trade Commission, Food and Drug Administration, Federal Communications Commission, and others. Each tries to keep unfair marketing activities from taking place. The FTC is the major overseer for marketing communications and gives special effort to stopping instances of unfair or deceptive practices. In conjunction with the courts, the FTC and other governmental agencies regulate the majority of companies and industries in the United States. The FTC regulates cases of fraudulent practices targeted at individual consumers as well as conflicts between businesses. Through the use of consent orders, administrative complaints, cease and desist orders, and full commission hearings, the FTC is able to make its findings and rulings known to the parties concerned. Court actions and corrective adver-

tising programs are utilized in more severe cases. Trade regulation rulings apply when an entire industry is guilty of an infraction.

In the attempt to build a favorable image of the company, the public relations department develops special events such as altruistic activities and cause-related marketing programs. Due care must be given to making certain these acts are not perceived with cynicism and skepticism. This means being certain than any good deed matches with company products and other marketing efforts. A natural fit between an altruistic event and the company's brand is more readily accepted by various members of the public.

The public relations team is also responsible for damage control when negative publicity arises. Both proactive and reactive tactics are available to maintain a positive image for the company. Socially responsible activities are also emphasized as part of the overall IMC program.

To reach all intended audiences, the public relations department has a series of tools available. These include company newsletters, internal messages, public relations releases, correspondence with stockholders, annual reports, and various special events. Even the bulletin board in the company's break room can be used to convey messages to internal stakeholders.

Sponsorship programs enhance and build the company's image and brand loyalty. A sponsorship of an individual or group involved in some kind of activity—whether it is a sporting event, a contest, or a performance by an artistic group—can be used to link the company's name with the popularity of the player involved. Sponsorships should match with the firm's products and brands.

Event marketing occurs when a firm sponsors an entire event. A strong physical presence at the event is one of the keys to successfully linking an organization's name with a program. To do so, the firm must determine the major objective of the event sponsorship, match it with company customers and publics, and make sure the firm's name is prominently displayed on the literature accompanying the event.

Managing public relations, sponsorships, and event marketing programs requires company leaders to carefully assess both the goals and the outcomes of individual activities. A cost–benefit approach may not always be feasible, but the marketing team should be able to track some form of change, whether it is increased inquiries, the number of samples passed out at an event, or a shift in the tenor of news articles about the organization. The primary task of public relations is to be the organization's "watchdog," making sure those who come in contact with the company believe the firm is working to do things right and to do the right things.

REVIEW QUESTIONS

1. Describe the role of the public relations department. How is it related to the marketing department? Should both departments be called the "department of communications"? Why or why not?

2. What is a stakeholder?

3. Name the major internal stakeholders in organizations. Describe their interests in the company.

4. Name the major external publics in organizations. Describe the major interest in the company of each one.

5. Name and describe the internal public relations tools that the department can utilize.

6. Name and describe the public relations tools the department uses to reach external publics.

7. What damage-control techniques are available to the public relations team? How are they related to social responsibility?

8. How can the company make sure public relations efforts are being integrated with the larger IMC program?

9. When does an ad or message become false or misleading, according to the Lanham Act of 1947?

10. What is "puffery"? Should a company use a great deal of puffery in its ads? Why or why not?

11. What role does the FDA play in marketing communication?

12. What roles does the FCC play in marketing communication?

13. What role does the U.S. Postal Service play in marketing communication?

14. What are the steps of the process when the Federal Trade Commission investigates a claim of false or misleading advertising?

15. What is a consent agreement?

16. What is a trade regulation ruling? How is it different from other FTC rulings?

17. What does the term "substantiation" mean? How does a company know it has met the substantiation test in an advertisement?

18. What is sponsorship marketing? Name a pro athlete, musician or musical group, and performer of some other type who has been featured in a sponsorship program. Was the program effective or ineffective? Why?

19. Describe an event marketing program. What must accompany the event in order to make it a success?

20. What are cross-promotions? How are they related to event marketing programs?

KEY TERMS

public relations (PR) department a unit in the firm that manages items such as publicity and other communications with all of the groups that make contact with the company.

hit the mention of a company's name in a news story.

stakeholder a person or group that has a vested interest in a firm's activities and well-being.

altruistic activities company-sponsored efforts designed to build goodwill with both internal and external publics.

cause-related marketing matching marketing efforts with some type of charity work or program.

green marketing the development and promotion of products that are environmentally safe.

crisis management either accepting the blame for an event and offering an apology, or refuting those making the charges in a forceful manner.

apology strategy presenting a full apology when the firm has made an error.

impression management the conscious or unconscious attempt to control images that are projected in real or imagined social situations.

entitlings attempts to claim responsibility for positive outcomes of events.

enhancements attempts to increase the desirable outcome of an event in the eyes of the public.

Internet interventions confronting negative publicity on the Internet, either in Web site news releases or by entering chat rooms.

social responsibility the obligation an organization has to be ethical, accountable, and reactive to the needs of society.

news release a message sent out by the public relations department regarding an aspect of a company's operation.

puffery when a firm makes an exaggerated claim about its products or services, without making an overt attempt to deceive or mislead.

Federal Trade Commission the most powerful federal agency with control over marketing communications.

consent order issued when FTC believes a law has been violated. If company leaders sign the consent order, they have agreed to stop the disputed practice without admitting guilt.

administrative complaint a formal proceeding similar to a court trial held before an administrative law judge regarding a charge filed by the FTC.

corrective advertisements ads that bring consumers back to a neutral state, so consumers once again hold beliefs they had prior to being exposed to a false or misleading advertisement.

trade regulation ruling findings that implicate an entire industry in a case of unfair or deceptive practices.

substantiation firms must be able to prove or back up any claims made in their marketing communications.

sponsorship marketing when the company pays money to sponsor someone or some group that is participating in an activity.

event marketing when a company pays money to sponsor an event or program.

cross-promotion a tie-in between a company's product and an event.

CRITICAL THINKING EXERCISES

Discussion Questions

1. Watch the news on television or read your local paper for news about a local or national business. Was the report positive or negative toward the firm? Did the news report affect your attitude toward the company? Watch one of the many special investigative shows such as *60 Minutes*. What companies did it investigate? If you were the firm being featured, what would you do to counteract the bad press?

2. The public relations officer for a small but highly respected bank in a local community was charged with sexual harassment by a female employee. What type of communications should be prepared for each of the constituencies listed in Figure 13.2? Which of the constituencies would be the most important to contact?

3. How important is the local community for a manufacturing firm that sells 99 percent of its products outside of the area? Does it really matter what the local people say or believe about the manufacturer as long as the firm's customers are happy?

4. What causes do you support or are special to you? Do you know which corporations sponsor or support the causes? If not, see if you can find literature or Web sites that contain that information. Why do you think the corporations choose a particular cause to support? What benefit do you think the corporations receive from their sponsorships?

5. When Starbucks opened its first coffee shop inside of a public library, 10 percent of all proceeds from coffee sold there went to support the operation of the library. Do you think public libraries should allow for-profit organizations such as Starbucks to sell their products inside of their buildings? Is this a conflict of interest for governmentally sponsored organizations such as libraries? What if the local doughnut shop wanted to sell doughnuts at the library? Should it be allowed to do so? How does a library decide whom it will and will not partner with?

6. Managers often are the most difficult group for the public relations department to reach. To entice employees to reach departmental goals, managers often communicate using memos or verbal messages. These messages may conflict with the IMC theme. For example, in an effort to trim costs, a manager may send a memo to all employees telling them to use only standard production procedures. Through verbal communications, employees learn that anyone caught violating or even bending the policy to satisfy a customer will be immediately reprimanded. The manager's action suggests that even though he wants employees to provide customer service, in actuality, they had better not do anything that is not authorized. Employees soon get the message that management cares only about costs, not the customer. Employees will perceive any advertising message about customer service as a big joke. Write a memo to employees that supports the IMC goal of high customer service, yet alerts them to the need to follow standard operating procedures. Is there anything else you would do to ensure that this is not a conflicting message being sent to employees?

7. Baskin-Robbins recently utilized public relations efforts to reach potential new franchise operators. In each market targeted for expansion, Baskin-Robbins prepared news releases announcing plans to open a specified number of stores. These news articles normally appeared in the business section of the local newspapers, often on the front page. The news articles contained more details than the classified ads that Baskin-Robbins used to attract franchise operators.[34] What advantage does Baskin-Robbins gain by combining the articles with the ads? Why would newspapers print an article about Baskin-Robbins wanting to open franchises? Is this really newsworthy information?

8. Corporate sponsorships are very important to not-for-profit organizations. Without their financial assistance, many causes would not exist. Look up two organizations from the following list of not-for-profit organizations. Who are their corporate sponsors? What benefits do the profit seeking companies receive from these sponsorships?

   a. American Cancer Society (www.cancer.org)

   b. National Alliance of Breast Cancer Organizations (www.nabco.org)

c. Arthritis Foundation (www.arthritis.org)

d. Multiple Sclerosis Society (www.mssociety.org.uk)

e. United Cerebral Palsy (www.ucp.org)

f. Alliance for the Wild Rockies (www.wildrockiesalliance.org)

g. National Wildlife Federation (www.nwf.org)

h. Trout Unlimited (www.tu.org)

Generating Positive Publicity and Considering Sponsorships

A fully integrated marketing communications program considers all of the means by which customers and other publics make contact with an organization. These messages travel in several directions, including from inside the organization to those outside of the firm, from customers and others to those inside the company, and among members of various departments within the organization. Positive public relations involves all of these publics through planned messages, inferred messages, maintenance messages, and unplanned messages. Publicity campaigns such as cause-related marketing and other altruistic activities can help build the firm's image. Further, event sponsorships that reflect the company's image and theme can be highly valuable. Go to the Prentice-Hall Web site at **www.prenhall.com/clow** or access the IMC Plan Pro disk that accompanied this textbook to complete the exercise for this chapter. It will help you learn how to incorporate your public relations department in with other marketing efforts and promotional activities.

CASE 1

FOURTH OF JULY MARKETING: MORE FIREWORKS THAN THEY NEEDED

Station manager Jim Jefferson decided it was time to pull the plug. For the past 12 years, his television station (KSNN) proudly sponsored the local annual Fourth of July Festival. Until recently, the event had been a solid promotional marketing tool that generated sales and goodwill for a variety of vendors. Now, however, Jim has decided the hassles outweigh the benefits.

The first KSNN Fourth of July Festival was a modest affair. One sponsor, a dynamite factory located in the community, chipped in money for a small fireworks display, and the local college allowed the event to be held in an open area of the campus. As time passed, the scale and scope had grown into the single largest attraction in the area each year.

First, corporate sponsors were added. Each provided funding for various aspects of the program. Some paid for the actual fireworks and were rewarded with the company's logo lit up in a display to start each year's show. Other sponsors kicked in money so that relatively famous entertainers could be brought in. Vendors paid money to sell their food and drink products during the course of the event.

When the event initially began, the festivities started at about 7:00 P.M. with only a fireworks display. As the show evolved, the gates were opened at 2:00 P.M., and programs started around 4:00 P.M., led by a welcoming proclamation from the mayor. Bands played, local choirs sang patriotic songs, parachute jumpers swooped into the arena. The local college opened its football stadium to accommodate parking, seating, rest room facilities, and other amenities.

KSNN developed a tie-in with an area radio station. Beginning in the sixth year of the event, the fireworks were set up in time with music piped through

(continued)

stadium speakers with a simulcast on the radio. KSNN even broke into network programming to provide pictures of the fireworks show for the city.

The event generated a considerable amount of money for KSNN. Sponsors were required to buy ads promoting the event for two weeks prior to the Fourth of July weekend. The college was given free advertising time throughout the year in exchange for opening its facilities. By the 10 year, nearly 40,000 people were at or near the school, seeing the ads and visiting the booths and displays set up by the various sponsors.

KSNN also benefited from the football stadium setup. Key sponsors and their guests were given seats inside the air-conditioned press box during the day. KSNN served food and drinks to these individuals as part of their pampered exposure to the show. The guests could then move to the roof of the press box when the actual fireworks display took place. The school's president was thrilled to be able to schmooze with major corporations in the area each year and in fact had generated donations to the college based on these relationships.

Unfortunately, in the 11th year, vandalism associated with the event reached an all-time high. The school's football field, which was made of AstroTurf, was badly damaged by hoodlums who infested the event. Traffic jams caused so many problems that the local police department began asking to be reimbursed for all the overtime it was forced to pay to keep officers on duty to direct traffic and solve other problems.

Also, some of the sponsors began to object to the rising fees they were being charged to be associated with the event. KSNN's revenues had risen, but the station was also paying higher expenses each year.

The tide turned when the college rejected KSNN's bid to return for a 13th show. The president reported that replacing the football field surface made it too cost prohibitive for the college to be involved. KSNN was forced to move the event to a local city golf course, over the objections of golfers and several members of the city council, who feared destruction of the greens, fairways, and tee-boxes would be a major expense.

In the same year, two sponsors dropped out, citing costs as their key concerns. Food and drink vendors expressed frustrations that they would not have good places to set up to sell their products, and the remaining sponsors balked at bad locations for their booths. Many attendees had to ride shuttle buses to get close enough to see the show, and they completely bypassed the booths on the ride.

The growing number of headaches with the city, sponsors, and others caused the local newspaper to write articles about problems the show created. Jim decided the negative publicity was not what his station needed.

Following intense negotiations, KSNN withdrew after the show. Another local television station took over sponsorship of the event, but pared it down to a simple fireworks display at a local auto racetrack, to be held in conjunction with a day of racing.

1. Did KSNN wait too long before pulling out? Should the company's leaders have tried to solve the problems on their own, rather than just giving up?

2. What benefits accrued to KSNN, the sponsors, and the college when the show was going well?

3. Do you think the college was wise to withdraw from the show? Why or why not?

CASE 2

MINOR LEAGUE TEAM, MAJOR LEAGUE PROBLEMS

Drew Burns was excited and depressed at the same time. He had just been named as director of public relations for the Tulsa Mustangs, the newest entry into the Arena Football Association. Arena football has been a relatively successful venture for a number of smaller cities and teams for over a decade. The small field, the fast pace, high-scoring games, and the opportunity to attend football games in the off-season had attracted a number of fans.

Arena football relies heavily on sponsorships to succeed. Various companies provide giveaways at games, from seat cushions to caps and other team memorabilia. Local restaurants provide coupons for price discounts on food when the team wins. Soft drink bottlers from individual cities provide drinks and other enticements to keep fans involved.

Players in arena football are required to stay after the game and make contact with fans. They sign autographs, shake hands, and fans go onto the field so that they may feel more part of the action. Sponsors love the one-on-one contact between individuals.

Drew's problem was trying to become established in his new market. Tulsa has a major college with its own sports teams and, more importantly, minor league baseball. Minor league baseball has experienced a resurgence of interest due to the high ticket prices major league teams charge. Families on budgets find they can go to a game, eat a hot dog, and still have some change left over. A typical family excursion to a major league game may cost over $150 for a family of four, with parking, ticket prices, and concessions being relatively expensive for the normal-size family. A beer at most major league ballparks costs around $4.

With a major competitor for the "Joe Average" sports fan, Drew knew he would have to make a positive impact on the community right away for the team to succeed. Arena football faced two problems as he began the venture. First, the "Kurt Warner effect" was wearing off. The rags to riches story of Kurt Warner's journey from arena football to the NFL Superbowl had lost its impact. Fans did not expect a player from the arena league to regularly become well-known at a higher level, and Warner was viewed mostly as a fluke.

Second, too many football players had made headlines for misbehavior. In one year, two professional players had been accused of murder, and numerous accounts of violence and crime had taken over the sports page. In fact, a book entitled *Pros and Cons* detailed all of the pro players who had some kind of brush with the law. Consequently, the Tulsa team needed to distance itself from those kinds of bad boys and try to establish a more squeaky-clean reputation.

Drew had a very limited budget. He simply could not advertise his way to success. He knew he would need the cooperation of the owners, the league, his players, the local media, and several sponsors to garner the attention his team needed. The players may be his biggest asset. Many had voiced the willingness to appear at promotional events on behalf of local charities to help the team gain an audience. At the same time, many other sports programs (rodeos, little leagues, soccer leagues, etc.) could attract potential customers away from the idea of summer football. Tulsa also had an active social life in terms of band concerts and other summertime events.

(continued)

1. Will the Tulsa Mustangs succeed in this environment? Why or why not?

2. What kinds of events should Drew schedule for his players who are willing to help the team?

3. How can Drew generate positive publicity for the Mustangs, beyond personal appearances by players? What should the IMC theme be for this team?

4. Most sporting events develop corporate sponsors for giveaways to fans and as a means of attracting fans to the games. What type of corporate sponsors should Drew solicit? What benefits would corporate sponsors expect from Drew?

ENDNOTES

1. Emily Fromm, "Good, Clean Entertainment," *Adweek,* Vol. 40, No. 4 (January 25, 1999), p. 3. Kelly Shermach, "Wrestling on a Peak Keeps One Eye on Valley," *Marketing News,* Vol. 31, No. 10 (May 12, 1997), p. 24; John Agoglia and Cory Bronson, "Outside the Ring," *Sporting Goods Business,* Vol. 32, No. 3 (February 8, 1999), pp. 68–69.

2. Donald Baack, *Organizational Behavior* (Houston: Dame Publications, 1997).

3. Charles Maclean, "For-Profit/Nonprofit Alliances Benefit Both Sides," *Business Journal Serving Greater Portland,* Vol. 16, No. 43 (December 17, 1999), p. 28.

4. Brad Edmondson, "New Keys to Customer Loyalty," *American Demographics,* Vol. 16, No. 1 (January 1994), p. 2.

5. Sarah Lorge and Geoffrey Brewer, "Is Cause-Related Marketing Worth It?" *Sales & Marketing Management,* Vol. 150, No. 6 (June 1998), p. 72.

6. Brian K. Miller, "Many Companies Give Generously, But With a Catch," *Business Journal Serving Greater Portland,* Vol. 14, No. 43 (December 19, 1997), pp. 28–29.

7. Marvin E. Shaw and Philip R. Costanzo, *Theories of Social Psychology,* 2nd edition, McGraw-Hill, 1982, p. 334.

8. Ibid, p. 329.

9. Ibid, p. 333.

10. Ibid, p. 330.

11. Shaw and Costanzo, *Theories of Social Psychology,* p. 334.

12. James A. Calderwood, "False and Deceptive Advertising," *Ceramic Industry* (August 1998), Vol. 148, No. 9, p. 26.

13. "Fish Claims Wendy's Deceived," *Marketing News* (August 17, 1998), Vol. 32, No. 16, p. 1.

14. Doug Halonen, "30% Disobey Kids Ad Limit," *Electronic Media,* (March 2, 1998), Vol. 17, No. 10, p. 3.

15. "FTC Upholds Charges: Automotive Breakthrough Services, Inc. Ordered Not to Use Term 'ABS' to Market Add-on Brakes,"

Federal Trade Commission (September 30, 1998), http://www.ftc.gov/1998/9809/abs.htm.

16. "FTC Wins Permanent Injunction Against Talent Broker," *Federal Trade Commission* (June 7, 1999), http://www.ftc.gov/opa/1999/9905/talent4.htm.

17. "Bogus 'Talent Scouts' Use Smoke Screen to 'Screen Test' Consumers," *Federal Trade Commission* (May 27, 1999), http://www.ftc.gov/opa/1999/9905/screen.htm.

18. R. Serafin and G. Levin, "Ad Industry Suffers Crushing Blow," *Advertising Age* (November 12, 1990), Vol. 61, No. 47, p. 1, 3.

19. "FTC Reviews Funeral Rules," *Federal Trade Commission* (April 30, 1999), http://www.ftc.gov/opa/1999/9904/fun-rule.rev.htm.

20. Jack Redmond, "Marketers Must be Familiar with FTC Guidelines," *Inside Tucson Business,* (March 18, 1996), Vol. 5, No. 51, pp. 18–19.

21. Ibid.

22. "NAD Rules in GM, Ford Ad Dispute," *Advertising Age,* (September 1, 1997), Vol. 68, No. 35, p. 32.

23. "Minute Maid Complains, but NARB Forces Change," *Advertising Age* (April 14, 1997), Vol. 68, No. 15, p. 51.

24. "AT&T Wins NARB Case Over Collect-Call Ads," *Advertising Age* (February 24, 1997), Vol. 68, No. 8, p. 2.

25. "Priority Mail Ads Win NARB Appeal," *Advertising Age* (February 3, 1997), Vol. 68, No. 6, p. 38.

26. "NARB Sends Winn-Dixie Complaint to FTC," *Advertising Age* (December 23, 1996), Vol. 67, No. 52, p. 2.

27. "Cultural Sponsorship Can Help Reach the Affluent," *Bank Marketing,* Vol. 26, No. 10 (October 1994), p. 7.

28. Kate Fitzgerald, "TNN Hits the Country Roads," *Electronic Media,* Vol. 18, No. 16 (April 19, 1999), p. 50.

29. Harvey Meyer, "And Now, Some Words About Sponsors," *Nation's Business* (March 1999), Vol. 87, No. 3, pp. 38–41.

30. Kate Fitzgerald and Nick Lico, "The Big Event," *Automotive News* (March 29, 1999), Vol. 73, No. 5812, pp. AM24–25.

31. Kim Pryor, "Events as Incentives," *Incentive,* Vol. 173, No. 8 (August 1999), pp. 102–103.

32. Kate Fitzgerald and Nick Lico, "The Big Event," *Automotive News,* Vol. 73, No. 5812 (March 29, 1999), pp. AM24–25.

33. "Cultural Sponsorship Can Help Reach the Affluent," *Bank Marketing,* Vol. 26, No. 10 (October 1994), p. 7.

34. Betsy Nichol, "Integrated Marketing: The Cluster-Buster," *Franchising World* (September/October 1994), Vol. 26, No. 5, pp. 15–17.

Internet Marketing

14

Chapter Objectives

Understand who uses the Internet and how it is used.

Adapt all of the marketing communications functions to Internet programs.

Develop a strong e-commerce program to complement and supplement other selling and promotional activities.

Make sure every component of an e-commerce approach is carefully integrated and designed to attract customers to a Web site and to eventually make purchases.

Be aware of the ramifications of Internet programs for business-to-business customers and for international marketing efforts.

E-BAY SOARS AS DOT-COMS DROP

In 2001, e-Bay beat all forecasts with a 71 percent jump in sales, to $194.4 million, resulting in profits of $18 million. This occurred in spite of a strong downturn following the September 11 terrorist attacks and a mild recession. How has e-Bay managed to not only survive, but thrive, while other Internet companies continue to struggle and die?

In part, the efforts of CEO Meg Whitman have caused the company to move forward. Rather than remaining what was essentially a worldwide flea market, e-Bay now represents a global marketplace for items as small as compact discs selling for $1 apiece to $5 million jets. Whitman herself purchased a car online and sold the contents of her Colorado vacation home through the company.

E-Bay currently hosts over 38 million customers. The company has achieved an almost cult-like status with those who sell and bid for items. Online purchases and auctions are held with e-Bay collecting listing fees and commissions that vary by the price of the item. In 2001, the total dollar figure of items sold through e-Bay topped $2 billion.

Whitman believes the key feature of e-Bay is the business model itself. Rather than selling merchandise, e-Bay is a marketplace. Competitors such as Amazon.com (which has launched an online auction site) primarily represent products that they own and sell. The result is a much higher cost of goods sold. Amazon also must process and ship items, creating more costs. In contrast, the e-Bay model is one where fees are charged for putting buyers and sellers together.

E-Bay is not designed to replace brick and mortar stores, Whitman notes. In fact, the company is not an online vendor in any sense. Instead, the company has chosen to focus on individual sellers and buyers. The business-to-business side of e-Bay is small and not a major source of revenue.

Many observers wondered how well e-Bay would fare in a post September 11 world. After all, the company relies on individual honesty and trust. On September 11, e-Bay's

new listings plunged 25 percent. Very few customers were interested in selling merchandise or bidding on goods. Instead, e-Bay message boards were filled with statements of grief.

Responding quickly, the e-Bay executive team decided to turn part of the site into the world's biggest fund-raising effort on behalf of the victims of the attacks. The program, called Auction for America, was designed to raise $100 million in 100 days. Customers were invited to sell off anything possible, with proceeds donated to the fund. E-Bay waived all fees, as did Visa, an active partner of the company.

The Auction for America program was launched on September 17, just six days after the attacks. CEO Meg Whitman stood with New York Mayor Rudolph Giuliani and Governor George Pataki to announce the drive. The NFL offered to sell football memorabilia and Jay Leno volunteered to sell one of his Harley-Davidson motorcycles, covered with autographs of numerous celebrities. Everything from Vietnam War medals to dinosaur teeth became part of the program.

The success of the Auction for America program helped restore confidence in the rest of e-Bay's operations. The company continued expansion plans into new markets, meeting with great success.

The new global atmosphere has caused some change. The company has taken gun listings off the board, as well as firecrackers, police badges, and tobacco products. Anything that might be considered "hate commerce" is also off-limits.

The continuing success of e-Bay must be attributed, in part, to the kind-hearted nature of the company and the family-like atmosphere of its clients. While the World Trade Center is gone, Meg Whitman and many others believe that e-Bay has become the virtual World Trade Center that represents all of the positive ingredients of a "global economic democracy."[1]

KAOLIN CALEFACTORS

An Internet marketing program has two sides. One is the part devoted to individual customers. The other is the business-to-business component. E-commerce programs as well as advertising, sales support, customer service, and public relations are all elements of an Internet marketing program. These items must remain consistent with the IMC approach used throughout the company.

Kaolin Calefactors is a company that sells dishware in several markets. Read the Executive Summary, Promotions Opportunity Analysis (Section 2.0), and the Competitive Analysis (Section 2.1.1) for this company. After gaining a sense of the nature of the business and the key players, examine the Internet marketing plan being utilized by the marketing team in Section 4.4. Notice that Kaolin's approach is designed to match the Internet program with the various types of customers the firm intends to reach. Both specialized and standardized designs are offered through the firm's Web site. To successfully compete in the market, Kaolin must rely heavily on the Internet to reach as many new and existing customers as possible.

overview

Two inventions had a profound impact on the nature of business in the latter half of the twentieth century: (1) the computer and (2) the Internet. Through the Internet, a business of any size can compete in the global marketplace. In fact, on the Internet, the size of an organization's operation makes little difference, because the Internet is an open environment. Similar companies compete against one another while being only a click of the mouse away. In other words, a buyer can locate numerous sellers offering similar merchandise, similar prices, and similar offers in a very short time period. As more people and businesses become comfortable with the Internet, the marketing landscape will continue to evolve quickly in the coming years.

The influence of the Internet on various businesses and industries has been noted throughout this text. In practically every chapter, some kind of impact or implication has been described. The presence of the Internet and e-commerce is so sweeping that the various applications of Web technology are now essential elements of a fully integrated marketing communications program.

The final section of this book is called "Integration Tools." The name denotes the uppermost level of the IMC pyramid shown as Figure 14.1. In this section, the roles of the Internet and e-commerce are described first. Next, a small chapter is devoted to the special issues and IMC concerns present in entrepreneurial and small business ventures. Finally, methods to evaluate IMC programs are examined. The goal is to provide a complete picture of the final ingredients in an IMC program. When these fundamentals are successfully applied, the company, whether small or large, is in the best position to know and understand its customers, and to meet their needs efficiently and effectively.

This chapter explores the Internet and e-commerce in greater detail. The specific topics to be addressed begin with an examination of the nature of Internet users as well as marketing functions on the Internet. Next, a description of e-commerce and the elements necessary to build a successful e-business, including the types of incentives required to build a base of customers, is provided. Then, an analysis of various IMC topics, such as brand development, brand loyalty, sales support, service efforts, and promotional programs, is presented. In each of these areas, implications for business-to-business marketing programs as well as international concerns are discussed.

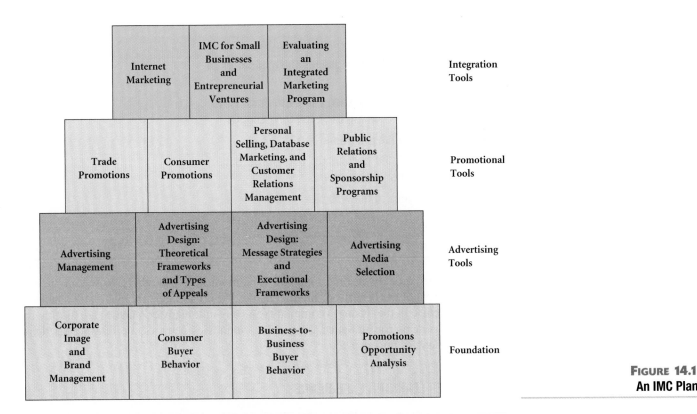

FIGURE 14.1
An IMC Plan

WHO USES THE INTERNET?

Use of the Internet has exploded during the last few years in both the consumer and business-to-business markets. Although the experts still debate the future of the Internet, no one doubts it will have an impact on how business will take place in the twenty-first century, even with all of the "dot.crashes" of the late 1990s. Here are some facts about the Internet that highlight its tremendous growth and presence in society:

▶ The most common products consumers research online and purchase off-line (at the store or outlet) are: automobiles, computer hardware, travel, electronics, books, appliances, music, sporting goods, and clothing.[2]

▶ Over 25 percent of all business-to-business purchases are placed through some type of Internet connection.

▶ The five top business-to-business e-commerce products are computers and electronics, motor vehicles, petrochemicals, utilities, and paper and office products.

▶ By 2004, 10 percent of business-to-business advertising dollars will be spent on the Internet. The total amount spent will be $8.7 billion.

▶ About 54 percent of the e-mail users have responded to an e-mail advertisement. Almost half purchased a product.

▶ Internet retail sales account for almost 2.5 percent of all retail sales.[3]

Business-to-business marketers were among the first companies actually to make profits using the Internet. In today's marketplace, the Web is becoming the communication tool of choice for many business-to-business companies. The Internet provides opportunities for communication, customer service, sales support, collaboration, and e-commerce. Some companies use the Internet for every aspect of their business including taking orders, inventory control, production scheduling, communications plans, sales programs, service departments, and support programs. The change from traditional communication channels such as salespeople, telephone, and "snail mail" to the Internet and

> ▶ **Building databases for e-mail campaigns**
>
> ▶ **Designing e-mail campaigns linking customers to Web site information**
>
> ▶ **Creating fun and innovative games to attract and keep customers coming back to the Web page**
>
> ▶ **Creating incentive programs**
>
> ▶ **Translating printed documents, catalogs, brochures, and newsletters for the Internet**
>
> ▶ **Adding graphics to the Web site**

FIGURE 14.2
Internet Services Offered by Marketing Agencies

Source: Ellisor, "Business-to-Business Offer WWW Opportunities," *Houston Business Journal* (September 17, 1999), Vol. 30, No. 7, p. 18B.

e-mail happened quickly in some companies and more slowly in others. Now, convincing top management of the benefits of Internet marketing is essential. There is a still a lack of Internet expertise in the business community. As a result, many companies are turning to marketing agencies for guidance. Figure 14.2 identifies some of the Internet services marketing agencies now provide.

INTEGRATED LEARNING EXPERIENCE

STOP

To get a feel for who is using the Internet as well as current Web news, the best source may be the CyberAtlas at **cyberatlas.com**. The "Stats Toolbox" page contains a large volume of statistics concerning Internet usage, top Web advertisers, and major e-retailers. Access this part of the CyberAtlas to discover the large number of categories listed. The sections entitled "Demographics," "Geographics," and "Traffic Patterns" reveal the "big picture," in terms of who is using the Internet. Then, to examine various markets, review the subcategories B-to-B, Finance, Small Biz, Retailing, and Travel.

MARKETING FUNCTIONS ON THE INTERNET

The greatest impact of the Internet is on sales, marketing, and distribution systems for various businesses. These three activities typically account for 20 percent to 30 percent of the final cost of a good or service. What makes the potential of the Internet so exciting is that e-commerce companies have the potential to save 10 percent to 20 percent of these costs. Thus, instead of paying for packing, shipping, and transporting the product to a retail site, the firm has the option to send it directly to customers and can pocket the markup a retailer would receive. Also, the company can choose to mark down the price of an item, saving customers money and enticing more purchases. Shipping costs may be charged to customers for e-commerce purchases. As a result, the manufacturer does not need to absorb these costs, which are normally part of the price charged to retailers.[4]

This section describes the various marketing activities that can be served by the Internet. Figure 14.3 identifies the primary functions a business Web site can provide.

> ▶ **Advertising**
>
> ▶ **Sales support**
>
> ▶ **Customer service**
>
> ▶ **Public relations**
>
> ▶ **E-commerce (retail store)**

FIGURE 14.3
Functions of the Internet

The marketing team should carefully consider each of these components when designing and managing an Internet program.

The design of a Web site should be guided by the IMC plan and the specific objectives the site seeks to accomplish within the overall IMC program. A flashy Web site designed to attract attention is created when the goal is *advertising*. Many firms use Web sites to promote individual products as well as the overall company. For instance, most movies now are advertised through traditional media (television, magazines) but also have Web sites for e-moviegoers to view.

Still, advertising is rarely presented by itself without being incorporated with other marketing functions. Some Web sites are for *sales support*. In those instances, information about the products should be accessible through either a salesperson or a direct link from the Web page. These types of Web sites are used more routinely for the business-to-business customers rather than retail consumers. Effective sales support sites must be useful for engineers and other members of the buying center who need additional product information. The actual sale is normally made via a salesperson. Then, the price and terms can be negotiated separately.

A *customer service* Internet site provides a different function. The goal of a customer service Web site is to support the customer after the sale. In this instance, documentation and operating information are provided. Customers who have questions can use the e-mail function to obtain information or scroll through the **FAQs**, or **frequently asked questions**, people have about various items or services. Portions of these sites may be password protected in order to ensure that only customers who have purchased products can access certain information.

Another purpose for a Web site is to create a positive *public relations* image. Some companies place information about not-for-profit and philanthropic causes they support on their Web sites. Individuals not only see what the company is doing but also may be able to volunteer for or donate money to a cause. At times these sites are separate from the company's primary site. In others, a link within the site is developed. Preparing a public relations site may be used by a firm in order to react to bad publicity. This gives the firm the opportunity to refute a charge or to explain the company's side of the story.

These marketing functions clearly indicate the potential of the Internet to be a valuable component of the company's IMC program. The next section provides a more complete description of the final item in Figure 14.3, e-commerce.

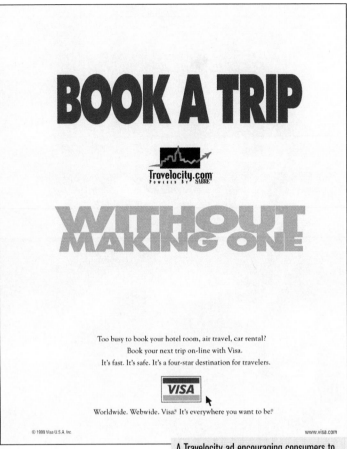

A Travelocity ad encouraging consumers to make travel arrangements using the Internet.
Source: Courtesy of Visa USA, Inc.

E-COMMERCE

Many times a Web site is designed for **e-commerce**, or selling goods on the Internet. E-commerce can take on many different forms. A retail store can vend items to consumers through the Internet when there is no handy outlet nearby or simply as a convenience for some shoppers. E-commerce also can be a retail operation that sells entirely on the Internet without any physical store or even inventory. Services are offered, deals are mediated, and products are shipped through this range of e-commerce operations. Instead of investigating all of the various forms of e-commerce, the purpose of the section is to provide a short synopsis of why and how setting up an e-commerce site benefits an organization.

Individual businesses have approached e-commerce in various ways. At one extreme is the business that jumped into e-commerce immediately, because the organization's

tuesday, 11:15 p.m.
buying a new dress.

bluefly™

Women's, men's and kid's designer fashions.
Save up to 75%.   90-day money back guarantee.

www.bluefly.com℠
the outlet store in your home℠

E-commerce retailers like Bluefly.com provide the opportunity for consumers to shop in the convenience of their homes, at any hour of the day or night.
Source: Courtesy of Bluefly.com.

leaders decided it was the trend of the future. These individuals concluded that the day would come when there would be no retail stores, and everything would be purchased over the Internet or through an interactive television setup. The other extreme includes those who decided that e-commerce is a fad that soon will pass away. These business leaders believe that consumers prefer dealing with people and therefore always will go to retail stores to make purchases. In reality, neither extreme seems very likely.

To the established retail operation, e-commerce offers customers an alternative mode for making purchases. Not every customer uses the Internet, but many do. As time passes, more people will become more comfortable with Web site shopping. Without an e-commerce site, these customers are lost to other retail operations who have established online retail sites.

Many times consumers make purchases at retail stores after first using the Internet to gather information. For example, a shopper may research stereos on the Internet and then go to the store with a list of "finalists." Another person may get on the Internet and find a fishing rod with a special set of features. Using the Internet store locator, the individual identifies the closest store offering the product to make the actual purchase. In that case, even though the customer did not make the purchase via e-commerce, he or she has used the Internet as part of the buying decision-making process. Consequently, the leaders of most established businesses know they must develop high-quality e-commerce sites in order to remain competitive in the twenty-first century.

E-Commerce Components

All e-commerce sites have three components. The first is some type of *catalog*. A catalog can vary from just a few items to a complex presentation of thousands of products. The nature of the firm's operation determines the type of catalog required. In every case, customers should be able to find the products of interest. Photos and product information are important in creating appealing online catalogs.

Second, each site must have some type of **shopping cart** to assist consumers as they select products. Again, the shopping cart can range from just checking a circle for an item when only a few products are offered to more complicated shopping carts that keep records of multiple purchases.

Third, each site must establish some way for customers to make *payments* for the things they purchase. For consumers, this normally is a credit card system. For business-to-business operations, payments are normally made through a voucher system. In other situations, a bill is generated or a computerized billing system is used so that the invoice goes directly to the buyer. In more trusting relationships, the invoice is added to the customer's records without a physical bill ever being mailed.

Remember, many consumers are still wary of purchasing products over the Internet. There are two reasons for this reluctance: (1) security issues and (2) purchase behavior habits.

Security Issues

Consumer fears about security are based on worries about a credit card number being stolen. Others are concerned about fraud, where a retailer takes the money but does not ship the merchandise. Both can cause people to resist making Internet purchases.

To resolve these problems, a review of the past may be helpful. When telephone orders were first encouraged by mail-order firms, people were hesitant because of fears about giving out a phone or credit card number to a stranger they couldn't see. Now, nearly everyone is willing to provide the information while placing orders on the phone. Also, it wasn't that many years ago that credit card holders expressed anxiety about various store employees stealing those numbers. Originally, customers were instructed to "take the carbon" from a credit card purchase to make sure it was torn into shreds in order to prevent an employee from using the credit card number later.

The same pattern is likely to follow with Internet shopping. As consumers become accustomed to using the Web, fears about giving out credit card information will be no greater than they are for telephone orders or credit card sales. IBM and MasterCard have created a series of independent television commercials designed to calm and reassure people about the quality of their Internet security program; however, these efforts are set back each time a major virus is turned loose. Also, the Verified by Visa program is designed to create additional security for online credit card purchases.

Purchasing Habits

The second issue has strong ramifications regarding the ultimate success of e-commerce. Currently, many consumers are most comfortable when they buy merchandise at retail stores. Some are also comfortable buying through catalogs. It will take time to change these habits, especially the preference for retail shopping.

At the retail store, consumers can view and touch the merchandise. They can inspect it for defects and compare brands. Clothes can be tried on to make sure they fit. In addition, the customer can see how the clothing item looks while being worn. Changing these habits requires the right kinds of incentives. Consumers and businesses must have valid reasons for switching to making purchases via e-commerce instead of through traditional methods (at the retail store or following a call from a salesperson). To overcome this handicap, many e-commerce firms are trying to develop incentives that will attract customers to make purchases in this new format.

E-COMMERCE INCENTIVES

Three incentives must be present for consumers to consider making a purchase online. They are the same incentives that lead people to use ATMs and to phone in mail-order purchases. The three incentives are: (1) financially based, (2) convenience based, and (3) value-based.

Financial Incentives

First, persuading an individual or business to change to buying via e-commerce requires some type of financial incentive. The first-time purchaser may be attracted to a price incentive, which can be in the form of a reduced price, an introductory price, or an e-coupon. Financial incentives are profitable for most firms because of the reduced costs of doing business online. Once the individual or company makes the switch, continuing the financial incentive may not be necessary because of the convenience or added-value features of an e-commerce program.

When consumers or businesses buy over the Internet, the company often can save both time and money. The e-company is then able to pass along savings. Customers placing orders via the Internet save the firm money in several ways, such as:

▶ Lower long-distance telephone bills

▶ Reduced shipping costs, because they are passed along to the buyer

▶ Decreased labor costs associated with stocking shelves

▶ Lower personnel costs (sales force) paid for waiting on in-store customers

In business-to-business settings, purchases via e-commerce also make it possible to offer financial incentives. The company may be saving the cost of a sales call, which

By providing an interactive Web site, Preference Video Introductions makes it convenient for consumers to gather information about the company before deciding to use it to meet some special.
Source: Courtesy of www.singlez4u.com.

often runs over $300 per call. Passing these savings on to customers can be a very effective means of encouraging customers to switch from their current mode of purchasing to e-commerce.

One special type of financial incentive is known as cyberbait. **Cyberbait** is some type of lure or attraction that brings people to the Web site. The bait may be a special offer such as a pair of jeans that is sold as a loss leader. It may be a game that consumers can play, or it can be a weekly or daily tip on some topic. For example, for a business-to-business health site, a weekly tip on how to reduce health risks and job-related injuries may be a cyberbait that attracts prospects to the site. To entice consumers and businesses to return to the site on a regular basis, additional cyberbait is needed. E-shoppers find it easy to surf the Internet and search competing sites. Therefore, these individuals need some reason to return on a regular basis.

Convenience Incentives

The second incentive to encourage customers to switch to e-commerce is convenience. Instead of making a trip to a retail store, a consumer can place the order while remaining at home. More importantly, the order can be placed at any time, which is a major reason why ATMs became so popular. Looking for information about various products can be quicker and easier on the Internet than using *Consumer Reports* or talking to salespeople. For businesses, ordering merchandise, supplies, and materials over the Internet can save purchasing agents considerable time. In addition to ordering, businesses can check on the status of an order, shipment information, and even billing data. In most cases, doing so online is considerably quicker than making a telephone call. In the fast-paced world of business, convenience is a highly attractive incentive for many consumers and businesses.

To get consumers to return, a Web site must be updated and changed regularly. It is important to keep the site current. Prices and product information must always be up-to-date. In addition, the appearance of the site should be routinely changed so consumers will return to see what is new. The front page of a Web site should be revised just as a display at a retail store is regularly altered. The difference, however, is that in changing the Web site, the marketing team must be careful not to change links or location of merchandise. Consumers become accustomed to finding things on the site. It is best not to make it hard for them to locate familiar items. Just as a grocery store seldom moves merchandise around just to create a different look, designers also must be aware that shoppers will become annoyed if they can't find their favorite products. Consequently, convenience remains an important feature as a Web site is being redesigned.

As company leaders become more Internet-savvy, new types of e-commerce programs have emerged. For example, Target now establishes sites for couples who are about to marry so that wedding gifts can be examined, purchased, and registered online. This convenience helps the couple receive gifts without duplicates, and out-of-town friends can conveniently choose, wrap, and ship presents to the couple.

COMMUNICATION ACTION

Getting Involved with Soap and Sauce

Most people see a logical connection between the Internet and companies that can sell products directly to consumers. Products such as music CDs, books, and airline tickets sell well over the Internet. But what about low-involvement products such as Tide or Ragu spaghetti sauce? These products would not be purchased over the Internet, because it is not financially feasible for the consumer or the company to offer them. No one particularly needs a box of detergent shipped in by FedEx or UPS. Still, the Internet can be a valuable tool for both products in terms of brand development.

Tide has sites at **www.clothesline.com** and **www.tide.com**. Instead of offering information about Tide and using the Internet site as an advertisement for Tide, Procter & Gamble uses the Tide Web site to assist consumers. The Web site provides helpful hints on removing stains from garments as well as other laundry tips. Consumers can ask the "Stain Detective" for help on specific stains by providing information about the type of fabric, color, and other information.

Ragu spaghetti sauce, on the other hand, has a highly entertaining site where a made-up personality known as "Mama" nags you about eating right. Browsers have the option of giving their e-mail address so they can receive coupons, updates on the site, and information about new products that are introduced.

The key, in both cases, is creativity. Firms that can discover ways to augment their communication programs with quality Web sites gain a major advantage in the marketplace. Thus, even soap and sauce are quality candidates for an Internet presence.

Value-Added Incentives

Financial incentives are often used to encourage customers to switch to e-commerce. At the same time, however, to completely change their purchasing habits in the long term will require some kind of value-added incentive. The added value may be personalization, whereby the firm becomes acquainted with the customer and his or her purchasing behaviors. Further, specialized software can be used to inform customers about special deals. These offers are based on past purchase behaviors or the customer's search patterns. For example, a consumer going through the mystery section of an online bookstore may see a banner pop up advertising a special deal on a new mystery novel. In addition to instant banners, consumers and businesses also may receive e-mails offering new information and other special deals that are available. Again, these are based on past purchase behaviors contained within a database. These tools can make it much easier for e-commerce programs to created added values for customers.

INTEGRATED LEARNING EXPERIENCE

An excellent Internet advertising and promotion resource is Ad Resource at **adres.internet.com**. Read the headlines at this Web site. Next, access the various sections such as "Advertising," "Articles," "Business," "Events," and "Marketing." What types of information are provided to help a company with a Web site?

BUSINESS-TO-BUSINESS E-COMMERCE

For business-to-business organizations, e-commerce may be as critical as it is in consumer markets. For routine rebuy situations, purchasing agents can go to the Internet and compare prices and product information. Once a business account is established, a business customer finds it very easy to place orders. This type of situation works well for products such as office supplies, maintenance supplies, as well as for repair and operation products. These orders are simple, because the product does not have to be modified for the buyer. Also the dollar cost per item is relatively low. For these purchasing situations, a strong brand name may be the one factor that will swing purchases when all other factors are considered equal. Companies are willing to purchase from strong brands that they know provide superior service, on-time delivery, and other more intangible attributes. As a result, to compete in e-commerce, business-to-business firms not only must provide strong e-commerce sites but also must develop strong brand names that stand out among competitors.[5]

Just as with consumers, to encourage businesses to use the Internet for e-commerce involves offering financial, convenience, or value-added incentives. In the iGo.com Internet advertisement in this section, a 10 percent discount is offered for orders placed via the Internet or by telephone. Also, there is a 10 percent discount on any product or service purchased through the Web site **employeesavings.com**.

A growing field of e-commerce in the business-to-business sector is online exchanges and auctions. These exchanges allow businesses to purchase a variety of commodities and goods at bargain prices. Businesses now use the Internet to enable them to speed up time to the market, to sell directly to other businesses, and to cut transaction and inventory costs. Companies can buy nonproduction goods such as office supplies but also purchase production-related supplies, raw materials, and equipment. There are also sites where companies can purchase oil, natural gas, electricity, coal, chemicals, steel, and other raw materials. Commodity-type products especially have become popular on the Internet. For example, the average business-to-business sale through a salesperson costs about $300. In the process of wining and dining, a company can spend several thousand dollars to get the sale and then spend additional money on sales commissions. These costs can be greatly reduced through the Internet. Still, it is very important to maintain sales support staff for Internet programs. In-house salespeople are often needed to handle online negotiations.[6]

Many of the online markets are neutral companies that simply match buyers and sellers. For example, **PaperExchange.com** recently arranged the sale of 250 tons of container-board grade paper. The paper was owned by a Finnish firm. It had been made for a Japanese firm but was being stored in Kansas City, where it was shipped to its final destination in Tokyo.

PaperExchange receives about 15,000 hits a day from prospective buyers and sellers. This means these types of transactions occur almost daily for various companies. PaperExchange receives 1 percent to 3 percent of the transaction costs for arranging sales.[7]

E-Commerce operations have other advantages. For example, most consumers still want to make purchases at a physical store. Therefore, it is important to provide store information for buyers. Vicinity Corporation is a company that dispenses store location information to consumers.

A similar process takes place in the business-to-business marketplace. Many businesses want merchandise to be shipped quickly when they use the Internet to obtain information and choose products. Vicinity Corporation's SiteMaker and Business Finder software display locations of the closest store for these businesses, complete with a map and directions showing how to get to there. A business needing specialized

An Internet advertisement for iGo.com featuring a financial incentive to encourage business or consumer purchases.
Source: Courtesy of iGo.com.

parts, supplies, or maintenance equipment is able to access the Vicinity Web site in order to find the nearest location where the merchandise is sold.[8]

Many other innovations are part of the business-to-business landscape. For instance, a new form of software makes it possible for firms to track shoppers on the Internet as they move to retail stores. To do so, consumers are presented with special offers and promotions. The offers are purchased on the Internet using credit cards. They then must be picked up at a store within a specified period, which creates the path from the Web to the store. In a variation of this approach, the consumer reserves the item on the Web site and then pays for and picks it up at the retail store. Again, the firm can track the consumer from the Internet to the store. Also, these programs generate excellent feedback regarding the types of promotions that work best on the Internet.

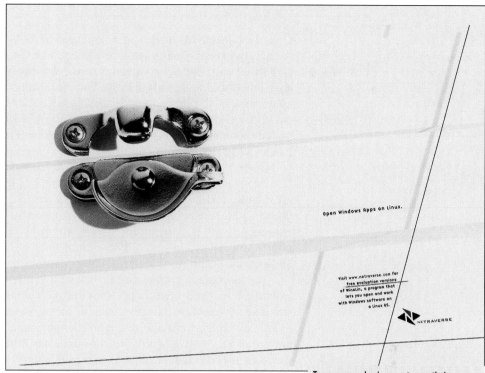

Open Windows Apps on Linux.

Visit www.netraverse.com for free evaluation versions of Win4Lin, a program that lets you open and work with Windows software on a Linux OS.

NETRAVERSE

To encourage businesses to use their software, Netraverse allows a company to access a demonstration version on the firm's Web site.

Source: Courtesy of West & Vaughan.

Several manufacturers are also involved in e-commerce. The actual methods used by the manufacturer depend on the distribution channel structure. Retailers and wholesalers become concerned if too many manufacturers establish e-commerce sites, because they sell products directly to consumers. Manufacturers must be aware that bypassing other channel members can cause a degree of alienation that is difficult to overcome when the manufacturer wants channel members to support a brand. Some manufacturers set up an e-commerce site and sell directly to consumers. Others develop sites that enhance the brand but then refer customers to the retailers and wholesalers actually selling the product. Establishing a link to these sites where the customer can continue with an online order is important to tying the customer to the brand.

In all of these applications, it has become clear that e-commerce is a major force in business-to-business marketing programs. It seems highly likely that there will be continual growth in the uses of the Internet in business-to-business transactions.

INTEGRATED LEARNING EXPERIENCE

Two business-to-business sites mentioned in this section were PaperExchange at **www.paperexchange.com** and E-Steel at **www.employeesavings.com**. Access both Web sites. What types of services does each provide for sellers? What types of services are provided for buyers? Which member(s) of the buying center would utilize these Web sites? For Web sites that wish to provide retail outlet information, a prominent firm is Vicinity at **www.vicinity.com**. For a company looking for specific products and for companies trying to sell products to other businesses, **www.BusinessFinder.com** provides a database for both buyers and sellers. Access both of these Web sites and review the types of business-to-business services provided.

STOP

INTERNATIONAL E-COMMERCE

One of the major advantages of e-commerce over the brick and mortar of a retail store is the ability to reach consumers everywhere, even in other countries. Still, almost 46 percent of current Internet companies turn away international orders because they do not have processes in place to fill them. Therefore, although the Internet makes it possible for a company to sell items in an international marketplace, many companies are not prepared to go global. Many obstacles to selling across national boundaries exist. They include communications barriers, cultural differences, global shipping problems due to a lack of sufficient infrastructure, and varying degrees of Internet capability in countries.[9]

Companies preparing to launch global e-commerce sites should keep in mind that a key step is to prepare for international shipments. Smaller products mean air transport is affordable, and DHL Worldwide Express, FedEx, and UPS offer excellent shipping options. Larger merchandise normally is shipped by some type of freight forwarder. Both express delivery and freight forwarding companies usually will be of assistance in shipping to countries they serve. These companies offer specialized logistics software and also provide the proper documentation and forms to meet the regulations of each country.

Making shipping arrangements is not all that must be done. Internet companies must examine both export and import laws in the countries involved. After working on the shipping, payment mechanisms must be installed. Each country differs not only in terms of type of currency but also in methods of payment. For example, in Europe, debit cards are preferred to credit cards. Europe also has a high rate of credit card theft, which increases the risks associated with accepting them.

Another challenge in the international arena is developing Web sites that appeal to the audiences of each country. This entails adding information that someone in another country would need, such as the country code for telephone numbers. It also requires removing or changing any colors, words, or images that might be offensive to a particular group of people in another country. Figure 14.4 identifies some cultural disasters to avoid. As has been discussed previously, simply translating an English site into another language is not sufficient. The company must have someone who understands both the language and the culture of the target area in order to ensure no one is offended by a company's marketing efforts. Also the cultural assimilator should check to make sure the proper meaning is being disseminated for each communication effort. Using local firms to translate the Web pages often prevents these types of communications problems from occurring.

Probably the most difficult challenge companies face in the international market is the technical side of the e-commerce site. Software compatibility is a major technical issue that has not yet been resolved. Countries vary in terms of how they handle e-commerce, and these various technologies must be merged into one system. Also, the bandwidth for handling Internet traffic varies considerably. Information technology (IT) people must be involved in every step of an internationalization process.

> ▶ **Using black in backgrounds and graphics has sinister connotations in Asia, Europe, and Latin America.**
>
> ▶ **The thumbs-up sign and the waving hand are rude gestures in Latin America and the Middle East, respectively.**
>
> ▶ **Showing a woman with exposed arms or legs is offensive in the Middle East.**
>
> ▶ **Using a dog as a company logo is not successful in Korea because dogs are used for food.**

FIGURE 14.4
Cultural Disasters to Avoid in International Internet Marketing

Source: Lynda Radosevich, "Going Global Overnight," *InfoWorld* (April 19, 1999), Vol. 21, No. 16, pp. 1–3.

Another major key to successful global e-commerce is a coherent IMC strategy utilizing local input from the various countries involved. The branding on the Internet site must be consistent from one country to the next and must leverage the brand's main marketing message. For IBM, this meant using local companies in each country to design the Web site and provide the information used on the site. To ensure consistency, IBM designs the main marketing messages at its central office, but then local companies translate the messages and add reseller contact and pricing information.

A unique aspect of e-commerce is that small companies can compete as effectively as large companies. For example, Trebnick Systems is a printing business located near Dayton, Ohio. Trebnick employees 10 people, yet its Web site has attracted customers from Japan, Germany, Spain, and Ireland. Similarly, Greyden Press employs only 25 people but uses the Internet as a primary tool of operation. Customers can request quotes and submit jobs online. Most customers Greyden serves are not located in Columbus, Ohio, where the organization's facility is physically located. E-commerce allows small companies like this to expand their customer bases beyond their local regions.[10]

In the future, the growth of international e-commerce is likely to be explosive. Firms that "get in on the ground floor" may have a major marketing advantage in the years to come.

IMC AND THE INTERNET

The Internet should be an important component of the integrated marketing communications plan. As the Internet continues to grow in usage in both consumer and business-to-business markets, its importance will continue to rise. The most critical decision facing businesses is what function the Web site should serve. It is extremely difficult to design a Web site that provides all of the functions mentioned earlier in Figure 14.3. If multiple functions are to be served, it may become necessary to create separate Web sites. These different sites can be connected by links, but a company must resist the temptation to create a Web site that attempts to be everything to everyone.

In addition to incorporating the Internet into the IMC plan, it is vital that the information technology (IT), human resource, production, and shipping departments are included as the marketing team develops the program. If they are not, disasters can happen. For example, marketers at a major consumer goods company launched a highly successful Web site that created 3,000 customer queries a day. The problem was that no one was hired by HR to handle these queries. Victoria's Secret announced its Internet fashion show during the Super Bowl. The site drew more than one million hits. The problem was that no one told the IT department the commercial was going to air. In fact, members of the IT department found out about the Internet fashion show while they were watching the Super Bowl themselves. The result was that the Victoria's Secret system crashed. This type of disaster illustrates why it is essential to communicate with other departments within the company when formulating an Internet strategy.[11]

The Internet is a critical component of BMW Motorcycles' IMC plan.
Source: Courtesy of BMW Motorcycles.

START LOOKING FORWARD TO RUSH HOUR

Introducing the F 650 CS. Just try not to snicker at those guys in sports cars hitting a top speed of 5 mph as you whip by. And if that doesn't turn heads, there are a few other things about this bike that will. Like an optional audio system with waterproof loudspeakers. Or if you prefer, use the built-in storage bay to hold an overnight bag (trust us, you'll be spending a lot less time at home). Put it this way: for you, getting around town is about to be the best part of city living.

To find out when and where you can get ahold of the new F 650 CS just call 1-800-345-4BMW, or visit bmwmotorcycles.com.

Coordination between the IT department and other areas involves a variety of activities. Changes can be made quickly on individual Web sites within hours, and marketers must think about how each change can impact other activities in the company. The marketing department should coordinate each advertising campaign with the IT department, so that software capabilities are addressed to ensure smooth operations. The company must work hard to avoid glitches that affect operations. Also, members of the call center need to know when additional telephone calls and e-mail inquiries may result from a special Internet offer. It takes time and effort to coordinate marketing changes with IT and other departments, but any delay in implementation will be offset by a smoother, more efficient operation.

A recent research poll, called the World Wide Internet Opinion Survey, examined the factors that drove people to Internet Web sites for the first time. These results are highlighted in Figure 14.5. As shown, a search engine is the primary method consumers use to discover new Web sites. As a result, it is important for companies to make sure they are listed under as many search engines as possible and also the correct keywords. Notice that television and print ads are the least successful in driving someone to an Internet site for the first time, finishing far behind word of mouth.

Many experts believe the traditional banner ad has little influence on people. Not surprisingly, Web designers are trying to attract attention through fancier banners. Graphics, flashing images, and streaming videos are used to garner attention. Interstitial or popup ads were created, which forced Web browsers to react. Unfortunately, these types of ads have become highly controversial and many view them as offensive. The truth, however, is that these popup ads work significantly better at attracting buyers than do traditional banner ads. This success has led many Internet companies to develop superstitials that work after a person leaves a Web site or even shuts off the computer. The ad appears the next time the person logs onto the Internet. E-mail advertisements also are being created with full graphics and videos that are sent overnight to customers who were on a particular Web site. Although the ethical implications of such advertising tactics are being debated, the fact is that they work. Since they do, their use will continue to increase.

E-mail advertisements have begun to lose their luster. A recent survey indicated that over the last two years, the number of individuals who complain that they receive too many e-mail ads rose from 44 percent to 70 percent. The number who report they delete the ads without even looking at them rose from 31 percent to 55 percent during the same time period. In the same survey, the percentage of respondents who agreed that e-mail offers were "a great way to find out about new products and promotions" declined from 48 percent to 25 percent. Therefore, marketing managers must be wary of the shifting feelings toward e-mail advertisements. As an alternative, businesses have shifted to b-to-b newsletters, which have enjoyed some success. These newsletters, which are sent monthly, have the benefit of being more filled with information and are perceived as better than both banner ads and e-mail.[12]

▶ Internet content search	38%
▶ Word-of-mouth	30%
▶ Internet banner	20%
▶ Television ad	7%
▶ Print ad	5%

FIGURE 14.5
What Drives People to a New Site?

Source: Don Jeffrey, "Survey Details Consumer Shopping Trends on the Net," *Billboard,*
(May 29, 1999), Vol. 111, No. 22, p. 47.

In business-to-business markets, the number of hits at a b-to-b Web site is directly related to the amount of off-line advertising and sales promotions. A large business-to-business company went from 20,000 visits per month to 80,000 visits per month during a six-month period by doubling the company's annual Internet advertising budget for print, direct mail, and trade shows. A small company went from 2,000 to 6,000 hits per month by increasing their budget for print ads from $25,000 to $65,000 per year. Dynamic Web, a high-tech Web company, saw company Web site traffic increase 250 to 300 hits per week immediately following participation in a trade show featuring the company's Web site.[13]

The Internet affects a firm's IMC program in numerous ways. In this section, the nature of Internet activities in response to various parts of the IMC program are described, including the impact on:

- Branding
- Brand loyalty
- Sales support
- Customer service
- Consumer promotions

These and other topics highlight the value of bringing the firm's Internet programs in line with the rest of its marketing communications efforts. A review of these IMC topics follows.

Branding

In Chapter 2, the importance of brand image was discussed. Powerful brands are vital to Internet success. The design of a Web site and the information it provides are key variables that affect perceptions of the brand. An IMC plan that emphasizes brand quality should maintain the same theme on the Web site. Also, a Web site should reinforce the integrated communications theme that is presented in other media. When this is accomplished, the Internet becomes a valuable tool in the development of the brand.

INTERNET MARKETING

Spamming, Cookies, and Ethics

Technology is a two-edged sword in the area of marketing. On the one side, it creates marvelous new ways to precisely reach a set of consumers with a key message and to keep in continuous contact with those customers. On the other, it can be invasive and intrusive and presents ethical dilemmas for those working on the Web.

There have been long and loud complaints about spamming. As with telemarketing calls, many consumers are frustrated with being forced to deal with so many unwanted messages. Is this an ethical issue or simply a practical matter? Either way, the marketing team must assess the viability of spamming programs.

At a more dramatic level, cookie technology allows a Web site to look into consumers' computers to see which sites they have visited. Is this ethical? Should an Internet company be allowed to gather this information? Should the company be allowed to sell the information to other companies? Answers fall into two categories: (1) legal, and (2) moral. While it may still be legal to collect and transfer consumer information in this manner, the ethical issue remains.

Marketing professionals will continue to face the need for quality information. They must balance this need with the ethical ramifications of invading privacy rights and customer sensibilities. Failing to do so may have long-term implications for both the company and those who use the Internet to shop for products and services.

I remember her in blue jeans and a T-shirt in high school.
I remember her in a thrift store leather jacket in college. I remember her in a rain jacket in
Oregon. I remember her in a swimsuit on the beach in Florida. I remember her without a
swimsuit on the beach in Greece. I remember her in a sleeping bag in a tent in Yellowstone,
refusing to come out. But I can't say that I remember ever seeing her in a dress like that.

Date set: *May 20th*

Plan your wedding | Buy a gift | Find your dress | Book your honeymoon | More

Thousands of gowns. And everything else you need to plan the perfect wedding.

WeddingChannel.com™

A magazine advertisement for
WeddingChannel.com designed to encourage
visits to its Web site.
Source: Courtesy of Della.com.

Creating an effective brand presence online requires more than a Web site with an e-commerce capability. Cyberbranding involves integrating online and off-line branding tactics that reinforce each other and that speak with one voice. The most common method of building an online brand presence is through an off-line technique called brand spiraling. **Brand spiraling** is the practice of using traditional media to promote and attract consumers to an online Web site. From television, radio, newspapers, magazines, and billboards to simple shopping bags, consumers are encouraged to visit the firm's Web site. One goal of each advertising campaign should be to encourage traffic to the site and enhance brand recognition. The interactive nature of the Internet makes it possible for a firm to learn more about each customer. This information can then be used to target more specific messages. The magazine advertisement in this section by WeddingChannel.com is designed to encourage traffic to the Web site. Once there, WeddingChannel.com requests information from viewers in an effort to learn more about them and their particular needs.

Adobe, a desktop publishing software company, uses billboard, Internet, and print ads to drive traffic to its Web site. Adobe uses print ads in magazines such as *Details, Spin, Wallpaper, and Wired* to target young, 20- to 25-year-old professionals who do not have strong backgrounds in graphic arts but, for some reason, have jumped into desktop publishing. Once at the site, a person can test and try different versions of Adobe's products.[14]

Figure 14.6 identifies some of the techniques business-to-business firms use to advertise their Web sites. As shown, the most common method is displaying the Web address on all printed and promotional material. Next is placing ads promoting the Web address in various trade publications. Over 70 percent of the companies register keywords with search engines, because business buyers often look for a specific product. The odds of making a sale increase substantially when a firm's Web site is cited after a keyword is typed into the search engine. The least used method is placing banners on other sites. Seldom do business customers go to a site when they are at another site. The primary effect of placing banners on other sites is to develop brand awareness and brand knowledge rather than to attract customers.

Companies with strong off-line brands benefit from what is called a **halo effect**. A well-received brand leads more customers to try new products and services that are being offered by the company on the Internet. These same customers are also more willing to

FIGURE 14.6
B-to-B Techniques to Boost Web Site Awareness

> ▶ Putting the Web address on printed materials and promotional items — 91%
> ▶ Advertising in trade journals — 74%
> ▶ Registering the Web site with search engines for keywords — 72%
> ▶ Buying banners on other sites — 25%

provide information that can be used for greater personalization of messages. This halo effect results from the credibility of the firm's brand being transferred to an individual's evaluation of the Web site. Barnes & Noble and Toys "R" Us were late entrants into e-commerce. Still, both companies built successful Internet businesses because of the strong brand names transferred to their Web site programs.

A company such as Amazon.com, which was an Internet start-up, is likely to use traditional advertising media to help develop a brand name. Brand-name power cannot be created solely through advertising on the Internet. To achieve a strong brand name, Amazon.com invested a half-billion dollars in traditional media. The Internet must be one component of the total IMC program if a strong brand name is to emerge.[15]

Brand Loyalty and IMC Internet Programs

A series of benefits may be realized when a firm effectively utilizes the Internet. For example, the Internet makes it easier for firms to communicate with loyal consumers. This makes it possible to solidify the relationships they have with the company. To secure this advantage, the process begins by identifying the heavy product users. Remember, being a heavy user is not always synonymous with feeling strong brand loyalty. Some individuals or companies are heavy users because of price or convenience or for some other reason. When another firm emerges offering a better price or an improved delivery schedule, the heavy user often will switch while the brand-loyal consumer will not.

Brand-loyal consumers make purchases for reasons beyond the price, the convenience, or the product itself. Often they experience a type of "psychic" or affective feeling toward the brand or company. Also, in nearly every instance of brand loyalty, consumers believe the brand is superior in quality. Inferior items are not likely to create brand loyalty. Lower quality products are more likely to capture repeat purchase behavior rather than loyalty.

The experience or feelings a consumer develops toward a brand are often the result of marketing communications between the firm and the consumer. Although advertising is a major component or communication channel used to develop brand loyalty, the Internet is becoming increasingly valuable.

The Internet provides three opportunities that are not possible with advertising. First, the Internet can be designed to make shopping and other contacts more pleasurable experiences. Buyers return to the Web sites because they enjoyed the experience previously. These feelings may be similar to what a customer encounters at Starbucks. Consumers are loyal to Starbucks because of the total experience and atmosphere of the establishment. Not only is the coffee good, but much more is involved in the feelings of loyalty toward the company.

The second opportunity the Internet provides is the ability to establish one-to-one communication between the consumer and the firm. As discussed earlier in the text, database technology permits the company to retain a detailed history of groups of consumers as well as information about individual shoppers. Using these data, the company can develop a one-on-one relationship that ties the consumer to the firm. These communications (special offers, customized ads, etc.) often move heavy users toward brand loyalty.

Third, the Internet offers the potential to contact niche customers. Computer Economics research analyst

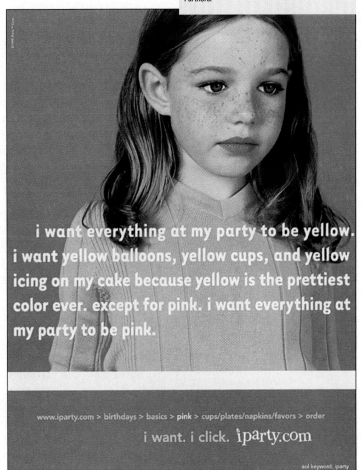

This advertisement by iparty.com highlights the convenience of finding all of the party needs a consumer would need to have that special event.
Source: Courtesy of iparty.com/ Kirsenbaum Bond's Partners.

Adam Harris notes that, "The Internet . . . offers a unique opportunity for companies to target market." Potential niches include African Americans, gays, women, Latinos, persons of Asian descent, and even Christian Web-surfers.[16]

In communicating with consumers, it is important to provide rewards for loyalty. These rewards are not promotions, but actual rewards. The gift or offer may be the same as for a promotion, but the dialogue with the consumer is different. For loyal consumers, these rewards are mentioned as a way to say "thank you" for that loyalty. On the other hand, consumer promotions are merely used to entice the price-sensitive consumer or the light user to make a purchase. A reward helps the firm to say that the person or business is important, and the psychological impact of this type of message can be very strong.

Sales Support on the Internet

One key feature of any IMC program is sales support. The Internet can be used in various ways to help with this effort. Manufacturers that sell their products through retailers and wholesalers must be careful to avoid having a Web site that is viewed as a threat. Many retailers and wholesalers are wary of manufacturing Web sites where customers can place orders. To prevent damaging relationships with retailers, manufacturers can offer product information, but actual orders for merchandise should go through the retailer or wholesale vendor.

The strategy of using a Web site for information only rather than for direct sales is found more frequently in the business-to-business sector. In that arena, each manufacturer has fewer customers. Therefore, it is critical for a manufacturer to maintain positive relationships with its retail or wholesale vendors. When a manufacturer sells through multiple vendors, it may be wise to offer a locator on the manufacturer's Web site that shows customers the nearest vendor. For example, a manufacturer of a depth finder for fishing boats could list the retail stores where that particular brand can be purchased. Through locator software, customers can find the closest retail store.

Often, the most important use of the Internet in the area of sales support is providing information about clients and products to the sales staff. The salesperson should be able to access all of the information the company has in its database about any given customer. In addition, data can be collected regarding which products are being examined by individual customers on a Web site. This gives the salesperson insight regarding what product to pitch and how to make the sales approach. The information also helps the company when a number of customers are accessing details about specific products. The **Web master** can then add materials regarding that product in order to increase the odds of making a sale.

Further, the sales staff can utilize the Internet as a valuable resource tool in another way. Although experienced salespeople may have complete knowledge of all of the products sold, new salespeople may not. The salesperson can use the Internet to provide the information a client requests. Often this can be done in the client's office or within a short period of time while on the phone. The Internet also can be used when a customer is ready to place an order. The order can be sent immediately, and the salesperson with access to the firm's database can inform the customer of the shipping date. If the item is out of stock, the salesperson informs the customer that the item must be back ordered. Being given this information at the time the order is placed is much better than receiving a phone call or note later.

Customers can go online and receive another kind of sales support. As noted previously, it has the advantage of being available 24 hours a day, 7 days a week. Customers can access a Web site to obtain product information at the time that best suits them. A Web site can provide extensive sales support that can be transmitted to customers and prospects even when the salesperson is not available.

Both prospecting for and qualifying prospects can be facilitated through the effective use of the Internet. A salesperson can locate companies that may be interested in a certain product. For example, Trebnick Systems, the printing service mentioned earlier in this chapter, discovered customers in Japan, Germany, Spain, and Ireland from examining 160 Web sites. Trebnick made contact and obtained orders. Once prospects have been located, whether through the Internet or through the traditional channels, the Internet can help qualify prospects to see if they are good candidates for sales calls. If they are not, the salesperson may want to try an e-mail contact or turn the lead over to telemarketers to explore.

The Internet provides valuable information for preparing a sales call. By examining a prospect's Web site first, the salesperson can discover information about the company, its products, and the personnel at the firm. Also, the sales rep can use a search engine to locate articles and press releases about a prospect or company. Financial information is available for publicly held corporations. All of this information can be useful in the preparation of a sales call, as the sales rep is able to individualize and personalize a presentation.

Customer Service and the Internet

The Internet is a highly cost-effective method for companies to provide customer service. Examples that illustrate how well this can be done are found at FedEx, the U.S. Postal Service, and Visa. Customers of FedEx and the USPS can track packages they have sent through the Internet. It is more efficient to use the Internet, and the costs of telephone calls are reduced, because fewer human operators are needed. Visa provides an ATM finder program for its consumers, which gives directions to the closest ATM when one is needed.

The key to using the Web effectively to enhance customer service is found in the design of the Web site. The site must be easy for the consumer to use and provide some benefit over using the telephone. Speed is one primary benefit the Internet offers. Making it easier and faster to get the information encourages consumers to use a Web site. Providing additional information that is not normally given over the telephone can be another advantage.

A major part of customer service is answering questions. Designed properly, a Web site can be a valuable resource for responding to common consumer inquiries. One method is to provide a series of responses to FAQs. They must be indexed or arranged by topics so customers can access answers quickly. Otherwise, consumers become frustrated and call a toll-free number instead. Asking users to go through a long list of FAQs does not work well. This is because customers often look for specific information. Consequently, it is important to provide as much information as possible on the Internet.

An option that should always be available to customers is e-mail. Consumers who have specific questions should have the option of sending an e-mail. If these e-mails are answered immediately and completely, it saves the company from making a telephone call. E-mail must be managed carefully. A recent survey conducted by JMM indicated that customer service e-mail response times, when the customer e-mails the company for information or with a complaint, are a significant factor in future purchase decisions. The management team must be certain e-mails are answered quickly and effectively.[17]

Another approach some companies use to enhance customer service on the Internet is to put together discussion groups or chat rooms. Many public relations people dislike chat rooms, even though they provide the opportunity for customers to interact with each other and with the firm in a somewhat controlled environment. One of the best ways for a firm to react to negative comments by consumers is through replying to the complaint directly. Everyone reading the chat conversation sees the response. A discussion group also allows consumers to interact with each other and may provide solutions to problems that the company had not considered. This type of situation can occur with computer software and highly technical products. Such open communication with customers tends to build a stronger bond between the customer and the firm.

For business-to-business marketing, granting access to information within the seller's database can be especially beneficial. Each company with access has a password to gain entry. Providing information in this manner can save everyone considerable time, especially when there is a strong bond between the two companies. For example, a shipping company may allow its customers access to all of its database information concerning location of shipments and availability of trucks, trains, and ocean vessels. In scheduling shipments, this information is helpful to the logistics coordinator responsible for planning and coordinating movement of goods from the manufacturer to the retailer or wholesaler. Thus, by knowing that an ocean vessel currently has capacity for a 25-ton shipment, a logistics manager can reserve the space to ensure a large shipment of merchandise arrives on time. Without the Internet, the logistics manager must make a series of telephone calls to obtain the needed information.

Many retailers now give manufacturers access to databases via the Internet. Manufacturers study which products are selling. They also can see which colors, sizes, and styles are the most popular. They even can find out which stores have the highest levels of sales. Then the manufacturer can modify or set production schedules in order to make sure retailers have a steady supply of just the right size, color, and so forth.

Customer service is an important part of an IMC program. Quality service conveys key information to the customer that the company cares. Servicing programs also help every member of the marketing channel build strong bonds with its constituents.

Consumer Promotions and the Internet

A popular cyberbait used in attracting consumers to a site is some type of consumer promotion. To build traffic, a firm must decide whether to have one major event or many smaller events. It is the difference between giving one person $100,000 or 500 people cash or merchandise worth $200. The large promotion attracts the type of person who enters a lottery or contest with the hope of winning the big prize. In contrast, smaller promotions often draw individuals who are more interested in the company's merchandise. For example, a music site could offer every person who buys a CD a chance of winning $100,000, and the odds of winning may be one in a million. On the other hand, the same company can offer free CDs as prizes with the chances of winning being only one in 10. These two promotions would attract different types of potential customers. Consequently, the choice of the promotional form should be based on the goals of the firm's IMC plan and oriented toward the type of person the company seeks to attract to the site.

The Internet provides a convenient method for companies such as Danish Porcelain Imports to track customer purchases and interests.
Source: Used with permission of the *Joplin Globe,* Joplin, Missouri.

It is important to change promotions on a regular basis. For example, one month individuals who purchase merchandise may receive 10 percent off. The next month, they may have a 1 in 10 chance of winning a free gift. In the third month, the promotion may change to receiving a third item free if the person buys two. Changing promotions encourages consumers to return to the site. Each promotion may also appeal to slightly different consumers. Thus, a coupon may appeal to one consumer while a premium may be more appealing to another.

A major advantage of offering promotions is the

opportunity to build a database. Contests and sweepstakes are effective means of building a database, because no purchase is required. Consumers receive a chance at winning simply by entering. With the lure of a prize in place, most individuals are willing to provide information about themselves. This basic information can be used to start a database. The company can then build records of individual purchases and even the items on the Web sites consumers browse.

E-commerce and the Internet play a vital role in the marketing successes and failures of numerous businesses. Company leaders must account for the role the Internet plays as they develop overall IMC programs. A Web site should reflect the image and theme portrayed in all other marketing communications efforts. A consistent message strengthens the brand and builds the potential for greater brand loyalty. Promotions, sales efforts, advertisements, and every other marketing activity should constantly remind the consumer of the major theme that drives the company. When this is accomplished, the Internet is more likely to fulfill its potential of becoming a strong new channel in the marketplace. Beyond these more general IMC efforts, direct sales to consumers can be used to build traffic and increase profits. These types of programs are presented next.

INTEGRATED LEARNING EXPERIENCE

Web sites serve a number of different functions such as advertising, sales support, customer service, public relations, and e-commerce. Access the following Web sites for firms that have been mentioned in this chapter. What is the primary purpose of the Web site? What do you like about the Web site? What do you dislike?

MVP.com (www.mvp.com)
Travelocity (www.travelocity.com)
Trebnick Systems (www.trebnick.com)
Greyden Press (www.greydenpress.com)
Victoria's Secret (www.victoriasecret.com)
WeddingChannel.com (www.weddingchannel.com)
Saturn (www.saturnbp.com)
Harley-Davidson (www.harley-davidson.com)
DiscountDomain (www.discountdomain.com)

DIRECT MARKETING ON THE INTERNET

The Internet is an ideal medium for direct marketing. Consumers and businesses now order directly from numerous companies through the Internet. Internet patrons can also be sent e-mails promoting specific products. Businesses, however, have to be careful about sending unsolicited e-mails, because many consumers and businesses are frustrated by the practice of spamming, or sending out mass unwanted e-mails. Spamming on the Internet is equivalent to sending out junk mail to an untargeted audience. Instead, the firm should develop a more targeted Internet e-mail direct-marketing program. To do so, the first step is to get the customer's permission. Obtaining this permission is easier when some type of reward is offered.

In the iGo.com direct-mail piece shown on page 456, notice the box customers can check in order to receive the free iGo e-newsletter. Also, individuals making purchases can receive two months' free service. To get more details about Pocketmail, individuals are encouraged to visit the iGo.com Web site at www.igo.com/pocketmail. This direct-mail piece is designed to encourage consumers to act quickly. Also, from the firm's perspective, the mailing is designed to obtain names for a database, which may then be used in later direct-mail and e-mail marketing programs.

Some florists have been successful using e-mail to encourage direct sales. These companies obtain the client's permission and then send reminders about anniversaries,

A direct-mail piece encouraging consumers to visit the iGo.com Web site and to receive the iGo e-newsletter.
Source: Courtesy of iGo.com.

birthdays, and other important dates. Many customers find these personalized e-mails to be beneficial. It takes time to develop this type of program, because the company needs a great deal of information from customers. When the plan is established, however, it can be a very strong direct-marketing technique.

The most recent trend in direct marketing via the Internet is **interactive marketing**. Interactive marketing is individualizing and personalizing everything from the Internet Web content to the products being promoted to e-mail messages. NCR produces a software called Relationship Optimizer and Prime Response that uses powerful data analysis techniques to personalize direct offers. The NCR software analyzes customer interactions such as click-stream data traffic, any type of customer interaction with the firm, and combines it with demographic information from external or internal direct-marketing databases. As the data are being processed, the software can launch complex interactive and personalized Web and e-mail campaigns.

Levi-Strauss uses a similar software, called Blue Martini E-Merchandising, to customize both the Levis.com and the Dockers.com Web sites. The Home Shopping Network uses Edify's Smart Options software to track user preferences and suggest products based on the customer's past activities and current purchases. These technologies blur the line between selling and marketing because the messages and products a customer sees are based on past purchasing activities. These programs are designed to increase the odds that the customer will see something he or she wants rather than being forced to wade through scores of products he or she has no interest in purchasing at a more standardized Web site.[18]

As the technology improves and grows, other forms of direct-marketing programs through the Internet will emerge. Also, as more people access the Web while on the move (through pagers and other carry-around devices), Web marketers undoubtedly will develop methods to reach customers with on-demand goods and services. It is likely that direct marketing has only scratched the surface of the potential the Internet offers.

INTEGRATED LEARNING EXPERIENCE

STOP

Customer interactive software is becoming an important component of many Web sites. Access the Blue Martini Software Company at **www.bluemartini.com** and Edify at **www.edify.com**. What types of services do these companies offer? How can their services be used in conjunction with an e-commerce Web site?

VIRAL MARKETING ON THE INTERNET

Today's technology has created a new form of marketing. **Viral marketing** is preparing an advertisement that is tied to an e-mail. It is also a form of advocacy or word-of-mouth endorsement marketing. In other words, viral marketing takes place as one customer passes along a message to other potential buyers. The name *viral* is derived from the image of a person being infected with the marketing message, then spreading it to friends like a virus. The major difference, however, is that the customer voluntarily sends the message to others.

Viral marketing messages include ads for goods and services, hyperlinked promotions that take someone immediately to a Web site, online newsletters, and various games. Statistics indicate that 81 percent of recipients who receive a viral marketing message pass it along to another person. Almost 50 percent pass it along to two or more people. The marketing message can be more deliberate such as when an individual recommends something to a friend. It can also be transmitted passively, when the message is simply attached to an e-mail. Viral marketing allows a firm to gain rapid product awareness at a low cost.[19]

Blue Marble, a viral marketing company, created a program for Scope mouthwash. Consumers were able to send a customized, animated e-mail "kiss" to their friends. The attached marketing message reinforced the brand message that Scope brings people "kissably close." People who received the e-mail kiss could then forward the message to someone else. Scope's tracking technology indicated most did forward the message.

The term *viral* may connote the negative image of a computer *virus*. Consequently, care should be given when offering to create such a program for a firm. Company leaders may want to find some other term to describe the technique to the general public so that no undue suspicion or fear arises.

INTERNET DESIGN ISSUES

The primary issue in the design of a Web site is to make sure it functions properly. E-commerce companies spend an average of $100 to acquire each new customer, and some companies spend up to $500.[20] It may appear that developing an effective Web site is cheap. In reality it is not. As a result, it is essential that the firm specify the key function to be served by the Web site before it is created. In addition, the site should then be designed to support the function, but from the user's point of view. For example, if the function is to *support e-commerce,* then the site needs to be designed so it is easy for customers to navigate, select products, and order them. If the key function is to *support selling,* then the person designing the Web site needs to talk with salespeople and determine their needs.

Companies spend almost $20 billion per year on Internet advertising of Web sites. Just as with the other components of advertising, consideration must be given to where these advertisements will be placed. One approach is to focus on targeted Web sites with similar customer profiles. For example, a Web site for John Deere may also advertise on other agriculture-related Web sites. Another approach is to advertise on a broader array of sites to develop brand awareness. For example, a company can advertise on a variety of Web sites in order to encourage different people to visit its Web site. Even if a person does not go to the site, the ad enhances brand awareness.[21]

A Web site should match the constituency it will serve. Too often, a site is designed by a computer whiz who likes fancy graphics and images, the users of the site hate it because they cannot find what they are looking for or the pages take too long to load. To summarize these kinds of flaws, Figure 14.7 provides some clues to poor Web site design.

The proliferation of e-commerce Web sites is a challenging problem by itself. The marketing team should avoid as many pitfalls as possible to achieve the goal of building a stronger company through Internet activities. In contrast to the don'ts listed in Figure 14.7, Figure 14.8 highlights some tips for creating winning Web sites.

▶ **Clueless banners**

▶ **Slow loading front pages**

▶ **Forcing people to go through numerous screens**

▶ **Too much verbal information**

▶ **Too many technical terms**

▶ **Sites that are hard to navigate**

FIGURE 14.7
Clues to Poor Design

> ▶ The Web site should follow a strategic purpose such as to acquire new customers, serve existing customers, cross-sell, and so forth.
>
> ▶ Make the Web site easy to access and quick to load.
>
> ▶ Written content should be precise with short words, short sentences, and short paragraphs.
>
> ▶ Content is the key to success, not fancy graphics and design.
>
> ▶ Graphics should support content, not detract from it.
>
> ▶ Make some type of marketing offer to encourage a response.
>
> ▶ Ask for site evaluation.
>
> ▶ Provide easy-to-use navigation links on every page.
>
> ▶ Use gimmicks such as moving icons or flashing banners to gain attention at the beginning but do not use them deeper in the Web site.
>
> ▶ Change the Web site on a regular basis to keep individuals coming back.
>
> ▶ Measure results continually, especially designs and offers.

FIGURE 14.8
Tips to Creating Winning Web Sites

Source: Based on Ray Jutkins, "13 Ideas That Could Lead to Successful Web Marketing," *Advertising Age's Business Marketing* (June 1999), Vol. 84, No. 6, p. 27.

INTEGRATED LEARNING EXPERIENCE

A very interesting site is the Cool Site of the Day at **www.coolsiteoftheday.com**. Access the Web site each day for at least a week. Read the cool site of the day. Write down why you thought it was chosen as the cool site of the day. What winning strategies outlined in Figure 14.8 did it follow? What other interesting pieces of information are available at this site? How could a small business trying to develop a Web site use this site?

SUMMARY

Increased usage of the Internet by both consumers and businesses has led most marketing teams to develop some type of Internet site. Sometimes Web designers are being asked to design a Web page because it's the "thing to do," and little or no thought is given to the functions the Web site should perform. This chapter is designed to explain how an Internet Web site can be integrated into the overall integrated marketing communications plan and why it should.

The primary goals of various Web sites are for advertising, sales support, customer service, public relations, and e-commerce. E-commerce ventures normally require a catalog, a shopping cart, and a method to collect payments. In e-commerce and other Internet ventures, customers must feel the process is secure and be enticed to change their buying habits. Three incentives that help people alter buying patterns are financial incentives, greater convenience, and added value.

The Internet changes the traditional ways that buyers and sellers deal with each other. In business-to-business markets, field salespeople have traditionally called on customers and prospects. Information is shared, prices are negotiated, and orders are taken. On the Internet, buyers can purchase directly from suppliers.

Middlemen can be eliminated. Buyers can obtain quotes from a number of vendors and obtain product information from each, all on the Internet. While it saves the selling company money in terms of sales calls, it also risks losing customers. Loyalty and strong relationships are endangered as buyers search the Web to meet their corporation's needs.

International markets may also be served by e-commerce enterprises, especially when cultural differences, shipping problems, and Internet capability problems can be solved. Information technology departments will play a key role in solving the Internet problems. Taxation issues and language differences also require attention in this lucrative and growing marketplace.

The Internet blurs many internal functional boundaries. An effective Internet Web site can advertise, send sales messages, provide public relations announcements, offer press releases to the media, talk about the company, provide answers to frequently asked questions, provide information to investors, dispense product catalogs complete with product descriptions and prices, take orders from customers, process payments, receive e-mail messages, handle customer service queries, and entertain Web viewers.

As always, the primary goal of an Internet program is to expand and enhance the message portrayed by the company's IMC plan. Careful attention must be paid to issues of brand image and loyalty, and Web sites must be designed to support selling efforts and customer service programs, and deliver consumer promotions of value to potential buyers. Brand spiraling may be used to combine the Internet program with advertising in traditional media. The quality of a Web site is a primary factor in the success of the entire Internet program. Many company leaders are beginning to grasp the potential of these marketing efforts, as interest and activity on the Web continue to grow. In the end, the capacity of the Internet may be limited only by what the company decides to do.

REVIEW QUESTIONS

1. Which age group is most likely to use the Internet? Which is the least? Does this have implications for IMC programs?
2. Name the five marketing functions that can be provided on the Internet that were described in this chapter.
3. Define e-commerce. What are the three common components of e-commerce programs?
4. What two issues must e-commerce providers overcome in order to build successful businesses?
5. Name and describe the three main incentives used to attract shoppers to e-commerce Web sites.
6. What is cyberbait? How must it be used over time to maintain it as an effective marketing tactic?
7. In business-to-business e-commerce operations, what obstacles occur? How can they be overcome?
8. What problems exist for international e-commerce operations? What can companies do to resolve them?

9. How can the Internet affect a brand? Brand loyalty?
10. What is brand spiraling? What is the primary goal of brand spiraling programs?
11. How can the Internet be used to provide sales support?
12. How can the Internet be used to provide customer service?
13. How can consumer promotions be offered over the Internet? What is the goal of a major prize giveaway as opposed to smaller prizes given to larger numbers of consumers?
14. How can direct marketing be used most effectively to reach customers?
15. What is interactive marketing?
16. What is viral marketing? What is the goal of a viral marketing program?
17. What tactics should companies avoid in designing Web sites? What should they do to make effective Web pages?

KEY TERMS

FAQs (frequently asked questions) questions people have about various items or services.

e-commerce selling goods on the Internet.

shopping cart a component of e-commerce operations that allows the individual to mark items to purchase later as part of a complete order.

cyberbait some type of lure or attraction that brings people to a Web site.

brand spiraling the practice of using traditional media to promote and attract consumers to an online Web site.

halo effect occurs when a well-received brand leads customers to try new company products and services that are being offered over the Internet.

Web master the person who manages a firm's Web site.

interactive marketing individualizing and personalizing Web content and e-mail messages for various consumers.

viral marketing preparing an advertisement that is tied to an e-mail in which one person passes on the advertisement or e-mail to other consumers.

CRITICAL THINKING EXERCISES

Discussion Questions

1. What types of goods or services have you purchased over the Internet during the last year? Have your parents purchased anything using the Internet? If so, compare your purchases and attitudes toward buying over the Internet to theirs. If you or your parents, or both, have not used the Internet to make purchases, why not?

2. Access four different Web sites for one of the following products. Locate the FAQ section. Was the FAQ section difficult to find? How is the FAQ section organized? Does it provide effective answers for questions? Do the four sites have similar questions listed?
   a. Antivirus software
   b. Cosmetic surgery

c. Automobile parts

d. Cameras

e. Financial services

3. Best Buy Company was a late e-commerce entry, but has developed strong e-commerce component. The key to Best Buy's success, according to Barry Judge, vice president of marketing, is, "We do a lot of one-to-one marketing. We're not overly focused on where the consumers buy." The Web site carries every product that Best Buy stocks. It uses personalized services, along with convenient pickup and solid return policies to entice consumers to shop. The consumer can purchase items on the Internet and either have them shipped directly to them or pick them up at the closest store. Shoppers can use the Internet to see if Best Buy stocks a particular item, what the item costs, and to gather product information.[22] What is the advantage to this philosophy? Access the Web site at www.bestbuy.com. Evaluate it in terms of ease of use, product information, and then locate the Best Buy closest to you. Next, access Circuit City's Web site at www.circuitcity.com. Compare it to Best Buy's site. Select one product such as a camcorder to compare the two Web sites.

4. Ironox at www.ironox.com is a business-to-business Internet auction service. Access the Web site to see what types of products it sells. Examine the buyer's corner. What tips are given for buyers? What services does Ironox offer to buyers? What tips and services are listed on the Web site for sellers? What are the advantages and disadvantages of using Ironox for buyers? For sellers? Which members of the buying center would be the most likely to use Ironox?

5. First Energy Corporation, the nation's twelfth largest utility, purchases about 30 percent of its coal over the Internet. The purchasing process that normally took 60 days to complete has been compressed to just two weeks. Bidding takes place on one day, and suppliers know within two to three days whether they have won the order.[23] What risks does First Energy take in purchasing coal over the Internet? How can those risks be minimized? Why would a supplier want to sell coal over the Internet instead of developing a strong personal relationship with First Energy Corporation?

6. Credit card security is an issue with many people. Interview 10 people you know of various ages and genders. Does age or gender make any difference in the person's feelings, especially about the fear of using a credit card over the Internet? Are there specific products or Web sites that people do not trust? More importantly, how do you judge whether a Web site provides the necessary credit security?

7. Pick one of the following product categories. What types of financial incentives are offered on the company's Web site to encourage you to purchase? What about the other two types of incentives: greater convenience and added value? What evidence do you see for them?

a. Contacts or eyeglasses

b. Water skis

c. Jeans

d. Computers

e. Camping supplies

8. The primary companies businesses use to ship small packages either overnight or two-day delivery are FedEx, UPS, and the U.S. Postal Service. Access each of these Web sites (Federal Express at www.fedex.com; UPS at www.ups.com; U.S. Postal Service: at www.usps.com). What guarantees do they make about delivery? Which site is the most user-friendly? Which site appears to offer the best customer service? In looking at the different functions of a Web site discussed in this chapter, indicate the function for which each Web site was designed.

Creating Internet Marketing Plans

How does the Internet apply to your company, product, or service? You should be able to discover how to use e-commerce effectively as part of an overall IMC program. Or, will you use your Web site for other purposes? Individual products may have local as well as international distribution points. Therefore, they should be effectively promoted on the Web and sold using e-commerce tactics whenever possible. The exercise provided for Chapter 14 on the IMC Plan Pro disk that accompanied this textbook or at www.prenhall.com/clow is to design your product or company's Web site and to consider all of the potential e-commerce possibilities for the item you are vending. Consideration must also be given to understanding the ways selling your product through the Internet may affect relationships with wholesalers and retailers that also are selling the item.

BUILDING AN
IMC
CAMPAIGN

IMC PlanPro

CASE 1

THE CIRCULATION GAME

William Johnson was about to embark on a major new phase of his publishing career. He had begun as a writer for a small newspaper in New York oriented to an African American readership. From there, William had become an editor and eventually a publisher of a chain of small-town newspapers in Georgia. The cities the chain served also were predominantly African American. Now, however, William's company had just made a successful bid to acquire newspapers in six cities in the upper Midwest. Suddenly William was about to become one of the largest minority owners in the United States.

The newspaper business has changed dramatically in the past half century. From a time when papers were the primary source of news for most Americans until the new millennium, where citizens are bombarded with news formats of all types, a major shake-out of news chains had occurred. Smaller local papers were forced to compete with national offerings, such as *USA Today* and the *Wall Street Journal.* Readership has changed as well. In the latter half of the twentieth century, editors knew their readers were largely over 18 and reasonably well educated.

Currently, newspapers appear in several formats: tabloids, traditional papers, weekly magazines, and Internet news. They compete with radio news stations, network news, and cable news stations such as CNN, ESPN, and other more specific program formats. African Americans also can tune in to one cable channel devoted more exclusively to them, with the BET (Black Entertainment Channel) offering some news programming. Satellites allow breaking news stories to appear instantly around the world, and people can access news via the Internet when a television is not nearby.

William's company, like most other paper chains, derives income from several sources. First, the "old-fashioned" subscriber forms the basis of the company's circulation numbers. Businesses buy advertising space, and many individuals and companies run classified ads. Weekly newspapers sell additional advertising space in these magazine-type papers. The newest source of revenue is advertising on Internet editions of the paper.

The biggest change in the newspaper business is the partnerships involved. Most papers are owned by media giants that also own radio and television stations. There is a cross-mix of reporting, polling, and other activities. In addition, most newspapers, even in small towns, find they must advertise their product in other markets. Thus, newspapers buy ads on television and on the radio promoting readership. The circulation department conducts telephone sales campaigns designed to entice people to buy home delivery. Others are distributed in vending machines and in newsstands throughout each city.

In this complex marketplace, William looks for ways to expand the reach of the paper and to compete with other media. He knows the future will witness increasing use of the Internet by most households, but there will continue to be a strong base of readers who want to wake up in the morning, go out to the front yard, pick up a paper, and read it over coffee or breakfast.

1. How can William's company cater to various minorities in its Internet division of the newspaper? Or should he avoid this type of tactic?

2. What special marketing and IMC challenges affect newspapers in both circulation (retail) and business-to-business (advertising) areas?

3. Look up your local city's newspaper on the Internet. How is it different from a traditional "paper" newspaper? How is it similar?

4. Design an advertising program for William Johnson's local newspaper's Internet edition.

CASE 2

CONTRACT HAULERS

Mike Testman has served as the computer operator for a local trucking company, Contract Haulers, for the past 10 years. His job is to help the company keep track of inventories, deliveries, and billings for companies served by the firm. These companies are located in a 500-mile region and are considered short trips. Contract Haulers does not perform cross-country deliveries.

Mike knows that 40 percent of the customers who utilize his company ask for less than a full trailer load shipment. This means the driver must combine two to five customers to complete a trailer load. His company can charge more per customer because the service is more specialized. The primary target markets for Contract Haulers are small manufacturers and small distributors. A secondary target market is larger manufacturers that need to make shipments to small businesses.

George Coffman, the CEO of Contract Haulers, recently stated that he believes the firm needs a Web site. He convened a meeting of his marketing team to decide what the Web site should feature. At the meeting, the marketing manager spoke first. She stated that the site should help promote the company's name and image. Her argument was that even though it was a short haul server, not enough businesses in the area knew about it. Building the name and image would increase sales due to visibility and loyalty.

The VP of sales spoke next. He believed the site should be used primarily to provide sales support for his 18-person sales force. He said his reps could use the site when making sales calls. If the Web site were properly set up, customers could get information regarding price rates, availability of trucks, and special deals. Contract Hauler's customers would also be able to arrange shipments on the spot while the sales rep was in the prospective customer's office. This would give Contract Haulers a unique competitive advantage in the local market.

The logistics manager then spoke up. He said there is no way the company can do what the sales manager was suggesting on the Internet. Only his office knows where each of the 125 company trucks are located at any given time and which ones are available for shipments. He stated that it would be far too complicated to provide that information on the Internet.

Then the VP of operations suggested that the primary purpose of a Web site should be additional customer support. Customers could access the Web site at any time to find out where a shipment is and when it will arrive. The salespeople could use it to see where trucks are and how soon a truck could come by. In other words, in his mind the site should be used for both sales support and customer service.

The VP of marketing responded. She did not believe the Web site should be so oriented to such an operational use. Instead, sales support and customer service should be handled over the phone with human operators. She emphasized that Contract Haulers had developed a reputation for personalized service. This advantage would be lost using the Internet instead of real people.

Mike was confused and concerned. He watched as the various individuals in the meeting become more engaged in a heated argument over how to use the Web site, and he knew he was going to have to keep many people happy as he designed the site. As the debate appeared to be getting out of hand, George, the CEO, called the meeting to a halt. George told Mike to "do his best" and to "bring me a proposal within the next couple of weeks."

1. What should be the primary purpose of Contract Hauler's Web site?

2. Does the VP of marketing have a valid point? Are logistics issues better handled in person? What are the advantages and disadvantages of doing all scheduling over the telephone or in person at the office?

3. Using a search engine, access at least four Web sites of shipping companies that Mike could take to the next meeting to show what other companies are doing. Make sure Mike is prepared to justify the selection of Web sites as comparable companies.

4. Outline the functions of the Contract Haulers' Web site and how it should be designed.

ENDNOTES

1. George Anders, "EBay learns to Trust Again," *Fast Company,* issue 53 (December 2001), pp. 102–107. Steve Smith, "E-Bay's Whitman Shares Opinions on Web at Annual CEA Dinner," *This Week in Consumer Electronics,* 17, issue 3 (January 28, 2002), pp. 1–2. "Meg Whitman," *Business Week,* issue 3631 (May 31, 1999), p. 134.

2. "Click First, Buy Later," *Marketing News,* 35, issue 11 (May 21, 2001), p. 5.

3. Alf Nucifora, "There Are Lots of Good Reasons for All the Internet Hype," *Pittsburgh Business Times,* 18, no. 42 (May 7, 1999), p. 20; Al Nucifora, "Are You Preparing for the e-Business Revolution?" *Business First,* Louisville, 16, no. 28 (February 11, 2000), p. 17; Don Jeffrey, "Survey Details Consumer Shopping Trends on the Net," *Billboard,* 111, no. 22 (May 29, 1999), pp. 47–48.

4. Alan Mitchell, "Marketers Must Grasp the Net or Face Oblivion," *Marketing Week,* 22, no. 3 (February 18, 1999), pp. 30–31.

5. Bob Donath, "Web Could Boost Branding in B-to-B Marketing," *Marketing News,* 32, no. 10 (May 11, 1998), p. 6.

6. John Evan Frook, "Trading Hubs Drive Changes," *B to B,* 85, no. 4 (April 24, 2000), p. 33.

7. Edward Teach, "World Wide Bazaar," *CFO,* 15, no. 5 (May 1999), pp. 113–16.

8. Karen E. Hussel, "New Service Helps Brand Clicks with Bricks," *Advertising Age's Business Marketing,* 84, no. 11 (November 1999), pp. 40–41.

9. Lynda Radosevich, "Going Global Overnight," *InfoWorld,* 21, no. 16 (April 19, 1999), pp. 1–3.

10. Todd McCollough, "Online Services Make Ordering, Billing, Printing a Snap," *Business First,* Columbus, 15, no. 24 (February 5, 1999), pp. 19–20.

11. Julia King, "Online Marketing Tools Can Cause IT Disasters," *Computerworld,* 33, no. 46 (November 15, 1999), p. 49.

12. "A Little Restraint, Please," *Marketing News,* 36, issue 11 (May 21, 2002), p. 4; "E-mail Newsletters Click Better With Customers," *Marketing News,* 35, issue 6 (March 12, 2001), p. 3.

13. Carol Patton, "Marketers Promote Online Traffic Through Traditional Media," *Advertising Age's Business Marketing,* 84, no. 8 (August 1999), p. 40.

14. Beth Snyder, "Adobe Drive Aims to Build Image as a Web Company," *Advertising Age,* 70, no. 41 (October 4, 1999), p. 28.

15. Robert Harvin, "In Internet Branding, the Off-Lines Have It," *Brandweek,* 41, no. 4 (January 24, 2000), pp. 30–31.

16. "Not Scratching the Niche," *Marketing News,* 34, issue 14 (June 19, 2000), p. 3.

17. "Yes, I Would Like Some Help, Thank You," *Marketing News,* 26, issue 4 (February 18, 2002), p. 3.

18. Jeff Sweat and Rick Whiting, "Instant Marketing," *Information Week,* no. 746 (August 2, 1999), pp. 18–20.

19. Alf Nucifora, "Viral Marketing Spreads by 'Word of Net,' " *Business Journal,* Central New York, 14, no. 18 (May 5, 2000), pp. 25–26.

20. Donna L. Hoffman and Thomas P. Novak, "How to Acquire Customers on the Web," *Harvard Business Review,* 78, no. 3 (May–June 2000), pp. 179–85.

21. Mie-Yun Lee, "Goal-Based Strategy Can Make Banner Ads Click," *Puget Sound Business Journal,* 30, no. 21 (October 1, 1999), p. 18.

22. Tobi Elkin, "Best Buy Takes Cue from Retail Shops," *Advertising Age,* 71, no. 10 (March 6, 2000), p. 8.

23. Hussel, "New Service Helps Brand Clicks with Bricks."

IMC for Small Businesses and Entrepreneurial Ventures

Chapter Objectives

Develop **an understanding of the challenges facing entrepreneurs and small business owners, especially in the area of marketing communications.**

Explain **the tactics used to reach small business customers effectively.**

Utilize **programs, such as guerilla marketing, to manage costs while designing an effective message.**

Take **advantage of alternative media, lifestyle marketing, and other advertising programs to reach a small-business target market.**

THE PASTA HOUSE CO.:
Neighborhood Marketing Builds Big Profits

"The Hill" in St. Louis, Missouri, is nationally known for fine Italian dining. In the neighborhood where baseball legends Yogi Berra and Joe Gargiola grew up, numerous low-cost restaurants are sprinkled among the houses and small businesses. In the middle of this competition, The Pasta House Co. has grown from a single unit in 1974 to more than 20 locations in St. Louis alone, along with franchises throughout the United States and internationally.

J. Kim Tucci, Joseph Fresta (shown in the photo on page 465, respectively) and their deceased partner John Ferrara, all sons of Italian immigrants, founded The Pasta House Co. The original decor featured Italian pop culture in a setting of an imaginary pasta factory. Nearly 30 pasta dishes, 10 entrees, and an all-you-can eat salad are on the menu. The company grew in part due to a suggestive selling program in which add-ons such as appetizers, wines, specialty drinks, specialty breads, and desserts created larger ticket totals per customer. The Pasta House Co.'s cheese garlic bread is a major seller each year.

When it became apparent that demand was great enough to expand, a site selection group helped pick the next six locations. To make sure that each unit was successful, owners of The Pasta House Co. began a neighborhood marketing program. "It's a family-oriented business, and basically we do things for families," says J. Kim Tucci about the operations.

To build loyalty to individual stores, a frequent diner program was instituted in which a person who buys $250 worth of food is given a $25 gift certificate. The certificate can only be redeemed at the location where the person is a frequent diner member, to encourage neighborhood loyalty. Members of the club also get free spaghetti and a dessert on their birthdays and a special-offer candlelight dinner for two on their anniversaries.

The Pasta House Co's. outreach program has been another major source of brand recognition and customer loyalty. One plan, called the "Reading, Writing, and Ravioli" program is targeted to elementary students. A child reads a book, writes a book report, and receives a free dish of spaghetti or ravioli with a salad and Coca-Cola as a prize. Coca-Cola is a co-sponsor of the program.

More than 400 schools and 4,000 teachers participate in the program. Since it began, over six million book reports have been turned in. Participating teachers receive a 50-percent discount coupon each month. "Inside every classroom is our logo and Coca-Cola's logo, a list of students, and how many books they've read," Tucci reports. He believes students are more loyal to The Pasta House Co. than to McDonald's as a result.

At the high school level, The Pasta House Co. sponsors a student art contest. To enter, students must recreate a great work of art with one addition—a plate of pasta. Winners and their schools receive prizes up to $1,000.

The Pasta House Co. also participates each year in the Jerry Lewis Muscular Dystrophy program, giving 30 cents for each order of toasted ravioli to "Jerry's Kids." Every five years The Pasta House Co. sets up a "RavoMeter" thermometer to show how much money has been raised. The company also maintains its own not-for-profit organization, The Caring and Sharing program. The organization raises money and canned goods to distribute to locals during the Christmas season. Individual employees have a payroll plan in which money is given to St. Jude's Hospital in Memphis, Tennessee.

The interior of a Pasta House Co. facility.

Further expansion now comes from franchising. There are 29 additional units beyond St. Louis. The first foreign franchise was established in the Dominican Republic. "The taste for Italian food is as universal as hamburgers and pizza, no question about it," Tucci says. Franchising agreements combined with local sales generated over $55 million. Licensee training takes place in St. Louis.

In the future The Pasta House Co. will expand into both domestic and foreign locations. From humble beginnings, many success stories similar to The Pasta House Co. have emerged. Each one contains common elements of quality, reputation, specialization in one unique competitive advantage area, community outreach, an energetic and visionary ownership group, and a strong message theme that reaches the target market effectively.[1]

KAOLIN CALEFACTORS

It is just as important for a small business to reach a target set of customers with a distinct voice as it is for a large organization. Using an IMC plan to move forward makes this possible. A small business must identify a unique market niche, find customers, and develop ways to attract those customers in order to survive. The IMC approach should be used with a major emphasis on the company's name and brand. These ingredients must be understandable and help the consumer believe that little purchase risk is involved in giving the company a try.

The Kaolin Calefactors plan on the IMC Plan Pro disk is an example of a small-business operation. Read the entire plan. Notice the emphasis on quality, a strong brand, and well-developed relationships with customers. Kaolin must compete with both specialty shops and standardized designs. Kaolin has chosen to compete with quality rather than price. Finding ways to reach all possible customers is the challenge. Using a well-thought-out IMC program will help Kaolin gain ground in the marketplace.

IMC PlanPro!

IMC PLAN PRO

s owning your own business still the "Great American Dream"? The answer may depend on whom you ask. Projections are that new business ventures will create a substantial number of new millionaires in the next two decades. On the other hand, the implosion of the dot-com marketplace sent thousands to unemployment lines. While starting, owning, and maintaining a small business is a higher-risk/higher-return venture, it remains an attractive option for many individuals.

One of the keys to success in creating a new business is to stand out in the marketplace. Doing so means careful planning and disciplined implementation. A well-thought-out IMC program is an essential tool in the pursuit of success.

The purposes of this chapter are: (1) to describe the challenges associated with running a small business or entrepreneurial venture, (2) to spell out how to create an IMC plan for this unique situation, one that is especially oriented to finding and attracting customers, and (3) to present methods for creating and keeping loyal customers. As is the case in any size organization, it is vital for the operation to speak with one clear and distinct voice to cut through the clutter of the marketplace. For a new start-up business, it is even more critical.

o v e r v i e w

TYPES OF VENTURES

All small businesses and new ventures are not the same. In fact, the range of types is quite large. Here are a few common types:

▶ A small family-owned business, such as a dry cleaner, a restaurant, a specialty shop (e.g. photo studio), or a one-stop convenience store, designed to provide the family with income.

▶ A business start-up with growth in mind, either through increased product sales, multiple locations, or franchise agreements.

▶ Corporate start-ups of entrepreneurial ventures, such as Genuity.com, and wireless phone and Internet access services offered by long-distance companies.

▶ Groups of physicians, dentists, or other professionals who go into practice together.

Typically, **entrepreneurship** means a company is being formed with the express goal of becoming larger through an aggressive growth agenda. **Intrepreneurship** is a corporate spin-off or start-up. A **small business** is a family-owned company or consortium of professionals that is formed with specific objectives in mind. In most cases, aggressive growth is not as important as providing adequate income for the owners.

INTEGRATED LEARNING EXPERIENCE

A number of Web sites, consulting firms, and organizations offer information, ideas, and support for entrepreneurs. Access the Entrepreneurship Centre at **www.entrepreneurship.com**. What type of assistance does the Entrepreneurship Centre provide? Be sure to examine seminars and events sponsored by the Entrepreneurship Centre and some of the success stories. Examine one of the successful companies listed on the site.

STOP

MAJOR CHALLENGES

The common denominator of all forms of start-up and new businesses is that they are unknown in the marketplace. This is the major challenge to any new business. For example, the launch of MLife at a recent Super Bowl created a substantial amount of confusion as to what exactly was being offered. While the company's Web site was flooded with

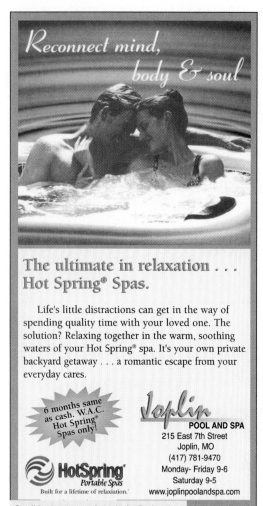

Small businesses, such as Joplin Pool and Spa, are an important component of each community's local economy.

Source: Used with permission of the *Joplin Globe,* Joplin, Missouri.

inquiries (so much so that it crashed), most people did not bother to find out, and the take-off was slow.

Many consumers are cautious about trying new goods, services, or companies. Purchases are often based on known brand names and familiar purchasing patterns. It is much easier for customers to purchase the same brand they have always purchased or another brand name they recognize or have used. To be considered, a new business must move the brand into a person or business's evoked set of brands, or at least into the inert set.

This dilemma is heightened by the massive amount of marketing clutter that all companies face. Overcoming clutter is especially difficult for new firms with limited budgets for marketing and promotion. Traditional methods of advertising and consumer promotions may not be enough to get recognized.

Company leaders must be sure to deliver on promises and provide a high-quality experience, especially on the customer's first purchase. One bad encounter will often lead to negative word-of-mouth. A new business will probably not get a second chance if the customer has a bad experience.

To overcome these problems, a new company must develop a unique selling point and find a way to inform consumers about that advantage.[2] Everything from the brand name to the logo to company advertisements must capture the interest and attention of the consumer. It is important to remember that customers are interested in *benefits* as opposed to product or service *features,* or as one writer put it, "What's in it for me?" The new company must be able to clearly answer this question in order to survive and grow.[3] The following is a list of some of the major challenges for new businesses.

▶ Consumers are not aware of the business.

▶ Consumers are cautious or wary of trying a new good, service, or company.

▶ Advertising and promotional clutter make it difficult to be recognized.

▶ Small budgets for marketing, advertising, and promotional activities make it difficult to compete.

▶ New businesses are especially vulnerable to negative word of mouth communications.

STARTING A COMPANY: THE MARKET ANALYSIS

Businesses are started for many reasons, including one as simple as turning a hobby into something more profitable. Thus, someone who loves computers may decide to open a computer retail store or computer repair service. They can either go it alone, form a part-

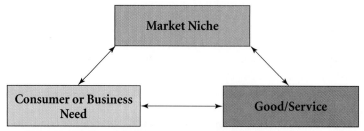

FIGURE 15.1
The Target Market

Finding a target market means matching the needs of consumers or businesses with a good or service in a unique way.

In this advertisement, Merry Maids offers house-cleaning services to consumers.
Source: Used with permission of the *Joplin Globe*, Joplin, Missouri.

nership with someone who has the same interest, or seek a franchise facility from a franchising operation such as Geeks On Call. By purchasing a franchise from Geeks On Call, an individual will gain access to marketing materials, a business plan, and an established customer base.[4] In any case, no matter how the business begins, a careful market analysis is in order. This includes three steps:

1. Understand and define consumer needs.
2. Establish a clearly defined product.
3. Develop a unique market niche.

These three tasks are intermingled as the creation of a business moves forward. For example, one ongoing and successful dot-com business is VIPdesk, which is an Internet-based concierge service. The company acquires theater tickets, sends flowers, and provides numerous "gofer" chores for customers of corporate clients such as MasterCard International and Citibank.[5] VIPdesk was formed based on the idea that some people can make better use of their time when certain tasks are "farmed out," which is the consumer need. In this case, the service is one that had never before been offered over the Internet. Its market niche is corporate customers and individuals with greater levels of disposable income. While the market analysis steps are combined in the development of a business such as VIPdesk, each is presented here separately.

INTEGRATED LEARNING EXPERIENCE

Many entrepreneurs will go into business by purchasing a franchise. Examine the following Web sites for information about franchise opportunities. Pick a franchise and look it up on all four Web sites. What did you learn about the franchise? How did the Web sites differ in terms of material presented?

S T O P

   Franchise Solutions (www.franchisesolutions.com)
   Own Your Own Franchise (www.ownyourownfranchise.com)
   Franchise.com (www.franchise.com)
   Franchises 4U (www.franchises-4u.com)

Understanding and Defining Consumer Needs

Understanding and defining needs means knowing more than just the name, demographic characteristics, or psychological tendencies of a target market segment. It means understanding what a particular group desires from a good or service that is not currently available.

Chris Otto identified an unmet need when she created a mobile dog-grooming business and named it "Your Fairy Dogmother." First, Otto understood that customers did not like transporting a dirty dog to a grooming shop, leaving it all day in a cage, then rushing back after work to pick the dog up and take it home. In response, Your Fairy Dogmother would go to the customer's residence in a brightly painted van with the company's name boldly featured and groom the dog. Otto says, her customers, "love the service. They love the fact that the dog doesn't have to leave the house."

An advertisement for the Magnolia House informing customers of the type of merchandise the company sells.

Source: Used with permission of the *Joplin Globe*, Joplin, Missouri.

A Cut-N-Heaven understands the needs of their customers.

Source: Used with permission of the *Joplin Globe*, Joplin, Missouri.

For Your Fairy Dogmother, the major factor in the decision to purchase the service was convenience. Once customers discovered that Your Fairy Dogmother would come to their homes, it was easy to decide to give the company a try. Also, the company's name suggested that the family dog would be treated with extra special care. By understanding and then defining the needs of her customers, Otto has been able to develop a successful small business.[6]

Through careful research, marketing professionals in businesses such as Your Fairy Dogmother, VIPdesk, and Geeks On Call have been able to identify a target market. Demographic characteristics are vital, but the research must go beyond demographics to include psychographic and purchasing behavior information. Understanding the attitudes, interests, and opinions of individuals in the target market is important in developing a product. It is also important in developing an IMC plan that will reach those consumers.

Creating a Clearly Defined Product

A clearly defined product means that everyone knows exactly what the company intends to deliver. As Leslie Godwin, a career and life-transition counselor pointed out, it is just as important to say what your company *won't do* as what it will do.[7] She noted that a psychotherapist participating in a new group of doctors with a business card that says, "Specializes in treating children, adults, adolescents, groups, and individuals" is overstating the professional's talents. Compared to an ob/gyn who claims she specializes in "women struggling with menopause," the differences are obvious. One professional is trying to be all things to all people. The other has more logically spelled out a form of expertise that would be attractive to a specific set of people.

Any form of new company is liable to fall into the trap of trying to please every potential customer. Unfortunately, this leads to no clear sense of identity for employees, customers, and company leaders. A simple question to ask is, "What do we do well?" The goal is to feature that good, service, or skill.

Once the product is clearly defined, it is important to carefully create a brand name, logo, and other word-based marketing elements such as the company's slogan and advertising tag line. These items must communicate the nature of the clearly defined good or service, or other efforts will not be as likely to succeed. Brand names such as The Pasta House Co. or Champion Dry Cleaners clearly spell out to customers what the business is all about. While VIPdesk and Geeks On Call are easy to remember, it is less clear to consumers exactly what type of service is being provided. These companies will have to expend greater effort in defining the business so that customers see the advantage in giving the firm a try.

Developing a Unique Market Niche

This process is also known as having a **unique selling position (USP)**. A USP is some feature that allows the newly formed company to stand alone and be distinct from all other competitors. This may be based on price, the offer of a service not previously available, or some other feature that is not easily duplicated in the market. VIPdesk, which is used by 10.5 million people, offers services via the Internet, phone, or through a wireless device. No other concierge service is unique in this way. The difference must be important enough for the customer to "stand up and take notice."

Simply competing with a minor price difference will not be enough, it must be a major difference. The success of the Midwestern chain Eureka Pizza was, in part, based on the "buy one—get two free" price advantage. This unique selling position was enough to get the company noticed in the strongly competitive pizza delivery market.

When the market analysis process is complete, other aspects of the IMC plan more readily fall into place. Finding a voice for a small business starts with defining the actual business and its market. Notice the relationship between these activities and the IMC foundation (see Figure 15.2). From there, other elements of the marketing plan can be delivered more effectively.

Butcher's Block offers the goods and services that meet the needs of target markets, both consumers and businesses.
Source: Used with permission of the *Joplin Globe*, Joplin, Missouri.

INTEGRATED LEARNING EXPERIENCE

Understanding your customers' needs, finding the right market niche, and clearly defining your good or service are the basics of establishing a new business. Examine the Web sites of Geeks On Call at **www.geeksoncall.com** and VIPdesk at **www.vipdesk.com**. In your opinion, why are these two businesses successful?

S T O P

FINDING CUSTOMERS: A CRUCIAL ELEMENT OF THE IMC PLAN

A new company's IMC plan must be created while bearing in mind the challenges present to entrepreneurial ventures. The person in charge of marketing, whether it is the new business owner or some member of the company, often operates with limited resources trying to reach a cautious and skeptical public. Beyond the tasks completed in forming the company (need, niche, and good or service) the most crucial activities

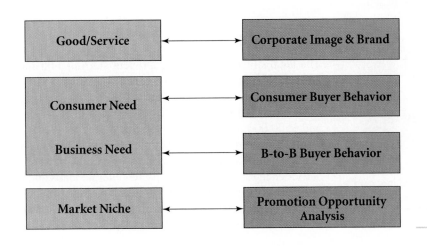

FIGURE 15.2
The Relationship of a Target Market to an IMC Plan

IMC FOR SMALL BUSINESS AND ENTREPRENEURIAL VENTURES

Building an Ethical Reputation

Word-of-mouth is a key ingredient the success or failure of a new business. It works in both directions. Negative word-of-mouth can quickly ruin the reputation of a company and make survival difficult, if not impossible. Positive word-of-mouth can build a customer base and help establish the entrepreneur in the community so that other strong relationships can be created, with suppliers, employment agencies, and the local government.

Two ethical issues emerge as a firm begins to grow. One is the use of reciprocal relationships. Is it ethical to set up a series of "I'll buy from you if you buy from me" connections with other companies? It is legal, but it may build the perception that a firm doesn't mind competing in an unfair manner.

The other issue is hiring away employees. Many times entrepreneurs became disenchanted with their company. The individual goes into the exact same business that he or she left. When this happens, there is a strong temptation to drag along customers and former employees. Is it ethical to do so? Will it hurt the reputation of the new firm?

These and other tricky issues, such as not fully reporting income, surround the new business operator. This person often has a lifetime of savings invested. Remaining ethical is important, both for personal well-being and the long-term standing of the new operation.

involved in creating an IMC plan for a small business or entrepreneurial venture include:

▶ Locating customers

▶ Making it easy for customers to reach the new company

▶ Reducing purchase risk for customers

Remember that all of the IMC activities must be performed. In the case of a new company, however, it is sometimes difficult to carry them out in traditional ways. A small business or start-up venture does not have $10 million budgeted for marketing. There may only be $1,000 or $5,000 for very small firms or maybe $75,000 for a larger start-up. It is essential that a small business allocate sufficient resources to ensure success. A minimum of 3 percent to 5 percent of the firm's revenues should be devoted to marketing. Failing to provide sufficient funding for marketing spells almost certain death for the new firm.

Marketing funds are spent differently for small firms as opposed to multinational firms such as Proctor & Gamble.[8] The number of potential customers is often lower and more concentrated in a particular geographic area. Therefore, those responsible for marketing must be creative and careful in using resources.

Locating Customers

The ideal situation for an entrepreneur starting a business is to hire a market research firm to assist in locating customers. While some small businesses and start-ups may be able to afford this service, it can be expensive. A well-developed market research effort is likely to cost between $25,000 and $500,000. Consequently, alternative methods may have to be used for locating customers and determining the level of demand.

One good way to start is by assessing the various types of marketing activities in terms of their ability to generate leads and then the probability of the leads turning into sales. If possible, it is often helpful to examine the market for comparable goods or services to gather an approximate estimate of the market size. For example, to compete in the dine-in restaurant

This advertisement for Mix 95.1 highlights the market niche served by the station.
Source: Used with permission of the *Joplin Globe,* Joplin, Missouri.

COMMUNICATION ACTION

Ethnic Targets

Many small-business owners have discovered that ethnic populations represent a rich new source of customers. In the next 20 years, the number of African Americans in the United States is expected to increase by 25 percent, while the Asian American population will grow by 68 percent, and Hispanic Americans will increase by 64 percent. In the past, marketing to ethnic groups was largely the domain of major companies; however, this is beginning to change.

To effectively reach an ethnic target market, Ken Greenberg of AC Nielsen Homescan recommends several key practices. First, create or participate in special events that reflect an ethnic heritage. Sponsorships are one angle, but creativity should be used. For instance, DaimlerChrysler offers a "ride and drive" program that provides vehicles to those who attend the National Association of Black Journalists convention each year. The vehicles make it possible for attendees to see local attractions in the convention city. Free samples and demonstrations of products at ethnic fairs provide firsthand contacts with potential new customers.

Second, personalize products and services by incorporating language (such as Spanish) and endorsements from local community leaders. Also, it is crucial to employ individuals from various ethnic backgrounds within the company.

Third, target media that reaches the ethnic communities in a given location. In San Diego, a firm seeking to reach Hispanics and Latinos should be targeted to radio, newspaper, and other media that reach Spanish-speaking people from the area.

Fourth, and most importantly, carefully review all messages so they do not offend or alienate the target market. Patronizing language is just as bad as culturally insensitive messages. Be certain the intended message is the one that is likely to be received.

Source: Chuck Paustian, "Anybody Can Do It," *Marketing News,* 35, issue 7 (March 26, 2001), p. 23.

The Pasta House Co. has successfully reached its local customers with both food products and quality services.
Source: Courtesy of The Pasta House Co.

market, an entrepreneur could study sales of comparable companies, such as TGIFriday's, Applebee's, or the Outback. The Pasta House Co. can estimate the market for its restaurant in a new city by looking at sales of other chain Italian restaurants, such as the Olive Garden. The primary objective is to be certain the market is large enough and viable enough to sustain operations over time.[9]

Locating customers involves finding a road map to them that is cost-effective. Doing so with limited resources is challenging, but can be done. One approach, known as **guerrilla marketing**, focuses efforts on low-cost, creative strategies to reach the right people. The approach was first described by Jay Conrad Levinson following his success in changing the image of Marlboro cigarettes from a woman's product into the now famous "Marlboro Man" approach. Levison argues that guerrilla marketing is designed to obtain instant results with limited resources using tactics that rely on creativity, good relationships, and the willingness to try different approaches.

One recent notable example of guerrilla tactics involved Van's Harley-Davidson franchise in Gloversville, New York. The company advertised a "cat shoot," to be held at the store. Local police, the Humane Society, the mayor, and the Society For Prevention of Cruelty to Animals all inquired, and the event generated front-page stories for three straight days in local papers. The event was actually a three-for-a-dollar (paintball) shoot at a 6-foot high cartoon cat, with proceeds benefitting the local Humane Society. It was a

Sponsoring events such as the Joplin Airfest can be beneficial in locating new customers and building brand name recognition.
Source: Used with permission of the *Joplin Globe,* Joplin, Missouri.

tremendous success in helping customers find their way to the store. While bizarre, the approach used by Van's Harley-Davidson illustrates the concept of guerrilla marketing. The contrast between guerrilla marketing and traditional marketing are summarized in Figure 15.3.[10]

Guerrilla marketing is not so much a method of marketing as a mentality or approach to marketing. It looks at ways of reaching individuals and small groups with a unique message that will cause them to take notice. Most small businesses do not have the money to send a marketing message to millions of potential customers. Consequently, the owner must look for ways to make an impression. Every dollar that is spent on marketing should have a strong potential for locating potential customers. Techniques that can be successful include:

▶ Participation in trade shows
▶ Involvement in sponsorships
▶ Participation in public relations programs
▶ Use of alternative media

Depending on the type of business, *trade shows* can be a major source of locating customers. The key, according to Doug Ducate, president of the Center for Exhibition Industry Research, is to follow up on sales leads created at the show. For example, an exhibitor may offer "show prices," which are discounts given if trade show participants make purchases within 30 days of the exhibit. Also, many exhibitors will have some type of contest or drawing. The goal is to generate names of perspective customers in addition to generating interest in the business and the company's products. Leads obtained at a trade show make an excellent start for a database while also leading to some purchases.[11]

Before participating in a trade show, it is important to define the primary objective. The goals can include generating leads, introducing a new good or service, finalizing deals with prospective customers who will be attending, and generating

▶ Requires money	▶ Requires energy and imagination
▶ Geared to large businesses with big budgets	▶ Geared to small businesses and big dreams
▶ Measure by sales	▶ Measure by profit
▶ Based on experience and guesswork	▶ Based on psychology and human behavior
▶ Increases production and diversity	▶ Grows through existing customers and referrals
▶ Grows by adding customers	▶ Cooperates with other businesses
▶ Obliterates the competition	▶ Aims messages at individuals and small groups
▶ Aims messages at large groups	
▶ Uses marketing to make sales	▶ Uses marketing to gain customer consent
▶ "Me Marketing" which looks at "My" company	▶ "You Marketing" which looks at how can we help "You"

FIGURE 15.3
Traditional vs. Guerilla Marketing

awareness of the company. The objective defines how the trade show booth will be constructed and manned. For example, if the goal is to generate awareness, then the exhibit should include an attention-getting feature. Bright lights, characters in colorful costumes, and music are ways to attract attention. If instead the goal is to generate customer interest in company products, then the products should be displayed in a manner that makes it easy for prospective customers to examine them. Also, the booth should be manned by personnel with expertise and product knowledge.

Sponsorships can be another creative way to locate customers and place the name of the company in the consumer's mind. For a small business, a sponsorship program should be a local event or organization. It is important to make sure the image is consistent with the IMC theme of the sponsoring company. When established carefully, various goals may be reached, such as winning new customers or creating a positive image to attract new employees.[12]

Cost is a concern with sponsorships; however, there are many options. A restaurant or dairy store can sponsor a little league baseball or soccer team at a low cost. A furniture store may develop a relationship with an art gallery without spending significant funds. The primary objective in a sponsorship is to make certain the right people are exposed to the company. The right people are potential customers. It does not make sense to sponsor an event that does not match the firm's target customers. For example, sponsoring an infant beauty contest is not a logical fit for a music store aimed at teenagers.

Public relations programs are often closely tied to sponsorships. They may also be separate. For example, a company that offers an in-house cancer screening for employees may wish to notify the local paper and count on word-of-mouth to send the signal that the firm cares about its workers. Public relations can be heightened when the owner or manager agrees to speak at a public event or writes articles for local newspapers. An article about a new or trendy event in a particular industry and how it affects consumers can be an effective means of getting some free news coverage. For example, a construction company owner may offer some tips about roof safety just before a forecasted major snowstorm. A clothing retailer may offer information about new fashions and how fashion shows in New York and Paris translate into fashions seen on the street in a local community.[13]

A firm must look creatively for ways to garner visibility. Offering promotions during for Valentine's Day, Mother's Day, July fourth, Halloween, and Christmas are not likely to make a new business stand out. Compared to what the big businesses offer, a small business will probably not be noticed, and the money spent on promotions is virtually wasted. Instead, the manager should look for unique opportunities for promotions. For example, Geeks On Call could offer a special promotion during October, which is Computer Learning Month. The company could offer free seminars to senior citizen groups or at a local elementary school. This

This award-winning ad ("Best Use of 4-color" and "Best of Show," Missouri Press Association Award Ceremony) is an excellent method for creating brand awareness of an automobile Web site.
Source: Used with permission of the *Joplin Globe,* Joplin, Missouri.

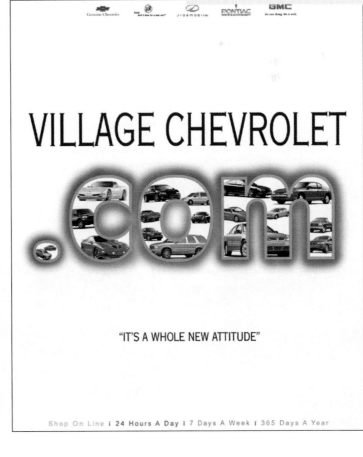

This advertisement by Bob's Furniture Gallery after the September 11 terrorist attacks highlights the company's support of the American Red Cross.
Source: Courtesy of Bob's Furniture Gallery.

would not only generate goodwill in the community but should also provide some free publicity for the firm.[14]

Alternative media are an excellent resource for small businesses. These include company logos on vehicles, ads on mall kiosks, billboards on little league baseball parks and soccer fields, T-shirt or baseball cap giveaways, and any other creative method for reaching potential customers. Many local firms will fax coupons or special deals to targeted customers. Restaurants may use faxes to offer specials to employees of various businesses.

One program that has captured the attention of many small-business owners is called **lifestyle marketing**. Rather than standing on a street corner giving out flyers or placing them on cars in a parking lot, lifestyle marketing means finding grass-roots contact points for potential customers. For example, Flip Records in Los Angeles gives free sample tapes of new music to specialty stores, tattoo shops, and at rock concerts in order to reach young people most likely to make purchases.[15]

Lifestyles that may be reached in this unique way include contacting consumers who attend farmers markets, bluegrass festivals, large citywide garage sales, flea markets, craft shows, stock car races, and other distinct groups that are limited in size but contain large concentrations of potential customers. For example, a fuel additive that makes cars run more smoothly may be marketed at both a drag race or stock car oval with good results. A new fertilizer may sell well at a farmers market. The key is to match the product to the distinct group.

Locating customers must involve both traditional and nontraditional elements. The marketing team cannot simply pursue standard methods, such as advertising, because of clutter and cost problems. Creativity and energy are tremendous assets in the introduction of a new good, service, or company to a local community.

ADVERTISING SMALL BUSINESSES

Advertising a small business is a major challenge for the owner, due to limited funds and lack of clout in the media marketplace. The tasks of advertising management, ad design, and media selection are often complicated because the company may not be able to afford an advertising agency. Even those with budgets large enough to afford an agency

Source: Courtesy of PhotoEdit.

may not have as much money as the business would wish to spend on advertising. At the same time, advertising should not be abandoned. Careful and selective use of advertising funding is the most important issue.

Ad design is critical to getting noticed among national ads that are created with large budgets. While a national advertiser can spend a million dollars creating a 30-second spot, a local advertiser may be able to spend only $500. The challenge is to design an ad that speaks clearly and effectively. Under these circumstances, small businesses are tempted to put too much into the ad, trying to present all of the reasons consumers should purchase from them. This type of ad is too cluttered and overwhelms the viewer.

A small-business manager should develop a creative brief to aid in the development of company advertisements. When business is new, the objective of advertising should be to create awareness. Creating persuasive or reminder ads should wait until there is a higher level of brand or company awareness.

Realizing its brand name was relatively unknown, Southland Cleaning Services of Springdale, Arkansas, decided to tie the company's brand name to other companies that were well known in the area. At a cost of only $400, a 45-second ad was created featuring four local businesses that were Southland's clients. Two included short testimonials from the client, while the other two featured

A billboard advertisement promoting Valley Harley-Davidson as a place for sales, service, and fashions.
Source: Courtesy of DJ Media.

Southland workers cleaning the facility. The ads ran on local television on a rotating schedule. Soon, Southland was getting phone calls from businesses asking "Are you the company that cleans Sears?" They were, because the ad featured Sears in the opening spot. While businesses could not always remember the Southland brand name, they did tie it to Sears and the message clearly came across to the right people, who concluded, "If this company could keep Sears clean, they could keep my business clean."[16]

Once the ad message is defined, various media can be selected. A brief review of advertising media selection follows.

Television ad time is expensive, especially national and prime-time slots. Many small businesses are shut out unless they can utilize the forms designed for them. These include

Cheek Auto Mall has been successful because the company understands its target market and promotes its female ownership as a competitive advantage.
Source: Used with permission of the *Joplin Globe*, Joplin, Missouri.

cooperative ads, where more than one company is featured in the same spot as well as rotate buys from cable providers. When a company buys a set of rotating spots on cable, they are shown at all hours and on a variety of programs. Therefore, it is not possible to target the ad to a specific viewer audience. It may be run on shows that do not reach the target market or at times when members of target market are not watching television. Under these circumstances, some of the advertising money is wasted, but this loss is offset by the low cost. For example, an ad on national television show such as *Friends* will cost as much as $200,000 for 30 seconds. A rotated cable spot may cost as little as $5.00 through a long-term contractual agreement in which the advertiser agrees to purchase a certain number of spots over a period of time, such as one year.

Retailers should explore cooperative advertising opportunities with manufacturers. Many manufacturers have co-op advertising programs that pay a portion of the cost of a local ad if the manufacturer's brand is prominently displayed. This can help the small business in managing the cost of advertising. Also, cooperative advertising with a national brand makes the small retailer more credible to the public.

Radio spots can be prepared at a relatively low cost, especially if a local DJ reads the copy. Listeners tend to build an affinity with radio personalities. This can create credibility when a DJ endorses a local company or brand.

For local companies, radio is an excellent advertising medium because most radio stations have a limited broadcast area and tend to provide local coverage. For small businesses serving other businesses, radio can provide an opportunity to reach business buyers or other members of the buying center while at work or traveling in their vehicles.

Radio stations have a solid knowledge of their station's listening audience. A local business owner can determine which station offers the best match. The cost of radio spots runs higher during prime drive time in the morning and afternoon. For smaller national start-up companies, purchasing national radio advertising time is virtually impossible because there are limited national radio networks other than news and sports.

Most *newspaper* advertising is relatively expensive when compared to local cable television and radio. While there are discounts for buying more space, the cost of a half-page or full-page ad is often prohibitive when compared to local cable TV or radio ads. For retail businesses, however, newspapers are an important advertising medium. This is especially true if a firm's target market consists of baby boomers or older Americans who are the primary readers of newspapers. It is also the best medium for reaching a local geographic area around a retail store.

Newspapers can be used to build brand awareness and to generate store traffic. Offering coupons and specials in newspaper ads can bring customers into a store. Newspaper advertising is more likely to be effective when it is tied to a consumer promotion and the ad encourages action.

Magazines have limited uses for local business advertising because it is expensive. Magazine ads can be used by national start-up or entrepreneurial ventures. Some magazines do offer regional editions that allow a business to advertise in a particular area. Also, if a business sells products over the Internet, magazine advertising can be used if the magazine readership matches the target market of the business and more importantly, if the target market is willing to purchase the product over the Internet. In that situation the company must select highly targeted specialty magazines.

The newspaper is an ideal medium for both local consumer and business markets.
Source: Used with permission of the *Joplin Globe*, Joplin, Missouri.

Billboard advertising features low CPM with long-term exposure. For local businesses, billboards are an excellent method of building brand awareness of the firm as well as informing local consumers where the business is located. Billboard space should be purchased along routes where potential customers live, work, and commute. Ads on vehicles such as buses, cabs, or in subways can reach a great deal of potential patrons. Many small businesses are able to make package buys on billboards that are rotated throughout a city. Advertisements placed on the store itself may be effective if the business is located on a major road.

For some small and start-up businesses, *Internet* ads may be effective. A local company can often purchase ads on the community's Chamber of Commerce site or city's Web site. If ads cannot be purchased, having the firm's name on the site or linked to the site is important. For example, a new restaurant should make sure it is mentioned by the local visitor's bureau and Chamber of Commerce materials. Providing a link to the restaurant's Web site is even better because it allows locals as well as visitors or tourists to access the company directly. Another option is a reciprocal arrangement with another business. For example, a local pet store may offer to list local veterinarians on its Web site in exchange for the veterinarians listing the pet store on theirs.

The Internet can be a very powerful tool to provide information for prospective customers that cannot be placed in an advertisement. On the Web site, a firm can place information about the business, its products and services, guarantees, current customers or clients, and special offers as well as prices. Television, radio, newspaper, magazine, and billboard ads all can identify the firm's Web site and encourage consumers and businesses to access it. If done properly, the Internet can be a beneficial form of advertising once consumers have been directed to it by some other form of advertising.

INTEGRATED LEARNING EXPERIENCE

Guerilla Marketing Online is a resource for online marketing using the concepts of guerilla marketing. Access the Web site at **www.gmarketing.com**. Examine the resources available and the search engines provided on the Web site. How might this Web site be useful to a small business owner?

The company considering local advertising must consider the "bang for the buck" criterion. Dollars must be spent judiciously. Also, low-quality ads may injure the reputation of the company. It is better to spend more money on developing a quality ad and less on the media reach of the ad than to create a poor advertisement that is the brunt of local jokes. Small and start-up companies must advertise, even though it is often a major challenge for the entrepreneur or business owner.

Helping Customers Reach the Company

The other side of a communications channel is the venues by which consumers can contact the new business. These include:

- Traditional methods
- Networking
- Lifestyle marketing
- Web sites

Traditional methods of helping customers reach the company include the firm's telephone service, mail, and in-store visits. Having a phone number that spells a word, such as 231-AUTO, or 555-SHOP will help the customer remember the number. Some firms ask for sequences of numbers, such as 885-1234 to assist in recall. Mail and e-mail to the business should be opened and answered quickly, in order to maintain the perception of service quality.[17] Phone numbers, Internet addresses, and mail addresses should be prominently featured in all marketing communications when a new business opens. Customers must know how to reach and find the company in order to make purchases. When a customer visits a retail store, it is vitally important to maintain the same prompt, courteous, and sincere service.

Networking begins with something as simple as attending a Chamber of Commerce, Lions Club, or some other local civic group meeting with a handfull of business cards. It is important to develop contacts and relationships with other local businesspeople, city officials, and other key citizens in the community. One method of strengthening these bonds is to become involved in committees and projects.

Networking provides the opportunity to meet other businesspeople, create leads, and personally promote a new company. Networking also offers an avenue for feedback from customers as well as other businesspeople. Relationships can be formed in many ways. A business owner's doctor, lawyer, butcher, dry cleaner, family, and friends should all be made aware of the new operation. They can pass along referrals and positive word-of-mouth.[18] When making new contacts, the business owner should exhibit tact and diplomacy. Seeming pushy is a negative in these kinds of relationships.[19]

Quality networks offer the possibilities of word-of-mouth endorsements and referrals. They can lead to not only more customers but also quality employees. Business-to-business sales of anything from flowers, to food, to computer repair and consulting services can greatly increase company revenues.

Lifestyle marketing is a guerilla marketing technique that is an excellent method of reaching customers and also represents a major opportunity to hear back from them. A booth at a special event such as local street fair offers the chance to visit firsthand with potential customers along with those who have done business with the company. Suggestions concerning product modifications as well as methods of delivering those items may come from direct users.

The "Buy One Pair and Get Two Pair Free" promotion is an excellent method of reducing purchase risk for new customers.
Source: Used with permission of the *Joplin Globe*, Joplin, Missouri.

Businesses that use the Internet or are involved in e-commerce should select a *Web site* address that is easy to remember and related to the business. For instance, The Pasta House Co. has the Web site address **www.pastahouse.com**. The goal is to make it easy for customers to find and communicate with the company. A quality Web site is easy to navigate and provides pertinent information. It should be an easy method for making purchases. An e-mail feedback option is vital. It is important to monitor e-mails and respond to them quickly.

Reducing Purchase Risk

Even after potential customers know about the company, there is still the issue of moving them to buy. Purchasing from someone new normally creates a higher level of perceived risk. In some cases, such as a new restaurant, the risk is relatively low. One bad meal is pretty easily dismissed. At times, however, utilizing a new vendor is a major investment of time, energy, and money. The marketing plan must be adjusted to the degree of perceived risk. Typical enticements designed to entice the first purchase include:

- Samples
- Coupons
- Price discounts
- Referral discounts (for gaining a new customer)
- Free first consultation visits
- Money-back guarantees

Each must be structured to fit the price/quality relationship. Thus, an attorney opening a practice would not use coupons. Money-back guarantees work well with new services, such as hair care. The goal is to ease the worry that a purchase is somehow a gamble.

Once the initial purchase has been made, the focus shifts to return business. Small business owners and especially new businesses spend considerable time, money, and effort in attracting and finding customers. To hold down future costs, the goal must be to keep those who have visited the location. Return business is vital to the long-term well-being of almost all small businesses.

MAKING CUSTOMERS ADVOCATES

A solid customer base is the difference between success and failure of a new business. It simply costs too much money and takes too much time to keep enticing new customers if old ones fall away. Once a customer base has been established, the goal is then to turn them into advocates for the business. An **advocate** is a customer who is loyal to the business and draws others through positive communications. Several methods can be used to keep customers and turn them into advocates. A discussion of these techniques follows.

Database Management

A crucial feature of a new or small business is the development and maintenance of a database. Unfortunately, many small businesses and start-up ventures neglect this important component of the IMC plan. It is the quickest and most cost-effective method of keeping customers and turning them into advocates.

Developing a database does not have to be difficult and does not require a high level of expertise. For a small retail operation, owners will discover that there are many idle hours while the store is open. Employees can use this time to help create a database. This can be accomplished by collecting business cards for drawings, pulling names and addresses from the tops of personal checks written for purchases, soliciting information at the time of a purchase, or buying lists from credit card companies. The goal should be made to try to enter every person who makes a purchase into the database. Once the customer is entered in the database, every purchase that customer makes should also be recorded. Developing a history of each customer is a valuable asset in marketing one-to-one.

An old rule of thumb in business is that 80 percent of the business comes from 20 percent of the customers. Company personnel need to know who those 20 percent are, by name. These individuals should be notified of special discounts and sales, the arrival of new merchandise, or when a new service is being offered. For example, a hair salon may run a one-week discount on perms. Longstanding customers should know about the special through some type of personal contact so they can take advantage of it. The small business database is an invaluable resource for helping keep tabs on customers, purchasing patterns, and for making contacts.

Direct Marketing

One of the major benefits of a database is the ability to use direct marketing, which can be in the form of mail, e-mail, telephone, or personal contacts. Most small businesses think of only direct-mail, but the customer base should be examined carefully. A telephone call, a fax, or an e-mail may be a more effective way of contacting the customer.

According to the Direct Marketing Association, the average dollar spent on direct-mail brought in $10 in sales.[20] When carried out correctly, direct mail is an effective method to increase revenues and build relationships with customers. Patrick Dineen suggests the following steps when creating a direct marketing program:

1. Define the goals of the program and make sure those goals are more than simply generating sales.
2. Define the audience. A solid database helps this process.
3. Target the prospective customers to be contacted. Once again, a database is crucial to providing relevant information about customer characteristics.
4. Produce the art and copy. Make it simple, direct, and professional.
5. Print and mail the package.
6. Track responses for the future.

There is some debate as to whether or not a follow-up phone call is advisable. Dineen believes it will generate additional sales. Others disagree, believing calls about mailings are viewed as a nuisance.[21] Keep in mind that while Dineen made these suggestions for direct-mail campaigns, the same principles would apply to e-mail, telephone, or fax campaigns.

Personal Selling

The "personal touch" remains as an integral part of keeping customers, regardless of the size of the company. In the case of a small business, it is absolutely vital. Knowing the names of customers, their preferences, and other key information makes a sales call or visit to a retail operation a much more positive experience.

Employees who are trained to recall names and go the extra mile in delivering service, and who exhibit positive manners on the phone as well as in person are a major asset to a small business. Uncaring and unprepared salespeople and service personnel may cost the company business it simply cannot afford to lose.

Trade and Consumer Promotions

Customers of small businesses need to know they are appreciated. To strengthen relationships with customers, company marketing leaders must be creative in the use of consumer

Romantic Delights offers a "free gift" with a purchase as a means of generating store traffic.

Source: Used with permission of the *Joplin Globe*, Joplin, Missouri.

and trade promotions, because marketing dollars are so limited. Specialty advertising is often helpful in trade promotions. Calendars, pens, cups, and other items help remind the customer of the small business. As the company grows, it will logically expand into other types of trade promotions such as discounts.

Consumer promotions should go beyond coupons. Creative use of premiums, contests or sweepstakes, samples, refunds, and rebates should be developed whenever possible. When created effectively, contests and sweepstakes help the company build a database. Contestants should be asked to provide names and addresses in order to enter. A store owner may find it extremely helpful to deliver samples beyond the store. For instance, a small-town chocolate company that provides samples to other businesses and residences may expect increased traffic in return.

There are several things to remember when developing trade and consumer promotions. First, they should be cost-effective. Second, goals should be stated for the program (awareness, image, sales, etc.). Third, these promotions should reflect the position, image, and theme of the company.

SUMMARY

Entrepreneurship means a company is being formed with the express goal of becoming larger through an aggressive growth agenda. Intrepreneurship is a corporate spin-off or start-up. A small business is a family-owned company or consortium of professionals formed with specific objectives in mind. In most cases, aggressive growth is not as important as providing adequate income for the owners.

Typical challenges to new businesses include the problem that consumers are not aware of the business. They are often cautious or wary of trying a new product, service, or company. Also, advertising and promotional clutter make it difficult to be recognized, and small budgets for marketing, advertising, and promotional activities make it difficult to compete. New businesses are especially vulnerable to negative word-of-mouth communications.

Starting a company consists of three intertwined activities: (1) understanding and defining consumer needs, (2) establishing a clearly defined product or service, and (3) developing a unique market niche. When finding customers, it is crucial to employ methods of research to locate interested clients, make it easy for consumers to reach the company, and reduce purchasing risk to whatever degree is possible.

Guerrilla marketing is a focus on low-cost, creative marketing strategies to reach the right people. Other methods include trade show participation, involvement in sponsorships, participation in public relations programs, and the use of alternative media. Lifestyle marketing is an alternative program designed to find grass-roots contact points for potential customers.

Advertising a small or start-up business includes all standard media; however, limited budgets means the dollars must be spent carefully. When attempting to reach customers, traditional methods of phone, mail, and in-store visits must be accompanied by networking, lifestyle marketing, and use of a Web site and e-mail.

Purchase risk can be reduced by using samples, coupons, price discounts, referral discounts, free first consultation visits, money-back guarantees, and other methods. The goal is to turn customers into advocates who are loyal to the business and draw others through positive comments.

Turning customers into advocates includes use of database management programs, direct-marketing tactics, quality personal selling, and effective trade and consumer promotions. All of the elements of an IMC program should be used in a small business setting; only the emphasis changes. Creativity, energy, quality, reputation, specialization, community outreach, and a visionary owner are the major assets in creating a successful new business operation.

REVIEW QUESTIONS

1. Describe the differences between entrepreneurship, intrepreneurship, and a small business.

2. What are the major challenges to new businesses? What is the difference between a product benefit and a product feature?

3. What are the three components of a market analysis?

4. When defining a product, why is it important to say what a company *won't* do as much as what it *will*?

5. What is a unique selling position? Why is a USP so crucial to a new business?

6. What is guerrilla marketing? How is it different from traditional marketing?

7. Discuss the role trade shows, sponsorships, public relations programs, and alternative media play in locating customers.

8. What is lifestyle marketing? Name some local events or activities that could be used in lifestyle marketing programs.

9. Describe the use of television in advertising a small business.

10. How can radio be used effectively in advertising a small business?

11. What types of customers are best targeted with newspaper advertising in a small business setting? What do newspapers offer that other media cannot?

12. Describe the limitations and uses of magazine advertising for small businesses.

13. What are the advantages of billboard advertising for small businesses?

14. How can Internet advertising enhance a small-business IMC program?

15. How can a small-business owner maintain two-way communication with customers?

16. Describe the tactics small businesses can use to reduce purchasing risk.

17. What is an advocate? How can small businesses turn customers into advocates?

KEY TERMS

entrepreneurship the organization and operation of a business venture.

intrepreneurship a corporate spin-off or start-up.

small business a family-owned company or consortium of professionals which is formed with the primary objective of providing adequate income for the owners.

unique selling position (USP) a feature that allows a newly formed company to stand alone and be distinct from all other competitors.

guerrilla marketing a focus on low-cost, creative marketing strategies to reach a firm's target market.

lifestyle marketing finding grass-roots contact points for potential customers.

advocate a customer who is loyal to the business and draws others through positive communications.

CRITICAL THINKING EXERCISES

1. Identify a small business in your area. Talk to the owner of the business about how he or she markets the business. Compare your findings with those of your classmates. Are there any underlying themes?

2. Look at five advertisements in your local newspaper for small, local businesses. What consumer or business need are they attempting to meet? Does the advertisement do a good job of presenting the company's expertise?

3. In a group of three to five students, discuss needs or wants you have that are not being met adequately by a local business. Choose one need that stands out among you. Describe the unique market niche that a start-up business could develop to meet that need. Is the market large enough to support a business? How could other consumers with the same need be reached?

4. Pick one of the following types of businesses listed below. Conduct an informal market analysis to determine if there is a sufficient market for a new business. Who would be the firm's primary competitors? What unique selling proposition could they use to differentiate themselves from the competitor?

   a. Dry cleaners

   b. Tanning salon

   c. Laundromat

   d. Car wash

   e. Lawn service

5. Pick one of the services listed in Question 4. Discuss guerilla marketing techniques that a new start-up business could use to locate customers.

6. Pick one of the services listed in Question 4. Discuss an advertising approach that would allow the small business to get the most "bang for its buck."

7. Pick one of the services listed in Question 4. Discuss ways the small business could turn their customers into advocates for the firm.

8. Access one of the following Web sites. Discuss what types of information is available and how a new business could use the Web site.

   a. Yahoo! Small Business (www.smallbusiness.yahoo.com)

   b. Business Week Online (Small Business) (www.businessweek.com/smallbiz/)

   c. Small and Home-Based Business Links (www.bizoffice.com)

CASE 1

FRED AND RED'S IMPORT MEATS

Fred and Johnny "Red" Johnson encountered a troublesome discovery just as their new business was about to take off. The Christmas season was about to begin, and it was supposed to be the largest season for sales in their newly opened company.

The two young entrepreneurs (Fred was 25, Red was 31) had been grocery store employees for several years, working for a major grocer in Minneapolis. During their breaks, the two men had long talks with various department managers. These coworkers revealed an exciting piece of information: Import meats have the luxury of generous markups, because many customers are willing to pay premium prices for exotic foods or tastes from their homelands.

After preparing a business plan, applying for a small-business loan, and finding a location convenient for shipping and receiving, the two entrepreneurs agree to the name "Fred and Red's Import Meats," even though they would sell more than just meat products. Still, the primary product was imported meat from all over the world. The store was small but well lit and clean.

To build sales, the company was expanded to include catalog sales and Internet-based orders. The location in Minneapolis meant many customers were of Scandinavian descent. One of the best-selling items was meat from Finland. Fred and Red established a strong relationship with Bjorkland meats and even met their counterparts on a business junket to Finland. Both companies were highly satisfied with the relationship.

While examining news from foreign Web sites, Red came across a controversy. He read that Finnish people prefer to buy Finnish foods, especially meat, because of strong concerns about how animals have been fed and how they are transported. Finnish people worry about the animal's living conditions and, most importantly, controls for animal diseases. Mad cow disease in England had spiked interest in this issue.

A consumer group had discovered that the country-of-origin laws in Finland allow local supermarkets to place the Finnish country-of-origin label on any meat that had been sliced, marinated, or in any way processed in the store, even if the meat came from another country. Although the practice was not illegal, it would be considered unethical if the intent of the label were to mislead the customer into believing the meat was of Finnish origin.

Bjorkland foods regularly marinated, spiral sliced, and repackaged meats for delivery to Fred and Red's store. The Johnsons worried that they might have violated truth-in-packaging and advertising laws by selling meats represented as being Finnish, when the only thing Finnish about them was where they were cut, packaged, and shipped.

More importantly, the Johnsons worried about customer reactions if they found out about the real nature of the meat. A young, struggling business cannot afford bad publicity, they concluded. Still, Fred and Red didn't like the idea of accusing their friends, the Bjorklands, of unethical behaviors, because no law had been violated.

Fred considered contacting the Federal Trade Commission, but Red talked him out of the idea, stating there was no point in "inviting trouble." They also considered printing a disclaimer in their catalog ads and on the Web site, noting what the Finnish law said and what it means about their products.

With the Christmas season coming and the company desperately needing revenues, the Johnsons knew they had a problem.

1. What are the primary small-business issues in this case? What is the IMC dilemma?
2. Are there any ethical issues to resolve in this case?
3. What should Fred and Red do?

CASE 2

BONUS PLAN OR MAJOR PAIN?

The grocery store business is rapid moving and risky. Customer preferences can evolve slowly or develop quickly. Hot new items can capture the fancy of some customers, while others remain staunchly devoted to old "standbys." The entry of Wal-Mart into the grocery business has also changed the dynamics of the industry. Smaller stores find they must create and dominate a niche if they want to remain in business.

In each major city, one or more grocery chains continually battle to retain a base group of loyal customers while enticing others to at least occasionally visit the store. Heavy promotion of loss-leader pricing has been the standard in the industry for many years. At the same time, various chains and local stores have tried other gimmicks to keep and build a share of the market.

Bobby's Market was associated with an independent grocer chain. Bobby Mulvaney inherited the store from his father, Bobby Senior, 20 years ago. Bobby had watched as stores opened and closed, and fretted as Wal-Mart's Supercenter, located on the edge of town, began taking away business from his store and others in the area.

The grocer chain associated with Bobby's Market was wary of magnet-card, VIP programs that several groups had tried. These programs, which provided a great deal of data about individual customers and their purchases, seemed to create a kind of "backlash" effect. Those who didn't have the cards wondered why they couldn't receive the more favorable discounts given to VIP cardholders, and those holding the cards soon were bombarded with extra promotions besides the regular weekly ads placed in the newspaper and on television. Consequently, this chain decided not to become involved in any kind of VIP card promotion.

Instead, Bobby was sent a series of materials for a "Bonus Buy" club promotion. Each customer was given a punch card that contained a series of dollar amounts. As the individual bought items from the store, the value of the total purchase was hand-punched into the card. A fully punched card was an entry into a contest, where the prizes ranged from $1 to a $1,000 grand prize, given out each week. To make the process more enticing, various items throughout the store were marked as "Bonus Buy" items, and dollar values on the punch card were increased by $1, $5, or $10, depending on the item. Thus, a package of T-bone steaks was marked with a $10 bonus punch, so the customer received the value of the total purchase plus $10 for that trip to the store, meaning the person was going to gain more entries into the contest for frequently shopping at Bobby's Market: The person gained an even greater advantage if he or she were willing to buy larger numbers of bonus buy items.

(continued)

One main feature of the contest was that cashiers would give punch cards to every shopper, unless the individual said he or she did not want one. A person who forgot his or her card was allowed to "combine" punches from a series of cards to gain an entry in the sweepstakes. Therefore, even absent-minded customers could still win.

Two negatives were associated with this program. First, the company could not collect any data from those who did not participate. The punch cards did not require the customer to disclose anything until an entry was redeemed. Then, the individual was asked to add his or her address and phone number to the punch card. Still, this meant many people did not provide information, and their actual purchases could not be tracked. Only increases in sales of bonus buy items could be studied.

Second, punching each individual card dramatically slowed the checkout times for all shoppers. Those who didn't want to mess with the contest became increasingly annoyed as cards were being punched and cash prizes were given by cashiers, who weren't ringing up items or sacking groceries while they took care of contest details. Even contest participants shopping at peak hours noticed the lines were longer and checkout times were rising.

As the contest wound down, Bobby wondered if it had been a good idea. He tried to figure out ways to discover if he should try the Bonus Buy plan again in six months. The grocery chain liked the program, because the marketing team could offer bonus buy points for overstocked items. Yet Bobby needed to know how all of his customers were reacting.

1. From a small-business perspective, which is more important, knowing more about customers or making some of those customers unhappy?

2. Are there any guerrilla marketing tactics Bobby could use to build the business?

3. What are the goals associated with the Bonus Buy promotion? Are these goals compatible with those of a small independent grocer trying to compete with Wal-Mart and other larger chains?

4. What type of message theme would work best for Bobby's Market? How can he get that message out to the right people?

ENDNOTES

1. Carolyn Walkup, "Pasta House Co. Signs Licensees to First Foreign-Expansion Pacts," *Nation's Restaurant News,* 34, issue 20 (May 15, 2000), p. 8; Bret Thorn, "The Pasta House," *Nation's Restaurant News,* 36, issue 4 (January 28, 2002), p. 152–54.

2. Arthur A. Thompson, Jr. and A. J. Strickland III, *Strategic Management: Concepts and Cases* (New York: Mc-Graw-Hill/Irwin), 2002, twelfth edition.

3. Meir Liraz, "Ten Marketing Mistakes Small Businesses Make," *Air Conditioning, Heating, & Refrigeration News,* 214, issue 9 (October 29, 2001), p. 24.

4. Debra Williams, "How To Turn Your Hobby Into A Business," *Air Force Times,* 62, issue 42 (May 13, 2002), pp. 2–3.

5. Toddi Gutner, "A Dot-Com's Survival Story," *Business Week,* Issue 3782 (May 13, 2002), p. 122.

6. Lee Zion, "Fairy Dogmother Service Carries on a Favorite Tradition," *San Diego Business Journal,* 22, issue 2 (January 8, 2001), p. 32.

7. Karen E. Klein, "Find Your Niche—and Stick With It," *Business Week Online* (March 22, 2002), p. N.PAG.

8. Jack Fanders, "Marketing on a Shoestring Requires Energy, Logic," *Business Press,* 10, issue 25 (October 1997), pp. 34–35.

9. Bo Burlingham, "Where Are The Customers?" *Inc.,* 24, issue 5 (May 2002), p. 110.

10. Shari Caudron, "Guerilla Tactics," *Industry Week,* 250, issue 10 (July 16, 2001), p. 52.

11. Bob Lamons, "Trade Shows Still a Good Bet for Small Firms," *Marketing News,* 36, issue 7 (April 1, 2002), p. 10.

12. Jenny Hirschkorn and Richard Cree, "The Perfect Match," *Director,* 55, issue 8 (March, 2002), p. 19.

13. Lisa Schalon, "Marketing Programs That Make Every Dollar Count," *San Diego Business Journal,* 22, issue 18 (April 30, 2001), p. 19.

14. Risa B. Hoag, "Tips to Increase Visibility for Any Size Business," *Westchester County Business Journal,* 36, issue 39 (September 29, 1997), pp. 15–16.

15. Jane Applegate, "Succeeding in Small Business," *Enterprise: Salt Lake City,* 30, issue 5 (August 7, 2000), p. 11.

16. Interview with Kenneth E. Clow, President of Southland Cleaning Services (June 8, 2002).

17. Kenneth E. Clow, Donald Baack, and Jerry D. Rogers, "The Impact of Effective Service Recovery Procedures on Satisfaction with City Services and Citizen Complaints About City Services, *Proceedings,* American Marketing Association Summer Educator's Conference, Washington, D.C., 2001, p. 54.

18. Karen E. Klein, "Want New Customers? Go Guerrilla," *Business Week Online* (April 29, 2002), p.N. PAG.

19. Alf Nucifora, "Networking Groups Still Best Source of Leads," *Fort Worth Business Press,* 13, issue 37 (January 5, 2001), p. 7.

20. Patrick Dineen, "Improving Direct Mail Prospecting," *Franchising World,* 33, issue 7, (October, 2001), p. 42.

21. John R. Graham, "Marketing and Sales Strategy: Ten Ways to Push Your Company Forward—By Doing It Backwards," *American Salesman,* 46, issue 11 (November, 2001), p. 6.

Evaluating an Integrated Marketing Program

Chapter Objectives

Recognize the various levels at which IMC programs should be assessed, from the successes of individual ads and coupon campaigns to long-term survival and growth of the company.

Develop both evaluations of messages and measures of behavioral responses when marketing tools are used.

Assess the quality of public relations efforts in conjunction with studies of other marketing programs.

Develop a series of short- and long-term goals that are linked to the company's voice and theme.

PRETESTING FOR EFFECTIVENESS:

The New High-Tech World of Advertising Design

For many years, management and marketing specialists have known that the easiest way to fix many problems is to prevent them from occurring in the first place. The "rocket" analogy usually follows. If a rocket is off course in the first few minutes of the ride, it will drift much farther off course as the trip proceeds. A correction right away puts the rocket back on track, and the ride goes much more smoothly.

The same is true in advertising design. If the ad is off course at the beginning, the company spends additional funding to develop a campaign that is doomed from the start. One new approach to making ads more effective is to send them through a series of pretests before the campaign begins. A company known as Decision Analyst is one of the leading international marketing firms in the world of advertising testing.

One program the company uses is based on Internet research. It is called CopyScreen™. To test an ad, a sample is drawn using 200 to 300 target audience consumers who are identified by the Internet. The subjects are shown preliminary versions of print ads and asked for opinions in four areas: (1) attention value, (2) Internet value, (3) purchase propensity, and (4) brand recognition. The responses are given mathematical scores, and a total is generated for the test ad. Those who go beyond a threshold score are deemed worthy of further development.

The ads moving on to the next stage may be tested through a program called CopyCheck®. This program provides more specific feedback concerning the ad's probable effectiveness. Questions CopyCheck attempts to answer include:

1. Will the ad capture the viewer's attention?
2. Will the brand name be noticed and remembered?

3. Does the ad increase the consumer's interest in buying the brand?

4. Does the ad trigger the intent to purchase?

5. How memorable is the brand name?

6. What are the key ideas in the ad?

7. What is missing from the ad (things viewers would like to know)?

8. What did viewers like about the commercial?

9. What did viewers not like about the commercial?

10. How could the commercial be improved?

The Decision Analyst company provides ad feedback in about a week after an advertiser purchases the CopyCheck program. This type of program gives the company preparing the ad two major advantages. First, money is not wasted on ineffective ads. Second, the final ads have a much greater chance of inducing the desired response.

The same company provides feedback regarding the potential for effectiveness of a completed ad as well as tests of recall for ads that have run. Even a rocket that is "in orbit" occasionally needs to have its course adjusted.

The use of computers, the Internet, and more sophisticated research techniques have made it possible for many companies to spend their advertising dollars more wisely. In a world where marketing departments and advertising account managers are being asked to produce tangible results, the use of these types of programs is likely to continue to rise.[1]

KAOLIN CALEFACTORS

An evaluation program for an IMC plan is an ending point and a starting point. It ends the presentation of a campaign or year of sales with the goal of seeing if various IMC objectives have been reached. It is the beginning point for the new season, year, or campaign. Evaluations should be made for brand loyalty, position, image, and all other factors related to the firm's well-being.

In the Kaolin Calefactors plan on the IMC Plan Pro disk, the overall evaluation process is described in section 3.7. The company's marketing team is interested in brand awareness and company image along with the effectiveness of consumer programs, database programs, trade promotions, and personal selling. These evaluations take place on a year-round basis. They will allow the marketing team at Kaolin to discover how each component of the overall IMC plan is faring in the market. Evaluations of individual objectives are also described in sections 5.4, 6.4, and 7.4 of the plan. Each element is assigned to a group or agency for assessment. This should provide invaluable information as Kaolin moves into the future.

o v e r v i e w

John Wanamaker, a well-known nineteenth-century department store owner, was one of the first to use advertising to attract customers to his store. He once remarked, "I know half the money I spend on advertising is wasted, but I can never find out which half." It is difficult to evaluate advertising effectiveness.

Millions of dollars are spent each year on marketing communications programs. Consequently, it is very important for each company to attempt to evaluate these efforts. To spend a major amount on a marketing campaign without trying to find out if it had positive impact does not make sense. The problem, however, as pointed out by John Wanamaker, is figuring out how to evaluate the effectiveness of a marketing communications plan.

This final chapter is devoted to the various methods available for evaluating components of an IMC program. At the most general level, two broad categories of evaluation tools can be used to evaluate IMC systems:

▶ Message evaluations
▶ Evaluating respondent behaviors

An overview of these two broad categories of evaluation programs is presented in this chapter.

Message Evaluations

Message evaluation techniques are used to examine the creative message and the physical design of the advertisement, coupon, or direct-marketing piece. Message evaluation procedures include the study of actors in advertisements as well as the individuals who speak in radio ads. A message evaluation program is designed to consider both the cognitive components associated with an ad (recall, recognition, etc.) as well as the peripheral cues (emotions, attitudes). In Chapter 3, cognitive and peripheral cues were explained in detail.

Evaluating Respondent Behaviors

The second category, evaluating **respondent behaviors techniques**, addresses visible customer actions including making store visits, inquiries, or actual purchases. This category contains evaluation techniques that are measured using numbers.

In today's IMC marketplace, many advertising companies are being asked to deliver compelling proof that the ads they design actually work. Respondent behaviors provide such evidence. Changes in sales, coupons redeemed, increases in store traffic, and other numbers-based outcomes appeal to many managers. Consequently, both forms of evaluation help the marketing manager try to build short-term results and long-range success.

MATCHING METHODS WITH IMC OBJECTIVES

When methods of evaluation are being chosen, they should match the objectives being measured. For example, if the objective of an advertising campaign is to increase customer interest in and recall of a brand, then the level of customer awareness should be measured. Normally this means the marketing team measures awareness before and after the ads are run. This procedure is commonly known as *pre-* and *posttest* analysis. At other times objectives vary. For instance, redemption rates measure the success of a campaign featuring coupons, so the behavior (purchasing) rather than the cognitive process (recall) is being tested. Redemption rates can be studied to discover how many items were purchased both with and without coupons.

Several levels of analysis should be identified when evaluating an advertising program. They include the following factors:

- Short-term outcomes (sales, redemption rates)
- Long-term results (brand awareness, brand loyalty or equity)
- Product-specific awareness
- Awareness of the overall company
- Affective responses (liking the company and a positive brand image)

It is important to remember that many marketers can fall in love with only the first factor, short-term outcomes, without considering the long-term impact of a campaign. The company must maintain a voice that carries across campaigns over time. For example, consider the "I love you man" Budweiser ads of the late 1990s. The short-term success was indeed attractive because so many people thought it was funny. Over the years Anheuser-Busch has built a strong voice using humor to sell products, from the Budweiser frogs and lizards to the "Whazzup" team and the subsequent "True" campaign.

In light of these overall goals, then, the marketing manager can consider the various options for evaluating the advertising program. Often it is necessary to think about the evaluation procedure prior to launching a particular campaign. An ad placed in a trade journal may contain a code number, a special telephone number, or a special Internet site that can be used to track responses to a particular campaign. For coupons, premiums, and other sales promotions, code numbers are printed on each item to identify where it came from.

When assessing the effectiveness of an ad, even something as simple as the date or time the advertisement appeared is important. For example, an Internet banner ad campaign should be reviewed by keeping a record of inquiries or hits associated with the banner. In the same way, the dates a magazine reaches the newsstands and when subscribers receive copies are important items used in evaluating magazine ads.

In general, careful planning prior to initiating an advertising program makes evaluation of the campaign easier and more accurate. At the same time, the evaluation of a specific advertisement is difficult, because many factors affect the outcome being measured.

For instance, a retailer may run a series of newspaper and radio ads to boost store traffic. In order to measure the impact of the ads, the retailer keeps records of store traffic before, during, and after the ad campaign. Unfortunately, the traffic count may be affected by other factors, even something as simple as the weather. If it rains for two

One measure of effectiveness of this advertisement is the increase in the number of phone calls to schedule a Cool Touch consultation.

Source: Used with permission of the *Joplin Globe*, Joplin, Missouri.

days, the traffic count will probably be lower. Further, the store's chief competitor may be running a special sale during the same time period. This would also affect traffic. A TV program, such as the season finale of a major series, or even a special program (commencement, school play) at the local high school could have an impact. In other words, many extraneous factors have an effect on results. Thus, in reviewing an advertising program, it is important to keep these external factors in mind.

More importantly, perhaps, is that one specific analysis does not assess the influence the ad may have had on the larger company image. For example, even though store traffic was low, the ad may have been recalled and stored in the buyer's long-term memory. At some future point, this may make a difference. Conversely, the same ad may have been awkward or in some way offensive, and the store owner may believe the weather affected the outcome instead of a poor advertising design. Consequently, company leaders must be reminded to consider both short-term consequences and long-term implications when they assess overall IMC programs.

MESSAGE EVALUATIONS

Evaluation or testing of advertising communications can occur at any stage of the development process. They can be analyzed at the concept stage before an ad is ever produced. This testing normally involves soliciting the opinions of either a series of experts or from "regular" people. The ad can be tested after the design stage has been completed but prior to development. For example, a television ad may be produced using a story board. A **story board** is a series of still photographs or sketches that outlines the structure of a television ad. After the television commercial is produced, then experimental tests can be used to evaluate the ad. At that point, a group of consumers can be invited to watch the ad in a theater-type setting. When this is done, the test ad is placed in a group of ads to disguise it. Viewers are then asked to evaluate all of the ads (including the test ad) to see if it had the desired effect.

Before launching the campaign, the agency may show the ad in a test market area. Several tools can then be used to measure the quality and impact of the ad. These instruments will be presented in detail later in this chapter. The final stage of evaluation takes place after the marketing communication has been used. Information collected at this time helps the company's leaders and the advertising agency to assess what worked and what did not. These findings are then used in the development of future marketing campaigns.

Companies have several methods to investigate the message content of an advertisement or marketing communication piece. These methods are listed in Figure 16.1. While most of the methods deal with the verbal or written components of the communication piece, peripheral cues are also important and should be part of the message evaluation.

The best method to use in a message evaluation scheme depends on the objective of the communication plan. Most companies prefer to use more than one method to make sure the findings are as accurate as possible. Therefore, while each evaluation tool is dis-

> ▶ **Concept testing**
> ▶ **Copytesting**
> ▶ **Recall tests**
> ▶ **Recognition tests**
> ▶ **Attitude and opinion tests**
> ▶ **Emotional reaction tests**
> ▶ **Physiological arousal tests**
> ▶ **Persuasion analysis**

FIGURE 16.1
Message Evaluation Techniques

cussed separately in this section of the text, in reality multiple measures of evaluation are often used. Also, as mentioned earlier, pre- and posttests normally are used for the purposes of making comparisons before and after a series of ads has run.

Concept Testing

Concept testing is aimed at the actual content of the ad and the impact that content has on potential customers. Many advertising agencies conduct concept tests before spending money to develop an advertisement or promotional piece. A television ad may cost thousands of dollars to produce. Consequently, it is more cost effective to test a concept at the early stages of an ad's development rather than after the actual commercial is taped. Also, if changes must be made, it is less costly to complete them during the planning stage rather than after the marketing piece has already been created. More importantly, once the marketing communication item is finished, creatives and others who worked on the piece tend to take ownership and become more resistant to making changes.

The most common procedure used for concept testing is a focus group. *Focus groups* normally consist of eight to 10 people who are representative of the target market. These individuals are paid in cash or are given financial incentives such as gift certificates to entice them to participate. In most cases, it is wise to use independent marketing research firms to conduct focus groups. The goal is to prevent biased results. An independent company is more likely to report that a certain advertising approach did not work than is someone who developed the approach and has a vested interest in it.

The number of focus groups used to study an issue varies greatly. It can be as many as 50 or as few as one. Focus group reactions can be quite different. Results are affected by the makeup of the group and the way the session is conducted. As a result, it is risky to base a decision on just one focus group's final opinion. For example, a humorous ad may have a great deal of appeal to one group, yet another might not think the ad is funny or might even find it offensive. Therefore, it is a good idea to study the responses of several groups to see the impact of the humor on a series of individuals. Even trained focus group leaders experience varying results due to the composition of the group, the questions the group is asked to answer, and the degree of formality used in conducting a session. Also, one person's opinions may strongly influence the rest of the group. Therefore, most agencies use more than one group in order to ensure reliable results. When four different focus groups arrive at the same conclusion, the findings are probably reliable.

Several components of a marketing communications plan can be evaluated with concept tests. They include:

- ▶ Copy or verbal component of an advertisement
- ▶ Message and its meaning
- ▶ Translation of copy in an international ad
- ▶ Effectiveness of peripheral cues, such as product placement in the ad and props used
- ▶ Value associated with an offer or prize in a contest

A mall intercept technique is often used for copytesting of advertisements and other communication pieces.

Source: Courtesy of The Image Works. Photograph by Bob Daemmrich.

Two common testing instruments are called comprehension and reaction tests. *Comprehension tests* are used when participants in a study are asked the meaning of a marketing communication piece. The idea is to make sure viewers comprehend the message as intended. The moderator can then explore the reasons why the intended message was not comprehended correctly by the individual or the group.

Reaction tests are used to determine overall feelings about a marketing piece, most notably whether the response is negative or positive. If the focus group reacts negatively to an ad or particular copy in an ad, the agency can make the changes before it is too late. It is possible for an advertisement to be correctly comprehended but elicit negative emotions. Therefore, exploring any negative feelings provides creatives with input to modify the marketing piece.

Copytesting

A second form of message evaluation is copytesting. **Copytests** are used when the marketing piece is finished or in its final stages of development prior to production. They are designed to solicit responses to the main message of the ad as well as the format in which that message will be presented. For a television ad, a copytest could be conducted using a story board format or a version that is filmed by agency members rather than professional actors.

The two most common copytesting techniques are portfolio and theater tests. Both tests place the marketing piece in with others. A **portfolio test** is a display of a set of print ads, one of which is the ad being evaluated. A **theater test** is a display of a set of television ads, including the one being evaluated. The individuals who participate in these studies do not know which piece is under scrutiny. Both techniques mimic reality in the sense that consumers normally are exposed to multiple messages, such as when a radio or television station plays a series of commercials in a row or when a set of newspaper ads appears on a single page. The tests also allow researchers the opportunity to compare the target piece with other marketing messages. For these approaches to yield the optimal findings, it is essential that all of the marketing pieces shown are in the same stage of development (e.g., a set of story boards or a series of nearly completed coupon offers).

Copytesting can utilize focus groups as well as other measurement devices. An ad or coupon that is in the final stage of design can be tested with a **mall intercept technique**. The approach involves stopping people who are shopping in a mall. They are then asked to evaluate the item. The mall intercept technique can incorporate a portfolio approach. To do so, subjects are asked to examine the marketing piece, which is mixed in with others, normally six to 10 ads, coupons, or other marketing communications tools. This may be a better approach than showing an item by itself. The disadvantage of displaying only one item is that people tend to give it a more positive evaluation than if it is mixed in with others. Comprehension and reaction tests are commonly utilized in a mall intercept setting.

For television commercials, the theater tests mentioned earlier are used. The test ad is placed among other ads within a television documentary or a new show, such as a pilot episode of a new comedy or drama. The advantage of using a new show is that it is better able to hold the subject's interest. At the end of the program, the individuals participating in the study are asked for their reactions to the ads that were shown. For more valid results, those participating in the study should not know which ad is being tested.

Copytests are valuable instruments in the sense that they can help an agency or company avoid using an ad or marketing tool that isn't "quite ready" or one that receives negative reactions. They also help the advertiser understand if an ad is going to compete favorably when shown in a cluttered setting.

Recall Tests

Another popular method used to evaluate advertising is called a **recall test**. This approach involves asking an individual to recall what ads he or she viewed in a given setting or time period. Then, in progressive steps, the subject is asked to identify information about the ad. Figure 16.2 lists some of the parts of an advertisement that can be tested for recall.

The most common form of recall test is the **day-after recall (DAR)** test. The DAR method is often used to evaluate TV advertisements. Individuals who participate in the study are called by phone the day after the advertisement first appears. Normally, they are tested using an approach called **unaided recall**. In other words, the subjects are asked to name, or recall, the ads they saw or heard the previous evening, without being given any prompts or memory jogs. For magazines and newspaper ads, there are two approaches. In the first, consumers are contacted the day after the ad appeared. The individuals name the ads they recall and then are asked a serious of questions to discover the features of the advertisements they remember. In the second, an individual is given a magazine for a certain period of time (normally one week) and instructed to read it as he or she normally would during leisure time. Then, the researcher returns and asks a series of questions about which ads became memorable and what features the individual could remember. In the business-to-business sector, the second method is a popular way to test ads for trade journals.

The day-after recall method works best when the objective is to measure the extent to which consumers have learned or remembered the content of an ad. DAR is perceived to be a valuable test because advertisers know that increased recall enhances the probability that the brand is becoming a part of the consumer's evoked set, or the primary choices that are remembered when purchase alternatives are being considered. A brand that is part of the evoked set is much more likely to be chosen when the purchase is made.[2]

The second type of recall test is the **aided recall** method. Aided recall means that consumers are prompted by being told the product category and, if necessary, names of specific brands in that category. The respondent still does not know which brand or ad is being tested. When the consumer states that he or she does recall seeing a specific brand being advertised, the person then is asked to provide as many details as possible about the ad. At that point, no further clues are given regarding the ad content.

Most researchers believe the unaided recall approach is superior to other evaluative tests because it identifies the times that an advertisement has become lodged in the person's memory. Unaided recall is also better than aided recall, because some people may

▶ **Product name or brand**

▶ **Firm name**

▶ **Company location**

▶ **Theme music**

▶ **Spokesperson**

▶ **Tag line**

▶ **Incentive being offered**

▶ **Product attributes**

▶ **Primary selling point of communication piece**

FIGURE 16.2
Items Tested for Recall

"They've walked around our muddy scrap yard in three-piece suits and wing tips. They take care of us."

It takes a lot to surprise a guy like Bernard Steinberg. But just leave it to his bankers at BB&T. To them, it's all in a day's work.

"Without their backing and blessing, we probably wouldn't be here today. They're fast, they're responsive, and they understand what you need."

We appreciate the high praise, Bernard. Next time you see us, you can bet we'll all be wearing boots.

BB&T

You can tell we want your business.
www.bbandt.com Member FDIC. ©1998 BB&T

Recall tests would be a valuable measure of the effectiveness of this BB&T advertisement.

Source: Courtesy of Howard, Merrell & Partners.

respond to a prompt by saying they do indeed remember an ad, even when they are uncertain. Recall scores are almost always higher when the aided recall method is used. Some ad agencies use both methods. First, they use unaided recall to gather basic information. Then, the researcher follows up with prompts to delve deeper into the memories that are present, even if it takes a little help to dig them out.

In both aided and unaided recall tests, if incorrect information is provided, the researcher continues the questioning. Individuals are never told they have given inaccurate answers. Incorrect responses are important data to record. Memory is not always accurate in both aided or unaided recall situations. Consequently, people give incorrect answers. In other words, they may mention commercials that did not actually appear during the test period, but rather one that was viewed at some other time. Although this may seem strange, bear in mind that the average person sees between 50 and 100 ads on a typical night of television viewing. It is easy to become confused.

An incorrect response is often triggered by exposure to a similar ad. For example, a person may remember seeing a commercial for Firestone tires when it was actually presented by Uniroyal. Seeing the Firestone ad triggered the recall of the Uniroyal brand because the individual is more familiar with Uniroyal or holds the brand in higher esteem. This type of error is more common in aided recall tests. In that situation, the individual is being provided with potentially incorrect responses from a particular product category, which increases the odds of remembering the wrong brand.

Recall tests are used to evaluate many types of ads as well as other forms of sales promotions. The design of the recall test varies from one medium to another and from one type of promotional approach to another.

Recall tests are used primarily after ads are aired or have been shown in print. At the same time, however, they can be used in the early stages of communication development. In these instances, participants in the study are recruited, and the test is more of the standard experimental design variety. For example, an agency that has created a new business-to-business ad may wonder if the ad would work when aired with consumer ads. Using a theater lab setting, the new ad can be placed in a documentary with other ads. At the end, either the aided or unaided recall method can be used to measure ad and brand awareness.

It is important to take into consideration the age of the respondent used in the study when conducting recall tests. Recall scores tend to decline with age. This is because older people do not remember ads as well as those who are younger. Table 16.1 displays average recall scores for different age segments using both DAR and brand recall instruments.[3] There are several explanations for lower recall scores in older people:

▶ They have reduced short-term recall capacity.

▶ Older persons are more fixed in terms of brand choices, making them less easily influenced by advertisements.

▶ The TV ads used to develop Table 16.1 may have been targeted more toward youth.

For whatever reason, it appears that age does affect recall scores. Still, recall tests are valuable instruments used in testing to see if the ad has the potential to move into a person's long-term memory and affect future purchase decisions.

Day-After Recall		Brand Recall	
Age Segment	**Average Recall**	**Age Segment**	**Average Recall**
12–17	34%	13–17	70%
18–34	29%	18–34	53%
35–49	24%	35+	36%
50–65	22%		

TABLE 16.1

Impact of Age on DAR and Brand Recall

Source: Based on Joel S. Debow, "Advertising Recognition and Recall by Age–Including Teens," *Journal of Advertising Research*, 35, no. 5 (September–October 1995), pp. 55–60.

INTEGRATED LEARNING EXPERIENCE

A leading provider of advertising research is Decision Analyst, Inc. at **www. decisionanalyst.com**. Examine the various sections, including "Published Articles" and "Published Data." Study the previous research conducted by Decision Analyst. Next, go to the "Advertising Research" section under "Company Services" to examine some of the research services such as CopyScreen, CopyCheck, CopyTest, CopyTrack, and CopyRecall. How does Decision Analyst conduct concept and copy testing? What type of organizations would utilize these services? How would they help a creative in designing an advertisement?

RECOGNITION TESTS

A **recognition test** is a format in which individuals are given copies of an ad and asked if they recognize it or have seen it before. Those who say they have seen the ad are asked to provide additional details about when and where the ad was encountered (e.g., specific television program, the name of the magazine, the location of the billboard, etc.). This information is collected to validate that it was indeed seen.

EVALUATION

Evaluation and Ethics

Advertising agencies and companies will often hire research firms to evaluate the effectiveness of IMC campaigns as well as components of the IMC plan such as advertising, sponsorships, and consumer and trade promotions. Techniques such as recall tests, recognition tests, and attitude measures are used with a representative sample. Conducting these tests is costly and the future of an IMC or advertising campaign may be dependent upon the result.

Many opportunities for unethical behavior are possible, ranging from selecting the sample to interpreting the results. If a client wants the results to come out a certain way, it is tempting for a research firm to manipulate the data until the desired outcome is obtained. Rather than spend money on selecting a random, representative sample, a firm may use a judgment or convenience sample even though it may not be truly representative.

These concerns are heightened when the advertising agency that designed the ads is evaluating its own work. The recent difficulty with Enron and Arthur Andersen evaluating their own consulting work highlights the ethical concerns in these situations.

When evaluating an IMC campaign or individual parts of an IMC plan, those doing the research must act in a responsible and ethical manner. Results should be reported accurately even if they do not reflect what management or the client wants.

Next, the individual is asked a series of questions about the ad itself. This helps the researcher gather information and insights into consumer attitudes and reactions to the ad. Recognition tests are best suited to testing for comprehension of and reactions to ads. In contrast, recall tests tend to work well when testing brand and ad awareness. Recognition tests help when the advertiser is more concerned about how the ad is received and what information is being comprehended. This is especially important for ads using a cognitive message strategy, in which some type of reasoning process is invoked in persuading the consumer about the value of a product.

Recognition tests tend to measure how many people saw an advertisement, while recall tests tend to measure how many saw the ad and were also sufficiently interested to take the time actually to view or read the ad. Because recognition and recall tests measure different things, many firms and research teams do both with the same subject. First, recall measures are used to start the interview, and then recognition tests are given at the end of the session. For instance, a subject may have viewed an ad during a particular TV show but does not mention the ad when undergoing a recall test. In this situation the respondent can then be given a recognition test to see if he or she remembers seeing the ad. There are many similarities between recognition and recall tests, which means there is a high level of correlation between items identified in both tests. In a study of magazine recall and recognition tests, the average recall score was equal to 0.33 times the average recognition score. In other words, about one-third of those who recognized seeing a commercial when it was shown to them also recalled seeing the ad when asked in an unaided recall test. For newspapers, the average recall was equal to 0.32 times the average recognition score. With aided recall, the percentage is slightly higher because the respondent is given a cue.[4]

Many ingredients affect the degree of recognition of an ad. For print media, the size of the advertisement has a major impact. The larger the ad, the higher the level of recognition. For example, a full-page magazine ad is twice as likely to be noticed as a one-eighth-page ad.

Using celebrities such as Spike Lee increases recall and recognition through greater interest in and liking of the ad.
Source: Courtesy of Bozell Worldwide, Inc.

Further, when the consumer uses the brand being displayed in the ad, the likelihood of recognizing the ad rises. A person who uses a brand is about 50 percent more likely to recognize the ad than an individual who does not use the brand. It is not surprising that people tend to notice ads for products they use.

Similar results occur when the test is used to determine if the ad is liked or deemed interesting. An ad that a person likes is about 75 percent more likely to be recognized than an ad the individual did not like. This is one reason celebrities are selected for ads, such as the milk ad in this section featuring Spike Lee. If an individual likes the celebrity in the advertisement, then he or she will be more likely to recognize the ad. For ads the respondent thought were interesting, the odds of recognition were about 50 percent higher than for ads that were not deemed interesting. Although percentages vary, similar results occur in recall tests.

Therefore, in using recognition (and recall) tests, it is important to consider these key factors that can affect the results of the study. Firms must look beyond the number of respondents who recognize a particular ad. Questions should be asked about which brands the subjects normally buy in the product category, if they liked the ad, and if they found the ad to be interesting. Also, the size of the print ad and the length of the broadcast ad will impact recognition. Larger print ads and longer broadcast ads tend to boost recognition.

Over time, recall and recognition help to establish the brand in the consumer's mind. Loyalty and brand equity are more likely to result. Therefore, even though recall and recognition are more oriented toward the short-term impact of a given ad or campaign, the long-term consequences of a series of successful and memorable ads should be considered.

Attitude and Opinion Tests

Many of the tests used to measure advertisements are designed to examine the attitudinal components. These types of instruments may be used in conjunction with recall or recognition tests. Attitude tests deal with both the cognitive and affective reactions to an ad. They are also used to solicit consumer opinions. Opinions are gathered from surveys or focus groups. They can also be obtained as part of a mall intercept plan or even in laboratory settings.

The content and formats of attitude tests vary widely. Sometimes specific responses are requested in what are called **closed-end questionnaire** formats. Scales such as *1 = highly unfavorable* to *7 = highly favorable* are often prepared for respondents to answer. In other tests, the individual is allowed to discuss whatever comes to mind regarding some aspect of a product or its advertisements. These are called **open-ended questions**.

Roper Starch Worldwide developed a testing system called ADD + IMPACT. It was created to study consumer reactions to advertisements before they are launched. As part of the testing process, Roper conducts one-on-one interviews with 60 or more consumers. Each participant responds to open-ended questions as well as more standardized closed-ended attitudinal questions. The results of the test, transcripts, and a quantitative analysis of the numbers-based responses are provided to clients within two weeks of the test. By testing the ad prior to a launch, advertisers are more likely to know what people think about the ad and what type of reaction to expect. Changing an ad at this point is much less costly than after a campaign has been launched.[5]

Attitude and opinion studies also can be used to evaluate sales promotions devices such as direct-mail pieces. Although most companies use response rates to measure effectiveness levels for direct-mail programs, one company, de Kadt Marketing and Research, Inc., of Ridgefield, Connecticut, has developed an alternate method. The goal of de Kadt Marketing is to identify the best direct-mail design, not just the design that produces the largest response rate. The firm tries to find out why some direct-mail pieces work and others do not.[6]

De Kadt Marketing begins by recruiting the same types of consumers that would be found in a typical focus group. Subjects are selected based on demographics matching the target market characteristics for the products and the firm being studied. The subjects are asked to collect and classify all of the direct-mail coming into their homes for 10 days. During this period, the test piece is mailed to them. The subjects do not know which piece is the test piece. Sometimes more than one test piece is mailed to test different designs.

To complete the test, the subjects are given four large envelopes and instructed to place each piece of direct-mail into one of the four envelopes. In the first envelope they place the letters that they normally would have thrown away without even opening. The second envelope holds direct-mail offers that the subjects would have opened but then discarded. The third envelope is for pieces that were opened and read, but then would have been discarded. The difference between the second and third envelopes is that the third

Conducting attitude tests would be important for *Family Circle* to ensure this advertisement will accomplish its stated objective.
Source: Used with permission of Gruner & Jahr USA Publishing (G&J).

envelope contains pieces that were read while the second does not. The fourth envelope is used to collect direct-mail pieces that were opened and either acted upon or kept to be acted on later.

At the end of the 10 days, the respondents bring all four envelopes to the research site. One-on-one interviews are then conducted. Each respondent is asked questions about the types of direct-mail pieces that were typically discarded as well as the ones that were read. Then, the moderator goes through each envelope and discusses each item with the subject, seeking the reasons why the piece was placed where it was. When the moderator arrives at the test piece, a few additional questions are asked to discover more detail about why it was placed in a particular envelope. The results not only help the firm understand how consumers react to various direct-marketing pieces but also provide the firm with information about its specific mailing. This means reactions to the test piece can be compared to other direct-mail offers.

As noted in Chapter 3, there are many parts of a consumer buying decision-making process. Attitudes and opinions are connected to short-term behaviors and longer-term assessments of a company and its products. Therefore, in addition to simply remembering that a firm exists, advertisers and IMC planners should try to understand how people feel about the company in the context of larger, more general feelings.

Emotional Reaction Tests

Many ads are designed to elicit emotional responses from consumers. Emotional ads are based on the idea that ads that elicit positive emotions are more likely to be remembered. Also, consumers who have positive attitudes toward ads would logically develop more positive attitudes toward the product. This in turn should result in increased purchases.[7]

It is difficult to measure the emotional impact of an advertisement. The simplest method is to ask questions about an individual's feelings and emotions after viewing a marketing communication piece. This can be performed in a laboratory setting theater test, or the ad can be shown to focus groups. In both circumstances the test ad should be placed with other ads rather than by itself.

A **warmth monitor** is an alternative method developed to measure emotions. The concept behind the warmth meter is that feelings of warmth are positive when they are directed toward an ad or a product. To measure warmth, subjects are asked to manipulate a joystick while watching a commercial. The movements track reactions to a commercial by making marks on a sheet of paper containing four lines. The four lines are labeled:

1. Absence of warmth
2. Neutral
3. Warmhearted or tender
4. Emotional

The warmth meter was developed to evaluate TV ads. It can be adapted to radio ads.[8]

A more sophisticated warmth meter was developed by the University of Hawaii. Individuals watch advertisements in a theater-type lab featuring big screen television. Those who feel negatively about what they are seeing pull a joystick downward. Those who feel more positively push the joystick in the opposite direction. Thus, as they are watching the commercial, they are constantly moving the joystick forward or backward, thereby conveying their feelings at every moment of the ad. The results of the 20 participants are tallied into one graph and then placed over the commercial. This technology allows an advertiser to see which parts of the ad elicit positive emotions and which parts elicit negative emotions. After graphing the test results, the group can then be used as a focus group to discuss the ad and why group members felt the way they did at various moments during the viewing.[9]

A similar technology has been developed by DiscoverWhy. The major difference is that DiscoverWhy provides the service on the Internet. DiscoverWhy can poll 1,000 or more people who look at an advertisement as it is shown on the Internet. As they watch the ad on streaming video, participants use a mouse to move a tab on a sliding scale from one to 10. If they like what they see, they slide the scale toward the 10. Those who don't slide the scale toward the one. After the data have been collected, a graph can be superimposed over the advertisement. This shows the advertiser the likable and nonlikable parts of the commercial. A major advantage of using the Internet is that subjects selected for the study can provide their ratings at any time that is convenient. If the agency needs a focus group to discuss the ad, subjects can be selected from the participants. The focus group session can even be held online.[10]

Most of the time, emotions are associated with shorter-term events, such as the reaction toward a given advertisement. At the same time, emotions are strongly held in the memory banks of most consumers. Therefore, an ad that made a viewer angry may be retrieved, and the anger recreated, every time the individual remembers either the ad or the company. As a result, it is wise to attempt to discover emotional responses to various ads before they are released to be shown to the general public.

Emotional advertising based on a substantial amount of pretesting led to a highly successful antismoking campaign in Minnesota. Based on focus group information, ads were structured to show the devastating effects of smoking (lost vocal chords) and of secondhand smoke on children. The ads were shown to groups of smokers and nonsmokers before being released because they were so dramatic and graphic. The net result was much stronger attitudes favoring smoke-free environments and additional calls to the state's quit-smoking hot-line.[11]

INTEGRATED LEARNING EXPERIENCE

Roper Starch Worldwide is one of the leaders in advertising research. Access its Web site at **www.roper.com**. In the "Products and Services" section, examine the various industries in which Roper has expertise. Examine the services the company provides, especially the ADD + IMPACT. How would Roper's services help an advertising department or advertising agency? While Roper is a worldwide, full-service research agency, Datum Analysis focuses only on the Hispanic market. Access its Web site at **www.d-source.com** to see the types of ad and concept tests this firm offers.

Physiological Arousal Tests

Emotional reaction tests are *self-report* instruments. In other words, individuals report their feelings as they see fit. Although this may or may not be a flawed instrument, many marketing researchers were interested in finding ways to measure emotions and feelings without relying on people to report how they feel.

Physiological arousal tests measure fluctuations in a person's body functions that are associated with changing emotions. The primary physiological arousal tests are:

1. The psychogalvanometer
2. A pupillometric test
3. Voice-pitch analysis

A **psychogalvanometer** measures a person's perspiration levels. As an individual reacts emotionally to a situation (in this case an advertisement), the amount of perspiration present changes. Perhaps you have noticed that you sweat quite a bit more when watching an exciting movie or sports event. This arousal indicates you are interested and involved emotionally. An ad producing these effects may be more memorable and powerful than one that is boring or receives no emotional response.

The psychogalvanometer works by evaluating the amount of perspiration located in the palm and fingers. A very fine electric current is sent through one finger and returns to the galvanometer through another finger. Remember, a reaction can be negative or positive. The galvanometer simply measures the individual's physiological reaction. One benefit of the psychogalvanometer is that it can be used to assess emotional reactions to many different types of marketing communication pieces including television commercials, consumer promotions, and trade promotions.

A **pupillometric meter** measures the dilation of a person's pupil. Dilation levels also change with emotional arousal. A person who is frightened displays much wider pupils, as does someone who is excited. Pupil dilation can be studied as the subject views a television or print advertisement. Pupils dilate more when the person reacts positively to the ad or marketing communication. Pupils become smaller when the subject reacts negatively.

When conducting a test, the subject's head can be set in a fixed position. The dilation of the pupil can then be measured throughout the ad. In this way, each aspect of the message can be evaluated for positive or negative responses. A graph can be superimposed on the commercial to show evaluators how each person responded to the advertisement.

The **voice-pitch meter** examines changes in the pitch of a person's voice as he or she reacts with emotion. A more shrill or higher-pitched voice indicates a stronger response. A voice-pitch device utilizes special computer software. A person's voice pitch is monitored as the individual answers a series of questions. Vocal chords tighten and pitch is higher when a person is emotionally affected. The amount of change in the pitch is an indicator of how strongly the person has been affected.

All three of these tests are based on the theory that emotions affect people physiologically and that these physical responses can be measured. Some researchers believe physiological arousal tests are more accurate than emotional reaction tests, because physiological arousal cannot easily be faked.

To demonstrate how physiological tests work, consider an advertisement with a sexually attractive male or female. In a focus group, respondents may enjoy the ad but cover up these feelings, stating the ad is sexist and inappropriate. These reactions may be due to social pressure or because the subjects want to be accepted by those around them. The same individual may not move the joystick to report his or her true feelings when participating in a study using the warmth monitor. The stigma attached to sex in advertising often affects self-reported reactions. Thus, a physiological arousal test may be a better indicator of a person's true feelings.

Emotions are short-term reactions that also are stored in long-term memory. Therefore, a feeling of love or affection associated with a song returns each time the song is played. If the relationship goes sour, the same song may elicit strong negative feelings. Therefore, advertisers must continually be aware of the emotions associated with brands and products. It is not surprising, for example, that ValueJet eventually changed its name to AirTran. This may be in part due to negative emotions that continually surfaced following reports of unsafe maintenance practices that eventually led to a crash in Florida.

Physiological arousal tests could be used to test the impact of this advertisement by Maidenform.
Source: Courtesy of Maidenform, Inc.

Persuasion Analysis

The final type of message evaluation tool is designed to appraise the persuasive ability of a marketing communication item. While other measures evaluate awareness, emotions, liking, and physical reactions, they do not measure the ability of the marketing piece to persuade the consumer. Persuasion techniques require a pre- and posttest assessment.

A researcher analyzing the persuasiveness of a television ad would start by gathering a group of consumers in a theater. Measures of brand attitudes and purchase intentions are then gathered for the test brand and other brands put in the study. A series of commercials is shown as part of a program. Next, measures are taken to see if any changes in attitude or purchase intentions resulted from exposure to the ads. The amount of change indicates how well the persuasion in the advertisement worked.

One company that conducts persuasion analysis programs is called ASI Market Research. The company normally recruits a sample of 250 consumers to attend a new television program. Once they are in the ASI theater, the consumers are informed that prizes will be given away through a drawing. These individuals are asked to identify the specific brand they prefer in each product category. The subjects are then shown two new TV programs complete with commercials. At the end, the subjects are told that a product was inadvertently left off the initial survey, and they are asked to fill the form out again in order to enter the drawing. ASI compares before and after responses to the same questions in order to see if there was any changes in attitudes, and the subjects are not aware of the intention of the study.[12]

Knowing the ad actually has persuasive power is a major advantage for the advertiser. Attempts to assess the impact of such ads before they are released to a wider audience are solid investments of marketing dollars.

INTEGRATED LEARNING EXPERIENCE

DiscoverWhy offers ad testing through the warmth meter technology discussed in this chapter as well as through Internet interactive services. Access the "Product" section of its Web site at **www.discoverwhy.com**. Examine the virtual client room to see how DiscoverWhy conducts research. Examine the other products and services offered by DiscoverWhy. Next, access the "Products and Services" section of Ipsos-ASI at **www.ipsos-asi.com**. Under ad testing, examine the Ipsos-ASI Next TV. What types of services are offered and how is ad testing conducted? Do the same for some of the company's other products such as Ipsos-ASI Next Print. Compare this to the methodologies used by DiscoverWhy.

EVALUATION CRITERIA

For all of the programs mentioned thus far, it is important to establish quality evaluation criteria. One program helpful in doing so is called **PACT, or positioning advertising copytesting**. PACT was created to evaluate television ads. It was formulated by 21 leading U.S. advertising agencies.[13] Even though PACT was designed to examine the issues involved in copytesting television ads, the principles can be used for any type of message evaluation system and all types of media. Figure 16.3 lists the nine principles that were developed. They should be followed when a written or verbal marketing communication piece is being tested. A discussion of these principles follows.

First, no matter which procedure is used, it should be *relevant to the advertising objective being tested*. For example, if the objective of a coupon promotion is to stimulate trial purchases, then the test should evaluate the coupon's copy in order to determine its ability to stimulate trial purchases. On the other hand, an evaluation of attitudes toward a brand would require a different instrument.

▶ **Testing procedure should be relevant to the advertising objectives.**

▶ **In advance of each test, researchers should agree on how the results will be used.**

▶ **Multiple measures should be used.**

▶ **The test should be based on some theory or model of human response to communication.**

▶ **The testing procedure should allow for more than one exposure to the advertisement, if necessary.**

▶ **In selecting alternate advertisements to include in the test, each should be at the same stage in the process as the test ad.**

▶ **The test should provide controls to avoid biases.**

▶ **The sample used for the test should be representative of the target sample.**

▶ **The testing procedure should demonstrate reliability and validity.**

FIGURE 16.3
Copytesting Principles of PACT

Source: Based on PACT document published in the *Journal of Marketing*, (1982), Vol. 11, No. 4, pp. 4–29.

Researchers should agree on how the results are going to be used when selecting test instruments. They should also agree on the design of the test in order to obtain the desired results. This is especially true for the preparation stage in an advertisement's development, because many tests are used to determine whether the advertisement eventually will be created.

The research team should also decide on a cutoff score to be used following the test. This will prevent biases from entering into the findings about the ad's potential effectiveness. Many ad agencies use test markets for new advertisements before they are launched in a larger area. A recall method used to determine if people in the target market remember seeing the ad should have a prearranged cutoff score. In other words, the acceptable percentage may be established so that 25 percent of the sample should remember the ad in order to move forward with the campaign. If the percentage is not reached, the ad has failed the test.

Using multiple measures allows for more precise evaluations of ads and campaigns. It is possible for a well-designed ad to fail one particular testing procedure yet score higher on others. Consumers and business buyers who are the targets of marketing communications are complex human beings. Various people may perceive individual ads differently. As a result, advertisers usually try to develop more than one measure so that there is greater agreement on whether the ad or campaign will succeed and reach its desired goals.

The test to be used should be *based on some theory or model of human response to communication.* This makes it more likely that the test will be a predictive tool of human behavior. The objective is to enhance the odds that the communication will actually produce the desired results (going to the Web site, visiting the store, making a purchase, etc.) when the ad is launched.

Many testing procedures are based on a single exposure. Although in many cases this is sufficient for research purposes, there are times that *multiple exposures* are necessary to obtain reliable test results. For complex ads, more than one exposure may be needed. The human mind can comprehend only so much information in one viewing. It is vital to make sure the person can and does comprehend the ad in order to determine whether the ad can achieve its desired effects.

Often ads are tested in combination with other ads to disguise the one being examined. Placing the test marketing piece in with others means the test subjects do not know which ad is being evaluated. This prevents personal biases from affecting judgments. To ensure valid results, *the alternative ads should be in the same stage of process development.* Thus, if ad copy is being tested prior to ad development, then the alternative ads should also be in the ad copy development stage rather than established ads.

Next, adequate controls must be in place to *prevent biases and external factors from affecting results.* To help control external factors, experimental designs are often used. When conducting experiments, researchers try to keep as many things as constant as possible and manipulate only one variable at a time. For instance, in a theater test, the temperature, time of day, room lighting, television program, and ads shown can all be the same. Then, the researcher may display the program and ads to an all-male audience followed by an all-female audience. Changing only one variable (gender) makes it possible to see if the ad, in a very controlled environment, is perceived differently by men as opposed to women.

This does not mean field tests are ineffective. Testing marketing communications in real-world situations is

For testing complex ads such as this Weight Watchers ad, multiple exposures will be necessary.

Source: Courtesy of Weight Watchers International, Inc.

extremely valuable because they do approximate reality. Still, when conducting field tests, such as mall intercepts, those doing the testing must try to control as many variables as possible. Thus, the same mall, same questions, and same ads are shown. Then, age, gender, or other variables can be manipulated.

As with any research procedure, sampling procedures are important. It is crucial for the *sample being used to be representative of the target population.* For example, if a print ad designed for Spanish-speaking Hispanic Americans is to be tested, the sample used in the test normally will be in Spanish.

Finally, researchers must continually try to make tests *reliable and valid.* Reliable means "repeatable." In other words, if the same test is given five times to the same person, the individual should respond in the same way over time. If a respondent is "emotional" on one iteration of a warmth test and "neutral" when the ad is shown a second time, the research team will wonder if the test is reliable.

Valid means "generalizable." Valid research findings can be generalized to other groups. For instance, when a focus group of women finds an ad to be funny, and then a group of men reacts in the same way, the finding that the humor is effective is more valid. This would be an increasingly valuable outcome if the results were generalizable to people of various ages and races. Many times an ad may be reliable, or repeatable in the same group, but not valid or generalizable to other groups of consumers or business buyers.

The PACT principles are helpful when designing tests of short-term advertising effectiveness. They are also helpful when seeking to understand larger and more long-term issues such as brand loyalty and identification with the company. The goal is to generate data that documents what a company is doing works. When this occurs, the company and its advertising team have access to invaluable information.

In evaluating this television advertisement for Maidenform, it is important that the sample used in the evaluation represent the target market of Maidenform.
Source: Courtesy of Maidenform.

BEHAVIORAL EVALUATIONS

The first part of this chapter has been devoted to message evaluations. These techniques provide valuable insights into what people think and feel. Still, some marketing reports contend that the only valid evaluation criterion should be *actual sales.* To these critics it is less important for an ad to be well liked. If an ad does not increase sales, then it is not effective. The same type of argument is often presented regarding the other marketing communication tools such as sales promotions, trade promotions, personal selling, and direct marketing. There is some validity to this position; however, not all communication objectives can be measured using sales figures.[14]

A company with low brand awareness may be most interested in the visibility and memorability aspects of a communication plan, even though a marketing program designed to boost brand awareness may not result in immediate sales. Further, measuring the results of a sales promotion campaign featuring coupons using sales figures is easier to do than measuring the results of an advertising campaign on television. Consequently, effective promotions evaluations should involve the study of both message and behavioral elements. In this section, various behavioral measures are discussed. Figure 16.4 lists these techniques.

▶ Sales

▶ Redemption rates

▶ Test markets

▶ Purchase simulation tests

FIGURE 16.4
Behavioral Measures

COMMUNICATION ACTION

A Quick Quiz

Knowing what works and what doesn't is the key to assessing any IMC promotional piece effectively. A magazine entitled *Tested Copy* appeared on a monthly basis for several years. It was oriented toward discovering the best methods for reaching customers. In one issue, the following quiz appeared. See if you can select the correct answers, which appear at the bottom of the page.

Question 1: Which of the following does *Tested Copy* most consistently find as a failure in print advertising? The failure to:

    a. Animate the product and bring it to life

    b. Thoroughly describe the characteristics of the product

    c. Tell the readers what the product will do for them

    d. Give the readers sufficient information about the advertisers

Question 2: Which type of advertising is the most believable?

    a. Ads that feature real people who have used the product

    b. Ads that cite the results of user surveys

    c. Ads with a money-back guarantee

    d. Ads that name the competition and make comparisons

Question 3: What proportion of readers of women's magazines agree with this statement: *I like the way scented ads make magazines smell?*

    a. 29%

    b. 44%

    c. 68%

    d. 80%

Question 4: On average, an ad with sans-serif type is more likely to earn higher readership scores than an ad with serif type.

    a. true

    b. false

To learn more about this type of marketing information, go to the Web site of Roper Starch Worldwide. Information about the *Tested Copy* magazine is also available online.

Source: Alan Rosenspan, "ROPER Starch Worldwide, Inc.," *Direct Marketing*, 61, no. 4 (August 1998), p. 4.

Answers:

1. c

2. c

3. d

4. a

Sales and Redemption Rates

Measuring changes in sales following a marketing campaign is easier now than it was in the past. Universal product codes and scanner data are available from many retail outlets. These data are available on a weekly basis and, in some situations, on a daily basis. Some retail outlets even have access to sales information on a real-time basis, and the information can be accessed at any point during the day.

Scanner data make it possible for companies to monitor sales and help both the retailer and the manufacturer discover the impact of a particular marketing program. Bear in mind, however, that extraneous factors can affect sales. For instance, in a multimedia advertising program, it would be difficult to know which ad moved the customer to action. Further, a company may be featuring its fall line of jackets, and a cold snap may affect the region. If so, which caused the customer to buy—the ad or the weather? Firms utilizing trade and consumer promotion programs must account for the impact of both the promotion and the advertising when studying sales figures. Sales are one indicator of effectiveness; however, they may be influenced by any number of intervening factors.

Advertisements are probably the most difficult component of the IMC program to evaluate, for several reasons. These include:

1. The influence of other factors
2. A delayed impact of the ad
3. Consumers changing their minds while in the store
4. Whether the brand is in the consumer's evoked set
5. Brand equity considerations

First, as just discussed, it is difficult to distinguish *the effects of advertising from other factors.* This is because ads have short- and long-term effects, and consumers and businesses see ads in so many different contexts. Thus, the direct impact of one ad or one campaign on sales is difficult to decipher.

Second, *advertising often has a delayed impact.* Many times consumers encounter ads and are persuaded to purchase the product, but will not actually make the buy until a later time, when they need the item. Thus a woman may be convinced that she wants to buy undergarments due to a sexy and effective presentation by Victoria's Secret. Still, rather than buying them herself, she leaves several well-placed hints for her husband before her next birthday, which could be several months later. The problem is that her husband may have purchased another brand or a different gift. So, then she must wait until Christmas or Valentine's Day, but still the ad worked and led to a purchase. Measuring the impact of an ad in that setting is almost impossible.

Third, many times consumers may decide to make purchases based on an advertisement but *change their minds when they arrive at the retail store.* A competing brand may be on sale, the store could be out of the desired brand, or the salesperson could persuade the customer that another brand is better. In each case, the ad was successful on one level but another factor intervened in the purchase.

Fourth, *the brand being advertised may not be part of the consumer's evoked set.* Upon hearing or seeing the ad, however, the brand is moved into the evoked set. Thus, even when the brand is not considered at first, it will be in the future when the need arises or when the consumer becomes dissatisfied with a current brand.

Fifth, advertising is an essential component of building brand awareness and brand equity. Although sales may not be the result immediately, *the ad may build brand equity,* which in turn will influence future purchases.

Scanner data could be used as one measure of the effectiveness of this Jim Beam advertisement.
Source: Courtesy of Jim Beam Brands Worldwide, Inc.

You always come back to the basics.

> ▶ Changes in sales
> ▶ Telephone inquiries
> ▶ Response cards
> ▶ Internet inquiries
> ▶ Direct-marketing responses
> ▶ Redemption rate of sales promotion offers—
>   Coupons, premiums, contests, sweepstakes

FIGURE 16.5
Responses to Marketing Messages That Can Be Tracked

Counting the number of phone calls requesting a free copy of the "Investment Strategy" report could be used as a measure of the effectiveness of this A.G. Edwards advertisement.
Source: Courtesy of A.G. Edwards.

You can't catch the wave if you're standing on the beach.

Volatility in the stock market has certainly made many investors think twice about investing again. But it's important to remember that with each month or year that goes by, you're that much closer to needing your retirement income ... or sending your child or grandchild off to college. Could you be missing current opportunities that would help you meet those needs?

Call today to request a free copy of A.G. Edwards' "Investment Strategy" report and learn about our long-term economic outlook.

A.G.Edwards
INVESTMENTS SINCE 1887

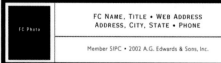
FC NAME, TITLE • WEB ADDRESS
ADDRESS, CITY, STATE • PHONE

Member SIPC • 2002 A.G. Edwards & Sons, Inc.

It is easier to measure the effects of trade and consumer promotions, direct-marketing programs, and personal selling on actual sales. For example, manufacturers can study the impact of trade promotions by observing changes in sales to the retailers at the time the promotions are being offered. The same is true for consumer promotions such as coupons, contests, and point-of-purchase displays. Many manufacturers push retailers to use their POP displays. At the same time, the retailer will be interested in the effects of the display on sales. Using scanner data, both the retailer and the manufacturer can measure the impact of a POP display. Retailers normally use POPs that have demonstrated the ability to boost sales.[15]

To track the impact of POP displays, Anheuser-Busch, Frito-Lay, Procter & Gamble, and Warner-Lambert joined together as initial sponsors of a program developed by *Point-of-Purchase Advertising International (POPAI).* In the initial study, POPAI tracked 25 different product categories in 250 supermarkets nationwide. Sponsors paid between $50,000 and $75,000 to receive customized data about the POP displays featuring particular brands. One advantage of using POPAI data is that each firm not only can see the impact of the POP for its brand but also receives comparative data showing how well the display fared against other displays. The major advantage of the POPAI program is its low cost. Sponsors of the POPAI program attained valuable data at a much lower cost than if they had sought the information on their own.[16]

There are a wide variety of responses to marketing communications programs besides sales. Figure 16.5 lists some of the responses that can be tracked. These items are described in the remainder of this section.

One method of measuring the impact of an advertisement, direct mailing, TV direct offers, or price-off discounts to a business customer is to assign a *toll-free number* to each marketing piece. A great deal of information can be collected during an inbound call. Sales data can be recorded and demographic information gathered. Psychographic information then can be added by contacting various commercial services.

In business-to-business situations, a toll-free number provides contact names to help the vendor discover who is performing the various functions in the buying center. As a result, a toll-free number provides sales data to determine which marketing program is the best and also can be used to generate valuable customer information that can be tied to the sales data. Knowing who is responding to each offer helps a firm better understand its customers and the approach that should be used for each target group.

Another method for measuring behaviors comes from *response cards.* These customer information forms are filled out at the time of a purchase. The primary disadvantage of response cards is that less data are obtained. Consequently, commercial sources will be needed to obtain additional demographic and psychographic information. This is because response cards solicited from current customers contain information the firm is already likely to have in its database.

Internet responses are excellent behavioral measures. By using "cookies," a firm can obtain considerable information about the person or business making the inquiry. Many times the person or business responding also is willing to provide a great deal of helpful information.

To evaluate Internet advertising campaigns, AdKnowledge introduced an online management tool called MarketMatch Planner. The MarketMatch Planner software includes two components: (1) Campaign Manager and (2) Administrator. Campaign Manager records traffic to a site as well as performing postbuy analysis. Administrator integrates Web ad-buy data and performance analysis with the firm's accounting and billing systems. In addition, MarketMatch Planner has the capability of integrating third-party data including audience demographics from the following sources:

▶ MediaMetrix for basic demographics

▶ NetRatings for GRP and other ratings instruments

▶ Psychographic data from SRI Consulting

▶ Web site ratings and descriptions from NetGuide

▶ Web traffic audit data from BPA Interactive.

More recently, a new form of focus group has emerged based on videoconferencing. Webcasting now comprises about 15 percent of the total for focus group video broadcasts, up from zero in 1999. One major provider of this type of service is FocusVision Worldwide.[17]

In international settings, the use of visuals and a shorter time period for the actual setting have increased the quality of information derived from focus groups. Pictures help identify common themes for the group. Because translation time is part of the focus group process when multinationals are involved, shorter sessions help the participants keep focused while waiting for words to be translated.[18]

In Moslem countries, focus groups routinely are dominated by males. In some Moslem nations, it is against the law to have mixed-gender focus groups, and in others the participants are simply not comfortable in a mixed setting. Therefore, research in these circumstances is still difficult, though many sources indicate that it is no more nor less difficult after September 11 than it was prior to the attacks on the United States and subsequent military operations in Moslem countries.[19]

All of this means that a firm can now quantitatively analyze Internet advertising. An e-company can see exactly how many hits an ad brings to a site. The company also can identify how many sales result and how much is spent per sale. Thus, individual e-businesses can identify demographic and psychographic information about each customer. Internet advertising is much easier to evaluate with hard numbers than is any other advertising medium because of the computer technology contained within individual computers.[20]

Individual companies must be careful how they use Internet data. They should be reviewed in light of the IMC objectives present. An IMC objective of building brand awareness requires something other than Internet sales data to be assessed. An Internet ad can bring awareness to a brand yet not lead to an online purchase. This might occur, for example, when a consumer or business uses the Internet to gather information but then makes the actual purchase at a retail store, over the telephone, or by fax. When that happens, the impact of an Internet advertising campaign may not be able to reflect all of the brand awareness or sales that the campaign generated.

By using technology such as MarketMatch Planner, a company such as McCormick can track who goes to its Web site for recipes.
Source: Courtesy of McCormick & Co., Inc.

Various kinds of redemption rates can be used as behavioral effectiveness measures. *Coupons, premiums, contests, sweepstakes,* and *direct-mail pieces* are marketing communications devices that can be coded to record redemption rates. Comparing a current campaign with previous campaigns makes it possible for a firm to examine changes made in the design or execution of an ad. The results are reviewed in light of positive or negative changes in redemption rates.

Immediate changes in sales and redemptions are one form of behavioral evaluation. It is tempting for the advertiser and company to use them and fail to see "the forest for the trees." One campaign, advertisement, or promotions program should be viewed in the context of all other marketing efforts. Behavioral measures are best when the team sees them as part of the "big picture."

STOP

INTEGRATED LEARNING EXPERIENCE

Tracking Internet traffic is an excellent method of measuring the effectiveness of Internet advertising. AdKnowledge is a leader in this technology. Access this Web site at **www.engage.com**. What type of services does AdKnowledge offer? Review the Media Metrix Global Landing Web site at **www.mediametrix. com**. How can AdKnowledge use the information provided by Media Metrix to develop a more complete profile of the Internet customers being tracked? How can these two firms measure the effectiveness of an Internet ad campaign?

Test Markets

A second form of behavioral response can be studied using a test market. Test markets are used when a company examines the effects of a marketing effort on a small scale before launching a national or international marketing campaign. The primary advantage of using a test market is that an organization can examine several elements of a marketing communication program. If the test market is successful, then it is likely that the national or global campaign also will be effective. It is also an excellent method of testing a campaign in a new country before launching it full scale. Test market programs are used to assess:

1. Advertisements
2. Promotions and premiums
3. Pricing tactics
4. New products

When one of these is tested and is not successful, the communication program can be changed. A product may be pulled before it is even released. For instance, McDonald's decided not to go forward with plans to sell onion rings, steak sandwiches, and a sandwich called a McFeast, because sales in a test market program did not warrant a national launch.

Test markets are cost-effective methods to analyze and make changes in marketing efforts before millions of dollars are spent on something that will not accomplish the intended objectives. Ads can be modified, premiums revised, and pricing policies revisited before a more widespread program is undertaken.

One major advantage of a test market is that it resembles an actual situation more than any of the other tests discussed thus far. The key is to make sure that the site selected for the test market strongly resembles the target population. For example, if a product is targeted toward senior citizens, then it is important to conduct the study in an area that has a high concentration of senior citizens.

It is also important to design the test marketing campaign as close to the national or full marketing plan as possible. A lengthy time lapse may cause a company to experience differing results. The goal is to make sure the test market is a mirror image of the actual marketing program.

A test market can be as short as a few days or as long as two to three years. The longer the test market program runs, the more accurate the results. A test that is too short may yield less reliable results. On the other hand, if the test market is too long, the national market situation may change and the test market may no longer be a representative sample. The greatest fear, however, is that the competition is able to study what is going on, giving them time to react to the proposed marketing campaign.

A competitor can respond to a test market program in one of two ways. First, the competition may introduce a special promotion in the test market area in order to confound the results. This may reduce the sales for the product or campaign, making it appear less attractive. The second approach is not to intervene in the test market, but to use the time to prepare a counter marketing campaign. Firms that use this tactic are ready when the national launch occurs and the impact may be that the test market results are not as predictive of what will happen.

The Botany Shop could use Joplin as a test market by promoting a price-off sale.
Source: Used with permission of the *Joplin Globe*, Joplin, Missouri.

Scanner data make it possible for results from test market campaigns to be quickly available. The figures can be studied to determine if test market results are acceptable. A firm also can design several versions of a marketing campaign in different test markets. Through scanner data, the firm can compare the sales from each test market to determine which version is the best. For example, in test market one, the firm may present an advertising campaign only. In test market two, the firm may add coupons to the ad program. In test market three, a premium and advertising can be used. Examining the results from each market helps the firm grasp which type of marketing campaign to use. Other test markets can be used with different prices in different regions to determine the price to charge and the elasticity associated with that price. It is also possible to vary the size of the coupon or premium to discover the impact. Rather than making a change at the national level, a firm can modify the consumer promotion in selected markets to see what happens.

Through test marketing, firms have the opportunity to test marketing communication ideas in more true-to-life settings. Test markets work best for trade and consumer promotions, direct marketing, and other marketing communication tools. They are not quite as accurate when assessing advertising because changes in sales take longer, and the test market program may not be long enough to measure the full impact. In any case, test markets are valuable instruments to use when examining specific marketing features and more general communications campaigns.

Purchase Simulation Tests

A third behavioral approach available is purchase simulation tests. Consumers can be asked in several ways if they would be willing to buy products. For instance, they could be asked about purchase intentions at the end of a laboratory experiment. In this situation, however, intentions are self-reported and tend not to be an accurate predictor of future purchase behaviors. Test markets examine actual purchases, but are more costly because the marketing piece must be completed first. TV commercials cost from several thousand to over a million dollars to prepare. Even then, the impact of purchasing intentions and behaviors is hard to measure.

A feasible and cost-effective approach to examine purchase behaviors is called a *simulated purchase test.* A leading marketing research firm that specializes in purchase simulation studies is Research Systems Corporation (RSC). RSC tests commercials by studying consumer behaviors in a controlled laboratory environment.

RSC does not ask consumers to render opinions, describe their attitudes, or even if they plan to purchase the product. Instead, RSC creates a simulated shopping experience. Subjects are able to choose from a variety of products they would see on a normal store shelf. After completing a simulated shopping exercise, the subjects are seated and watch a television preview containing various commercials. The participants are asked to watch the TV preview as they would watch any TV show at home. The test ad is placed in with other ads, and the subjects do not know which ad is being tested.

When the preview is over, the subjects are asked to participate in a second shopping exercise. Researchers then compare the products chosen in the first shopping trip to those selected in the second. Shifts in brand choices are at least partly due to the effectiveness of the advertisement because it is the only variable that has changed.

A major advantage of this methodology is that the test procedures do not rely on opinions and attitudes. Among other things, this means that RSC's procedure can be used in international markets as well as domestic markets.[21] In some cultures, subjects tend to seek to please the interviewer who asks questions about opinions and attitudes. As a result, the answers are polite and socially acceptable. The same subjects may also seek to provide answers they think the interviewer wants to hear. By studying purchases instead of soliciting opinions, subjects are free to respond in a more accurate fashion.

Any methodology designed to tap into behaviors rather than emotions and feelings has a built-in advantage. Opinions and attitudes change and can be quickly affected by other variables in a situation. Observing behaviors and changes in behaviors gets more quickly to the point of the experiment, which is, can the buyer be influenced in a tangible way by a marketing communications tool?

In summary, the three systems designed to examine respondent behaviors are response rates, test markets, and purchase simulation tests. Many of these programs are used in conjunction with one another and also with the message evaluation techniques described earlier. None of these approaches is used in a vacuum. Instead, the data generated and findings revealed are tested across several instruments and with numerous groups of subjects. In that manner, the marketing departmental manager and the advertising agency can try to heighten the odds that both short- and long-term goals can be reached through the ads, premiums, coupons, and other marketing communications devices used. Even then, the job of evaluation is not complete.

EVALUATING PUBLIC RELATIONS ACTIVITIES

Most public relations can be studied using one or more of the evaluation techniques that have already been described. Many times, however, company leaders use three additional methods. These evaluation techniques are:

1. Counting clippings
2. Calculating the number of impressions
3. The advertising equivalence technique

Counting clippings occurs when a company subscribes to what is called a *clipping service.* The service scours magazines, journals, and newspapers looking for a client company's name. The number of clippings found is then compared to the number of news releases that were sent out. A firm that sends out 400 news releases and is told there are 84 clippings would conclude that the *percent return* is 21 percent.

The second approach, which became popular in the 1990s, is to calculate impressions. *Impressions* are counted as the total number of subscribers and purchasers of a print medium in which the client company's name has been mentioned. For example, when a company's name is mentioned in a newspaper article with a circulation of 800,000 and newsstand sales of 150,000, then the total number of impressions is 950,000.

Some problems are associated with counting clippings and impressions as methods for evaluating public relations efforts. Clippings ignore whether the article spoke positively or negatively about the company. Any clipping is counted when the company's name is mentioned no matter the context. Unfortunately, this means an article criticizing the company counts as much as one praising the company. With impression counts, everyone who subscribes to or buys a magazine or newspaper is part of the total. No effort is made to see what percentage of those who bought the paper or magazine actually saw the company name or read the article.

Firms that continue to use clippings and impressions should modify these techniques when possible. Clippings should be sorted into piles of positive and negative articles in order to see which occurs more frequently. Also, readers should summarize what was said in the article rather than simply noting that the company's name was mentioned. It is also wise to note if the article, whether negative or positive, appeared in a setting that would reach the company's customers, or if it is "buried" somewhere with less importance.

For impressions, surveys should be conducted to indicate the percentage of the total audience (readership of a magazine) that saw the company's name. This can be accomplished by using recall or recognition tests, or both. In addition, attitude questions can be posed to see how people reacted to what was in the story. Again, merely counting impressions does not provide adequate feedback about a PR campaign.

The problems associated with clippings and impressions have led to a third method used to measure public relations effectiveness. The approach, called *advertising equivalence,* involves finding every place the company name was mentioned in print and broadcast media. Then, the market researcher calculates the cost of the time or space if it was a paid advertisement. For example, if the company is discussed in an article that occupies one-half page of a magazine, the firm finds out the cost of a half-page ad. A similar approach is used for TV publicity. The cost of an ad running for the amount of time the company was discussed on the air is calculated. Again, this method makes the most sense only if positive publicity stories are counted.

The least used but best method involves examining the public relations piece in comparison to the company's PR objectives. Many times, the objective of a particular PR campaign is to increase awareness of the firm or product's name. Evaluation includes developing an index of awareness before a PR campaign begins. Then, after the PR event, awareness is measured a second time to see if it actually increased. This kind of information is valuable in the motion picture industry. When celebrities make personal appearances and visits to talk shows in the effort to generate publicity, awareness should increase.

In other situations, the goal of a PR campaign is to build a positive image for the company because of bad publicity or some other negative event. Again, the image should be measured before and after the PR campaign. The goal is to see if the image changed and, if so, to what degree. This approach is time-consuming and difficult. It may take time for a PR campaign to have a full impact. Still, many firms are interested in knowing if their public relations efforts are working.

Each of these methods is based on the goal of discovering the impact of the PR program. When combined with assessments of the effectiveness of advertisements and behavioral responses, the company has a fairly solid grasp regarding what is going on in the current marketplace. Completion of a full IMC evaluation involves one more crucial process.

EVALUATING THE OVERALL IMC PROGRAM

Many years ago, Peter Drucker outlined a series of goal areas that are indicative of organizational health. In other words, the goals shown in Figure 16.6 are solid measures of the overall well-being of a company. These goals match very well with the objectives of an IMC program.[22]

Market share has long been linked to profitability. It demonstrates consumer acceptance, brand loyalty, and a strong competitive position. A promotions opportunity analysis, as described in Chapter 3, should help the marketing team understand both its market

▶ **Market share**

▶ **Level of innovation**

▶ **Productivity**

▶ **Physical and financial resources**

▶ **Profitability**

▶ **Manager performance and development**

▶ **Employee performance and attitudes**

▶ **Social responsibility**

FIGURE 16.6
**Measures of Overall
Health of a Company**

Source: Peter Drucker, *Management: Tools, Responsibilities, Pratices* (New York: Harper and Row, 1974).

share and the relative strengths and weaknesses of the competition. IMC programs are designed to hold and build market share.

Innovation is finding new and different ways to achieve objectives. This applies to many marketing activities, including new and unusual trade promotions devices (Chapter 10), consumer promotions (Chapter 11), public relations events and sponsorships (Chapter 13), Internet and e-commerce programs (Chapter 14), and, of course all of the firm's advertising efforts.

Productivity is reflective of the industry's increasing emphasis on results. IMC experts are being asked to demonstrate tangible results from IMC campaigns. Both short- and long-term measures of the effects of advertisements and promotions demonstrate the "productivity" of the organization, in terms of gaining new customers, building recognition in the marketplace, by sales per customer, and through other measures.

Physical and financial resources are also important to an IMC program. Physical resources include the most up-to-date computer and Internet capabilities. The firm must provide sufficient financial resources to reach this goal. Scanner technologies and other devices that keep the firm in contact with consumers are vital elements in the long-term success of an IMC plan.

Profitability is vital for the marketing department and the overall organization. Many IMC managers know that more than sales are at issue when assessing success. Sales must generate profits in order for the company to survive and thrive over time.

Manager performance and development is possibly an overlooked part of an IMC program. Effective marketing departments and advertising agencies must develop pipelines of new, talented creatives, media buyers, promotions managers, database Web masters, and others in order to succeed in the long term. Also, new people must be trained and prepared for promotion for more important roles over time.

Employee performance and attitudes reflect not only morale within the marketing department but also relations with other departments and groups. As noted in Chapter 1, an effective IMC plan consists of building bridges with other internal departments so that everyone is aware of the thrust and theme of the program. Satisfied and positive employees are more likely to help the firm promote its IMC image.

Social responsibility was described in Chapter 13. It is clear that the long-term well-being of an organization rests, in part, in its ability to eliminate negative activities and expand its positive programs. Brand equity and loyalty hurt when the firm is known for illegal or unethical actions. Therefore, marketing leaders should encourage all of the members of an organization to act in ethical and socially responsible ways.

When these goals are being reached, it is likely that the firm's IMC program is working well. Beyond these targets, IMC plans continually should emphasize the evolving nature of relationships with customers. Retail consumers and business-to-business buyers should be constantly contacted to find out how the company can best serve their needs.

Simply stated, every chapter in this book implies a series of key performance targets for IMC programs that should guide the actions of the marketing department and the advertising agency both in the short term and over the long haul. Firms that are able to maintain one clear voice in a cluttered marketplace stand the best chance of gaining customer interest and attention as well as developing long-term bonds with all key publics and stakeholders. An effective IMC program helps set the standards and measure performance and, in the end, becomes the model for marketing success for the entire organization.

SUMMARY

Assessing an IMC program often involves examining the effects of individual advertisements. These efforts are conducted in two major ways: (1) message evaluations, and (2) evaluating respondent behaviors. A wide variety of techniques can be used. Most of the time marketing managers and advertisement agencies use several different methods in order to get the best picture of an ad's potential for success. Advertisements are studied before they are developed, while they are being developed, and after they have been released or launched.

The guiding principles for any marketing tool include agreement on how test results will be used, preestablishing a cutoff score for a test's results, using multiple measures, basing studies on models of human behaviors, using multiple exposures, testing marketing instruments that are in the same stage of development, and preventing as many biases as possible while conducting the test. Many times it is difficult for certain members of the marketing team to be objective, especially when they had the idea for the ad or campaign. In these instances, it is better to retain an outside research agency to study the project.

Public relations programs should be assessed in light of not only how many times a company is mentioned in the media but also what various ads and stories said about the company. Also, public relations efforts should be compared with the goals for the department in order to see if the company is achieving the desired effects with its publicity releases and sponsorship efforts.

IMC plans are general, overall plans for the entire company. Therefore, more general and long-term criteria should be included in any evaluation of an IMC program. When the IMC theme and voice are clear, the company is achieving its long-range objectives, the principles stated in this book are being applied efficiently and effectively, and the company is in the best position to succeed at all levels.

REVIEW QUESTIONS

1. What is the difference between a message evaluation and respondent behaviors when assessing the effectiveness of an advertisement?

2. What does a concept test evaluate? How are story boards and focus groups used in concept tests?

3. Describe the use of portfolio tests and theater tests in copytesting programs.

4. What is DAR? How are aided and unaided recall tests used in conjunction with DAR evaluations? What problems are associated with both types of tests?

5. What is a recognition test? How is it different from a recall test?

6. How are closed-ended questions and open-ended questions used in attitude and opinion tests?

7. What is a warmth monitor? What does it measure?

8. Describe how psychogalvanometers, pupillometric meters, and voice-pitch analysis techniques are used in evaluating advertisements.

9. How do the positioning advertising copytesting principles help advertisers to prepare quality ads and campaigns?

10. What are the three forms of behavioral evaluations that can be used to test advertisements and other marketing pieces?

11. Name the measures of behavioral responses described in this chapter.

12. What items can be evaluated using test markets?

13. Describe a purchase simulation test.

14. Describe counting clippings and calculating the number of impressions as methods for assessing public relations effectiveness. What problems are associated with these two techniques?

15. Describe the advertising equivalence approach to assessing public relations programs.

16. Name and describe the criteria that can be used to assess the impact of the overall IMC program, as noted in this chapter.

KEY TERMS

message evaluation techniques   methods used to examine the creative message and the physical design of the advertisement, coupon, or direct-marketing piece.

respondent behaviors techniques   methods used to examine visible customer actions including making store visits, inquiries, or actual purchases.

story board   a series of still photographs or sketches that outlines the structure of a television ad.

concept testing   an evaluation of the content or concept of the ad and the impact that concept will have on potential customers.

copytests   tests that are used to evaluate a marketing piece that is finished or is in its final stages prior to production.

portfolio test   a display of a set of print ads, one of which is the ad being evaluated.

theater test   a display of a set of television ads, including the one being evaluated.

mall intercept technique   a test where people are stopped in a shopping mall and asked to evaluate a marketing item.

recall tests   an approach in which an individual is asked to recall ads he or she has viewed in a given time period or setting.

day-after recall (DAR)   individuals participating in a study are contacted the day after an advertisement appears to see if they remember encountering the ad.

unaided recall   subjects are asked to name, or recall, the ads without any prompts or memory jogs.

aided recall   consumers are prompted by being told the product category and, if necessary, names of specific brands in that category to see if they recall an ad.

recognition tests   a format in which individuals are given copies of an ad and asked if they recognize it or have seen it before.

closed-end questionnaire   subjects are asked to give specific responses to questions, and the answers are usually rated using some type of scale.

open-ended questions   subjects are allowed to discuss whatever comes to mind in response to a question.

warmth monitor   a method to measure emotional responses to advertisements.

psychogalvanometer   a device that measures perspiration levels.

pupillometric meter   a device that measures the dilation of a person's pupil.

voice-pitch meter   a device that examines the pitch of a person's voice as he or she reacts with emotion to an advertisement or situation.

positioning advertising copytesting (PACT)   principles to use when assessing the effectiveness of various messages.

CRITICAL THINKING EXERCISES

Discussion Questions

1. Create an idea for advertising one of the following products. Put that idea down in three or four sentences. Organize a small focus group of four other students in your class. Ask them to evaluate your advertising concept. What did you learn from the exercise?

   a. Retail pet store

   b. Baseball caps

   c. Computers

   d. Sweaters

   e. Watches

2. A very popular form of recall testing is the day-after recall (DAR). Write down five advertisements you remember seeing yesterday. In addition to writing down the product and brand, note whatever else you can remember. Form into groups of four students. Compare your lists. How many commercials were recalled? How much could each of you remember about the commercial?

3. Pick out five advertisements you like. Conduct an aided recall test of these five ads. Ask 10 individuals, independently, if they saw the commercial. Mention only the brand name. If so, ask them to recall, in an unaided fashion, as much about the ad as they can. If they do not remember the ad immediately, give them cues. Be sure to record how much each person

remembers unaided and how much each person remembers with aided information. Report your results to the class.

4. Form into a group of five students. Ask students to write down two advertisements they really like and their reasons. Ask students to write down two advertisements they dislike and their reasons. Finally, ask students to write down an advertisement they believe is offensive and their reasons. Ask each student to read his or her list comparing ads that were liked, disliked, and offensive. What common elements did you find in each category? What were the differences?

5. How important are sales figures in the evaluation of integrated marketing communications? How should hard data such as redemption rates and store traffic be used in the evaluation of marketing communications? In terms of accountability, how important are behavioral measures of IMC effectiveness?

6. In some Asian countries it is improper to talk about oneself. Therefore, questions about feelings and emotions would be too embarrassing for citizens to answer. Those who answer the questions tend to provide superficial answers. Explain the advantages of a simulated purchasing test methodology in this situation. What other methods of evaluating feelings and emotions could an agency use in Asian countries?

7. From the viewpoint of a marketing manager of a large sporting goods manufacturer, what types of measures of effectiveness would you want from the $500,000 you pay to an adver-

tising agency to develop an advertising campaign? Knowing that evaluation costs money, how much of the $500,000 would you be willing to spend to measure effectiveness? What type of report would you prepare for your boss?

8. A clothing manufacturer spends $600,000 on trade promotions and $300,000 on sales promotions. How would you measure the impact of these expenditures? If an agency were hired to manage these expenditures, what type of measures would you insist the company should utilize?

9. Look through a magazine. Record how many advertisements have a method for measuring responses. How many

list a code number, a toll-free number, or a Web site? Just listing a toll-free number or a Web site does not ensure the agency or firm will know where the customer obtained that information. How can the ad agency or firm track the responses from a specific advertisement in the magazine you examined?

10. Pick five print or television advertisements that provide Web sites. Go to each site. Was the Web site a natural extension of the advertisement? What connection or similarities did you see between the Web site and the advertisement? Do you think your response was tracked? How can you tell?

Evaluating Your IMC Program

There are several levels to consider when evaluating the success of your advertising and promotions activities. They include short-term outcomes (sales, redemption rates), long-term results (brand awareness, brand loyalty, or equity), product-specific awareness, awareness of the overall company, and affective responses (liking the company and a positive brand image). In the exercise for this chapter, various approaches such as counting coupon redemptions, reviewing viewer responses to advertisements, and others are considered as possible methods to evaluate outcomes. It is possible that you may have to go back and modify a component of your IMC program because of inability to evaluate it effectively. Go to the Web site at **www.prenhall.com/clow** or access the IMC Plan Pro disk that accompanied this textbook to complete this final stage of your IMC plan.

BUILDING AN

IMC

CAMPAIGN

IMC PlanPro !

CASE 1

CRUISING FOR INCREASED PROFITS

Adventure Cruises owns a fleet of ships that tour the Caribbean and the Bahamas and make trips to Hawaii. The company has been in operation for over 20 years. Recently, there has been a drop in passengers on each voyage. Adventure's leadership believes increasing competition in the cruise ship industry combined with additional new leisure-time activities have led to the decline. Some worry that cruise ship tours are viewed as something "old people" do and that Disney has taken away the family cruise business.

To combat these problems, Adventure Cruises has decided on two tactics. First, the marketing department will present a new ad campaign highlighting the advantages the company holds over other lines. Second, a new type of passenger will be recruited, a "working business vacationer."

Adventure rebuilt the state rooms on 10 of its ships to accommodate business travelers. These individuals can be members of a company or guests of the company. The idea is to get the customer alone on a ship to conduct business over a series of days, all the while being able to enjoy the many features of cruise travel, including fine dining, gambling, shows, and stops at various ports. The advantage to the company is that it has essentially a "captive audience" when a customer is given a free cruise in exchange for doing business with the company footing the bill. Adventure intends to take out ads in business magazines and journals, selling these new packages to various business buyers. Adventure president Henry

(continued)

Crouch points out, "Lots of companies pay really big bucks to rent luxury boxes in football stadiums. They get the customer for what, four or five hours? We can offer them a chance to keep a customer for four or five *days*."

Henry hired a large international advertising agency to prepare ads for both regular passengers and the new business-to-business market. Lauren Patterson was the account executive who signed the deal, by emphasizing that she would follow the Roper Starch test copy principles. For cruise ship passengers, the ads would pass muster only if they met the following criteria:

1. *The eyes have it.* The ads must be clear and easy to follow.
2. *Never place copy above an illustration.* People see the picture first, so if the copy is higher, it's ignored.
3. *Great visuals work.* The idea is to capture attention and interest.
4. *Make sure the headlines and visuals blend with the copy.* Don't confuse the reader.
5. *Don't use confusing visuals.*
6. *Don't use confusing headlines.*
7. *Testimonials increase believability and readership.*
8. *Size matters.* The ad must be big.
9. *Keep it simple.* Readers are not as interested in the product as you are, so make the ad easy to follow.
10. *Break the rules.* Be creative.

In the business-to-business marketplace, three problems routinely occur. Lauren is going to insist that the ads avoid these problems. She calls them the ABC sins in business-to-business marketing. The problems are:

A. Ads that are not visually appealing
B. Ads that are abstract rather than designed with a human appeal
C. Ads that fail to emphasize the benefit to the business buyer

Henry realizes that these two markets (regular passengers and business customers) are somewhat distinct. Still he believes Adventure Cruises should speak with one voice. He believes his company has three major advantages over the competition: better food, unusual entertainment, and excellent service. He wants to be sure Lauren incorporates those three elements into the ads that appear on television and in the trade journals that they select.

1. Design a print ad for Adventure Cruises' regular passengers.
2. Design a print ad for Adventure Cruises' business customers.
3. What type of testing should be done during the design phase of the advertisement?
4. What type of testing should be done after the ad is designed but prior to placing it in a magazine or other print media?
5. What type of testing should be done after the advertisement is launched? How can the effectiveness of the advertisement be measured?

CASE 2

When Judy Mims was assigned the account for a major Midwestern cellular phone company, she knew the task would be both exciting and challenging. Cellular service was rapidly moving into the mature stage of the product life cycle. There had been many early entries and explosive growth in sales during the past decade, and the shake-out was beginning. Costs, economies of scale, technological advantages, and superior marketing programs were forcing some companies to the sideline.

Clear Voice had been able to set up services in a five-state region, including Missouri, Kansas, Oklahoma, Arkansas, and Texas. The company provided high-quality service at a competitive price. Roaming charges were low, and many long-term contracts had been signed. The company had built alliances with other major providers, giving them national access for the confirmed cell phone user.

Judy knew several issues were currently dominating the industry. First, each company needed a "voice" in the marketplace. The question Judy asked her client to answer was "Why do people use cell phones? And, how do we speak to them as a result?" Cell phones can be used for convenience, for safety reasons, and as status symbols, though the latter was rapidly losing its appeal, because so many people could now afford the phones and the service. "Is the cellular lifestyle different than a noncellular style?" Judy continued. "If so, how do we win over the nonusers? And how do we keep them from signing on with another company?"

Two other issues were daunting the cell phone marketplace. The first was health. There were disturbing reports of links between extensive cell phone use and cancer of the brain, not an appealing prospect. The second, flying just "under the radar screen," as Judy put it, is the backlash factor.

There was little doubt that some people hold cell phone users in contempt. They interrupt lunches in restaurants and annoy the patrons trying to have a quiet meal. Cell phone users seem to go deaf when airline flight attendants announce that the phones must be turned off so that a plane can take off. Every flight now involves a trip down the center aisle of the plane just to shut down cell phone fanatics. Further, insurance agencies and law enforcement departments have begun to question the safety of driving a car while talking on the phone. Nearly every driver has had a near miss or accident because someone was more distracted by a phone call than attentive to driving. A few municipalities have even made it a traffic offense to drive while talking on a cell phone.

Against this backdrop, cell phone purchases continue to rise and user fees offer lucrative sources of revenue for various companies. Judy knew an effective campaign would be one that differentiated Clear Voice from other servers as offering a noticeable advantage. Although the short-term prospects of Clear Voice were good, Judy was being asked to develop and maintain an IMC and advertising program to build a strong company over the long term.

1. Name four major goals that Clear Voice should emphasize in the next decade.

2. Define the theme that will drive Clear Voice during those 10 years.

3. Develop an immediate advertising campaign for the company. Select the methods of assessment for the ads to evaluate the advertising campaign. Justify the choices.

4. How should Clear Voice deal with the "negatives" associated with cell phone use? How would you measure the effectiveness of such an effort?

ENDNOTES

1. www.decisionanalyst.com; Patricia Riedman, "DiscoverWhy Tests TV Commercials Online," *Advertising Age,* 71, no. 13 (March 27, 2000), pp. 46–47.

2. David W. Stewart, "Measures, Methods, and Models in Advertising Research," *Journal of Advertising,* 29, no. 3 (1989), pp. 54–60.

3. Joel S. Debow, "Advertising Recognition and Recall by Age—Including Teens," *Journal of Advertising Research,* 35, no. 5 (September–October 1995), pp. 55–60.

4. Jan Stapel, "Recall and Recognition: A Very Close Relationship," *Journal of Advertising Research,* 38, no. 4 (July–August 1998), pp. 41–45.

5. Christina Merrill, "Roper Expands Testing," *Adweek, Eastern Edition,* 37, no. 45 (November 4, 1996), p. 6.

6. Jack Weber and Mary Ann Morgan, "Why It Is Important to Assess Direct Mail Effectiveness," *Marketing News,* 32, no. 9 (April 27, 1998), p. 11.

7. Steven P. Brown and Douglas M. Stayman, "Antecedents and Consequences of Attitude Toward the Ad: A Meta-Analysis," *Journal of Consumer Research,* 19 (June 1992), pp. 34–51.

8. Douglas M. Stayman and David A. Aaker, "Continuous Measurement of Self-Report or Emotional Response," *Psychology and Marketing,* 10 (May–June 1993), pp. 199–214.

9. Freddie Campos, "UH Facility Test Ads for $500," *Pacific Business News,* 35, no. 23 (August 18, 1997), pp. A1–A2.

10. Riedman, "DiscoverWhy Tests TV Commercials Online."

11. Steve Jarvis, "Minnesota Campaign Grabs Smokers By Throat," *Marketing News,* 36, issue 8 (April 15, 2002), pp. 5–6.

12. David W. Stewart, David H. Furse, and Randall P. Kozak, "A Guide to Commercial Copytesting Services," *Current Issues and Research in Advertising,* ed. James Leigh and Claude Martin, Jr. (Ann Arbor: Division of Research, Graduate School of Business, University of Michigan, 1983), pp. 1–44.

13. Based on PACT document published in *Journal of Marketing,* 11, no. 4 (1982), pp. 4–29.

14. "Aiming for an Accurate ROI," *Marketing News,* 35, issue 15 (July 16, 2001), p. 11.

15. James Heckman, "Better Measures Could Make a Noise in Retail," *Marketing News,* 32, no. 25 (December 7, 1998), p. 6.

16. Amanda Beeler, "POPAI Initiates Study Tracking Effectiveness of Displays," *Advertising Age,* 71, no. 15 (April 10, 2000), p. 54.

17. "Two Technologies Vie for Piece of Growing Focus Group Market," *Marketing News,* 36, issue 11 (May 27, 2002), p. 4.

18. Jackie Todd, "Visuals, Wording Help Lower Language Barriers in Multinational Tests," *Marketing News,* 36, issue 9 (April 29, 2002) p. 38.

19. Steve Jarvis, "Status Quo=Progress," *Marketing News,* 36, issue 9 (April 29, 2002), pp. 37–38.

20. Kim M. Bayne, "AdKnowledge Rolls Out Web Ad Evaluation Tool," *Advertising Age,* 69, no. 23 (June 8, 1998), p. 38.

21. Tim Triplett, "Researchers Probe Ad Effectiveness Globally," *Marketing News,* 28, no. 18 (August 29, 1994), pp. 6–7.

22. Peter Drucker, *Management Tools, Responsibilities, Practices* (New York: Harper & Row, 1974).

Credits

Chapter 1
Courtesy of PhotoEdit. Photograph by Michael Newman.

Chapter 2
Courtesy of AP/Wide World Photos.

Chapter 3
Courtesy of Woodfin Camp & Associates. Photograph by Bernard Boutrit.

Chapter 4
Courtesy of Getty Images, Inc.

Chapter 5
Courtesy of Woodfin Camp & Associates. Photograph by Chuck Nacke.

Chapter 6
Courtesy of LWA-JDC/Corbis.

Chapter 7
Courtesy of Procter & Gamble Company. © The Procter & Gamble Company. Used by permission.

Chapter 8
Courtesy of Getty Images, Inc–Liaison. Photograph by Joe Polillio.

Chapter 9
Courtesy of Corbis/Sygma. Photograph by Frank Trapper.

Chapter 10
Courtesy of AP/Wide World Photos. Photograph by Chris O'Meara.

Chapter 11
Courtesy of Corbis/Stock Market. Photograph by R. B. Studio.

Chapter 12
Courtesy of Corbis/SABA Press Photos, Inc. Photograph by Greg Smith.

Chapter 13
Courtesy of Getty Images, Inc.–Liaison. Photograph by Newsmakers.

Chapter 14
Courtesy of SuperStock, Inc. Photograph by Lisette Le Bon.

Chapter 15
Courtesy of the Pasta House Company.

Chapter 16
Courtesy of Toshiba America Information Systems, Inc.

Name/Organization Index

Subject Index

Notes

Notes

Notes

Notes

Notes

Notes

Notes

Notes

Notes